D1442141

Dictionary of Literary Biography

1 *The American Renaissance in New England,* edited by Joel Myerson (1978)

2 *American Novelists Since World War II,* edited by Jeffrey Helterman and Richard Layman (1978)

3 *Antebellum Writers in New York and the South,* edited by Joel Myerson (1979)

4 *American Writers in Paris, 1920-1939,* edited by Karen Lane Rood (1980)

5 *American Poets Since World War II,* 2 parts, edited by Donald J. Greiner (1980)

6 *American Novelists Since World War II, Second Series,* edited by James E. Kibler Jr. (1980)

7 *Twentieth-Century American Dramatists,* 2 parts, edited by John MacNicholas (1981)

8 *Twentieth-Century American Science-Fiction Writers,* 2 parts, edited by David Cowart and Thomas L. Wymer (1981)

9 *American Novelists, 1910-1945,* 3 parts, edited by James J. Martine (1981)

10 *Modern British Dramatists, 1900-1945,* 2 parts, edited by Stanley Weintraub (1982)

11 *American Humorists, 1800-1950,* 2 parts, edited by Stanley Trachtenberg (1982)

12 *American Realists and Naturalists,* edited by Donald Pizer and Earl N. Harbert (1982)

13 *British Dramatists Since World War II,* 2 parts, edited by Stanley Weintraub (1982)

14 *British Novelists Since 1960,* 2 parts, edited by Jay L. Halio (1983)

15 *British Novelists, 1930-1959,* 2 parts, edited by Bernard Oldsey (1983)

16 *The Beats: Literary Bohemians in Postwar America,* 2 parts, edited by Ann Charters (1983)

17 *Twentieth-Century American Historians,* edited by Clyde N. Wilson (1983)

18 *Victorian Novelists After 1885,* edited by Ira B. Nadel and William E. Fredeman (1983)

19 *British Poets, 1880-1914,* edited by Donald E. Stanford (1983)

20 *British Poets, 1914-1945,* edited by Donald E. Stanford (1983)

21 *Victorian Novelists Before 1885,* edited by Ira B. Nadel and William E. Fredeman (1983)

22 *American Writers for Children, 1900-1960,* edited by John Cech (1983)

23 *American Newspaper Journalists, 1873-1900,* edited by Perry J. Ashley (1983)

24 *American Colonial Writers, 1606-1734,* edited by Emory Elliott (1984)

25 *American Newspaper Journalists, 1901-1925,* edited by Perry J. Ashley (1984)

26 *American Screenwriters,* edited by Robert E. Morsberger, Stephen O. Lesser, and Randall Clark (1984)

27 *Poets of Great Britain and Ireland, 1945-1960,* edited by Vincent B. Sherry Jr. (1984)

28 *Twentieth-Century American-Jewish Fiction Writers,* edited by Daniel Walden (1984)

29 *American Newspaper Journalists, 1926-1950,* edited by Perry J. Ashley (1984)

30 *American Historians, 1607-1865,* edited by Clyde N. Wilson (1984)

31 *American Colonial Writers, 1735-1781,* edited by Emory Elliott (1984)

32 *Victorian Poets Before 1850,* edited by William E. Fredeman and Ira B. Nadel (1984)

33 *Afro-American Fiction Writers After 1955,* edited by Thadious M. Davis and Trudier Harris (1984)

34 *British Novelists, 1890-1929: Traditionalists,* edited by Thomas F. Staley (1985)

35 *Victorian Poets After 1850,* edited by William E. Fredeman and Ira B. Nadel (1985)

36 *British Novelists, 1890-1929: Modernists,* edited by Thomas F. Staley (1985)

37 *American Writers of the Early Republic,* edited by Emory Elliott (1985)

38 *Afro-American Writers After 1955: Dramatists and Prose Writers,* edited by Thadious M. Davis and Trudier Harris (1985)

39 *British Novelists, 1660-1800,* 2 parts, edited by Martin C. Battestin (1985)

40 *Poets of Great Britain and Ireland Since 1960,* 2 parts, edited by Vincent B. Sherry Jr. (1985)

41 *Afro-American Poets Since 1955,* edited by Trudier Harris and Thadious M. Davis (1985)

42 *American Writers for Children Before 1900,* edited by Glenn E. Estes (1985)

43 *American Newspaper Journalists, 1690-1872,* edited by Perry J. Ashley (1986)

44 *American Screenwriters, Second Series,* edited by Randall Clark, Robert E. Morsberger, and Stephen O. Lesser (1986)

45 *American Poets, 1880-1945, First Series,* edited by Peter Quartermain (1986)

46 *American Literary Publishing Houses, 1900-1980: Trade and Paperback,* edited by Peter Dzwonkoski (1986)

47 *American Historians, 1866-1912,* edited by Clyde N. Wilson (1986)

48 *American Poets, 1880-1945, Second Series,* edited by Peter Quartermain (1986)

49 *American Literary Publishing Houses, 1638-1899,* 2 parts, edited by Peter Dzwonkoski (1986)

50 *Afro-American Writers Before the Harlem Renaissance,* edited by Trudier Harris (1986)

51 *Afro-American Writers from the Harlem Renaissance to 1940,* edited by Trudier Harris (1987)

52 *American Writers for Children Since 1960: Fiction,* edited by Glenn E. Estes (1986)

53 *Canadian Writers Since 1960, First Series,* edited by W. H. New (1986)

54 *American Poets, 1880-1945, Third Series,* 2 parts, edited by Peter Quartermain (1987)

55 *Victorian Prose Writers Before 1867,* edited by William B. Thesing (1987)

56 *German Fiction Writers, 1914-1945,* edited by James Hardin (1987)

57 *Victorian Prose Writers After 1867,* edited by William B. Thesing (1987)

58 *Jacobean and Caroline Dramatists,* edited by Fredson Bowers (1987)

59 *American Literary Critics and Scholars, 1800-1850,* edited by John W. Rathbun and Monica M. Grecu (1987)

60 *Canadian Writers Since 1960, Second Series,* edited by W. H. New (1987)

61 *American Writers for Children Since 1960: Poets, Illustrators, and Nonfiction Authors,* edited by Glenn E. Estes (1987)

62 *Elizabethan Dramatists,* edited by Fredson Bowers (1987)

63 *Modern American Critics, 1920-1955,* edited by Gregory S. Jay (1988)

64 *American Literary Critics and Scholars, 1850-1880,* edited by John W. Rathbun and Monica M. Grecu (1988)

65 *French Novelists, 1900-1930,* edited by Catharine Savage Brosman (1988)

66 *German Fiction Writers, 1885-1913,* 2 parts, edited by James Hardin (1988)

67 *Modern American Critics Since 1955,* edited by Gregory S. Jay (1988)

68 *Canadian Writers, 1920-1959, First Series,* edited by W. H. New (1988)

69 *Contemporary German Fiction Writers, First Series,* edited by Wolfgang D. Elfe and James Hardin (1988)

70 *British Mystery Writers, 1860-1919,* edited by Bernard Benstock and Thomas F. Staley (1988)

71 *American Literary Critics and Scholars, 1880-1900,* edited by John W. Rathbun and Monica M. Grecu (1988)

72 *French Novelists, 1930-1960,* edited by Catharine Savage Brosman (1988)

73 *American Magazine Journalists, 1741-1850,* edited by Sam G. Riley (1988)

74 *American Short-Story Writers Before 1880,* edited by Bobby Ellen Kimbel, with the assistance of William E. Grant (1988)

75 *Contemporary German Fiction Writers, Second Series,* edited by Wolfgang D. Elfe and James Hardin (1988)

76 *Afro-American Writers, 1940-1955,* edited by Trudier Harris (1988)

77 *British Mystery Writers, 1920-1939,* edited by Bernard Benstock and Thomas F. Staley (1988)

78 *American Short-Story Writers, 1880-1910,* edited by Bobby Ellen Kimbel, with the assistance of William E. Grant (1988)

79 *American Magazine Journalists, 1850-1900,* edited by Sam G. Riley (1988)

80 *Restoration and Eighteenth-Century Dramatists, First Series,* edited by Paula R. Backscheider (1989)

81 *Austrian Fiction Writers, 1875-1913,* edited by James Hardin and Donald G. Daviau (1989)

82 *Chicano Writers, First Series,* edited by Francisco A. Lomelí and Carl R. Shirley (1989)

83 *French Novelists Since 1960,* edited by Catharine Savage Brosman (1989)

84 *Restoration and Eighteenth-Century Dramatists, Second Series,* edited by Paula R. Backscheider (1989)

85 *Austrian Fiction Writers After 1914,* edited by James Hardin and Donald G. Daviau (1989)

86 *American Short-Story Writers, 1910-1945, First Series,* edited by Bobby Ellen Kimbel (1989)

87 *British Mystery and Thriller Writers Since 1940, First Series,* edited by Bernard Benstock and Thomas F. Staley (1989)

88 *Canadian Writers, 1920-1959, Second Series,* edited by W. H. New (1989)

89 *Restoration and Eighteenth-Century Dramatists, Third Series,* edited by Paula R. Backscheider (1989)

90 *German Writers in the Age of Goethe, 1789-1832,* edited by James Hardin and Christoph E. Schweitzer (1989)

91 *American Magazine Journalists, 1900-1960, First Series,* edited by Sam G. Riley (1990)

92 *Canadian Writers, 1890-1920,* edited by W. H. New (1990)

93 *British Romantic Poets, 1789-1832, First Series,* edited by John R. Greenfield (1990)

94 *German Writers in the Age of Goethe: Sturm und Drang to Classicism,* edited by James Hardin and Christoph E. Schweitzer (1990)

95 *Eighteenth-Century British Poets, First Series,* edited by John Sitter (1990)

96 *British Romantic Poets, 1789-1832, Second Series,* edited by John R. Greenfield (1990)

97 *German Writers from the Enlightenment to Sturm und Drang, 1720-1764,* edited by James Hardin and Christoph E. Schweitzer (1990)

98 *Modern British Essayists, First Series,* edited by Robert Beum (1990)

99 *Canadian Writers Before 1890,* edited by W. H. New (1990)

100 *Modern British Essayists, Second Series,* edited by Robert Beum (1990)

101 *British Prose Writers, 1660-1800, First Series,* edited by Donald T. Siebert (1991)

102 *American Short-Story Writers, 1910-1945, Second Series,* edited by Bobby Ellen Kimbel (1991)

103 *American Literary Biographers, First Series,* edited by Steven Serafin (1991)

104 *British Prose Writers, 1660-1800, Second Series,* edited by Donald T. Siebert (1991)

105 *American Poets Since World War II, Second Series,* edited by R. S. Gwynn (1991)

106 *British Literary Publishing Houses, 1820-1880,* edited by Patricia J. Anderson and Jonathan Rose (1991)

107 *British Romantic Prose Writers, 1789-1832, First Series,* edited by John R. Greenfield (1991)

108 *Twentieth-Century Spanish Poets, First Series,* edited by Michael L. Perna (1991)

109 *Eighteenth-Century British Poets, Second Series,* edited by John Sitter (1991)

110 *British Romantic Prose Writers, 1789-1832, Second Series,* edited by John R. Greenfield (1991)

111 *American Literary Biographers, Second Series,* edited by Steven Serafin (1991)

112 *British Literary Publishing Houses, 1881-1965,* edited by Jonathan Rose and Patricia J. Anderson (1991)

113 *Modern Latin-American Fiction Writers, First Series,* edited by William Luis (1992)

114 *Twentieth-Century Italian Poets, First Series,* edited by Giovanna Wedel De Stasio, Glauco Cambon, and Antonio Illiano (1992)

115 *Medieval Philosophers,* edited by Jeremiah Hackett (1992)

116 *British Romantic Novelists, 1789-1832,* edited by Bradford K. Mudge (1992)

117 *Twentieth-Century Caribbean and Black African Writers, First Series,* edited by Bernth Lindfors and Reinhard Sander (1992)

118 *Twentieth-Century German Dramatists, 1889-1918,* edited by Wolfgang D. Elfe and James Hardin (1992)

119 *Nineteenth-Century French Fiction Writers: Romanticism and Realism, 1800-*

1860, edited by Catharine Savage Brosman (1992)

120 *American Poets Since World War II, Third Series,* edited by R. S. Gwynn (1992)

121 *Seventeenth-Century British Nondramatic Poets, First Series,* edited by M. Thomas Hester (1992)

122 *Chicano Writers, Second Series,* edited by Francisco A. Lomelí and Carl R. Shirley (1992)

123 *Nineteenth-Century French Fiction Writers: Naturalism and Beyond, 1860-1900,* edited by Catharine Savage Brosman (1992)

124 *Twentieth-Century German Dramatists, 1919-1992,* edited by Wolfgang D. Elfe and James Hardin (1992)

125 *Twentieth-Century Caribbean and Black African Writers, Second Series,* edited by Bernth Lindfors and Reinhard Sander (1993)

126 *Seventeenth-Century British Nondramatic Poets, Second Series,* edited by M. Thomas Hester (1993)

127 *American Newspaper Publishers, 1950-1990,* edited by Perry J. Ashley (1993)

128 *Twentieth-Century Italian Poets, Second Series,* edited by Giovanna Wedel De Stasio, Glauco Cambon, and Antonio Illiano (1993)

129 *Nineteenth-Century German Writers, 1841-1900,* edited by James Hardin and Siegfried Mews (1993)

130 *American Short-Story Writers Since World War II,* edited by Patrick Meanor (1993)

131 *Seventeenth-Century British Nondramatic Poets, Third Series,* edited by M. Thomas Hester (1993)

132 *Sixteenth-Century British Nondramatic Writers, First Series,* edited by David A. Richardson (1993)

133 *Nineteenth-Century German Writers to 1840,* edited by James Hardin and Siegfried Mews (1993)

134 *Twentieth-Century Spanish Poets, Second Series,* edited by Jerry Phillips Winfield (1994)

135 *British Short-Fiction Writers, 1880-1914: The Realist Tradition,* edited by William B. Thesing (1994)

136 *Sixteenth-Century British Nondramatic Writers, Second Series,* edited by David A. Richardson (1994)

137 *American Magazine Journalists, 1900-1960, Second Series,* edited by Sam G. Riley (1994)

138 *German Writers and Works of the High Middle Ages: 1170-1280,* edited by James Hardin and Will Hasty (1994)

139 *British Short-Fiction Writers, 1945-1980,* edited by Dean Baldwin (1994)

140 *American Book-Collectors and Bibliographers, First Series,* edited by Joseph Rosenblum (1994)

141 *British Children's Writers, 1880-1914,* edited by Laura M. Zaidman (1994)

142 *Eighteenth-Century British Literary Biographers,* edited by Steven Serafin (1994)

143 *American Novelists Since World War II, Third Series,* edited by James R. Giles and Wanda H. Giles (1994)

144 *Nineteenth-Century British Literary Biographers,* edited by Steven Serafin (1994)

145 *Modern Latin-American Fiction Writers, Second Series,* edited by William Luis and Ann González (1994)

146 *Old and Middle English Literature,* edited by Jeffrey Helterman and Jerome Mitchell (1994)

147 *South Slavic Writers Before World War II,* edited by Vasa D. Mihailovich (1994)

148 *German Writers and Works of the Early Middle Ages: 800-1170,* edited by Will Hasty and James Hardin (1994)

149 *Late Nineteenth- and Early Twentieth-Century British Literary Biographers,* edited by Steven Serafin (1995)

150 *Early Modern Russian Writers, Late Seventeenth and Eighteenth Centuries,* edited by Marcus C. Levitt (1995)

151 *British Prose Writers of the Early Seventeenth Century,* edited by Clayton D. Lein (1995)

152 *American Novelists Since World War II, Fourth Series,* edited by James and Wanda Giles (1995)

153 *Late-Victorian and Edwardian British Novelists, First Series,* edited by George M. Johnson (1995)

154 *The British Literary Book Trade, 1700-1820,* edited by James K. Bracken and Joel Silver (1995)

155 *Twentieth-Century British Literary Biographers,* edited by Steven Serafin (1995)

156 *British Short-Fiction Writers, 1880-1914: The Romantic Tradition,* edited by William F. Naufftus (1995)

157 *Twentieth-Century Caribbean and Black African Writers, Third Series,* edited by Bernth Lindfors and Reinhard Sander (1995)

158 *British Reform Writers, 1789-1832,* edited by Gary Kelly and Edd Applegate (1995)

159 *British Short Fiction Writers, 1800-1880,* edited by John R. Greenfield (1996)

160 *British Children's Writers, 1914-1960,* edited by Donald R. Hettinga and Gary D. Schmidt (1996)

161 *British Children's Writers Since 1960, First Series,* edited by Caroline Hunt (1996)

162 *British Short-Fiction Writers, 1915-1945,* edited by John H. Rogers (1996)

163 *British Children's Writers, 1800-1880,* edited by Meena Khorana (1996)

164 *German Baroque Writers, 1580-1660,* edited by James Hardin (1996)

165 *American Poets Since World War II, Fourth Series,* edited by Joseph Conte (1996)

166 *British Travel Writers, 1837-1875,* edited by Barbara Brothers and Julia Gergits (1996)

167 *Sixteenth-Century British Nondramatic Writers, Third Series,* edited by David A. Richardson (1996)

168 *German Baroque Writers, 1661-1730,* edited by James Hardin (1996)

169 *American Poets Since World War II, Fifth Series,* edited by Joseph Conte (1996)

170 *The British Literary Book Trade, 1475-1700,* edited by James K. Bracken and Joel Silver (1996)

171 *Twentieth-Century American Sportswriters,* edited by Richard Orodenker (1996)

172 *Sixteenth-Century British Nondramatic Writers, Fourth Series,* edited by David A. Richardson (1996)

173 *American Novelists Since World War II, Fifth Series,* edited by James R. Giles and Wanda H. Giles (1996)

174 *British Travel Writers, 1876-1909,* edited by Barbara Brothers and Julia Gergits (1997)

175 *Native American Writers of the United States,* edited by Kenneth M. Roemer (1997)

Documentary Series

1 *Sherwood Anderson, Willa Cather, John Dos Passos, Theodore Dreiser, F. Scott Fitzgerald, Ernest Hemingway, Sinclair Lewis,* edited by Margaret A. Van Antwerp (1982)

2 *James Gould Cozzens, James T. Farrell, William Faulkner, John O'Hara, John Steinbeck, Thomas Wolfe, Richard Wright,* edited by Margaret A. Van Antwerp (1982)

3 *Saul Bellow, Jack Kerouac, Norman Mailer, Vladimir Nabokov, John Updike, Kurt Vonnegut,* edited by Mary Bruccoli (1983)

4 *Tennessee Williams,* edited by Margaret A. Van Antwerp and Sally Johns (1984)

5 *American Transcendentalists,* edited by Joel Myerson (1988)

6 *Hardboiled Mystery Writers: Raymond Chandler, Dashiell Hammett, Ross Macdonald,* edited by Matthew J. Bruccoli and Richard Layman (1989)

7 *Modern American Poets: James Dickey, Robert Frost, Marianne Moore,* edited by Karen L. Rood (1989)

8 *The Black Aesthetic Movement,* edited by Jeffrey Louis Decker (1991)

9 *American Writers of the Vietnam War: W. D. Ehrhart, Larry Heinemann, Tim O'Brien, Walter McDonald, John M. Del Vecchio,* edited by Ronald Baughman (1991)

10 *The Bloomsbury Group,* edited by Edward L. Bishop (1992)

11 *American Proletarian Culture: The Twenties and The Thirties,* edited by Jon Christian Suggs (1993)

12 *Southern Women Writers: Flannery O'Connor, Katherine Anne Porter, Eudora Welty,* edited by Mary Ann Wimsatt and Karen L. Rood (1994)

13 *The House of Scribner, 1846–1904,* edited by John Delaney (1996)

14 *Four Women Writers for Children, 1868–1918,* edited by Caroline C. Hunt (1996)

Yearbooks

1980 edited by Karen L. Rood, Jean W. Ross, and Richard Ziegfeld (1981)

1981 edited by Karen L. Rood, Jean W. Ross, and Richard Ziegfeld (1982)

1982 edited by Richard Ziegfeld; associate editors: Jean W. Ross and Lynne C. Zeigler (1983)

1983 edited by Mary Bruccoli and Jean W. Ross; associate editor: Richard Ziegfeld (1984)

1984 edited by Jean W. Ross (1985)

1985 edited by Jean W. Ross (1986)

1986 edited by J. M. Brook (1987)

1987 edited by J. M. Brook (1988)

1988 edited by J. M. Brook (1989)

1989 edited by J. M. Brook (1990)

1990 edited by James W. Hipp (1991)

1991 edited by James W. Hipp (1992)

1992 edited by James W. Hipp (1993)

1993 edited by James W. Hipp, contributing editor George Garrett (1994)

1994 edited by James W. Hipp, contributing editor George Garrett (1995)

1995 edited by James W. Hipp, contributing editor George Garrett (1996)

Concise Series

Concise Dictionary of American Literary Biography, 6 volumes (1988-1989): *The New Consciousness, 1941-1968; Colonization to the American Renaissance, 1640-1865; Realism, Naturalism, and Local Color, 1865-1917; The Twenties, 1917-1929; The Age of Maturity, 1929-1941; Broadening Views, 1968-1988.*

Concise Dictionary of British Literary Biography, 8 volumes (1991-1992): *Writers of the Middle Ages and Renaissance Before 1660; Writers of the Restoration and Eighteenth Century, 1660-1789; Writers of the Romantic Period, 1789-1832; Victorian Writers, 1832-1890; Late Victorian and Edwardian Writers, 1890-1914; Modern Writers, 1914-1945; Writers After World War II, 1945-1960; Contemporary Writers, 1960 to Present.*

Dictionary of Literary Biography® • Volume One Hundred Seventy-Five

Native American Writers of the United States

Dictionary of Literary Biography® • Volume One Hundred Seventy-Five

Native American Writers of the United States

Edited by
Kenneth M. Roemer
University of Texas at Arlington

A Bruccoli Clark Layman Book
Gale Research
Detroit, Washington, D.C., London

Printed in the United States of America

The paper used in this publication meets the minimum requirements of American National Standard for Information Sciences–Permanence Paper for Printed Library Materials, ANSI Z39.48-1984. ∞™

Library of Congress Cataloging-in-Publication Data

Native American writers of the United States / edited by Kenneth M. Roemer.
p. cm. – (Dictionary of literary biography; v. 175)
"A Bruccoli Clark Layman book."
Includes bibliographical references and index.
ISBN 0-8103-9938-5 (alk. paper)
1. American literature – Indian authors – Bio-bibliography – Dictionaries. 2. Indian authors – United States – Biography – Dictionaries. 3. American literature – Indian authors – Dictionaries. 4. Indians of North America – Biography – Dictionaries. 5. Indians in literature – Dictionaries. I. Roemer, Kenneth M., 1945- . II. Series.
PS153.I52N39 1997
810.9'897'03 – dc21 96-52414
[B] CIP
r96

10 9 8 7 6 5 4 3 2 1

This book is dedicated to my paternal grandfather, Herbert Curtis Roemer, and to my parents, Arthur and Mildred Roemer, whose willingness to learn from and to help American Indians inspired my interest in Native American literatures. It is also dedicated to Larry Evers, Paula Gunn Allen, Terry Wilson, John Rouillard, and Dexter Fisher Cirillo, whose 1977 summer seminar helped to inspire a generation of scholars. And to Micki for her continuing love and patience.

Contents

Plan of the Series

. . . Almost the most prodigious asset of a country, and perhaps its most precious possession, is its native literary product – when that product is fine and noble and enduring.

Mark Twain*

The advisory board, the editors, and the publisher of the *Dictionary of Literary Biography* are joined in endorsing Mark Twain's declaration. The literature of a nation provides an inexhaustible resource of permanent worth. We intend to make literature and its creators better understood and more accessible to students and the reading public, while satisfying the standards of teachers and scholars.

To meet these requirements, *literary biography* has been construed in terms of the author's achievement. The most important thing about a writer is his writing. Accordingly, the entries in *DLB* are career biographies, tracing the development of the author's canon and the evolution of his reputation.

The purpose of *DLB* is not only to provide reliable information in a convenient format but also to place the figures in the larger perspective of literary history and to offer appraisals of their accomplishments by qualified scholars.

The publication plan for *DLB* resulted from two years of preparation. The project was proposed to Bruccoli Clark by Frederick C. Ruffner, president of the Gale Research Company, in November 1975. After specimen entries were prepared and typeset, an advisory board was formed to refine the entry format and develop the series rationale. In meetings held during 1976, the publisher, series editors, and advisory board approved the scheme for a comprehensive biographical dictionary of persons who contributed to North American literature. Editorial work on the first volume began in January 1977, and it was published in 1978. In order to make *DLB* more than a reference tool and to compile volumes that individually have claim to status as literary history, it was decided to organize volumes by topic, period, or genre. Each of these freestanding volumes provides a biographical-bibliographical guide and overview for a particular area of literature. We are convinced that this organization – as opposed to a single alphabet method – constitutes a valuable innovation in the presentation of reference material. The volume plan necessarily requires many decisions for the placement and treatment of authors who might properly be included in two or three volumes. In some instances a major figure will be included in separate volumes, but with different entries emphasizing the aspect of his career appropriate to each volume. Ernest Hemingway, for example, is represented in *American Writers in Paris, 1920–1939* by an entry focusing on his expatriate apprenticeship; he is also in *American Novelists, 1910–1945* with an entry surveying his entire career. Each volume includes a cumulative index of the subject authors and articles. Comprehensive indexes to the entire series are planned.

With volume ten in 1982 it was decided to enlarge the scope of *DLB*. By the end of 1986 twenty-one volumes treating British literature had been published, and volumes for Commonwealth and Modern European literature were in progress. The series has been further augmented by the *DLB Yearbooks* (since 1981) which update published entries and add new entries to keep the *DLB* current with contemporary activity. There have also been *DLB Documentary Series* volumes which provide biographical and critical source materials for figures whose work is judged to have particular interest for students. One of these companion volumes is entirely devoted to Tennessee Williams.

We define literature as the *intellectual commerce of a nation:* not merely as belles lettres but as that ample and complex process by which ideas are generated, shaped, and transmitted. *DLB* entries are not limited to "creative writers" but extend to other figures who in their time and in their way influenced the mind of a people. Thus the series encompasses historians, journalists, publishers, and screenwriters. By this means readers of *DLB* may be aided to perceive literature not as cult scripture in the keeping of intellectual high priests but firmly positioned at the center of a nation's life.

**From an unpublished section of Mark Twain's autobiography, copyright by the Mark Twain Company*

DLB includes the major writers appropriate to each volume and those standing in the ranks immediately behind them. Scholarly and critical counsel has been sought in deciding which minor figures to include and how full their entries should be. Wherever possible, useful references are made to figures who do not warrant separate entries.

Each *DLB* volume has a volume editor responsible for planning the volume, selecting the figures for inclusion, and assigning the entries. Volume editors are also responsible for preparing, where appropriate, appendices surveying the major periodicals and literary and intellectual movements for their volumes, as well as lists of further readings. Work on the series as a whole is coordinated at the Bruccoli Clark Layman editorial center in Columbia, South Carolina, where the editorial staff is responsible for accuracy of the published volumes.

One feature that distinguishes *DLB* is the illustration policy – its concern with the iconography of literature. Just as an author is influenced by his surroundings, so is the reader's understanding of the author enhanced by a knowledge of his environment. Therefore *DLB* volumes include not only drawings, paintings, and photographs of authors, often depicting them at various stages in their careers, but also illustrations of their families and places where they lived. Title pages are regularly reproduced in facsimile along with dust jackets for modern authors. The dust jackets are a special feature of *DLB* because they often document better than anything else the way in which an author's work was perceived in its own time. Specimens of the writers' manuscripts are included when feasible.

Samuel Johnson rightly decreed that "The chief glory of every people arises from its authors." The purpose of the *Dictionary of Literary Biography* is to compile literary history in the surest way available to us – by accurate and comprehensive treatment of the lives and work of those who contributed to it.

The *DLB* Advisory Board

Introduction

The sweep of American Indian literature encompasses thirty thousand years of history and a geographical area that stretches from the Arctic Circle to the tip of South America. Spoken and written in hundreds of Native and non-Native languages, it includes such oral genres as ceremonial performance and liturgy; narratives as old as creation and trickster stories as new as an elaborate joke told at an intertribal powwow; oratory; "as-told-to" autobiography; and many written genres, including autobiography, history, journalism, critical essays, fiction, poetry, and drama. The most accessible and wide-ranging introductions to these many forms of literature are Andrew Wiget's *Native American Literature* (1985); A. LaVonne Brown Ruoff's *American Indian Literatures* (1990); Wiget's *Dictionary of Native American Literature* (1994), republished as *Handbook of Native American Literature* (1996); and Janet Witalec's *Native North American Literature* (1994).

In a highly selective way, this volume of the *Dictionary of Literary Biography* examines one important segment of Native American literature: Indian authors, most of whom live or lived in the United States and who wrote or write primarily in English. (Although the Ojibwe George Copway and the Mohawk E. Pauline Johnson were Canadians, their works had a significant impact in the United States; to exclude them would have meant preserving artificial boundaries while ignoring literary and cultural realities.) Deciding which thirty-five to forty-five authors would best illustrate the complex issues and literary diversity of Native American writing was a difficult task. More than half of the authors treated in this volume are still living; the increasing number of Native American writers justifies this imbalance. Another reason for including so many modern authors is that it was the work of a few of them during the late 1960s and the 1970s – notably, the Standing Rock Sioux Vine Deloria Jr.; the Kiowa/Cherokee N. Scott Momaday, who won the 1969 Pulitzer Prize for Fiction for *House Made of Dawn* (1968); the Laguna Leslie Marmon Silko; the Acoma Simon J. Ortiz; and the Blackfeet/Gros Ventre James Welch – that first gained widespread and sustained recognition for Indian oral and written literatures.

While the emphasis on modern writers is certainly justified, so is the criticism of an almost exclusive focus on them and on a few genres, such as fiction, poetry, and autobiography. There were important late-nineteenth- and early-twentieth-century authors, such as the Sioux Charles Eastman, the Creek Alexander Posey, the Okanogan Mourning Dove, the Osage John Joseph Mathews (whose *Wah'Kon Tah,* 1932, was a Book-of-the-Month Club selection), and the Flathead D'Arcy McNickle. To gain even more historical perspective it is necessary to represent some of the eighteenth- and nineteenth-century pioneers in particular genres: in sermons, the Mohegan Samson Occom; in autobiography and essays, Occom and the Pequot William Apess; in history, Copway; in fiction, the Creek S. Alice Callahan and the Cherokee John Rollin Ridge; and in poetry, the Ojibwe Jane Johnston Schoolcraft. Finally, to suggest the genre diversity of Native American writing, several types of writing often neglected by literary critics are represented in this volume: academic writing and translations, from the Omaha Francis La Flesche's early Bureau of American Ethnology Annual Reports to the Miwok-Pomo Greg Sarris's *Keeping Slug Woman Alive* (1993); and drama, including the well-known plays of the Cherokee Lynn Riggs, author of *Green Grow the Lilacs* (1931), and the less well-known plays of the Kiowa Hanay Geiogamah and the Cherokee Diane Glancy.

This introduction will deal with three basic issues. First, how have Native Americans been defined? Second, are there distinctive characteristics and responsibilities of Native American authors and texts? Third, how have historical and institutional forces shaped the roles of the authors and texts?

The question of who is an Indian is fundamental to the study of Native American authors, since a text written by an Indian about Indians is typically perceived as being based on personal knowledge. Also, since practically all of the well-known Indian writers today, and many of those of the past, have mixed heritages, it is not surprising that a recurring topic in Native American writing is the construction of Indian identities. As the Osage Robert Allen Warrior warns in his *Tribal Secrets* (1995), however, an overly narrow focus on "questions of identity" can "reduce" and "constrain" concepts of Indian literature.

Of course, the history of Native American identity creation has all too often involved reduction and constraint. The multiculturalism and dynamism of pre-Columbian cultures were transformed by the invention of the notion of the "Indian." As the Anishinaabe Gerald Vizenor argues in his essay "Trickster Discourse" in *Narrative Chance* (1989), a volume that he edited, part of the tragic irony of this invention was that its "inventor is unaware of his act of invention . . . the invention then becomes the basis of his world view and actions." This "basis" was often perceived in extreme terms either of transparency or opaqueness. Deloria opens his *Custer Died for Your Sins* (1969) by satirizing the former extreme: "Our foremost plight is our transparency. People can tell just by looking at us what we want, what should be done to help us, how we feel, and what a 'real' Indian is really like." A striking example of the other extreme – the forever unknowable or forbidden-to-be-known Indian – is captured by Richard Drinnon in *Facing West* (1980): "Indian-hating identified the dark others that white settlers were not and must not under any circumstances become."

One response to the problem of defining Native Americans, taken by Native and non-Native writers and by tribal and federal agencies, has been to use the individual's quantum of Indian blood. Blood quantum is a major factor in such important early-twentieth-century novels as Mourning Dove's *Cogewea, the Half Blood* (1927), Mathews's *Sundown* (1934), and McNickle's *The Surrounded* (1936), as well as in modern works such as Silko's *Ceremony* (1977), the Turtle Mountain Chippewa Louise Erdrich's *Tracks* (1988), and the Chickasaw Linda Hogan's *Mean Spirit* (1990). In *Tracks* and *Mean Spirit* the effects of the 1917 federal Declaration of Policy that held that only Indians with more than 50 percent white blood could get fee patents for their land allotments are seen in fierce inter- and intrafamily fighting, legal swindles, and murders.

As Jack Utter points out in his *American Indians* (1993), the complexities of blood-quantum identity policies are not limited to laws and Bureau of Indian Affairs (BIA) policies: today tribes have the authority to establish membership criteria, though they can be overruled by Congress. While many of the approximately 550 recognized tribal governments use a minimum one-quarter blood requirement; others require one-half or more Indian blood while still others ask for only a trace. But even the existence of official Certificates of Degree of Indian Blood (CDIBs) and BIA 4432 forms verifying Indian descent that meets tribal expectations does not eliminate identity problems. It has only been during the twentieth century that tribes have had authority over their own membership rolls; in the past there may have been different criteria, and "mistakes" – some of them intentional – have been made on tribal rolls. Moreover, tribes may have criteria that go beyond blood-quantum requirements; for instance, some require birth on the reservation. And certain individuals, no matter what their blood quanta, may not want to be on the official rolls.

Controversies about blood quantum and tribal membership have motivated many Native authors to consider broader measures of identity, such as community opinion. The Cherokee/Quapaw/Chickasaw Geary Hobson has been a particularly strong proponent of community opinion. In his introduction to *The Remembered Earth* (1979), one of the most comprehensive collections of contemporary Native American writing, and again in "Indian Country," a survey of modern Indian literature that appeared in the Spring 1989 issue of *Wicazo Sa Review,* Hobson emphasizes "the Indian tribe's, or community's, judgment" as "the most essential" measure of which writers are Native Americans. The least documentable methods of determining identity, commitment and self-concept, may be the most important complements to blood quantum and community opinion. When questioned about their mixed heritages in interviews, Erdrich and her husband, the Modoc Michael Dorris, emphasize the importance of choosing a commitment to the Indian element in a multicultural background. In *The Names* (1976) Momaday offers a striking example of such a choice:

> In 1929 my mother was a Southern belle; she was about to embark on an extraordinary life. It was about this time that she began to see herself as an Indian. That dim native heritage became a fascination and cause for her . . . it became her. She imagined who she was. This act of imagination was, I believe, among the most important events of my mother's early life, as later the same essential act was to be among the most important of my own.

Momaday's own imaginative choice is detailed in his well-known essay "The Man Made of Words," which first found wide distribution in Abraham Chapman's *Literature of the American Indians* (1975): "We are what we imagine. Our very existence consists in our imagination of ourselves. Our best destiny is to imagine, at [last and] completely, who and what and *that* we are. The greatest tragedy that can befall us is to go unimagined."

These imaginings "won't be easy," to quote a refrain from Silko's *Ceremony,* especially for writers who, unlike Momaday, Ortiz, and Silko, were not raised in or near Indian communities. The complexities and ambiguities of modern Native American identity can be overwhelming. It is not surprising that some of the most powerful self-images and character portrayals in Indian autobiographies, fiction, and poetry express the anguish of imagining Indian selves. But some of the most perceptive fiction, poetry, and essays such as Deloria's "Indians Today, the Real and the Unreal" in *Custer Died for Your Sins* have transformed this "identity crisis" into forms that help readers to understand past and present tragedies, as well as the triumphs of Indian survival.

In regard to the second issue – whether there are distinctive characteristics and responsibilities of Native American authors and texts – the Hopi/-Miwok Wendy Rose offers a revealing insight about Indian identity and Indian authors in her interview with Laura Coltelli in Coltelli's *Winged Words* (1990): "I think most Indian writers probably are more similar to each other than they are to other members of their tribe who are not writers." One of the similarities that this "tribe of writers" has shared since Occom's *A Sermon Preached at the Execution of Moses Paul* (1772) – thought to be the first book published in English by a Native American – is an ironic relationship with the notion of authorship. Much has been made, and rightly so, of the influence of oral traditions on works by Native Americans. Yet with the exceptions of a few forms of oral presentation – for instance, the Plains coup narratives – most oral literature is communal: the individual performing the song, ceremony, or narrative is usually not considered the creator of the work. Thus, there is the irony of authors drawing authority and authenticity from traditions to which individualized notions of authorship are foreign. In Native American essay writing and journalism this irony is not as obvious, because authors of such works often do not explicitly draw on communal oral traditions – though the Creek Alexander Posey mimicked Native speech patterns in his Fus Fixico Letters (1902–1908).

In historical writing, autobiography, poetry, and fiction Indian writers have found creative ways to incorporate the paradoxes of communal-oral and individual-written authorship into their texts. Copway used oral narratives as the foundation of his *Traditional History and Characteristic Sketches of the Ojibway Nation* (1850), one of the earliest histories by an Indian. From Eastman's popular *Indian Boyhood* (1902) and Apess's *A Son of the Forest* (1929) to more literary and experimental autobiographies, such as Mathews's *Talking to the Moon* (1945), Momaday's *The Way to Rainy Mountain* (1969), Silko's *Storyteller* (1981), and Glancy's *Claiming Breath* (1992), Indian writers have incorporated oral traditions into their life stories. In poetry communal oral traditions often appear in chantlike cadences of repetition with variation, as in the Creek Joy Harjo's frequently anthologized poems "I Give You Back" and "She Had Some Horses," or in successful attempts to capture the cadences of "Red English."

In short stories the traditional communal voice can frame and interpret contemporary events. In novels the major characters, the narrative structure, and the implied reading experience can reflect communal oral traditions: the trickster Coyote and his dreams open, pervade, and close the Cherokee Thomas King's *Green Grass, Running Water* (1993); Vizenor's many novels team with tricksters, and his rapid-fire wordplay and abrupt transitions often reflect the chaotic, creative transformations of trickster narratives; and Silko's *Ceremony* is an ambitious and successful attempt to juxtapose oral and written narrative processes of healing to produce a ceremonial reading experience. One of the most important contributions of Native American writing has been to transform the tensions between communal-oral origins and individualized authorship into creative invitations to perceive history, autobiography, poetry, and fiction in ways new to both Native and non-Native readers.

At least since Ridge was identified as "a 'Cherokee Indian,' born in the woods" in the "Publishers Preface" to his *The Life and Adventures of Joaquín Murieta, the Celebrated California Bandit* (1854), most publishers of books by Native Americans about Native Americans have capitalized on the authority conferred by the writers' insider status. One way to define the role of Indian authors is to portray them as mediators and translators between Native and non-Native cultures; another is to portray them as representatives, spokespersons, or advocates of Indian culture. Since the recognition of Native American writing as literature during the late 1960s, questions of authorial role and implied audience have become central to much of the discussion of writing by Indians.

Several of the most influential critics, including Arnold Krupat, James Clifford, James Ruppert, and David Murray, have emphasized the mediator-cultural translator functions. In *The Voice in the Margin* (1989) Krupat argues that the term *Indian literature* should be limited to oral performances in tribal languages; for writing in English by Indians he adopts the term *indigenous literature,* which he defines as "a form of literature which results from the *interaction* of local, internal, traditional, tribal, or 'Indian' literary modes with the dominant literary modes of various nation-states in which it may appear." In

Forked Tongues: Speech, Writing and Representation in North American Indian Texts (1991) Murray points out that a Native writer who publishes a poem, newspaper article, or novel would have had years of English-language and non-Indian cultural training that would force and make possible a multicultural representation of "Indian" experience. Murray observes that all writing in English by Indians has occurred "within the terms made available by the cultural situation and surroundings." His comments about Occom's sermon and Apess's autobiographical writing can be applied to most writing in English by Native Americans since 1772: a published text, he says,

> was likely to reflect the tastes of a white audience, and conform to a large extent to what at least some of them thought it was appropriate for an Indian to write. Indian *writers* are mainly going to materialize, therefore, only when what they say meets a white need.

A glance at two quite different nineteenth-century novels tends to support Murray's view. Ridge's *Joaquín Murieta* reflects escape-and-recapture adventure conventions, while the domestic romance strongly influenced Callahan's *Wynema* (1891). Similar points could be made about twentieth-century novels, as the modernistic elements of Momaday's *House Made of Dawn* suggest.

As *House Made of Dawn* also demonstrates, however, the role of the Indian author is not simply to plug Indian topics and characters into familiar non-Indian literary conventions. Historical and cultural conditions blocked the development of a tradition of writing based entirely on Native languages and concepts of literature, but these conditions have also allowed talented writer-mediators to imitate, appropriate, and exploit familiar conventions for their own purposes. But then the question arises: should these mediators strive primarily to reach large multicultural audiences, should they reinforce traditional Indian views and translate non-Indian cultures mainly for Indian readers, or should they see themselves as representing or even advocating specific Indian views first for Indians and then for a wider reading audience?

Versions of the latter two views have been forcefully argued by the Renapa/Lenape/Saponi Jack Forbes and the Dakotah/Crow Creek Sioux Elizabeth Cook-Lynn in *Wicazo Sa Review*. Forbes's "Colonialism and Native American Literature" (Fall 1987) defines Native American literature as "works produced by persons of Native identity and/or culture for primary dissemination to other persons of Native identity and/or culture." Today, he says, the most typical examples of this literature in Indian communities appear in "weeklies, monthlies, newsletters." In "The American Indian Fiction Writer" (Fall 1993) Cook-Lynn assails a misuse of "cultural authority" by Indian authors, including herself. She maintains that Indian and non-Indian readers often look to Indian authors as respected insiders who offer valid representations of Native American views and experience. Instead, these readers often get "cosmopolitan" representations in which Indian issues are transformed by literary conventions that make the text accessible to a wide reading audience and to critics with preconceived notions of the kinds of subtlety, complexity, and ambiguity that make great literature.

Many Native American writers are well aware of the problems of authority, role, representation, and audience raised by Forbes and Cook-Lynn. Nevertheless, in collections of interviews, such as Coltelli's *Winged Words* and Joseph Bruchac's *Survival This Way* (1987), they frequently express a strong reluctance to view their authorial roles too narrowly, especially if doing so would limit their topics, styles, tones, or audiences. Such restrictions, they argue, would hamper their creativity and could lead to a ghettoization of Indian writing. To be authoritative, responsible, representative, mediative, and still free "won't," as Silko says, "be easy." But as the American population becomes more multicultural, the ways Native American authors adapt to their challenges may make them important role models who can show other authors how to speak to diverse audiences while remaining true to their people and to themselves.

As writing by Indians has received more attention, a recurrent question has been whether there are features of such works that distinguish them from works by non-Indians. Considering the diversity of writings by Indians, it is not surprising that Indian authors and responsible critics have been hesitant to construct rigid definitions of Indian texts. Many of these authors and critics are aware, however, that the process of literary canonization demands that newcomers (an ironic misnomer in the case of Indians) define their distinctiveness so that room can be made in the canon for the "new" body of literature. Points of distinctiveness discussed by authors and critics since the publication of Momaday's *House Made of Dawn* include the assumptions that Indian works should be about Indians and that they are distinguished by particular concepts of language, place or community, sovereignty, and survival. There are, however, disadvantages to using these characteristics to define Indian texts. Even the almost self-evident "about Indians" criterion has drawbacks. This requirement implies that all Native American writers are inherently experts on things Indian and that they should concentrate on depictions of Indians. The assumption also leads to exclusions: many critics have placed less emphasis on works or parts of works by Indians that do not focus on Indians – for example, Riggs's Oklahoma plays, including *Green Grow the Lilacs,* which was the basis for the musical *Oklahoma!* (1943); most of the Cherokee John Milton Oskison's fiction; Momaday's poems about Russia; and much of Erdrich's *The Beet Queen* (1986). In general, contemporary Native American authors have been against rigid subject definitions and restrictions. In *The Remembered Earth* Hobson depicts the "about Indians" prerequisite as being "as myopic as wishing Joseph Conrad had written 'Polish' novels."

Two critics who attempt to avoid overly rigid prescriptions of subject matter for Native American literature are Warrior and the Choctaw/Cherokee Louis Owens. In *Other Destinies* (1992) Owens depicts Ridge's *Joaquín Murieta* as "a disguised act of appropriation, an aggressive and subversive masquerade" that is as much about oppression of Indians as it is about the adventures of a Mexican bandit. In *Tribal Secrets* Warrior demonstrates that Deloria's American Indian perspectives on land and community shape his analyses of European religion and philosophy. For Ridge and Deloria these approaches are convincing. But the assumption that whenever an Indian writer portrays a non-Indian topic he or she is performing either an act of appropriation for Native purposes or a reshaping of the non-Indian topic from a Native perspective is almost as restrictive as the "about Indians" requirement. A better approach would be to define "about Indians" flexibly enough to include the huge diversity of the topic (past and present; tribal, pan-tribal, mixed-blood; rural and urban), the possibility of appropriation, and the transformative power of Native American perspectives. But it is clearly preferable to examine each author within the context of his or her personal development as a Native American and as a writer.

Another distinguishing characteristic of Native American texts is a focus on defining Indian identity. Again, flexible boundaries are the most appropriate. Owens praises Indian novelists' ability to capture "an affirmation of a syncretic, dynamic, adaptive identity," and one certainly finds this dynamic syncretism in modern Indian poetry and fiction. It can also be found in the early autobiographies by Occom, Apess, and Copway, as these authors imagined Christian-Indian identities, and later in personal narratives by La Flesche and the Sioux Zitkala-Ša as they combined Plains and boarding-school cultures. The syncretism also exists in the early novels. In the late nineteenth century, Callahan's Wynema Harjo is a full-blood Creek but shapes her identity from Creek, Methodist, and Southern white value systems. In the early twentieth century Mourning Dove's Cogewea, Mathews's Chal Windzer, and McNickle's Archilde Leon all work to create identities out of mixed racial and cultural backgrounds. The syncretic identities portrayed in more than two hundred years of Native American prose and poetry represent a powerful counterstatement to the invention of the "pure" or static Indian and to simplistic images of the Indian pathetically caught between two worlds.

In their discussions of Indian writing authors and critics probably refer to language, sense of place or community, sovereignty, and survival more than to any other motifs or issues. One should not, of course, expect that every newspaper article, historical essay, autobiography, play, poem, or novel by a Native American will be full of references to oral traditions and sacred places that have helped Indians to survive and to articulate their desire for sovereignty. Still, some familiarity with traditional concepts of words, land, and survival is crucial to understanding much of the best Indian writing.

Traditional Native American concepts of language move far beyond describing, communicating, and explaining to encompass generative powers of creating and interconnecting. In their essays and fiction Silko, Momaday, and Erdrich have offered especially provocative discussions of these concepts. Silko's *Ceremony* begins with the dynamic image of the Keresan Pueblo creator Ts'its'tsi'nako (Thought Woman) thinking; what she thinks becomes the stories that the reader reads. The stories associated with Thought Woman and her avatars Night Swan and Ts'eh allow the protagonist, Tayo, to re-create himself, but not before he has been severely tested by the negative generative powers of other stories, including Betonie's narrative of how a story told by an Indian witch created destructive European civilizations; war veterans' self-deluding stories of the good old days when they had sex with white women; and medical stories that would type Tayo as a shell-shocked, alcoholic, Indian veteran. Momaday also stresses the generative force of words. In *House Made of Dawn* Tosamah's "*In principio erat Verbum*" sermon links Abel's disease and potential for being cured to the absence and the development, respectively, of a voice; in "The Man Made of Words" Momaday recalls how writing about an old one-eyed woman enables her to step out of the language and appear before him, and how an arrow maker was willing to allow his and his wife's lives to hang upon a few words. In Erdrich's *Tracks* Nanapush, explaining why he talks so much, offers a moving statement on the power of words:

> Talk is an old man's vice. I opened my mouth and wore out the boy's ears, but that's not my fault. I shouldn't have been caused to live so long, shown so much of death, had to squeeze so many stories in the corners of my brain. They're all attached, and once I start there is no end to telling because they're hooked from one side to the other, mouth to tail. During the year of the sickness, when I was the last one left, I saved myself by starting a story. . . . I got well by talking. Death could not get a word in edgewise, grew discouraged, and traveled on.

Word power and sense of place are intimately connected. In a letter to James Wright that is reproduced in *The Delicacy and Strength of Lace: Letters between Leslie Marmon Silko and James Wright* (1986), edited by Anne Wright, Silko observes that "it was as if the land was telling the stories" in *Ceremony*. Erdrich, in her 28 July 1985 *New York Times Book Review* essay "Where I Ought to Be: A Writer's Sense of Place," maintains that a strong attachment to place is essential to good writing. She quotes Isak Dinesen – "Here I am, where I ought to be" – and continues: "A writer must have a place where he or she feels this, a place to love and to be irritated with."

Native American writers of nonfiction also draw attention to the importance of place. In *God Is Red* (1973) Deloria argues that a fundamental difference between Native American and Western Christian worldviews is that the former is grounded in spatial relationships, the latter in history ("linear time"). Deloria and other Native writers also link place with sovereignty. In " . . . on Sovereignty" in *Akwesasne Notes* (Fall 1995) the Seneca John Mohawk outlines the complex overlapping and conflicting notions of sovereignty associated with feudal European societies, the Euro-American legal system, and Native concepts of nationhood. The last "for the most part" represented "something 'owned,' not by an individual or a class of land owners, but by all of its citizens in common." Despite disagreements among Indian leaders and writers about how to resolve the various concepts of sovereignty, all assume that self-determination should be a basic element of any "Indian place."

The diversity of the sense of place in Native American writing can be suggested by examining four perspectives: the traditional grounding of oral literatures and worldviews in place, the "homing" motif in nineteenth- and twentieth-century writing, Mathews's biological/ecological concepts in *Talking to the Moon,* and the references to absent landscapes in many Indian genres. Momaday dramatizes the grounding in place of stories and worldviews in the introduction to *The Way to Rainy Mountain* when he imagines that the Kiowa responded to their first view of Devil's Tower (or Bear Lodge) in Wyoming by creating a story, "because they could not do otherwise." The nature of the landscape thus often determined the nature of the stories that oriented Indian cultures; as Robert Nelson puts it in *Place and Vision: The Function of Landscape in Native American Fiction* (1993), "geographical landscapes . . . precede and at least partially determine social and cultural ones." A key element in this determination was the perception of landscape as a reflection of the necessary and proper order that should guide the lives of the people. In *Western American Literature* (Winter 1977) Larry Evers's "Words and Place" offers an example: "The extraordinary interest in geography exhibited in Navajo oral literature then may be seen as an effort to evoke harmony in those narratives by reference to the symbolic landscape of the present world." Sometimes this profound sense of place is addressed in descriptions of monumental settings, such as the vast Montana landscapes in McNickle's *The Surrounded,* or Devils Tower in "Spiritual ride to culminate at Devils Tower," an unsigned article in the 4–11 June 1996 issue of the newspaper *Indian Country Today.* Ortiz has shown how it can also be evoked by images of small, ordinary places and objects, such as a juniper root in a New Mexico dry wash. The persona in "Dry Root in a Wash" in Ortiz's collection *Going for the Rain* (1976) is impatient for rain; the root's presence speaks of a cyclical order bred of "centuries" of waiting and a deeply grounded knowledge that "Underneath the fine sand / it is cool / with crystalline moisture, / the forming rain."

The homing motif is crucial to many genres of Native writing: for instance, in autobiographies as different as the "A Trip Westward" and "My Mother's Curse upon White Settlers" sections of Zitkala-Ša's "An Indian Teacher among Indians" (1900), Mary TallMountain's "You *Can* Go Home Again" in Brian Swann and Arnold Krupat's *I Tell You Now* (1987), or the recollections in *Home Places* (1995), edited by Evers and Ofelia Zepeda; in the departures for Oklahoma, Kansas, and Hawaii and the returns to Navajo Country in the Navajo Luci Tapahonso's poems in *Sáanii Dahataał* (1993); and in many works of fiction, such as Wynema Harjo's nineteenth-century return from the white South to the Creek Nation in Callahan's *Wynema,* Archilde's early-twentieth-century return to the Salish reservation in McNickle's *The Surrounded,* and the late-twentieth-century returns of Will in King's *Medicine River* (1990) and Lipsha in Erdrich's *The Bingo Palace* (1994). These returns offer dramatic stages for cross-cultural identity creations. As William Bevis argues in "Native American Novels: Homing In" in *Recovering the Word* (1987), edited by Swann and Krupat, and as J. Frank Papovich contends in *Approaches to Teaching Momaday's* The Way to Rainy Mountain (1988), edited by Kenneth M. Roemer, the homing motif also presents a distinctive alternative to the "leaving" and "frontier" narratives of non-Indian American literature.

In *Talking to the Moon* Mathews presents another place-related cultural contrast, which is examined by Warrior in *Tribal Secrets.* Mathews identifies the urge toward ornamentation that, in human civilizations, expresses itself in creations that are not directly necessary for the satisfaction of the primal urges of reproduction and survival. Unfortunately, in many non-Indian cultures these creations became divorced from the primal processes, resulting in an "irreversible effect on the land." In contrast, the traditional Osage had expressed their urge toward ornamentation in relation to the primal processes. Warrior cites a crucial passage from *Talking to the Moon* that clarifies this alternative: "Their religion, their concept of God, came out of my blackjacks [the oaks], out of the fear inspired by the elements, and it was colored just as the animals were colored for perfect adjustment." The Osage "mental processes" Matthews continues, "were still under the influence of the natural background, and the Osage religion of Wah-Kon-Tah was as much a product of the blackjacks and the prairie and the physical [human]."

Today, more than half of the two million Indians live in urban areas; nevertheless, the sense of place expressed by Native writers has something to say to them. Many writers demonstrate sympathy for the difficulty of establishing a sense of place by stressing an awareness of the absence of former tribal lands and the absence of Indian sovereignty in Indian country. This awareness can take the form of a painful daily consciousness of places lost. In Silko's *Ceremony* Betonie reminds Tayo that "Indians wake up every morning of their lives to see the land which was stolen, still there, within reach, its theft being flaunted." This awareness can address the effects of past and present removals and relocations, as do many of Rose's powerful "half-breed chronicles" that dramatize the persona's separation from and connection to Hopi landscapes. And in some of the bleakest depictions, the absence of the traditional place or community implies the desperate need for combinations of old and new senses of place. For example, in Geiogamah's play *Body Indian* (1972), which is set in a noticeably unsacred and grubby apartment, the abuse suffered by Bobby (including the theft of his artificial leg) at the hands of his Indian friends obviously implies, as Jeffrey Huntsman says in the introduction to Geiogamah's *New Native American Drama* (1980), that "if Indian people are to survive with a measure of decency and dignity, they must stick together." Place must still mean community.

A fundamental issue confronted by Native American writers is survival – "We all want to survive" is a refrain in the works of the Spokane/Coeur d'Alene Sherman Alexie. Considering Indian survival involves acknowledging both the fact of near extinction and the fact of continuity. In "Where I Ought to Be" Erdrich searches for ways to convey this duality and discovers two striking images: "Many Native American cultures were annihilated more thoroughly than even a nuclear disaster might destroy ours," and it was "as if the population of the United States were to decrease from its present level to the population of Cleveland." Many Indian authors have found ways to incorporate a sense of Native American identity into lives that their ancestors could not have imagined five hundred years ago. Erdrich proclaims that in "the light of enormous loss" Indian writers "must tell the stories of contemporary survivors while protecting and celebrating the cores of cultures left in the wake of catastrophe." The ending of Harjo's poem "Anchorage" is such a telling:

> Everyone laughed at the impossibility of it,
> but also the truth. Because who would believe
> the fantastic and terrible story of all of our survival
>
> those who were never meant
> to survive?

The third issue to be discussed concerns the historical and institutional forces that have shaped the roles of Native American authors and texts. The concepts of identity, authorship, words, place, and survival defined by Native American writers grow out of a historical context that is both rich and tragic. This history includes pre-Columbian tribal cultures, as well as the Native multiculturalism of pre-Columbian intertribal contacts. It includes centuries of extermination by disease, war, and colonialism. It includes the ironic contrast of legal status as sovereign nations, on the one hand, and broken treaties and forced removals, on the other hand. It includes thousands of federal acts, regulations, and policies, such as the 1887 Dawes Act, which resulted in a tremendous reduction of tribal lands; the granting of citizenship to Indians in 1924; the Indian Reorganization Act of 1934; the termination and relocation policies initiated in the 1950s; the Alaskan Native Claims Settlement Act of 1971; and the American Indian Religious Freedom Act of 1978. It includes a complex web of popular culture in film and print. It includes the political activism of Indian organizations such as the Society of American Indians, the Association on American Indian Affairs, the National Congress of American Indians, the National Indian Youth Council, and the American Indian Movement. It also includes the ethnic-studies and women's movements. Various aspects of this history have been examined by Indian authors; among them are Copway, in his *The Traditional History and Characteristic Sketches of the Ojibway Nation* (1850), and, in the twentieth century, McNickle and Dorris. Historical perspectives can be found in novels such as Welch's *Fools Crow* (1986) and Hogan's *Mean Spirit,* as well as in protest literature from Apess's *Indian Nullification of the Unconstitutional Laws of Massachusetts, Relative to the Marshpee Tribe* (1835) to Deloria's *Custer Died for Your Sins; We Talk, You Listen* (1970); *God Is Red;* and *Red Earth, White Lies* (1995). Even if a work does not confront Native American history explicitly, the arguments of an essayist, the actions of the characters in a novel or short story, or the attitudes of a poem's persona can usually be traced back to historical situations.

For Native American authors another aspect of Indian history is the fact that publication has almost always required writing in English, which, in turn, often meant attendance at boarding, mission, or small reservation schools. Daniel F. Littlefield Jr. and James W. Parins's *A Biobibliography of Native American Writers, 1772–1924* (1981) reveals a predominance of tribes that either had early histories of English-based education or were "displaced by non-Native populations" in the East and thereby "cut off from their traditional lifestyles or homelands." Thus, "literary production in English is a direct indication of the degree of acculturation of the tribes." This situation helps to explain the tribal affiliations of the authors of some of the "firsts" in Native writing: the work that was both the first best-seller and the first sermon by an Indian was written by Occom, a Mohegan and a Methodist missionary; the first autobiography was by Apess, a Pequod and Methodist missionary; the first poetry was by Schoolcraft, an Ojibwe; the first novel was by Ridge, a Cherokee; and the first dialect satires were by Posey, a Creek.

Education has been just as important for Native American writing in the second half of the twentieth century. In *Voice of the Turtle: American Indian Literature 1900–1970* (1994) the Laguna/Lakota Paula Gunn Allen draws attention to the GI Bill, which "educated thousands of Native vets." The Indian Education Act of 1972, the Indian Self- Determination and Educational Assistance Act of 1975, and a growing number of tribal colleges all contributed to the pool of potential Indian authors. Academic mentors and programs also played crucial roles in the training and discovery of many of the best-known authors: for example, Ivor Winters of Stanford University fostered and proclaimed Momaday's talents; John Herrmann and Richard Hugo of the University of Montana helped Welch; Erdrich and Harjo attended two of the finest writing programs in the country, at Johns Hopkins University and the University of Iowa, respectively; Kenneth Lincoln of UCLA mentored Sarris; and Alex Kuo of Washington State University at Pullman mentored Alexie.

Even the best educated, most talented writers remain invisible if their works are not published, and which books find publishers depends on the tastes of non-Indian readers. The contrast between two early authors is revealing in this regard: except for *Indian Nullification,* all of Apess's books were self-published; Ridge's *Joaquín Murieta,* on the other hand, found a commercial publisher, W. B. Cooke, who printed Ridge's Cherokee name (Yellow Bird) on the title page and emphasized Ridge's Indian identity in the publisher's preface. Apparently the demand for adventure stories by a "real Indian" was greater than for Apess's biographies of and eulogies for Indian leaders such as King Philip. Nineteenth-century Native American authors were not, however, limited to non-Indian commercial publishers. There were several American Indian newspapers, notably *The Cherokee Phoenix,* begun in 1828, and later *The Cherokee Advocate,* established in 1844, and the short-lived *Copway's American Indian,* published from 10 July to 4 October 1851. After the Civil War there were mission publications, such as the White Earth Reservation's *Progress,* and publications supported by the Hampton Institute and by government schools such as Carlisle and Haskell. By the turn of the twentieth century prestigious non-Indian journals were publishing Indian works; Zitkala-Ša's stories and autobiographical essays, for example, appeared in *Harper's* and the *Atlantic Monthly*. Political journals edited by Indians began to appear during the early years of the century. The second half of the century witnessed an explosion of publications, ranging from Indian Center newsletters and local papers, such as South Dakota's *Shannon County News,* to large tribal and national papers, including *The Navajo Times* and *Indian Country Today* (formerly *The Lakota Times*), and national magazines, such as *Akwesasne Notes,* which in 1995 changed from a tabloid to a slick-paper magazine format. A notable characteristic of many of these publications is their openness to commentary and creative writing, particularly poetry.

For fiction and poetry – especially poetry – small presses and periodicals and special issues of regional journals have been essential outlets for many Indian writers. Particularly noteworthy for introducing important poets are Greenfield Review Press; Strawberry Press; Contact II Publications; the West End Press; the Sun Tracks book series, which began as a journal in the mid 1970s; and the *Blue Cloud Quarterly* chapbooks, edited by Benedictine monks in Marvin, South Dakota. Special issues devoted to "Indian literature" extend back at least to 1917, when *Poetry Magazine* published a collection of "re-creations" by non-Indians of translated songs and chants. Among modern special issues on Native writers, none had a greater initial impact than the Summer 1969 and Summer 1971 issues of the *South Dakota Review,* edited by John R. Milton. Both issues were republished as handsome illustrated paperback books, *The American Indian Speaks* (1969) and *American Indian Two* (1971). The University of Oklahoma Press, the University of Arizona Press, and UCLA Press have series of Native American fiction, poetry, or both. Support for Indian studies at the University of New Mexico, which published Momaday's *The Way to Rainy Mountain;* the University of Nebraska; and, on a more limited scale, at Navajo Community College has fostered interest in Native writing. In 1971 Harper and Row established a Native American series that included Welch's *Winter in the Blood* (1974) and the poetry anthology *Carriers of the Dream Wheel* (1975), edited by Duane Niatum. These works were landmarks in establishing the legitimacy of Native American writing.

Anthologies have had a profound effect in determining which authors and which genres are recognized as important. Silko's dominance of Kenneth Rosen's short-story collection *The Man to Send Rain Clouds* (1974) helped to launch her career, and Niatum's *Carriers of the Dream Wheel* and his *Harper's Anthology of 20th Century Native American Poetry* (1988) helped to convince many critics and English teachers that poetry by Indians was "good" literature. The collection and translation of Native North American oral literature were begun by Jesuits in the early 1600s, but, as Evers points out in "Cycles of Appreciation" in Allen's *Studies in American Indian Literature* (1983), George Cronyn's anthology *The Path on the Rainbow* (1918) "marks one of the first real efforts to offer American Indian oral literature to a general audience as imaginative literature." Mary Austin introduced the collection, and other writers and critics wrote interpretations, often noting similarities between the translations and Imagist poetry. Through the early 1970s the approaches taken by anthologies of oral literature varied greatly; some, such as Margot Astrov's *The Winged Serpent* (1946) and A. Grove Day's *The Sky Clears* (1951), placed emphasis on ethnographic contexts, while others, such as William Brandon's *The Magic World* (1970) and Jerome Rothenberg's *Shaking the Pumpkin* (1972), stressed literary qualities. Despite the differences, these collections demonstrated that Indian literature had existed for centuries and could be appreciated in the form of written English.

One of the differences between the comprehensive anthologies of Native American writing that appeared just after Momaday's 1969 Pulitzer Prize, on the one hand, and the literary anthologies of the 1990s, on the other, suggests a possible disadvantage of bestowing the term *literature* on Indian texts. There were serious flaws in the collections of the early 1970s, but Milton's *The American Indian Speaks,* Shirley Hill Witt and Stan Steiner's *The Way* (1972), Jeannetta Henry's *The American Indian Reader: Literature* (1973), Thomas E. Sanders and Walter W. Peek's *Literature of the American Indian* (1973), and Frederick W. Turner III's *The Portable North American Indian Reader* (1973, 1974) included essays by Indians. The more recent multigenre anthologies, such as Alan R. Velie's revised *American Indian Literature* (1991) and Vizenor's *Native American Literature* (1995), are in many ways superior to the earlier collections, but they include no essays. A possible reason for the difference is that in the early 1970s "Red Power" activism made the inclusion of social and protest essays relevant, while, at the same time, there was not much rediscovered or recognized new fiction or poetry available; thus, there was room for the inclusion of essays. In *Tribal Secrets,* however, Warrior identifies another possible reason: "an unfortunate prejudice among scholars against American Indian critical, as opposed to fictional, poetic, oral, or autobiographical, writings." In other words, as Indian texts came to be perceived as literature, editors tended to lean toward the familiar genres of fiction and poetry.

Even though anthologists have occasionally succumbed to generic blind spots, the collections have made visible and have legitimized particular genres of writing by Indians. Niatum's two anthologies clearly helped to make Indian poetry respectable. Because the best-known novels by Native Americans are readily available, the role of fiction anthologies has been less critical. Still, Rosen's *The Man to Send Rain Clouds* gained recognition for a major author – Silko – and for contemporary Native fiction, and more-recent collections from major commercial publishers, such as Dell's *Talking Leaves* (1991), edited by Craig Lesley, continue to draw attention to both established and new fiction writers. Earlier fiction writers are also being rediscovered in collections such as Bernd Peyer's *The Elders Wrote* (1982) and *The Singing Spirit: Early Short Stories* (1989) and Allen's *Voice of the Turtle.* These rediscovery efforts have been enhanced by Helen Jaskoski's essay collection *Early Native American Writing* (1996). Until the mid 1990s the only multitribal collection of autobiographical writing was Swann and Krupat's *I Tell You Now,* which was limited to memoirs by contemporary writers, but that situation changed with the appearance of Krupat's *Native American Autobiography* (1994), Arlene Hirschfelder's *Native Heritage: Personal Accounts by American Indians, 1790 to the Present* (1995), and Jane B. Katz's *Messengers of the Wind* (1995). Three of Geiogamah's plays are available in his *New Native American Drama;* Vizenor and Witalec include drama in their respective anthologies, *Native American Literature* and *Smoke Rising* (1995); *Gathering Our Own* (1996) collects three Institute of American Indian Arts plays; and Momaday, Riggs, and Glancy have received praise for their plays. There are several collections of Native American women's writing and oral narratives, including Katz's *I Am the Fire of Time* (1977), Rayna Green's *That's What She Said* (1984), and Allen's *Spider Woman's Granddaughters* (1989); and Dexter Fisher's *The Third Woman* (1980) includes a major section on Native women writers. There is at least one anthology devoted to gay Native American literature, Will Roscoe's *Living the Spirit* (1988). The various types of anthologies helped the editors of anthologies of general American literature, especially those published by Heath, HarperCollins, Prentice Hall, and W. W. Norton, by prescreening the Native writing.

Although journals, small presses, university and commercial publishers, and anthologies are the most visible forces in shaping the discovery, rediscovery, and recognition of writing by Native Americans, scholarly influences have also played an important role. Ruoff's *American Indian Literatures* includes bibliographies, overviews, and studies of individual authors that have helped to shape the canon of Native American literature. Theoretical analyses can be found in Murray's *Forked Tongues,* Owens's *Other Destinies,* the early chapters of Ruppert's *Mediation in Contemporary Native American Fiction* (1995), and Krupat's *The Voice in the Margin.* The increasing use of poststructuralist critical approaches is evident in collections of critical essays, especially Vizenor's *Narrative Chance* and Krupat's *New Voices in Native American Literary Criticism* (1993). This theoretical approach, succeeding the use of ethnographic contextualizations and the New Criticism to interpret writings by Indians, has raised questions about the appropriateness of applying non-Indian interpretive concepts to Indian texts. Of course, the authors themselves were influenced not only by their Native heritages but also by their extensive schooling in their eras' non-Indian critical perspectives – Christian iconography for Occom and Apess, Romanticism for Eastman, feminism for Allen, modernism for Momaday, and postmodernism for Vizenor. Still, critics such as Warrior in *Tribal Secrets* and Sarris in *Keeping Slug Woman Alive* point out that there is a history of writing by Native American intellectuals that can provide quite different critical models; and, of course, there are the centuries-old paradigms of aesthetic, ethical, and narrative structures to be found in Indian oral literatures.

The scholarship that has facilitated the movement of Native writing into the canon and the classrooms has benefited from institutional support and scholarly organizations. Two key events were the formation of the Association for the Study of American Indian Literatures (ASAIL) at the 1972 Modern Language Association Convention and the MLA/National Endowment for the Humanities "Native American Literature: Criticism and Curriculum" Summer Seminar in Flagstaff, Arizona, in 1977. Outgrowths of the former were the journal *SAIL* and the newsletter *ASAIL Notes.* These two publications, along with *American Indian Quarterly, American Indian Culture and Research Journal,* and *Wicazo Sa Review,* carry most of the articles on Native writers. Two institutions, in particular, have fostered writing by American Indians. Seven years before Momaday won the Pulitzer Prize, the Institute of American Indian Arts (IAIA) was formed in Santa Fe with Bureau of Indian Affairs support. IAIA was especially effective in encouraging poetry; it sponsored one of the first anthologies of contemporary Indian poetry for classroom use, Terry Allen's *The Whispering Wind* (1972). Twenty years later the largest gathering ever of American Indian writers and storytellers was held at the University of Oklahoma, when around three hundred attended Returning the Gift, the first North American Native Writers' Festival. Among the many results of the festival were Bruchac's anthology *Returning the Gift* (1994); a newsletter, *Moccasin Telegraph,* that includes leads for publication and Internet addresses; and the Wordcraft Circle of Native Writers and Storytellers.

Despite the accomplishments that have been made since the late 1960s, as late as 1995 a catalogue, *Films for the Humanities and Sciences,* could feature a Native American novelists section in which Momaday is described as "Best known, of course, for *Bury My Heart at Wounded Knee*" – a 1970 work that was actually written by Dee Brown, a non-Indian. Such an error is a reminder that the existence and nature of Native American writing are still unknown to many readers. Still, recognition has been impressive. Besides Momaday's Pulitzer Prize, accolades for individual authors include Silko's 1981 MacArthur Foundation grant and Erdrich's National Book Critics Circle Award for *Love Medicine* (1984). Indian writers appear in virtually every current college and high-school anthology of American literature. Just as important, scholarly work is enabling teachers to get beyond the stereotype, curiosity, and tokenism stages so that they and their students can grapple with the challenging identity, authorship, language, land, sovereignty, and survival issues that make Native American writing so distinctive and significant. This *DLB* volume is intended to contribute to this continuing process of recognition and definition.

– *Kenneth M. Roemer*

Acknowledgments

This book was produced by Bruccoli Clark Layman, Inc. Karen L. Rood is senior editor for the *Dictionary of Literary Biography* series. Philip B. Dematteis was the in-house editor.

Production manager is Samuel W. Bruce. Photography editors are Julie E. Frick and Margaret Meriwether. Photographic copy work was performed by Joseph M. Bruccoli. Layout and graphics supervisor is Pamela D. Norton. Copyediting supervisor is Laurel M. Gladden Gillespie. Typesetting supervisor is Kathleen M. Flanagan. Systems manager is Chris Elmore. Laura Pleicones and L. Kay Webster are editorial associates. The production staff includes Phyllis A. Avant, Stephanie L. Capes, Ann M. Cheschi, Melody W. Clegg, Patricia Coate, Joyce Fowler, Brenda A. Gillie, Rebecca Mayo, Kathy Lawler Merlette, Jeff Miller, Marie Parker, Delores Plastow, Patricia F. Salisbury, William L. Thomas Jr., and Allison Trussell.

Walter W. Ross, Steven Gross, and Mark McEwan did library research. They were assisted by the following librarians at the Thomas Cooper Library of the University of South Carolina: Linda Holderfield and the interlibrary-loan staff; reference-department head Virginia Weathers; reference librarians Marilee Birchfield, Stefanie Buck, Stefanie DuBose, Rebecca Feind, Karen Joseph, Donna Lehman, Charlene Loope, Anthony McKissick, Jean Rhyne, Kwamine Simpson, and Virginia Weathers; circulation-department head Caroline Taylor; and acquisitions-searching supervisor David Haggard.

The editor would like to acknowledge his debt to A. LaVonne Brown Ruoff, who contributed three entries to this volume, made extensive suggestions about which authors to include, and evaluated an early draft of the introduction. Another debt of gratitude goes to all the other contributors, who also gave advice about including particular writers. Other scholars, editors, and authors who offered valuable suggestions about which writers should be treated include Peggy Ackerberg, Helen Bannan, Betty Bell, Joseph Bruchac, Dexter Fisher Cirillo, Laura Coltelli, Larry Evers, Lee Francis, Jeff Huntsman, Arnold Krupat, Lanniko Lee, Andrea Lerner, Daniel Littlefield, Jack Marken, Jim Payne, Carter Revard, Kay Sands, Greg Sarris, Rodney Simard, Donald B. Smith, Joseph Stout, Brian Swann, Clifford Trafzer, Lawana Trout, Alan R. Velie, Robert Warrior, Andrew Wiget, and Charles Woodard.

The publishers acknowledge the generous assistance of William R. Cagle, director of the Lilly Library, Indiana University, and his staff, who provided many of the illustrations in this volume. Their work represents the highest standards of librarianship and research.

Dictionary of Literary Biography® • Volume One Hundred Seventy-Five

Native American Writers of the United States

Dictionary of Literary Biography

Sherman Alexie

(7 October 1966 -)

Susan B. Brill
Bradley University

BOOKS: *I Would Steal Horses* (Niagara Falls, N.Y.: Slipstream, 1992);

The Business of Fancydancing: Stories and Poems (Brooklyn, N.Y.: Hanging Loose, 1992);

Old Shirts & New Skins (Los Angeles: American Indian Studies Center, University of California, Los Angeles, 1993);

First Indian on the Moon (Brooklyn, N.Y.: Hanging Loose, 1993);

The Lone Ranger and Tonto Fistfight in Heaven (New York: Atlantic Monthly, 1993);

Seven Mourning Songs for the Cedar Flute I Have Yet to Learn to Play (Walla Walla, Wash.: Whitman College Book Arts Lab, 1994);

Water Flowing Home (Boise, Idaho: Limberlost, 1995);

Reservation Blues (New York: Atlantic Monthly, 1995);

Indian Killer (New York: Atlantic Monthly, 1996);

The Summer of Black Widows (Brooklyn, N.Y.: Hanging Loose, 1996).

RECORDING: *Reservation Blues: The Soundtrack,* by Alexie and Jim Boyd, Thunderwolf Productions, TWPRB95, 1995.

RADIO: "The Indian Fighter," *The Sound of Writing: National Public Radio's Literary Magazine of the Air,* NPR, 1995.

SELECTED PERIODICAL PUBLICATIONS – UNCOLLECTED: "White Men Can't Drum," *New York Times Magazine,* 4 October 1992, pp. 30–31;

Sherman Alexie at the time of Indian Killer *(photograph by Marion Ettlinger)*

"Sweet Sioux," review of Joseph Iron Eye Dudley's *Choteau Creek, New York Times Book Review,* 11 October 1992, p. 24;

"Flight," *Ploughshares,* 20 (Spring 1994): 38–43;

"A Few Reservation Notes on Love and Hunger," *Left Bank,* 6 (Summer 1994): 94–103;

"The Writer's Notebook," *Zyzzyva,* 10 (Fall 1994);

"Beyond Talking Indian Chiefs," *New York Times,* 23 October 1994, II: 1, 44;

"Generation Red," *Seattle Weekly,* 20 (15 February 1995): 16–23;

"Airplane, Airport, Airline, Error in the Bottom of the Ninth Inning," "Remembering the Last Great War," "Why I Am Afraid," and "Indian Woman, Asleep," *Forkroads,* 1 (Fall 1995): 25–27.

Sherman Alexie is the "Indian du jour" of the mainstream publishing industry, as he notes in his 1995 *Tonic* interview with Kelly Myers. Alexie has published seven books and three chapbooks in less than five years; while such productivity is remarkable in itself, Alexie's rapid-fire writing and publishing are all the more extraordinary because each work builds on the previous writings, showing ever-increasing degrees of polish and control as well as experimentation with diverse literary forms and styles.

Sherman Joseph Alexie Jr. was born on 7 October 1966 in Spokane, Washington, to Sherman Joseph Alexie, a Coeur d'Alene Indian, and Lillian Agnes Cox Alexie, of Spokane, Flathead, Colville, and white descent. A registered member of the Spokane tribe through his mother, Alexie lived and attended school on the Spokane reservation in Wellpinit, Washington, until he transferred to the white high school in Reardan. He studied at Gonzaga University from 1985 to 1987 and at Washington State University from 1988 to 1991. At Washington State he took a creative-writing class with Alex Kuo; he has not stopped writing since that class, publishing in such periodicals as the *Beloit Poetry Journal, Caliban, Esquire, Forkroads, Hanging Loose, The Journal of Ethnic Studies, The Kenyon Review, Left Bank, New York Quarterly, Ploughshares, Slipstream,* and *Zyzzyva.* As Kuo notes in his introduction to Alexie's second book, *The Business of Fancydancing: Stories and Poems* (1992), "Alexie's work has escaped the pervasive influence of writing workshops, academic institutions and their subsidized intellect." Hailed by James R. Kincaid in *The New York Times* (3 May 1992) as "one of the major lyric voices of our time," Alexie writes from his own experiences, his own heritage and traditions, and in his own distinctive storytelling voice.

Alexie's work has already garnered many honors and awards. In 1991 he received a Washington State Arts Commission poetry fellowship. In 1992 his first book, *I Would Steal Horses,* won Slipstream's fifth annual chapbook contest; the National Endowment for the Arts awarded him a poetry fellowship; and *The New York Times* named *The Business of Fancydancing* Notable Book of the Year. In 1993 *The Lone Ranger and Tonto Fistfight in Heaven* received a PEN/Hemingway Award for Best First Book of Fiction and the Great Lakes College Association Best First Book of Fiction Award. In 1994 Alexie received a Lila Wallace–Reader's Digest Award. Although he had left Washington State University three credits short of a degree, in 1995 the university gave Alexie a B.A. in American studies and an Alumni Achievement Award.

Alexie's first four books appeared in little more than a year. *The Business of Fancydancing* appeared in 1992 and was followed in 1993 by *Old Shirts & New Skins, First Indian on the Moon,* and *The Lone Ranger and Tonto Fistfight in Heaven.* Like many of his fellow Indian writers, Alexie is a storyteller. His powerful stories about contemporary Indian life in the United States deal with such themes as pain and humor, hunger and survival, love and anger, broken treaties, Manifest Destiny, basketball, car wrecks, commodity food, U.S. Department of Housing and Urban Development houses, smallpox blankets, and promises and dreams.

The Business of Fancydancing is a collection of stories and poems about reservation life – a life of alcoholism, commodity food, broken families, and a pervasive racism that offers "Crazy Horse dreams, the kind that / don't come true." The volume is divided into three sections: "Distances," "Evolution," and "Crazy Horse Dreams." Perhaps the bleakest of Alexie's published works, it holds out no hope for improvement in the lives of the characters.

Old Shirts & New Skins, a volume of poetry, also expresses a bleak outlook and follows a tripartite division. The first section, "Indian Education," centers around the clash of the dominant and Indian cultures in various educational, religious, and social institutions. "Songs from the Film" looks at popular-culture media images of Indian America. "Drought" depicts the effects of racism on Indians.

First Indian on the Moon is a collection of short prose pieces and poetry that, while not exactly hopeful, offers a fuller image of Indian life. Divided into five sections – "Influences," "A Reservation Table of the Elements," "Tiny Treaties," "The Native American Broadcasting System," and "All I Wanted to Do Was Dance" – the book ends with a degree of optimism that reflects Alexie's growing success as a writer. One of the final poems in the volume, "Song," ends with a confidence and faith that are largely absent from Alexie's earlier work: "Believe me, the Indian men are rising from alleys and doorways, rising from self-hatred and self-pity, rising up on horses of their own making. Believe me, the warriors are coming back." Reviewing *First Indian on the Moon* in *The Bloomsbury Review* (May–June 1993), Carl L. Bankston III says that "Alexie's

Dust jacket for Alexie's first novel, the story of an Indian rock band

new book will be familiar in its characters, style, themes, and atmosphere to all of his readers. He is not exploring new territory. But he is reworking the old ground productively, like a gardener who sticks to his own backyard."

The Lone Ranger and Tonto Fistfight in Heaven, a collection of short prose pieces, each of which combines fiction with nonfiction, also presents more-realistic and well-rounded images of contemporary Indian America. While many of the images are harsh and raw, they are counterbalanced by passages depicting the love and laughter of people whose human connections enable them to survive in a world that seems increasingly bleak and hopeless.

A writer who is willing to take risks, Alexie transforms traditional Western literary forms and models into new ones. His work is part of an Indian storytelling tradition that resists disappearing through its expected transformation into written literature. Here Alexie is following in a developed tradition of other American Indian writers who have struggled against the Western literary tradition in order to convey their own stories, words, and worlds on paper in ways that do not compromise their selves and their vision. Other Indian writers whose work is especially important to Alexie include Simon Ortiz, Leslie Marmon Silko, Adrian C. Louis, and Luci Tapahonso.

Many of the strategies used by such writers are to be found in Alexie's writing. Occasional shifts to a second-person voice, for example, allow the writer-narrator to speak directly to his or her listener-reader – in some cases providing information non-Indian readers need in order to understand the story. In the oral storytelling tradition that is prevalent throughout Indian America, the listeners are as much a part of the story and of the storytelling event as are the storyteller and the story's characters. In "My Heroes Have Never Been Cowboys" (*First Indian on the Moon*) Alexie begins in a protective and distancing third-person voice, commenting on the contrast between the history taught in the reservation schools and the lived history of the students' own lives. In the second section Alexie switches to the second person: "Did you know that in 1492 every Indian instantly became an extra in the Great American Western?" This shift personalizes Alexie's telling, bringing it and the reader closer together as the diverse worlds of the reservation and the dominant culture not only clash but also begin to converge.

Alexie invites his readers into the worlds he creates in his writing, but this invitation is fraught with the history of five hundred years of welcomings and betrayals. As he says in "My Heroes Have Never Been Cowboys," "Every frame of the black and white western is a treaty; every scene in this elaborate serial is a promise" – treaties repeatedly broken, promises rarely kept. He writes in the final section of the poem,

> Every song remains the same here in America, this country of the Big Sky and Manifest Destiny, this country of John Wayne and broken treaties. Arthur, I have no words which can save our lives, no words approaching forgiveness, no words flashed across the screen at the reservation drive-in, no words promising either of us top billing. Extras, Arthur, we're all extras.

A work that initially opens itself up to its white readers thus concludes by pushing them back into the more expected literary role of voyeurs, of outside observers. In the end the speaker in the poem directs his words to Arthur, a fellow Indian. Here Alexie is no longer speaking directly to his readers but indirectly as the telling narrows to a world that includes the storyteller, Arthur, and other Indians. This shift in voice underscores the complexity of the entire history of Indian and non-Indian relations. At times Alexie's writing is open and welcoming to all, Indian and non-Indian alike; at other times it is more cautious and protective and even overtly distancing with an anger that reflects generations of oppression.

Alexie's works include variations on the formulaic introductions and conclusions that traditionally bound oral stories. The beginnings establish the time and place of the story, usually situating it in a mythic past: "Beginning somewhere near the reservation . . . " ("Breaking out the Shovel," *Old Shirts & New Skins*); "It was the summer of grasshoppers . . . " ("Indian Summer," *Old Shirts & New Skins*); "I remember when . . . " ("Indian Boy Love Song [#3]" and "Indian Boy Love Song [#4]," *The Business of Fancydancing*); "During the sixties . . . " ("Because My Father Always Said He was the Only Indian Who Saw Jimi Hendrix Play 'The Star-Spangled Banner' at Woodstock," *The Lone Ranger and Tonto Fistfight in Heaven*); "In the one hundred and eleven years since the creation of the Spokane Indian Reservation . . . " (*Reservation Blues,* 1995). The endings provide the transition from the story world back to the world of the listener-reader, but in such a way that the story is shown to be relevant to the listener-reader. In many of the endings the voice shifts to the second person and speaks directly to the listener-reader; in others it shifts to a first-person plural voice of inclusion; and in other cases the endings provide helpful explanations for the reader-listener's understanding of the poems and stories: "Imagine a story that puts wood in the fireplace" ("A Train Is an Order of Occurrence Designed to Lead to Some Result," *The Lone Ranger and Tonto Fistfight in Heaven*); "you can't stop a man from trying to survive, no matter where he is" ("War All the Time," *The Business of Fancydancing*); "we all get to choose" ("When I Die," *The Business of Fancydancing*); "And we laughed" ("The Approximate Size of My Favorite Tumor," *The Lone Ranger and Tonto Fistfight in Heaven*); "Jesus, we all want to survive" ("Family Portrait," *The Lone Ranger and Tonto Fistfight in Heaven*); "you must remember that Muhammad Ali was still standing / he stood up" ("Split Decisions," *First Indian on the Moon*); "it meant we were all alive and that was enough" ("Influences," *First Indian on the Moon*).

One poignant example can be seen in the short story "Witnesses, Secret and Not," which concludes the collection *The Lone Ranger and Tonto Fistfight in Heaven.* Like virtually all of Alexie's writing, it focuses on the struggles of Indians to survive in a world that transforms everyday experiences into traumas. A thirteen-year-old boy, presumably Alexie, learns what it means to be a man and, more specifically, an Indian man; as Alexie writes, "there ain't no self-help manuals for that last one." The boy accompanies his father to Spokane to meet with the police: Jerry Vincent, one of the father's friends, had disappeared ten years earlier and had later been found shot and buried; the police have called the father in for his annual questioning about the murder. Vincent's disappearance serves as a metaphor for Indian survival and loss: " 'He wasn't the first one to disappear like that. No way,' my father said. . . . 'All those relocation programs sent reservation Indians to the cities, and sometimes they just got swallowed up.' "

The trip to Spokane demonstrates the pervasive threats to Indian survival that surround even seemingly simple and straightforward events. Their car "fancydanced across the ice" on the road into town; the brown air of Spokane tastes like mud in their mouths; an old Indian man asks them for money on the street; and their diet sodas reveal the father and son as diabetics. "Sometimes it does feel like we are all defined by the food we eat, though. My father and I would be potted meat product, corned beef hash, fry bread, and hot chili. We would be potato chips, hot dogs, and fried bologna." Government-subsidized commodity food is one of the signs of Indian America that appear throughout Alexie's writing – a sign of particular significance to the writer, whose diabetes manifests the effects of his childhood diet.

As the boy watches "his father walk toward the police station, wearing old jeans and a red T-shirt," he looks "as Indian as you can get. . . . As soon as I get off the reservation, among all the white people, every Indian gets exaggerated. My father's braids looked three miles long." The boy learns that being an Indian man means being a second-class citizen in a world that defines a man as white. When the questioning is over, the boy and the father return home to have dinner with the rest of the family. "When we got home everybody was there, everybody. My father sat at the table and nearly cried into his food. Then, of course, he did cry into his food and we all watched him. All of us." "All of us" reaches out to include the reader-listener, who joins the family in watching the father's tears. The narrator goes on to say, "My father got completely out of control once because he lost the car keys. Explain that to a sociologist." Alexie's reader-listener is thus welcomed into the story as a close friend, one who is offered an intimate understanding of the story beyond that available to a sociologist observing from a scientific distance.

Alexie's first four books are tied together by his conscious use of repetition from story to story and from volume to volume. Characters, events, and even sentences are resurrected and transformed. As Kristan Sarvé-Gorham notes in a review of *The Business of Fancydancing* in *Studies in American Indian Literature* (Summer 1995), "like repetition in oral literature, memorable lines from *Fancydancing* – 'There is nothing as white as the white girl an Indian boy loves' ('Distances') – surface in *Old Shirts & New Skins* ('Red Blues')."

Old Shirts & New Skins includes a poem written for Alexie's younger brother: "Poem for James Who Asked Me Why Everything Hurts so Much." In the poem James creates a trap for wasps: a large jar of water with floating marshmallows for bait. The trap is ten-year-old James's revenge for the pain of his life. The wasps, symbols of an abusive world, "struggle against water and drown. / *Look,* he said. *One of those wasps is using another one / like a raft.*" The wasps, like James and his brother, struggle to survive. Alexie ends the poem by explaining to the reader-listener, "It was the smallest possible war and still / too large."

As they watch the wasps, Alexie reflects: "We all want to survive." This line returns with greater insistence in "Family Portrait" in *The Lone Ranger and Tonto Fistfight in Heaven.* As Alexie remembers his family, his most vivid recollection is of the ever-present intrusion of the television set, which "was always loud, too loud, until every emotion was measured by the half hour" as the children "waited for the conversation and the conversion, watched wasps and flies battering against the windows. We were children; we were open mouths. Open in hunger, in anger, in laughter, in prayer. Jesus, we all want to survive." Thus, Alexie's explanation at the end of "Poem for James" becomes in "Family Portrait" a prayer of desperation.

As Louis Owens points out in the *Boston Sunday Globe* (29 August 1993), "In 'Family Portrait,' language always means what it does not say or seems to say what it refuses to mean. The discourse of the invaders dominates and distorts." For example:

> The television was always loud, too loud, until
> every conversation was distorted, fragmented.
> "Dinner" sounded like "Leave me alone."
> "I love you" sounded like "Inertia."
> "Please" sounded like "Sacrifice."

Survival is perhaps the omnipresent theme of these four books. In the poem "War All the Time" (*The Business of Fancydancing*), in which Crazy Horse serves as a metaphor for an Indian Vietnam veteran, Alexie writes: "you can't stop a man / from trying to survive." At the end of "The Game Between the Jews and the Indians Is Tied" (*First Indian on the Moon*) Alexie tells his reader "every once in a while / we can remind each other / that we are both survivors and children / and grandchildren of survivors." In "The Only Traffic Signal on the Reservation Doesn't Flash Red Anymore" in *The Lone Ranger and Tonto Fistfight in Heaven,* a story about a promising high-school basketball player who is beginning to find his future at the bottom of beer bottles, Alexie emphasizes the capacity of reservation Indians to survive:

> It's hard to be optimistic on the reservation. When a glass sits on a table here, people don't wonder if it's half filled or half empty. They just hope it's good beer. Still Indians have a way of surviving. But it's almost like Indians can easily survive the big stuff. Mass murder, loss of language and land rights. It's

the small things that hurt the most. The white waitress who wouldn't take an order, Tonto, the Washington Redskins.

Throughout Alexie's works themes, images, and phrases recur with a resurrective power that reflects Alexie's own transformation of the oral tradition. The image of waiting – a metaphor for promises, treaties, and dreams deferred, if not altogether broken – pervades Alexie's writing. "I'm waiting. / I'm waiting for someone to tell the truth," in "Shoes" (*Old Shirts & New Skins*), becomes in "Split Decisions" (*First Indian on the Moon*) the more insistent "I / am / waiting / for / someone / to tell / the / truth." In "Traveling," the short story that begins *The Business of Fancydancing,* the goal of the waiting is more modest: "I turned back to the van [that had run out of fuel], put my shoulder to the cold metal and waited for something to change." But little ever changes in the lives of Alexie's characters. Commodity food, alcoholism, and desperation are constants in the stories. In "Indian Education" (*The Lone Ranger and Tonto Fistfight in Heaven*) Alexie tells of a punishment he received in the third grade: "I stood alone in the corner, faced the wall, and waited for the punishment to end. I'm still waiting." The futile waiting for dreams to be fulfilled, promises to be kept, and treaties to be honored explains why Alexie writes in "Amusements" (*The Lone Ranger and Tonto Fistfight in Heaven*), a story about an old drunk Indian tormented by two younger Indians: "We wear fear now like a turquoise choker, like a familiar shawl." As he further explains in "Year of the Indian" (*First Indian on the Moon*), "We've all got so many reasons, real and imagined, to drink."

Two events that recur throughout the early volumes seem to epitomize Alexie's worldview and the realities of reservation life. One is the death of his sister and her husband in a trailer fire – the smoke alarm was insufficient to wake the two, who were passed out from alcohol. As Alexie poignantly says in "Fire Storm" (*First Indian on the Moon*), "*The cause of the blaze is still under investigation*": while the authorities search for the immediate cause of the fire, Alexie's italics underscore the fact that the ultimate causes extend back through five hundred years of history. The other event is also an alcohol-related death; as Alexie describes it in "A Reservation Table of the Elements" (*First Indian on the Moon*): "An Indian man drowned here on my reservation when he passed out and fell face down into a mud puddle. There is no other way to say this." In the story "Every Little Hurricane" (*The Lone Ranger and Tonto Fistfight in Heaven*) a boy named Victor – one of several characters who, along with Thomas Builds-the-Fire and Junior, are loosely based on Alexie – considers the significance of the man's death: "Even at five, Victor understood what that meant, how it defined nearly everything." But as Thomas Builds-the-Fire protests in "Special Delivery" in *The Business of Fancydancing,* "This isn't how the story is supposed to be." Human lives are not meant to be continuously under siege. Alexie's stories are told starkly and directly, and yet, throughout, there is the constant theme of survival. As Jennifer Gillan comments, "The twentieth-century fancydancer makes music by fingering all the discordant strings of his life; his survival is entwined with fancydancing, the stickgame, even alcoholism, government dependence, and basketball. And it is by playing his music that Alexie tries to find his way home."

The response of reviewers to Alexie's first four books has been strongly positive. In *Western American Literature* (Summer 1993) Andrea-Bess Baxter says that *The Business of Fancydancing* "is an outstanding collection of poetry, prose, vignettes and epigrams that will surely launch him firmly into the Native American literature scene." Leslie Ullman points out in *The Kenyon Review* (Summer 1993) that *The Business of Fancydancing* "is tautly written and versatile in its use of forms, which include prose vignettes, two villanelle, and several delicately constructed, songlike poems, making skillful use of white space." James R. Kincaid writes in *The New York Times Book Review* (3 May 1992) that *The Business of Fancydancing* "is so wide-ranging, dexterous and consistently capable of raising your neck hair that it enters at once into our ideas of who we are and how we might be, makes us speak and hear his words over and over, call others into the room or over the phone to repeat them. Mr. Alexie's is one of the major lyric voices of our time." The critics have consistently pointed to the power of Alexie's writing to evoke Indian life. Baxter says that "Sherman Alexie's powerful voice exemplifies how imagination and the power of words, native or not, can be the most potent weapon of all. His writing challenges the reader to listen and listen well and to confront an honest portrait of the contemporary Indian world, a world where, all too often, 'suddenly, nothing happens.' " Regarding *Old Shirts & New Skins,* Bankston says that "Alexie . . . combines a gift for startling associations and a fluid ease of literary style with an intimate familiarity with the quotidian facts of modern reservation life."

Perhaps more than any other Indian writer today, Alexie presents a clear and stark portrayal of reservation America. As J. R. Hepworth notes in *Choice* (May 1994), "Alexie's retellings may just be the right mix to civilize a savage mainstream culture, for they bridge the gulf between popular misperceptions and the realities of contemporary Indian life." Hepworth particularly points to Alexie's "affection for the icons of popular culture and its institutions – Elvis, 7-Eleven, AT&T, film, television, automobiles, neon – as well as the depth of his knowledge about history and myth, [that permit] him to play freely with traditional European literary forms (including the captivity narrative) and create his own unmistakable style." And Joseph Bruchac, reviewing *First Indian on the Moon* in *Small Press* (Winter 1994), writes that Alexie's depictions of "contemporary Native life" are "so seldom caught in print that I found myself holding my breath as I raced from poem to poem."

The Lone Ranger and Tonto Fistfight in Heaven has garnered the most critical attention. In *The New York Times Book Review* (17 October 1993) Reynolds Price comments on the simplicity of Alexie's prose, noting that "the reader is expected to perform a number of jobs that are generally assumed by the writer." The interrelational act of storytelling, in which teller and listener work together to cocreate the story, is part of Alexie's literary method. Owens says that "Alexie's prose startles and dazzles with unexpected, impossible-to-anticipate moves, like the perfect reservation pointguard whose passes sometimes catch you flatfooted and right in the face. It is a prose that takes risks and seldom stumbles." In the *Edmonton Journal* (9 January 1994) Paula Simons claims that "Alexie's deep dark humor and his tremendous delight in wordplay make even the most bleak and hopeless of stories a joy to read." She particularly appreciates Alexie's "tough-minded, funny, postmodern vision." In *Review of Contemporary Fiction* (Fall 1993) Brian Schneider praises Alexie's "original narrative voice, which mixes mythmaking with lyrical prose and captures the nation-within-a-nation status of American Indians and the contradictions such a status produces, and more important, the survival of a people through mythmaking rooted in their everyday lives."

Critical response to *Reservation Blues* has been more restrained. While some reviewers of the earlier works found fault with Alexie's use of repetition, undeveloped characters, and lack of plot – all elements that differentiate literary forms that are more influenced by oral traditions from those that are more strictly literary – reviewers have tended to find in *Reservation Blues* both the strengths and weaknesses of a first novel. Silko, reviewing the work in *The Nation* (12 June 1995), says: "It is difficult not to imagine *Reservation Blues* as a reflection of the ambivalence that a young, gifted author might have about 'success' in the ruthless, greed-driven world of big publishing."

The novel centers around the brief career of an Indian rock-and-roll band named Coyote Springs. Playing in reservation bars, the band is scouted by two Cavalry Records executives, George Wright and Phil Sheridan – named after two notorious nineteenth-century U.S. Army generals who fought the Spokanes and slaughtered thousands of their horses – and brought to a recording studio in New York City. There the band disintegrates. Coyote Springs's failed recording session and the members' retreat to the reservation demonstrate that Indians should never expect much from a racist country built on the legacies of Manifest Destiny, genocide, and greed. One band member commits suicide; another turns to alcohol; the remaining three leave the reservation for Spokane, where one of them has been promised a job with the telephone company.

Each chapter of the novel begins with the lyrics of one of the band's blues songs, and the titles of the songs double as chapter titles: a song about being poor and hungry is titled "Reservation Blues"; another, about a broken heart and broken promises, is called "Treaties"; and a song about government relocation policies is "Urban Indian Blues." Although each chapter begins with a song, there is no song ending the novel – an absence that underscores an ending that, while not totally bleak, is hardly upbeat and hopeful. (The songs have been put to music by Alexie and Jim Boyd and are available on cassette and compact disc as *Reservation Blues: The Soundtrack,* 1995.) Brief appearances by the blues guitarist Robert Johnson serve as the framing device for the novel; it is Johnson's magical guitar that transforms Victor, a member of the band, into a brilliant guitar player. The band's songs focus on broken hearts; distant fathers; illness; death by accident, murder, and suicide; the abuses of "the black robes . . . in the name of Jesus"; and the strength of Indian women, especially grandmothers. Alexie's gift for memorable aphoristic statements is on display in the novel:

> "Sometimes," Checkers said, "I hate being Indian."
> "Ain't that the true test?" Chess said, "You ain't really Indian unless there was some point in your life that you didn't want to be."
> "Enit," Thomas said.

Dust jacket for Alexie's second novel, a murder mystery set in Seattle

Alexie's second novel, *Indian Killer* (1996), is a murder mystery that builds its events on the foundations of racism, alienation, and lost and confused notions of self. The plot centers around a series of murders of white men in Seattle. In the media the murderer is dubbed the "Indian Killer," further exacerbating tensions between the white and Indian communities in the area. Alexie includes and plays on romanticized stereotypes held by white people about Indians as a means of exploding those preconceived notions as dramatically as the "Indian Killer" murders white men. In the chapter "Introduction to Native American Literature" Marie, an Indian student enrolled in a University of Washington class in Native American literature, clashes with her white professor, Dr. Mather, whose syllabus "included three anthologies of traditional Indian stories edited by white men, two nonfiction studies of Indian spirituality written by white women, a book of traditional Indian poetry translations edited by a Polish-American Jewish man, and an Indian murder mystery written by some local white writer named Jack Wilson, who claimed he was a Shilshomish Indian." Dr. Mather's syllabus, lectures, and interpretations of Indian literature demonstrate his erroneous and disturbingly romanticized misconceptions about Indians and their cultures and literatures.

The Summer of Black Widows (1996), Alexie's most recent volume of poetry, continues the threads interwoven throughout his earlier poetry collections, but in a decidedly more hopeful vein. "The First and Last Ghost Dance of Lester Falls Apart" tells of the return of the buffalo and their defiance on being sent to a zoo. Even in the buffaloes' removal Alexie sees hope in their intelligent stares that make white people nervous. Alexie ends the poem: "Everything beautiful / begins somewhere." In "The Exaggeration of Despair" Alexie points to the power of the sacred to overcome the horrors of the world. He ends this poem: "and this is my grandmother who saw, before the white men came, / three ravens with white necks, and knew our God was going to change / I open the door / and invite the wind inside." Throughout this volume, as in all of his other works, Alexie demonstrates the creative and destructive power of stories. When allied with truth, stories have a healing power to bring back the buffalo and the sacred. As Alexie begins "Sonnet: Tattoo Tears": "No one will believe this story I'm telling, so it must be true." Alexie is committed to telling his readers truths about their words, worlds, and lives – which is the responsibility of any storyteller.

Sherman Alexie is one of the most prolific and promising writers working today. The pace of his work does not appear to be letting up: he is currently working on his third novel; a new collection of poetry; and a screenplay, *Powwow,* based on material from *The Lone Ranger and Tonto Fistfight in Heaven.* As Silko says, "Make no mistake: Alexie's talent is immense and genuine. . . . On this big Indian reservation we call the United States, Sherman Alexie is one of the best writers we have."

Interview:

Kelly Myers, "Reservation Stories with Author Sherman Alexie," *Tonic,* 1 (11 May 1995): 8–9.

Reference:

Jennifer Gillan, "Reservation Home Movies: Sherman Alexie's Poetry," *American Literature,* 68 (March 1996): 91–110.

Paula Gunn Allen

(24 October 1939 -)

Ann E. Reuman
Tufts University

Paula Gunn Allen

BOOKS: *The Blind Lion: Poems* (Berkeley, Cal.: Thorp Springs, 1974);
Coyote's Daylight Trip (Albuquerque, N.Mex.: La Confluencia, 1978);
A Cannon between My Knees (New York: Strawberry Hill, 1981);
Star Child: Poems (Marvin, S.Dak.: Blue Cloud Quarterly, 1981);
Shadow Country (Los Angeles: American Indian Studies Center, University of California, 1982);
The Woman Who Owned the Shadows (San Francisco: Spinsters, Ink, 1983);
The Sacred Hoop: Recovering the Feminine in American Indian Traditions (Boston: Beacon, 1986; revised, 1992);
Wyrds (San Francisco: Taurean Horn, 1987);
Skins and Bones: Poems 1979–87 (Albuquerque, N.Mex.: West End, 1988);
Grandmothers of the Light: A Medicine Woman's Sourcebook (Boston: Beacon, 1991);
As Long as the Rivers Flow: The Stories of Nine Native Americans, by Allen and Patricia Clark Smith (New York: Scholastic, 1996);
Life Is a Fatal Disease: Selected Poems 1964–1994 (Albuquerque, N.Mex.: West End, 1996).

OTHER: "*Iyani*: It Goes This Way," in *The Remembered Earth,* edited by Geary Hobson (Albuquerque: University of New Mexico Press, 1979), pp. 191–193;
From the Center: A Folio, Native American Art and Poetry, edited by Allen (New York: Strawberry Hill, 1981);
Studies in American Indian Literature: Critical Essays and Course Designs, edited by Allen (New York: Modern Language Association of America, 1983);
"All the Good Indians," in *The '60s Without Apology,* edited by Sohnya Sayres, Anders Stephanson, Stanley Aronowitz, and Fredric Jameson (Minneapolis: University of Minnesota Press, 1984), pp. 226–229;
"This Wilderness in My Blood: Spiritual Foundations of the Poetry of Five American Indian Women," in *Coyote Was Here: Essays in Contemporary Native American Literary and Political Mobilization,* edited by Bo Schöler (Århus, Denmark: Seklos, Department of English, University of Århus, 1984), pp. 95–115;
"From *Raven's Road,*" in *The New Native American Novel: Works in Progress,* edited by Mary Dougherty Bartlett (Albuquerque: University of New Mexico Press, 1986), pp. 51–63;
"The Autobiography of a Confluence," in *I Tell You Now: Autobiographical Essays by Native American Writers,* edited by Brian Swann and Arnold

Krupat (Lincoln: University of Nebraska Press, 1987), pp. 141–154;

"American Indian Fiction, 1968–1983," in *A Literary History of the American West,* edited by J. Golden Taylor and Thomas J. Lyon (Fort Worth: Texas Christian University Press, 1987), pp. 1058–1066;

"Bringing Home the Fact: Tradition and Continuity in the Imagination," in *Recovering the Word: Essays on Native American Literature,* edited by Swann and Krupat (Berkeley: University of California Press, 1987), pp. 563–579;

"Selections from *Raven's Road,*" in *Living the Spirit: A Gay American Indian Anthology,* edited by Will Roscoe (New York: St. Martin's Press, 1988), pp. 134–152;

Spider Woman's Granddaughters: Traditional Tales and Contemporary Writing by Native American Women, edited by Allen (New York: Fawcett Columbine, 1989);

"Deer Woman," in *Talking Leaves: Contemporary Native American Short Stories,* edited by Craig Lesley (New York: Dell, 1991), pp. 1–11;

" 'Border' Studies: The Intersection of Gender and Color," in *Introduction to Scholarship in Modern Languages and Literatures,* edited by Joseph Gibaldi (New York: Modern Language Association of America, 1992), pp. 303–319;

Voice of the Turtle: American Indian Literature 1900–1970, edited by Allen (New York: Ballantine, 1994);

Song of the Turtle: American Indian Literature 1974–1994, edited by Allen (New York: Ballantine, 1996).

SELECTED PERIODICAL PUBLICATIONS – UNCOLLECTED: " 'The Grace That Remains': American Indian Women's Literature," *Book Forum: An International Transdisciplinary Quarterly,* 5, no. 3 (1981): 376–382;

Review of *This Bridge Called My Back: Writings by Radical Women of Color,* edited by Cherríe Moraga and Gloria Anzaldúa, *Conditions Eight,* 3 (Spring 1982): 127.

Acclaimed essayist, poet, theorist, novelist, educator, editor, political activist, and recipient of the 1990 Native American Prize for Literature and the 1990 American Book Award, Paula Gunn Allen is a leading Native American scholar in the literary world today. Her groundbreaking book *The Sacred Hoop: Recovering the Feminine in American Indian Traditions* (1986) is an important feminist analysis of Native American history that focuses on the centrality of women and ritual to indigenous cultures and Native American narrative tradition. Her novel, *The Woman Who Owned the Shadows* (1983), was one of the first to choose a complex female Indian protagonist and to emphasize not just alienation but also continuity and the potency of relationship in the character's development. Her four chapbooks and four major volumes of poetry established her prominence as a Native American poet. Her public readings, active service on academic panels, dedication to curricular development that supports ethnic and racial minority literary studies, and research on world religious traditions continue to place her as a major voice in American studies, Native American studies, women's studies, gay studies, and American literature today. Her collections of Native American literature – *Spider Woman's Granddaughters: Traditional Tales and Contemporary Writing by Native American Women* (1989), *Voice of the Turtle: American Indian Literature 1900–1970* (1994), and *Song of the Turtle: American Indian Literature 1974–1994* (1996) – show her commitment to putting her power to use in the community by giving voice to other Native American writers.

In all of her works Allen struggles to negotiate multiple, often contentious, worldviews and urges white, Western, patriarchal culture to revalue and remember a Native American worldview from which it has become estranged and from which it has much to learn. In a draft of "This Wilderness in My Blood: Spiritual Foundations of the Poetry of Five American Indian Women" published in 1984 before it appeared in edited form in *The Sacred Hoop,* Allen asserts: "merging is a feature of my life. . . . Making [multiple settings and perspectives] come together in my work is the primary impulse that governs it. For me . . . finding metaphors that unify diverse and conflicting experience is more than an aesthetic exercise, it is a matter on which survival is based. A half-breed . . . is not in a position to accept either-or viewpoints. . . . We are 'the women of daylight,' and daylight makes multitudes of darks and lights, of patterns that move and change constantly."

Allen's power as a mediator derives from her upbringing in what she referred to in *I Tell You Now* (1987) as a "confluence of cultures." Born 24 October 1939 in Albuquerque to Ethel Haines Gottlieb ('Tu'u-we'tsa, "like a song") and Elias Lee Francis, Paula Marie Francis was raised in Cubero, a small town in northern New Mexico that abuts the Laguna Reservation, the Acoma Reservation, and the Cibola National Forest. Her mother's Laguna, Métis, and Scottish ancestry and her father's Lebanese-American heritage provided a home environment that blended religions, languages, foods, music, traditional stories, thought structures, and worldviews. As Allen says with characteristic humor in an autobiographical essay in *I Tell You Now*: "My life was more chaos than order in any ordinary American, Native American, Mexican-American, Lebanese-American, German-American, any heathen, Catholic, Protestant, Jewish, atheistic sense. Fences would have been hard to place without leaving something out." At the same time, she explains in a 1982 review of Cherríe Moraga and Gloria Anzaldúa's anthology *This Bridge Called My Back,* she saw herself as a "multicultural event" who could "attest to the terrible pain of being a bridge." Allen's help in her father's small business (the Cubero Trading Company), where people exchanged goods and stories alike, and her public role as daughter of an elected official (her father was lieutenant governor of New Mexico from 1967 to 1970) further developed Allen's mediating skills, as did perhaps her position as the middle of five children between two older sisters, Carol Lee Sanchez and Kay Swanquist, and two younger brothers, Lee Francis III and John Francis. Allen's versatility in many narrative forms – essay, short story, poetry, novel – grew out of her family's traditions of storytelling and reflect her capacity to negotiate multiple voices.

Allen attended mission schools in Cubero until the age of six, when she transferred to Saint Vincent Academy, run by the Sisters of Charity, in Albuquerque. There she boarded until she was twelve, leaving for her seventh-grade year to go to the mission school in San Fidel run by the Sisters of Saint Francis, then returning to the convent to attend classes while living off campus with her grandfather until she graduated in 1957. From 1957 to 1958 Allen took courses at Colorado Women's College, then left to marry a Lebanese-American, Eugene Hanosh; gave birth to a son, Gene, and a daughter, Lauralee; divorced in 1962; went back to school; and completed her B.A. in English at the University of Oregon, Eugene, in 1966. She later married Darrel Brown, a white man from Kansas; divorced; married an Oklahoma Cherokee, Joe Charles Allen; and gave birth to twin sons, Sulieman and Fuad. Only after these marriages, Allen says, did she realize that she was a lesbian; and in the years that followed, she had long-term relationships with women, including the poet Judy Grahn. Several of Allen's experiences from this period in her life appeared in *The Woman Who Owned the Shadows* in fictionalized form: her Catholic schooling, the depths of anguish she suffered when one of her twins died as an infant, her gradual coming out, and her cross-cultural relationships.

Allen's move to Oregon in 1965 marked a turning point in her literary career. Until then she had been enamored of the works of white American and English writers, including Gertrude Stein, John Keats, Percy Bysshe Shelley, Charlotte Brontë, Jane Austen, William Carlos Williams, and Adrienne Rich, had studied writing with Robert Creeley, and felt considerably influenced by the Black Mountain School of poetry and by readings and works by Charles Olson, Allen Ginsberg, Robert Duncan, and Denise Levertov. Although she valued much of what she learned from these writers, Allen also felt confined by conventional Western literary standards. Poetry professors urged her to end her pieces more sharply. Book editors insisted that she eliminate or conflate complicated truths to fit a constrictive Eurocentric aesthetic because they were not willing to make the effort to understand her Indian consciousness; they wanted linear, industrial time as a structuring device, not achronological, ceremonial time; and they expected a foregrounded, isolate hero, with events, setting, heritage, and other characters used only as backdrops. Large, mainstream publishing firms preferred stereotyped, eminently marketable "media Indians," not complex, contradictory characters crossing "American" and Indian qualities; and they thought Native American writers should be relegated to a separate "Indian series." Small, liberal printing companies were often no less exploitative in their "benign" racism which for a long time primarily sought portraits of Indians-as-victims.

At an early point in her career Allen tried to fit the established norms. She truncated last lines, even though she thought that they should keep going, like a ceremonial drum. In order to get published, she excised sections from her novel which, though integral to her worldview, were confusing to Western readers. Yet at the same time she struggled to keep stylistic elements that were important to her sense of self as a twentieth-century American Indian woman writer. She felt, for instance, that instead of sequential ordering, a hierarchical construction that tends to privilege whatever comes at the end, her novel, like her thought, should be organized in accretive bursts; accumulating in ever-expanding, irregular loops; often returning to, rather than fleeing from, a center. She knew that art has a tremendous debt to oral culture; and she worked with the recognition that one of the main audiences she wrote for, her Pueblo people, considered writing to be detached from true feeling and therefore suspect

Title page for the first of three chapbooks Allen wrote in the late 1970s and early 1980s

as a form of expression. Moreover, as a "woman of daylight," she knew that ancient understandings and contemporary experience coincide: steel foundries, powwows, uranium mines, wildernesses, superhighways, vision quests, airports, rodeos, and spirit voices exist side-by-side. As she wrote in her poem "*Kopistaya* (A Gathering of Spirits)," in "This Wilderness in My Blood" (1984), even though the world is wrapped in glass and steel, "spirit voices are singing, / . . . / if we could listen. / If we could hear."

Allen's reunion in 1965 with an old friend, Dick Wilson, a Santee Sioux who had moved to Oregon to teach, helped her to see that the distress she felt from not fitting conventional Western literary and social standards was not simply her problem, and gradually she shifted away from her teachers to develop her own voice. Seeing Wilson, and reading N. Scott Momaday's *House Made of Dawn* (1968), which features a modern mixed-breed American Indian torn between Jemez Pueblo, Kiowa, Navajo, and Eurocentric ways of thinking, Allen said, probably saved her life: they told her she was not alone; that she, like Chickasaw poet Linda Hogan, was Indian, not crazy. As she said in an interview with Joseph Bruchac in 1983, Momaday's novel "brought *my land* back to me. . . . [If] that line hadn't been thrown in my direction, I wouldn't be here now." Allen's environment is a mythic, spiritual, integral aspect of her being. This reconnection with her tribal heritage helped ground her, and not long after this experience, she began what she called in an interview with Laura Coltelli in *Winged Words* (1990) "a thirteen-year conversation" that developed into *The Woman Who Owned the Shadows.*

The effect of Allen's shift in perspective is clear when one considers her great productivity after earning her bachelor's degree. In 1968 she completed an M.F.A. in creative writing at the University of Oregon, then taught at De Anza Community College and at the University of New Mexico while working on her doctorate. In 1974 her first book of poetry, *The Blind Lion,* was published; and in 1975 she earned her Ph.D. in American studies, with an emphasis on Native American studies, from the University of New Mexico. Her dissertation, *Sipapu: A Cultural Perspective,* laid the groundwork for the many essays she published in the late 1970s and early 1980s that were subsequently revised and collected in *The Sacred Hoop.* After finishing her doctorate, Allen taught at San Diego State University, the College of San Mateo, and San Francisco State University, where she became the department chair of American Indian Studies. In the summer of 1977 she directed a Modern Language Association–National Endowment for the Humanities curriculum-development seminar on American Indian literature, the results of which she later compiled and edited in *Studies in American Indian Literature: Critical Essays and Course Designs* (1983).

She published three chapbooks – *Coyote's Daylight Trip* (1978), *A Cannon between My Knees* (1981), *Star Child* (1981) – and one major volume of poetry, *Shadow Country* (1982), which received an honorable mention from the National Book Award Before Columbus Foundation; she completed *The Woman Who Owned the Shadows* while teaching American Indian studies at UCLA for a postdoctoral fellowship year (1981–1982); and she taught at the University of California at Berkeley (1982 to 1990). While at Berkeley she published her novel and *Studies in American Indian Literature.* In the academic year 1984–1985 she was awarded a postdoctorate fellowship from the Ford Foundation–National Research Council to study oral traditional elements in Native

American novels while privately teaching classes on women's spirituality and serving as an associate fellow at the Stanford Humanities Institute. Allen then went on to publish *The Sacred Hoop,* two books of poetry (*Wyrds,* 1987, and *Skins and Bones,* 1988), and a collection of contemporary and traditional writings by Native American women, *Spider Woman's Granddaughters,* which won the American Book Award in 1990. In 1991, continuing her interest in women and ritual transformation, Allen published *Grandmothers of the Light: A Medicine Woman's Sourcebook.* In 1994 she published *Voice of the Turtle: American Indian Literature 1900–1970,* which was followed in 1996 by a second volume of collected writings, *Song of the Turtle: American Indian Literature 1974–1994.* Also in 1996 Allen published a collection of poems, *Life is a Fatal Disease,* and collaborated with Patricia Clark Smith, her dissertation chair and longtime friend and colleague, to produce *As Long as the Rivers Flow: The Stories of Nine Native Americans.*

Allen established her reputation early in her career with her several books of poetry, her many readings and lectures, and the wide publication of her poetry in journals and anthologies, including *Calyx, Frontiers, Sinister Wisdom, SAIL (Studies in American Indian Literatures), That's What She Said, A Gathering of Spirit,* and *Songs from this Earth on Turtle's Back.* Themes and images that she developed in later works all emerge here: liminality and ritual transformation, land connection, sacred continuities and balance, the road and four directions, sisterhood, resilience, storytelling, and shadows that bring rain and comfort and the meeting of ways. Poetry, Allen shows, is performative: it enacts sacred truths and enables reconnective action. It is word medicine.

Surprisingly, Allen's novel, a mixed-genre collection of integrated stories that bases its form on a relational model of development and experience, has received much less critical attention than her other work. Allen dedicates the novel to three powerful female figures: her great-grandmother Meta Atseye Gunn (whose last name Allen uses as her middle name), the giver-of-rain Iyatiku, and Spider Grandmother. Allen opens *The Woman Who Owned the Shadows* with two ceremonial chants that identify the need of the focal character, Ephanie Atencio, to remember the spiritual world, specifically the sacred power of women. With repeated images of people abused and cut off from their sources of strength, Allen links racism, misogyny, and homophobia, and shows the psychic disequilibrium caused by alienation, silences, and self-doubt. While men figure prominently in this colonialistic impulse to divide, conquer, straighten, reduce, and obliterate, Allen also takes issue with divisiveness within the female community, confronting univocal feminism and complicitous silencing between women of color and between lesbians. Individual and social healing, Allen insists, depends on recognizing continuities as well as the ways in which individuals let illusions trick them into forgetting the essential interrelatedness of all people and all things.

The Woman Who Owned the Shadows is about a young woman, part Spanish and part Indian, who feels split, isolated, and profoundly disoriented. Violated by her cousin, her husband, and a culture that makes no room for mixed-breeds or for women who love women, and detached from her heritage, Ephanie despairs and slowly tries to kill herself – first with alcohol, then with drugs, then with a knife and a rope. Only in her last suicide attempt, when she has an epiphanic encounter with a spider that she finally understands is Grandmother Spider of Keres theology, does Ephanie come out of the closet (literally and figuratively), return to the living, and begin her journey toward healthy balance, or "right relationship." Through interconnected traditional tales and current peer relationships the novel shows how Ephanie gradually reclaims herself; and knowing herself, Allen shows, means knowing her "mother," or the entire generation of women whose psychic "shape" made the existence of the following generation possible. Balance, Allen contends, can only be restored by understanding one's place in the great web of which all living things are a part and which everyone helps to create. By the end of the novel Ephanie enters the mythic space of her spirit guide and becomes a tribally connected medicine woman who crosses several worlds.

A parable of gradual recovery through reconnection to a larger whole, *The Woman Who Owned the Shadows* takes its shape from a ritualistic aesthetic: the multidimensional medicine wheel, or what Oglala Lakota holy man Black Elk called "the nation's hoop." Dynamic and communal, Allen's collection of interrelated stories in *The Woman Who Owned the Shadows* resists what the author in *Spider Woman's Granddaughters* called the "intellectual apartheid" of Western literary aesthetics, which most highly values "purity" of genre, separates long pieces from short and contemporary from traditional, and critically distinguishes oral and written forms of expression. Instead, Allen's 1983 novel reenacts in literary form the ceremonial reintegration of different but interrelated traditions.

Rather than following a single thread, Allen weaves together several narrative lines into a cyclic shape that encompasses, but is not limited to, linear structure. Like a web, all parts connect at the center with the design emerging as it is made; and from the hub radiate many characters and events, all interdependent. Underscoring the centrality of multiplicity and hybrid combinations to her work and worldview, Allen also overlaps literary genres – theological tales, contemporary stories, therapist's notes, history, current events, letters, dreams, memories, and internal dialogue. Valuing performance, repetition, and oral/aural interchange, she blends musical rhythms (of Arabic chants and American Indian dance beats as well as of Mozart) into her work, developing multiple variations on themes. Balancing Indian thought that develops in accretive bursts with colonial, patriarchal language – which is for her always fragmented and incomplete – Allen uses metaphors and similes to create a mixed, punning language, embedding question and comment in every phrase. Furthermore, to show the confluence of the spiritual and material worlds, artificially divided in Western thought, Allen integrates into her novel many sacred realities: shawls, which figure Ephanie's evolving sense of self; spiders repairing webs in the shadows; a forked apple tree that carries Haudenoshonee (Iroquois) and Christian symbolic value; and the feminized landscape that coexists with the phallic sentinel peak Picacho. Each image links the human with the supernatural, the present with the past, dreams with "reality," for each, as Allen sees it, are "wings of the same bird": parts of a continuum, not binary opposites.

Linked to Allen's landscape of female promise and power is her map of a new literary terrain, based not on conquest but on confluence and transformation. Women writers, she contends, are healers, translators, mediators, transformers of consciousness; they are bringers-into-balance. In putting their thoughts on paper, they see the pieces, make connections, and work with the creative power of the spiritual world. With the sacred power of utterance, they set things in motion.

Although Allen is better known for her scholarly essays than for her poetry or her novel, *The Sacred Hoop* should really be read as a companion piece to *The Woman Who Owned the Shadows,* for the two tell the same story in different form, and each deeply enhances the reading of the other. "No balance is possible," Allen said in a 1983 interview with Franchot Ballinger and Brian Swann, "if the centrality of womanness is not clearly understood." As she explains in *The Sacred Hoop, context* and *matrix,* among the Keres, "are equivalent terms, and both refer to approximately the same thing as knowing your derivation and place. Failure to know your mother, that is your position and its attendant traditions, history, and place in the scheme of things, is failure to remember your significance, your reality, your right relationship to earth and society. It is the same as being lost – isolated, abandoned, self-estranged, and alienated from your own life."

The Sacred Hoop critiques erasure of women's power in male-dominant myths and culture, examines the ways in which patriarchal renderings of traditional tales have stressed heterosexual and Christian elements, and emphasizes the need for a shift in focus to nonauthoritarian, spirit-infused gynocentricity to reflect tribal worldviews more accurately. In keeping with her philosophy and cross-cultural perspective, Allen writes at the intersection of several fields – anthropology, history, theology, psychology, literary studies, culture studies, psychology, sociology, ethnic and gender studies – for her point in this book is to show how gynocratic tribes are dialogic – or, more exactly, polylogic – emphasizing diversity and complementarity rather than isolation or opposition.

In her study of mother-right cultures in Native America, Allen explores the tales of several ancient spirit-women, including Spider Grandmother. As she writes in the first chapter of *The Sacred Hoop,* merging Western and Native American narrative traditions: "In the beginning was thought, and her name was Woman. The Mother, the Grandmother, recognized from earliest times into the present among those peoples of the Americas who kept to the eldest traditions, is celebrated in social structures, architecture, law, custom, and the oral tradition. To her we owe our lives, and from her comes our ability to endure, regardless of the concerted assaults on our, on Her, being, for the past five hundred years of colonization. . . . She is the Old Woman Spider who weaves us together in a fabric of interconnection. She is the Eldest God, the one who Remembers and Re-members." Essays in the first section discuss female gods and the principles of kinship and cooperation that are central to woman-centered American Indian theology, chronicle the history of several Indian women in North America since white contact, and give a personal account of Allen's own resistance and survival as a contemporary Indian woman.

In the second section of the volume Allen explains in depth the Native American concepts of the

Dust jacket for the collection of Allen's creation stories from various religious traditions

sacred hoop and dynamic interrelationship that form the core of the book. In the chapter titled "Whose Dream Is This Anyway? Remythologizing and Self-definition in Contemporary American Indian Fiction," she analyzes Western and traditional tribal narratives as well as Westernized Indian novels to see how they shape options for living. Here, through the works of Mourning Dove, D'Arcy McNickle, Momaday, James Welch, Leslie Marmon Silko, Gerald Vizenor, and herself, she considers themes of engulfment, endurance, transition, transcendence, healing, ritual, regeneration, and continuity. Other chapters in this section of *The Sacred Hoop* discuss mythic vision, Indian concepts of time, alienation in Native American literature, genocide and continuance in poetry by American Indian women, feminized landscape in Silko's *Ceremony,* and spirituality in poetry by Joy Harjo, Hogan, Mary TallMountain, Wendy Rose, and Carol Lee Sanchez (Allen's sister). In the final section of *The Sacred Hoop,* Allen explores even more challenging themes, most notably the indebtedness of white feminism to Native American thought and the roles of gays and lesbians in American Indian cultures. A landmark study of female power in American Indian traditions, *The Sacred Hoop* is an important text in feminist scholarship.

Grandmothers of the Light (1991) continues to explore what Allen recognizes as the "living reality of the medicine world." The first section contains creation stories from various religious traditions – including the Keres S'ts'tsi'naku (Thinking Woman), Haudenoshonee Sky Woman, Mayan Xmucane (Grandmother of the Light), and Cherokee Selu (Corn Woman) – that reveal what she terms a "cosmogyny," or "multiverse" (diverse universe) in harmony with gynocratic principles of balance, relationship, and egalitarianism. Here she describes the seven ways of the medicine woman: the way of the daughter, the way of the householder, the way of the mother, the way of the gatherer, the way of the ritualist, the way of the teacher, and the way of the wise woman. As Allen says in the introduction to this section, drawing on the words of Lakota shaman Lame Deer in *Lame Deer: Seeker of Visions* (1972): those who "walk the medicine path" are "seated amidst the rainbow," "where the spiritual and the commonplace are one."

Dust jacket for Allen's anthology of works by Native American writers

In the Yellow Woman, Grandmother Spider, White Buffalo Woman, Qiyo Kepe, and other "ritual-magic-stories" included in the second section, Allen examines the role that goddesses play as mediators between the supernatural and the mortal worlds. The final section, "Myth, Magic, and Medicine in the Modern World," considers transformations of ritual tradition in the last few centuries, particularly the gradual movement toward patriarchy, Christianity, and heterosexual worldviews. Yet the power of women endures, as shown in the tales of Tonantzin, Shimana, Deer Woman, and Crystal Woman. While Allen acknowledges crucial distinctions between cultures represented by these theological tales, her focus in this "sourcebook" is their psychological, spiritual, and cultural continuity. For in the collection of these "myths," or medicine stories, Allen shows the cumulative power of interrelationship.

While some critics have argued that Allen has essentialized Native Americans, and reviewers have sometimes misinterpreted her Pueblo rhythms and thought structures, ignored the everyday reality of violence in many people's lives, or emphasized the theme of victimization over its complementary resilience and continuance, most literary critics have highly acclaimed the originality of Allen's scholarship, the rich narrative tradition in her poetry, and the lyricism and innovation in her fiction.

Allen's choice in the last few years to anthologize writings by other Native American writers reflects her political commitment to share power and contribute to the community. Noting the double marginalization of Native American women writers by the Western literary canon, Allen compiled *Spider Woman's Granddaughters,* a collection of traditional tales and contemporary writing. Divided into three sections – "The Warriors," "The Casualties," and "The Resistance" – this anthology challenges stereotypes of Indian warriors and testifies to women's ongoing struggle to resist the tyrannies that continue to be enacted against Native Americans. As Allen comments in the introduction, American Indians "are occupied peoples" who cannot afford the luxury of being unconscious of the state of war that persists for indigenous peoples today.

Voice of the Turtle brings together literature published by American Indians between 1900 and 1970, including pieces by E. Pauline Johnson, Charles Eastman, Mourning Dove, Pretty-shield,

Luther Standing Bear, Black Elk, Zitkala-Sa, McNickle, Momaday, and Simon Ortiz. Referring in the preface to the collection of stories as a "narrative Pot Luck," Allen believes that the varied forms and voices in this anthology nourish those who are starving to hear about multiple traditions of indigenous peoples. Her *Song of the Turtle* further develops the American literary canon by collecting American Indian literature since 1974. Here, through the works of Leslie Marmon Silko, James Welch, Patricia Clark Smith, Mary TallMountain, Linda Hogan, Louis Owens, Beth Brant, Diane Glancy, Anna Lee Walters, Louise Erdrich, Joseph Bruchac, Michael Dorris, Sherman Alexie, Joy Harjo, and Betty Louise Bell, she explores contemporary themes of war, loss, recovery, boundary crossing, and transformation as seen from Native American perspectives.

In *As Long as the Rivers Flow,* written in collaboration with Smith, Allen directs her attention to nine Native Americans in and out of literature who have made history and who have taught others how to survive, excellently: the Olympian Jim Thorpe; the entertainer Will Rogers; the first female principal chief of the Cherokee Nation, Wilma Mankiller; the acclaimed novelist Louise Erdrich; Sen. Ben Nighthorse Campbell; the Pocasset warrior Weetamoo; the Apache leader Geronimo; the dancer Maria Tallchief; and the artist Michael Naranjo.

In these anthologies as in all her work, Allen does not forget the many people who helped make her writing possible. As she mentions in "'Border' Studies: The Intersection of Gender and Color," an essay included in the Modern Language Association's *Introduction to Scholarship* (1992), she is a being "*in-communitas,*" or a self-in-relation; and her acknowledgments recognize the many "midwives" who have directly or indirectly helped bring her work into being: family members, friends, writers, and spirit people as well as typists, editors, and office and research assistants.

Currently, Allen is writing "Raven's Road," a "medicine-dyke novel," as she has described it in her interview with Coltelli, that is really "a bridge novel," joining Indian and lesbian communities. She is also working on what she called in her 1996 interview with Ann Reuman, a "family biomythography," which examines the Lebanese Maronite tradition.

Helpful as her works have been to Native Americans, particularly women, in validating their experiences, Allen's writings are not just for people of her own community. "I think that Native American literature is useful to everybody who's trying to move from one world to another," she said in an interview with Laura Coltelli in 1985. And reconnection with tribal traditions, she insists, is essential to everyone's survival. Where, as the Sioux say, "we are all relatives," the fate of one group or individual is the fate of all.

Interviews:

Franchot Ballinger and Brian Swann, "A MELUS Interview: Paula Gunn Allen," *MELUS,* 10 (Summer 1983): 3–25;

Joseph Bruchac, "I Climb the Mesas in My Dreams: An Interview with Paula Gunn Allen," in his *Survival This Way: Interviews with American Indian Poets* (Tucson: University of Arizona Press, 1987), pp. 1–21;

Katharyn Machan Aal, "Writing As an Indian Woman: An Interview with Paula Gunn Allen," *North Dakota Quarterly,* 57 (Spring 1989): 148–161;

Laura Coltelli, "Paula Gunn Allen," in her *Winged Words: American Indian Writers Speak* (Lincoln: University of Nebraska Press, 1990), pp. 10–39;

Annie O. Eysturoy, "Paula Gunn Allen," in *This Is about Vision: Interviews with Southwestern Writers,* edited by William Balassi, John F. Crawford, and Eysturoy (Albuquerque: University of New Mexico Press, 1990), pp. 94–107;

Donna Perry, "Paula Gunn Allen," in her *Backtalk: Women Writers Speak Out* (New Brunswick, N.J.: Rutgers University Press, 1993), pp. 1–18;

Ann E. Reuman, "An Interview with Paula Gunn Allen," in her "Narratives of Negotiation: Feminist Dialogics, Narrative Strategies, and Constructions of Self in Works by Four U.S. Women Writers," dissertation, Tufts University, 1997.

Bibliography:

A. LaVonne Brown Ruoff, *American Indian Literatures: An Introduction, Bibliographic Review, and Selected Bibliography* (New York: Modern Language Association of America, 1990), pp. 156–157, 175.

References:

Renae Bredin, "'Becoming Minor': Reading *The Woman Who Owned the Shadows,*" *Studies in American Indian Literatures,* 6 (Winter 1994): 36–50;

Elaine Jahner, "A Laddered, Rain-bearing Rug: Paula Gunn Allen's Poetry," in *Women and Western American Literature,* edited by Helen Winter Stauffer and Susan Rosowski (Troy, N.Y.: Whitston Press, 1982), pp. 311-326;

Ana Louise Keating, *Women Reading Women Writing: Self-Invention in Paula Gunn Allen, Gloria Anzalda and Audre Lorde* (Philadelphia: Temple University Press, 1996);

Kenneth Lincoln, "Southwest Shadows," in his *Native American Renaissance* (Berkeley: University of California Press, 1983), pp. 214–221;

Ann E. Reuman, "Walking in Balance: Dialogic Differences and the Potency of Relationship in Paula Gunn Allen's *The Woman Who Owned the Shadows,*" in *Border Crossings: World Feminisms in Dialogue,* edited by Merry Pawlowski (Urbana: University of Illinois Press, forthcoming, 1997);

James Ruppert, "Paula Gunn Allen and Joy Harjo: Closing the Distance Between Personal and Mythic Space," *American Indian Quarterly,* 7, no. 1 (1983): 27–40;

Patricia Clark Smith, "Coyote's Sons, Spider's Daughters: Western American Indian Poetry, 1968–1983," in *A Literary History of the American West,* edited by J. Golden Taylor and Thomas J. Lyon (Fort Worth: Texas Christian University Press, 1987), pp. 1067–1078;

Ann Van Dyke, "The Journey Back to Female Roots: A Laguna Pueblo Model," in *Lesbian Texts and Contexts: Radical Revisions,* edited by Karla Jay and Joanne Glasgow (New York: New York University Press, 1990), pp. 339–354.

William Apess

(31 January 1798 - April or May 1839)

Barry O'Connell
Amherst College

BOOKS: *A Son of the Forest: The Experience of William Apes, a Native of the Forest. Comprising a Notice of the Pequod Tribe of Indians. Written by Himself* (New York: Published by the author, 1829; revised edition, New York: Printed for the author by G. F. Bunce, 1831);

The Increase of the Kingdom of Christ: A Sermon (New York: Printed for the author by G. F. Bunce, 1831) – includes "The Indians: The Ten Lost Tribes";

The Experiences of Five Christian Indians of the Pequod Tribe (Boston: Printed by James B. Dow, 1833); also published as *The Experiences of Five Christian Indians of the Pequod Tribe; or, An Indian's Looking-Glass for the White Man* (Boston: Printed for the author by James B. Dow, 1833); revised as *Experience of Five Christian Indians of the Pequot Tribe* (Boston: Printed for the publisher, 1837);

Indian Nullification of the Unconstitutional Laws of Massachusetts, Relative to the Marshpee Tribe; or, The Pretended Riot Explained (Boston: Printed by Jonathan Howe, 1835);

Eulogy on King Philip, as Pronounced at the Odeon, in Federal Street, Boston (Boston: Published by the author, 1836; revised, 1837).

Editions and collections: *Indian Nullification of the Unconstitutional Laws of Massachusetts, Relative to the Marshpee Tribe; or, The Pretended Riot Explained,* foreword by Jack Campisi (Stanfordville, N.Y.: Coleman, 1979);

Eulogy on King Philip, as Pronounced at the Odeon, in Federal Street, Boston (Brookfield, Mass.: Dexter, 1985);

On Our Own Ground: The Complete Writings of William Apess, a Pequot, edited by Barry O'Connell (Amherst: University of Massachusetts Press, 1992).

William Apess's ordination as a minister in the Protestant Methodist Church preceded by only a few months the publication of his *A Son of the Forest* (1829), the first published autobiography – and one of the earliest books of any genre wholly written – by a Native American. In 1831 he was appointed a missionary to his people, the Pequots, and eventually settled with the Mashpees (the name was spelled Marshpee in the early nineteenth century), the inhabitants of the last remaining Indian town in Massachusetts. He quickly became a leader in their struggle to govern their town free of white guardians and to appoint a minister of their own choosing for the local church. The Mashpee Revolt broke out in 1833, and Apess's name became briefly known throughout the United States: he was, in effect, the leader of one of the first Indian rights movements. In large part because of Apess's brilliance as a polemicist and a tactician, the Mashpees achieved most of their demands by 1834. Apess was once more in the public eye in January 1836 when he delivered his controversial *Eulogy on King Philip* in the largest hall in Boston. He died in New York City three years later.

William Apes – he would change the spelling of his surname in his last publications and in a series of court cases brought against him in 1836 for unpaid debts – was born on 31 January 1798 in a tent in the woods near the town of Colrain in the northwestern corner of Massachusetts. His father, also named William, was a shoemaker who moved back and forth throughout his life between Colrain and Colchester, Connecticut, near the homelands of the Pequots in southeastern Connecticut. Apess's mother was probably named Candace; if so, she was a bound servant or perhaps even a slave in the household of Capt. Joseph Taylor, also of Colchester. Although she may have married Apess's father before Apess's birth – no record of the marriage exists – she was not formally freed by her master until 1805. There is no evidence that either parent had any formal education, although Apess's father seems to have been able to read and write. Apess refers in his autobiographical writings to two brothers and two sisters; two additional brothers were born after Apess was no longer living with his parents.

Apess's parents' racial identities were mixed, a common situation among Native Americans in the northeast by the late eighteenth century. By Apess's account in *A Son of the Forest* his father, the child of a Pequot woman and a white father, chose to affiliate with his mother's people and to marry "a female of the tribe, in whose veins a single drop of the white man's blood never flowed." Despite this claim, his mother's race is uncertain. In an inventory of Taylor's estate Candace is identified as "Negro," while in the 1820 federal census schedule she is characterized as "a free white woman." This uncertainty shows how unreliable and in flux were categories of racial identity, especially as applied to Native Americans, in this period. In any case, his parents identified themselves as Pequots and were apparently accepted as such by their fellows.

By the time of Apess's birth native peoples in the northeast had been severely reduced in numbers by European diseases to which they lacked immunity; by removals from their homelands to the West; and, ironically, by having joined white Americans in fighting the Revolutionary War, in which many Native American men died. Those who remained in close proximity to white settlements had lost most of their land in the eighteenth century through deeds that Indians understood as maintaining their rights to continue to use the land for planting, hunting, and fishing but that European Americans enforced as giving themselves exclusive ownership; white guardians and overseers who abused their positions to steal the land; and, when these tactics failed, the use or threat of force to compel Indian removals or signatures on agreements that took the land away forever. What little land was left was insufficient to support the surviving Native Americans, who eked a bare living from some of the older ways of trapping, hunting, and fishing; making brooms and baskets for sale to whites; and working as day laborers for white farmers, who often cheated them out of their wages. Many of the men went to sea on long whaling voyages; the women often worked in domestic service to white gentry households, to which, not uncommonly, their children were bound out as indentured servants. Apess summarizes these conditions, some of their causes, and their consequences at the beginning of *The Experiences of Five Christian Indians of the Pequod Tribe* (1833):

> the land of my fathers was gone; and their characters were not known as human beings but as beasts of prey. We were represented as having no souls to save, or to lose, but as partridges upon the mountains. All these degrading titles were heaped upon us. Thus, you see, we had to bear all this tide of degradation, while prejudice stung every white man, from the oldest to the youngest, to the very center of the heart.

Much of Apess's writing focuses on the conditions of Native Americans in the northeast in the first third of the nineteenth century and on the racism against which they struggled. Apess was a historian, though he depended on the research of others, and in *A Son of the Forest* and the *Eulogy on King Philip* his analysis of contemporary Native American life is embedded in a detailed reading of Indian-European relations from the time of first contact.

It is Apess's evangelical Christianity that most immediately strikes many readers today, however, and, given still-dominant notions about what constitutes Indian identity, baffles their expectations. Of his five publications, three largely concentrate on his conversion to Methodism, his ordination as a minister, and his work as a preacher. Only his last two books, *Indian Nullification of the Unconstitutional Laws of Massachusetts, Relative to the Marshpee Tribe; or, The Pretended Riot Explained* (1835) and *Eulogy on King Philip,* shift substantially away from this primary focus. Yet any understanding of the complexities of Native American identities, and of Apess himself as a person and as a writer, requires a grasp of the way in which his conversion to evangelical Christianity was integral to his capacity to affirm himself as a Pequot and as a person of color. Only through his experience of Christianity was Apess able to overcome in some measure the psychic wounds of racial and economic oppression and to create a public career dedicated to fighting the impact of this oppression on his fellow Indians. This complex story shapes all of his writing. Apart from its rhetorical power, the writing claims attention by its ability to make comprehensible how native peoples could adopt selected European or European American cultural modes as means of surviving and of maintaining a sense of their own distinctive identities.

Some time after Apess's birth his mother and father returned to the area around Colchester, where "our little family lived for nearly three years in comparative comfort." Then the parents quarreled and separated, and each, apparently, moved some distance away. Apess and two brothers and two sisters were placed with their maternal grandparents. Both grandparents "would drink to excess"; the house was cold and often bare of food; and the children lacked warm cloth-

M^r. WILLIAM APES,

A NATIVE MISSIONARY OF THE PEQUOT TRIBE OF INDIANS.

A SON OF THE FOREST.

THE EXPERIENCE OF WILLIAM APES, A NATIVE OF THE FOREST.

WRITTEN BY HIMSELF.

Second Edition, Revised and Corrected.

NEW-YORK:

PUBLISHED BY THE AUTHOR.

G. F. Bunce, Printer.

1831.

Frontispiece and title page for the revised edition of William Apess's autobiography, published before he added a second s *to his surname (courtesy of the Lilly Library, Indiana University)*

ing. Kindly white neighbors, the Furmans, saw to it that the children at least got milk. Apess contrasts their behavior to that of his own grandparents: " 'Once in particular, I remember that when it rained very hard my grandmother put us all down cellar, and when we complained of cold and hunger, she unfeelingly bid us dance and thereby warm ourselves – but we had no food of any kind; and one of my sisters almost died of hunger.' "

One day the grandmother returned home drunk after peddling baskets and brooms to white people and, without warning, turned on the four-year-old Apess and began to beat him with a club. Had it not been for the intervention of an uncle, Apess believed, he would have been beaten to death; even then, his grandfather took up a firebrand to try to prevent the uncle from stopping the beating. The next day the uncle, realizing how badly his nephew was injured, went to the Furmans. Mr. Furman petitioned the town selectmen in Colchester, and the children were removed from the house and bound out to nearby white families; Apess was placed with the Furmans. It took Apess a year to recover from the beating.

One wonders why Apess, who was abandoned by his Pequot parents, nearly beaten to death by his Pequot grandmother, kindly treated by white people, and was raised from the age of four entirely in white households came to think of himself as a Pequot – let alone to adopt a career as a writer and leader devoted to the cause of the Pequots and other northeastern native peoples. It is possible that he regularly saw his Pequot relatives – including his father, who returned to Colchester some time after Apess was beaten – but he does not say in his autobiography that he did so; he does say that after his parents separated he did not see his mother again for twenty years. In his eyes, the Furmans seem to have become his parents. When Mrs. Furman's mother, who lived in the household, died, Apess tells his readers: "She had always been so kind to me that I missed her quite as much as her children, and I had been allowed to call her mother."

Apess was especially close to Mrs. Furman, who brought him his first vivid awareness of Christianity. She was a Baptist and not only "esteemed as a very pious woman" but, in a distinction Apess recurrently draws in describing European American Christians, she was one who actually behaved like a Christian: "her whole course of conduct was upright and exemplary." He makes special note of a conversation they had when he was six about the importance of leading his life in such a way that he would go to heaven when he died. When he responded that "only old people died," she took him to the graveyard to show him otherwise. This experience produced his first spiritual crisis, and from this point onward his journey to Christian conversion, culminating in his ordination as a Methodist minister, becomes the primary theme in his autobiographical writings.

While it is plausible to read *A Son of the Forest* and "The Experience of the Missionary" in *The Experiences of Five Christian Indians of the Pequod Tribe* as conventional Protestant narratives of conversion, to do so is to miss the subtlety of Apess's autobiographical narrative. Here is an Indian whose conversion to Christianity was not a form of acquiescence or an acknowledgment of the superiority of European American culture or a sign of assimilation; the closer he moves to conversion the more he affirms his identity as an Indian and as a Pequot – precisely the reverse of the effect that European Americans expected when they used Christianity as a major tool in the colonizing enterprise. Each moment the autobiographical protagonist moves toward Christianity seems to remind him either of his irrevocable "Indianness" in white peoples' eyes or of their commitment to seeing native people as murderous and savage.

Perhaps only a shock akin to being beaten by his grandmother could have given Apess sufficient motive to reject white culture and assume an identity as a Pequot. Apess lived with the Furmans for six years, the only time he received any formal schooling. He mentions being "flogged" twice by Mr. Furman and called "an Indian dog," but these experiences did not provide the decisive shock; it occurred when, as a boyish fantasy, he made plans to run away that were discovered by Mr. Furman. Though the boy assured him that he did not actually wish to leave the family, Furman sold his indenture to the elderly Judge James Hillhouse, one of the most prominent and powerful members of the Connecticut elite. Apess says little in his narratives about this incident, but he says enough to make clear his shock at being expelled from a family he had come to regard as his own. He emphasizes that he was "*sold*" like a piece of property, an object; in the eyes of the Furmans he was, perhaps, a person, but he was one who would always be of less value than a white:

> I was alone in the world, fatherless, motherless, and helpless . . . and none to speak for the poor little Indian boy. Had my skin been white, with the same abilities and the same parentage, there could not have been found a place good enough for me. But such is the case with depraved nature, that their judgment for fancy only sets upon the eye, skin, nose, lips, cheeks, chin, or teeth and, sometimes, the forehead and hair; without any further examination, the mind is made up and the price set.

Apess's stay with Hillhouse was brief; he was soon "sold" to William Williams, another well-placed and prosperous Connecticut gentleman. Although he spent four years under Williams's supervision, the autobiographies never suggest that Apess felt any emotional attachment to his master. Christianity takes the central place in the narratives and functions literally to subordinate those who, in secular terms, could claim to be his masters and racial superiors.

The Methodists, then a "lowly" sect whose class meetings and open-air revivals no respectable person would attend, began holding meetings in the area. Apess began to attend the meetings: "the stories circulated about them were bad enough to deter people of 'character'. . . . But it had no effect on me. I thought I had no character to lose in the estimation of those who were accounted great." At the meetings he found poor white, African American, Native American, and mixed-race men and women, united by their awareness of themselves as among the despised of their society. In contrast to the stiff, formal, rote preaching and prayers and insistent reinforcement of the social and economic hierarchy in his masters' church, he discovered a community in which he was recognized as an equal:

> I could not see that they differed from other people except in their behavior, which was more kind and gentlemanly. Their countenance was heavenly, their songs were like sweetest music – in their manners they were plain. Their language was not fashioned after the wisdom of men. . . . The exercises were accompanied by the power of God.

Hillhouse and Williams were antievangelical Congregationalists, and their church membership reinforced their power and status. Apess's representation of these men is unabashedly sardonic: "For what cared they for me? They had possession of the red man's inheritance and had deprived me of lib-

"Mannner of Instructing the Indians": frontispiece for Apess's Indian Nullification of the Unconstitutional Laws of Massachusetts *(1835)*

erty." In Apess's portrayal their hypocrisy, their wealth and social standing, and their hostility to evangelical religion stand for white power itself. In the fervent egalitarianism of early Methodism, its informality of ritual, and its commitment to spontaneous preaching and prayer, Apess experienced a powerful affirmation of his human worth: "I felt convinced that Christ died for all mankind – that age, sect, color, country, or situation made no difference. I felt an assurance that I was included in the plan of redemption with all my brethren." Becoming an evangelical Christian became the means for him to affirm his identity as an Indian.

Williams eventually prohibited Apess from attending Methodist meetings. After being flogged several times, Apess ran away to New York with another boy in the early spring of 1813. Discovering that Williams had advertised a reward for his recovery, Apess enlisted in a New York militia unit bound for the Canadian campaign in the War of 1812. The two years in the military interrupted his journey to conversion: he took up the habits of the men around him, including swearing and drinking, and he would struggle with alcoholism for the rest of his life. Apess mustered out of the militia in the spring of 1815 and spent the next year working at a variety of jobs in northern New York and Canada, including farm laborer, bartender, and galley cook on a Great Lakes boat. During that time he became acquainted with several communities of Native Americans, probably members of the Mississauga Ojibwa nation, in eastern Ontario. These encounters seem to have strengthened his self-identification as an Indian.

After the year of moving from job to job, a period punctuated by bouts of heavy drinking, Apess decided to return to Connecticut. Traveling on foot because he had no money, he was finally reunited with his family in April 1817: "at last I arrived in safety at the home of my childhood. At first my people looked upon me as one risen from the dead. . . . They were rejoiced to see me once more in the land of the living, and I was equally rejoiced to find all my folks alive." He began attending Methodist meetings again, although his family rejected his urgings to join him. He supported himself again with a variety of jobs, including agricultural labor, keeping a tavern, and selling books. He lived for a time with his aunt, Sally George, a revered elder among the Pequots and one of those who seems to have held the nation together in the midst of poverty and white hostility. She and Apess held outdoor meetings that were attended by Native Americans from the surrounding area. George preached and Apess led prayers in a manner that seems to have combined customary Pequot spiritual practices with compatible ones from evangelical Christianity.

Apess was baptized in December 1818, and by the next spring he began to feel called to preach the Gospel. It was in the hill country of western Massachusetts, where he had gone to visit his reunited parents, that Apess began his preaching – provoking hostility from whites who opposed the idea of an Indian preaching Christianity. He obtained from the Methodist Conference a license to exhort, the first stage in gaining ordination as a regular preacher. In late 1820 or early 1821 he met Mary Wood of Salem, Connecticut, at a camp meeting; they were married in Salem on 16 December 1821. Apess's autobiographies do not mention the names or number of his children, but it is known that he and his wife had a son named William Elisha and two daughters; there may have been other children. During the eight years between his marriage and his ordination as a preacher in the Protestant Methodist Church in New York in 1829, he continued to work at a variety of laboring jobs. He and his family lived for a while in Providence, Rhode Island, where Apess was a class leader in a local Methodist society and was again licensed to exhort. Probably between 1827 and 1829 he traveled as an itinerant Methodist exhorter around Long Island; up the Hudson River valley as far as Albany and Troy; to Boston, New Bedford, and Martha's Vineyard; and north of Boston. His auditors appear to have been mostly African Americans and Native Americans.

Somehow in those years Apess, who had had only six winter terms of schooling when he lived with the Furmans, acquired impressive skills as a reader and writer. In one of his indictments of Hillhouse, Apess remembers the judge asking him to read: "I could make out to spell a few words, and the judge said, 'You are a good reader.'" Alive to the condescension of that long-ago moment, Apess adds, "I hope he was a better judge at law." Given his constant traveling and the necessity of finding jobs to support his growing family, obtaining books and finding time to read them would have been difficult. He did work as a book peddler, and one might assume that he read the works in his stock. And he would not be the first writer in English or American literature who came to impressive performance primarily from immersion in the Bible. His authorship of the books published in his name is virtually certain, although W. G. Snelling contributed some pages and perhaps editorial assistance to *Indian Nullification of the Unconstitutional Laws of Massachusetts.* If he had an amanuensis or an editor, it could only been one of the few white men and women who were then involved in reform and who had a special interest in Native Americans, such as Snelling and Lydia Maria Child – neither of whom ever wrote anything like Apess's works in style or sentiment. Only among other writers of color can one find similar critiques of white forms of domination and such clarity about racism and the hypocrisy of using Christianity as a means of humiliating and colonizing nonwhite peoples. Apess and the African American writer David Walker have much in common, but Walker's *Appeal to the Colored Citizens of the World* (1829), though it resembles Apess's *The Experiences of Five Christian Indians of the Pequod Tribe* in ideas and militancy, is distinctly different in style.

One must assume, however, that Apess had patrons: the printing of his first book was probably subsidized, and the rest may have been. Also, his writing shows enough care to suggest that he was able in the midst of his other labors enough to devote a good deal of time to it. His knowledge of American literature and of a large body of writing on Native Americans may show that he had access to the library of a person of some wealth and learning, such as Samuel Gardner Drake of Boston. Drake collected extensive documents on New England Indians and published several historical accounts; his *Biography and History of the Indians of North America* (1832) went through many editions under several titles, and, because of it, he was considered by his contemporaries the premier authority on eastern Indians. He knew Apess, and he mentions the *Eulogy on King Philip* in one of the later editions of the *Biography and History of the Indians of North America;* but his tone is not especially sympathetic or warm. New York City, rather than Boston, may be where Apess studied, wrote, and most consistently found support: his autobiography was registered for copyright there; he preached in and around the city with some frequency; and he returned there toward the end of his life. Future scholarship may turn up further information on these matters.

Apess visited Mashpee in May 1833. He reports that some people had told him that the Mashpees were well cared for by a decent minister and were vigilant against whites who wished to take their land, but that "Others asserted that they were much abused," and he apparently decided to see for himself. The inhabitants of Mashpee had long struggled against paternalistic institutions imposed on them by whites: the white overseers had unchecked power over land rentals and leases, woodlot rights, the conditions of labor, and who could enter and who could stay in the township. Although the townspeople had built their own church, Harvard College had control over who ministered to them. Periodically the

"King Philip Dying for His Country": frontispiece for Apess's eulogy on Metacomet, or King Philip, delivered in Boston in January 1836

Mashpees had gained greater control over their own affairs, only to lose it again. The community prospered when the Mashpees governed themselves and went into decline when forced to submit to white oversight.

Apess found Phineas Fish, the minister, to be an orthodox Old Light Calvinist whose congregation was almost entirely made up of whites from nearby towns; the whites were assigned the privileged pews, while the few Native Americans were seated behind them. Fish expressed no interest in learning Wampanoag, the first language of many of the Mashpees, and he was open about his conviction of the Mashpees' racial inferiority. A dull and patronizing preacher, Fish enraged the Mashpees by refusing access to the Old Indian Meeting House, which they had built, to the many Mashpees who worshiped with the Mashpee Baptist preacher Blind Joe Amos. The Indians had other grievances as well: whites from the nearby towns were obtaining rights to the best woodlots and pastures for minimal fees; men were leaving the community rather than submit to the overseers' dictates; and the people's standard of living was steadily worsening.

From the rapidity with which the community gathered around him one can get an idea of how charismatic Apess must have been, as well as for how aggrieved the Mashpees were. He was adopted into the community and promised a home along with fishing, farming, and wood rights. He organized a small Methodist meeting and also joined Amos in starting a temperance organization. By mid June, only six weeks after his arrival, the community agreed to two petitions that were almost certainly written by Apess. "The Indian Declaration of Independence," addressed to the governor of Massachusetts and his council, proclaimed that after 1 July 1833 "we, as a tribe, will rule ourselves, and have the right to do so; for all men are born free and equal, says the Constitution of the country." The document specified that no white man would be permitted to take wood or cut hay in Mashpee after 1 July without the Indians' explicit permission. The second petition, to the Corporation of Harvard College, requested Fish's dismissal, pointing out that the Mashpees had never been consulted about his appointment; it also announced that they had chosen Apess for their minister and that they intended to take control of their meetinghouse.

So unexpected was this assertion of Native American determination that many whites in Massachusetts and much of the rest of New England initially responded with hysteria, as though a new Indian war was about to break out; Levi Lincoln, the governor of Massachusetts, threatened to call out troops to put down what he believed was an insurrection. More-sensible temperaments, however, finally ruled the day. Apess was singled out as the outside agitator responsible for misleading an otherwise well-contented group of Native Americans, and the white strategy focused on removing his influence. On 1 July a group of whites entered Mashpee and loaded their carts with wood. Apess and several Mashpees confronted them, ordered them to leave without the wood, and, when they refused, unloaded the carts. The men had probably been sent to test the Indians' seriousness and possibly to justify the arrest of Apess, which followed on 4 July in the middle of a community meeting. He was charged with "riot, assault, and trespass," for which he served thirty days in jail, paid a $100 fine – an enormous sum in 1833 – and had to post bond for another $100 to guarantee that he would "keep the peace for six months."

Apess was not to be silenced so easily, nor were the Mashpees to prove simple creatures of what whites imagined as a demagogue in their midst. They made an appeal, probably written by Apess, through newspapers to the whole state and then directly petitioned the legislature to abolish the overseership, to incorporate the town, and to repeal all laws affecting the Mashpees, "with the exception of the law preventing their selling their lands." Apess and two Mashpees addressed the Massachusetts House in speeches that were, according to a contemporary newspaper account, "fearless, comprehensive and eloquent." In March 1834 the legislature granted the substance of the petition. Fish remained, as intransigent as his Harvard College patrons (he would be removed by force in 1840, after Apess's death). These events and documents and Apess's reflections form the matter of *Indian Nullification of the Unconstitutional Laws of Massachusetts.*

The Mashpees had won an impressive victory, thanks in good measure to Apess's polemical and tactical skills. His ability to appropriate the rhetoric of the age, formulating the Mashpees' demands as democratic ones in the spirit of the Declaration of Independence and the Constitution, indicate how thoroughly he had mastered contemporary politics. Nevertheless, after the crisis passed, Apess continued to be attacked in the press as an outsider. His last major public act was to deliver twice, in January 1836 in the largest hall in Boston, the *Eulogy on King Philip,* his principal exposition of his political thought. The eulogy proposes a fundamental revision of the conventional patriotic narrative of the creation of the United States. Apess maintains that there were two "fathers" of the country: George Washington and the seventeenth-century Wampanoag chief King Philip (Metacomet). His insistence on dual and symbolically antagonistic founders shows Apess's rejection of any notion of the inevitable demise of the Indian. American history, in his argument, is inescapably shaped by the conflict between Europeans and Native Americans. Instead of a sanitized, harmonious, and homogeneous myth of origin and progress, he spoke for a concept of nationhood founded on struggle, contradiction, and the presence of many nations with different and often irreconcilable interests.

Apess lost his house in Mashpee and all his possessions in a series of debt actions in 1836 and 1837. His next mention in print is his obituary in the *New York Sun* in May 1839. According to the obituary he died in New York City, where he had resided for some time after having "lost the confidence of the best portions of the community" because of frequent public bouts of drunkenness. The obituary suggests that he died from the effects of alcoholism, but the inquest report indicates that he died of complications from the medical treatment for a routine stomach ailment.

One might be tempted to pity Apess and other Indians for being victims of white oppression and of their own vulnerabilities, especially to alcohol. Apess's voice, represented powerfully in his writings, might warn off such a response. He was unsparing, tough-minded, and lucid about the many deceits and forms of domination practiced by whites, but he was equally clear and harsh about his own failings and those of his people. Apess did not want to make escape from responsibility easy for whites or Indians. His indictments of European American culture are, perhaps, as valid today as when he wrote them. His own story will always, one hopes, make people wonder how anyone so injured could survive and achieve so much. But it may be that Apess's most valuable contribution is to offer his fellow Americans a strain of political thought that contests the image of the New World as a paradisiacal and innocent new beginning. Instead, he asked his readers to accept the picture of a nation formed in conflict among separate but also inextricably related peoples. In such a history Native Americans have pride of place not only as the original inhabitants of the land but also as living people, shapers of the emerging nation and shaped by it, not as an "aboriginal" people but one as complexly modern and diverse as any other.

References:

H. David Brumble III, *American Indian Autobiography* (Berkeley: University of California Press, 1988), pp. 63, 122, 213;

Arnold Krupat, *Ethnocriticism: Ethnography, History, Literature* (Berkeley: University of California Press, 1992), pp. 220–229;

Krupat, *The Voice in the Margin: Native American Literature and the Canon* (Berkeley: University of California Press, 1989), pp. 143–149, 151, 188;

Kim McQuaid, "William Apes, A Pequot: An Indian Reformer in the Jackson Era," *New England Quarterly*, 50 (1977): 605–625;

David Murray, *Forked Tongues: Speech, Writing and Representation in North American Indian Texts* (Bloomington: Indiana University Press, 1991), pp. 57–62;

Barry O'Connell, "William Apess and the Survival of the Pequot People," in *Algonkians of New England: Past and Present,* The Dublin Seminar for New England Folklife Annual Proceedings, volume 16, edited by Peter Benes (Boston: Boston University Press, 1993), pp. 89–100;

A. LaVonne Brown Ruoff, "Three Nineteenth-Century American Indian Autobiographies," in *Redefining American Literary History,* edited by Ruoff and Jerry W. Ward Jr. (New York: Modern Language Association, 1990), pp. 251–269.

Jim Barnes

(22 December 1933 –)

Elizabeth Blair
Southwest State University, Minneapolis

BOOKS: *This Crazy Land* (Tempe, Ariz.: Inland Boat/Porch Publications, 1980);

The Fish on Poteau Mountain (Dekalb, Ill.: Cedar Creek Press, 1980);

The American Book of the Dead (Urbana: University of Illinois Press, 1982);

A Season of Loss: Poems (West Lafayette, Ind.: Purdue University Press, 1985);

La Plata Cantata: Poems (West Lafayette, Ind.: Purdue University Press, 1989);

Fiction of Malcolm Lowry and Thomas Mann: Structural Tradition (Kirksville, Mo.: Thomas Jefferson University Press, 1990);

The Sawdust War (Urbana: University of Illinois Press, 1992);

Paris (Urbana: University of Illinois Press, 1997);

On Native Ground; Memoirs and Impressions (Norman: University of Oklahoma Press, 1997).

Jim Barnes (photograph by Robert Tunney, courtesy of Jim Barnes)

OTHER: "These Damned Trees Crouch," "Last Look at La Plata, Missouri," "Camping Out on Rainy Mountain," "Tracking Rabbits: Night," "Bone Yard," "Sweating It Out on Winding Stair Mountain," "The Captive Stone," "Lying in a Yuma Saloon," "Paiute Ponies," "Halcyon Days," and "Autobiography: Last Chapter," in *Carriers of the Dream Wheel: Contemporary Native American Poetry,* edited by Duane Niatum (New York: Harper & Row, 1975), pp. 15–27;

Geary Hobson, ed., *The Remembered Earth: An Anthology of Contemporary Native American Literature,* contributions by Barnes (Albuquerque: Red Earth, 1979), pp. 46–51;

Five Missouri Poets, edited by Barnes (Kirksville, Mo.: Chariton Review, 1979);

Dagmar Nick, *Summons and Sign: Poems,* translated by Barnes (Kirksville, Mo.: Chariton Review, 1980);

"The Chicago Odyssey," in *The Pushcart Prize V: Best of the Small Presses,* edited by Bill Henderson (Yonkers, N.Y.: Pushcart, 1980), pp. 374–375;

"Autobiography, Chapter XVII: Floating the Big Piney," "Four Things Choctaw," "Concomley's Skull," "Four Choctaw Songs," and "Wolf Hunting Near Nashoba," in *Songs from This Earth on Turtle's Back: Contemporary American Indian Poetry,* edited by Joseph Bruchac (Greenfield Center, N.Y.: Greenfield Review, 1983), pp. 15–19;

"On Native Ground," in *I Tell You Now: Autobiographical Essays by Native American Writers,* edited by Brian Swan and Arnold Krupat (Lincoln: University of Nebraska Press, 1987), pp. 87–97;

Niatum, ed., *Harper's Anthology of 20th Century Native American Poetry,* contributions by Barnes (New York: Harper & Row, 1988), pp. 49–62;

"One for Grand Ronde, Oregon," "At the Burn on the Oregon Coast," "Near Crater Lake," and "Contemporary Native American Poetry," in *Dancing on the Rim of the World: An Anthology of Contemporary Northwest Native American Writing,* edited by Andrea Lerner (Tucson: University of Arizona Press, 1990), pp. 9–13;

John E. Smelcer and D. L. Birchfield, eds., *Durable Breath: Contemporary Native American Poetry,* contributions by Barnes (Anchorage, Alaska: Salmon Run, 1994), pp. 15–17;

Gerald Vizenor, ed., *Native American Literature,* contributions by Barnes (New York: HarperCollins, 1995), pp. 250–254.

Jim Barnes is an accomplished poet of the American landscape. Of Choctaw, Welsh, and English descent, he has published eight books of poems that explore land, loss, memory, and heritage. While he prefers not to be labeled a Native American poet, many of his best poems explore bones, rocks, rivers, plains, and glyphs that refer to Indian history.

Barnes was born on 22 December 1933 in Summerfield, Oklahoma, to the ranchers Bessie Vernon Adams Barnes and Austin Oscar Barnes. In a 1987 autobiographical essay, "On Native Ground," Barnes makes clear his spiritual debt to the hill country of eastern Oklahoma. He credits Le Flore County's Fourche Maline River and Holson Creek, and the woods and meadows that lay between them, with giving him the strong sense of place that characterizes his poetic imagination.

After graduating from high school in Oklahoma, Barnes moved to Eugene, Oregon, where he worked for nearly a decade in the deep woods, including the years 1954 to 1959 as a lumberjack for the Giustina Brothers Lumber Company. During this period he attempted to write poetry and fiction. He then returned to his home state to attend Southeastern Oklahoma State University, where he began to write poetry. He earned his B.A. in 1964; from the University of Arkansas he received an M.A. in 1965 and a Ph.D. in 1970 both in comparative literature. On 23 November 1973 he married Caroline Louise Ahlborn; they have two sons, Bret Alan and Blake Anthony. Since 1970 he has been at Truman State University in Kirksville, Missouri, where he is a professor of comparative and contemporary literature, writes and translates, and edits *The Chariton Review,* an international literary journal that publishes poetry, fiction, essays, and translations. Barnes is also the founding editor of the Chariton Review Press and a contributing editor of *Paintbrush: A Journal of Poetry, Translation, and Letters.*

In 1978 Barnes was awarded a National Endowment for the Arts Creative Writing Fellowship in poetry. In 1980 he published three books: *Summons and Sign,* a translation from the German poems by Dagmar Nick, for which he won a Columbia University Translation Award; *This Crazy Land;* and *The Fish on Poteau Mountain.* That same year Barnes's poem "The Chicago Odyssey" was included in *The Pushcart Prize V: Best of the Small Presses.*

His first major collection of poems, *The American Book of the Dead* (1982), takes as its subjects place, heritage, and loss, all of which remain prominent themes in his later books. Barnes has been called both a confessional poet and a Romantic poet. In a 1983 interview with Gretchen Bataille he rejected the first label out of hand: "I am sick of biographical criticism. It is not valid and has never been, from my point of view. Execution is all, intent is nothing." And while his poetry testifies to a deeply felt bond with nature, Barnes is hardly a traditional Romantic. He views nature not as a nurturing mother figure but as landscape, or place. In a 1986 interview with Heinz Woehlk, Barnes said, "Any poet worth his ink today has got to be grounded in a place."

Commitment to place is often neither comforting nor simple, as the poems in *The American Book of the Dead* amply illustrate. In "Autobiography, Chapter XIV: Tombstone at Petit Bay, Near Tahlequah," one of the twenty-one "autobiographical" poems that trace the speaker's wanderings from his childhood haunts in Oklahoma through his experiences as a logger in the Willamette Valley to his present home in Missouri, Barnes suggests that his quest for a sense of belonging is "a running search / for something still you cannot name." As hard as he might search for meaningful artifacts, "the trail always ends / on solid stone mute with glyphs" ("Tracking the Siuslaw Man"). In "Under Buffalo Mountain" Barnes studies the landscape to decipher the past: "Here the Choctaw stopped, forever, / staked the ground / with bones broken beyond rage." For those who would read them, Barnes implies, aboriginal claim stakes are etched into the landscape and echo in the prairie wind. For Barnes nature is a hard but revealing slate on which is written an indelible, often painful past.

One of the best poems in *The American Book of the Dead* is "Autobiography, Chapter II, Setting Out." "Leaving at last," the youthful speaker watches the Oklahoma landscape sailing past beneath his own shadow, cast from the window of a Greyhound bus. Another fine poem, "An Ex-Deputy Sheriff Remembers the Eastern Oklahoma Murderers," demonstrates Barnes's ability to invoke voices distinctly different from his own quiet and often melancholy lyricism, a melancholy so pervasive that the speaker sometimes doubts his own vision. "Old Soldiers' Home at Marshalltown, Iowa" concludes:

> You know that you've got it wrong, dead wrong,
> that life here is as vital as your organs.
> But somewhere in your head the old soldiers
> are dying, dying into the fullness of spring.

This vision of death and dying is especially prevalent in section 2 of the book, "Death by Water." In "For a Drowned Sailor, Age 4" the speaker appears to envy the child his "death / by water, the loveliest / of deaths by far." The speaker of "Sundown at Swan Lake, Missouri" also flirts with suicide but pulls back at the last minute, saying: "I will not drown / to know my life." *The American Book of the Dead* also includes what may well be the most incisive poem ever written on the special character of Native American poetry. Describing it as a scarecrow seen ragged across a field, Barnes writes: "You seldom think, at the time, / to get there it had to walk through hell."

The American Book of the Dead was well received by most reviewers. One critic dismisses what he calls Barnes's predilection for the "boneless anonymous poem," preferring those verses that display "a convincing native mean streak." A. Lavonne Brown Ruoff, writing in *American Indian Literatures* (1990), on the other hand, detects a Wordsworthian sensibility in Barnes's blend of recollected and immediate observations of nature. In a review in *World Literature Today* (Winter 1993) Charles R. Larson calls Barnes a master of ironic distance. Other critics take note of the poet's deep interest in his Native American heritage as well as his solid grounding in the British and American literary traditions.

Barnes's next book, *A Season of Loss* (1985), continues his concern with his lost heritage. In "Bone Yard" the speaker is a bard of ghostly presences. The poem memorializes a dried water hole that houses buffalo bones and "hoofs / that still tramp along / play on a hot wind." "Near Crater Lake" traces the lives of his ancestors:

> Ways my fathers walked are things I
> learn from hard stones. I lift my arms
> and hold the bear, the bull, the lost
> maidens.

Longing to know the land in the old way, the speaker would evoke ancestral knowledge about such intangibles as "why the path forks and the river / runs fast with fish." In other poems Barnes sings of Paiute ponies and eulogizes Charlie Wolf, a Choctaw acquaintance from his boyhood. The title poem details his continuing search for an Indian past:

> Our blood was now too thin to know
> the half-moon brother, our skin too pale;
> yet we, hands out, tried again to sow
> our spirit in the stars.

Such recovery efforts inevitably result in a sense of loss, but, Barnes argues, loss can be redemptive when it is affirmed and accepted.

Reception of *A Season of Loss* was varied. Ruoff is among the critics who admire Barnes's quest to recover the sense of unity with nature once held by his Indian ancestors, and Fred Chappell praises Barnes's "strong unsentimental lyricism." Other reviewers find the book uneven. In *Puerto Del Sol* (Summer 1989) Greg Kuzma argues that *A Season of Loss* alternates between "lean imagistic poems on the edge of silence" and "gabby" blank verse; but he appreciates the poet's self-appraisal, candor, and richness of sound, singling out for high praise one of Barnes's most personal poems. Because Barnes frequently employs traditional rhyme scheme, meter, and form, reaction to his work has been partially determined by the individual critic's response to such formalist practices. For example, Robert Peters asserts in *Paintbrush* (Spring–Autumn 1986) that the poet's "neatly tooled rhyme schemes" detract from his achievement. Nonetheless, Peters commends Barnes for his "rare and often powerful" depictions of landscape.

Barnes's next book, *La Plata Cantata* (1989), also explores loss and memory. As the speaker puts it in "Paraglyphs," "What's lost concerns me / more than what may be." *La Plata Cantata* is built around two strong sequences, a four-part poem called "Bombardier" and the twelve-part title poem. "Bombardier" is an understated elegy for Barnes's older brother, a pilot who disappeared over the Netherlands during World War II. Subtle and true in feeling, the poem evokes the child's memories of the exotic souvenirs his brother brought home during a leave. Barnes uses bald statement rather than lyric to convey his grief: "Then my brother was gone." Despite the telegram that eventually comes, the poet imagines his brother still alive, "passing out mementos of the world." But this fantasy proves to be cold comfort, as do the glimpses in pawnshops of war souvenirs he thought were private. He sees similar objects, "their bright mystery tarnished by hard hands / that cast them away to live." In "Bombardier" the poet searches for a way to live with a personal loss that is too deep to forget or to understand.

The title poem consists of twelve songs in terza rima in which Barnes imagines life in the present and in the past in La Plata, Missouri, a town midway between his home in Macon and his campus in Kirksville. In the opening poem the speaker stalks wild turkeys with a camera, capturing their image but not their spirit. Other poems in the sequence tally the losses of a midwestern town poised precariously between urban social problems and the decline of the family farm. A town "grown as practical as moles," La Plata struggles with divorce, suicide, a tornado, grain elevator explosions, heavy metal in the local lake, and economic decline yet refuses to acknowledge its more intangible losses of purpose and spirit.

Critics found much to praise in *La Plata Cantata*. In the *Bloomsbury Review* (May-June 1987) Ray Gonzalez pronounces it the poet's most moving book and calls Barnes a visionary historian. While Michael J. Bugeja, in *The Georgia Review* (1992), finds a few poems too contrived, he considers *La Plata Cantata* a strong book made even stronger by its varied diction, form, and meter and by the musical orchestration of the title sequence. In the same year in which *La Plata Cantata* was published Barnes received the Saint Louis Poetry Center's Stanley Hanks Memorial Poetry Award.

"The War over Holson Valley" in *La Plata Cantata* captures the vulnerability of a child growing up in the shadow of World War II. "And now it / roars back, the innocence you were guilty of. . . . You knew it wrong to like the war." Barnes's *The Sawdust War* (1992) picks up and extends this theme. In the title poem the speaker shapes theaters of war out of rain-wet sawdust, imitating the maneuvers that he hears about on his father's battery-powered radio each night. When a fire begins to smolder in the center of the sawdust pile, the speaker grows ashamed of his childish efforts to sculpt the war's course with a mason's trowel. While building an imaginary aircraft tower out of brush, indulging in aviator dreams, or building a playhouse on Nanny Ridge, the protagonist and his friends sing Choctaw and Cherokee hymns, "innocent of all / that we surveyed." It is only on returning to these haunts as an adult that the speaker recognizes how deeply the war affected his childhood and his adult life.

Barnes, circa 1975

Section 2 of *The Sawdust War,* "After the Great Plains," includes poems of travel, loss, and landscape that only superficially resemble those in Barnes's previous books. Here the speaker's sense of loss is tempered by philosophical forbearance. In "Driving through Missouri" the speaker contemplates a dust-dry autumn landscape and wishes that he could "sing the woods / rich in rainy, salmon leaves and new light." Using his imagination to leaven a bleak reality, he concludes: "Out of / this pale time there's still a thing or two to love." "Postcard to Alain-Andre Jourdier from the Longhorn Bar in Kirksville, Missouri" also reflects the speaker's new determination to transcend despair. Although the speaker, gazing out of a rain-glazed bar window, describes a darkened and desperate western landscape, he pledges to write lighter lines after the rain passes. "I'll say: there's something in the air, Indians / and songs are coming back to stay." These yearnings for traditional "song" and for the Indian past as it is manifested in the American landscape are some of the strongest features of Barnes's work. As he admits in "Forche Maline Bottoms," "No toy / could ever do what flint or milky chert / could do for my own small mauled imagination."

The last section of *The Sawdust War,* "In Another Country," is set in Lombardy, where Barnes enjoyed a 1990 Rockefeller Foundation Bellagio Residency Fellowship awarded for his translations from the German. While in Italy, Barnes was invited to give readings at the University of Florence and at the Palazzo delle Esposizioni in Rome. The most effective of the Italian poems is "In Another Country: A Suite for the Villa Serbelloni." In this poetic sequence the speaker enjoys contentment and companionship while laughing over a velvet painting of Francesca and Paolo, hiking mule tracks up to castles, and rowing a boat over the fallen tombs of monks. In "In the Melzi Gardens" the speaker writes in the shadow of a stone Dante, whose face has "grown / soft with love." In "Another Country" he finds a Celtic metate that "speaks of loss." But this Italian artifact does not have the same power to wound as do American runes: "In another country, I push / aside the leaves, and my own loss begins / to fade." In this far country, Barnes seems strangely content.

Barnes's best book to date, *The Sawdust War* has been well received by critics. In the *Cimarron Review* (October 1993) Samuel Maio praises the book's careful structuring, its redemptive wisdom, and its ambition. *Publishers Weekly* (27 January 1992) comments on Barnes's "lovely, concise imagery and philosophical asides that are . . . entirely true to life." *The Sawdust War* received a 1993 Oklahoma Book Award.

In his interview with Woehlk, Barnes expressed a desire to "soak up lots of good things in lots of exotic places." Little did he imagine then the amount of traveling that he was to do in the coming years. A year after his Bellagio residency Barnes was awarded a 1993–1994 Senior Fulbright Fellowship to Switzerland, where he read his poems in Lausanne, Basel, Geneva, and Fribourg. Between 1988 and 1995 he made several trips to France, where he was a featured poet at the Paris Writers Workshop, the Marche de Poesie, and the thirteenth Franco-Anglais Poetry Translation Festival. In 1995 Barnes was a translator in residence in Feldafing, Germany. From January to June 1996 Barnes was a Camargo Foundation fellow in Cassis, France, where he completed a new volume of poetry, *Paris* (1997). The poems pay homage to the American expatriates of the 1920s who lived and worked in Paris and to French novelists, poets, and painters of the nineteenth and twentieth centuries. The final poem concludes that "the failed work, the uncaptured melody, the frail effort" represented by the book is worthwhile because "the bard in all of us would like to sing."

Paris suggests that Barnes's poems will continue to reflect his deep connection to place. In his interview with Woehlk he said that a poet can write about any location, as long as it is accurately reflected in the poems that result: "I believe in active absorption. I look around me. I remember things I see, I hear." This intense interest in his immediate surroundings makes it likely that Barnes will be writing more poems based on his European travels. After all, as he wrote in "At 39: The View from Sycamore Tower" (*La Plata Cantata*), "Home is always ten thousand miles away." *Paris* also demonstrates his continued commitment to the "new formalist" branch of contemporary poetry. In *Native American Literature* (1985) Andrew Wiget sums up Barnes's literary contributions: "The maturity of his vision and the richness of his language command our assent."

Interviews:

Michael Sebald, "An Interview with Jim Weaver Barnes," in *The Magic of Names: Three Native American Poets,* edited by Patrick D. Hundley (Marvin, S.Dak.: Blue Cloud Quarterly Press, 1979);

Gretchen Bataille, "A *MELUS* Interview: Jim Barnes," *MELUS,* 10 (Winter 1983): 57–64;

Heinz Woehlk, "An Interview with Jim Barnes," *Paintbrush,* 13 (Spring–Autumn 1986): 52–61.

References:

Kenneth Lincoln, *Native American Literature* (Los Angeles: University of California Press, 1983), pp. 12–13, 69;

Linda Rodriguez, "Contemporary Profile: Jim Barnes," *Potpourri,* 5 (May 1993): 3;

A. Lavonne Brown Ruoff, *American Indian Literatures: An Introduction, Bibliographic Review, and Selected Bibliography* (New York: Modern Language Association, 1990), pp. 99–101, 114;

Andrew Wiget, *Native American Literature* (Boston: Twayne, 1985), pp. 105–106.

S. Alice Callahan

(1 January 1868 - 7 January 1894)

A. LaVonne Brown Ruoff
University of Illinois at Chicago

BOOK: *Wynema: A Child of the Forest* (Chicago: H. J. Smith, 1891).

Edition: *Wynema: A Child of the Forest,* edited, with an introduction and notes, by A. LaVonne Brown Ruoff (Lincoln: University of Nebraska Press, 1997).

S. Alice Callahan's *Wynema: A Child of the Forest* (1891) is probably the first novel published by an American Indian woman. Callahan's parents were Samuel Benton Callahan, who was one-eighth Creek and seven-eighths white, and Sarah Elizabeth Callahan, née Thornberg or McAllester (the names vary in different sources), a white woman. A captain in the First Creek Confederate Regiment, Samuel Callahan was a delegate to the Confederate Congress at Richmond, Virginia, representing the Creek and Seminole nations jointly. After the Civil War he joined his wife and children in Texas, where they had settled. Sophia Alice Callahan was born on 1 January 1868 in Sulphur Springs, Texas. In 1885 the family moved to the Creek Nation in Indian Territory (today Oklahoma), where Samuel held various positions with the tribe; farmed and ranched near Okmulgee; edited the *Indian Journal* in Muskogee; and served as superintendent of Wealaka Boarding School, a Methodist mission school for Creeks, from 1892 to 1894. The Callahans were members of the Creek aristocracy, a close-knit group that had large landholdings, had been slave owners, and built fine homes adorned with expensive furniture. As Angie Debo points out in *The Road to Disappearance* (1941), the Creek mixed-bloods were proud of their Indian heritage and sympathetic toward what they called the "real Indians."

By 1886 Alice Callahan seems to have been teaching in Okmulgee. The next year she went away to attend the Wesleyan Female Institute in Staunton, Virginia, returning in June 1888 after a ten-month stay. In February 1891 Callahan became a teacher at Harrell International Institute, a private Methodist high school for both Creek and white children in Muskogee. *Wynema* was published in the late spring of that year. In 1892–1893 Callahan taught at Wealaka Boarding School, where her father was superintendent. In letters written during this period she says that William Makepeace Thackeray's *Vanity Fair* (1847–1848) amused and entertained her more than anything else she had ever read but that she was more interested in Edward Bulwer-Lytton and Charles Dickens. Her feminism is revealed in her reaction to Thackeray's comments about women: "I don't like a great many things he says such as 'it's only women who get together and hiss and shriek and cackle,' or 'the best

S. Alice Callahan (courtesy of the Oklahoma Historical Society)

of women are hypocrites – a good housewife is of necessity a humbug.' " Callahan planned to return to the Wesleyan Female Institute to study languages, literature, and mathematics in preparation for opening her own school, but she returned to teach at Harrell in late 1893. Unwell after Thanksgiving, she developed pleurisy in December and died on 7 January 1894.

A mixed-blood raised away from the Creek Nation, Callahan was well aware of the issues facing the Creeks because of her father's involvement in tribal politics; she was, thus, both a part of and separate from Creek culture. *Wynema* reflects her position as both an insider and outsider. It also shows an Indian woman author both using and departing from the dominant literary trends in women's literature of the late nineteenth century.

The title character of *Wynema* is Wynema Harjo, a Creek girl; her first name is probably taken from that of the female Modoc subchief who saved the Indian commissioner, A. B. Meacham, from death in 1871 during the fight at the California Lava Beds. Wynema becomes the best student and close friend of the novel's other heroine, Genevieve Weir, a Methodist teacher from a genteel southern family.

The first part of the novel chronicles Genevieve's adjustments to life in the Creek Nation. Wynema and Gerald Keithly, a Methodist missionary, help her to understand Creek culture. That part and the second part also describe the "civilizing" of Wynema. A reverse acculturation theme is introduced in the second part, when Genevieve takes Wynema on a visit to her family home in the "sunny Southland" (no specific place is named); there the teacher must readjust, and the pupil must adjust, to the southern lifestyle. Genevieve has turned down Gerald's marriage proposal because she has an "understanding" with Maurice Mauran, a childhood friend; but she breaks off that relationship when she recognizes his prejudice against Indians and women. In the meantime, Wynema and Robin Weir, Genevieve's sensitive and enlightened brother, fall in love. Wynema and Genevieve return to the Creek Nation and marry Robin and Gerald, respectively. Two other romances, involving Genevieve's younger sisters, are introduced but not developed: between Bessie Weir and Carl Peterson, a missionary to the Creeks who formerly served the Sioux; and between Winnie Weir and a Dr. Bradford.

The third part of the book is an abrupt departure from the earlier romance plot and was obviously inspired by the Sioux hostilities, the murder of Sitting Bull on 15 December 1890, and the massacre at Wounded Knee, South Dakota, on 29 December 1890. The picture of domestic bliss, in which the married Wynema and Genevieve are surrounded by their loved ones and live in harmony with the Creeks, is interrupted when Carl announces that he must rejoin his Sioux friends, who are about to go to war. Accompanied by Robin, Carl acts as an intermediary between the Sioux chiefs and the army. Through the debate between Carl and Chief Wildfire over whether the Sioux should surrender, Callahan reveals her own mixed feelings about the events of that winter. Wildfire, his wife, and most of his followers die; through the stories of Chikena, a surviving widow, Callahan narrates how the Sioux were starved by Indian agents and massacred by the army. The details correspond to the events at Wounded Knee.

Callahan's bicultural background, her years in Staunton, her experiences as a teacher at a Methodist mission school for Creeks, and her support for women's rights inform the novel. She uses a plot formula that was common in American women's fiction from about 1820 to 1870, in which a heroine finds within herself the intelligence, will, resourcefulness, and courage to overcome the hardships that befall her. Also like other nineteenth-century women authors, Callahan uses sentimentality for political purposes. Genevieve is both a domestic heroine and woman of ideas: though wary of marriage, she is a shy, romantic woman who longs for a love based on mutual respect between a man and woman. Wynema, a bright and determined girl, shows the possibility of acculturating Indians through education. By the time Wynema visits Genevieve's southern home she has become a cultured, refined lady who speaks fluent English. Her relationship with Robin Weir exemplifies not only the ideal love of sentimental romantic tradition but also the ideal love between an Indian woman and a white man.

Callahan uses multiple voices and perspectives, Indian and non-Indian, female and male, to educate her readers. Gerald Keithly is the author's main vehicle for explaining the significance of Creek customs, but Genevieve and Wynema discuss such issues as the allotment of Indian land in severalty, authorized under the General Allotment Act, or Dawes Act, of 1887; corruption among Creek delegates; and the sale of whiskey to Indians in violation of federal law. In the third part of the novel Callahan quotes from contemporary newspapers that supported and opposed the Indian cause. Although most of the novel deals with Indian issues, Wynema, Genevieve, and Robin all express the author's commitment to the cause of equal rights for women.

Wynema was ignored by contemporary reviewers and critics. Only two copies of the original edition appear to be extant, one in the Library of Congress and the other at the Oklahoma Historical Society. Photocopies are in the library of the University of Illinois at Chicago. The book was not reprinted until the annotated edition, edited by A. LaVonne Brown Ruoff, was published by the University of Nebraska Press in 1997. Though the novel lacks a complex plot or multidimensional characters, it deals with issues generally ignored by white male authors of the period and is a significant contribution to the evolution of American Indian fiction.

References:

Angie Debo, *The Road to Disappearance* (Norman: University of Oklahoma Press, 1941);

Carolyn Thomas Foreman, "S. Alice Callahan: Author of Wynema: A Child of the Forest," *Chronicles of Oklahoma,* 33 (Autumn 1955): 306–315, 549;

A. LaVonne Brown Ruoff, "Justice for Indians and Women: The Protest Fiction of Alice Callahan and Pauline Johnson," *World Literature Today,* 66 (Spring 1992): 249–255;

Annette Van Dyke, "An Introduction to *Wynema, A Child of the Forest* by Sophia Alice Callahan," *Studies in American Indian Literatures,* 4 (Summer–Fall 1992): 123–128.

Elizabeth Cook-Lynn

(17 November 1930 -)

Norma C. Wilson
University of South Dakota

BOOKS: *Then Badger Said This* (New York: Vantage, 1977);

Seek the House of Relatives (Marvin, S.Dak.: Blue Cloud Quarterly, 1983);

The Power of Horses and Other Stories (New York: Arcade–Little, Brown, 1990);

From the River's Edge (New York: Arcade, 1991);

Why I Can't Read Wallace Stegner and Other Essays (Madison: University of Wisconsin Press, 1996).

OTHER: " 'You May Consider Speaking about Your Art . . . ,' " in *I Tell You Now: Autobiographical Essays by Native American Writers,* edited by Brian Swann and Arnold Krupat (Lincoln: University of Nebraska Press, 1987), pp. 55–63.

SELECTED PERIODICAL PUBLICATIONS – UNCOLLECTED: "Profile: Asa Primeaux, Sr.," *Wicazo Sa Review,* 1 (Spring 1985): 2–4;

"Survival in Hexasyllables," *Wicazo Sa Review,* 1 (Spring 1985): 49–52;

"The Rise of the Academic 'Chiefs,' " *Wicazo Sa Review,* 2 (Spring 1986): 38–40;

"A Case Study: The Black Hills Issue: A Call for Reform," *Wicazo Sa Review,* 4 (Spring 1988): 1–2;

"In the American Imagination, the Land and Its Original Inhabitants: An Indian Viewpoint," *Wicazo Sa Review,* 4 (Fall 1990): 42–47;

"A Monograph of a Peyote Singer: Asa Primeaux, Sr.," *Wicazo Sa Review,* 7 (Spring 1991): 1–15;

"The Radical Conscience in Native American Studies," *Wicazo Sa Review,* 7 (Fall 1991): 9–13;

"Elan (Poem for the Young Men Who Are the Big Foot Memorial Riders of 1990)," *Wicazo Sa Review,* 7 (Fall 1991): 13;

"Politics and the Native American Novel," *Wicazo Sa Review,* 7 (Fall 1991): 78–80;

"Deer at the Keshena Amphitheatre, 1993," *Wicazo Sa Review,* 9 (Fall 1993): 25;

Elizabeth Cook-Lynn (Studio of Carolyn Forbes)

"Some Thoughts about Biography," *Wicazo Sa Review,* 10 (Spring 1994): 73–74;

"A Few More River Poems: Deluge, The Cove, The Bleak Truth, They Seemed, City Games of Life and Death, Going Home," *Woyake Kinikiya,* 1 (Summer 1994): 8–13;

"A 'Desecration Tour' Now Awaits Travelers Who Visit the Sacred Black Hills," *Indian Country Today,* 18–25 November 1996, p. A7.

An author, editor, teacher, and scholar, Elizabeth Cook-Lynn is first and foremost a Dakota who speaks with the voice of her tribe. She is quick to point out, however, that she does not presume to speak *for* her tribe; she says in her autobiographical essay, "You May Consider Speaking about Your

Art . . ." (1987), that the real tribal poets are those "who sit at the drum and sing the old songs and create new ones." Cook-Lynn's deep respect for her culture is evident in her poetry, fiction, and expository prose. Out of her life, rich in the experience of the Dakota language, mythology, and history and of life on the northern plains, Cook-Lynn has developed a body of work that rings with uncompromising truth. She has no doubt about the power and worth of her ancestral heritage and its capacity for survival. As Kenneth M. Roemer says in *Native American Women: A Biographical Dictionary* (1993), Cook-Lynn "remembers the land," but it is more than the "visual images of skies and rivers . . . powerful animals . . . sounds as delicate as a meadowlark's call" that "define her sense of place. So do histories as old as Wounded Knee and as recent as wounded rivers . . . and stories as ancient as Dakotah creation narratives . . . and as recent as destruction narratives of brutal reservation murders."

Cook-Lynn was born Elizabeth Irving on 17 November 1930 at the government hospital in Fort Thompson, on the Crow Creek Sioux Reservation in South Dakota. Politics and writing were part of her family life and heritage: her grandfather Joe Bowed Head Irving and her father, Jerome Irving, served for many years on the Crow Creek Sioux Tribal Council. Her mother, Hulda Alma Peterson Irving, was a teacher. Elizabeth was named for her grandmother Eliza Renville Irving, who had written bilingual articles for Christian newspapers published in the late 1800s by the Dakota Mission at Sisseton, South Dakota; during Elizabeth Irving's childhood this grandmother lived only four miles away and sometimes stayed with Irving's family. Another grandfather, Gabriel Renville, who died before Irving was born, had been a linguist who was instrumental in developing early Dakota-language dictionaries. Cook-Lynn says in the autobiographical essay that she "read everything: the Sears catalog, *Faust,* Dick and Jane, *Tarzan of the Apes, The Scarlet Letter,* the First Letter to the Corinthians, *David Copperfield,* 'The Ancient Mariner,' Dick Tracy, 'Very Like a Whale,' *Paradise Lost, True Confessions,* and much more. . . . But I read nothing about the Dakotapi."

At South Dakota State College (now University) she took a history course titled "The Westward Movement," in which there was no mention of the Indian nations. As a result, she decided that she wanted to write and teach. She completed a B.A. in English and journalism in 1952. In 1953 she married a fellow student, Melvin Traversie Cook of Eagle Butte, South Dakota; the marriage ended in divorce in 1970. In 1975 she married Clyde Lynn, a Spokane Indian from Wellpinit, Washington. She worked as a journalist and taught at the secondary level before receiving a master's degree in educational psychology and counseling at the University of South Dakota in 1971. That year she began teaching English and Indian Studies at Eastern Washington University in Cheney while raising her four children from her first marriage: Mary, Lisa, Margaret, and David. She was a National Endowment for the Humanities fellow at Stanford University in 1976.

Cook-Lynn first gained a wide audience when excerpts from her first book, *Then Badger Said This* (1977), were included in Geary Hobson's *The Remembered Earth: An Anthology of Native American Literature* (1979). In a 1987 interview Cook-Lynn told Joseph Bruchac that in *Then Badger Said This* she was trying "to write the Sioux version of " N. Scott Momaday's *The Way to Rainy Mountain* (1969). Her choice of a title was based on the function of the badger in Sioux literature – to keep the plot moving. Comparing Cook-Lynn and Momaday, both of whom are profoundly influenced by the oral tradition, James Ruppert observes in the *American Indian Culture and Research Journal* (1980) that, "like Momaday's *The Way to Rainy Mountain,* her approach to history is not the cold unimaginative one of literal history, but a highly oral process where the personal and the cultural merge." This merging is evident in the prose and the poetry of the mixed-genre *Then Badger Said This* as she describes the destruction of the Missouri River country that resulted from the damming of the river in 1952. Though she writes from a Dakota worldview, Cook-Lynn's emphases on nature and family give the book a universal message – for example, in her description of a father's grief at the loss of his "middle son, the finest rider anywhere around," who died and was buried in France during World War I and whose bones "could not mingle with the bones of his grandfathers."

The loss of that young man in a foreign war is deeply ironic, for the U.S. government's policy toward the Sioux when they lived freely on the plains in the nineteenth century was designed to remove their spiritual and military leaders so that they would be forced to give up vast land areas and accommodate settlers. In her chapbook, *Seek the House of Relatives* (1983), Cook-Lynn takes the U.S. government and those who have used it to exploit the native nations to task in poetry and a short story that are more refined and complex treatments of the themes introduced in her first book. Discussing one

Dust jacket for Cook-Lynn's novel about an Indian rancher's futile attempt to gain justice through the American legal system

of the poems, "A Poet's Lament: *Concerning the Massacre of American Indians at Wounded Knee,*" she says in her autobiographical essay that "it is the responsibility of a poet like me to 'consecrate' history and event, survival and joy and sorrow, the significance of ancestors and the unborn; and I use one of the most infamous crimes in all of human history, which took place against a people who did not deserve to be butchered, to make that responsibility concrete." The identical first and last stanzas of the poem describe the government strategy: "All things considered, they said, / Crow Dog should be removed. / With Sitting Bull dead / It was easier said." In another poem in the chapbook, "My Grandmother's Burial Ground," she refers to the buying of Indian land as the "coins invaders played / which made you play your hand against your will," suggesting that the land speculators forced the Native American tribes to gamble away their future. The poem ends: "History, / that counterfeit absurdity / is no match for Buffalo bones / and dried skins of crows." "Seeking the house of relatives," Cook-Lynn searches for what is real and lasting amid the false history she exposes.

The Power of Horses and Other Stories (1990) continues this search. Its prologue, a recasting in verse of the essay that constitutes the second section of *Then Badger Said This,* contrasts the reshaping of the landscape caused by the damming of the river and the "steel REA / towers / stalking up and down / prairie hills" with the enduring reality "that this vast region / continues to share its destiny / with a people / who have survived hard winters / invasions / migrations / and transformations / unthought of / and unpredicted." The collection includes stories from her first two books. In the *American Book Review* (December 1992–January 1993) John Purdy compares the book to Sherwood Anderson's *Winesburg, Ohio* (1919) and William Faulkner's *Go Down, Moses and Other Stories* (1942): "*The Power of Horses* is a collage of individual characters' experiences that draws one into a specific landscape over a long period of time. We come very close to this place and the people who inhabit it."

Native Americans often point out that one of the most essential elements of cultural survival is one's native language; thus, in these stories, as in her earlier books, Cook-Lynn supplements English with Dakota words. In "Mahpiyato," which opens the book, a *kunchi* (grandmother) teaches her grandchild to observe and appreciate the rare and sacred quality of the blue-gray sky they are observing. Perhaps in speaking of the sky as feminine – which, in Dakota mythology, it is not – the grandmother wishes to instill in the child a feeling of reverence for the female as creator. As Paula Gunn Allen says in *The Sacred Hoop* (1986), "the centrality of the feminine power of universal being is crucial to" Cook-Lynn's work. Yet what is most apparent in her work is the general respect for the creation that her culture entails. In "Bennie," which ends the collection, Cook-Lynn presents an image of responsibility to, and appreciation for, even the smallest creatures. Other stories in the collection are overtly political. The narrator of "A Good Chance" is in Chamberlain, South Dakota, searching for Magpie, a young poet who has been offered a university scholarship. Magpie is on parole, having spent a year in jail for allegedly participating in the Custer Courthouse protest. With his talent and obvious commitment to his culture – he has been singing the traditional songs with his brothers – Magpie has a "good chance" to become a leader of his people; but he never gets a real chance. Picked up for breaking the conditions of his parole because he has not stayed away from his friends and relatives, Magpie is shot and killed in jail.

Cook-Lynn again exposes and condemns the misuse of the justice system in her novel, *From the River's Edge* (1991). The novel is set on the Crow Creek Sioux Reservation during the 1960s, the decade following the one in which the Missouri River was dammed for a hydroelectric project and many native families, including Cook-Lynn's relatives, were forced to relocate. On the surface the work is the story of John Tatekeya's attempt to use the court system to get back more than forty cattle that were stolen from him, but of more import is Tatekeya's search for an ethical life as his environment is destroyed. Purdy points out that the trial "provides the small event that illuminates the century for us." The attention shifts during the trial from determining who stole his cattle to probing Tatekeya's personal life. Tatekeya suffers the indignity of his excessive drinking and secret love affair being exposed, in the presence of his wife and daughter, by a fellow tribesman who testifies against him. At the end of the trial Tatekeya has not recovered any of his cattle, and the thief, a white man who has been released on bail, has probably set the fire that burns down Tatekeya's hay shed and a dozen of his haystacks. Yet there is hope: the ordeal makes Tatekeya more conscious of the value of his family and his tribe. At the end of the novel he is in the sweat lodge with Harvey Big Pipe, whose sons had cooperated with the rustler, acknowledging the "antiquities of the universe" and "his own triviality." Although Purdy thinks that "there are moments . . . when the narrator becomes too intrusive," he concludes that the novel "is compelling and relevant and wonderfully engaging." The Blackfeet critic Woody Kipp says that Cook-Lynn "writes with that surety of knowing what it is to be a stranger in your homeland. She knows also that the white man, his laws, his technology, his whole mode of existence, is perilously close to the river's edge."

In 1985 Cook-Lynn and three colleagues at Eastern Washington University – Roger Buffalohead, William Willard, and Beatrice Medicine – founded the *Wicazo Sa* [Red Pencil] *Review,* which is defined on its table of contents page as "a journal which has as its main focus the scholarship which accompanies the development of Native American Studies as an academic discipline." Since that time she has edited the journal and written many articles for it. Issues have been devoted to such topics as religious freedom for the Native American Church, the Black Hills Case, Native American Studies pedagogy and curricula, and Native American literature. Cook-Lynn's articles on Asa Primeaux Sr., the sacred pipe carrier and peyote singer, are particularly valuable in conveying the meaning of the Peyote Church to the Yankton Sioux and in exposing the U.S. government's violations of their religious freedom. Her articles on land issues, such as the Black Hills Case, expose the damage to native cultures that have resulted from breaking up land areas that had traditionally been held in common. Her articles on Native American studies stress that Native Americans ought to determine the content of the discipline and how it should be taught. Cook-Lynn offers a tribal perspective on these and other issues in her *Why I Can't Read Wallace Stegner and Other Essays* (1996).

Cook-Lynn was writer in residence at Evergreen College in Olympia, Washington in 1990; at West Virginia University in 1992; and at Atlantic Center for the Arts in New Smyrna Beach, Florida, also in 1992. During the fall of 1993 she and Momaday conducted a workshop for Sioux Nation writers at South Dakota State University, which resulted in the publication of the first issue of *Woyake Kinikiya: A Tribal Model Literary Journal* in 1994. (The title can be translated as "To Cause Our Ancestors To Live Again.") In the introduction to the journal, Elden Lawrence, a Sisseton-Wahpeton historian, says, "The true Indian authors are those who reach into their own culture, heed the voices of oral traditions still faintly heard, and accept the overwhelming challenge of trying to capture the oral traditions on the printed page." This high purpose is reflected not only in Cook-Lynn's own writing but also in her nurturing of the young Sioux writers, whose journal opens with six of Cook-Lynn's poems. Among Cook-Lynn's finest poems, they illustrate her gift for bringing together the history, places, and voices of her culture to speak the truths of human existence. They refer to the ancient water beings, the *unktechies;* to the flooding of a beloved cove; to the "glittering glass panes" of San Francisco; to lovers' quarrels; and to the remembered words of elders.

Professor emeritus at Eastern Washington University since 1989 and a visiting professor at the University of California, Davis, Cook-Lynn lives with her husband in Rapid City, South Dakota. Along with writing a sequel to her first novel, she is working with the Oglala attorney Mario Gonzalez on a nonfiction manuscript about Indian politics.

Interviews:

Joseph Bruchac, ed., *Survival This Way: Interviews with American Indian Poets* (Tucson: University of Arizona Press, 1987), pp. 57–71;

Jamie Sullivan, "Acts of Survival: An Interview with Elizabeth Cook-Lynn," *Bloomsbury Review,* 13 (January–February 1993): 1, 6.

References:

Paula Gunn Allen, *The Sacred Hoop: Recovering the Feminine in American Indian Traditions* (Boston: Beacon, 1986), p. 264;

Duane Champagne, *Native America: Portrait of the Peoples* (Detroit: Visible Ink, 1994), p. 686;

Woody Kipp, "Cultural Clash Reverberates 'From the River's Edge,' " *Lakota Times,* 21 August 1991, p. B6;

Kenneth M. Roemer, "Cook-Lynn, Elizabeth," in *Native American Women: A Biographical Dictionary,* edited by Gretchen M. Bataille (New York: Garland, 1993), pp. 62–64;

James Ruppert, "Elizabeth Cook-Lynn," in *Dictionary of Native American Literature,* edited by Andrew Wiget (New York: Garland, 1994), pp. 403–405;

Ruppert, "The Uses of Oral Tradition in Six Contemporary Native American Poets," *American Indian Culture and Research Journal,* 4, no. 4 (1980): 87–110.

George Copway (Kah-ge-ga-gah-bowh)

(1818 - January 1869)

A. LaVonne Brown Ruoff
University of Illinois at Chicago

BOOKS: *The Life, History, and Travels of Kah-ge-ga-gah-bowh (George Copway), a Young Indian Chief of the Ojebwa Nation, a Convert to the Christian Faith and a Missionary to His People for Twelve Years; with a Sketch of the Present State of the Ojebwa Nation, in Regard to Christianity and Their Future Prospects. Also an Appeal; with All the Names of the Chiefs Now Living, Who Have Been Christianized, and the Missionaries Now Laboring among Them* (Albany, N.Y.: Printed by Weed & Parsons, 1847); revised and enlarged as *The Life, Letters and Speeches of Kah-ge-ga-gah-bowh, or George Copway, Chief of the Ojibway Nation* (New York: Benedict, 1850); republished as *Recollections of a Forest Life; or, The Life and Travels of Kah-ge-ga-gah-bowh, or George Copway, Chief of the Ojibway Nation* (London: Gilpin, 1850);

Organization of a New Indian Territory, East of the Missouri River. Arguments and Reasons Submitted to the Honorable the Members of the Senate and House of Representatives of the 31st Congress of the United States: by the Indian Chief Kah-ge-ga-gah-bouh, or Geo. Copway (New York: Benedict, 1850);

The Traditional History and Characteristic Sketches of the Ojibway Nation. By G. Copway, or Kah-ge-ga-gah-bowh, Chief of the Ojibway Nation (London: Gilpin, 1850; Boston: Mussey, 1851); republished as *Indian Life and Indian History, by an Indian Author. Embracing the Traditions of the North American Indians Regarding Themselves, Particularly of that Most Important of All the Tribes, the Ojibways* (Boston: Colby, 1858);

Running Sketches of Men and Places, in England, France, Germany, Belgium, and Scotland. By George Copway (Kah-ge-ga-gah-bowh) (New York: Riker, 1851).

Editions: *Recollections of a Forest Life* (Toronto: Canadiana, 1970);

The Traditional History and Characteristic Sketches of the Ojibway Nation (Toronto: Coles, 1972);

Indian Life and Indian History (New York: AMS, 1978);

The Life, Letters and Speeches of Kah-ge-ga-gah-bowh, or G. Copway, Chief of the Ojibway Nation, edited by Donald B. Smith and A. LaVonne Brown Ruoff (Lincoln: University of Nebraska Press, 1997).

OTHER: Acts of the Apostles, translated by Copway and Sherman Hall as *Odizhijigeuiniua igou gaanoninjig* (Boston: Printed for the American Board of Commissioners for Foreign Missions by Crocker & Brewster, 1838);

Julius Taylor Clark, *The Ojibway Conquest: A Tale of the Northwest. By Kah-ge-ga-gah-bowh, or, G. Copway, Chief of the Ojibway Nation,* introduction, additional poem, and notes by Copway (New York: Putnam, 1850).

SELECTED PERIODICAL PUBLICATIONS – UNCOLLECTED: "The American Indians," *American Review,* 18 (June 1849): 631–638;

"The End of the Trail," *Saturday Evening Post* (30 March 1850); reprinted in *The Saturday Evening Post Special Bicentennial Issue: Best of the Post 1728 to 1976* (July–August 1976): 25.

George Copway, or Kah-ge-ga-gah-bowh, was one of the earliest Native American authors to write an autobiography and a history of his people. Though he translated his Indian name as "Firm Standing," it can also be interpreted as "Standing Firm" or "Committed." One of three children (he had an older sister and a younger brother), Copway was born in 1818 near the mouth of the Trent River in Upper Canada (today Ontario). Raised as a traditional Ojibwe (*Ojibwe,* rather than *Ojibwa,* is the spelling currently preferred by members of the tribe in Minnesota, Wisconsin, and Michigan; it is also the official spelling adopted by the Minnesota Chippewa Tribe), Copway was increasingly drawn into the white world after his parents converted to Methodism in 1827, and in 1830 he acceded to his mother's deathbed plea that he become a Christian.

George Copway

He occasionally attended the Methodist Mission School at Rice Lake, Ontario, and from 1834 to 1836 he helped Methodist missionaries spread the gospel among the Lake Superior Ojibwe. Two years later he entered Ebenezer Manual Labor School in Jacksonville, Illinois.

After he graduated from Ebenezer in late 1839 Copway traveled in the northeastern United States before returning to Rice Lake, where he met and married Elizabeth Howell, a white woman. The marriage was evidently opposed by her family, none of whom attended the wedding. Until 1842 the Copways served as missionaries to the Indian tribes of Wisconsin and Minnesota. Accepted as a preacher by the Wesleyan Methodist Canadian Conference, Copway was briefly a missionary in Upper Canada. In 1845 he was elected vice president of the Grand Council of Methodist Ojibwas of Upper Canada. Later that year the Saugeen and Rice Lake bands accused him of embezzlement; although Copway's mishandling of the funds may have been due less to dishonesty than to unfamiliarity with modern accounting procedures and to failure to communicate with the bands, he was imprisoned briefly in the summer of 1846 and expelled from the Canadian Conference. He went to the United States, where he was befriended by American Methodists and launched a new career as a lecturer and writer on Indian affairs.

In 1847 he published *The Life, History, and Travels of Kah-ge-ga-gah-bowh (George Copway),* which was reprinted seven times by the end of 1848. After the publication of his autobiography he lectured in the East, South, and Midwest on his plan for a separate Indian state. During this lecture tour he met the well-known scholars Henry Rowe Schoolcraft and Francis Parkman Jr. and the authors Henry Wadsworth Longfellow, Washington Irving, and James Fenimore Cooper, all of whom provided moral and financial encouragement for his later publishing projects. Three of the Copways' four children died between August 1849 and January 1850.

Copway advocated his plan for an Indian state in his pamphlet *Organization of a New Indian Territory, East of the Missouri River* (1850), in which he argues for the establishment of a Christian Indian territory to be called "Kahgega" (Ever To Be). The idea was derived from a plan for the Ojibwes advanced in 1841 by James Duane Doty, governor of the Wisconsin Territory, who proposed such a territory in the present-day Dakotas. Copway argued for a Dakota territory for the Ojibwes and other Great Lakes tribespeople, ignoring the fact that these lands were the hunting grounds of their archenemies, the Sioux. Copway submitted his plan to Congress, which never considered it. His work on his autobiography, this pamphlet, and his *Traditional History and Characteristic Sketches of the Ojibway Nation* (1850), the first published book-length history of that group written by an Ojibwe, coincided with government efforts from 1847 to 1850 to remove Ojibwes to land west of the Mississippi.

In 1850 the poem *The Ojibway Conquest* was published under Copway's name. It was actually written by Julius Taylor Clark, who gave Copway permission to publish the poem to raise funds for his missionary work. Copway added an introduction, a short poem of his own to Elizabeth, and notes.

An enlarged edition of Copway's autobiography, to which he added letters and speeches, appeared in 1850 in New York as *The Life, Letters and Speeches of Kah-ge-ga-gah-bowh, or George Copway* and in London as *Recollections of a Forest Life; or, The Life and Travels of Kah-ge-ga-gah-bowh, or George Copway.* (Although Copway referred to himself as a "chief" in his publications, he was not one.) His most important book, it incorporates material from earlier written personal histories and from Indian oral narratives. Copway seems to have felt that he had to prove he was an educated man capable of writing an autobiography, and he uses literary quotations and historical sources for this purpose. The first part of the autobiography is an ethnographic account of Ojibwe culture, in which Copway balances general descriptions with specific examples from his own experience; the second part is devoted to the conversions of his band, his family, and himself; the third to his role as mediator between Indians and whites; and the fourth to a history of Ojibwe-white relations in the recent past. Later American Indian autobiographers would imitate Copway's blending of myth, history, and recent events and his combining of tribal ethnohistory and personal experience.

By beginning his narrative with the description of his life as an Ojibwe, Copway demonstrates his strong identification with his tribal culture. His goal is not to give a detailed account of his life but rather to present himself as a typical Indian who, after conversion, exemplifies the ability of his tribe to become worthy members of mainstream society. In the ethnographic sections, which are designed to persuade his audience of the value of tribal culture and of the essential humanity of Indian people, he adopts an overwhelmingly romantic and nostalgic tone, unabashedly appealing to American affection for the stereotype of the Indian as a child of nature at the same time that he uses himself as an example of the Indian's adaptability to white civilization.

Copway's descriptions of his conversions and those of his band are meant to show the power of Christianity to uplift Indians from what the converts were taught was the darkness of tribal religion and from the degradation inflicted by whites who lured Indians into alcoholism. The description of his spiritual awakening follows the literary conventions of the confession; the passages that deal with his missionary work among the Great Lakes Ojibwes replace the conventional fall from grace and subsequent recapture of faith found in confessional narratives and reflect the influence of the missionary reminiscences that were popular in the mid nineteenth century. Indian-white relations are a major focus of the autobiography.

The Traditional History and Characteristic Sketches of the Ojibway Nation emphasizes the importance of oral tradition as a basis for Ojibwe history. The author describes his people's migrations as told in their legends and discusses their wars with such perpetual enemies as the Iroquois and the Sioux. He explains the tribe's religious beliefs, forms of government, language, pictograph writing, hunting, and games, illustrating them with anecdotes from his own experience. Especially valuable is his examination of the Ojibwes' oral history of their defeat of the Iroquois around 1700. In his comments on Indian-white relations Copway is far more critical of whites than in his autobiography. Like most historians at that time, he does not provide notes or always identify his sources. He reprints the report of the Bagot Commission of 1845 on the Canadian Indians and passages from works by Gen. Lewis Cass, William Warren (Warren's *History of the Ojibway Nation,* completed by 1852 or 1853 but not published until 1885, was known to Copway), and the Reverend Edward D. Neill. He also appends four letters on Indian civilization that he published in *The Saturday Evening Post* (30 March 1850) and an account of his lectures published in the *Liverpool Mercury* in the summer of 1850. The book disappointed his supporters, who expected more original work. In *The Writer and the Shaman* (1973) Elémire Zolla says that the history, "though chaotic on the surface, becomes coherent, carefully elaborated to demonstrate, without openly saying so, the superiority of the natives."

In 1850 Copway visited Britain and the Continent on his way to represent the Christian Indians at the World Peace Congress in Frankfurt am Main, Germany, where he created a great stir by delivering his lengthy antiwar speech in full Ojibwe regalia. Returning from Europe in December 1850, Copway hurriedly stitched together *Running Sketches of Men and Places, in England, France, Germany, Belgium, and Scotland* (1851), one of the first travel books by an Indian. Of particular interest are his impressions of such figures as Benjamin Disraeli, Lord John Russell, and Baron de Rothschild and his reactions to a concert by the Swedish singer Jenny Lind. Unfortunately, the book is padded with excerpts from his lectures, newspaper accounts of his triumphal lecture tours throughout Britain, and descriptions taken from other travel books. A review in the *New York Daily Tribune* (4 September 1851) commented that several of his "descriptions are very clever, and as naive confessions of the effect of European life on a native of the forest, may be read with interest." It concluded, however, that a "great portion of the extracts from common-place sources would have been better omitted."

Abandoned by most of his intellectual friends, who had become tired of his too-frequent appeals for money, Copway attempted to support his family by publishing a weekly newspaper, *Copway's American Indian,* in which he reprinted old lectures, rehashed previously expressed positions on issues pertaining to Native Americans, and published letters from influential acquaintances. The paper ran from 10 July to 4 October 1851. In 1852 Copway was elected to membership in the New York chapter of the Order of United Americans, an antiimmigrant, anti–Roman Catholic movement that was later reorganized as the Know-Nothing Party. He abandoned his family in the summer of 1856, but they were reunited in 1858. *The Traditional History and Characteristic Sketches of the Ojibway Nation* was republished that year under the title *Indian Life and Indian History*. Copway and his wife had a daughter, Frances Minnehaha, in 1860 or 1861. Along with his brother, David, Copway recruited Canadian Indians to serve in the American Civil War; he surfaced again in 1867 when he advertised himself in the *Detroit Free Press* as a healer. The following year, after apparently abandoning his family again, Copway arrived at Lac-des-deux-Montagnes, a large Algonquian and Iroquois mission about thirty miles northwest of Montreal. Describing himself as a pagan, he announced his intention to convert to Catholicism. On 17 January 1869 he was baptized Joseph-Antoine. He died a few days later, shortly before he was to receive his first communion; the exact date of his death is not known.

Undoubtedly, Elizabeth Howell Copway aided her husband in the preparation of his books. In his autobiography Copway acknowledges the assistance of a "friend" who corrected all "serious grammatical errors." The "friend" was probably his wife, an accomplished writer who wrote many articles for publications in Canada and the United States. She died in 1904.

George Copway is one of the most important figures in nineteenth-century American Indian literature. *The Life, History, and Travels of Kah-ge-ga-gah-bowh (George Copway)* is the first full-length autobiography by a Native American that deals with traditional tribal culture. *The Traditional History and Characteristic Sketches of the Ojibway Nation* is among the earliest histories written by an Indian. It is significant also because of the emphasis Copway places on the importance of incorporating oral tradition into tribal histories, a principle that historians of Native American history have increasingly acknowledged in the twentieth century. Both his autobiography and his history express a native point of view that is sorely missing in other accounts of Indian-white relations published in the nineteenth century. Nevertheless, readers should be aware that he sometimes substitutes imagination and enthusiasm for accuracy in his accounts of his life and of historic events. His style is, by turns, journalistic, discursive, romantic, and hortatory. He evokes the image of the "noble savage" who remembers fondly the golden age of Ojibwe and Indian cultures that has been superseded by white "civilization"; at the same time, by creating the image of the educated Native American he reminds his audience of his people's capacity for acculturation. While he often casts himself as a forest poet and rhapsodizes about the past, he also depicts himself as a "word warrior" who does not hesitate to point out the hypocrisy and cruelty with which Indians have been treated.

References:

Dale T. Knobel, "Know-Nothings and Indians: Strange Bedfellows?," *Western Historical Quarterly,* 15 (April 1984): 175–198;

A. LaVonne Brown Ruoff, "George Copway: Nineteenth-Century American Indian Autobiographer," *Auto/Biography,* 3 (Summer 1987): 6–17;

Ruoff, "Nineteenth-Century American Indian Autobiographers: William Apes, George Copway, and Sarah Winnemucca," in *Redefining American Literary History,* edited by Ruoff and Jerry W. Ward Jr. (New York: Modern Language Association, 1990), pp. 251–269;

Donald B. Smith, "The Life of George Copway or Kah-ge-ga-gah-bowh (1818–1869) – and a Review of his Writings," *Journal of Canadian Studies,* 23 (Autumn 1988): 5–38;

Elémire Zolla, *The Writer and the Shaman* (New York: Harcourt Brace Jovanovich, 1973), p. 238.

Papers:

Letters, receipts, and other papers of George Copway are in the Library of Congress.

Ella C. Deloria

(31 January 1889 - 12 February 1971)

Julian Rice
Florida Atlantic University

BOOKS: *Dakota Texts* (New York: Stechert, 1932);

Dakota Grammar, by Deloria and Franz Boas (Washington, D.C.: U.S. Government Printing Office, 1941);

Speaking of Indians (New York: Friendship Press, 1944);

Waterlily, with a biographical sketch by Agnes Picotte and an afterword by Raymond J. DeMallie (Lincoln: University of Nebraska Press, 1988).

Editions: *Dakota Texts,* edited by Agnes Picotte and Paul N. Pavich (Vermillion, S.Dak.: Dakota Press, 1978);

Dakota Grammar (Vermillion, S.Dak.: Dakota Press, 1982);

Speaking of Indians, edited by Picotte and Pavich (Vermillion, S.Dak.: Dakota Press, 1983).

OTHER: "Iron Hawk: Oglala Culture Hero" and "Dakota Play on Words," in *Ella Deloria's Iron Hawk,* by Julian Rice (Albuquerque: University of New Mexico Press, 1993), pp. 19–104, 209–216;

"A Sioux Captive," "Stake Carriers," "A Woman Captive and Her Baby," "The Prairie Dogs," and "The Buffalo People," in *Ella Deloria's The Buffalo People,* by Rice (Albuquerque: University of New Mexico Press, 1994), pp. 27–38, 45–93.

SELECTED PERIODICAL PUBLICATIONS – UNCOLLECTED: "The Sun Dance of the Oglala Sioux," *Journal of American Folklore,* 42 (1929): 354–413;

"Short Dakota Texts, Including Conversations," *International Journal of American Linguistics,* 20 (1954): 17–24.

Until the 1988 publication of her posthumous novel, *Waterlily,* Ella C. Deloria's reputation rested on her achievements in linguistics and ethnology. Few readers realized the literary talents that had produced the little-known collection of traditional stories titled *Dakota Texts* (1932), because most assumed that Deloria simply transcribed and translated tales that elderly Sioux people had agreed to tell her. These narrators, distrustful of non-Indian anthropologists, spoke freely to Deloria because she needed no interpreter and listened respectfully as a relative, without such inhibiting paraphernalia as a recorder or a notepad. Like generations of Indian storytellers before her, Deloria absorbed the spirit and feeling of the stories; but, unlike those earlier storytellers, she retold them in writing – first in Lakota, then in English. Essentially, however, she transmitted the stories as they had always been passed down, renewing them in her own words rather than duplicating a prior performance. Her

Ella C. Deloria

adaptation of the oral tradition to nuanced, written Lakota is a unique achievement.

The white term *Sioux* comprises three related groups of people, with members of each group speaking a language that can be understood by members of the other two groups: the Dakota of Minnesota and eastern South Dakota, the Nakota of south central South Dakota, and the Lakota of western South Dakota. Ella Cara Deloria's parents were Nakota speakers from the Yankton reservation, where she was born on 31 January 1889; but she grew up among Lakota people on the Standing Rock reservation in Fort Yates, North Dakota, where her father served as one of the first Indians ordained in the Episcopal Church. Philip Deloria had converted to Christianity at seventeen; though he respected the beliefs and ceremonies of his ancestors, he employed his forceful eloquence to help his people adapt to change by adopting Christianity and Western culture. Some of his willingness to abandon the spiritual practices of his father, Saswe, a great medicine man, may have arisen from his knowledge of his own mixed origins: his paternal grandfather, Philippe Des Lauriers, had established the first trading post among the Yankton around 1822 near the present city of Pierre, South Dakota. Ella Deloria's mother, Mary Sully Bordeaux, had been born and raised in the White Swan (Yankton) community but was three-quarters white. Both parents spoke Nakota as their primary language, so it was the first language of Deloria's childhood. The closely related Lakota dialect, however, would become the major vehicle of her adult work.

In line with her parents' Christian beliefs and their faith in the promise of assimilation, Deloria received a rigorous education in the fundamentals of reading and writing English, along with introductory French and German, at the Episcopalian Saint Elizabeth Mission School and All Saints School in Sioux Falls, South Dakota. After she spent the academic year 1911–1912 at Oberlin College in Ohio, her professors suggested that her particular talents would flourish at Columbia University under Franz Boas, the founder of American Indian linguistics. Having learned an orthography developed by Boas, Deloria was assigned the task of revising, translating, and annotating a thousand-page manuscript, most of it consisting of traditional stories, that a young, literate Lakota, George Bushotter, had written for the ethnologist James Owen Dorsey in 1887. She began work on the manuscript in 1918, the year after she received her B.S. from Columbia; after many interruptions, she would complete it around 1945. Still unpublished, the Bushotter manuscript is a major contribution to the study of Lakota narrative tradition.

After graduating from Columbia, Deloria taught at All Saints School and then, from 1923 to 1928, held a position as a physical education instructor at Haskell Institute, an Indian school in Lawrence, Kansas. Having learned to write Lakota by reworking previously transcribed texts, Deloria was encouraged by Boas to collect stories on her own at the Pine Ridge and Rosebud Lakota reservations. Deloria's research resulted in *Dakota Texts,* a remarkable bilingual collection of sixty-four short stories. It is unlikely that anyone else could have produced this volume. If she had not been fluent in the Lakota language, the stories would only have been summaries gleaned from verbally unsophisticated interpreters, such as traders or reservation employees, as are other anthropological versions of Indian oral narratives. If she had not been trained from childhood in the subtleties of kinship respect and deference, the storytellers would not have told the stories freely, with all the cultural nuances they knew that only she, among the visiting academic auditors, could understand. If she had not received linguistic training under Boas at Columbia she would not have been able to transcribe the stories in Lakota. And if her parents had not been progressive enough to see to her acquisition of polished English-language skills, Deloria could not have left a record that makes the renewal of traditional oral storytelling a possibility today.

Decades of indoctrination by missionaries and other "friends of the Indian" had caused many Lakota people to abandon such "backward" customs as storytelling. But Deloria was able to hear storytellers who were old enough to remember and convey an unbroken narrative tradition that reached back long before the reservation period began; several of these storytellers were already in their twenties by the time of the Little Bighorn Battle in 1876. Deloria divided the volume into tales that are considered mythical; those that are ancient and probably true, though they may include supernatural events; and those that are historically true and directly traceable for several generations back. The most-developed narratives are the trickster and culture-hero stories and the stories of courting, seduction, and jealousy.

The Lakota trickster is called Iktomi (Spider). By assuming this persona, the narrators warn of danger in human nature, so that the listener may learn to beware of self-deception or of unscrupulous enemies both domestic and foreign. Iktomi often incarnates an outrageous selfishness that could destroy a camp circle: in one story he pretends to die so that he can come back in disguise to marry his daughter, while in another he seduces his mother-in-law and has children by her – a violation of a taboo so strong that men and their mothers-in-law and women and their fathers-in-law were never even supposed to look at each other. In other stories Iktomi's threats to the social order are less drastic, though they represent wasteful diversions: Iktomi's curiosity about mice dancing in an elk's skull prompts him to get his head caught in the skull, from which only a concussion-producing blow with a rock can free him; his effort to silence scraping branches that disturb his sleep results in his getting stuck between them, while a wolf steals the roasting ducks he had earlier tricked into dancing with their eyes closed.

These trickster episodes have familiar analogues in many traditions, but Iktomi is an especially complex and contradictory figure. While he demonstrates the misuse of the mind, he also personifies an alertness that others may put to good use. In the first story in *Dakota Texts,* for example, Iktomi saves a tribe by eliciting a people-eating monster's confession that he fears rattles, drums, bells, and shouts – ceremonial expressions that banish brutality. Here, as in other stories, Iktomi acts selfishly but awakens the group's ability to act responsibly. Intelligence is only a beginning; it can be used selfishly, as Iktomi uses his, or creatively to assure the survival of the people. Iktomi goes his own merry, often devastating way at the end of the stories, but the tribe – both in the stories and in real life – benefits by imitating his alertness.

Some of Deloria's culture heroes employ trickster qualities on behalf of the people. Stone Boy pretends to apply a chiropractic treatment to a witch who has imprisoned his uncles; in the process he breaks all of her bones. Later he entices the buffalo nation to attack his family so as to establish human predominance and end his people's fear of the large, dangerous animal that will become the basis of their material and cultural life. Other culture heroes, such as White Plume Boy and Blood Clot Boy, are unlike Iktomi in any way. He immobilizes them for a time, but in the end they prevail and assume their adult responsibility of unstinting service to the group. The culture-hero stories typically follow a pattern: a young man is educated in hunting skills and social respect by a wise grandparent; his early triumphs lead to an overconfidence that makes him easy prey for Iktomi, who, after diverting him from his journey to marriage and joining of the people, usurps his role and steals his supernatural powers; the hero recovers and banishes Iktomi, marries, and attains leadership in his own community or in that of his wife.

While the culture-hero stories in *Dakota Texts* demonstrate male pitfalls and possibilities, the stories of courting, seduction, and jealousy concern the virtues that women may direct against the social and psychological dangers that they are likely to face. In "Double-Face Steals a Virgin" a young woman who has refused many suitors is swept off her feet by a handsome stranger. After running away with him she discovers that he is a cannibal who has eaten his previous wives. She escapes by employing the dexterity and concentration she had learned in the women's arts. After a long and dangerous journey, during which she is adopted and protected from the pursuing monster by a family of animals that includes a buffalo, bear, lynx, and snake, she arrives at her people's camp, having learned the hard way not to succumb to infatuation and ready to rely on her relatives to protect her. She endured initially, however, only because her upbringing had prepared her to be resourceful in times of danger. In other stories mature women, unable to escape human or animal attackers, deceive and kill them with only skinning knives for weapons.

In the course of an escape from an abusive husband, another of Deloria's women acquires supernatural powers usually reserved for men. While resting in a cave with her baby she is befriended by a pack of wolves, with whom she lives peacefully for the winter. They bring her meat, and she cracks the bones to feed marrow to their pups. In the spring she meets two Lakota scouts and returns, reluctantly at first, to her people. In return for her periodically leaving them piles of fat outside the camp, the wolves give the woman the ability to locate lost objects clairvoyantly and to heal diseases ceremonially. In the end, however, she abandons her supernatural powers to devote herself to raising the child of the man she had left.

Other stories in *Dakota Texts* show the consequences of adultery. In "A Bad Deed" a jealous husband who kills the lover of his youngest wife is banished from the group, along with his wives, because nothing can justify the murder of a fellow tribesman. He is adopted into the Crow tribe when he agrees to give his youngest wife in marriage to a kindly Crow war leader. The story illustrates the necessity of preserving a peaceful network of relationships within a camp circle: if an individual allows personal passions to threaten the peace, he –

and sometimes his immediate dependents – must depart to avoid an endless cycle of revenge. Without an extended family or tribe, an individual is as good as dead.

After leaving her position at Haskell Institute, Deloria derived an income of $100 to $200 a month for several months each year from Columbia University, where she gave occasional lectures on the stories she had heard in South Dakota. She also collaborated with Boas on *Dakota Grammar* (1941). In the preface Boas praises Deloria's Lakota language skills, her "perfect control of idiomatic usage," and her sensitivity to the "minute" shades of meaning produced by varying accents or particles that are almost inaudible to a non-Dakota linguist.

Deloria's most significant transformations of the narrative tradition remained unpublished for more than fifty years after she wrote them. By 1937 she had refined her technique of writing in the oral narrative style sufficiently to produce a series of tales that are much longer and more complex than those in *Dakota Texts*. "Iron Hawk: Oglala Culture Hero," published in 1993, combines all of the elements of the culture-hero genre that are usually distributed into many shorter stories; as Deloria puts it, it includes "all the usual incidents bound up and woven together around one hero." Few narrators told stories of this elaborateness and length, but the one on whom Deloria based "Iron Hawk" almost certainly did: he was the renowned Makula, who is called Left Heron in James R. Walker's collection *Lakota Myth* (1983).

Makula was about eighty-five when he spoke to Deloria, and the version Deloria produced contains much more dialogue and much more attention to the nature and propriety of kinship relations than the digests of Makula's stories that Walker had gathered almost twenty-five years earlier. But the story has a purpose and an effect that goes beyond the correct reporting of cultural details. For years Lakota culture had been subjected to unrelenting white pressure to reduce itself to nothing; Indian children were forced to attend boarding schools, where the potential "savages" could be turned into docile farmers, mechanics, and maids. Native languages and tribal identities were zealously suppressed to implement the programs of a series of commissioners of Indian affairs. The sentiments of J. D. C. Atkins, commissioner from 1885 to 1888, as given in an 1887 report to Congress, are typical:

> Their barbarous dialect should be blotted out and the English language substituted. . . . The object of greatest solicitude should be. . . . to blot out the boundary lines which divide them into distinct nations, and fuse them into one homogeneous mass. Uniformity of language will do this – nothing else will.

Through "Iron Hawk" Deloria disproves these self-serving beliefs. The story's existence as a complex literary expression of a highly developed mythology implies the effectiveness of traditional education, and the opening episode shows the wisdom of early nurture and growth in the camp circle. Deloria traces the development of the hero from his spiritual imprinting by wise and loving grandparents, through a series of triumphs and setbacks that remind him of his vulnerabilities and help to develop his strength. After the usual humiliation at the hands of Iktomi and captivity by a seductive Rock woman, Iron Hawk recovers and confers gifts of power and wisdom on the tribe. He brings the people their first horses after making an alliance with the grandfather of the West, and he succeeds in transmitting the best of the past to the present when he has his son, Red Calf, transport Iron Hawk's meadowlark parents from their old home in the East so that they can influence the growth of their great-grandson, Rattling Deer Hooves.

Like many Plains culture heroes, Iron Hawk begins life as an abandoned infant adopted by benevolent animals. The meadowlarks represent the courage and joy conferred by culture rather than by blood. Other important symbols of culturally created virtue include the red paint that his meadowlark father applies to the child as physical and spiritual protection and the clothing that Iron Hawk temporarily loses to Iktomi when he forgets that one's identity depends on remembering the makers of protective cover and on providing physical and spiritual shelter for one's relatives.

Directional symbols are important in the story. Like most culture heroes, Iron Hawk initially travels west to establish his social identity; but the story's final episode describes the eastward journey of Red Calf. Deloria reverses the usual direction because Red Calf's mission resembles her own efforts: first he travels eastward into the past; then, like many Lakota people of the generation that followed Deloria's, he brings the best of the past – his meadowlark grandparents – back to the West and the present. In Lakota culture meadowlarks embody social harmony, the will and ability to defend their nests, and the power of infusing humor, joy, and comfort into all who hear their songs. The separation of Iron Hawk from his meadowlark parents at the beginning and his son's successful mission to recover them symbolize Deloria's refusal to allow the discontinuity suffered by Indian culture in her time to become an insurmountable gap.

Another long story of 1937, "The Buffalo People," first published in 1994, demonstrates the effectiveness of tribal education in shaping character. Here, as in all of her ethnological, linguistic, and literary work, Deloria continues to fulfill the mission she described in a letter of 2 December 1952 to H. E. Beebe: to make her people "understandable as human beings" so as to counteract the assumption that they "had *nothing,* no rules of life, no social organization, no ideals." "The Buffalo People" reveals the far from primitive complexity of many Lakota customs by mythologizing their origins.

The first man and woman on earth, Waziya and Wakanka, receive no supernatural instruction and never refer to a creator, but they seem to know from the beginning that each of their five children should be born at no less than three-year intervals. Thus, they begin the age-old Lakota practice of ensuring that each child receives sufficient nurture to establish a strong separate identity, along with the spontaneous desire to reciprocate familial love. Later, Waziya not only teaches his two grandsons to walk at an earlier age than their overprotective aunts might have wished but also teaches them to walk the earth with reverence. Then he instructs them in how to play the hoop-and-stick game, not only to enhance their coordination and to teach them to count their scores but also to show them how to endure occasional defeat cheerfully.

The mother of one of the boys exemplifies the egotism that threatens to divide society when she overreacts to her son's minor injury during a game by taking the boy and leaving the camp. Returning to her original form as a buffalo, she easily outdistances her pursuing sisters-in-law with her calf. Her husband can at first do nothing but grieve for the loss of his son. He is equipped for the pursuit of his wife and son, however, by his selfless second wife, a corn spirit in the body of a beautiful blonde woman. To help him locate his buffalo wife the corn woman gives him four magic arrows, and to help him avoid danger she gives him a magic plume.

The father endures thirst and quicksandlike mud and finally arrives at the buffalo camp, where his mother-in-law tirelessly devises ways to kill him. First she tries to crush him in a stone door, but the corn woman's plume turns him into a feather and he wafts out of reach. Next she sends him to gather tepee pins from snake-infested bushes, but the plume generates a whirlwind that breaks the bushes and destroys the snakes. Then she sends him to take birdlings from a Thunderbird's nest, anticipating his destruction by lightning. This time the Great Spirit Judge intervenes, admonishing the Thunderbird and the man to have respect for each other.

Thereafter, the mother-in-law's plots suggest a desire to destroy society by seeking a false justice that condemns rather than the diplomatically arranged agreements that allow the group to endure. She sets up a test whereby the man must pick his wife from a group of identical buffalo women and his son from a group of identical buffalo calves; if he fails the first test he will show himself to be guilty of adultery, and if he fails the second he will reveal that he is not completely devoted to his family. Like the trickster, the mother-in-law lives to humiliate others while promoting the image of herself as a victim of injustice. Also like the trickster, she comically violates all the social taboos that promote harmony, not only facing her son-in-law directly but even calling him "son-in-law" frequently and with no compunction. (Deloria retains the humorous effect of this direct address, which only dialogue can supply, while summaries of the story by other anthropologists miss it.) After the man passes all of the tests, he kills his mother-in-law and the brutal chief Crazy Buffalo, who had conspired with her to tyrannize the buffalo nation. The buffalo elders then adopt and honor him. In the end he becomes the father of the Lakota people, enabling them to draw food, clothing, shelter, and visionary inspiration from their primary animal kin.

Waziya and Wakanka, their four daughters, the corn wife, and her son grieve for the man's absence for a time; but the corn wife, like the meadowlark grandparents in "Iron Hawk," has the cheerful resilience that allowed the Lakota people, and in this case their neighbors, the Arikara people, to survive. She teaches the remaining family members to grow corn, the plant that came to serve the Arikara as the source of life and spiritual meaning. The corn wife also institutes customs that the Arikara and Lakota shared: the respect-avoidance between parents and children-in-law of the opposite sex, rituals of appreciation before taking food from the earth or from animals, the food-preserving technique of digging deep caches for dried vegetables and meat, and, for the Arikara alone, the method of building large, firmly constructed dwellings of wood and packed earth. In the end the corn woman arranges marriages for her sisters-in-law; her son departs the camp and returns with a wife; and she herself finally marries a brother of her sister's husbands, thus strengthening the kinship bonds that held Plains communities together.

In her writing of oral narratives, as in her other works, Deloria emphasizes that the psychological integrity of Lakota society derived directly from kinship. All of a child's father's brothers were also the child's fathers, and all of his or her mother's sisters were the child's mothers. When any of a child's siblings – which included cousins – married, all the brothers-in-law and sisters-in-law became the child's in-laws. All respect relationships then had to be observed, even if the people involved barely knew each other, including the bold teasing relationship that was mandated between brothers-in-law and sisters-in-law. The kinship system permitted many expressions of respect and disrespect, decorum and mischief, but only within a larger pattern that was predictable enough to mitigate slights, insults, or rage. The buffalo mother-in-law in "The Buffalo People" represents the degree to which egotism can disrupt a society prior to the evolution of a complicated kinship order. In Lakota communities virtually everyone was related by marriage or adoption, and that is why young men in the stories always travel to find wives.

Two other stories from 1937, first published in 1994, are actually two versions of a story about a Lakota woman who rescued her husband from captivity by the Crow; while both storytellers accept the story as basically true, each modifies it to accord with his message, temperament, and audience. The narrator of the first version, "A Sioux Captive," is Deloria's brother by an adoption involving her brother, Vine Deloria Sr.; although they had never met before the interview, he addresses her as "Younger Sister" and several times makes interjections to distance himself from the incidents of torture and scalping in his story.

The woman in this story is initially fearful, but she secretly enters the Crow camp disguised as a Crow woman, carrying a piece of rotting wood wrapped to look like a baby, and, calming herself with a great effort, frees her husband while his guards sleep. The narrator calls the man's torture at the hands of the Crow "a nightmare"; after the woman drags her husband to the waiting horses and observes his wounds more clearly, she flies into a rage, returns to the camp, and kills and scalps the guards. At the end of the story the narrator describes the tribe's praise of her actions and comments that she "takes first prize in loving her husband."

In the other version of the story Deloria's narrator does not address her by a kinship term and is more concerned to show the recuperative powers of the "Indians the white men call Sioux." "Stake Carriers" begins with a description of the husband's prowess as a stake carrier, a warrior pledged to tie himself to a stake driven into the ground and hold off pursuers until the rest of the war party escapes. After his capture the stake carrier's wife sets out to track him to the Crow camp. Showing no fear, she not only carries the rotting-wood "baby" as a disguise but also speaks to it almost humorously, apparently using her imagination in an effort to repress her rage. While the hands of the first narrator's woman shake as she cuts her husband's ropes, the woman in this story coolly tells her husband to kill and scalp one of the sleeping guards in order to gain the honor he has earned. When he is too weak to do so, she cuts the throats of all six guards but does not take any scalps. On the way out of the camp she commandeers two especially swift buffalo-hunting horses, because, unlike the woman in "A Sioux Captive," she had traveled to the Crow camp on foot.

On their return to their own tribe the man and woman are praised and given new names: the man is called "Wearer of a Cloth Blanket" because his wife wrapped him in such a blanket when she brought him from the tepee, and the woman is called "Rotting Wood's Mother." At the end the narrator adds that the husband's rescue by a woman did not diminish his reputation as a warrior and that he went on to distinguish himself in many fights. The second narrator seems less concerned to show an individual woman's love for her husband than to recall the sort of tribal character trait that can defy the humiliation of defeat. Deloria sustains the quite different voice of each narrator throughout each story.

In "The Prairie Dogs," another of Makula's stories written down in 1937 and first published in 1994, Deloria recommends the revival of warrior-society ceremonies and dances as an antidote to the despair that gripped many Native Americans in the 1930s. The prairie dogs in the story, who dwell in "permanent houses" such as the reservation Lakota, have suddenly stopped dancing. Their village has become lethargic, as were many reservation communities. Six animals arrive in succession and exhort the prairie dogs to dance, describing their prowess in escaping hunters and driving off enemies. Such a "coup-talk" was a conventional means of assuring warriors that they had relatives ready and willing to defend them, and the recitation of an individual's deeds was invigorating to the onlookers. When the prairie dogs remain unmoved, the six

Dust jacket for Deloria's posthumously published novel about a Lakota woman

animals foretell the introduction of the two elders' societies and the four oldest-warrior societies of camp-circle days by individuals who will receive a vision instructing them to direct the group's distinctive rituals. The warrior societies, each of which had one of the six animals as its guardian, spent more time instilling symbolically dramatized confidence than in actual fighting; their purpose was primarily inspirational rather than military. Women played an important role in the performances by sounding the screech owl cry, an electrifying trill that followed talk about brave deeds and that concluded initiation ceremonies.

Among the societies' guardians, non-Lakota readers may be surprised to observe the skunk, protector of the Crow Owners society; the prairie chicken, guardian of the Brave Hearts society; and the rabbit, coguardian with the fox of the Kit Fox society; but the Lakota stressed intelligent survival rather than pure strength. The will to survive symbolized by these animals eventually led the Lakota to revive warrior-society songs and dances in the modern powwow. The story suggests that the Lakota must depend on their own traditions rather than allow their children to regard themselves as belonging to a vanquished people. The story also indicates that generosity is as important as the will to fight: the two elders' societies – the Owl Feather Headdress society for counselors and the Buffalo society for chiefs – had their own dignified dances that were supposed to suffuse the whole society with steadiness. The dances symbolize the obligation of Lakota men of all ages to teach and inspire, as well as to feed, clothe, and defend the tribe.

Deloria annotates many of the meanings her narrators left unspoken, but she does not alter the poetic suggestiveness of the oral style. In "Iron Hawk," "The Buffalo People," "The Prairie Dogs," and several still-unpublished stories, Deloria reached the highest development of her writing in the spoken style. In the 1940s she devoted herself to two major projects in English, one ethnographic, the other literary.

The still-unpublished "Camp Circle Society" is a long description of nineteenth-century Lakota life, derived directly from informants who could say "I saw" and "I did" or who had parents or grandparents who could say the same. In her 1954 introduction to the manuscript Margaret Mead emphasizes Deloria's ability to externalize the experience of the people she described: "Miss Deloria has produced a volume which supplements, in cadence and image, the formal descriptions with the introspective reality." In the oral narratives Deloria's adherence to the authentic storytelling forms had prevented her from spelling out a character's private thoughts.

In her novel, *Waterlily,* published more than forty years after its completion, Deloria was able to show "not only what a people do, but how they *think* and *feel* to make them do it," as she described her purpose in a grant application to the American Philosophical Society in 1944. *Waterlily* reflects Deloria's accumulated knowledge of social customs and material culture as well as her imaginative projection of a past when predictable habits balanced the ever-present possibility of devastation by enemies or natural forces. A valuable source of information about a nineteenth-century Indian community, it includes detailed descriptions of the obtaining and preparation of all kinds of food; the instruction of children; the making of tools, containers, clothing, and other objects; major ceremonies, such as the Ghost Keeping, Sun Dance, and *Hunka* (making of relatives, or, as in *Waterlily,* honoring of children); and games and amusements. The novel follows the title character's life from her birth, through a childhood that includes a deadly enemy raid, to a marriage that ends when her husband dies of smallpox spread by the whites, and finally to a promise of happiness in a second marriage that begins as the novel ends.

Waterlily's story transpires against a background of cultural integrity that was just beginning to feel the effects of white encroachment. Few of the characters have ever seen, let alone talked to, a non-Indian. But Deloria, the narrators she interviewed, and most of her Native American readers would understand *Waterlily* as an English-language refutation of stereotypic slanders that had been perpetrated against the Lakota in that language. In *Waterlily,* as in "The Prairie Dogs," Deloria shows how traditional values of sacrifice and generosity were manifested in a never-ending social theater. Its performances ranged from the profoundly sacred, as in the Sun Dance or Ghost Keeping, to the monologues of storytellers, to the spectacularly costumed and choreographed dances of the warrior societies.

In *Waterlily* the storyteller character, Woyaka, reflects Deloria's reverence for the vast memory and brilliant spontaneity she observed in men such as Makula. Since the society's ability to cohere depends on cultural memory, Woyaka's father has imbued him with a sense of mission: "If you fail them, there might be nobody else to remind them of their tribal history." This responsibility is a heavy and lonely burden: "His eyes were fierce and searching and he went about with a great preoccupation that everlastingly set him apart and made ordinary men uneasy in his company unless he was telling a story." The story Woyaka tells clarifies the role of the creative individual in Lakota society: a dreamer ends a famine when he intones a sacred language, learned in a vision, to summon a herd of buffalo. "A magnificent buffalo . . . led them; with eyes aglare he approached, frightening the people. But they knew they must stand their ground . . . everyone must cooperate, for that was where the power finally lay." The buffalo "entered the circle . . . to the accompaniment of the continuous clatter, clatter of wood on wood, which the women and children made, striking their clubs in rhythm on the dog-travois poles. The singing of the holy man, the clatter, and the pace of the buffalo never slackened. Meantime each hunter picked out his animal and shot it from over the women's shoulders." The sense of cooperative performance includes the auditors, who are the beneficiaries of the represented deeds.

When Waterlily is about twelve her fifteen-year-old brother, Little Chief, kills his first buffalo in a snowstorm. His recitation of the deed occurs at a feast for the male elders of his grandfather's generation. Little Chief's monologue has been eagerly awaited by these old men, because it affirms a future they have devoted their lives to ensuring. Little Chief remembers being blinded by "whipping snow" that cut through his naked body after he loses his robe; nevertheless, he cut a buffalo from the herd and killed it with only three arrows. The grandfathers perform their part in this drama of tribal continuity by rubbing their hands together to show satisfaction and placing them over their mouths to show wonder and praise. Repeatedly, Little Chief comments naively on his struggle: "I tell you it was hard," "It was very bad"; but the statements are not considered boastful because they reveal an emerging confidence in his ability to provide. An old man closes the performance with a gesture of renewal, holding up one finger as if to say, "This is only the beginning."

All of these ritualized events build confidence in the tribe's future. The description of a Kit Fox society initiation is so dramatic that it helps to explain why the prairie dogs were depressed when these ceremonies ended. The pageantry of the meeting between the massed Lakota and Omaha tribes, the conferring of an additional honor on Little Chief after he daringly tags along with a war party to earn the rank of "water carrier," the riveting episode of the "snake dreamer" coaxing a rattlesnake away from a sleeping child by showing "his brother" patience and respect – these and many other events offer variations, not found elsewhere in the written record, on how the male role required poised performance in both act and representation.

A man Waterlily does not know offers to buy her with horses that her family needs to replace stolen ones they had planned to give away at the Ghost Keeping ceremony. She agrees to marry him because she wishes to uphold her family's honor and to provide the uplifting ceremony for the camp circle, placing these duties before her personal happiness. Her husband proves to be intelligent, protective, and kind. But now she must reside in her husband's community rather than her own. Apart from homesickness, this uprooting necessitates many forms of kinship behavior that do not allow relaxed intimacy, from the avoidance relationship to her father-in-law, to the constant bantering between brothers- and sisters-in-law. The tension of playing the role of perfect daughter or sister-in-law is finally broken when Waterlily discovers a "mother" and "father" in her new camp circle: they are parents, in the extended-family sense, of her "brother," Red Leaf, who had entered into a formal adoption bond with her real brother, Little Chief, when they were children. Waterlily's freedom to express both the adult and childlike sides of her nature provides the psychological balance that the kinship system could ideally achieve; she is fortified to play the part her husband's relatives expect of her because she has found other members of the community in whom she can confide and with whom she can laugh, gossip, and relax. Because the kinship system extends benevolent feelings to virtual strangers, Waterlily is able to gain instant intimate connections to men, women, and children of several generations. She even has a "granddaughter" when her eldest sister's son becomes the father of a girl.

There are social rules regarding speech that require a range of verbal behavior from oration to silence. During her labor to give birth to Waterlily her mother, Blue Bird, suffers without a sound to sustain the awed respect that would vanish with a voiced complaint. Frequently in the novel the withholding of overt expression communicates support more effectively than words or explicit gestures would. When Blue Bird returns to her home camp circle after her husband's family is decimated in an enemy attack, she refrains from seeking out close relatives because she does not want to act "as an untrained puppy" that leaps up and soils a person's clothes. Children are taught to restrain their words; a girl must never call her brother "silly," for example, even if he is. Grandparents teach restraint by example; severe verbal or physical punishment is never countenanced. The usual reproof is simply a reminder of the social responsibility each individual has learned: "Nobody does that, Grandchild."

Withheld speech achieves its strongest expression at the novel's conclusion. Earlier in the book there is a performance of the Sun Dance, which involved various forms of suffering – body piercing, flesh offerings, and fasting – that lasted for three nights and two days. Wives and girlfriends would ritually slip small containers of water to the dancers during rest periods, as if they were secretly aiding captives. The "sneaking" dramatized the subordination of concern for oneself and one's immediate relatives to the universal life the Sun Dance renewed. Overt expression of personal feelings for loved ones was regarded as shameful; the shared life of the group came first. The young man to whom Waterlily "illicitly" gives water is a stranger at the time, but he eventually becomes her second husband. (He is also her first husband's "brother" in the extended-family sense: he is a brother of the first husband's cousin and is, therefore, automatically a father to Waterlily's children.) After they have been married for a time, he mentions that he hopes that Waterlily was the girl who gave him water at the Sun Dance long ago. Part of her wishes, romantically, to say yes, but she realizes that her husband might come to feel suspicious of one who had broken the rules before. She refuses to lower this "curtain of distrust" that might divide not only her marriage but also the families that marriage unites: "He shall never know! He must get along with a little less than perfect happiness. It will be best that way."

The Missionary Education Movement subsidized Deloria's informal ethnographical book, *Speaking of Indians* (1944), and the Wenner-Gren Foundation conferred a $600 grant that resulted in an article published in 1954 in the *International Journal of American Linguistics*. In 1955 Deloria had to accept the directorship of Saint Elizabeth Mission School, the same school where she had begun her own education, to support herself and her sister. In 1959 she was able to find employment more compatible with her training and experience at the Sioux Indian Museum in Rapid City, South Dakota, and in 1961 she became director of the W. H. Over Anthropological Museum at the University of South Dakota. In 1962 she received a major grant from the National Science Foundation to put together a dictionary based on the compilation of Lakota root words and their derivatives that she had begun in collaboration with Boas in 1929 and had continued for thirty years. The grant ran out in 1966, and the unpublished dictionary remains in the Boas Collection of the American Philosophical Society.

In failing health, Deloria had to return to teaching at Saint Mary's Indian School for Girls in Springfield, South Dakota. One student recalled how she made the students "tickled and happy" just to be in the same room with her. To stress the value of speaking their own language Deloria told the students stories that were amusing in English but hilarious in Lakota – as the English-only speakers had to judge by the laughter of their Lakota-speaking classmates. Deloria suffered a stroke in 1970 and died on 12 February 1971.

One of her students offered a tribute that could not have been better put by any of the experts Deloria's work now attracts. In *The Saint Mary's Bugle* (March 1966) Wanda Janis wrote of how reductive stereotypes in Deloria's class were replaced by enlightened respect: "Tecumseh is perhaps the greatest [chief], but I had only heard the name in a satirical poem and so thought it was made up. Too many people are ignorant of the Indian . . . including those of us who are Indian." Throughout her work Deloria counteracted the propaganda of the missionaries and boarding schools with encyclopedic knowledge and with principles of generosity and social cohesion that the future of the globe, as well as of the tribe, now demand.

Biography:

Janette K. Murray, "Ella Deloria: A Biographical Sketch and Literary Analysis," dissertation, University of North Dakota, 1974.

References:

Elaine Jahner, "Sources for Comparative Analysis," introduction to *Lakota Myth,* by James R. Walker (Lincoln: University of Nebraska Press, 1983);

Beatrice Medicine, "Ella C. Deloria: The Emic Voice," *MELUS,* 7, no. 4 (1980): 23–30;

John Prater, "Ella Deloria: Varied Intercourse," *Wicazo Sa Review,* 11 (Fall 1995): 40–46;

Julian Rice, *Deer Women and Elk Men: The Lakota Narratives of Ella Deloria* (Albuquerque: University of New Mexico Press, 1992);

Rice, *Ella Deloria's Iron Hawk* (Albuquerque: University of New Mexico Press, 1993);

Rice, *Ella Deloria's The Buffalo People* (Albuquerque: University of New Mexico Press, 1994);

Rice, "How the Bird that Speaks Lakota Earned a Name," in *Recovering the Word: Essays on Native American Literature,* edited by Brian Swann and Arnold Krupat (Berkeley: University of California Press, 1987), pp. 422–445;

Rice, "Narrative Styles in *Dakota Texts,*" in *On the Translation of Native American Literatures,* edited by Swann (Washington, D.C.: Smithsonian Institution Press, 1992), pp. 276–292.

Papers:

Manuscripts for most of Ella C. Deloria's unpublished writings are in the American Philosophical Society Library in Philadelphia. They include many bilingual stories (English with both Dakota and Lakota), ranging from the Gideon Pond papers of the 1830s to the stories Deloria herself collected in the 1930s; bilingual autobiographical texts by George Sword, George Bushotter, and many others; seventy-one letters from Deloria's correspondence with Franz Boas; large portions of the Lakota-English dictionary that she and Boas began; linguistic notes; her skeptical response to the James R. Walker texts; and personal reminiscences. More reminiscences, various drafts of major stories, including "Iron Hawk: Oglala Culture Hero," and extensive though fragmented descriptions of ceremonies and customs are in the Deloria Family Collection at the University of Colorado. The manuscript for "Camp Circle Society" is in the South Dakota State Archives, Pierre, South Dakota. Deloria's correspondence with H. E. Beebe is in the Southwest Museum, Los Angeles, California. Her correspondence with Ruth Benedict is in the Vassar College Library. Her correspondence with Virginia Dorsey Lightfoot is in the personal possession of Raymond J. DeMallie.

Vine Deloria Jr.

(26 March 1933 -)

Roger Dunsmore
University of Montana

BOOKS: *Custer Died for Your Sins: An Indian Manifesto* (New York: Macmillan, 1969; London: Collier-Macmillan, 1969; revised edition, Norman: University of Oklahoma Press, 1988);

We Talk, You Listen: New Tribes, New Turf (New York: Macmillan, 1970);

The Lumi Indians: A Special Report (Washington, D.C.: Smithsonian Institution, 1972);

God Is Red (New York: Grosset & Dunlap, 1973; revised edition, Golden, Colo.: Fulcrum, 1992);

Behind the Trail of Broken Treaties: An Indian Declaration of Independence (New York: Delacorte, 1974);

The Indian Affair (New York: Friendship Press, 1974);

Legislative Analysis of the Federal Role in Indian Education (Washington, D.C.: Department of Health, Education, and Welfare, Office of Education, 1975);

A Better Day for Indians (New York: Field Foundation, 1976);

Indians of the Pacific Northwest: From the Coming of the White Man to the Present Day (New York: Doubleday, 1977);

A Brief History of the Federal Responsibility to the American Indian (Washington, D.C.: Department of Health, Education, and Welfare, Office of Education, 1979);

The Metaphysics of Modern Existence (San Francisco: Harper & Row, 1979);

American Indians, American Justice, by Deloria and Clifford Lytle (Austin: University of Texas Press, 1983);

The Nations Within: The Past and Future of American Indian Sovereignty, by Deloria and Lytle (New York: Pantheon, 1984);

Indian Education in America: Eight Essays (Boulder, Colo.: American Indian Science and Engineering Society, 1991);

Red Earth, White Lies: Native Americans and the Myth of Scientific Fact (New York: Scribners, 1995).

OTHER: *Of Utmost Good Faith*, edited by Deloria (San Francisco: Straight Arrow, 1971);

"This Country Was a Lot Better Off When the Indians Were Running It," in *Red Power*, edited by Alvin Josephy (New York: McGraw-Hill, 1971; reprinted, Lincoln: University of Nebraska Press, 1985), pp. 235–247;

Jennings Cropper Wise, *The Red Man in the New World Drama: A Politico-Legal Study with a Pageantry of American Indian History*, edited and revised by Deloria (New York: Macmillan, 1971);

Indian Education Confronts the Seventies, 5 volumes, edited, with contributions, by Deloria (Washington, D.C.: Office of Indian Education, 1974);

Robert K. Dodge and Joseph B. McCullough, eds., *Voices of Wah-Kon-Tah: Contemporary Poetry of Native Americans*, introduction by Deloria (New York: International Publishers, 1974);

Edwin R. Embree, ed., *Indians of the Americas*, introduction by Deloria (New York: International Publishers, 1974);

George Manuel and Michael Poslums, eds., *The Fourth World: An Indian Reality*, introduction by Deloria (Don Mills, Ontario: Collier-Macmillan Canada, 1974);

Barbara Leitch, ed., *A Concise Dictionary of Indian Tribes of North America*, introduction by Deloria (Algonac, Mich.: Reference Publications, 1979);

John Neihardt, ed., *Black Elk Speaks*, introduction by Deloria (Lincoln: University of Nebraska Press, 1979);

Christopher Lyman, ed., *The Vanishing Race*, introduction by Deloria (New York: Pantheon, 1982);

Michael L. Lawson, ed., *Damned Indians*, introduction by Deloria (Norman: University of Oklahoma Press, 1982);

A Sender of Words: Essays in Honor of John G. Neihardt, edited by Deloria (Salt Lake City: Howe Brothers, 1984);

The Aggressions of Civilization: Federal Indian Policy Since the 1880s, edited by Deloria and Sandra L.

Vine Deloria Jr. at the time of Custer Died for Your Sins (1969)

Cadwalader (Philadelphia: Temple University Press, 1984);

American Indian Policy in the Twentieth Century, edited by Deloria (Norman: University of Oklahoma Press, 1985);

Peter Nabakov, ed., *Native American Testimony,* introduction by Deloria (New York: Viking, 1991);

Joseph Brouchac, ed., *Keepers of the Animals,* introduction by Deloria (Golden, Colo.: Fulcrum Press, 1991);

Adam Fortunate Eagle, ed., *Alcatraz Alcatraz,* introduction by Deloria (San Francisco: Heyday, 1992);

"The Application of the Constitution," in *Exiled in the Lands of the Free,* edited by Oren Lyons (Santa Fe: Clear Light, 1993), pp. 281–303;

Frank Waters: Man and Mystic, edited by Deloria (Athens, Ohio: Swallow Press, 1993).

SELECTED PERIODICAL PUBLICATIONS – UNCOLLECTED: "It Is a Good Day to Die," *Katallagete,* 4 (Fall–Winter 1972): 62–65;

"The Theological Dimension of the Indian Protest Movement," *Christian Century,* 90 (19 September 1973): 912–914;

"The Indian Movement: Out of a Wounded Knee Past," *Ramparts,* 13 (March 1975): 28–32;

"Escaping from Bankruptcy: The Future of the Theological Task," *Katallagete,* 6 (Summer 1976): 5–9;

"A Native American Perspective on Liberation," *Occasional Bulletin of Missionary Research,* 1 (July 1977): 15–17;

"Landlord to Welfare Client: The Decline of the Indian in National Consciousness," *Humbolt Journal of Social Relations,* 10 (Fall–Winter 1982–1983): 116–128;

"Indian Studies – The Orphan of Academia," *Wicazo Sa Review,* 2 (Fall 1986): 1–9;

"Traditional Education in the Modern World," *Winds of Change,* 5 (Winter 1990): 12–18;

"Traditional Technology," *Winds of Change,* 5 (Spring 1990): 12–17.

RECORDING: *Great American Indian Speeches,* edited by Arthur Junaluska, Caedmon TC 2082, 1976.

Most non-Indian readers probably know Vine Deloria Jr. as the author of his popular first book, *Custer Died for Your Sins* (1969); they recall the humor, wit, and bite of this "Indian manifesto" that deals with subjects as large as the Indian Wars by revealing how those wars continue today, and as specific as Indian tax exemptions by indicating that most tribes believe that "they paid taxes for all time when they gave up some two billion acres of land to the United States." Many non-Indians may not know that Deloria's many other books, his reports and articles, and his contributions as an organizer and leader have established him as the most significant voice of his generation in the presentation and analysis of contemporary Indian affairs. He has a great command of information about the "legislation" pertaining to Indian affairs, from Pope Alexander VI's *Inter Caetera* bull of 1493 – in which, as Deloria notes in *God Is Red* (1973), the pope did "give, grant, and assign forever to you and your heirs and successors, kings of Castile and Leon, all singular the aforesaid countries and islands . . . hitherto discovered . . . and to be discovered . . . together with all their dominions, cities, camps, places, and villages, and all rights, jurisdictions, and appurtenances of the same" – to the controversies over varying interpretations of the American Indian Religious Freedom Act of 1978, the 1978 demise and renewal of the Indian Claims Commission, and the need for congressional action on Indian rights. Deloria has a unique ability to cut through stereotypes, myths, and outright lies to arrive at the truth about Indian affairs.

Deloria was born to Vine and Barbara Eastbuin Deloria on 26 March 1933 in Martin, South Dakota, on the border of the Pine Ridge Indian Reservation. An enrolled member of the Standing Rock Sioux Tribe, he comes from a distinguished Sioux family on his father's side: his great-grandfather Saswe was a medicine man of the Yanktons; his grandfather was a Yankton chief who converted to Christianity in the 1870s and spent the rest of his life as a missionary on the Standing Rock Reservation. His father spent thirty-seven years as an Episcopal missionary in South Dakota. His aunt, Ella Deloria, an anthropologist, was trained by the great Franz Boas and had several distinguished books to her credit.

After serving in the U.S. Marine Corps and graduating from Iowa State University, Deloria worked as a welder in an auto body shop for four years while attending the Augustana Lutheran Seminary in Rock Island, Illinois; he earned his B.D. degree in 1963. He then worked for the United Scholarship Service in Denver, Colorado, developing a program to get scholarships for Indian students in eastern preparatory schools. In 1964 he became executive director of the National Congress of American Indians (NCAI) in Washington, D.C. In September 1967 he entered the University of Colorado law school, hoping that Indian legal programs could do for the tribes what the Legal Defense Fund had done for the black community. He has been a member of the Board of Inquiry on Hunger and Malnutrition in the U.S.A. and of the National Office for the Rights of the Indigent. He has served on the board of trustees of the Museum of the American Indian since 1977 and has also been chairman of the Collections Committee. He also served on the board of the Indian Rights Association. He appeared as an expert witness at the four Wounded Knee trials; founded the Institute for the Development of Indian Law in Washington, D.C.; served as a consultant on the movie *Soldier Blue* (1970); and was professor of law and political science at the University of Arizona in Tucson from 1978 to 1990, directing the graduate program in American Indian Policy Studies. At present he teaches in the departments of law, history, political science, and religious studies at the Center for Studies in Ethnicity and Race in America at the University of Colorado at Boulder. Above all, however, through his writing and actions Deloria has been a leading spokesperson for the Indian people.

In an unpublished letter of 21 December 1994 Deloria says that aside from his writing he considers his most important work to be his assistance to various small Indian communities in obtaining federal recognition. The tribes he has successfully assisted in gaining this recognition include the Nooksacks of western Washington, the Tonto Apaches of northern Arizona, the Tiguas of El Paso ("remnants of the Isleta group that went down to El Paso with the Spanish during the revolt"), the Tunicas of Louisiana, some of the Pequots of New England, and the Little Traverse Bay band of Odawa, Michigan. Deloria is also proud of the conferences he has helped organize that bring together people who hold some of the traditional knowledge that has been passed from generation to generation since precontact days: a conference on Sioux, Hawaiian, Tohono Oodham, Wichita, Blackfeet, and Navajo star knowledge in November 1992; an animal conference in September 1993; and another star conference, with Pueblo, Hoopa, Iroquois, and Pawnee tribe members, in November 1993. In August 1994 he hosted a conference on avoiding "New Age" connotations in writings about traditional knowledge.

Early in *Custer Died for Your Sins* Deloria tells his readers that the title was originally a bumper sticker, common in Indian country, that struck back with humor and bite at the sort of American religious consciousness that erected "Christ Died for Your Sins" signs across the landscape while, at the same time, building mission churches and schools on choice pieces of reservation land stolen through the Allotment Act. As the title indicates, sin is a major aspect of the American experience; the sinners are those who have stolen and desecrated the land, and Gen. George Armstrong Custer is the leading symbol of the greed, arrogance, aggression, and deceit that guide and fuel this desecration. Deloria realizes that orgies of guilt and confession over past sins have too often been substituted for significant change in whites' attitudes toward or treatment of Native Americans. As he points out, accepting responsibility for current and future oppression and abuse is much harder than wallowing in guilt.

In his second book, *We Talk, You Listen: New Tribes, New Turf* (1970), Deloria deals with issues and events of the 1960s: the Black Power movement; the bankruptcy of liberalism; the emergence of the New Left, the Woodstock Nation, and the

Dust jacket for Deloria's first book, the work for which he is best known

anti–Vietnam War movement; the stereotyping of Indians and other minorities by the media, especially motion pictures; the "fading mythology" of industrial technology; ethnic studies; the Poor People's Campaign; the idea that tribal individualism is based on shared social experience instead of competitive economics; the "artificial universe" of the urban world; the ecological crisis; and the failure of Christian churches to respond to the Foreman Manifesto calling for reparations to blacks for centuries of institutionalized racism. His thesis is that in the 1960s the notion of individualism so beloved by Americans gave way to "as yet unrelated definitions of man as a member of a specific group." Minority groups, especially blacks, were seen as the key to this transition, but so were Indian tribes, Chicanos, gangs, hippies, and antiwar protesters. He calls on his readers to take up the challenge to remake their society at this crucial historic juncture.

There are two particularly telling examples of the crisis in American life in *We Talk, You Listen.* The first comes from Deloria's service on the Board for Hunger and Malnutrition in 1967, when he discovered that black children in the Mississippi Delta were eating red clay on alternate days to prevent hunger pangs; at the same time, millions of tons of food in United States Department of Agriculture warehouses went undistributed. The other example is how the federal government cheated the Indians out of such vast holdings of treaty land in California that the government itself issued a report denouncing its own policy: "The report contained such detrimental material exposing the vast land swindles that it was pigeonholed in the Senate files and *has never been released and cannot be obtained today, nearly a century later!*" In contrast, he cites the Lummi tribe's development of a bay on the Washington coast as an aquaculture facility over the opposition of five powerful government agencies, especially the Army Corps of Engineers.

Reviewing *We Talk, You Listen* in *The New York Review of Books* (8 April 1971), N. Scott Momaday expressed a significant criticism of Deloria's first two books:

> Deloria is a thoughtful man . . . but his books are disappointing in one respect: they tell us very little about Indians, after all. In neither book is there any real evocation of that spirit and mentality which distinguishes the Indian as a man and as a race.
>
> The chapter on Indian humor in *Custer Died,* for example, is little more than a catalogue of ethnic jokes. In it, we are told nothing whatever of the essential humor, of that profound gaiety of vision and delight in being which has marked most Indians I have known. . . . In *We Talk,* there is a plea for the return to nature, in the interest of "tribalism," of course, but it is made in the interest of an economic and not an ethical ideal; we are told nothing of what the landscape is or of how it functions as a vital entity in Indian tradition.

It should be pointed out, however, that Deloria's theme of the Indian involvement with the land, which he would develop in later books, is present in *We Talk, You Listen:*

> a land-use plan for the entire nation should be instituted. The government should repurchase all marginal farmlands and a substantial number of farms in remote areas. This land should be planted with its original growth, whether forest or grassland sod. The entire upper midwest plains range area of the Dakotas and Montana and upper Wyoming should become open-plains range with title in public hands. Deer, buffalo, and antelope should replace cattle as herd animals.
> . . . .

> ... the call of the land brings a religious understanding that surpasses everything ever advocated by the religious-political combine that has directed this nation over its lifetime. Young people may mushroom the pollution issue completely out of hand because they may come to understand the necessity of religious people to be intimately related to their lands.

Deloria's next major publication, *God Is Red,* is his most controversial book. Many readers were especially disturbed by his recounting of the cultural genocide for which Christians bear a heavy responsibility and by his scathing account of the perverse condition of modern Christianity. In chapter 13, "Christianity and Contemporary American Culture," for instance, he says that modern Christianity "is chaos. . . . The question is not whether one can make Christianity relevant in the modern world. The question is whether the modern world can have any valid religious experience or knowledge whatsoever." The title, like *Custer Died for Your Sins,* plays with catchphrases from white society – in this case he takes the Nietzschean "God is dead" and the 1950s slogan "better red than dead" and turns them over in such a way as to affirm the vitality of Indian religion. This ability to play with popular ideas in incisive ways is crucial to his most popular books.

God Is Red is much more than a "highly telling polemic against Christianity," as it was called by George H. Fren, a reviewer for *The Nation* (9 February 1974); it is, rather, an insightful comparison of Indian religion and Christianity. According to Deloria, experience, rather than an intellectual acceptance of doctrine, is at the heart of Indian religion. Perhaps the most important distinction between the two forms of religion to which he points is that while Indian religion emphasizes space (that is, place), Christianity is fundamentally a religion of time (that is, history): "Unless the sacred places are discovered and protected and used as religious places, there is no possibility of a nation ever coming to grips with the land itself. Without this basic relationship, national psychic stability is impossible."

Deloria further defines the difference between Western civilization and Indian ways of thinking by looking at Albert Einstein's theory of relativity from the Sioux viewpoint of "all my relations":

> The theory of relativity ... hardly means that all things are relative. It rather means that all things are related. This fundamental premise undergirds all Indian tribal religions and determines the relationships of all parts of creation to one another.

When Deloria warms to his main theme, the connection to the "spirit of this continent, of all continents, that shines through the Indian anthologies and glimmers in the Indian communities in grotesque and tortured forms," he waxes poetic: "the lands of the planets" call out to humans for redemption – not an end-of-time redemption but a "redemption of sanity":

> Who will listen to ... the voice of the places of the land? As the long-forgotten peoples of the respective continents rise and begin to reclaim their ancient heritage, they will discover the meaning of the lands of their ancestors. That is when the invaders of the North American continent will finally discover that for this land, God is Red.

The spirit animating Indian religions, Deloria is saying, is the spirit of the land. Native Americans' religious traditions are not human centered; the human community is caught up in something much greater and more necessary than itself – the land, which includes the particular genius of each river, mountain range, lake, plain, and forest. The land is the central value of Indian life.

If Indian sovereignty and self-determination and the vigorous, sustained, and treacherous white attempts to destroy this sovereignty and self-determination are Deloria's most obvious themes, his deeper and more compelling preoccupation is the land. He perceives the land as the flesh of the continent, a vital and active landscape that has, as he says in *A Sender of Words* (1984), a "potential and therefore a 'passive-active' character in the great western epic." For Deloria the sovereignty of any nation is founded on the quality of that nation's life with the land, with the particular places where its national history has actually happened. All of his social, political, and historical commentary, analysis, and criticism depend on the understanding of this primal connection between the aboriginal peoples of North America and their lands. No amount of military or industrial might, no amount of consumer choice and titillation, no amount of political-religious fervor can restore the strength and flexibility that the land spirit supplied. In *God Is Red* Deloria delivers this sense of connection to land through the words of Curley, a Crow Indian leader, when he refused to cede yet more land to the government:

> "The soil you see is not ordinary soil – it is the dust of the blood, the flesh and the bones of our ancestors. We fought and bled and died to keep other Indians

Cover for the book in which Deloria and Clifford Lytle call for fundamental changes in Indian policies

> from taking it, and we fought and bled and died helping the Whites. You will have to dig down through the surface before you can find nature's earth, as the upper portion is Crow. The land as it is, is my blood and my dead; it is consecrated; and I do not want to give up any portion of it."

The lives and deaths of individuals such as Curley and of a people such as the Crow are part of the natural cycles that are the life of the land. One's death, rather than something to be feared or to be transcended in some other realm, is a return to the pool or reservoir of life that resides in the land: one eats and is eaten, and so one lives in gratitude for the reciprocal giving and taking that is the life process of the land. Every seed carries the scar of mortality where it was connected to the mother plant, and it carries future generations wrapped deep in itself. Deloria has great anger because he has witnessed repeated violations of the life of the land. He believes that whites, beginning by regarding the land as a commodity, have gone on to make Indian spiritual experience the ultimate commodity for a people who are in a radical state of religious hunger.

In an interview with Steve Crum, Geraldine Keams, and Steve Nelson in *Sun Tracks* (1978) Deloria doubts that it is possible to educate whites, or even to begin to communicate with them, unless the "fundamental premises" of white culture are critiqued. After all, he says, "these are people who destroyed two or three continents. They say they're sorry, and they think that's all there is to it." In his next major book, *The Metaphysics of Modern Existence* (1979), Deloria moves toward the most heretical thinkers in modern society – Immanuel Velikovsky, for example – to break up entrenched ideas, such as evolution (that is, progress), that have been used against Indians. For instance, Supreme Court cases have justified taking Indian land on the basis that it is in the natural order of things for farmers to supersede hunters and gatherers.

Deloria does not merely criticize the status quo; he also makes concrete suggestions for change. In *The Nations Within: The Past and Future of American Indian Sovereignty* (1984) Deloria and the attorney and political scientist Clifford Lytle recommend structural reform of tribal governments; a cultural renewal that will address the question of Indian identity in the modern world; reservation economic policies that are appropriate to Indian culture while still being efficient; and mutual respect in relations between tribes and the federal and state governments. The authors detail the prospects for and obstacles to each of their recommendations.

The Nations Within, like Deloria's other works, goes beyond the surface realities of contemporary Indian affairs or the history of white/Indian encounters in North America to reveal the dimensions of the rift between the spiritual "owners" of the land, the Indians, and the political owners of the land, the whites. He believes that until a reconciliation is achieved, American society will be unstable and dangerous; and his hopes for such a reconciliation are sustained by the civil rights and anti–Vietnam War movements, which revealed a moral fiber in American culture that was not yet entirely corrupted or dissipated. Deloria seeks a healing of the American body politic that will allow real justice for minorities and a positive sense of identity for the society that will free it from the "necessity" for imperialistic wars. This "solution" is possible, he holds, only in a "reconciliation" between the two ways of coming to grips with the land: the spiritual way of the Indian and the commodity way of the

Dust jacket for Deloria's attack on the biases of Western science

white. Deloria says he knows that in the land resides the wisdom, spirit, and will to establish a society that is whole and healed, for he is a member of such a society: the Sioux. Indian societies are the vehicles through which the will of the land can establish its rhythms in the American people. The land, he contends, is the only element that can produce cohesion in the dominant society.

In *The Nations Within* Indians, as well as whites, come in for criticism. Deloria and Lytle chide Indians for prostituting their wisdom by making it too readily available to whites. They also criticize some tribal chairmen for demanding a respect that they have not earned and do not merit.

Deloria's most recent book is *Red Earth, White Lies: Native Americans and the Myth of Scientific Fact* (1995). As in *God Is Red* and *The Metaphysics of Modern Existence,* Deloria here examines fundamental questions of belief and knowledge. He attacks Western written accounts for representing Indians as subhuman; to balance such misrepresentations he argues for alternative narratives of Indian history that are grounded in Native oral traditions. The heart and soul of all aboriginal society, he maintains, is the connection to the land. The choice is between history and nature, between the ideas of progress and evolution and the sacredness of place in the universe. As Deloria sees it, a belief in history allows one to act immorally toward anything or anyone that stands in the way of "progress." Morality is a matter of rootedness, of deep knowledge of and connection to place, of the capacity for establishing such a connection even when one's place must change. Deloria ponders the idea that specific places might be formative of particular kinds of personalities. He quotes from Carl Gustav Jung's "Mind and Earth" (1928): "Certain Australian primitives assert that one cannot conquer foreign soil, because in it there dwell strange ancestor-spirits who reincarnate themselves in the new born. The foreign land assimilates its conquerors." In this work, as in all of his writings, Deloria is aware of, and constantly strives to impress his readers with, the dangers of rootlessness and ruthlessness in societies that are cut off from conscious and unconscious links to the soil.

Vine Deloria's work – his writing, his teaching, and his political activity on behalf of Indian tribes and causes – has been crucial to both Indians and whites. His voice has done much to inform the American public of the long-term history and the contemporary state of Indian affairs, and their importance to the health of American society.

Interviews:

James R. McGraw, "God Is Also Red," *Christianity and Crisis,* 35 (15 September 1975): 196–206;

Michael McKale, "From Reservation to Global Society: American Culture, Liberation and the Native American," *Radical Religion,* 2, no. 4 (1976): 49–58;

Steve Crum, Geraldine Keams, and Steve Nelson, "A Conversation with Vine Deloria, Jr.," edited by Lawrence J. Evers, *Sun Tracks,* 4 (1978): 80–88;

Robert Allen Warrior, "Vine Deloria, Jr.," *Progressive* (24 April 1990): 24–27.

Reference:

Robert Allen Warrior, *Tribal Secrets: Recovering American Indian Intellectual Traditions* (Minneapolis: University of Minnesota Press, 1995).

Michael Dorris

(30 January 1945 –)

Hertha D. Wong
University of California, Berkeley

BOOKS: *Native Americans: Five Hundred Years After,* photographs by Joseph C. Farber (New York: Crowell, 1975);

A Guide to Research on North American Indians, by Dorris, Arlene B. Hirschfelder, and Mary Gloyne Byler (Chicago: American Library Association, 1983);

A Yellow Raft in Blue Water (New York: Holt, 1987; Bath, U.K.: Chavers, 1987);

The Broken Cord: A Family's Ongoing Struggle with Fetal Alcohol Syndrome (New York: Harper & Row, 1989; London: Futura, 1992); republished as *The Broken Cord: A Father's Story* (New York: Collins, 1990);

Route Two and Back, by Dorris and Louise Erdrich (Northridge, Cal.: Lord John, 1991);

The Crown of Columbus, by Dorris and Erdrich (New York: HarperCollins, 1991; London: Flamingo, 1992);

Morning Girl (New York: Hyperion, 1992);

Rooms in the House of Stone (Minneapolis: Milkweed Editions, 1993);

Working Men: Stories (New York: Holt, 1993);

Paper Trail: Essays (New York: HarperCollins, 1994);

Guests (New York: Hyperion, 1994);

Sees Behind Trees (New York: Hyperion, 1996);

Cloud Chamber (New York: Scribners, 1997);

The Most Wonderful Book (Minneapolis: Milkweed, 1997);

The Window (New York: Hyperion, 1997).

Michael Dorris (photograph by Louise Erdrich)

OTHER: Arlene B. Hirschfelder, ed., *American Indian Stereotypes in the World of Children,* introduction by Dorris (Metuchen, N.J.: Scarecrow Press, 1982);

"The Indian on the Shelf," in *The American Indian and the Problem of History,* edited by Calvin Martin (New York: Oxford University Press, 1987), pp. 98–105;

"Why I'm Not Thankful for Thanksgiving," in *Books Without Bias: Through Indian Eyes,* edited by Beverly Slapin and Doris Seale (Berkeley, Cal.: Oyate, 1989), pp. 17–20;

"Rayona's Seduction," in *The Lightning Within: An Anthology of Contemporary American Indian Fiction,* edited by Alan R. Velie (Lincoln & London: University of Nebraska Press, 1991), pp. 131–161.

SELECTED PERIODICAL PUBLICATIONS – UNCOLLECTED:

FICTION

"Change of Light," by Dorris and Louise Erdrich, as Milou North, *Redbook,* 158 (March 1982): 78–79;

"Hard Luck," *Seventeen,* 46 (March 1987): 262–263;
"The Best of Pen Pals," *Seventeen,* 46 (August 1987): 272;
"The Queen of Christmas," *Seventeen,* 46 (December 1987): 128–129;
"The Bench Mark," *Mother Jones,* 15 (January 1990): 19–21, 47–48.

NONFICTION

"Native American Literature in an Ethnohistorical Context," *College English,* 41 (1979): 147–162;
"The Grass Still Grows, the Rivers Still Flow: Contemporary Native Americans," *Daedalus,* 110 (Spring 1981): 43–69;
"Cows, Colleges, and Contentment," *New York Times,* 3 August 1986, X: 37;
"Why Mr. Ed Still Talks Good Horse Sense," *TV Guide,* 36 (28 May–3 June 1988): 34–36;
"Who Owns the Land? Chippewa Indian and the White Earth Indian Reservations," by Dorris and Louise Erdrich, *New York Times Magazine,* 4 September 1988, p. 32;
"Rite of Passage: A Man's Journey into Fatherhood Echoes His Son's Entry into Adolescence," *Parents' Magazine,* 64 (June 1989): 246–248;
"A Desperate Crack Legacy," *Newsweek,* 115 (25 June 1990): 8;
"Fetal Alcohol Syndrome," *Parents' Magazine,* 65 (November 1990): 238–245;
"The Minnie Mouse Kitchen," *Parents' Magazine,* 65 (December 1990): 234–235;
"Ode to an Author Escort," *Publishers Weekly,* 238 (7 June 1991): 34;
"What Men are Missing," *Vogue,* 181 (September 1991): 511.

In his fiction, scholarly and popular nonfiction, and poetry Michael Dorris repeatedly returns to a few major themes: the centrality of family relationships, the renarrating of American history from Native American perspectives, and the necessity for mixed-blood individuals to search for their identities and to situate themselves in relation to Indian and non-Indian communities. He is committed to destroying the dominant stereotypes of Native North Americans, to taking off the feathered headdresses and beaded vestments, the "noble and stoic / savage and passionate" masks imposed on Native people by non-Natives. He is best known for his novels, short stories, and essays and his collaborations with his much-acclaimed wife, the writer Louise Erdrich.

Born in Louisville, Kentucky, on 30 January 1945, Michael Anthony Dorris is of Irish and French descent on his mother's side and Modoc descent on his father's. When Dorris was two years old, his father, Jim, an army lieutenant, was killed in a jeep accident near Passau, Germany. Shortly thereafter, Mary Besy Burkhardt Dorris and her son returned from Germany to Louisville. She never remarried, and Dorris was raised as an only child in a house full of strong and loving women. "My role models," he says in *The Broken Cord* (1989), "were strong, capable mothers, aunts, and grandmothers." In 1967 Dorris graduated cum laude and Phi Beta Kappa with a B.A. in English and the classics from Georgetown University. After a year in the graduate program of the department of history of the theater at Yale University, he switched to anthropology, receiving an M.Phil. from Yale in 1970. He was an assistant professor at the University of Redlands in California in 1970 and at Franconia College in New Hampshire in 1971–1972. In 1971 the unmarried Dorris adopted a three-year-old Sioux boy whom he named Reynold Abel. In 1972 he accepted a position at Dartmouth College in Hanover, New Hampshire. In 1974 he adopted another son, also a Sioux, whom he named Jeffrey Sava after a deceased Native Alaskan friend; in 1976 he adopted a Sioux daughter, Madeline Hannah. In 1979 he became a full professor and chair of the Native American studies department. Dartmouth graduate Erdrich returned to the campus as a writer in residence in 1981, and on 10 October of that year she and Dorris were married. Together they have had three daughters: Persia Andromeda, Pallas Antigone, and Aza Marion.

As an anthropologist Dorris conducted fieldwork in Alaska, New Zealand, Montana, New Hampshire, and South Dakota and published *Native Americans: Five Hundred Years After* (1975) and, with Arlene B. Hirschfelder and Mary Gloyne Byler, *A Guide to Research on North American Indians* (1983). Among his academic articles, "Native American Literature in an Ethnohistorical Context" (1979) is notable for its call for Native literatures to be considered in their cultural and historical contexts rather than interpreted from a supposedly "objective" New Critical – that is, European American – perspective that conflates hundreds of tribal literatures into the monolithic category of American Indian literature. Notable also are his many essays and interviews, often addressed to educators, that challenge stereotypical representations of Native Americans. In a 1989 interview with Bill Moyers, included in *Conversations with Louise Erdrich and Michael Dorris* (1994), edited by Allan Chavkin and Nancy Feyl Chavkin, Dorris tells an anecdote about being approached by a Boy Scout leader whose "troop wanted to be absolutely

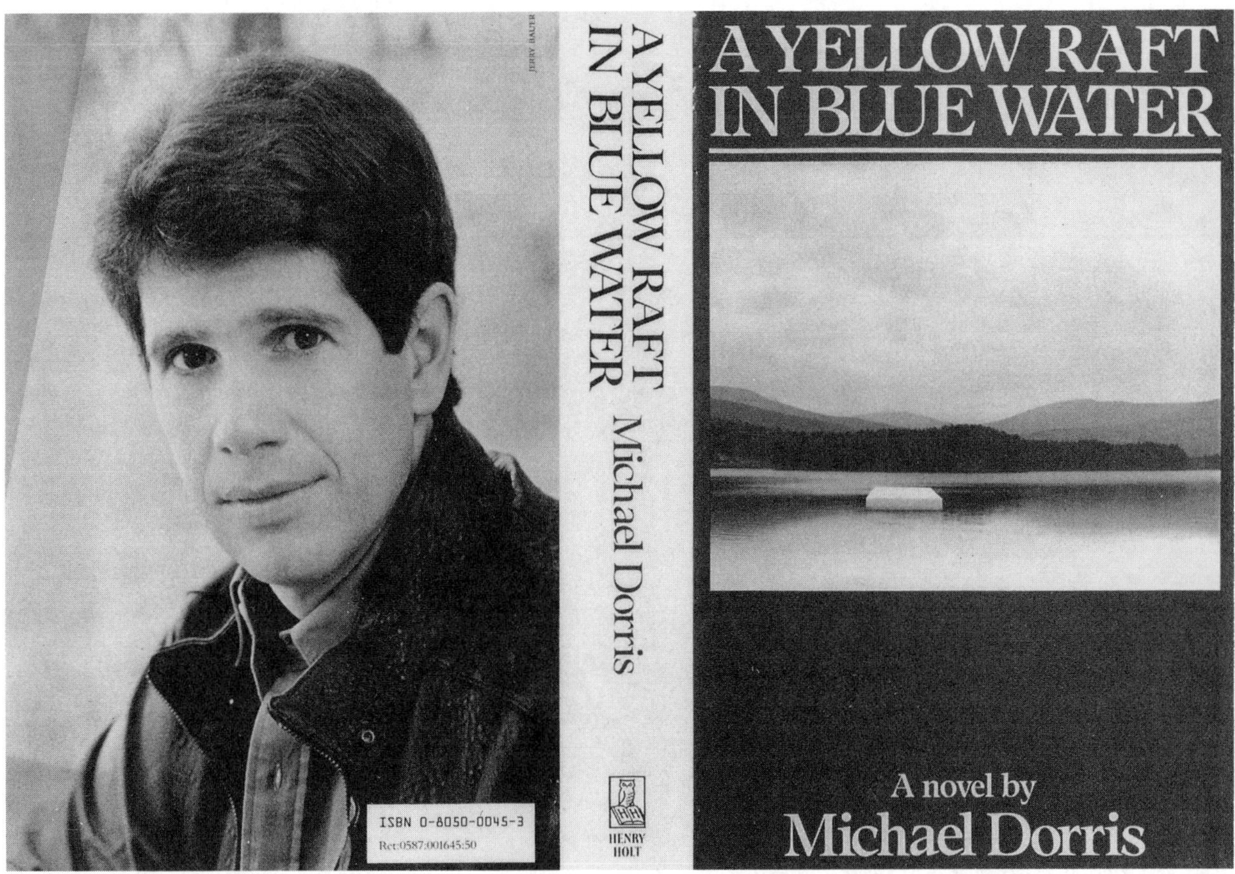

Dust jacket for Dorris's first novel, narrated by women from three generations of a Native American family

authentic Iroquois, so they were going to go live in the woods for a week." When asked what he would recommend for the boys to take along, Dorris, considering the matrilineal traditions of the Iroquois, replied: "Their mothers." The scouts were clearly disappointed, since "they wanted hatchets or something."

From 1977 to 1979 Dorris served on the editorial board of *MELUS: The Journal of the Society of Multiethnic Literatures in the United States;* he has served in the same capacity for the *American Indian Culture and Research Journal* since 1974. He received National Institute of Mental Health Fellowships in 1970 and 1971, a Guggenheim Fellowship in 1978, Woodrow Wilson Faculty Development Fellowships in 1971 and 1980, a Rockefeller Foundation Research Fellowship and an Indian Achievement Award in 1985, and a National Endowment for the Arts Grant in 1989. In 1989 Dorris stepped down from his academic position to devote more time to his writing.

Dorris's writing career began in earnest after his marriage to Erdrich. They published several short stories jointly under the pseudonym Milou North – the first name combines parts of their first names; the last refers to the part of the country in which they were living. The Dorris-Erdrich collaboration has been the topic of considerable curiosity; although they generally publish a book under the name of whichever of them is the primary author, they collaborate on every piece. By their own account, they discuss the story and characters long before they begin writing. After one of them writes the initial draft, the other reads it, offering comments and editorial suggestions; the originator revises it and gives it back to the reader. This process may be repeated many times before the work is complete. "We virtually reach consensus on all words before they go out, on a word by word basis," Dorris explained in a 1987 interview with Hertha D. Wong included in *Conversations with Louise Erdrich and Michael Dorris.* Dorris and Erdrich insist that their collaboration enhances, rather than limits, their individual creativity, and that it keeps them from suffering from writer's block.

Although his poetry has been published in such journals as *Sun Tracks, Akwesasne Notes, Wassaja,*

Dust jacket for Dorris's collection of fourteen short stories about characters who have illuminating experiences while going about their mundane, everyday tasks

and *Ploughshares,* Dorris is best known for his prose. His first novel, *A Yellow Raft in Blue Water* (1987), has received critical praise and is examined in literature courses at colleges and universities throughout the United States. In this novel, Dorris presents the interrelated but distinct narratives of three generations of women. In a typical modernist technique, each of the novel's three sections is narrated by a different character: the story begins with the fifteen-year-old, part-Indian Rayona; continues with her mother, Christine; and concludes with Rayona's "grandmother," Ida, who prefers, for reasons that are surprising and dramatic when they are finally revealed, to be called "Aunt Ida." Each of the narrators is entirely convincing and engaging, even when she contradicts or quibbles with what the others have said.

As in Dorris's short fiction, allusions to television abound in *A Yellow Raft in Blue Water.* In the 1987 interview with Wong, Dorris explains that he was "totally weaned on television" and that in the novel references to television serve as "a marker of time and class." In one comic scene Christine, leaving Seattle to return to the reservation in Montana to die, stops by a video store to buy a lifetime membership for her daughter even though they do not own a videocassette recorder and the sound on their television set is barely audible. Christine says to Rayona, "It's like something I'd leave you." She checks out two tapes, misinterpreting *lifetime* to mean that they can be kept permanently: *Christine* (1983), a horror film about a vengeful car that goes on a murderous rampage, and *Little Big Man* (1970), a movie image of Plains Indians, are all that Christine can bequeath to Rayona. Such moments led Louis Owens to say that in *A Yellow Raft in Blue Water* the video village replaces the tribal village.

Although mixed-blood identity is a common theme in twentieth-century Native American literature, Dorris is the first writer to present a mixed-blood character who is part Native American and part black: her father, Elgin, is an African American postal worker. Rayona imagines finding the "exact shades" of her family "on a paint mix-tone chart. Mom was Almond Joy, Dad was Burnt Clay, and I was Maple Walnut." She describes herself as "too big, too smart, not Black, not Indian, not friendly." With Rayona, Dorris complicates the generic plot of a mixed-blood protagonist torn between two

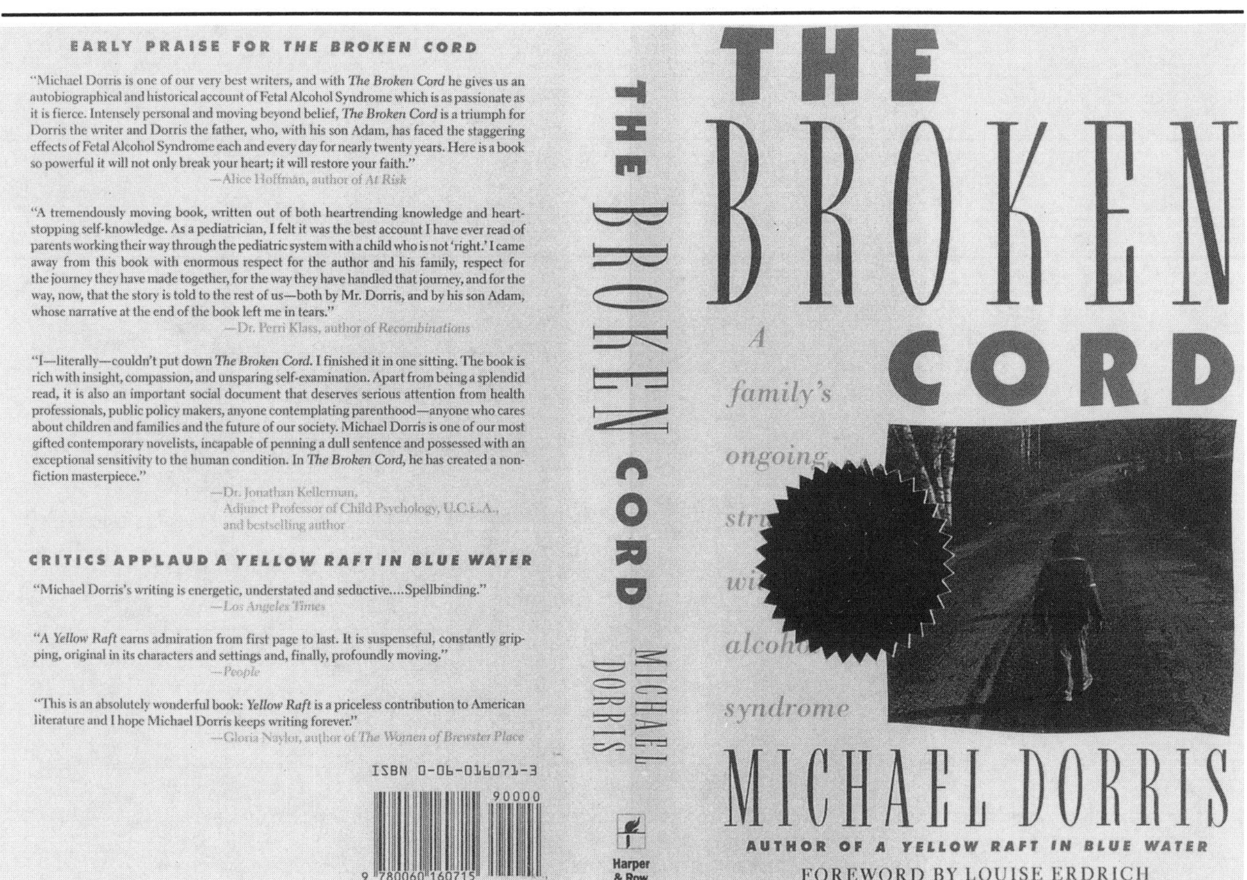

Dust jacket for Dorris's account of his adopted son's fetal alcohol syndrome

worlds. In his interview with Moyers, Dorris explains that "Rayona grows up very much an urban, black, Indian kid in a northwest city." When she ends up on the reservation, she is "inappropriate in every respect": wrong color, wrong background, wrong language. Nonetheless, Rayona's search, like the quests of so many other characters in Native American novels, is, as William Bevis has noted, a search for a home. Rayona can find her identity only by realizing the inappropriateness of the dominant society – she finally gives up her fantasy of having a family like the one the "perfect" Ellen DeMarco has; by returning "home" to the reservation that she visited only once, as a toddler; and by recovering her family history and learning how she fits into a much larger story. Although the plot sounds like a romantic search for a lost past, Dorris resists easy answers: going home does not guarantee a warm welcome or a gift-wrapped Indian identity.

His second novel, *The Crown of Columbus* (1991), carries both Dorris's and Erdrich's names on the title page. They planned the novel during a 1988 automobile trip across Saskatchewan; the publisher, HarperCollins, gave them a $1.5 million advance for the book on the basis of a brief outline. Inspired, they told Moyers, by a "translation of Bartolomé de Las Casas's sixteenth-century edition of Columbus's diary" and by the quincentennial of Christopher Columbus's arrival in America, they planned to take the almost unimaginable leap – for Native American authors – of writing the novel from Columbus's point of view. Instead, the book turned out to be an Indian version of American history, an ironic counterpoint to Columbus's "discovery" of the so-called New World, and a satire of academia. *The Crown of Columbus* received mixed reviews: some critics exulted over the comic adventure, while others, such as Nina King in the *Washington Post* (5 May 1991), criticized the melodramatic and romantic plot, the confusion of "romance, detective story, thriller, and revisionist history," and the "politically correct" didacticism.

In this novel two Dartmouth College professors – the forty-year-old, pregnant, Coeur d'Alene-Navajo-Irish-Hispanic and Sioux-by-marriage tenure-aspiring assistant professor of anthropology Vivian Twostar and the stuffy European American poet

31

who would watch over me. "If he shows his face on that windy hillside, it's as sure as a kiss."

"I don't get home often enough," my dad went on, getting teary in his cups.

"You do your best," I consoled him. "Like the rest of us."

#

For a thousand years, the story went, McGarrys had perched atop the farthest heights of Kilnamanagh, since the days when the monastery, in ruins before memory, tolled its bells for vespers. Once it must have been a proud spot, commanding as it did a wide and distant view of Kingsland. Pilgrims climbed here to deposit their prayers with the holy monks. Farmers gathered within the walls for safety against invading armies. Generations of young men, young men who themselves would never father sons of their own but rather had to recruit them through the Lord's intercession, fought their demons in this place, committed and confessed their sins of deed and more often of thought, toiled a soil so barren and rocky that no hope of abundance could be harbored, only a prayer for sufficiency, for enough to last the stormy winter.

The burial ground itself was a peaceful precinct, open to heaven and bound on all sides by crumbling stone walls. There, neighbors with the graves of priests long turned to dust, rested those McGarrys who had gone to their reward, arranged in death as they had lived in life, mother and

Two pages from the typescript for Dorris's novel Cloud Chamber, *with marginal suggestions and comments by Dorris's wife, Louise Erdrich, and revisions by Dorris (courtesy of Michael Dorris)*

33

pry the blown grit from the shallow engravings, to remember, for an hour's sweat, if not the particular actors in life's drama at least the buzz of their modest assembly. lonely

So absorbed was I in fulfilling this task once I begun it that the night's subterfuge was all but pushed to the back of my awareness. I pulled at overgrown grass, straightened tilted stones, whispered a *Requies in pacem* under my breath as I knelt at each probable tomb. The quiet that enveloped me was lush as the softest lambswool, the air ~~cool and~~, weightless, the stars close and familiar. There's a feeling you get alone on a hilltop on a clear night -- as though the music of a fine-tuned fiddle caresses and soothes your every thought -- a feeling that you're above the reach of anything ugly or coarse, safe with the angels. ~~purified.~~ The monks must have known this peace, I decided. It's what kept them here more than any churchly promise or stretch of faith. Beauty. No doubt such moments culled all mortal question ~~from the fact of beauty.~~

So concentrated was I in trying to translate this impression into words I could later repeat to myself that I didn't hear the footsteps of the two soldiers until they were upon me, and then it was too late to flee or even stand for my capture. They reached me still upon my knees, grabbed me under the arms and rousted me up.

"This is the one?" asked a voice stiff with England.

There was no answer.

"Speak up."

and tenured professor Roger Williams – are researching Columbus. Roger's name unambiguously recalls the seventeenth-century clergyman who was banished from Salem in the Massachusetts Bay Colony for his democratic views in 1635 and, a year later, founded Providence, the first white settlement in what would become Rhode Island; living among and preaching to the Indians of the area, he wrote *A Key into the Language of America* (1643), one of the first attempts to record a Native language and customs. Perfect opposites – she is vivacious, he is quiet; she is passionately down-to-earth, he is coolly intellectual; she is flexible, he is fastidious – Vivian and Roger are the mismatched parents of Violet, who represents the new generation of Indian-white relations. When Roger criticizes Vivian for having an underdeveloped sense of history, employing sloppy research methods, and being too emotional for "objective" and rational scholarship, the reader is presented with a recapitulation of Indian-white contact stories in which cross-cultural communication is nominal at best. In addition, Dorris and Erdrich seem to be criticizing the academic battles about gender, race, and ethnicity and the politics of supposedly objective scholarship. The chapters are narrated alternately by Vivian and Roger, a technique that, as Thomas Matchie argues in the *North Dakota Quarterly* (Fall 1991), "resembles a point/counterpoint debate." The plot moves on two levels: as King notes, the story is "a contemporary romance" and "a historical mystery" linked by "the contemporary couple's attempt to solve the old mystery."

A key theme is the search for Columbus: who was he then? Who is he now, five hundred years later? In a 1991 interview with Douglas Foster, included in *Conversations with Louise Erdrich and Michael Dorris,* Dorris explains that "Columbus is a metaphor"; he "stands for a notion of encounter of the unexpected." The novel is, thus, about unanticipated encounters: Vivian and Roger must open their minds and hearts to discover Columbus and each other. With their exaggerated differences, their stormy relationship becomes a metaphor for Indian-white interaction. Violet, the offspring of the two races, offers the promise of a better future.

Spending a night accidentally locked in the Dartmouth library, Vivian finds some clues about Columbus that she decides to follow up. Financed by a wealthy businessman with greedy motives, Vivian travels to Eleuthera in the Bahamas accompanied by Roger, her teenage son Nash, and the baby Violet. Outrageously dramatic scenes abound: the unscrupulous capitalist attacks the karate-kicking Vivian on his yacht; the helpless baby Violet floats alone on the ocean in a deflating raft; the stuffy, self-important Roger sacrifices himself to save the baby and, as in classical mythology, descends to the underworld – in this case, an underwater cave – where he gains self-understanding. All of these moments clarify what is truly important – not academic stardom but love, relationships, and self-knowledge.

The Crown of Columbus is a significant departure from the kind of writing Dorris and Erdrich have published independently, although it retains elements of their previous work: the dominant ironic vision, the emphasis on love and family, and the large-spirited humor. In addition, both *A Yellow Raft in Blue Water* and *The Crown of Columbus* dramatize a quest for personal identity and historical accuracy through remembering the past and imaginatively reconstructing it in the present.

Working Men (1993) is a collection of fourteen short stories, ten of which were published previously. The stories are narrated by diverse voices – Indian and non-Indian, young and old, gay and straight, male and female – and are set in locales as various as the states of Washington, Montana, New Jersey, New Hampshire, Kentucky, and Alaska. Most of the characters are going about their jobs as flight attendants, pharmaceutical salesmen, disc jockeys, pond designers, or snowplow drivers when something happens to trigger a self-revelatory moment. These are not grand experiences of enlightenment but tiny flickers of illumination. The minute and predictable rhythms of everyday life reflected in work patterns are jostled, transporting the characters, if only momentarily, from the ordinary to the extraordinary or revealing the remarkable within the mundane.

In typical Dorris style, the tone of the stories is often wry and the narrative voice naively self-reflexive. Humor abounds, even in the midst of pathos. Dorris never condescends to his down-to-earth characters, but part of the humor hinges on the gap between the readers' perspectives and those of the narrators, who are often not entirely conscious of their motives or feelings. In "Oui," for instance, Dwayne drifts from experience to experience, finally running off to Montana with a woman who happens to drive by and getting a job as a high-school French teacher even though the only word of French he knows is *oui.* Dwayne interprets his dream of "a man and a woman standing on a sticky bun, their feet planted in the icing" as an omen that he and his lover, Cecille, are "destined to get married. . . . There was no mistaking that breakfast roll, plain as a three-tiered cake." His interpretation is not only comic, it is conveniently pragmatic, since marrying Cecille solves his problems of a lack of lodging and employment. The supposedly clear borders between absurdly naive interpretations and brilliance, between chance and destiny, between true love and crafty self-interest are revealed to be ambiguous at best.

In "Earnest Money" Sky Dial, the draft-dodging hippie turned gas-station owner from *A Yellow Raft in Blue Water,* provides a good example of Dorris's one-liner humor: "Without Dad around, Mom was horsepower with nothing to move," he comments; later he says, "Mom was in a condition of mental arrest, the two causes for it tied for number one." Similarly, Sky describes the wedding reception when he marries the older Evelyn: "From the point of view of the guests it was a mixture of 'too bad' and 'it could be worse' with a little bit of 'what the hell' thrown in on the side." Dwayne, Sky, and many of the other characters in the stories have deep feelings but lack the ability to articulate them, even to themselves, except in simple language and prepackaged images taken from popular culture, especially television programs.

Only two of the stories, "Groom Service" and "Shining Agate," are explicitly about Native Americans. The first story is about the traditional courtship practices of an unspecified matriarchal community. In "Shining Agate" Dorris uses a translation of a Native Alaskan tale as the starting point for a story about an anthropologist's fieldwork in the Native Alaska community of Suscitna. The tale provides an interpretive context for the contemporary story of the anthropologist, who does not fit into the community – he endures "ritual avoidance" – but finally gains some insight into the people he is studying and, more important, into himself. In an ironic turnabout, at the end of the story Sergei Mishikoff, a Native Alaskan informant, tells the anthropologist: " 'I'll explain you your story.' "

Throughout these stories, Dorris is sensitive to common people of every sort, to lives lived within narrow constraints, to insights filtered through the popular media, and to the telling detail. In the short story "The Benchmark" the protagonist is a man who builds ponds. The pond designer, who reads the lay of the land, becomes a metaphor of the writer/anthropologist, both careful observers and shapers of experience. Elsewhere Dorris has compared the positions of writers and anthropologists to those of mixed-bloods who find themselves outsiders and mediators. As a mixed-blood anthropologist writer, Dorris is particularly mindful of his role as one who observes and translates.

In his award-winning novel *Morning Girl* (1992), aimed at young adult readers, Dorris imagines life among the pre-Columbian Taino Indians. Chapters are narrated alternately by twelve-year-old Morning Girl and her ten-year-old brother, Star Boy. Opposites in every way, Morning Girl and Star Boy at first antagonize each other as only siblings can: "I don't know how my brother came to see everything so upside down from me," says Morning Girl. But their relationship grows into friendship, and Star Boy gives his sister a new name: The One Who Stands Beside. The novel concludes with Morning Girl meeting a boatful of strange visitors speaking a strange language, whom the reader knows to be the so-called discoverers of America. In Dorris's treatment, however, it is really Morning Girl who discovers the strangers, and she heads for home to arrange for her family to welcome the newcomers with proper graciousness. The book closes with an ominous epilogue: an excerpt from Columbus's journal for 11 October 1492.

As in *Morning Girl,* in *Guests* (1994), another novel for young adults, Dorris offers a new perspective on a familiar American theme – in this case a Native boy's view of Thanksgiving. Also like *Morning Girl, Guests* is both a children's coming-of-age story and a contact narrative.

Dorris's *The Broken Cord* was named the Best Nonfiction Book of 1989 by the National Book Critics Circle and the Outstanding Academic Book by *Choice;* it also received the Heartland Prize and the Christopher Award. It is the story of Abel, Dorris's adopted son – called Adam in the book – who was diagnosed as suffering from fetal alcohol syndrome. Because of his "defensive optimism," it took Dorris a long time to realize that "the poor hearing, the convulsions, the hundreds of repetitions of even the most basic instructions, the abbreviated attention span, the many minor, dismissible incidents, mistakes, and shortfalls" were not the aberrations of a healthy child but the incurable condition of a child poisoned by alcohol in his mother's womb. In his essay collection *Paper Trail* (1994) Dorris writes that after twenty years of wavering between hope and despair, denial and acceptance, anger and understanding, he came to the conclusion that he "could not affect Abel's life, but [he could] document it"; so he wrote *The Broken Cord.* The book was made into an ABC television movie starring Jimmy Smits that aired on 3 February 1992.

As would be expected with such a painful and controversial topic, not all reviewers agreed with Dorris's condemnation of pregnant women who drink. Katha Pollitt, for example, accused him of blaming women – especially single mothers – who were themselves victims of oppressive social and economic conditions and consequent lack of medical care. Margit Stange claims that "the strain of antidisease logic" displayed in writing about fetal alcohol syndrome and alcoholism generally "enables a healing discourse to become an antiwoman discourse." Dorris is acutely aware of the history of Indian-white relations, including the introduction of alcohol to Native people. He points out that "socioeconomic deprivation" affects Indian alcoholism and that "alcoholism, over the past 150 years, had become so absorbed into the social systems of many American Indian groups that it could not be easily excised." Even so, dealing on a daily basis with the tragic consequences of a biological mother's alcoholism leads Dorris to present an impassioned, unromantic, and uncompromising denunciation of maternal drinking. Reynold Abel Dorris was hit by a car – a direct consequence of the diminished capacities produced by fetal alcohol syndrome – and died two years after *The Broken Cord* was published.

Because of *The Broken Cord,* Dorris is often invited to serve on national and international committees and boards devoted to children's health and welfare. He was a member of the board of directors of the Save the Children Foundation in 1991–1992 and now serves as an advisory board member; he became a member of the U.S. Advisory Committee on Infant Mortality in 1992. As a part of his work for the Save the Children Foundation, Dorris visited drought-ridden Zimbabwe, where thousands of men, women, and children die from lack of water, food, and medicine. To publicize the situation in Zimbabwe, Dorris wrote *Rooms in the House of Stone* (1993). The essays in the book address the burnout of donors, the alternation of the press from sensationalism to silence ("Is it a sexy drought?" one reporter asks him before agreeing to cover it), and the needs of those who are still alive in Zimbabwe. Dorris concludes: "We must give as if to ourselves. . . . To be fortunate is, in a deep moral sense, to be obliged."

Still relatively young, Dorris has written an impressive collection of fiction and nonfiction, much of it focused on identity formation, family ties, and setting the record straight about Native American history. He acknowledges diverse influences on his writing, from family storytelling and Native American oral traditions to the highly literary work of Albert Camus, Sinclair Lewis, Toni Morrison, Gloria Naylor, Barbara Pym, Paul Theroux, John Updike, Laura Ingalls Wilder, and Tennessee Williams; but he insists that the single most important influence on his writing is his wife. In intimate collaboration with Erdrich, Dorris combines everyday words into simple sentences that evoke a sense of the extraordinary, juxtapose simplicity and surprise with a sense of the mysterious, and seduce readers into fresh ways of perceiving the world.

Interviews:

"Louise Erdrich and Michael Dorris," in *Winged Words: American Indian Writers Speak,* by Laura Coltelli (Lincoln & London: University of Nebraska Press, 1990), pp. 40–52;

Allan Chavkin and Nancy Feyl Chavkin, eds., *Conversations with Louise Erdrich and Michael Dorris* (Jackson: University Press of Mississippi, 1994).

Bibliography:

Lillian Brewington, Normie Bullard, and Robert W. Reising, comps., "Writing in Love: An Annotated Bibliography of Critical Responses to the Poetry and Novels of Louise Erdrich and Michael Dorris," *American Indian Culture and Research Journal,* 10, no. 4 (1986): 81–86.

References:

William Bevis, "Native American Novels: Homing In," in *Recovering the Word: Essays on Native American Literature,* edited by Brian Swann and Arnold Krupat (Berkeley: University of California Press, 1987), pp. 580–620;

Thomas Matchie, "Exploring the Meaning of Discovery in The Crown of Columbus," *North Dakota Quarterly,* 69 (Fall 1991): 243–250;

Louis Owens, "Erdrich and Dorris' Mixedbloods and Multiple Narratives," in his *Other Destinies: Understanding the American Indian Novel* (Norman: University of Oklahoma Press, 1992), pp. 192–224;

Katha Pollitt, " 'Fetal Rights': A New Assault on Feminism," *Nation,* 250 (26 March 1990): 409–418;

Barbara K. Robins, "Michael (Anthony) Dorris," in *Dictionary of Native American Literature,* edited by Andrew Wiget (New York: Garland, 1994), pp. 417–422;

Ruth Rosenberg, *A Teacher's Guide to* A Yellow Raft in Blue Water (Jacksonville, Ill.: PermaBound, 1994);

Margit Stange, "The Broken Self: Fetal Alcohol Syndrome and Native American Selfhood," in *Body Politics: Disease, Desire, and the Family,* edited by Michael Ryan and Avery Gordon (Boulder, Colo.: Westview, 1993), pp. 126–136.

Charles A. Eastman (Ohiyesa)

(19 February 1858 - 8 January 1939)

Raymond Wilson
Fort Hays State University

BOOKS: *Indian Boyhood* (New York: McClure, Phillips, 1902);

Red Hunters and the Animal People (New York & London: Harper, 1904);

Old Indian Days (New York: McClure, 1907);

Wigwam Evenings: Sioux Folk Tales Retold, by Eastman and Elaine Goodale Eastman (Boston: Little, Brown, 1909);

Smoky Day's Wigwam Evenings: Indian Stories Retold, by Eastman and Elaine Goodale Eastman (Boston: Little, Brown, 1910);

The Soul of the Indian: An Interpretation (Boston: Houghton Mifflin, 1911);

Indian Child Life (Boston: Little, Brown, 1913);

Indian Scout Talks: A Guide for Boy Scouts and Camp Fire Girls (Boston: Little, Brown, 1914); republished as *Indian Scout Craft and Lore* (New York: Dover, 1974);

The Indian Today: The Past and Future of the First American (Garden City, N.Y.: Doubleday, Page, 1915);

From the Deep Woods to Civilization: Chapters in the Autobiography of an Indian (Boston: Little, Brown, 1916);

Indian Heroes and Great Chieftains (Boston: Little, Brown, 1918).

Collection: *The Soul of an Indian and Other Writings From Ohiyesa,* edited by Kent Nerburn (San Rafael, Cal.: New World Library, 1993).

SELECTED PERIODICAL PUBLICATIONS – UNCOLLECTED: "The Sioux Mythology," *Popular Science Monthly,* 46 (November 1894): 88–91;

"For Indian Young Men," *Young Men's Era,* 21 (16 May 1895): 323;

"The Story of the Little Big Horn," *Chautauquan,* 31 (July 1900): 353–358;

"Indian Handicrafts," *Craftsman,* 8 (August 1905): 658–662;

"The War Maiden of the Sioux," *Ladies' Home Journal,* 23 (August 1906): 14;

"The Indian and the Moral Code," *Outlook,* 97 (7 January 1911): 30–34;

"Education without Books," *Craftsman,* 21 (January 1912): 372–377;

"My People: The Indian's Contribution to the Art of America," *Red Man,* 7 (December 1914): 133–140;

"Stories Back of Indian Names," *Boys' Life* (December 1914): 21;

"The Indian as a Citizen," *Lippincott's Magazine,* 95 (January 1915): 70–76;

Eastman's father, Ite Wakanhdi Ota (Many Lightnings), known after his conversion to Christianity as Jacob Eastman

"The Indian's Gift to the Nation," *Quarterly Journal of The Society of American Indians,* 3 (January-March 1915): 17-23;

"The Indian's Health Problem," *American Indian Magazine,* 4 (April-June 1916): 139-145;

"The Sioux of Yesterday and Today," *American Indian Magazine,* 5 (Winter 1917): 233-239;

"The Indian's Plea for Freedom," *American Indian Magazine,* 6 (Winter 1919): 162-165;

"A Review of the Indian Citizenship Bills," *American Indian Magazine,* 6 (Winter 1919): 181-183;

"Justice for the Sioux," *American Indian Magazine,* 7 (Summer 1919): 79-81;

"The American Eagle: An Indian Symbol," *American Indian Magazine,* 7 (Summer 1919): 89-92;

"Great Spirit," *American Indian Teepee,* 1 (Winter 1920): 3-4;

"What Can the Out-of-Doors Do for Our Children?," *Education,* 41 (1920-1921): 599-605;

"Sacajawea's Lost Years," *Great Falls (Mont.) Tribune,* 27 March 1949, pp. 8-9, 13; 3 April 1949, pp. 12-13; 10 April 1949, pp. 10-11; 17 April 1949, pp. 10-11;

"A Half-Forgotten Lincoln Story," *Rotarian,* 76 (February 1950): 34.

Charles A. Eastman (Ohiyesa) was the most widely known Native American author in the United States and abroad during the first decades of the twentieth century. His eleven books and many articles for national magazines explained Indian customs, beliefs, and history to non-Indian Americans. Reformers held Eastman up as a model for other Indians to emulate; unlike most of these reformers, however, Eastman did not view Indian cultures with disdain but took pride in his Indianness. His writings frequently demonstrated the superiority of Indian ways to the practices of the dominant culture.

The child who would later be known as Charles Alexander Eastman was born near Redwood Falls, Minnesota, on 19 February 1858. His father, Ite Wakanhdi Ota (Many Lightnings), a hunter and warrior, belonged to the Wahpeton band of the Eastern, or Santee, Sioux. His mother, Wakantankanwin (Goddess) or Mary Nancy Eastman, was the granddaughter of Mahpiya Wichasta (Cloud Man), a leader of a Mdewakanton band of the Eastern Sioux, and the daughter of the artist Capt. Seth Eastman. As a result of complications in giving birth to Charles, Wakantankanwin died shortly thereafter. The motherless infant was given the name Hakadah (The Pitiful Last). Uncheedah (Grandmother), his father's mother, helped to raise him in the traditional ways of a Santee Sioux. In 1862 he received the name Ohiyesa (The Winner) when his band defeated another in a lacrosse game. He would use that name in conjunction with the English name he would acquire later in his life.

In August 1862 many Santee Sioux fled to Canada after an unsuccessful and short-lived uprising over conditions on the reservation. Among them was Ohiyesa's father's younger brother, who adopted the boy – Ite Wakanhdi Ota was believed to have been killed – and raised him as a warrior and hunter. Returning from a hunt in 1873, Ohiyesa was startled to meet his father, who had been sentenced to death for his actions during the Minnesota uprising but had been pardoned by President Abraham Lincoln. While in confinement, Many Lightnings had become a Christian and had adopted the name Jacob Eastman. After his release he had rejected reservation life and established a homestead at Flandreau in Dakota Territory. He had then traveled to Canada to find his son.

Jacob Eastman persuaded Ohiyesa to accompany him to the homestead. The renamed Charles Alexander Eastman attended Flandreau Mission School; Santee Normal Training School; and the preparatory departments of Beloit College, Knox College, and Kimball Union Academy. He received a B.S. degree from Dartmouth College in 1887 and an M.D. from Boston University in 1890. The Indian Rights Association and the Lake Mohonk Conference of Friends of the Indian, powerful Indian reform groups, hailed Eastman as an example of what an Indian could achieve.

The thirty-two-year-old Eastman accepted an appointment as government physician at Pine Ridge Agency in South Dakota. There he witnessed the massacre at Wounded Knee and also met Elaine Goodale, a social worker who supervised education for the Sioux. They were married in New York City in June 1891 and had six children: Dora Winona, Irene Taluta, Virginia, Ohiyesa II, Eleanor, and Florence. Eastman and the Indian agent at Pine Ridge exchanged accusations regarding policy violations and payments to Indians who suffered property losses during the Ghost Dance, an Indian revitalization movement. Frustrated with the situation, Eastman resigned in 1893. He moved to Saint Paul, Minnesota, and opened a private medical practice, but it was unsuccessful.

It was in 1893, while living in Saint Paul, that Eastman began writing sketches of his childhood. His wife edited the pieces and encouraged him to have them published. The monthly *St. Nicholas: An Illustrated Magazine for Young Folks,* to which Elaine Eastman had contributed previously, published the six articles between December 1893 and May 1894; they would become chapters in Eastman's first book, *Indian Boyhood* (1902).

Eastman served as field secretary of the Young Men's Christian Association from 1894 to 1898, establishing Indian associations on reservations. His article "The Sioux Mythology," published in *Popular Science Monthly* in November 1894 – he had presented it as a paper at the 1893 World Columbian Exposition in Chicago – helped establish Eastman as an authority on Indian religion. His major treatise on Indian religious beliefs, *The Soul of the Indian: An Interpretation,* would appear in 1911.

In 1896 Eastman became a representative of the Santee Sioux in their efforts to secure the restoration of annuities that had been taken from them after the Minnesota uprising in 1862; he would continue to fight for the Santee claims in Washington, D.C., for more than twenty-five years. He served as "outing agent" for the Carlisle Indian School in Pennsylvania in 1899, helping Indian students adjust to life among whites. He became government physician at the Crow Creek Agency in South Dakota in 1900.

Eastman at the time he received his M.D. from Boston University in 1890

In July 1900 Eastman's "The Story of the Little Big Horn" was published in *The Chautauquan.* It provided information on broken treaties and white encroachment into the Black Hills and criticized white accounts of the battle that inflated the number of Indians engaged and ignored the strategy the Indians employed against George Armstrong Custer. Eastman apparently interviewed several Indians who had participated in the battle.

Eastman's first book appeared in 1902. Written for children, *Indian Boyhood* became extraordinarily popular; more than twenty editions, some in foreign languages, had been published by the early 1990s. One of the first Indian autobiographies, the book describes Eastman's fifteen years of training in the traditional ways of a hunter and warrior in Minnesota and Canada. Because time and place are not as important to Indians as to non-Indians, events in *Indian Boyhood* are not presented chronologically; Indians primarily record events by reference to the changing seasons. In addition, Indians do not separate historical facts and oral traditions as distinctly as do non-Indians.

Eastman does not ignore the harsh realities of the life he led as a youth: he describes famine, disease, confrontations with other Indian bands, and conflicts with whites. But he devotes most of his attention to the more gratifying aspects of his childhood, idealizing and romanticizing his past and investing it with an atmosphere of childlike simplicity. In an informal, at times intimate tone, Eastman conveys a longing to return to a world in which nearly every activity helped develop courage, endurance, generosity, or patience. Among his recollections is the story of how boys had to prove their courage by sacrificing a prized possession to Wakan Tanka (The Great Mystery); Eastman sacrificed his beloved dog. (Because he is writing for a white readership, he neglects to mention that eating the dog was an important part of the ceremony.)

In the book Eastman praises his grandmother Uncheedah for providing for his early education as a Sioux. Elaine Goodale Eastman, an ardent assimilationist, felt differently: she delivered a paper at the 1895 Lake Mohonk Conference of Friends of the Indian that attacked the role Indian grandmothers played as teachers of old customs and traditions and impediments to assimilation. One wonders what Charles Eastman thought about his wife's speech.

As he had at Pine Ridge, Eastman became embroiled in controversy with the Indian agent at Crow Creek. He resigned in 1903, and the Eastmans moved to Amherst, Massachusetts. Charles Eastman became head of a project to select surnames for the Sioux to protect their property rights. He worked on the project until 1909, renaming about twenty-five thousand Sioux.

Between 1904 and 1909 Eastman published three collections of short stories that depict Sioux customs, values, and history. Eastman had heard many of these stories as a youth, as he sat around the campfire with other boys listening to the elders relate Indian traditions and history. Although the books are written for young readers, adults found them fascinating as well.

The twelve stories in *Red Hunters and the Animal People* (1904) illustrate the Sioux respect for animals, such as the white bison in "The Mustering of the Herds" and eagles in "The Sky Warrior." In "On Wolf Mountain" Indians show respect for wolves by offering them food, whereas whites kill the wolves by giving them poisoned food; in "The River People" Indians admire the industrious beaver, while whites destroy the beaver dams; in "Wild Animals from the Indian Stand-Point" Indian hunters learn from animals in the hope of acquiring their resourcefulness, while whites indiscriminately kill the animals. Eastman provides a glossary of Sioux words and phrases at the end of the book.

Eastman's wife and collaborator, Elaine Goodale Eastman

Old Indian Days (1907) has more emphasis on plot, character development, and ethnology than *Red Hunters and the Animal People,* and the stories have more excitement and suspense. In eight of the fifteen stories the protagonists are women; Eastman was one of the first authors to provide a comprehensive and accurate view of the major roles women played in Sioux society. "Winona, The Woman-Child" and "Winona, The Child-Woman" depict the training of a Sioux girl. In "Snana's Fawn" an Indian woman's love for a baby deer is

The old woman screamed and wept as she rowed him across the river

OLD INDIAN DAYS

BY

C. A. EASTMAN

(Ohiyesa)

AUTHOR OF INDIAN BOYHOOD

Illustrations in color by Dan Sayre Groesbeck

NEW YORK

THE McCLURE COMPANY

MCMVII

Frontispiece and title page for Eastman's second collection of stories (courtesy of the Lilly Library, Indiana University)

later transferred to a warrior. In "The Faithfulness of Long Ears" a mule saves a woman's twin babies from the Crow Indians, the enemies of the Sioux. In "Blue Sky" a Sioux woman finds her lover, who has been captured by the Crow; later the Crow allow them to return to their village. "The Peace-Maker" concerns the brave deeds of a Sioux woman against the Sac and the Fox tribes; she also speaks out against the use of liquor by her people. In "She Who Has a Soul" a Sioux woman persuades her father to spare the life of a Catholic priest, while the exploits of a woman warrior are detailed in "The War Maiden." "The Chief Soldier," "The Famine," and "The White Man's Errand" concern the Minnesota Uprising of 1862 and provide information on real people such as Little Crow, one of the Santee leaders. Stories about Indian warriors deal with such subjects as peer approval and honor ("The Madness of Bald Eagle"), marriage and mourning customs and the practice of counting coup ("The Love of Antelope"), a Canadian métis (mixed-blood) on a buffalo hunt ("The Singing Spirit"), and the close bond between a hunter and his dog ("The Grave of the Dog"). *Old Indian Days* also includes a glossary of Sioux words.

Eastman's wife is listed as co-author of *Wigwam Evenings: Sioux Folk Tales Retold* (1909). Smoky Day, a wise Indian storyteller, narrates most of the twenty-seven "evenings," or chapters, to an audience of Sioux children. Like Aesop's fables and Joel Chandler Harris's Uncle Remus tales, many of the stories involve animals who behave in human fashion, and all of them provide a moral. In one story a turtle has been captured by his enemies. They discuss burning him to death, but the turtle replies that he will scatter the burning coals and kill them all. Next they consider boiling him, but the turtle warns them that he will dance in the boiling kettle, and the steam will blind them forever. Finally, the turtle's captors suggest drowning. When the turtle has nothing to say about this form of death, his enemies throw him into the water; the turtle, of course, escapes. The moral of the story is the importance of being patient and of using quick wit. In another story a drake outwits a falcon; later, believing that the falcon is dead, the drake is boasting of this feat when he is overtaken and killed by the falcon. The message of the story is that one should not boast too soon or too loudly. Other stories communicate such morals as working hard, keeping promises, doing one's best, avoiding greediness, and being positive. The temptations, frustrations, and adventures of Little Boy Man and Star Boy provide information about Sioux origin beliefs and other concepts of the cosmos.

In 1910 Eastman began his long association with the Boy Scouts of America. He wrote articles for *Boys' Life,* the organization's magazine; spoke at scout meetings; and served as a camp director and national councilman. During the summer of 1910 Eastman conducted fieldwork for the University of Pennsylvania among the Ojibwa, hereditary enemies of the Sioux, in northern Minnesota and Canada. Chosen to represent North American Indians at the First Universal Races Congress in London from 26 to 29 July 1911, Eastman read a paper that presented a historical and sociological overview of Indians before and after European contact, stressed the need for Indians to participate in mainstream American life, and condemned the paternalistic policies of the Bureau of Indian Affairs. W. E. B. Du Bois, representing African Americans, spoke at the same session.

In 1911 Eastman was one of the founders of the Society of American Indians, an organization that attempted to improve reservation conditions, to protect Indians from injustice, and to gain citizenship for all Indians. Eastman contributed several articles to the society's journal, the *American Indian Magazine;* he would serve as president of the organization in 1918. The society's effectiveness was limited by divisions among its leaders regarding such issues as the use of peyote in religious ceremonies, the role of the Bureau of Indian Affairs, and the relationship between the society and the journal.

Also in 1911 Eastman published *The Soul of the Indian,* an account of Indian religious beliefs. Although a convert to Christianity, Eastman was proud of his ancestral religion, which seemed to give meaning and perspective to his life. The Indian expression for God is *Wakan Tanka* (The Great Mystery), an all-powerful force to be worshipped in silence and solitude. Spiritual training was provided mainly by Indian women, who instructed children about the wonders of nature, respectfulness and other values, and the importance of prayer. Eastman fondly recalls the religious instruction he received from his surrogate mother, Uncheedah. Indians accepted the supernatural

Cover for Eastman's collection of retellings of Sioux folktales, one of two books for which his wife is named as co-author (courtesy of the Lilly Library, Indiana University)

and, consequently, readily believed biblical accounts of miracles; they could not understand why their creation stories were not equally accepted by Christians. Eastman takes to task white missionaries who condemn Indian beliefs and laments that the tenets of Christianity are professed in theory but not practiced; modern Christianity, he believes, is linked too closely with white society's emphasis on competition and materialism. He is shocked to hear whites use God's name in vain, something that Indians would never do. A problem in this book, as in his other works, is that Eastman frequently neglects to make it clear whether he is discussing traits of Indians in general or only of the Sioux.

In 1914 Eastman published *Indian Scout Talks,* a guide for Boy Scouts and Campfire Girls on such topics as how to make bows and arrows, tepees, and canoes and how to survive in the wilderness. In 1915 the Eastmans established a girls' summer camp, Camp Oahe, at Granite Lake, near Munsonville, New Hampshire. They printed elaborate brochures that showed campers engaged in activities directed by a "real" Indian. The camp was an instant success.

In *The Indian Today: The Past and Future of the First American* (1915) Eastman offers a broad overview of Indian history, customs, and beliefs, and he documents the devastating results of ill-conceived government policies toward the Indians. He declares that the two greatest white "civilizers" were whiskey and gunpowder and shows how white contact destroyed Indian societies. Drawing on his personal experience, Eastman vehemently criticizes the reservation system, condemning unqualified Indian agents, the locating of reservations on poor agricultural land, unhealthful living conditions, and inadequate educational facilities. He calls for the abolition of the Bureau of Indian Affairs and its replacement by a commission of which at least half the members would be Indians. Like many other reform-minded individuals, Eastman supports the Dawes Act of 1887, which provided for land allotments in severalty and the breakup of reservations; he particularly favors a provision that granted citizenship to Indians who accepted allotments. By becoming citizens, he thinks, Indians can obtain more rights – especially suffrage, which will give Indians more influence in decisions affecting their lives. Eastman also reminds his readers of the many contributions Indians have made to American society. There was discussion of Eastman's becoming commissioner of Indian affairs under President Woodrow Wilson in 1915, but nothing came of the idea.

In 1916 Eastman published his second autobiographical work, *From the Deep Woods to Civilization: Chapters in the Autobiography of an Indian,* which starts where *Indian Boyhood* ended. Readers soon become aware that the youthful optimism and idealism that Eastman possessed when he began his passage into an alien culture diminished with the sobering experiences of adulthood. He attacks the evils of white society and laments the sorrows Indians endured as a result of cultural contact. *From the Deep Woods* includes valuable information about Eastman's education and career in the white world. Certain omissions are noteworthy, however. For example, his account of his confrontations with the Indian agent at the Pine Ridge Reservation are entirely one-sided, and he does not even mention the turmoil he experienced at the Crow Creek Reservation.

In 1918 Eastman published his final book, *Indian Heroes and Great Chieftains.* The work comprises biographical sketches of fifteen Indian leaders, several of whom he interviewed. Most of the subjects are Sioux, including Sitting Bull, Red Cloud, Crazy Horse, and Spotted Tail; among the non-Sioux leaders included are the Cheyenne chiefs Roman Nose and Dull Knife, and Chief Joseph of the Nez Percé. Eastman's portrayal of these men is sympathetic and, in the main, accurate, although the historian George A. Hyde found several errors in Eastman's account of Spotted Tail. Eastman shows how these leaders struggled to protect their people and maintain their Indian ways. He condemns the economic warfare whites waged on the Plains Indians and frequent breaking of treaties by whites. He again criticizes white accounts of Indian victories, such as the Battle of the Little Big Horn, for not recognizing Indian military prowess. Nearly all Indian wars, he laments, ended with the loss of tribal lands and Indian imprisonment on reservations.

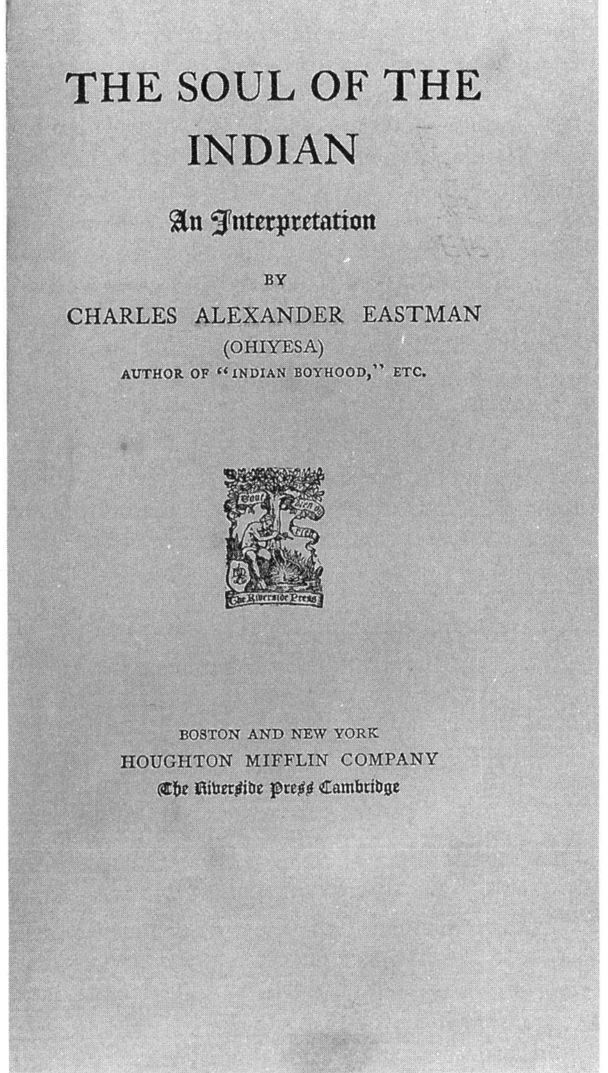
THE SOUL OF THE INDIAN

An Interpretation

BY

CHARLES ALEXANDER EASTMAN

(OHIYESA)

AUTHOR OF "INDIAN BOYHOOD," ETC.

BOSTON AND NEW YORK
HOUGHTON MIFFLIN COMPANY
The Riverside Press Cambridge

Title page for Eastman's account of Indian religious beliefs

Although Eastman's books sold well, and he delivered many paid lectures, by 1920 he was having financial problems. The summer camp fell on hard times, attracting fewer campers. There were also mounting tensions between Eastman and his wife. Rumors of their incompatibility had been circulating since the mid 1890s, and the couple secretly separated in August 1921. The reasons for the separation remain shrouded in mystery. Possible causes include Eastman's prolonged absences from home and his alleged promiscuity; the conflict between Elaine's staunch assimilationist views and his emphasis on acculturation; her overbearing manner; and disagreements arising from their collaboration on Eastman's writings. Although he was working on several projects, including a novel about Pontiac, a biography of Sacajawea, and a book on Sioux history and legends, Eastman published no major works after the separation. Although Elaine did continue to publish, her works never achieved the popularity or recognition of his. They had been, despite their problems, an excellent writing team: he had furnished the experiences and ideas, and she had supplied the literary skill.

In 1923 Eastman finally received payment – perhaps $5,000 – for the work he had performed since the 1890s in the Santee Sioux claims case. He had expected more. He reentered the Indian service for the fifth and final time in August 1923, becoming a U.S. Indian inspector. In his new job Eastman investigated charges against Indians and government employees at reservations and inspected general conditions and health problems. He played major roles in entertaining Prime Minister David Lloyd George of Great Britain, who wanted to meet some Indians during his October 1923 visit to the United States, and in the controversy concerning the year of death of Sacajawea, in which Eastman supported 1884 over 1812.

In December 1923 Eastman was one of the prominent figures invited by Secretary of the Interior Hubert W. Work to study federal Indian policy. Called the Committee of One Hundred, the group made several recommendations that included development of comprehensive Indian educational programs, improvement of health and sanitary conditions on reservations, and continued study of the peyote issue and granting Indian citizenship.

The grueling schedule of an Indian inspector took its toll on the sixty-five-year-old Eastman, and he resigned in March 1925. After spending the next several months regaining his strength Eastman resumed his lecture schedule, traveling to New York City; Washington, D.C.; and Chicago. Also in 1925 Eastman accepted an offer to become a director of the Brooks-Bryce Foundation, which promoted better relations between the United States and Great Britain. His speeches for the foundation so impressed its founder, Florence Brooks-Aten, that she asked him to represent the organization on a two-month speaking tour in England. Eastman sailed for England for the second time in January 1928. He gave popular talks before large audiences and presented special lectures on Indian culture at the University of Oxford, Eton College, and the Royal Colonial Institute.

Eastman, circa 1918, in Sioux costume at Camp Oahe, the girls' summer camp he and his wife established in New Hampshire in 1915 (courtesy of James D. Ewing)

Returning from Britain, Eastman purchased a site on the shore of Lake Huron near Desbarats, Ontario, and built a cabin there. He spent the warmer months there, enjoying the solitude, and spent the winters with his son in Detroit. In 1933 the Indian Council Fire, a national fraternal Pan-Indian organization, chose Eastman to receive its first annual award recognizing distinguished achievements by an Indian. In spite of failing health, he continued to give lectures in 1938. He died on 8 January 1939 and was buried in an unmarked grave at Evergreen Cemetery, Detroit. After his death his estranged wife acquired his manuscripts; she published his work on Sacajawea under his name in a series of articles in the *Great Falls Tribune* in 1949. She died in December 1953, at age ninety, and was buried in Northampton, Massachusetts. Raymond Wilson and the Dartmouth Club of Detroit erected a stone on Charles Eastman's grave in 1984.

Many prominent Indian reformers of the late nineteenth and early twentieth centuries considered Eastman the prime example of what an Indian could achieve. Most reformers failed, however, to realize that Eastman was an acculturated rather than an assimilated Indian: as his writings attest, he did not forsake his Indianness. Nearly every aspect of his long, varied, and controversial career was related to Indian-white relations. He was the first major Indian author to write Indian history from the Indian perspective; the main objective of his publications was to tear down the wall of prejudice that separated Indians and whites.

Biographies:

Marion W. Copeland, *Charles Alexander Eastman (Ohiyesa)* (Caldwell, Idaho: Caxton Printers, 1978);

David R. Miller, "Charles Alexander Eastman, The 'Winner': From Deep Woods to Civilization, Santee Sioux, 1858–1939," in *American Indian Intellectuals,* edited by Margot Liberty (Saint Paul, Minn.: West, 1978), pp. 61–73;

Raymond Wilson, *Ohiyesa: Charles Eastman, Santee Sioux* (Urbana: University of Illinois Press, 1983);

Bernd C. Peyer, "Charles Alexander – Ohiyesa Eastman," in *Dictionary of Native American Literature,* edited by Andrew Wiget (New York: Garland, 1994), pp. 231–237.

References:

Ruth A. Alexander, "Building a Cultural Bridge: Elaine and Charles Eastman," in *South Dakota Leaders,* edited by Herbert T. Hoover and Larry J. Zimmerman (Vermillion: University of South Dakota Press, 1989), pp. 355–366;

Alexander, "Elaine Goodale Eastman and the Failure of the Feminist Protestant Ethic," *Great Plains Quarterly,* 8 (Spring 1988): 89–101;

Elaine G. Eastman, "All the Days of My Life," *South Dakota Historical Review,* 2 (July 1937): 171–184;

Kay Graber, ed., *Sister to the Sioux: The Memoirs of Elaine Goodale Eastman, 1885–91* (Lincoln: University of Nebraska Press, 1978);

Hazel W. Hertzberg, *The Search for an American Indian Identity: Modern Pan-Indian Movements* (Syracuse, N.Y.: Syracuse University Press, 1971);

George A. Hyde, *Spotted Tail's Folk: A History of the Brule Sioux* (Norman: University of Oklahoma Press, 1961), pp. 13, 15, 20, 33, 35, 39–40;

Ethel Nurge, ed., *The Modern Sioux: Social Systems and Reservation Culture* (Lincoln: University of Nebraska Press, 1965), p. 37;

Anna L. Stensland, "Charles Alexander Eastman: Sioux Storyteller and Historian," *American Indian Quarterly,* 3 (Autumn 1977): 199–208;

Raymond Wilson, "The Writings of Ohiyesa – Charles Alexander Eastman, M.D., Santee Sioux," *South Dakota History,* 6 (Winter 1975): 55–73.

Papers:

Charles A. Eastman's official government correspondence as an employee of the Bureau of Indian Affairs can be found at the National Archives and Records Service in Washington, D.C., in Record Group 75, as well as at the Federal Archives and Records Center in Kansas City, Missouri, in Record Group 75, Pine Ridge Agency, 1890–1893, and Crow Creek Agency, 1900–1903. His status records are at the National Personnel Records Center in Saint Louis. Other depositories containing valuable information on Eastman are the New York State Museum at Albany; Jones Public Library, Amherst, Massachusetts; and the records of Dartmouth College and Yale University.

Louise Erdrich

(7 June 1954 –)

Peter G. Beidler
Lehigh University

See also the Erdrich entry in *DLB 152: American Novelists Since World War II, Fourth Series.*

BOOKS: *Imagination* (Westerville, Ohio: Merrill, 1981);

Jacklight (New York: Holt, Rinehart & Winston, 1984; London: Abacus, 1990);

Love Medicine (New York: Holt, Rinehart & Winston, 1984; London: Deutsch, 1985; revised edition, New York: Holt, 1993; London: Flamingo, 1993);

The Beet Queen (New York: Holt, 1986; London: Hamilton, 1986);

Tracks (New York: Holt, 1988; London: Flamingo, 1994);

Baptism of Desire (New York: Harper & Row, 1989);

The Crown of Columbus, by Erdrich and Michael Dorris (New York: HarperCollins, 1991; London: Flamingo, 1992);

Route Two, by Erdrich and Dorris (Northridge, Cal.: Lord John, 1991);

The Bingo Palace (New York: HarperCollins, 1994; London: Flamingo, 1994);

The Blue Jay's Dance: A Birth Year (New York: HarperCollins, 1995);

Tales of Burning Love (New York: HarperCollins, 1996);

Grandmother's Pigeon (New York: Hyperion, 1996).

OTHER: "American Horse," in *Earth Power Coming: An Anthology of Native American Fiction,* edited by Simon Ortiz (Tsaile, Ariz.: Navajo Community College Press, 1984), pp. 59–72;

Michael Dorris, *The Broken Cord: A Family's Ongoing Struggle with Fetal Alcohol Syndrome,* foreword by Erdrich (New York: Harper & Row, 1989; London: Futura, 1992);

Desmond Hogan, *A Link with the River,* preface by Erdrich (New York: Farrar, Straus & Giroux, 1989);

Erdrich at the time of The Blue Jay's Dance

The Best American Short Stories 1993, edited, with an introduction, by Erdrich (Boston: Houghton Mifflin, 1993).

SELECTED PERIODICAL PUBLICATIONS – UNCOLLECTED: "The True Story of Mustache Maude," *Frontiers,* 7 (Summer 1984): 62–67;

"Where I Ought to Be: A Writer's Sense of Place," *New York Times Book Review,* 28 July 1985, pp. 1, 23–24;

"Mister Argus," *Georgia Review,* 39 (Summer 1985): 379–390;

"Pounding the Dog," *Kenyon Review,* new series 7 (Fall 1985): 18–28;

"Who Owns the Land?" *New York Times Magazine,* 4 September 1988, pp. 32–35, 52–54, 57, 65;

"A Wedge of Shade," *New Yorker,* 65 (6 March 1989): 35–40;

"Mauser," *New Yorker,* 67 (8 April 1991): 38–42;

"Line of Credit," *Harper's,* 284 (April 1992): 55–61;

"A Woman's Work: Too Many Demands and Not Enough Selves," *Harper's,* 286 (May 1993): 35–46.

Louise Erdrich is one of the most important contemporary Native American writers. She writes poetry and some of the most sophisticated fiction and nonfiction being produced in the United States; her novels, particularly, deserve to be read, discussed, and appreciated. She shows every promise of rising to star status not merely among Native American writers but among contemporary writers in general. Although most of her characters and themes grow out of her background as a Native American woman who grew up off the reservation, her writing is accessible to any reader willing to put forth a bit of effort. Like life itself, her writing sometimes appears disjointed, but she raises virtually all of the issues important to an understanding of the human condition: accidents of birth and parentage, falling in love, generosity, greed, psychological damage, joy, alienation, vulnerability, differentness, parenting, aging, and dying.

Karen Louise Erdrich was born on 7 June 1954 in Little Falls, Minnesota, the eldest of seven children of Ralph Louis and Rita Joanne Gourneau Erdrich. Her father was of Germanic descent, her mother of Chippewa and French descent. Three-eighths Chippewa, Erdrich is related through her mother to Kaishpau Gourneau, who was tribal chairman of the Turtle Mountain Band of Chippewa in 1882, and she is an enrolled member of that band in the reservation town of Belcourt, North Dakota. Although she has never lived on the reservation, she has visited it often with her family. Both of her parents worked for the Bureau of Indian Affairs at a boarding school in Wahpeton, North Dakota, where she spent most of her youth. Her parents encouraged her writing: her father paid her a nickel for each story she wrote, and her mother gathered the stories together and sewed them into little books.

After being educated in various schools in Wahpeton, in 1972 Erdrich enrolled at Dartmouth College as a member of the first class of women admitted into the previously all-male institution. She arrived the same day as Michael Dorris, a mixed-blood of Modoc descent who was nine years her senior and a new professor of anthropology; their romantic interest in each other would not begin until some years later. In a 1988 interview Erdrich told Kay Bonetti that she began writing seriously when "I was in college and had failed at everything else. I kept journals and diaries when I was a kid, and I started writing when I was nineteen or twenty. After college I decided that that's absolutely what I wanted to do. Part of it was that I did not prepare myself for anything else in life." At Dartmouth, Erdrich won the Cox Prize in fiction, as well as a prize from the American Academy of Poets. While in college and immediately after receiving her B.A. in English in 1976, she worked at a variety of jobs: hoeing sugar beets, picking cucumbers, selling popcorn at a movie theater, babysitting, lifeguarding, selling fried chicken and pastries, waitressing, short-order cooking, shelving books in a library, weighing dump trucks, writing advertising copy, and developing photographs. In 1976 she returned to North Dakota to conduct poetry workshops through the Poetry in the Schools program sponsored by the North Dakota Arts Council. In 1978 she entered Johns Hopkins University's creative writing program, directed by Richard Howard. Her 1979 master's thesis was a collection of poems titled "The Common Mercies and Run of Hearts." She then went to Boston and edited the Boston Indian Council newspaper, the *Circle.*

Erdrich received fellowships in 1980 to the MacDowell Colony and in 1981 to the Yaddo Colony. In 1981 she was named writer-in-residence at Dartmouth and became involved with Dorris, who by then had become the founding director of the college's Native American studies program. When they married on 10 October 1981, Erdrich became the adoptive mother of the three Native American children Dorris had earlier adopted as a single parent: Reynold Abel, Jeffrey Sava, and Madeline Hannah. Together they have had three more children: Persia Andromeda, Pallas Antigone, and Aza Marion. Abel, a victim of fetal alcohol syndrome, was to become the subject of Dorris's *The Broken Cord* (1989), for which Erdrich wrote a moving foreword in which she admits that "I drank hard in my twen-

Dust jacket for the second novel in Erdrich's North Dakota Saga

ties, and eventually got hepatitis. I was lucky." She refers to this period again in "Skunk Dreams," first published in the *Georgia Review* in 1993 and collected in *The Blue Jay's Dance: A Birth Year* in 1995, where she refers to "spells of too much cabernet and a few idiotic years of rolling my own cigarettes out of Virginia Blond tobacco."

Erdrich and Dorris say that most of their writing is collaborative, though they usually publish a particular piece under the name of the one who writes the first draft. Although she published a children's writing textbook, *Imagination,* in 1981, Erdrich's literary book-length publications began in 1984 with a collection of poems, *Jacklight.* The jacklight of the title poem is the bright light that hunters use illegally to draw deer from the forest; it becomes a metaphor for the destructive lure of European American culture, with its money, alcohol, cars, religion, and offer of military heroism.

One set of poems in *Jacklight* concerns the legendary Indian trickster Potchikoo, who is born of the sun, marries a cigar-store Indian, and emits flatulence in church. More memorable is the set of fifteen connected narrative poems titled "The Butcher's Wife." Mary Kröger marries the butcher, Otto, after his first wife – who is also Mary's best friend – dies, asking her to take care of Otto and their four sons. Many of the poems in "The Butcher's Wife" are about Mary's relationships with the people she "inherits" from her friend: Otto, the sons, Otto's proud sister Hilda, the scavenging woman known as Step-and-a-Half Waleski, the priest. After Otto dies she has to deal with the dog who loved him and with Rudy J. V. Jacklitch, whose courting she does not encourage and for whose suicide she feels responsible. In a 1985 interview with Jan George, Erdrich said that her grandmother's life "vaguely resembles the life lived by Mary Kröger." An intense exploration of the interconnected lives of a family, "The Butcher's Wife" is a preview of a major theme of Erdrich's fiction.

The final poem of *Jacklight,* "Turtle Mountain Reservation," dedicated to Pat Gourneau, her grandfather, is a collection of reservation images and people: the heron, the owl, drunken Uncle Ray, Theresa, and, most of all, the senile Grandpa, "crazy / as the loon that calls its children / across the lake." Grandpa's hands are twisted and useless, but they are her hands as well: "Hands of earth, of this clay / I'm also made from."

In a 1990 interview with Laura Coltelli, Erdrich said that she soon found poetry too confining: "I just began to realize that I wanted to be a fiction writer; that's a bigger medium, you know. I have a lot more room and it's closer to the oral tradition of sitting around and telling stories." She published some short stories in collaboration with her sister, Heidi Erdrich, under the name Heidi Louise and with her husband under the name Milou North; then she and Dorris, seeing a notice about the Nelson Algren Award for stories of five thousand words, worked for two weeks to put together the "The World's Greatest Fishermen." It won the $5,000 Algren Award for 1982. The next year Erdrich received a Pushcart Prize for one of her poems and a National Magazine Fiction Award for "Scales," which was included in *The Best American Short Stories 1983.* With the help and advice of her husband she revised "The World's Greatest Fishermen" as the lead story in the novel *Love Medicine* (1984).

In her introduction to *The Best American Short Stories 1993* Erdrich writes that "the best short stories contain novels." *Love Medicine* is a series of fine short stories revised and augmented into a fine novel; the stories are not so much chapters in a novel as they are a complex entangling of families, histories, and themes into a richly diverse narrative. *Love Medicine* bears comparison with Sherwood Anderson's *Winesburg, Ohio* (1919) and William Faulkner's *Go Down, Moses and Other Stories* (1942) as a bringing together of stories that work individually but are enriched when read in the context provided by the other stories. By setting her most important work on and around a North Dakota Indian reservation and by depicting its German-French-Irish-Scandinavian-Mexican-Chippewa-Cree-Catholic characters through several generations, Erdrich has created her own Winesburg and her own Yoknapatawpha County.

The first novel in what may be called her North Dakota Saga, *Love Medicine* is about the members of five families of Indians and mixed-bloods – the Nanapushes, the Kashpaws, the Pillagers, the Lazarres, and the Morrisseys – that are bound by ties of blood, love, jealousy, hate, religion, death, history, and politics. The novel begins in 1981 when June Morrissey Kashpaw, after being picked up in a bar and seduced in a pickup truck by a drunken white engineer, walks off toward her home on the reservation but freezes to death on the way. Some of the other characters see her death as having been caused by an exploitative white society; some are jealous of her beauty and differentness; some are fascinated by her life story; some miss their lost mother, aunt, or lover; some appear to be interested only in the new car her son buys with her life insurance benefit. Above all, however, there is love for June. The ripples of love that her death sets in motion serve as a kind of medicine for the others.

Love Medicine introduces many of the concerns Erdrich would explore in her later works, one of which is the question of parentage. Albertine Johnson never knew her white father. Since Lipsha Morrissey does not know that June was his mother, he knows neither that King Kashpaw is his half-brother nor that Gerry Nanapush is his father. Lulu Lamartine has so many lovers that it is difficult to know who fathered which of her children: is Henry Lamartine Jr. really Henry's son or the son of Henry's brother Beverly? Marie Kashpaw thinks that her parents are Ignatius Lazarre and an alcoholic woman, but her real mother turns out to be a nun. Although the novel climaxes with Lipsha's discovery of his real parents, in the context of the larger family relationships that make up *Love Medicine,* biological parentage matters far less than love parentage. What concerns Lipsha most is not that his biological mother, June, tied him into a weighted potato sack when he was a baby and threw him into the lake but that his "real" mother is Marie, who took him in as she had earlier taken in June. What matters to him is that he gets along far better with Albertine, who is not really his blood cousin, than he does with King, who is really his half-brother. Blood relationships are sometimes far more full of hate and pain than of joy. June, one of Marie's favorite "take-ins," was really the daughter of her sister and was later educated in the ways of the wild by Eli Kashpaw, Marie's brother-in-law. The woman who turns out to be Marie's "real mother" either ignores her or seems bent on destroying her.

Another theme in *Love Medicine* is the role of alcohol in Indian families. One of Marie's chief functions as a wife has been to try to keep Nector Kashpaw away from drink. Henry Lamartine dies drunk when he drives his car along the railroad tracks. June is drunk when she sets off across the plains to her death after being seduced by the drunken engineer. At the family gathering some months later, June's son King's love, guilt, and anger are accentuated by his being drunk. Albertine, June's niece, is almost as drunk as Henry Jr. when, at age fifteen, she loses her virginity to him. After June's death Albertine drinks beer and wine to numb the pain of memory and of family frictions. And Gordie Kashpaw is drunk when he confuses the dead June with a car-struck deer. Alcohol is not far from most of the significant actions of the novel, and it serves as a kind of jacklight, luring the characters into danger and sometimes to destruction.

In her 1985 essay "Where I Ought To Be" Erdrich emphasizes the importance of place in her writing:

> I grew up in a small North Dakota town, on land that once belonged to the Wahpeton-Sisseton Sioux but had long since been leased out and sold to non-Indian farmers. Our family of nine lived on the very edge of town in a house that belonged to the Government and was rented to employees of the Bureau of Indian Affairs boarding school, where both my parents worked, and where my grandfather, a Turtle Mountain Chippewa named Pat Gourneau, had been educated. . . . I often see this edge of town – the sky and its towering and shifting formations of clouds, that beautifully lighted emptiness – when I am writing.

It is apparent that much of the setting for *Love Medicine* comes from Erdrich's memories of her early life near this Bureau of Indian Affairs boarding school, as well as from her memories of frequent visits to the Turtle Mountain reservation in northern North Dakota, just below the Canadian border. The existence of most of her characters is controlled by the fact that they are

Dust jacket for Erdrich's third novel, set chronologically prior to Love Medicine *and* The Beet Queen

Indians surrounded by a white culture. Issues of race and ethnicity, though in some ways they dominate *Love Medicine,* are finally rather insignificant: the novel is about being human, not about being Indian. Nor is *Love Medicine* an antiwhite novel. There are some subtle jabs at the federal government's policies of allotment and termination on Indian reservations; June's seducer is a white man; and Gerry is thrown in jail the first time for kicking a white cowboy in the crotch during a barroom argument about whether Indians are "niggers." But racial prejudice runs both ways. The mostly white Albertine is thought inferior by some Indians who are more pure-blooded than she, and most of the Indians in the novel seem united in their dislike of the mostly white, no-good Morrisseys and the mostly white, dirty Lazarres. Still, in *Love Medicine* one's quantum of Indian blood matters less than one's quantum of love.

That love takes on grotesque dimensions at times. Sister Leopolda – possibly angry that Marie is living proof of her own nonvirginity – shows her motherly hate/love for Marie by attacking her with a bread poker and pouring boiling water on her. Nector poses in a diaper for a white artist who wants to show her love of Indians by painting one jumping naked off a cliff. Fat Dot Adare is impregnated by fat Gerry Nanapush while sitting astride him with a hole ripped in her pantyhose in the visiting room of a prison. Lulu picks for her husband the brother who, standing naked before her after a game of strip poker, has the better erection. Nector and Lulu make love smeared in butter and, later, in the laundry room of the senior citizens' center. Nector chokes on a turkey heart that has been blessed by Lipsha and is supposed to be a "love medicine."

In an interview with Joseph Bruchac shortly after the publication of *Love Medicine* (collected in *Conversations with Louise Erdrich and Michael Dorris,* 1994), Erdrich said that the writer's conscious role in writing is almost passive:

> I really don't control the subject matter, it just takes me. I believe that a poet or a fiction writer is something like a medium at a seance who lets the voices speak. Of course, a person has to study and develop technical expertise. But a writer can't control subject and back-

ground. If he or she is true to what's happening, the story will take over.

She even uses the passive voice in speaking about writing: "Maybe I'm just crazy. But I sit down and, if something is there, it will be written."

Love Medicine won the National Book Critics Circle Award, the Virginia McCormick Scully Prize as the best book of 1984, the Best First Fiction Award from the Great Lakes College Association, the Sue Kaufman Prize for best first fiction from the American Academy and Institute of Arts and Letters, the American Book Award from the Before Columbus Foundation, and the *Los Angeles Times* Award for fiction. It was widely praised by critics and was listed as one of the best books of the year by *The New York Times Book Review*. The success of *Jacklight* and *Love Medicine* no doubt influenced the judges who awarded her a Guggenheim Fellowship for 1985–1986.

Erdrich's *The Beet Queen* (1986) is the story of the life of Dot Adare, whose between-prisons affair with Gerry Nanapush provides a measure of humor in *Love Medicine*. The main setting of *The Beet Queen* is the little town of Argus, a few miles south of the reservation, but it moves to the reservation, to Fargo, and to Minneapolis. In this second novel in her North Dakota Saga, Erdrich introduces a white family, the Adares, who are just as fragmented as many of the Indian families in the earlier novel. The fragmentation begins with the death of the white businessman who, though he has another family, keeps Adelaide Adare as his mistress and fathers her three children. His death at the beginning of the Great Depression leaves Adelaide so desperate that she abandons her three children and impulsively flies away with a stunt pilot, never to return. Her daughter Mary goes to Argus to be raised by her Aunt and Uncle Kozka. Adelaide's son Karl, after having been rescued by the Indian peddler Fleur Pillager, winds up in an orphanage in Minnesota. The newborn baby is kidnapped by another family and raised as Jude Miller. On its most literal level, *The Beet Queen* is the story of how these three children are brought back together – physically, if not emotionally – forty years later, when Karl's daughter, Dot, repeats the family history by flying off with another stunt pilot.

Many of the chapters in this novel, like those in *Love Medicine,* had been published first as short stories. The effect of *The Beet Queen,* however, is far more focused. It covers only forty years instead of the seventy of *Love Medicine,* and it keeps the reader's attention on a single family rather than dividing it among five families, as the earlier novel did. It shares with *Love Medicine,* however, the theme of the search for one's parents. The counterpart of Lipsha in this novel is Jude Miller, the infant abandoned by his mother and raised by someone else. By becoming a priest Jude delivers a different kind of love medicine on his stumbling, reluctant, and abortive path toward discovery.

The Beet Queen is not a novel about Indians, but Indians play roles in it. Eli is caretaker to his ailing half-brother, Russell Kashpaw. The novel introduces Fleur Pillager, who will play a larger role in Erdrich's next novel, *Tracks* (1988). The part-Indian heritage of Celestine James, Dot's mother, makes Dot at least one quarter Indian. Again, however, blood quantum is not nearly as important as love quantum. Most of the strange characters in *The Beet Queen* are incapable of love: men use women; mothers abandon or kidnap children; fathers abandon daughters; sons abandon sisters; and daughters reject mothers. Dot, however, grows in the final chapter to feel something like love for her mother, Celestine: "In her eyes I see the force of her love. It is bulky and hard to carry like a package that keeps untying. . . . I walk to her, drawn by her, unable to help myself."

If Dot is uncomfortable showing love, the circumstances of her engendering and upbringing help to explain why. Her father, Karl, is an effeminate homosexual who has come reluctantly to Argus to establish contact with his sister and makes love with the masculine Celestine. When Celestine becomes pregnant she marries him but then immediately banishes him so that she can raise Dot alone. Karl does little more in the way of fatherly duty than buy Dot a breakfast and send her a motorized wheelchair she does not need. In raising Dot, Celestine is aided by Mary Adare, who seems to feel a lesbian attraction to Celestine, and by Wallace Pfef, a homosexual who had had a brief affair with Karl. Wallace helps in the emergency delivery of Dot and then acts as a surrogate father, throwing occasional birthday parties for her and rigging the voting for queen of the sugar beet festival so that Dot wins. At first glance it seems that Mary's cousin Sita is the only person who displays normal love; but she is a pretentious and anorexic model whose two marriages were based more on need than on love and whose addiction to painkillers eventually leads to her suicide. In such surroundings, it is not surprising that Dot seems immune to love.

There are grotesque incidents in *The Beet Queen*. After each of his homosexual encounters – one with a railroad bum, Giles Saint Ambrose, the other with Wallace Pfef – Karl Adare leaps from high places, nearly to his death. Mary slides face-first down the school sliding board in midwinter; when her face cracks a sheet of ice at the bottom in such a way that it seems to resemble the face of Christ, she is hailed as the bringer of a "manifestation." Sita's death, far from being tragic, is almost comic: Mary and Celestine find her body in her yard, sitting against a yew bush. Too busy to call an undertaker, they take her with them, propped up in the middle of the pickup seat, to the beet festival. A policeman who stops them for speeding says a few words to the corpse, never realizing that it is dead. Later Karl gets into the pickup, talks to Sita, and takes a nap – also never realizing that she is dead.

The Beet Queen has not earned the critical praise that *Love Medicine* did, perhaps because Erdrich's readers want Native American writers to write about Native American characters and subjects. It may also be that Erdrich's narrative voice loses some of its vigor when she begins to step away from an Indian milieu. Leslie Marmon Silko, a Native American writer, began what some scholars call "the Silko-Erdrich controversy" by criticizing Erdrich's novel for not being more revealing of the racism of North Dakota society. She calls particular attention to Russell Kashpaw, the wounded veteran:

> We don't have a clue to what Russell feels about all the blood and bone he's lost defending a government and people who will always exclude him. We never know what reasons or feelings make Russell volunteer for two foreign wars. In the entire 338 pages, only once is any bitterness over racism ever expressed.

Erdrich regained her voice and her audience in 1988 with her third novel, *Tracks.* It is one of her most powerful works and the favorite of many of her readers. It is not as choppy and disjointed as *Love Medicine;* it focuses more narrowly on Indian characters and themes than *The Beet Queen;* and it is more overtly political than its predecessors. Its main events precede those of the earlier novels. Readers who want to know how Sister Leopolda came to be a nun will find out here that Leopolda is half-crazy, that she is several times over a near-murderer, and that she had become a reluctant mother before becoming an eager bride of Christ. It is revealed that the brothers Eli and Nector are so different because they are not twins after all but nearly a decade apart in age and the product of quite different educational environments: Eli was raised by Nanapush to know the land, while the younger Nector was raised by Margaret Kashpaw to know white ways. While in *Love Medicine* Eli seems to have had no women in his life, in *Tracks* one learns that he had fallen in love early in his life with the wild Fleur, apparently the only romantic attachment he ever had. Fleur, the peddler who rescues Karl in *The Beet Queen,* is shown to have had supernatural, almost witchlike powers as a young woman. Lulu and Marie are rivals for Nector in *Love Medicine;* here it is revealed that Lulu was born of the union of Fleur with one of four possible fathers, while Marie is the child of the partly deranged Pauline Puyat, who later becomes Sister Leopolda, and the drunk Napoleon Morrissey.

In the 1988 interview with Bonetti, Dorris mentions that a draft of *Tracks* was in existence at the time that he and Erdrich were trying to get a publisher for *Love Medicine.* By the time it appeared as a novel many of its chapters had been published as separate stories. Even so, the chapters fit together more seamlessly than do those of the earlier novels. Not only is the dozen-year time span of the novel more narrow, but with only two narrators, both speaking in the first person, *Tracks* feels far more circumscribed and controlled than either *Love Medicine* or *The Beet Queen.* There is still a confusingly rich array of characters, but the focus is more clearly on only a few of them: Nanapush and his lover Margaret, Fleur Pillager and her lover Eli Kashpaw, and Pauline, or Sister Leopolda.

Tracks is at once both Erdrich's most humorous novel and her most political one. The humor comes primarily in Nanapush's comic exchanges about sex with Margaret and in his genial criticism of Pauline. Vowing to urinate only at dawn and at dusk, Pauline is tricked by Nanapush into a midafternoon release – much to her consternation and his amusement. Nanapush's humor serves generally to place Pauline's strange behavior into a friendly, rather than an antagonistic, frame. She is deranged, of course: in addition to her peculiar urinary habits, she mortifies her flesh by putting her shoes on the wrong feet, starving herself almost to death, and refusing to bathe or change her clothes. And yet, in part because of Nanapush's loving humor, the reader sees her as solidly human rather than as merely weird. Even though she is probably a murderer, Nanapush helps the reader to love rather than condemn her.

The condemnation in this novel is reserved for the white political forces that destroyed the forests and altered families and a tribe almost beyond recognition, but Indians are also held responsible. The real villains are young Nector and his mother, Margaret, who violate Fleur's trust by using her money to pay the taxes on their own Kashpaw land. Even so, Erdrich seems not to want her readers to hate any of these people but rather to share with Nanapush a sense of sadness that the tribe has been changed forever into "a tribe of file cabinets and triplicates, a tribe of single-space documents, directives, policy. A tribe of pressed trees. A tribe of chicken-scratch that can be scattered by a wind, diminished to ashes by one struck match."

One of Erdrich's most impressive attributes as a novelist is her experimentation with narrative point of view: each of the narrators in her novels speaks with authentic individuality. Erdrich's skill with point of view is especially impressive in *Tracks*. Nanapush is a generally truthful narrator; he is motivated to tell Lulu the story of those early days by his desire to convince her that she should not hate her mother, Fleur, for abandoning her, and by his desire that she not marry the Morrissey man she thinks she loves. Pauline's motives for telling her story and the story of Fleur are not so clear, but it seems that, in her half-crazed and fanatical way, she wants to justify her own violent and probably murderous actions. If Nanapush seems intent on telling the truth, Pauline seems intent on concealing it – or, at least, concealing the full truth about her part in the events. Both narrators focus so effectively, and so differently, on Fleur that the reader comes to know the wild young woman deeply. Nanapush loves Fleur, and Pauline is jealous of her; together they reveal Fleur to the reader more clearly than she could have revealed herself if she had been the speaker. The indomitable Fleur can be buffeted by nature but can control the wind. She can be beaten but never defeated. She can drown but survive again and again. She sounds like a spirit, but the reader knows her as human and can understand why she attracts not only men but also the lake creature who lives in Matchimanito. The reader never enters Fleur's mind directly, and she says little. But the reader knows her and comes to love her through Erdrich's skillful narrative indirection.

Baptism of Desire (1989), Erdrich's second book of poetry, returns to some of the themes and personages of *Jacklight;* Mary Kröger and the delightful Potchikoo are present, for example. But the poems in *Baptism of Desire* will have special appeal for Roman Catholics. The poems are not pious, at least not in the usual sense. Saint Clare, for example, is referred to as the "patron saint of television," while Christ's twin was "formed of chicken blood and lightning." The poem "Mary Magdalene" ends with Mary driving boys to "smash empty bottles on their brow": "It is the old way that girls get even with

Dust jacket for a collection of interviews with Erdrich and her husband and collaborator, Michael Dorris (courtesy of the Lilly Library, Indiana University)

their fathers – / by wrecking their bodies on other men." Many of the poems in *Baptism of Desire* were written, according to a note, "between the hours of two and four in the morning, a period of insomnia brought on by pregnancy," and several of them refer to pregnancy, birth, growth, and loneliness.

The Virgilian "Potchikoo's after Life" takes the trickster-hero's soul to the Pearly Gates. Saint Peter sends him on to the Indian heaven, in which Potchikoo is rather disappointed: it is just a place where the chokecherries give him diarrhea and the people sit around and eat venison that is not as tasty as his wife's had been. He returns home, stopping off to see the white people's hell – a warehouse where souls drag around old Sears Roebuck catalogues. More realistic is "Poor Clare," in which the title character defies her mother by sneaking out at night to go to the carnival. She earns money for the ferris wheel by giving sex in the bushes: "She wasn't bad, just dull, and much too eager / for a man's touch as she had no father." Nine months later she kills her baby, who dies without benefit of baptism – of desire or any other kind.

Dust jacket for Erdrich and Dorris's novel about the adventures of two Dartmouth professors in the Bahamas

The year 1991 brought the publication of two fully collaborative books, in which both Erdrich's and Dorris's names appear on the title page. *Route Two* is a reminiscence of the Dorris-Erdrich family trip along route 2 through Minnesota, North Dakota, and Montana to visit relatives. It is of interest for its descriptions of landscape, its language, and the glimpses it affords of family life. *The Crown of Columbus,* a novel published to capitalize on the five-hundredth anniversary of Christopher Columbus's arrival in America, relates the unlikely adventures of two Dartmouth professors who fall in love: Vivian Twostar, a part-Navajo assistant professor of anthropology who hopes to get tenure, and Roger Williams, an English professor who already has it. She has a "difficult" teenage son, whom he learns to father, and together they have a baby daughter. This unlikely family heads to the Bahamas and encounters movielike adventures that ought to be more hair-raising and more convincing than they are.

Though *The Crown of Columbus* has some of the Erdrichian delight in language and character, reviewers called it a potboiler that is not as good as the best work that the two writers have done individually. After the first spate of reviews, literary scholars generally ignored the book. The narration is reminiscent of that in *Tracks,* with the looser Vivian telling some chapters, the stiffer Roger telling others. There are some surprising moments, as when the lazy Bahamian native Valerie Clock suddenly begins to look at the sea not in terms of her boring job but as an opportunity – "It was a while before Valerie started to think of the sea as a place to cross, but once she did, she couldn't stop" – and some funny scenes, but *The Crown of Columbus* rarely overcomes the fundamental unbelievability of its plot. Erdrich can make unlikely internal adventures seem real; this work requires that she do the same for unlikely external adventures involving evil capitalists, attempted murder, and shark-infested waters. The theme of internal psychological discovery, of people finding themselves, is overshadowed by the political theme of the "discovery" of a land that did not need to be discovered. As for the crown itself, readers tended to be either not surprised that it turns out to be a crown of thorns or disappointed that it is, after all the waiting, merely that. In a 1991 interview with Douglas Foster (reprinted in *Conversations with Louise Erdrich and Michael Dorris*) the authors were asked about their biggest fears in regard to the publication of their new book. Erdrich replied, "My biggest fear is always nasty reviews. I'm a real chicken." Her husband's response was that his "biggest fear is that people will say, 'She ought to write by herself.' " Both of their fears were realized. *The Crown of Columbus* seems to have taught Erdrich that her strongest voice as a writer comes out in a Western reservation setting rather than in an Eastern academic one, and the $1.5 million advance she and her husband received for it allowed them to give up the Eastern academic establishment and move back to the Minnesota–North Dakota environs that have been so important to her.

After being disappointed in *The Crown of Columbus,* Erdrich's readers were delighted to see her return to her solo voice and her old themes in a revised and enlarged version of *Love Medicine* (1993). Many of the changes are innocuous: Erdrich adds a hyphen to the compound adjective *just-born* at the end of "The Good Tears," changes the name of Lake Turcot to Matchimanito Lake, makes it clear that Old Man Pillager is Moses Pillager, changes Old Lady Blue to Old Lady Pillager in one place and Old Man Pillager to Old Lady Pillager in another, and changes the French word *merde* (shit) to the Indian word *ka-ka.* Some of the changes are more substantial: Gordie now dies, and Eli and Nector are no longer twins but, as in *Tracks,* are nearly a decade apart in age.

The most fundamental change is that Marie and Nector do not have sex on their first encounter on the hillside road leading away from the convent; Nector merely touches her with his hand. There are four and a half additional chapters that look back to the events of *Tracks* ("The Island" and part 2 of "The Beads"), resolve issues left unresolved in the original version ("Resurrection"), or prepare the way for Lyman Lamartine's capitalistic shenanigans in Erdrich's next book, the 1994 novel *The Bingo Palace* ("The Tomahawk Factory" and "Lyman's Luck"). In these last chapters Lyman Lamartine changes from the loving and good-hearted friend of Henry Jr.'s that he was in the 1984 version to a much more cynical, political, and calculating person:

> They gave you worthless land to start with and then they chopped it out from under your feet. They took your kids away and stuffed the English language in their mouth. They sent your brother to hell, they shipped him back fried. They sold you booze for furs and then told you not to drink. It was time, high past time the Indians smartened up and started using the only leverage they had – federal law.

One wonders why Erdrich decided to revise and add to a novel that had already been completed and published. In an epistolary interview she gave to Nancy Feyl Chavkin and Allan Chavkin between September 1992 and April 1993 she says that "there is no reason to think of publication as a final process. I think of it as temporary storage." She admits that she hates "the process of finishing anything"; when asked why, she answers, "because I don't want to die, I hate death, and living things keep growing. I hope I live long enough to cultivate a civilized attitude about the end of things, because I'm very immature, now, about letting go of what I love."

Erdrich's concern with death is never far below the surface of her poetry, fiction, and nonfiction. In her 1992 poem "Foxglove" (reprinted in *The Blue Jay's Dance*), for example, she speaks of her resentment of old New England houses because they "have contained many deaths." The following year, in "Skunk Dreams" (also reprinted in *The Blue Jay's Dance*), she says, "I want something of the self on whom I have worked so hard to survive the loss of the body." She comes almost to admire the skunk because its odor makes it nearly immune to danger: "If I were an animal, I'd choose to be a skunk; live fearlessly, eat anything, gestate my young in just two months. . . . I wouldn't walk so much as putter, destinationless, in a serene belligerence – past hunters, past death overhead, past death all around."

At one point Erdrich and her husband envisioned the North Dakota Saga as a tetralogy based on the four classical elements. As Dorris put it in their 1988 interview with Bonetti, they had "thought of each of these books as having kind of an element central to its symbolism, *Love Medicine* being water, *Beet Queen* being air, *Tracks* being earth, and the last book being fire, because there are missiles in it." That symbolism has not played itself out in the actual fourth novel in the series, in which there are no missiles or fire (unless a sweat lodge counts as fire). And there is no indication that the fourth novel was ever meant to be the last of the series. *The Bingo Palace* leaves the usual number of loose threads to be picked up in subsequent stories and novels. Even before finishing *The Bingo Palace,* Erdrich spoke to the Chavkins about her next book, *Tales of Burning Love* (1996), "about women and the complexity of their love for one man, for their children, for God, for other women." She also mentioned that she was working on a book to be called "The True Story of Mustache Maude," about "a real person, a North Dakota maverick." It would be based on the early 1984 story of the same title, which was "an experiment in voice and form."

The Bingo Palace picks up where the 1993 version of *Love Medicine* leaves off. Lyman Lamartine's dream of a bingo establishment on the reservation not only comes true but also spawns a new dream of a full-blown casino resort to be built on the banks of Matchimanito Lake. Albertine Johnson is back, this time as a medical student home for a visit. Her mother, Zelda, is trying to control the lives of those around her. Fleur Pillager is an old woman who is about to be displaced once again from her land on the Matchimanito shore. Gerry Nanapush is still escaping from the law. His mother, Lulu Lamartine, is doing what she can to keep the tribe functioning as a unit. Marie is still at genial odds with Lulu. Lipsha Morrissey is playing his biggest role yet as a lovestruck drifter who loses his medical powers when he decides to charge for them. Even June is back, playing a ghostly cameo role.

There is one important new character in *The Bingo Palace:* Shawnee Ray Toose, a lovely young unmarried mother. A major feature of the plot is the love triangle involving Shawnee Ray, Lipsha, and Lyman. Lyman loves Shawnee Ray and may be the father of her child, Redford; but Lyman's nephew, Lipsha, loves her as well, and both men seek to marry her. Zelda also lays claim to Shawnee Ray, or at least to her son, Redford. Shawnee Ray, however, is not much interested in cementing any of these relationships and goes off at the end to the university, Redford in tow, to study design. Lipsha, meanwhile, helps his father, Gerry, to escape the police yet again, this time in a car chase across the snow-swept plains northwest of Fargo as they head home to the reservation. Just as *Love Medicine* had begun with June's death by freezing on her way home from an off-reservation town, *The Bingo Palace* ends with her son's apparent death by freezing on his way home from another one.

Readers who remember Erdrich's story "American Horse" (1984), about a boy named Buddy who is stolen away from his mother, Albertine American Horse, will recognize the basic plot, with the names changed, of chapter 15, "Redford's Luck." Some characters in *The Bingo Palace* appear to be taking over roles occupied by other characters in *Love Medicine.* Lyman is the new Nector, an educated, sophisticated, politically astute but unprincipled leader who tramples the rights of others as he pursues his ambitions. Zelda is the new Marie, taking in stray people and trying to manage their lives. Shawnee Ray is the new Lulu, smiting men with her beauty and giving birth to children of whose paternity she cannot be sure.

The Bingo Palace continues the trend in Erdrich's novels toward tighter focus. *Love Medicine* covers seventy years; *The Beet Queen* covers forty years; *Tracks* covers twelve years. The events in *The Bingo Palace,* on the other hand, extend over only a year, from one winter to the next. Though there is still a rich array of characters, the main figure here is, unquestionably, Lipsha. He is central to most of the events of the plot, from the comic vision quest that ends in a female skunk spraying him to the climactic car chase, complete with his enormous stolen stuffed bird. The other characters exist in this novel primarily to provide meaningful interactions with Lipsha. Lipsha struggles to find or define himself in relationship with Gerry, his father; June, his mother; Lyman, his uncle; Marie and Lulu, his grandmothers; and Shawnee Ray, his lover.

Lipsha's struggle to come to terms with June – the dead woman who had tied him, as a newborn baby, into a cloth sack with some rocks and had thrown him into the lake – is the central drama of the novel. It gradually becomes clear that though Lipsha thinks he loves Shawnee Ray for her beauty and sexuality, he loves her at least as much for her motherhood:

> I see her rocking Redford, kissing him, touching his face with her finger, and it presses a panic jolt. First off, there is no way I can imagine June Morrissey doing that to me, and my thoughts veer away in longing. The subject makes my throat choke up with envy. . . . I wish I was that little boy, I wish I was Redford.

The novel ends with Lipsha becoming a kind of mother himself. When he and Gerry head for home, they find a baby in the car they steal. When Gerry leaves to join the ghostly June in her ghostly car, Lipsha is left with the baby in a freezing snowstorm. Lipsha wraps the baby warmly and zips him into his own coat. The outcome of the scene is ambiguous, but it appears that Lipsha may freeze to death, while the baby, unzipped in a grotesque parody of a caesarean birth, lives. Lipsha seems to have been able to give this baby the love and life that his own mother, June, had denied him.

Erdrich's nonfiction has taken the form of short magazine pieces; those pieces, augmented by several previously unpublished ones, appeared in 1995 as *The Blue Jay's Dance: A Birth Year.* Many of the articles – which include essays, thoughts, reflections, recipes, and assorted snippets – are built around her thoughts about being pregnant and about raising her three daughters. The title piece is about a blue jay that audaciously faces or "dances" down an attacking hawk and wins its own right to life. *The Blue Jay's Dance* is full of surprises: "Reliable birth control is one of the best things that's happened to contemporary literature"; "Death is the least civilized right of passage"; "It seems unfair that because I am a mammal I am condemned to give birth through the lower part of my body while flowers, though brainless, have the wisdom to shoot straight upward"; "Why is no woman's labor as famous as the death of Socrates?"; "A woman needs to tell her own story, to tell the bloody version of the fairy tale."

Erdrich's most recent novel, *Tales of Burning Love,* is made up of forty-six stories. Some of them are narrated by women telling about their experiences with Jack Mauser, a construction contractor in Fargo, North Dakota. Jack is of somewhat uncertain origin, but his father is of German heritage and Jack is an enrolled member of the Chippewa tribe through his mother, Mary Stamper. Jack is "Andy," the engineer who seduces June Morrissey Kashpaw in the opening sequence of "The World's Greatest Fishermen" in *Love Medicine.* That sequence is retold from Jack's point of view in the opening chapter of *Tales of Burning Love.* He gives June a false name in the bar in Williston because he does not want her to guess that his mother was from the same reservation as June's. The reader learns in this novel that Jack and June had been married in the bar in a quasi-legal "ceremony" performed by a "preacher" who had ordered

Dust jacket for Erdrich's collection of nonfiction

his divinity degree from a matchbook cover, with beer can pop-tops as wedding rings. The "bride" and "groom" fail in their attempt to consummate their "marriage" before June sets out on her walk to her death.

Apparently ridden with guilt for June's death and frustrated in his burning love for her, Jack subsequently marries, successively, Eleanor Schlick, a college professor; Candice Pantamounty, a dentist; Marlis Cook, a waitress and would-be singer; and Dot Adare Nanapush, an accountant in his construction firm, Mauser and Mauser. When Jack's financial troubles grow too big for him – partly because Marlis had stolen his huge loan check from the bank – the intoxicated Jack allows his house to burn down around him, thinking vaguely that his insurance adjustment will help him get back on his feet financially. He almost dies in the fire, and when he escapes he leaves behind evidence that he has, in fact, perished.

Three of his four surviving wives attend his funeral in early January 1995. Later they join the fourth wife in a bar. As they are driving home together a blizzard starts, and they become stranded in a snowbank alongside the road. To keep each other awake, they agree to tell "scorching" true tales about their own lives. The situation of four widows trapped in a car in a blizzard provides the frame for a series of tales, many of them focused on or leading up to each woman's relationship with Jack Mauser.

The blizzard in which the four wives are caught is the same one that nearly entombs Lipsha Morrissey and the baby at the end of *The Bingo Palace*. Lipsha and the baby, who turns out to be Jack's son by his fourth wife, Marlis, survive the blizzard when they are rescued in the nick of time by the snowplow-driving Jack. Gerry Nanapush, who has just escaped from an airplane crash, is behind the back seat of the car in which Jack's four wives are telling their stories. Gerry is the former husband of Jack's fifth wife, Dot, and seems to overhear much of what the women say before he again narrowly escapes capture, this time on a stolen snowmobile. In this last escape he is perhaps aided by the ghost of June, which hovers over many of the chapters in *Tales of Burning Love*. Lyman Lamartine plays a small role as the man who pays off Jack Mauser's debts and offers Jack the job of building the new casino on the reservation.

Dust jacket for Erdrich's novel about a part-Indian contractor and his various wives

Tales of Burning Love is Erdrich's least realistic, and at the same time her most optimistic, novel. Contrivances, coincidences, and improbabilities abound, yet the reader willingly suspends disbelief. Would Jack really marry so often and with such foolish haste? Could he be so blind both to his own needs and to the needs of his wives? Could so poor a businessman succeed as well as he seems to have? Would an undertaker hold a funeral for a man if the only evidence of his having been killed in a fire was a partial dental plate? Is it likely that Jack's third and fourth wives would wind up as lesbian parents of his only child? Could Jack survive, almost without a scratch, having a marble statue of the Blessed Virgin dropped on him? The various activities on the night of the blizzard seem more like the shenanigans of a group of comedians than the life-threatening encounters of frail humans with powerful natural forces. Almost all of the stories have happy endings: Candice and Marlis find true love with one another; Dot and Gerry are reconciled and make love once again; Gerry, tricksterlike, escapes yet again; and Eleanor and Jack seem to find true happiness together at last. Jack has grown up to an awareness of his role as a father and a knowledge of what love is all about.

In some ways *Tales of Burning Love* can be considered a feminist novel. Jack Mauser can be regarded as standing for most men in their dealings with women – insensitive, self-oriented, fickle, inconstant, childish, lust-driven, immature. By the design of her novel, Erdrich keeps the point of view of women in the forefront of her reader's consciousness; the result is that the novel is far less about Jack than it is about the reactions of women to him. Those reactions are often moving, sometimes memorable, sometimes funny, but never really unfair. No one who reads the novel will forget the richly comic scene in which Marlis hog-ties Jack, plucks his eyebrows, and rips the hair off his legs, then glues high-heeled shoes onto his feet. She wants him to know firsthand some of the pain women endure to attract the likes of him and keep them happy.

In 1996 Erdrich published, in addition to the 452-page *Tales of Burning Love,* the 30-page *Grandmother's Pigeon,* with lush illustrations by Jim LaMarche. *Grandmother's Pigeon* is an almost-mythical children's story about a grandmother who rides off on a dolphin to Greenland, leaving behind in her room eggs that later hatch into homing pigeons of an extinct species. Her two grandchildren help to raise the pigeons, then tie messages to their legs and release them. Later they get a letter from their grandmother in Greenland, thanking them for the messages.

It would be a mistake to label Erdrich exclusively a woman's writer; she speaks with deep understanding about what it is to be male, as well. But there can be no doubt that women readers find much to connect with in Erdrich's poetry, fiction, and nonfiction. Whether or not her own life and personality are reflected in Mary Kröger or Albertine Johnson or Vivian Twostar or Shawnee Ray Toose, Erdrich speaks with an unquestionable authority about what it is to be a woman. In her 1993 essay "A Woman's Work: Too Many Demands and Not Enough Selves" she speaks of the situation of a woman who hopes to pursue a career as well as raise children:

> I'm being swallowed alive. On those days suicide is an idea too persistent for comfort. "There isn't a self to kill," I think, filled with melodramatic pity for who I used to be. That person is gone. Yet once I've established that I have no personal self, killing whatever remains seems hardly worth the effort.

Men and women both can rejoice that Erdrich has found ways, especially through her writing, to rise above such grim feelings.

Asked by the Chavkins why she writes her early drafts longhand, Erdrich replied, with her typical mixture of seriousness and humor, "Longhand feels more personal, as though I'm physically touching the subject. If I get a good idea in a bar I can walk back to Women, Females, Damsels, Does, etc., shut and lock the stall, then jot." Asked if she feels like an outsider, she answered unequivocally, "Sure, always an outsider, but that's a gift for a writer. . . . People who belong don't become writers, they're immersed and have no edge." Louise Erdrich has the edge.

Interviews:

Jan George, "Interview with Louise Erdrich," *North Dakota Quarterly,* 53 (Spring 1985): 240–246;

Miriam Berkley, "Louise Erdrich," *Publishers Weekly,* 230 (15 August 1986): 58–59;

Kay Bonetti, "An Interview with Louise Erdrich and Michael Dorris," *Missouri Review,* 11 (1988): 79–99;

Laura Coltelli, "Louise Erdrich and Michael Dorris," in her *Winged Words: American Indian Writers Speak* (Lincoln & London: University of Nebraska Press, 1990), pp. 40–52;

Nancy Feyl Chavkin and Allan Chavkin, eds., *Conversations with Louise Erdrich and Michael Dorris* (Jackson: University Press of Mississippi, 1994).

Bibliographies:

Lillian Brewington, Normie Bullard, and R. W. Reising, "Writing in Love: An Annotated Bibliography of Critical Responses to the Poetry and Novels of Louise Erdrich and Michael Dorris," *American Indian Culture and Research Journal,* 10, no. 4 (1986): 81–86;

A. LaVonne Brown Ruoff, *American Indian Literatures: An Introduction, Bibliographic Review, and Selected Bibliography* (New York: Modern Language Association of America, 1990), pp. 84–88;

Gretchen M. Bataille and Kathleen M. Sands, *American Indian Women: A Guide to Research* (New York: Garland, 1991);

Debra A. Burdick, "Louise Erdrich's *Love Medicine, The Beet Queen,* and *Tracks:* An Annotated Survey of Criticism through 1994," *American Indian Culture and Research Journal,* 20, no. 3 (1996): 137-166.

References:

Hans Bak, "Toward a Native American 'Realism': The Amphibious Fiction of Louise Erdrich," in *Neo-Realism in Contemporary American Fiction,* edited by Kristiaan Versluys (Amsterdam: Rodopi, 1992), pp. 145–170;

Julie Barak, "Blurs, Blends, Berdaches: Gender Mixing in the Novels of Louise Erdrich," *Studies in American Indian Literatures,* 8 (Fall 1996): 49–62;

Marianne Barnett, "Dreamstuff: Erdrich's *Love Medicine,*" *North Dakota Quarterly,* 56 (1988): 82–93;

Nora Barry and Mary Prescott, "The Triumph of the Brave: *Love Medicine*'s Holistic Vision," *Critique: Studies in Contemporary Fiction,* 30 (Winter 1989): 123–138;

Gretchen M. Bataille, "Louise Erdrich's *The Beet Queen:* Images of the Grotesque on the Northern Plains," in *Critical Perspectives on Native American Fiction,* edited by Richard F. Fleck (Washington, D.C.: Three Continents, 1993), pp. 277–285;

Peter G. Beidler, "Three Student Guides to Louise Erdrich's *Love Medicine,*" *American Indian Culture and Research Journal,* 16, no. 4 (1992): 167–173;

Gloria Bird, "Searching for Evidence of Colonialism at Work: A Reading of Louise Erdrich's *Tracks,*" *Wicazo Sa Review,* 8 (Fall 1992): 40–47;

Susan Pérez Castillo, "Postmodernism, Native American Literature, and the Real: The Silko-Erdrich Controversy," *Massachusetts Review,* 32 (Summer 1991): 285–294;

Catherine M. Catt, "Ancient Myth in Modern America: The Trickster in the Fiction of Louise Erdrich," *Platte Valley Review,* 19, no. 1 (1991): 71–81;

Joni Adamson Clarke, "Why Bears Are Good to Think and Theory Doesn't Have to Be Murder: Transformation and Oral Tradition in Louise Erdrich's *Tracks,*" *Studies in American Indian Literatures,* 4 (Spring 1992): 28–48;

Daniel Cornell, "Woman Looking: Revis(ion)ing Pauline's Subject Position in Louise Erdrich's *Tracks,*" *Studies in American Indian Literatures,* 4 (Spring 1992): 49–64;

Claire Crabtree, "Salvific Oneness and the Fragmented Self in Louise Erdrich's *Love Medicine,*" in *Contemporary Native American Cultural Issues,* edited by Thomas E. Schirer (Sault Ste. Marie, Mich.: Lake Superior State University Press, 1988), pp. 49–56;

James Flavin, "The Novel as Performance: Communication in Louise Erdrich's *Tracks,*" *Studies in American Indian Literatures,* 3 (Winter 1991): 1–12;

Louise Flavin, "Gender Construction amid Family Dissolution in Louise Erdrich's *The Beet Queen,*" *Studies in American Indian Literatures,* 7 (Summer 1995): 17–24;

Flavin, "Louise Erdrich's *Love Medicine:* Loving over Time and Distance," *Critique,* 31 (Fall 1989): 55–64;

William Gleason, " 'Her Laugh an Ace': The Function of Humor in Louise Erdrich's *Love Medicine,*" *American Indian Culture and Research Journal,* 11, no. 3 (1987): 51–73;

Elizabeth Hanson, "Louise Erdrich: Making a World Anew," in her *Forever There: Race and Gender in Contemporary Native American Fiction* (New York: Peter Lang, 1989), pp. 79–104;

Roberta Makashay Hendrickson, "Victims and Survivors: Native American Women Writers, Violence against Women, and Child Abuse," *Studies in American Indian Literatures,* 8 (Spring 1996): 13–24;

Michelle R. Hessler, "Catholic Nuns and Ojibwa Shamans: Pauline and Fleur in Louise Erdrich's *Tracks,*" *Wicazo Sa Review,* 11 (Spring 1995): 40–45;

Debra C. Holt, "Transformation and Continuance: Native American Tradition in the Novels of Louise Erdrich," in *Entering the 90s: The North American Experience,* edited by Thomas E. Schirer (Sault Ste. Marie, Mich.: Lake Superior State University Press, 1991), pp. 149–161;

Jane Howard, "Portrait: Louise Erdrich," *Life,* 18 (April 1995): 27–28, 34;

Wendy K. Kolmar, "Dialectics of Connectedness: Supernatural Elements in Novels by Bambera, Cisneros, Grahn, and Erdrich," in *Haunting the House of Fiction: Feminist Perspectives on Ghost Stories by American Women,* edited by Kolmar and Lynette Carpenter (Knoxville: University of Tennessee Press, 1991), pp. 236–249;

Karl Kroebler and others, "Louise Erdrich's *Love Medicine,*" in *Critical Perspectives on Native American Fiction,* pp. 263–276;

Ellen Lansky, "Spirits and Salvation in Louise Erdrich's *Love Medicine,*" *Dionysos: The Literature and Addiction Triquarterly,* 5 (Winter 1994): 39–44;

Sidner Larson, "The Fragmentation of a Tribal People in Louise Erdrich's *Tracks,*" *American Indian Culture and Research Journal,* 17, no. 2 (1993): 1–13;

A. Robert Lee, "Ethnic Renaissance: Rudolfo Anaya, Louise Erdrich, and Maxine Hong Kingston," in *The New American Writing: Essays on American Literature since 1970,* edited by Graham Clarke (New York: St. Martin's Press, 1990), pp. 139–164;

Kenneth Lincoln, "Bring Her Home: Louise Erdrich," in his *Indi'n Humor: Bicultural Play in Native America* (New York: Oxford University Press, 1993), pp. 205–253;

Marvin Magalaner, "Louise Erdrich: Of Cars, Time, and the River," in *American Women Writing Fiction: Memory, Identity, Family, Space,* edited by Mickey Pearlman (Lexington: University Press of Kentucky, 1989), pp. 95–112;

Kathleen E. B. Manley, "Decreasing the Distance: Contemporary Native American Texts, Hypertext, and the Concept of Audience," *Southern Folklore,* 51, no. 2 (1994): 121–135;

Julie Maristuen-Rodakowski, "The Turtle Mountain Reservation in North Dakota: Its History as Depicted in Louise Erdrich's *Love Medicine* and *Beet Queen,*" *American Indian Culture and Research Journal,* 12, no. 3 (1988): 33–48;

Thomas Matchie, "Exploring the Meaning of Discovery in *The Crown of Columbus,*" *North Dakota Quarterly,* 59 (Spring 1991): 243–250;

Matchie, "*Love Medicine:* A Female *Moby-Dick,*" *Midwest Quarterly,* 30 (Summer 1989): 478-491;

James McKenzie, "Lipsha's Good Road Home: The Revival of Chippewa Culture in *Love Medicine,*" *American Indian Culture and Research Journal,* 10, no. 3 (1986): 53-63;

Paulo Medeiros, "Cannibalism and Starvation: The Parameters of Eating Disorders in Literature," in *Disorderly Eaters: Texts in Self-Empowerment,* edited by Lilian R. Furst and Peter W. Graham (University Park: Pennsylvania State University Press, 1992), pp. 11-27;

Susan Meisenhelder, "Race and Gender in Louise Erdrich's *The Beet Queen,*" *Ariel,* 25 (1995): 45-57;

David Mitchell, "A Bridge to the Past: Cultural Hegemony and the Native American Past in Louise Erdrich's *Love Medicine,*" in *Entering the 90s: The North American Experience,* pp. 162-170;

Louis Owens, "Erdrich and Dorris's Mixedbloods and Multiple Narratives," in his *Other Destinies: Understanding the American Indian Novel* (Norman: University of Oklahoma Press, 1992), pp. 193-217;

Nancy Peterson, "History, Postmodernism, and Louise Erdrich's *Tracks,*" *PMLA,* 109 (October 1994): 982-994;

John Lloyd Purdy, "Karen Louise Erdrich," in *Dictionary of Native American Literature,* edited by Andrew Wiget (New York: Garland, 1994), pp. 423-429;

Catherine Rainwater, "Reading between Worlds: Narrativity in the Fiction of Louise Erdrich," *American Literature,* 62 (September 1990): 405-422;

Ann Rayson, "Shifting Identity in the Work of Louise Erdrich and Michael Dorris," *Studies in American Indian Literatures,* 3 (Winter 1991): 27-36;

James Ruppert, "Celebrating Culture: *Love Medicine,*" in his *Mediation in Contemporary Native American Fiction* (Norman: University of Oklahoma Press, 1995), pp. 131-150;

Ruppert, "Mediation and Multiple Narrative in *Love Medicine,*" *North Dakota Quarterly,* 59 (Spring 1991): 229-242;

Greg Sarris, "Reading Louis Erdrich: *Love Medicine* as Home Medicine," in his *Keeping Slug Woman Alive: A Holistic Approach to American Indian Texts* (Berkeley: University of California Press, 1993), pp. 115-145;

Lissa Schneider, "*Love Medicine:* A Metaphor for Forgiveness," *Studies in American Indian Literatures,* 4 (Spring 1992): 1-13;

Lydia A. Schultz, "Fragments and Ojibwe Stories: Narrative Strategies in Louise Erdrich's *Love Medicine,*" *College Literature,* 18 (18 October 1991): 80-95;

Lee Schweninger, "A Skin of Lakeweed: An Ecofeminist Approach to Erdrich and Silko," in *Multicultural Literatures through Feminist/Poststructuralist Lenses,* edited by Barbara Frey Waxman (Knoxville: University of Tennessee Press, 1993), pp. 37-56;

Jennifer Sergi, "Storytelling: Tradition and Preservation in Louise Erdrich's *Tracks,*" *World Literature Today,* 66 (Spring 1992): 279-282;

Jennifer Shaddock, "Mixed Blood Women: The Dynamic of Women's Relations in the Novels of Louise Erdrich and Leslie Silko," in *Feminist Nightmares, Women at Odds: Feminism and the Problem of Sisterhood,* edited by Susan Ostrov Weisser and Jennifer Fleishner (New York: New York University Press, 1994), pp. 106-121;

Robert Silberman, "Opening the Text: *Love Medicine* and the Return of the Native American Women," in *Narrative Chance: Postmodern Discourse on Native American Literatures,* edited by Gerald Vizenor (Norman: University of Oklahoma Press, 1989), pp. 101-120;

Leslie Marmon Silko, "Here's an Odd Artifact for the Fairy-Tale Shelf," *Studies in American Indian Literatures,* 10 (Fall 1986): 178-184;

Nicholas Sloboda, "Beyond the Iconic Subject: Re-Visioning Louise Erdrich's *Tracks,*" *Studies in American Indian Literatures,* 8 (Fall 1996): 63-79;

Jeanne Smith, "Transpersonal Selfhood: The Boundaries of Identity in Louise Erdrich's *Love Medicine,*" *Studies in American Indian Literatures,* 3 (Winter 1991): 13-26;

James D. Stripes, "The Problem(s) of (Anishinaabe) History in the Fiction of Louise Erdrich," *Wicazo Sa Review,* 7 (Fall 1991): 26-33;

Margie Towery, "Continuity and Connection: Characters in Louise Erdrich's Fiction," *American Indian Culture and Research Journal,* 16, no. 4 (1992): 99-122;

Annette Van Dyke, "Questions of the Spirit: Bloodlines in Louise Erdrich's Chippewa Landscape," *Studies in American Indian Literatures,* 4 (Spring 1992): 15-27;

Alan R. Velie, "American Indian Literature in the Nineties: The Emergence of the Middle-Class

Protagonist," *World Literature Today,* 66 (1992): 264–268;

Velie, "The Trickster Novel," in *Narrative Chance: Postmodern Discourse on Native American Literatures,* pp. 121–149;

Victoria Walker, "A Note on Narrative Perspective in *Tracks,*" *Studies in American Indian Literatures,* 3 (Winter 1991): 37–40;

Dennis M. Walsh and Ann Braley, "The Indianness of Louise Erdrich's *The Beet Queen:* Latency as Presence," *American Indian Culture and Research Journal,* 18 (1994): 1–17;

Hertha D. Wong, "Adoptive Mothers and Thrown-Away Children in the Novels of Louise Erdrich," in *Narrating Mothers,* edited by Brenda O. Daly (Knoxville: University of Tennessee Press, 1991), pp. 174–192;

Wong, "Louise Erdrich's *Love Medicine:* Narrative Communities and the Short Story Cycle," in *Modern American Short Story Sequences: Composite Fictions and Fictive Communities,* edited by J. Gerald Kennedy (New York: Cambridge University Press, 1995), pp. 170–193.

Hanay Geiogamah

(22 June 1945 –)

Sue M. Johnson

BOOKS: *New Native American Drama: Three Plays,* introduction by Jeffrey Huntsman (Norman: University of Oklahoma Press, 1980);

The American Indian Resource Guide: Compiled for the Entertainment Industry, by Geiogamah and others (Los Angeles: American Indian Registry for the Performing Arts, 1987).

PLAY PRODUCTIONS: *Body Indian,* New York City, La Mama Experimental Theatre Club, 25 October 1972;

Foghorn, West Berlin, Reichskabaret, 18 October 1973;

Coon Cons Coyote, New York City, La Mama Experimental Theatre Club, December 1973;

49, Oklahoma City, Oklahoma City University, 10 January 1975;

War Dancers, New York City, Native Americans in the Arts, March 1981;

Grandma and *Grandpa,* New York City, American Folk Theatre, August 1984;

Land Sale, Tulsa, American Indian Theatre Company of Oklahoma, 1985;

American Indian Dance Theatre, Los Angeles, Beverly Theatre, June 1987.

TELEVISION: *The Native Americans,* by Geiogamah and Michael Grant, Turner Network Television, October 1994.

OTHER: "The New Native American Theatre," in *The Dictionary of Native American Literature,* edited by Andrew Wiget (New York: Garland, 1994), pp. 377–381.

Hanay Geiogamah (photograph courtesy of Hanay Geiogamah)

Although he fills many roles – director, producer, screenwriter, editor, teacher, and mentor – Hanay Geiogamah is mainly recognized as the most important Native American playwright of the late twentieth century. In his plays Geiogamah strives to portray contemporary American Indian life for both Indians and non-Indians.

Geiogamah was born in Lawton, Oklahoma, on 22 June 1945 to Lola Clark, of Irish and Delaware Indian descent, and Claude Geiogamah, a Kiowa. He grew up in nearby Anadarko and attended Fort Sill Indian School near Lawton and Chilocco Indian School near Newkirk, Oklahoma. Unlike many of his contemporaries, Geiogamah has positive memories of his boarding-school experiences. The educators at the school encouraged cultural exchange among the students, and Geiogamah learned about his own Kiowa heritage as well as those of the thirty-eight other Oklahoma tribes. In an unpublished 1996 interview he recalled that he and his friends acted out "life shows": "Since we were poor, we didn't have a TV and couldn't afford to go to the movies. . . . These were serious kids' plays."

In 1963 Geiogamah received a Charles MacMahon Foundation Scholarship to study journalism at the University of Oklahoma, where he won a William Randolph Hearst National Writing Award. As part of his studies he worked as an intern in the office of Sen. Edward M. Kennedy of Massachusetts. He left the university, without completing a degree, in 1968. During this time, he told McCandish Phillips in 1972, he conceived the idea of creating an all-Indian acting troupe: "For decades American Indians have been portrayed in films and on television in a manner entirely derogatory to their cultural and mental well-being. Who wants to see themselves and their race depicted as fiendish savages and murderers?" Geiogamah told Phillips that he wanted to write "plays for and about Indians, their past, their despairing present, their hopes and dreams and daily lives, presented by Indian artists for the 850,000 Indians in the United States today."

He achieved his goal with the organization of the Native American Theatre Ensemble, whose first production, Geiogamah's *Body Indian,* opened on 25 October 1972 at the La Mama Experimental Theatre Club in New York City. The performance received accolades from Clive Barnes in *The New York Times* (29 October 1972). After a two-week engagement in New York the Native American Theatre Ensemble took *Body Indian* on tour throughout the United States, followed by a six-week run at the Reichskabaret in West Berlin. Geiogamah's second play, *Foghorn,* opened at the Reichskabaret on 18 October 1973, and his third, *49,* premiered on 10 January 1975 at Oklahoma City University.

Geiogamah enrolled in 1979 at Indiana University, majoring in theater with a minor in journalism. He received his B.A. in 1980; that same year he published his first three plays as *New Native American Drama.*

A short play in five scenes, *Body Indian* depicts a group of Indians living off the reservation in Oklahoma and engaging in heavy drinking, singing, and dancing. Everyone seems to be having a great time despite the poverty and degradation in which they live. The main character, Bobby Lee, arrives at the beginning of the play with more wine and a large sum of money from cashing the check he has received for leasing his allotment of reservation land to a farmer. Some years earlier Bobby Lee had passed out drunk on the railroad tracks and a train had severed his leg. At the end of each scene he passes out again, and his friends and relatives search him for money to buy more wine. In the fifth scene, finding no more money, they take his artificial leg. After Bobby Lee gets "rolled" in each scene, the action freezes while an image of railroad tracks is projected on a screen and a train whistle is heard.

In his review of Geiogamah's plays in *American Indian Quarterly* (November 1979) Jack W. Marken says that "*Body Indian* presents a situation of near hopelessness" but that its theme is one of survival: "despite the bleakness of the play, Geiogamah is pointing out that Bobby Lee has survived, and he, like all crippled Indians (that is, of course, all of them), can survive. They do have a chance to overcome." In *Studies in American Indian Literature* (Winter 1983), on the other hand, Norma Wilson views *Body Indian* as "a bleak dramatization of the effects of alcoholism," a "somber warning . . . that all alcoholics are in danger of being maimed." The characters are too "weak-willed" to help themselves or each other. The train "symbolizes the culture that invaded their land, dislocating the Indians from their source of life." Kenneth Lincoln describes *Body Indian* as "dangerously humorous, something tribally akin to dark comic theatre of conscience." He finds in it "losers humor," Brechtian humor, trickster humor, and mythic humor. Bobby Lee "has some pride left," holds out "for better, even at the bottom," and will not "give in to victimization." Lincoln interprets the train motif as showing that "the railroad historically ran over the backs of Bobby's people." Jeffrey Huntsman presents yet another perspective in his introduction to *New Native American Drama,* saying that for Bobby Lee the train is a horrible reminder of the accident that took his leg, while for the others it is "a persistent reminder of their guilt." Huntsman describes Bobby Lee as dignified, as "a man of character and decency." Like Marken, Huntsman believes that Bobby's "suffering has been redemptive, and this realization makes *Body Indian* a play of optimism and triumph."

In the unpublished interview Geiogamah revealed his original intention for the theme of *Body Indian:* the train "represents the guilt of the characters stealing from Bobby." In an interview with Lincoln he explained that he was trying to expose Indians' lack of a sense of community: "I realized that there were just real problems, real things with Indians that needed to be brought to their attention. . . . Indi'n brotherhood, Indi'n love, all this Indi'n kind of thing . . . to me was a hypocrisy that I felt very strongly about." While there is humor in the play, it is the sad and pathetic humor of drunks: "We all thought that we were all doing a big tragedy. We were playing it that way. . . . I thought that I was just writing about an alcoholic setting. I guess for me all the humor had gone out of that – out of my experiences and my trafficking in the alcoholic aspects of life." Any laughter from an audience is probably a nervous reaction to a harsh reality.

Bobby Lee survived the train accident, but living the life of an alcoholic is not heroic; the ending holds no triumph. No one has changed; although various characters have talked about going to Alcoholics Anonymous, no one has actually begun treatment. The addiction will continue.

In contrast to the gloomy *Body Indian,* Geiogamah's second play, *Foghorn,* is a vaudeville show; but it has a serious message. As Marken says, "the author's mirror reflects the history of stupidity and racism in American society in dealing with Native Americans in cases of education, religion, sex, television, treaties, and the areas of human and governmental relationships. The play is a purgation of Indian resentment." Geiogamah does not have to preach to get his message across; the absurdity of stereotyping Native Americans is made obvious in the play. In his production notes Geiogamah says that the stereotypical characters should be "almost . . . pushed to the point of absurdity" and that the "satire" should be "playful mockery rather than bitter denunciation." The basic seriousness of the play is more obvious "if the heavy hand is avoided" and a "light, almost frivolous" atmosphere is created.

Foghorn has a circular structure: the first two scenes are serious in tone; they are followed by scenes that become progressively more hilarious, until the eleventh, and final, scene closes the play on a somber note. This style of writing symbolizes the circle of the Indian nations, the strength of the people. To enhance this concept the traditional drum is played at various times; the beat of the drum is the heartbeat of the people who are the circle. The play opens with Indians on a forced journey similar to the Trail of Tears. The journey is interrupted by Christopher Columbus "discovering" America, European settlers screaming derogatory comments at the travelers, and congressmen plotting to move the Indians onto reservations. The forced journey continues into the beginning of scene 2, which is set on Alcatraz Island during the 1972 Thanksgiving Day occupation. The narrator steps forward and proclaims:

> We, the Native Americans, reclaim the land, known as America, in the name of all American Indians, by right of discovery. We wish to be fair and honorable with the Caucasian inhabitants of this land, who as a majority wrongfully claim it as theirs, and hereby pledge that we shall give to the majority inhabitants of this country a portion of their land for their own to be held in trust by American Indian people – for as long as the sun shall rise and the rivers flow down to the sea! We will further guide the majority inhabitants in the proper way of living. We will offer them our religion, our education, our way of life – in order to help them achieve our level of civilization, and thus raise them and all their white brothers from their savage and unhappy state.

A traditional song follows the speech. With the final beat of the drum still echoing, scene 3 begins with the blast of a church organ, and the play progresses into the lighter, more satiric scenes. In scene 3 a Catholic nun arrives to bring "the one true religion" to the "pagans." Her Bible is the Yellow Pages of the telephone book, and her cross is made of paper money. One hysterical scene follows another. A white teacher waves tiny American flags while attempting to teach English, "the most beautiful language in all the world," to the children of the tribe. The first word she wants them to learn is *hello* because it is the one word they "must know to become civilized." Another scene depicts Pocahontas and her handmaidens laughing at the color of the white man's skin and his lack of manliness. In another scene it is revealed that Tonto is the real hero and that the Lone Ranger has been taking undue credit for their good deeds all these years. The First Lady announces that more land will be taken from the Indians to build a national park. A scene about a possible tribal revolution parodies the Watergate scandal.

These scenes build to the tenth, the most riotous of all. With carnival music playing in the background, Indians with brightly colored headdresses, stick horses, rubber knives, and children's bows and arrows frolic on the stage in a chaotic parody of the old-style Wild West show. But the tone suddenly changes when a single gunshot is heard. Scene 10 merges into scene 11, and the audience finds itself at Wounded Knee, South Dakota, during the 1973 occupation. The circle is complete.

In contrast to *Body Indian* and *Foghorn,* Geiogamah's third play, *49,* has a sparse set and calls for few props. The actors create their environment in pantomime, compelling the audience to use their imaginations. The play is set on a Native American ceremonial ground in two time periods: 1888 and the present. Night Walker, an ageless, timeless ceremonial figure who represents the spirit of the people, connects the two eras. A "49" is a modern celebration that begins around midnight, after a powwow. Huntsman describes it as "a time when Indian people gather for a night of singing, dancing and conversation, predictably leavened, like most parties everywhere, by the promise of intoxicants and sex." In the scene set in the past Night Walker introduces Singing Man and Weaving Woman. These characters teach the youth to be creative, patient, and hopeful and to see good things in the future. In the scene set in the present the voices of highway patrolmen are heard attempting to break up the party; the patrolmen fail because the youths band together and defy them.

49 "has a theme of hope and resurrection," according to Marken. "It recommends unity to the Indian people with a stress on the old values of love and beauty and following the Indian ways of the past in the present and future. . . . The Indian people should see the truths in the old myths rather than succumb to the seductions of white society." Wilson, who attended the premiere performance, says that

> *49* is the most hopeful of the three plays, for it dramatizes a group of contemporary youth with purpose and meaning in relation to the cycle of life. . . . In seeing and reading the play I was closer to a shared ritual experience than is usual in contemporary American stage drama. While its structure is fragmented, and Night Walker's first speech is weak, the play overall has great vitality.

In 1984 Geiogamah began teaching in the theater department at the University of California at Los Angeles. From 1984 to 1988 he was executive director of the American Registry for the Performing Arts in Los Angeles. In 1988 he cofounded the American Indian Dance Theatre, which tours throughout the United States and abroad. He wrote the company's two specials for the Public Broadcasting System's *Great Performances: Dance in America* series, directing "Finding the Circle" in 1989 and codirecting and producing "Dances for the New Generations" in 1992. In 1989 he served as technical adviser for the Wildwood Productions feature film *Dark Wind.* With Michael Grant he wrote *The Native Americans,* a six-part historical series broadcast by Turner Network Television in October 1994. For Turner he also produced the films *Broken Chain* (December 1993), *Geronimo* (December 1993), *Lakota Woman* (October 1994), *Tucumseh* (June 1995), and *Crazy Horse* (July 1996).

Geiogamah has written several plays since *New Native American Drama* was published. Asked in the unpublished interview why he had not published them, Geiogamah explained that he did not feel that they were polished enough; he said that he "now understands the writing process to be one of changing and refining," that plays need to be perfected on stage as well as on paper. He spoke enthusiastically about the prospects for a Native American theater movement: "The writers are there, but it's difficult to find actors with the level of performing talent" necessary for professional productions. While "waiting for the actors," Geiogamah is "maturing, refining, and reflecting. Today, I am a mentor, a guide now for other Native Americans in the theater." He edits UCLA's *American Indian Culture and Research Journal.* He has adapted for television his play *Land Sale,* originally produced by the American Indian Theatre Company of Tulsa in January 1985; the television version will be broadcast in 1998. He and Paula Gunn Allen are adapting stories by a variety of authors for a television series to be titled *American Indian Masterpiece Theatre.* He will serve as the producer of the Drama Development Project of the Native American Telecommunication Consortium, which will begin producing a series of scripts for television and feature films in 1997. Geiogamah has his own production company, Native American Media enterprises, in Los Angeles.

Interview:

Kenneth Lincoln, "Appendix C: Interview with Hanay Geiogamah," in his *Indi'n Humor: Bicultural Play in Native America* (New York & Oxford: Oxford University Press, 1993), pp. 326–377.

References:

Sue M. Johnson, "Hanay Geiogamah," in *The Dictionary of Native American Literature,* edited by Andrew Wiget (New York: Garland, 1994), pp. 431–435;

Kenneth Lincoln, "Indi'ns Playing Indians," in his *Indi'n Humor: Bicultural Play in Native America* (New York & Oxford: Oxford University Press, 1993), pp. 162–170;

McCandish Phillips, "Indian Theatre Group: Strong Beginning," *New York Times,* late city edition, 9 November 1972, I: 56, cols. 1–4.

Diane Glancy

(18 March 1941 –)

Julie LaMay Abner
California State University, San Bernardino

Diane Glancy (photograph by Mike Long)

BOOKS: *Traveling On* (Tulsa: Myrtlewood, 1980);

Brown Wolf Leaves the Res and Other Poems (Marvin, S.D.: Blue Cloud Quarterly, 1984);

One Age in a Dream (Minneapolis: Milkweed Editions, 1986);

Offering: Aliscolidodi (Duluth, Minn.: Holy Cow!, 1988);

Iron Woman: Poems (Minneapolis: New Rivers, 1990);

Trigger Dance (Boulder, Colo.: Fiction Collective Two, 1990);

Lone Dog's Winter Count (Albuquerque: West End, 1991);

Claiming Breath (Lincoln: University of Nebraska Press, 1992);

Firesticks: A Collection of Stories (Norman: University of Oklahoma Press, 1993);

Boom Town (Goodhue, Minn.: Black Hat, 1995);

Monkey Secret (Evanston, Ill.: Triquarterly/Northwestern University Press, 1995);

War Cries: A Collection of Plays (Duluth, Minn.: Holy Cow!, 1996);

Pushing the Bear (New York: Harcourt Brace Jovanovich, 1996);

The Only Piece of Furniture in the House (Wakefield, R.I.: Moyer Bell, 1996);

The West Pole (Minneapolis: University of Minnesota Press, 1997).

PLAY PRODUCTIONS: *Segwohi,* Tulsa, Oklahoma Theater, March 1987;

Testimony, Tulsa, Heller Theater, 2 April 1987;

Weebjob, Tulsa, Performing Arts Center, 8 April 1987;

Stick Horse, Aspen, Colorado, Aspen Summer Theater, August 1988;

The Lesser Wars, Minneapolis, Playwrights' Center, November 1989;

Halfact, San Diego, Modern Language Association Conference, San Diego Convention Center, 30 December 1994.

OTHER: "Two Dresses," in *I Tell You Now: Autobiographical Essays by Native American Writers,* edited by Brian Swann and Arnold Krupat (Lincoln: University of Nebraska Press, 1987), pp. 167–183;

"Aunt Parnetta's Electric Blisters," in *Talking Leaves: Contemporary Native American Short Stories,* edited by Craig Lesley (New York: Dell, 1991), pp. 118–124;

"The Firedragon and Sweat" and "Without Title," in *Braided Lives: An Anthology of Multicultural American Writing* (Saint Paul: Minneapolis Humanities Commission, 1991), pp. 13–15, 67;

"The First Indian Pilot," in *Stiller's Pond: New Fiction from the Midwest,* edited by Jonis Agee, Roger Blakely, and Susan Welch (Minneapolis: New Rivers, 1991), pp. 392–393;

"October/From the Backscreen of the Country," in *The Heartlands Today,* edited by Larry Smith and Nancy Dunham (Huron, Ohio: Bottom Dog, 1991), pp. 11–12;

"Lead Horse," in *Earth Song, Sky Spirit: Short Stories of Contemporary Native American Experience,* edited by Clifford Trafzer (Garden City, N.Y.: Doubleday, 1993), pp. 217–233;

"Saturday Night Radio," in *Inheriting the Land: Contemporary Voices from the Midwest,* edited by Mark Vinz and Thom Tammaro (Minneapolis: University of Minnesota Press, 1993), pp. 135–138;

"Christopher," in *The Pushcart Prize XVIII: Best of the Small Presses, 1993–1994,* edited by Bill Henderson (New York: Pushcart, 1994), p. 411;

Two Worlds Walking: Short Stories, Essays, and Poetry by Writers with Mixed Heritages, edited by Glancy and C. W. Truesdale (Minneapolis: New Rivers, 1994);

"Speaking the Corn into Being," in *Freeing the First Amendment: Critical Perspectives on Freedom of Expression,* edited by Robert Jensen and David Allen (New York: New York University Press, 1995), pp. 278–282.

The strength of Diane Glancy's writing is summarized in her award-winning autobiographical work *Claiming Breath* (1992): "The ordinary life I write about from the harshness, the fullness of this land." Her work is a refreshingly honest depiction of contemporary American Indian life with common themes that are easily accessible to Indian and non-Indian readers alike: mixed-bloodedness, heritage, colonialism, middle age, feminism, divorce, death, power, and survival.

Helen Diane Hall was born in Kansas City, Missouri, on 18 March 1941 to Edith Wood Hall, of English and German descent, and Lewis Hall, a Cherokee. She attended school in Kansas City, Indianapolis, and Saint Louis, where she graduated in 1959 from Normandie High School. She received her B.A. from the University of Missouri in 1964. That same year she married Dwane Glancy – "the wrong man," she says in *Claiming Breath* – with whom she had two children: David, born on 10 December 1964; and Jennifer, born on 19 December 1967. The marriage ended in divorce in 1983. Glancy received an M.F.A. from the University of Iowa in 1988. She taught part-time from 1982 to 1992 as artist in residence for the Oklahoma Arts Council; since then she has been a professor of English, specializing in creative writing, scriptwriting, and Native American literatures, at Macalaster College in Saint Paul, Minnesota.

Paula Gunn Allen asserts in *The Sacred Hoop* (1986):

> Traditional American Indian literature is not similar to western literature because the basic assumptions about the universe and, therefore, the basic reality experienced by tribal peoples and by Western peoples are not the same, even at the level of folklore. This difference has confused non-Indian students for centuries.

The difference in Glancy's writing has to do with her attempts to construct Native American texts by combining oral and written traditions, fusing the visual and verbal, mixing poetry and prose, and experimenting with the arrangement of the text on the page. In N. Scott Momaday's *The Way to Rainy Mountain* (1969) each two-page spread includes three paragraphs that relate an experience from a mythic, a historical, and a personal viewpoint, respectively. Similar techniques are present in Glancy's *One Age in a Dream* (1986), which won the Lakes and Prairies Prize; *Offering: Aliscolidodi* (1988); *Trigger Dance* (1990), which won the Charles H. and Mildred Nilon Excellence in Minority Fiction Award; *Iron Woman* (1990); *Lone Dog's Winter Count* (1991); *Claiming Breath,* which won the Native American Prose Award; and *Firesticks* (1993).

Lone Dog's Winter Count, Glancy's fourth collection of poetry, is autobiographical, but Glancy breaks generic distinctions by incorporating myth, nonlinear time, and mixed poetry and prose and by painting a visual landscape through pictographs. The theme of *Lone Dog's Winter Count* and of much of Glancy's other work is made explicit in "February 10, Late Afternoon," in which she asks, "Is all of life this barely making it through?" *Lone Dog's Winter Count* opens with "Here I am Standing Beside Myself," which describes the isolation of one who is not fully accepted in either the Anglo or the Indian world. Glancy has suffered ostracism from the Indian community because of a misdeed committed by her great-grandfather: "My father said his grandfather fled Indian / Territory *kuna' yeli st'di* [claw-scratch-like] / when he'd done something wrong. We were outcast now as well as Indian."

Firesticks, probably Glancy's best-known work, is a collection of nineteen novellas and short stories about contemporary urban Indian life. Her Indians are not glamorous, romanticized figures; she shows that Indians are often indistinguishable from the rest of the population and suffer from similar problems, such as victimization and loneliness. Glancy's nonlinear tales blur the distinctions between poetry and prose and emphasize the power of words. *Firesticks* is filled with characters such as the color-blind Louis, who yearns to be "The First Indian Pilot." He learns that "no Indian was a pilot. . . . No Indian was anything but in the way. A leftover walking in two worlds." Louis tries to imagine what other people see; he wonders if colors are similar to musical instruments: "Maybe it was the way the banjo was different from the guitar." By implication, Glancy is exploring how differences among people are perceived.

The pieces in *Firesticks* are tied together by the character Turle Heppner, whose story is interspersed throughout the various tales. In Turle, Glancy has created a voiceless and powerless woman who is dominated and used by the men in her life. She is forty-two and one-eighth Cherokee, works long hours as a waitress at a truck stop, and is desperate to escape from the small Oklahoma town of Guthrie. She meets the selfish thirty-nine-year-old drifter Navorn, who drives her from Guthrie to Frederick, Oklahoma, to visit her father, where she learns from his caretaker that he is close to death. On the way, Turle comments about her father: " 'What did he ever cause me but grief?' " Navorn asks why, then, she is visiting him; she replies that she visits her father because he is her father. Navorn is insensitive to Turle's emotional and physical needs; he does not even appear to listen to her when she speaks. He forces his way into her apartment and has sex with her after Turle repeatedly says no and asks him to leave. When Navorn asks Turle if she liked their sexual encounter, she laments, "It was easy to do, just uncomfortable a moment and somewhat messy, like spilling soup down my chin."

Turle tells Navorn that she does not want to see him anymore; but when he is gone, she misses him. Still, she realizes that if she had allowed Navorn to stay, "I would be stuck with someone I didn't want to be with." She makes a similar comment about her father just before she finds out that he has died: he never called her on her birthdays, even after saying that he would, but "I didn't want to be with him."

Turle is finally free from her father when he dies, but she must rely on Navorn to drive her back to Frederick to bury him. Turle sleeps in her father's bed and has visions of her dead father, wild horses, and buffalo herds and awakes with the thunder. Navorn leaves Guthrie after returning Turle to her apartment, but he soon returns and has fierce sex with her on the floor. After their second sexual encounter, he asks Turle what she thinks about when he touches her. She responds, "I think that I would like for you to leave me alone." When they have sex a third time, Navorn finally pays attention to Turle's sexual needs, and she actually enjoys the experience. Turle is disappointed when Navorn

Dust jacket for Glancy's award-winning collection of short stories

leaves for a few days to work in Yukon, Oklahoma; yet when he returns, she feels smothered. She begins to have dreams about her father and persuades Navorn to take her to Frederick one more time, to bury his pipe and belt buckle on Mount Scott. As was the case with Momaday's pilgrimage to his grandmother's grave in *The Way to Rainy Mountain,* Turle's three journeys to deal with her father heal her: she begins to chant and sing ancient songs, realizing that her connection to the past and to her heritage can set her free.

Glancy's play *Halfact* (1994; published in *War Cries,* 1996) mixes poetry, prose, myth, and drama. The work has only three characters – Coyote Girl; her brother, Coyote Boy; and the Narrator – and the set consists of three chairs on a bare stage. Coyote Girl lives in a world of incest, patriarchy, isolation, and fear, but she empowers herself despite her helplessness: she discovers the power and communication of silence. She escapes life's injustices through her imagination, meandering through the play intertwining the real and surreal.

At the beginning of the play Coyote Girl is trying to climb up on the roof, which symbolizes equality and freedom: there her father and Coyote Boy will no longer be "above" her. Before riding into town, Coyote Boy tells her that if she falls off the ladder and smashes her head no one will want to dance with her. After he leaves, she says: "He could have taken me to town / under these cream-pitcher clouds." When he returns from town, Coyote Boy tells Coyote Girl that her role is to help with the cooking and that if she does not acquiesce he will carry her into the kitchen "like wood for the stove." Coyote Girl's mother has accepted the submissive role symbolized by the kitchen, and she actually dies there while making bread. Coyote Girl is then forced to assume the incestuous position of wife to her father. The Narrator observes that "Coyote Girl's Father is glad / to have a new wife. Ah the sex of it – / the fine smooth crotch, the divided fold of skin." Coyote Girl is voiceless and powerless in this male-dominated world. Nevertheless, like many women, she finds power in herself and continually attempts to climb the ladder to the roof; she knows that if she gives up her climb and goes into the kitchen, she will die.

Diane Glancy exposes her readers and audiences to a realistic Indian worldview. In *Claiming Breath* she summarizes her goals as a Native American writer: preserving "myths that are being forgotten" and providing "new myths by which we survive this world." Glancy's characters survive with courage and determination and by returning to and embracing the old Indian ways.

References:

Paula Gunn Allen, *The Sacred Hoop: Recovering the Feminine in American Indian Traditions* (Boston: Beacon, 1986), p. 58;

Gerald Vizenor, *Manifest Manners: Postindian Warriors of Survivance* (Hanover, N.H.: Published for Wesleyan University Press by University Press of New England, 1994), pp. 58, 91, 93.

Janet Campbell Hale

(11 January 1946 -)

Gretchen M. Bataille
University of California, Santa Barbara

BOOKS: *The Owl's Song* (Garden City, N.Y.: Doubleday, 1974);

Custer Lives in Humboldt County and Other Poems (Greenfield Center, N.Y.: Greenfield Review, 1978);

The Jailing of Cecelia Capture (New York: Random House, 1985);

Bloodlines: Odyssey of a Native Daughter (New York: Random House, 1993).

Janet Campbell Hale at the time of Bloodlines *(photograph by Scott Britain)*

Janet Campbell Hale began her literary career with two poetry awards – the Vincent Price Poetry Competition in 1963 and the New York Poetry Day Award in 1964 – but her first major work, the novel *The Owl's Song,* was not published until 1974. Her single collection of poems, *Custer Lives in Humboldt County and Other Poems,* appeared in 1978. Her second novel, *The Jailing of Cecelia Capture* (1985), was nominated for many literary awards, including the Pulitzer Prize. Hale received the American Book Award for *Bloodlines: Odyssey of a Native Daughter* (1993), a personal chronicle in which she traces the effects of her Coeur d'Alene heritage on her present.

Janet Campbell was born on 11 January 1946 in Riverside, California, to Nicholas Patrick Campbell, a carpenter and full-blood Coeur d'Alene Indian, and Margaret Sullivan Campbell, a Kootenay with some white and Chippewa ancestry. Campbell is the Anglicized version of Cole-man-née, the name of her great-grandfather. Hale's great-grandparents on her mother's side were Dr. John McLoughlin, a fur trader for the Hudson's Bay Company who was the chief factor in the Northwest Territory, and Annie Grizzly, a Kootenay woman. Hale is a member of the Coeur d'Alene tribe of northern Idaho and spent parts of her childhood on the Coeur d'Alene and Yakima reservations.

Campbell attended high school in Wapato, Washington, before transferring to the Institute of American Indian Arts in Santa Fe, New Mexico. On 23 June 1964 she married Harry Arthur Dudley III; they have a son, Aaron Nicholas, and were divorced in 1965. She attended the City College of San Francisco in 1968. On 23 August 1970 she married Stephen Dinsmore Hale; they have a daughter, Jennifer Elizabeth. Janet Campbell Hale received a B.A. in rhetoric from the University of California at Berkeley in 1972 and studied law there for two years. In 1984 she earned an M.A. in English at the University of California at Davis, where she has taught literature courses. She also has taught at the University of California at Berkeley; DQ University near Davis, California; Western Washington University in Bellingham; the University of Oregon; and the Centrum Foundation in Port Townsend,

Dust jacket for a collection of essays in which Hale examines her Native American heritage

Washington. She currently teaches at Lummi Community College, an Indian-controlled school in Bellingham. She was writer-in-residence at the University of Washington in 1985–1986.

Written for younger readers, *The Owl's Song* is the story of Billy White Hawk, who at age fourteen leaves the reservation in Idaho and his alcoholic father to live with his sister, Alice Fay, in California. Although he has escaped the malaise of the reservation, he encounters prejudice from his fellow students, both white and black – Hale here addresses a subject seldom mentioned in American Indian literature: prejudice among races rather than just between whites and Indians. His sister turns out to be a self-loathing hypocrite who wants nothing to do with Indians and curses the drunken Indians from the reservation while sipping sherry. The only adult who seems to understand Billy and offer him support is his homosexual art teacher. Above all, this is a novel about death – physical, spiritual, and cultural; for many tribes the owl is the bringer of death, and its song is one of despair. A tribal elder tells Billy, "There is little left of what once was. The time is coming when even this will be gone, taken away. And we will be no more. The time is coming when the owl's song will be for our race." Billy White Hawk's cousin, a troubled Vietnam veteran, commits suicide, and his father dies at the end of the novel.

In the title poem of *Custer Lives in Humboldt County and Other Poems* Hale calls Anglo interpretations of Indian history "justifiable genocide" and "involuntary manslaughter." After mentioning Little Bighorn, Steptoe, and Wounded Knee, she ends the poem: "The past is best forgotten"; but the reader is keenly aware that Hale has not forgotten and does not intend to. In "My Sisters the Summer of '53" Hale remembers envying her sisters going to dances with Indian cowboys. In "Desmet, Idaho, March 1969" she writes of returning to the reservation for her grandfather's wake and of hearing the old people speaking a language she only vaguely remembered from her childhood. In "Tribal Cemetery" she shows her children the grave of their grandfather. Hale, like many other American Indians, is a product of a Catholic upbringing; in "On a Catholic Childhood" she introduces humor into what is otherwise a serious collection of memories:

> I'd never confess:
> I stole my sister's
> plastic glows-in-the-dark Virgin Mary

> And hid it deep within the lilac bush.
> God would never understand.

Her tribute to the late Supreme Court justice William Douglas, a man who had "respect for Human Dignity," traces her own life as well as his.

The protagonist of Hale's second novel, *The Jailing of Cecelia Capture,* is a far better developed and much stronger character than Billy White Hawk; Hale seems more at ease with a female character closer to her own age and experiences. Cecelia Capture, an American Indian woman, is a law student at Berkeley who is jailed on her birthday for drunk driving. During her incarceration Capture reflects on her past, a past she tried to forget by moving to the city and marrying a white man. Alcohol was ever present on the reservation and in her own home: her father was frequently drunk and verbally abusive. Her upbringing exposed her to a love/hate relationship with whites: they were models to emulate but were still despised by her father, who sent Cecelia to white schools and encouraged her to leave the reservation. Her father is unhappy that she is an Indian and equally unhappy that she is female: "too bad that you're a girl, Cece, because, you know, men just don't like smart women." Her mother also communicates to Cecelia a sense of her worthlessness, calling her a girl "no real life man would ever want." Leaving the reservation to seek a new life, Cecelia finds only poverty and an unhappy marriage to Nathan, "who didn't look like a man who would be her husband. He looked more like her dad." She seeks the escape she saw as a child: alcohol.

The *jailing* of the title clearly refers to more than Cecelia's incarceration: she has been imprisoned by negative attitudes and by a system that has not allowed her to grow and to thrive. Her surname is also significant: she is "captured" by her environment. At the beginning of the novel Hale quotes the philosopher Friedrich Nietzsche: "The thought of suicide is a great consolation. By means of it one gets through many a bad night." Cecelia's decision not to kill herself is a turning point in her life: she learns to take control of her destiny, and she can then regain the positive reference of the name that was passed on to her by her grandfather, Eagle Capture, who was skilled at snaring eagles. Cecelia's father had criticized her for wearing red as a child, a sign to whites that she was an Indian. As an adult she decides that "red was always going to be her favorite color . . . her whole wardrobe would consist of nothing but red."

Bloodlines, Hale's most recent book, is a collection of essays in which she tries to gain a sense of the meaning of her own life. Hale's story is reminiscent of the life of her character Cecelia Capture; Hale calls herself a "broken-off piece" of her family. As the only one of five siblings who was born off the Coeur d'Alene reservation in northern Idaho, she has always felt alienated from the land of her tribe. Her mother, a light-skinned woman who could pass for white, was older than most mothers of young girls her age; Hale remembers her mother as "a master, an absolute master, of verbal abuse." Hale's grandmother seemed to reject her because of her dark skin. By the time she was fifteen, Hale was writing poetry and sending it to magazines in New York. None of it was published, but through writing Hale could cope with her status as an outcast in her own family. In May 1986, while on a speaking tour in Montana, Hale traced the route of her father's mother, a Coeur d'Alene who had been with Chief Joseph during his attempt to escape to Canada. She recaptured in the memories of her grandmother her connections to her Indian past:

> I felt the biting cold. I was with those people, was part of them. I felt the presence of my grandmother there as though two parts of her met each other that day: the ghost of the girl she was in 1877 (and that part of her will remain forever in this place) and the part of her that lives on in me, in inherited memories of her, in my blood and in my spirit.

By the time of her mother's death in 1987, Hale came to realize that "In the end there are no resolutions. Only an end." Finally, in 1992, Hale returned to the reservation with her daughter. There she came to terms with the lies she had created, the fantasies she had passed on to her children about her childhood. She now understands that for "an Indian, home is the place where your tribe began. . . . Home is the place where your people began, and maybe where your family began and your family still is"; but she still feels alienated: "I will remain, as I have long been, estranged from the land I belong to." Nevertheless, "I am as Coeur d'Alene in New York as I am in Idaho, that is something that is an integral part of me." In tracing her ancestry, she made a discovery: "The Kootenay was the only tribe in the region that had been matrilineal, the only one that had had women warriors." Hale continues that warrior tradition, but she uses words as her weapons.

Reference:

Michelle Savoy, "Janet Campbell Hale," in *Native American Women: A Biographical Dictionary,* edited by Gretchen M. Bataille (New York: Garland, 1993), pp. 101–102.

Joy Harjo

(9 May 1951 -)

Norma C. Wilson
University of South Dakota

See also the Harjo entry in *DLB 120: American Poets Since World War II, Third Series.*

BOOKS: *The Last Song* (Las Cruces, N.Mex.: Puerto del Sol, 1975);

What Moon Drove Me to This? (New York: Reed Books, 1979);

She Had Some Horses, edited by Brenda Peterson (New York: Thunder's Mouth, 1983);

Secrets from the Center of the World, by Harjo and Stephen Strom (Tucson: Sun Tracks/University of Arizona Press, 1989);

In Mad Love and War (Middletown, Conn.: Wesleyan University Press, 1990);

Fishing (Browerville, Minn.: Ox Head, 1992);

The Woman Who Fell from the Sky (New York: Norton, 1994);

Reinventing the Enemy's Language: Contemporary Native Women's Writing of North America (New York: Norton, 1997).

MOTION PICTURE: *Origin of Apache Crown Dance,* screenplay by Harjo, Silver Cloud Video, 1985.

RECORDINGS: *Furious Light,* Watershed, 1986;

Harjo and Poetic Justice, *Letter from the End of the Twentieth Century,* Red Horse Records, 1996.

OTHER: "Ordinary Spirit," in *I Tell You Now: Autobiographical Essays by Native American Writers,* edited by Brian Swann and Arnold Krupat (Lincoln: University of Nebraska Press, 1987), pp. 263–270;

"The Flood" and "Northern Lights," in *Talking Leaves: Contemporary Native American Short Stories,* edited by Craig Lesley (New York: Dell, 1991), pp. 133–138;

"Writing with the Sun," in *Where We Stand: Women Poets on Literary Tradition,* edited by Sharon Bryan (New York: Norton, 1993), pp. 70–74;

"Fire," in *The Woman That I Am: The Literature and Culture of Contemporary Women of Color,* edited by D. Soyini Madison (New York: St. Martin's Press, 1994), p. 3.

Joy Harjo (photograph by Paul Abdoo)

SELECTED PERIODICAL PUBLICATIONS – UNCOLLECTED: "Bio-poetics Sketch for Greenfield Review," *Greenfield Review,* 9 (Winter 1981–1982): 8–9;

"The Woman Hanging from the Thirteenth Floor Window," *Wicazo Sa Review,* 1 (Spring 1985): 38–40;

"Three Generations of Native American Women's Birth Experience," *Ms.,* 2 (July–August 1991): 28–30;

"Family Album," *Progressive,* 56 (March 1992): 22–25.

The poetry of Joy Harjo has consistently evolved toward an increasingly diverse and complex vision of contemporary America. In her poems the land speaks through the voices of people who are intimately connected to it. Seeking a state of balance, Harjo attempts to resolve such polarities as love/hate and male/female.

Joy Foster was born on 9 May 1951 in Tulsa, Oklahoma, to Allen W. and Wynema Baker Foster; she is of French, Irish, and Cherokee descent on her mother's side and Muskogee (Creek) on her father's. His family included a long line of tribal leaders and orators, including Monahwee, who led the Red Stick War against Andrew Jackson's army. In 1970, with the permission of her family, Joy Foster took the surname of her paternal grandmother, Naomi Harjo. An enrolled member of the Muskogee tribe, Harjo credits her great-aunt, Lois Harjo Ball, who died in 1982 and to whom Harjo dedicated her book *She Had Some Horses* (1983), with teaching her about her Indian identity.

Harjo attended high school at the Institute of American Indian Arts in Santa Fe, New Mexico, graduating in 1968. She walked four blocks to the Indian hospital in Tahlequah, Oklahoma, to give birth to her son, Phil Dayn, when she was seventeen; her daughter, Rainy Dawn, was born four years later in Albuquerque. Between the children's births Harjo worked as a waitress, a service-station attendant, and a nursing assistant; cleaned hospital rooms; and led a health-spa dance class. She completed a B.A. in English at the University of New Mexico in 1976 and an M.F.A. in creative writing at the University of Iowa in 1978. She taught at the Institute of American Indian Arts in 1978–1979 and at Arizona State University in 1980–1981, studied filmmaking at the Anthropology Film Center in Santa Fe in 1982, and taught at the University of Montana in 1985, the University of Colorado in 1985–1988, and the University of Arizona in 1988–1990. Since 1991 she has taught at the University of New Mexico. She has served as a contributing editor of *Contact II* and *Tyuony* and as poetry editor of *High Planes Literary Review;* she has also served on the boards of directors of the National Association for Third World Writers and the Native American Public Broadcasting Consortium and on the policy panel for the National Endowment for the Arts.

Hearing the poet Simon Ortiz read from his works on the University of New Mexico campus in 1971 inspired Harjo to change her major from painting to poetry. Other influences she has mentioned include Leslie Marmon Silko, Flannery O'Connor, James Wright, Pablo Neruda, Meridel Le Sueur, Galway Kinnell, Leo Romero, Audre Lorde, Louis Oliver, and June Jordan. Harjo told Marilyn Kallet in a 1993 interview, "I made the decision to work with words and the power of words, to work with language, yet I approach the art as a visual artist."

Cover for Harjo's first book

The poetry in Harjo's first book, *The Last Song* (1975), reflects her strong connection to the landscape, history, and native people of the Southwest. In the title poem she says that her breath evolved from "an ancient chant" that her mother knew. She acknowledges that the land she left behind is still part of her: "oklahoma will be the last song / i'll ever sing." (Most of the poems in the book use minimal capitalization and punctuation.) Other poems hearken back to memories, transmitted by her mother, of life in Georgia, Tennessee, Mississippi, and Alabama, areas from which Harjo's Muskogee and Cherokee ancestors were forcibly moved to Indian Territory (now Oklahoma) in the late 1830s on the Trail of Tears. Still other poems indicate Harjo's feeling of relatedness to Native Americans of other tribes. In "3AM" she writes of "trying to find a way back" to "a part of the center / of the world": Old Oraibi, a Hopi village in Arizona that may be the oldest settlement in the United States. In "Conversations Between Here and Home" she expresses concern and respect for women who have suffered abuse from men and are struggling to rebuild their lives:

angry women are building
houses of stones
they are grinding the mortar
between straw-thin teeth
and broken families.

Harjo expresses frustration with communication in contemporary America, which increasingly takes place by telephone rather than face-to-face. In "Are You Still There" the narrator finds it hard to talk to the man she has called; his voice overwhelms her when he says, "'i have missed you'"; the narrator's voice, "caught / shredded on a barbed wire fence," "flutters soundless in the wind." In a similar poem, "Half-Light," from her second book, *What Moon Drove Me to This?* (1979), the narrator is awakened by a telephone call from a man with whom she cannot live but whom she still loves: "even in the emptiness we are mad for each other, / but it twists me the fear his voice makes."

Since the publication of *What Moon Drove Me to This?,* Harjo's poetry has received acclaim from critics, and her work has been included in anthologies of Native American poetry. While Harjo's poetry has evolved from her own experience, her vision has consistently moved outward. In *Native American Literature* (1985) Andrew Wiget says that "at her best the energy generated by this journeying creates a powerful sense of identity that incorporates everything into the poetic self, so that finally she can speak for all the earth." In *The Sacred Hoop* (1986) the Native American writer and critic Paula Gunn Allen calls Harjo "a poet whose work is concerned with metaphysical as well as social connections."

In the title poem of *She Had Some Horses,* kinds of horses represent types of people, from those who willingly serve others to those who are aloof and self-centered. Horses also represent the various elements of nature, from "blue air of sky" to "bodies of sand." In "Bio-poetics Sketch for Greenfield Review" (1981–1982) Harjo says that digging in the "dark rich earth" as a child was a formative experience in her development as a poet, and through the voices in her poems in *She Had Some Horses* the ground speaks. In "For Alva Benson and for Those Who Have Learned to Speak" Harjo writes,

And the ground spoke when she was born.
Her mother heard it. In Navajo she answered
as she squatted down against the earth
to give birth.

Women like Alva Benson, who know that the land is their source of life, are symbols of strength and continuity in Harjo's poetry.

Harjo does not romanticize the lives of Indians in *She Had Some Horses,* however. In "Night Out" she considers some of the reasons for Indian alcoholism. As they try "another shot, anything to celebrate this deadly / thing called living," Indians find that

You have paid the cover charge thousands of times over
with your lives
and now you are afraid
you can never get out.

The speaker in "The Friday Before the Long Weekend" expresses frustration in trying to teach a "drunk child."

In "White Sands" a woman driving to Tulsa for her sister's wedding knows that she does not fit her mother's image of what she should be. But the woman's image of herself – "I will be dressed in / the clear blue sky" – gives her, as Allen says in *The Sacred Hoop,* an "unbroken and radiant connection with something larger and more important than a single individual" such as her mother.

Women in Harjo's poems long for the security of a family and a home, a security that is often lost to people who live in cities. In the powerfully moving poem "The Woman Hanging from the Thirteenth Floor Window" in *She Had Some Horses* Harjo describes a woman "hanging by her own fingers, her / own skin, her own thread of indecision," "crying for / the lost beauty of her own life." Not just one suicidal woman in Chicago, she becomes a metaphor: "all the women of the apartment / building who stand watching her, stand watching themselves." The image of the woman hanging, though imagined, seems so real that women have often told Harjo that they have known or read a newspaper article about the woman in the poem.

Harjo's frequent use of repetition in the poems in *She Had Some Horses* creates a chantlike impression; in "The Woman Hanging from the Thirteenth Floor Window," for example, Harjo writes:

She thinks of Carlos, of Margaret, of Jimmy.
She thinks of her father, and of her mother.

She thinks of all the women she has been, of all
the men. She thinks of the color of her skin, and
of Chicago streets, and of waterfalls and pines.
She thinks of moonlight nights, and of cool spring storms.

In an article about the poem in the *Wicazo Sa Review* (1985) Harjo says that in poetry, as in ceremonies, stories, and oratory, the use of repetition can transform a statement into a "litany," giving the reader "a way to enter in to what is being said and a way to emerge whole but changed." The repetition not only of words but also of sounds and rhythms energizes Harjo's poetry. C. B. Clark notes that "A cadence marks her work that is reminiscent of the repetitions of the Indian ceremonial drum."

The character Noni Daylight appears in many of the poems in *She Had Some Horses.* In "Kansas City" Harjo writes that "Noni Daylight's / a dishrag wrung out over bones." There could be no more precise metaphor for a worn-out woman. Yet Noni accepts her life, choosing

to stay
in Kansas City, raise the children
she had by different men,
all colors. Because she knew
that each star rang with separate
colored hue, as bands of horses
and wild
like the spirit in her.

Harjo's poetry includes many references to the history of colonization and oppression of Native Americans and other people of color in the United States. Through surrealistic imagery her poem "Backwards" in *She Had Some Horses* alludes to the colonizers' wasteful disregard of nature and women:

The moon came up white, and torn
at the edges. I dreamed I was
four that I was standing on it.
A whiteman with a knife cut pieces
away and threw the meat
to the dogs.

As Allen points out in *The Sacred Hoop,* Harjo's poetry "finds itself entwining ancient understandings of the moon, of relationship, of womanhood, and of journeying with city streets, rodeo grounds, highways, airports, Indian bars, and powwows. From the meeting of the archaic and the contemporary the facts of her life become articulate." John Scarry refers to the "poetic fluidity of Harjo's simultaneous physicality and spirituality, and her ability to combine the eternal past and the continuing present."

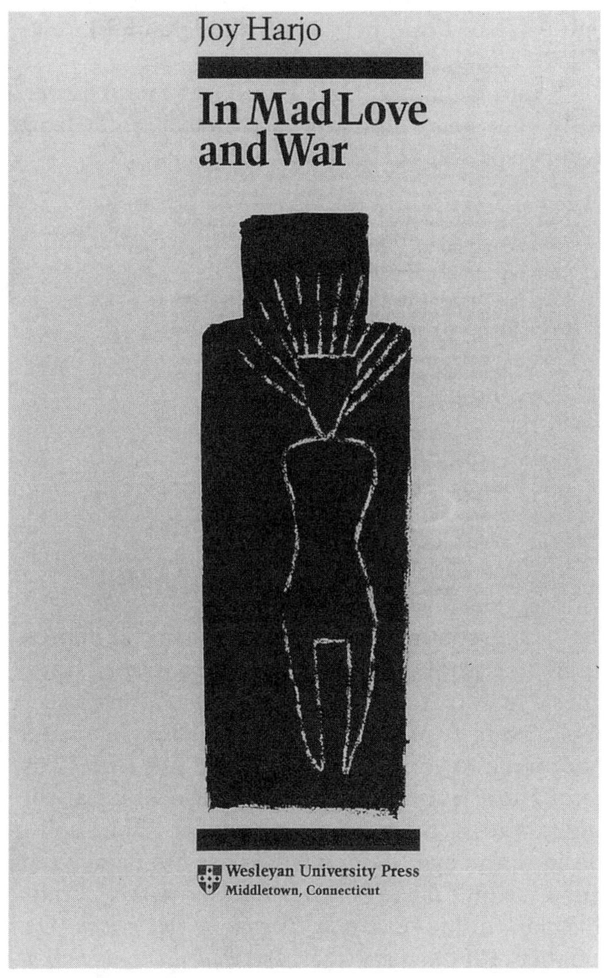

Title page for Harjo's 1990 collection of poems, which won several major literary awards

Another poem in *She Had Some Horses,* "New Orleans," comments more directly on the colonization of Harjo's Creek culture. She describes the Spanish conquistador Hernando de Soto as "one of the ones who yearned / for something his heart wasn't big enough / to handle. / (And DeSoto thought it was gold)." But the Creeks, she says, "lived in earth towns, / not gold, / spun children, not gold." According to the poem, the Creeks drowned de Soto in the Mississippi. Nevertheless, the narrator says,

I know I have seen DeSoto,
having a drink on Bourbon Street
mad and crazy
dancing with a woman as gold
as the river bottom.

The poem presents an image of reverse assimilation, in which the influence of the land and native culture has been pervasive, though unacknowledged, on the colonizers.

In the chant "I Give You Back" Harjo powerfully confronts oppressors past and present from two perspectives. The first is individual:

I am not afraid to be hungry.
I am not afraid to be full.
I am not afraid to be hated.
I am not afraid to be loved.
to be loved, to be loved, fear.

The second perspective is cultural:

I give you back to the white soldiers
who burned my home, beheaded my children,
raped and sodomized my brothers and sisters.
I give you back to those who stole the
food from our plates when we were starving.

Overcoming fear of various forms of oppression is a central theme in *She Had Some Horses.* Harjo goes even further in her poem "Transformations," included in *In Mad Love and War* (1990). In a letter addressed to someone who "would like to destroy me," she rejects revenge, calling instead for a willingness to transform hatred to love: "Bone splintered in the eye of one you choose / to name your enemy won't make it better for you to see." Frank Parman, in his review in *The Gayly Oklahoman* (December 1990), says that *In Mad Love and War* "demonstrates the range of her poetic development, from the 1979 narratives of Indian bar and powwow flirtations to a visionary mixture of past and present." From the blues lament "Strange Fruit" to "Resurrection," set in Nicaragua, the powerful poems in this collection tell the horrible truth about oppression while at the same time celebrating the beauty of the natural world.

Scarry compares one of the poems in *In Mad Love and War* to the visionary poetry of William Butler Yeats: "'Deer Dancer' may be seen as something of a Native American 'Second Coming'"; the "sterility of the landscape and the objective yet involved tone of Harjo's speaker" are similar to the landscape and tone of Yeats's poem. Yet, Scarry says, "'Deer Dancer' more directly invites the reader to share in the humanity of the 'Indian ruins' sitting so desolately in our native landscape." Unlike Yeats, who questions and fears the coming of the new age, Harjo's "Deer Dancer" interprets the woman in a dingy bar as a symbol of promise and her dance as a blessing.

The title of another poem in the volume, "Strange Fruit," is taken from a song by Lewis Allan that Billie Holiday recorded in 1939; the song is a graphic and metaphoric description of lynching and a lamentation for the "strange fruit hangin' from the poplar trees." Harjo's poem emphasizes that too much remains unchanged since those days. Harjo dedicated the poem to Jacqueline Peters, who was hanged from an olive tree in Lafayette, California, in 1986. Peters had been working to organize a local chapter of the National Association for the Advancement of Colored People in response to the 1985 lynching of a twenty-three-year-old black man. Written from the point of view of a woman being lynched, the poem ends with an extremely long line followed by a short one: "I only want heaven in my baby's arms, my baby's arms. Down the road through the trees I see the kitchen light on my lover fixing supper, the baby fussing for her milk, waiting for me to come home. The moon hangs from the sky like a swollen fruit. / My feet betray me dance anyway, from this killing tree."

"For Anna Mae Pictou Aquash, Whose Spirit is Present Here and in the Dappled Stars (for we remember the story and must tell it again so we may all live)" memorializes a Micmac woman whose body was found in February 1976 on the Pine Ridge reservation in South Dakota. When her body was buried, Aquash had not been identified, and the coroner attributed her death to exposure. When it was discovered that the body was that of Aquash, a member of the American Indian Movement, the body was exhumed, and a second autopsy was performed. The autopsy revealed that Aquash had been killed by a bullet fired at close range into the back of her head, and many were outraged to learn that the first coroner had cut off the woman's hands and turned them over to an FBI agent. Harjo speaks to Aquash's ghost:

Anna Mae,
everything and nothing changes.
You are the shimmering young woman
who found her voice,
when you were warned to be silent, or have your body cut away
from you like an elegant weed.
You are the one whose spirit is present in the dappled stars.

In Mad Love and War won the William Carlos Williams Award from the Poetry Society of America, the Delmore Schwartz Memorial Prize from New York University, and the Josephine Miles Award from the Oakland, California, branch of PEN.

In "The Place the Musician Became a Bear," included in *The Woman Who Fell from the Sky* (1994), Harjo links her interest in jazz to her Indian heritage: "*I've always believed us Creeks . . . had something to do with the origins of jazz. After all, when the African peoples were forced here for slavery they were brought to the traditional lands of the Muscogee peoples.*" When she was in her thirties Harjo taught herself to play the saxophone with the help of the Muskogee and Kaw jazz saxophonist Jim Pepper, and she plays soprano and alto saxophone with Poetic Justice, an all-Native American band. The music of Poetic Justice accompanies Harjo's reading of ten of the poems from *The Woman Who Fell from the Sky* on an audiocassette that is sold with the book. In reading the poems Harjo makes alterations that clarify the poems' meanings.

Many of the poems in the collection are myths created by Harjo, and they are followed by prose accounts of the people, ideas, or events that inspired them. Believing that "*the word* poet *is synonymous with truth-teller,*" Harjo tells the poetic and mythical truth, followed by the literal truth. The title poem is the story of Lila and Johnny, who meet as children at an Indian boarding school. After graduation Johnny joins the army and goes to Vietnam; Lila works days cleaning houses and nights at the Dairy Queen. While the two are apart Johnny names himself "Saint Coincidence," and Lila has three children. Having leaped into the "forbidden place," Lila has fallen; but she is caught "in front of the Safeway" by Saint Coincidence. Love, then, places the two in a spiritual state of grace. In the comment that follows the prose poem, Harjo says that she understands "*love to be the very gravity holding each leaf, each cell, this earthy star together.*"

"The Naming" links Harjo's granddaughter Haleigh Sara Bush to Harjo's maternal grandmother, Leona May Baker. Haleigh was born out of "wind bringing rain," and "My grandmother is the color of night as she tells me to move away from the window when it is storming. *The lightning will take you.*" But when the poem ends, "The earth is wet with happiness." In the italicized prose passage following the poem Harjo says that as a child she did not like her grandmother; but she was "*prompted to find out more*" about the woman before her granddaughter's birth. After hearing her mother's story about her grandmother, Harjo "*began to have compassion for this woman who was weighted down with seven children and no opportunities.*" When Haleigh was born, Harjo "*felt the spirit of this grandmother in the hospital room*" and "*welcomed her.*" Leona May Baker's story, like many others in the book, is violent. Returning home from working on the railroad for nine months, Harjo's grandfather found her grandmother pregnant with another man's child. He beat her so severely that she "*went into labor and gave birth to the murdered child.*" After that, the two "*attempted double suicide. They stood on the tracks while a train bore down on them as all the children watched in horror.*" At the last second Harjo's grandfather pushed her grandmother off the tracks and leaped to safety.

In "Letter from the End of the Twentieth Century" Harjo records another story of violence, this one told to her by "Rammi, an Igbo man from northern Nigeria," as he drove her "in his taxi to the airport." Rammi's friend was shot in the back of the head early one morning as he was "filling his taxi with gas." In the commentary following the prose poem Harjo says that she finds that she has "*much in common with many of the immigrants from other colonized lands who come here to make a living, often as taxi drivers.*" The final poem in the book, "Perhaps the World Ends Here," however, is a peaceful one. The speaker is seated at the kitchen table: "The gifts of the earth are brought and prepared, set on the table. So it has been since creation, and it will go on." Here, in the mundane center of the house, the cosmic meaning of life is revealed.

Harjo narrated the six-part series *The Native Americans,* broadcast on Turner Network Television in October 1994. In late 1996 she was working on "A Love Supreme," a poetry collection to be published by W. W. Norton; "The Goodluck Cat," a book for children, to be published by Harcourt Brace Jovanovich; and "Reinventing the Enemy's Language," an anthology of Native American women's writing. She was also writing a screenplay, "When We Used to Be Humans," for a motion picture to be produced by the American Film Foundation.

Interviews:

Joseph Bruchac, ed., *Survival This Way: Interviews with American Indian Poets* (Tucson: University of Arizona Press, 1987), pp. 87–103;

Laura Coltelli, "Joy Harjo," in her *Winged Words: American Indian Writers Speak* (Lincoln: University of Nebraska Press, 1990), pp. 54–68;

Marilyn Kallet, "In Love and War," *Kenyon Review,* 15 (Summer 1993): 57–66;

Stephanie Izarek Smith, "Joy Harjo," *Poets and Writers Magazine,* 21 (July-August 1993): 22–27;

Coltelli, ed., *The Spiral of Memory: Interviews. Joy Harjo* (Ann Arbor: University of Michigan Press, 1996).

References:

Paula Gunn Allen, *The Sacred Hoop: Recovering the Feminine in American Indian Traditions* (Boston: Beacon, 1986), pp. 124, 160–166;

Allen, ed., *Studies in American Indian Literature* (New York: Modern Language Association of America, 1983), p. 123;

Allen and Patricia Clark Smith, "Earthly Relations, Carnal Knowledge: Southwestern American Indian Woman Writers and Landscape," in *The Desert Is No Lady,* edited by Vera Norwood and Janice Monk (New Haven: Yale University Press, 1987), pp. 174–196;

Dan Bellm, "Ode to Joy," *Village Voice,* 2 April 1991, p. 78;

C. B. Clark, "Joy Harjo (Creek) b. 1951," in *The Heath Anthology of American Literature,* volume 2, edited by Paul Lauter and others (Lexington, Mass.: Heath, 1994), p. 3049;

Laura Coltelli, "Harjo, Joy," in *Native American Women: A Biographical Dictionary,* edited by Gretchen M. Bataille (New York: Garland, 1993), pp. 105–106;

Maura McDermott, "Joy Harjo: Poetic Justice," *Oklahoma Today,* 43 (September–October 1993): 46–47;

John Scarry, "Representing Real Worlds: The Evolving Poetry of Joy Harjo," *World Literature Today,* 66 (Spring 1992): 286–291;

Andrew Wiget, *Native American Literature* (Boston: Twayne, 1985), pp. 116–117;

Wiget, "Nightriding with Noni Daylight: The Many Horse Songs of Joy Harjo," in *Native American Literature,* edited by Coltelli (Pisa: SEU, 1989), pp. 185–196;

Norma C. Wilson, "Joy Harjo," in *Dictionary of Native American Literature,* edited by Wiget (New York: Garland, 1994), pp. 437–443.

Lance Henson

(20 September 1944 –)

Norma C. Wilson
University of South Dakota

BOOKS: *Keeper of Arrows* (Johnstown, Pa.: Renaissance, 1971; revised edition, Chickasha, Okla.: Renaissance / Walking Badger, 1972);

Naming the Dark: Poems for the Cheyenne (Norman, Okla.: Point Riders, 1976);

Mistah: New Poems (New York: Strawberry, 1977);

Buffalo Marrow on Black (Edmond, Okla.: Full Court Press, 1979);

In a Dark Mist (New York: Cross-Cultural Communications, 1979);

A Circling Remembrance: Poems (Marvin, S.Dak.: Blue Cloud Quarterly, 1982);

Selected Poems, 1970–1983 (Greenfield Center, N.Y.: Greenfield Review, 1985);

Tonger ut Stiennen / Thunder from Stones, with Frisian translation by Jelle Kaspersma (Leeuwarden, Netherlands: Fryske Nasjonale Partij, 1987);

Teepee (Chivasso, Italy: Cooperative La Parentesi / Soconos Incommindios, 1987);

Another Song for America (Norman, Okla.: Point Riders, 1987);

This Small Sound / Dieser kleine Klang, with German translation by Hartmut Lutz (Berlin: Institut für Indianische Kulturen Nordamerikas, 1988);

Le Orme del Tasso / The Badger Tracks (Turin: Soconos Incommindios, 1989);

Another Distance: New and Selected Poems (Norman, Okla.: Point Riders, 1991);

A Motion of Sudden Aloneness (Little Rock: American Native Press Archives / University of Arkansas at Little Rock, 1991);

A Cheyenne Sketchbook (Greenfield Center, N.Y.: Greenfield Review, 1992);

Trail Buio e la Luce / Between the Dark and the Light (Milan: Selene Edizioni, 1993);

Poems for a Master Beadworker (Osnabrück: OBMA, 1993).

PLAY PRODUCTIONS: *Winter Man,* by Henson and Andy Tierstien, New York, Dance Theatre Workshop, February 1991;

Lance Henson

Coyote Road, by Henson and Jeff Hooper, West Liberty, Ohio, Mad River Theatre Works, 27 June 1992.

SELECTED PERIODICAL PUBLICATION – UNCOLLECTED: "Journal Entries," *Poetry East,* 32 (Fall 1991): 51–52.

One of the few contemporary Native American poets who writes bilingual poetry, Lance Henson has received international recognition for his knowledge of Cheyenne language and culture and his skill as a poet in English. Seventeen collections of his poetry have been published, including five that appeared in Europe with translations into German, Frisian, and Italian. Having traveled and read widely, Henson acknowledges influences from European, Latin American, and Oriental literature; but he remains Cheyenne in his basic outlook, returning to Oklahoma each June for the Sun Dance. In a 1993 article Maura McDermott quotes Henson as saying, "Western Oklahoma will always be my home." He served as an official representative of the Southern Cheyenne Nation at the European Free Alliance in Leeuwarden, Netherlands, in 1985 and at the United Nations Indigenous People's Conference in Geneva in 1988.

Of Cheyenne, Oglala, and French ancestry, Lance David Henson was born in Washington, D.C., on 20 September 1944 but was raised on a farm near Calumet, Oklahoma, by his great-aunt Bertha Cook, a tepee maker, and his great-uncle Bob Cook, who kept the grounds for Chapter One of the Native American Church in Oklahoma. The last of five boys the couple raised, Henson grew up living the Southern Cheyenne culture.

After graduating from Calumet High School he served in the marines. On his return to Oklahoma he began writing poetry while attending the Oklahoma College of Liberal Arts (now University of Science and Arts of Oklahoma) in Chickasha. His first book, *Keeper of Arrows,* was published in 1971, while he was still a student. After graduating in 1972, he attended the University of Tulsa as a Ford Foundation scholar, receiving an M.F.A. in creative writing in 1975. Since then he has taught and given workshops in more than five hundred schools and colleges across the United States and in Europe. His poems have been included in major anthologies of Native American literature and in a wide range of magazines, including *National Geographic, World Literature Today, Studies in American Indian Literatures,* and *Contact II.* Henson is a member of the Cheyenne Dog Soldier Society, the Native American Church, and the American Indian Movement. He has three children: a daughter, Christian; and two sons, Jon David and Michael.

At a 27 September 1991 session of the Native American Writers' Forum in Telluride, Colorado, Henson stated his view that "Indians are linked to metaphysical reality, live lives of heightened imagery, tell stories in images." Without capitalization, punctuation, or an extraneous word, his poems create images of historical and contemporary places, people, and events. They make impressions on the mind that are like the fleeting perceptions that constantly enter and leave one's thoughts; the reader or hearer responds to them intuitively.

"Morning," the first poem in *Keeper of Arrows,* introduces one of Henson's most prevalent poetic themes – the spiritual presence of those who have died. Henson describes steam rising from frost as "rising from the / backs of the / sleeping old," from the bodies of his buried ancestors or of the animals who had lived in those earlier times. Variations on this theme are particularly evident in Henson's early poetry. "Wherever I go I carry my relatives with me," he has said.

One of Henson's most moving and complete expressions of this theme is "homecomings," in *Naming the Dark: Poems for the Cheyenne* (1976). While Henson was in the marines, his grandfather died; two days before his death, the grandfather had mailed Henson some photographs he had taken of a March snowstorm in Oklahoma. When Henson returned to the base from attending the funeral, he found the photographs. In one of them his grandfather was standing by a pump house at noon with only whiteness around him. In the final section of the poem Henson describes the photograph and its meaning to him:

you are in a photograph
standing in the snow
without a shadow
your words go into themselves
they reach a silent country where
we will meet
i have been going there forever.

Death is the ultimate homecoming; life is a progression toward the final home. The only way one can be fully aware of life is to come to terms with the "silent country," to accept that one is going there.

Alongside reflections about his personal life in *Naming the Dark* are poems informed by the cultural heritage of the Cheyenne. As Robert L. Berner says, "Henson's best poems reveal a remarkable symbiosis of the personal and the traditional; they are the results of a process by which he receives power from his traditions while simultaneously enriching those traditions, helping them evolve, and ensuring their survival." For example, "anniversary poem for the cheyennes who died at sand creek" commemorates the place where a peacefully camped band was massacred by cavalry troops in 1864. Henson believes, he says in this poem, that one can come close to the ghosts of the past by speaking "to the season / to the ponds / touching the dead grass."

Loneliness, emptiness, death, and silence fill the poems in Henson's third book, *Mistah* (1977). The title is the Cheyenne word for "owl," and the title poem is spoken by one of those birds, "calling toward a house / in which / no one lives." Henson's Cheyenne name means Walking Badger; prefacing his interview with Henson in *Survival This Way* (1987), Joseph Bruchac says, "Like the badger he is capable of holding stubbornly to the things he believes in, even when confronted by those seemingly more powerful than he." In the poem "song for warriors" Henson finds a dead badger on the road one night, "after hours of beers at fats place." He refers to the scent of the "carcass of badger" as "the blessing on my hands"; Berner interprets the passage to mean that since "the badger, tough, independent, possessing courage and strength all out of proportion to its size, the courage and strength, that is, of the Cheyenne warriors and of the Cheyenne tribe itself, is a warrior by definition," the badger's carcass "suggests a threat to the warrior ideal."

This Small Sound / Dieser kleine Klang (1988) includes poems in English and Cheyenne with German translations. The title of the collection is from the poem "woodpecker song"; the last line, "i make this small sound," calls attention to the similarity between the sound of the woodpecker and that of the typewriter. The woodpecker, a sacred power entity of the Sun Dance ceremony, uses the small gift of his sound perfectly.

The title poem of *Another Song for America* (1987), which is also the last selection in the book, is a record of Henson's response to driving "just past the kent state turnoff." Remembering the killing of four student Vietnam War protesters and the wounding of eight others by National Guardsmen on the Ohio campus in 1970, he asks, "god damn you america / what have you done to your children." The poem concludes, "the wind speaks their names / anyway you breathe it." That the speaker is a Vietnam veteran intensifies the poem's impact. The first poem in the collection, "for white antelope," is the death song that the warrior White Antelope sang before being killed in the Sand Creek Massacre and includes the lines "nothing endures / only the earth and sky." By bracketing the volume with these two poems, Berner says, "Henson wants to suggest . . . that America's self-wounding at Kent State was an inevitable consequence of a history that has been written in the blood of his people." Marveling at the variety of poems in the book, Roger Weaver comments poetically in his review in *Studies in American Indian Literatures* (Winter 1992): "Within a single poem, like a candle lit in a dark window, a life sings. Outside, the great silence of the prairie moves within to shape the language. It's as if an enormous moment has been registered, giving significance and resonance to the words."

Title page for Henson's second volume of poetry

In his review in *American Indian Quarterly* (Winter 1993) Craig Womack calls the poems in Henson's *Another Distance* (1991) "mini-ceremonials that merge words, movement, and meaning and culminate in restored relationship and renewal." Rena Cook, Bob Cook's sister-in-law, inspired the first two poems in the book. Her words in "poem from a master beadworker" poignantly reveal how much the act of creating means to an artist:

i close my eyes and bead in my head
and then i cry
i cry
and i guess my tears are the beads.

Many of the poems in *Another Distance,* including "a dream of european stones," emerge from Henson's travels in Italy, the Netherlands, Denmark, Sweden, Germany, Austria, and Luxembourg and demonstrate his ability to describe foreign landscapes in terms of his Native American sensibility. In "two poems at elisabettas house" he says:

my life is the dark sound
of someone walking on bruised stars
fallen to ground
as shards of stone
lit by the sun
and the seas tears.

There is a wide range of language and settings in the book, from "she wolf song," written in Cheyenne and English, to "talking truckstop blues," which is filled with the images and words of contemporary America.

"Journal Entries," in the fall 1991 issue of *Poetry East,* may indicate the direction Henson's writing is taking. Compared to his earlier work, the lines in this poem are longer and their meanings more expansive:

there are ancestral horses underneath us warning us to be careful
with what is left
the dreaming horses echoing in the marrow of this land.

Conscious of the necessity of respecting and protecting the environment if the human race is to survive, Henson includes himself in the collective *us.* The poem ends:

i lean back feeling my real name and close my eyes to the
pure and collective dark
that knows all our names.

Henson has also written for the theater. An opera, *Winter Man,* co-authored with Andy Tierstien and dealing with the Sand Creek Massacre, premiered at the Dance Theatre Workshop in New York in February 1991; it was also produced at La Mama Experimental Theater Club in New York in March 1995. *Coyote Road,* co-authored with Jeff Hooper, premiered at the Mad River Theatre Works in West Liberty, Ohio, on 27 June 1992 and ran until 9 August. The play was also produced at the University of New Guinea in Papua.

Interviews:

Patrick D. Hundley, ed., *The Magic of Names: Three Native American Poets. Norman H. Russell, Lance Henson, Jim Weaver Barnes* (Marvin, S.Dak.: Blue Cloud Quarterly, 1979), n.p.;

Joseph Bruchac, ed., *Survival This Way: Interviews with American Indian Poets* (Tucson: University of Arizona Press, 1987), pp. 105–117;

Jacob Freydont Attie, "Interview with Lance Henson," *Cuyahoga: The Oberlin Quarterly* (Spring 1993): 24–29;

T. D. Cameron, "The Conceptions Southwest Interview with Lance Henson," *Conceptions Southwest* (Spring 1993): 24–28.

References:

Caroll Arnett, "Lance (David) Henson," in *Dictionary of Native American Literature,* edited by Andrew Wiget (New York: Garland, 1994), pp. 441–443;

Robert L. Berner, "Lance Henson: Poet of the People," *World Literature Today,* 64 (Summer 1990): 418–421;

Maura McDermott, "A Harvest of Native Poets," *Oklahoma Today,* 43 (September–October 1993): 42–47.

Linda Hogan

(17 July 1947 –)

Kathryn W. Shanley
Cornell University

BOOKS: *Calling Myself Home* (Greenfield Center, N.Y.: Greenfield Review, 1978);

Daughters, I Love You (Denver: Research Center on Women, 1981);

Eclipse (Los Angeles: American Indian Studies Center, University of California, 1983);

Seeing through the Sun (Amherst: University of Massachusetts Press, 1985);

That Horse, by Hogan and Charles Colbert Henderson (Acoma Pueblo, N.Mex.: Pueblo of Acoma Press, 1985);

Savings: Poems (Minneapolis: Coffee House, 1988);

Mean Spirit (New York: Atheneum / Toronto: Collier Macmillan Canada, 1990);

Red Clay: Poems and Stories (Greenfield Center, N.Y.: Greenfield Review, 1991);

Book of Medicines (Minneapolis: Coffee House, 1993);

Dwellings: A Spiritual History of the Living World (New York: Norton, 1995);

Solar Storms (New York: Scribners, 1995).

PLAY PRODUCTION: *A Piece of Moon,* Stillwater, Oklahoma State University, October 1981.

OTHER: *The Stories We Hold Secret,* edited by Hogan, Carol Bruchac, and Judith McDaniel (Greenfield Center, N.Y.: Greenfield Review, 1986);

"The Two Lives," in *I Tell You Now: Autobiographical Essays by Native American Writers,* edited by Brian Swann and Arnold Krupat (Lincoln: University of Nebraska Press, 1987), pp. 233–249;

"Aunt Moon's Young Man," in *The Best American Short Stories 1989,* edited by Margaret Atwood and Shannon Ravenel (Boston: Houghton Mifflin, 1989), pp. 195–215;

Between Species: Women and Animals, edited by Hogan, Brenda Peterson, and Deena Metzger (New York: Ballantyne, forthcoming, 1997).

Linda Hogan at the time of Mean Spirit *(photograph by Jennifer Barton)*

SELECTED PERIODICAL PUBLICATIONS – UNCOLLECTED: "The 19th Century Native American Poets," *Wassaja,* 13, no. 4 (1980): 24–29;

"Who Puts Together," *Denver Quarterly,* 14 (Winter 1980): 103–110.

As a writer of Chickasaw heritage, Linda Hogan centers herself and, consequently, her readers on what nature has to teach human beings and on the regenerative female forces that shape the world. The Chickasaw were matrilineal and matrilocal in precontact times; other tribes, though patriarchal, revered their women as the creative life force of the universe. Domination by Christian Europeans has altered the traditional tribal balance between male and female power in American Indian life. In her works Hogan seeks to restore that balance and to offer ancient wisdom about nature in mythological yet contemporary terms.

Born in Denver on 17 July 1947 to Charles Henderson, a Chickasaw, and Cleona Bower Henderson, a white, Hogan was raised in various locations as her father was transferred from post to post by the army. But she has always regarded Oklahoma, where her father's family lives, as her home. In a 1990 interview she told Patricia Clark Smith that her

> idea of what a home is, is *there,* in south-central Oklahoma. . . . I felt *loved* there, cared for, wanted. I kissed my cousins in the hay, and played spin-the-bottle. That's where I first got attacked by a tarantula, and fell apart, where I caught a blue racer snake, and a turtle . . . where I heard my own history, and stories, and gossip about other Chickasaw people.

In her autobiographical essay, "The Two Lives" (1987), she writes of her mother's ancestors, who settled in the Nebraska Territory. Drawing on a journal she inherited, Hogan describes the settlers' desperation after crop failures and grasshopper plagues, which was compounded by the government's policy of killing the buffalo that both Indians and non-Indians needed for survival. At the same time, Native Americans were being forced off their lands, removed to new places, crowded together, and sometimes killed outright. As Hogan notes, "It was a continuing time of great and common acts of cruelty and violence."

In her recitation of her job history in "The Two Lives" one can readily see why she feels loyalty toward the working poor: "I worked at many . . . low-paying jobs, in nursing homes, in dental offices, and filing for a collection agency where I occasionally threw away the files of people who called to tell how hard their lives were." She obtained her undergraduate degree as a commuter student at the University of Colorado at Colorado Springs and other schools, only to find much of the educational experience lacking in relevance to her own life. Nonetheless, she became aware of working-class writers whose stories run parallel to those of her family and the family of her former husband, Pat Hogan.

Hogan received her M.A. in English and creative writing from the University of Colorado at Boulder in 1978. A recipient of many distinguished research awards – among them a D'Arcy McNickle Memorial Fellowship at the Newberry Library in 1980, a Yaddo Colony Fellowship in 1982, a National Endowment for the Arts grant in fiction in 1986, a Guggenheim for fiction in 1990, and a Lannan Award in 1994 – Hogan has also been honored by a Five Civilized Tribes Playwriting Award in 1980 for *A Piece of the Moon* (produced in 1981), the short-fiction award from *Stand Magazine* in 1983, and an American Book Award from the Before Columbus Foundation in 1985 for *Seeing through the Sun.* She was a finalist for a Pulitzer Prize for her novel *Mean Spirit* (1990), and her *Book of Medicines* (1993) was a National Book Critics Circle finalist. She taught at the University of Colorado from 1977 to 1979, at Colorado Women's College in Colorado Springs in 1979, and at the Rocky Mountain Women's Institute of the University of Denver in 1979–1980. She was a poet-in-residence for the Colorado and Oklahoma Arts Councils from 1980 to 1984 and taught at the University of Minnesota–Twin Cities from 1984 to 1989. Since 1989 she has taught in the American Indian Studies Program and the English department at the University of Colorado at Boulder. In addition, she gives lectures, readings, and workshops at other universities and in Native American communities and for Native American organizations. As a poet, fiction writer, essayist, and playwright Hogan has been committed to environmental preservation; she has worked as a volunteer in wildlife rehabilitation clinics in Minnesota and in Colorado.

Hogan adopted two daughters of Oglala Lakota heritage, Sandra Dawn Protector and Tanya Thunder Horse, in 1979. Many of the poems in her collection *Eclipse* (1983) portray a mother's sense of helplessness in shielding her children from such destructive forces as war and nuclear waste. In the poem "A Prayer for Men and Women" the women are sleepless, on guard while the men and children rest. It is a prayer

> To save the eyes
> that watched flowers on wallpaper
> ignite like a thousand suns.
> . . . .
> A prayer against heat
> that burns dark roses from shirts into skin.

Other poems in *Eclipse* are more hopeful; for example, the narrator in "Blessing the Children" tells how

> the wind in leaves
> feeds fire
> gives you dreams
> and words
> to move your lives.

Other kinds of light surround the family in "Black Hills Survival Gathering, 1980": the "fragile fire" of a child's life, the "warm sun" in a child's hair, the "reflecting light" that celebrates the wife's love for her husband, the "center of light" and "expanding light" at daybreak, and, finally, "the burning hills," where, "in flaring orange cloth / men are singing and drumming / Heartbeat." Dark enters the poems in relation to tragedy and loss, such as in the following lines from "Daybreak": "staring at her innocence of what is dark / her fear at night of nothing. . . ." and "In her dark eyes / the children of Hiroshima / are screaming." By contrast, dark in this collection speaks to the sorts of activities that occur at night, as in "Small Animals At Night," when "Dark hills move / through wire and highways / and the soft black leaves / that slip through our eyes / to trees growing at the edge of the world." In addition to the light/shadow motif, the balance *Eclipse* offers can be found in the movements from fearful and sorrowful silence to an ardent voice, a voice the poet learns from the heartbeat drum of human ritual as well as from animals and insects, "night's music / which means we are safe / we are never alone."

Hogan's fourth collection of poems, *Seeing through the Sun,* is divided into four sections: "Seeing through the Sun," "Territory of Night," "Daughters Sleeping," and "Wall Songs." "The Truth Is," the second poem in the book, has frequently been cited for its honesty and agony over the author's mixed-blood heritage. That heritage is symbolized by two hands, one Chickasaw and one white; "they are masks / for the soul." The "sinister" left hand is Indian, always concerned with who killed whom; the right hand is white, distinctly female, the hand of a woman who "falls in love too easily." Neither hand finds money in its pocket. A reconciliation comes in the last poem of the first section, "Evolution in Light and Water," in which the narrator unites the macrocosmic view of the earth from an airplane, "flying in gravity's teeth," with the microcosm that is the human body:

> Dark amphibians
> live in my skin.
> I am their country.
> . . . .
> the radiant vault of myself,
> this full and broken continent of living.

The second section, "Territory of Night," ends, rather than begins, with its title poem and progresses from a white, "innocent" light to a "black alphabet of the horse" darkness. In "Watch Me" the speaker says, "This year I was suddenly old, / a mother, / and without a single cow to my name." Despite her loneliness and lack of possessions, this woman is a warrior on her own behalf and on the behalf of other women when she says,

> I won't weep at tables
> at home or in cowboy bars.
> I am done with weeping.
> The bones of this body say, dance.

With that cavalier gesture, she admonishes other weeping women to "just watch" her dance, to learn how to make being alone a celebration of life. In "Desert," in the third section, human tissues are viewed as contiguous with the earth:

> This is the earth
> skin stretched bare
> like a woman who teaches her daughters to plant,
> leaving the ants in their places,
> the spiders in theirs.
> She teaches them to turn the soil
> one grain at a time.
> They plant so carefully
> seeds grow from their hands.

The seven poems in the final section, "Wall Songs," express anguish over the false barriers individuals, "races," and communities draw between themselves and others. In "Cities Behind Glass" Hogan reflects that throughout history people have migrated toward the promise of a better life, whether by choice or by necessity; having arrived at their new home, "Mothers open the sills and shake the old world / from lace tablecloths." All the while, others pretend that they cannot see the newcomers, the poor, the workers. In "Bees in Transit: Osage Country" the narrator speaks of northeastern Oklahoma as the place "where dark women, murdered for oil / under the ground / still walk in numbers." She would like the bees, driven from the hives of home and toward madness by a brush fire, to know that "there is a way back home."

In addition to poetry, Hogan also writes short stories and novels. In a 1988 interview Bo Schöler asked Hogan how she perceives the distinctions among "fact, history, fiction and truth." "Fiction may be a dance along the razor's edge of paradox," she replied. Fiction at its best functions much as myth does, as a spotlight on greater truths than who did what, where, and why, according to Hogan. In response to Schöler's query whether the pieces in *That Horse* (1985), by Hogan and her father, Charles Colbert Henderson, reflect an interest in re-creating ethnic history, Hogan replied:

> In *That Horse,* my father's story and my story are about the same horse, but they're very different sto-

> ries. I wanted to show the history of the time. I don't know if it's ethnic history, or if it's the history of that particular place and the people in that place. . . . I'm tired of reading stories about Indian people that don't seem to me to be true: no bumper-stickers, no events going on. . . . I'm telling it from an Indian perspective that happens to be Chickasaw, Southern. . . . In that way it's ethnic history, but we are all history. We are history taking place right now.

As Arnold Krupat writes in *The American Book Review* (July/August 1990), Hogan's poetry collection *Savings* (1988) offers an "awareness that spiritual consciousness and material political action may stand in complementary, not antithetical, relation to one another." The book comprises poems written while Hogan was at the University of Minnesota in Minneapolis. In her interview with Smith, Hogan said:

> The racism here – it's kind of like Gallup, in some ways. The divisions between the color of people are very sharp. And the racism here seems primarily focused on Indian people. At the same time that Minneapolis prides itself on being liberal, radical, progressive, it romanticizes Indian people, as Jimmie Durham says, "to death." It's hard to teach here, in Indian Studies, because of the combination of spiritual, romantic, destructive stereotypes.

During the 1950s the government had decided that Indians would be better off if they blended into the populations of cities than if they remained on reservations, and many of them had been relocated to Minneapolis, Denver, Oakland, Seattle, Chicago, and other cities. There they found abundant racism. The Minneapolis police were notorious in the 1970s for their abuse of Native Americans, who, in the interval between being picked up on the street – usually for drunkenness – and arriving at the jail, would often be severely beaten; in response, Indian patrols were organized to give people rides home. In "The New Apartment: Minneapolis" Hogan tells of "how last spring white merchants hung an elder / on a meathook and beat him / and he was one of The People." (He was accused of stealing a bottle of Lysol – a detail that Hogan reveals in her interview with Smith but that does not find its way into the poem.) The poem ends in the timelessness of ritual, where "there are no apartments, / just drumming and singing: / The Duck Song, The Snake Song, / The Drunk Song."

Broken bodies, some mending and some too weighted down to rise again, populate the last section of *Savings*. The sense of enclosure in "The New Apartment: Minneapolis" is found in many of these poems as well. "Neighbors" portrays the watching, listening city dweller; "This is the truth, not just a poem" and "This is a poem and not just the truth," the narrator declares, describing a desperate man who "holds his wife and children hostage / from life and bills." The will to live and to be whole resounds in the last lines:

> and hearts with their own chambers
> of living, hearts
> that want nothing,
> not paychecks
> on nightstands, not guns in the drawer,
> nothing
> but to know on walls of the body,
> let me in,
> let me travel veins to the eyes,
> light a candle
> with the arteries in nervous hands,
> and let me look out
> on the beating world.

As if to match the heart's looking out in this poem, the last poem of the collection, "What Gets In," ends with images of the world wanting in – into the world of the narrator and into the consciousness housed by the body and mind speaking: "No place is safe from invasion / and everything wants to live, even the moth with eyes on its wings flying in on light."

First published in the *Missouri Review* in 1989 and selected for inclusion in *The Best American Short Stories* the same year, "Aunt Moon's Young Man" is narrated by a Chickasaw girl who is fascinated by her "Aunt Moon," Bess Evening. Although she is not a blood relative of the girl, Aunt Moon treats the child with tenderness and respect, teaching her about the herbalist traditions through which she produces tonics, remedies, and cures, as well as passing along her philosophy to the youngster. Aunt Moon tells the narrator that "the soul is a small woman inside the eye who leaves at night to wander new places." Later, in speaking of her mother's limited life, the girl remarks, "the small woman inside her eye was full and lonely at the same time." Aunt Moon also tells her that "Women like us weren't meant to live on golden streets [in heaven]. We're Indians." Women who lust after gold, Aunt Moon says, have hearts like withered raisins; Indians know that they come from the mud, as all living creatures do.

A stranger, Isaac Cade, a full-blooded Indian, arrives in the town, where his father once lived. He brings out the lusty dreams of youth and lovemaking in the women and the carefree

Dust jacket for Hogan's novel about treachery and exploitation during the Osage oil boom in Oklahoma in the 1920s

belief in luck at cards in the men, but he beats them all at both: he becomes Bess Evening's lover, leaving the other women feeling shame for their unfulfilled lives; he takes money and treasured possessions from the men in card games, leaving them feeling foolish for their false hopes. He symbolizes all that the townspeople fear and suppress in themselves.

"Aunt Moon's Young Man" is remarkable for its finely honed language, its intriguing characterizations, and its vivid imagery. For example, the narrator describes the gossip Mrs. Tubby as "the town's chief social justice. She sat most days on the bench outside the grocery store. Sitting there like a full-chested hawk on a fence, she held court." Hogan captures the sensibility of budding womanhood in her young protagonist's struggles to understand sex and family; through conversations and interactions between the protagonist and her mother, Hogan delicately presents the mother's valiant efforts at parenting, in spite of her feelings of unfulfillment. Throughout, the reader sees the little things people do – for better or for worse – to make themselves feel important and useful.

In her novel *Mean Spirit* Hogan takes the reader on a journey to the heart of America, showing it not as a land of opportunity but as a land of the American Dream gone dreadfully and shamefully wrong. The novel is set in northeastern Oklahoma in the 1920s, during the Osage oil boom – known among the Indians as the Osage Reign of Terror or "the great frenzy" – and follows the Graycloud and Blanket families through a time when whites were exploiting, oppressing, and killing Native Americans to obtain the tribe's oil wealth. Since the income from oil was divided equally among all enrolled Osage tribe members, marrying an Osage woman could make a non-Indian man rich, particularly if the couple had children. Hogan quotes from an actual letter written by a young white man, C. J. Plimer of Joplin, Missouri, to the Indian agent in Pawhuska, Oklahoma, on 16 October 1907; in the novel the writer is unnamed and the agent is in the fictional town of Watona, Oklahoma. The writer says that he is seeking an Osage wife, "not a full blood, but . . . one as near white as possible." In exchange for helping him find a woman, the man offers to pay a fee: "for every Five Thousand Dollars she is worth I will give you Twenty-Five Dollars." Such blatantly materialistic grasping went hand-in-hand with spiritual intrusion on the part of the government, in its assimilation policies and its encouragement of missionaries among the Indians.

The novel opens in the summer of 1922. Belle Graycloud sleeps amid the herbs in her garden, where she has set up her bed for the summer while her more modern-minded family members sleep inside:

> That night the lights of fireflies and the songs of locusts were peaceful, as if nothing on earth had changed. How strange that life was as it had been on other summer nights with a moon rising behind the crisscross lines of oil derricks and the white stars blinking in a clear black sky.

Three groups of Indians are portrayed in the novel: the Watona town Indians; Indians living in shacks on the outskirts of the cities; and the Hill people, who live in a set-apart community. The presence in the novel of Stace Red Hawk, a bureaucrat sent from Washington, D.C., to investigate the troubles, suggests the Pan-Indian implications of the Osage people's resistance and struggle. The Hill people have sent one of their own, Grace Blanket, to live with Belle Graycloud in Watona, so that Grace can learn the new ways of the white people and function as an intermediary between the Hill people and the Indian and non-Indian communities around them.

As the dominance of the Osage people by whites increases, speech diminishes in effectiveness and is replaced by written documents that tell little of the truth. Indian complaints fall on deaf bureaucratic ears, and legally appointed white guardians become the spokesmen for Osages who are determined by the white-dominated courts to be incompetent to handle their own affairs. When a Bureau of Indian Affairs man and a nurse arrive to take Belle Graycloud's daughter, Nola, off to school, Belle's "arguments" fall "on closed ears." The matter is finally settled with a piece of paper: an order signed by the Indian agent demanding that Nola attend school.

Another kind of "speech" appears in the story, however: the older people beckon new life with words and songs, and the "old corn would tell the new corn how to grow." This quiet speech is contrasted throughout the novel with violent noise, as when Hale's girlfriend, China, witnesses an oil-rig fire:

> From where she stood, she saw Hale run toward the men, yelling. . . . Despite the roaring fire, China thought she could make out Hale's words. "It's burning out all the oil in the goddamned earth," he screamed. "Plug it! We've got to plug it." And they did. . . . the vision of it changed her. It was like watching hell rise up. She knew then that the earth had a mind of its own. She knew the wills and whims of men were empty desires, were nothing pitted up against the desires of earth.

Hogan's 1993 poetry volume *Book of Medicines* is divided into two long sections, "Hunger" and "Book of Medicines," preceded by a section titled after and including a single poem, "The History of Red." *Red* signifies the exposed, exploited earth and the rising up of a righteous revenge for its wounding:

> Red is this yielding land
> turned inside out
> by a country of hunters
> with iron, flint and fire.
> Red is the fear
> that turns a knife back
> against men, holds it at their throats,
> and they cannot see the claw on the handle,
> the animal hand.

A woman-centered environmentalist view emerges in Hogan's interview with Smith:

> I've often thought about how one of the things that was probably necessary for the woman's movement – the dominant culture woman's movement – was to break free of the duty of being a caretaker. . . . But then, for women to *return* to being caretakers, because it's important to offer service to the living, and to the planet. . . . I see a direct relationship between how we care for the animal-people and the plants and insects and land and water, and how we care for each other, and for ourselves. Part of our work here is to care for life.

As the bearers of life, women have, says Hogan, a special responsibility in taking care of life. *Book of Medicines* lays out a plan, much as the New Testament Gospels do, in which a new vision of the world takes shape; in Hogan's poem, however, God resides not above, but within nature. Biblical events from the Creation to the Fall from Grace to the Redemption are reinterpreted. "The History of Red" presents a vision of the first humans' harmony with animals and the rest of creation; the sections that follow, "Hunger" and "The Book of Medicines," represent the Fall and the Redemption, respectively.

Dust jacket for Hogan's novel about a teenage girl's journey to find her heritage

One poem in "Hunger," titled "The Fallen," depicts a narrator with godlike powers who declares,

I threw the fallen stone [comet] back to sky
and falling stars
and watched it all come down
to ruined earth again.

The narrator cannot, by an act of will, set right what has already been done; the desecrated earth requires its own time of regeneration. The wanton destruction of the she-wolf, "the mother of all women" in Native American belief, calls down the Great Wolf from the sky; but the Great Wolf descends to earth not, as the "new people" imagine, as Lucifer. Rather, it sees "with yellow eyes" how they have failed and knows "that they could kill the earth, / and they would kill each other." "Crossings," another poem in this section, tells of "the clan of crossings," real and metaphorical amphibians between sea and land, life and death:

There is a place at the center of the earth
where one ocean dissolves inside the other
in a black and holy love;
It's why the whales of one sea
know songs of the other,
why one thing becomes something else
and sand falls down the hourglass
into another time.

"Milk" ends the section, hunger and milk representing need and its satiation. Here Hogan's themes of women's power and nature's balance coalesce:

At the river one day
the women were washing cloth
blue as the flowing light of milk.
It could have been stolen by water,
carried away, except for the hands that held it.
Something must hold me this way,
and you,
and the thin blue tail of the galaxy,
to keep us from leaving.

What many would see as the power of God holding the universe in place, the poet metaphorically links to female tasks, the most ordinary of daily chores.

In the last section, "Book of Medicines," the poem "Flood: The Sheltering Tree" exemplifies the unifying powers of water:

Land takes back the forgotten name of rain
and speaks it
like a roar, dark and running
away from breaking sky.

The last poem, "The Origins of Corn," provides a finely crafted circling back to the themes of creation and continuance that were set up in the first poem, "The History of Red." "Old people with yellowed hair" become the bearers of medicines; seeds planted with love bring back the abundance to satisfy hunger.

Two books appeared late in 1995. *Dwellings: A Spiritual History of the Living World* gathers seventeen essays that express Hogan's belief in the interconnectedness of all life forms. In the preface she says that she writes "out of respect for the natural world, recognizing that humankind is not separate from nature." The opening sentences of the first essay, "The Feathers," capture the book's blending of personal experiences and general beliefs: "For years I prayed for an eagle feather. I wanted one from a bird still living. A killed eagle would offer me none of what I hoped for. A bird killed in the name of human power is in truth a loss of power from the world, not an addition to it." In the novel *Solar Storms* seventeen-year-old Angela Jensen leaves her foster home in Oklahoma and travels to a rural village in Minnesota called Adam's Rib. There she meets her great-grandmother, her great-great-grandmother, and Bush, the woman who cared for her when she was a baby. Together they journey in canoes searching for the great-great-grandmother's birthplace, which will be destroyed by a proposed hydroelectric dam. Both *Dwellings* and *Solar Storms* continue Hogan's celebration of the natural world and her powerful critique of those who scar that world.

Interviews:

"To Take Care of a Life," in *Survival This Way: Interviews with American Indian Poets,* edited by Joseph Bruchac (Tucson: University of Arizona Press, 1987), pp. 119–133;

Bo Schöler, "A Heart Made out of Crickets: An Interview with Linda Hogan," *Journal of Ethnic Studies,* 16 (Spring 1988): 107–117;

Laura Coltelli, "Linda Hogan," in her *Winged Words: American Indian Writers Speak* (Lincoln: University of Nebraska Press, 1990), pp. 71–86;

Patricia Clark Smith, "Linda Hogan," in *This is about Vision: Interviews with Southwestern Writers,* edited by William Balassi, John F. Crawford, and Annie O. Eysturoy (Albuquerque: University of New Mexico Press, 1990), pp. 141–155.

References:

Janet St. Clair, "Uneasy Ethnocentrism: Recent Works of Allen, Silko, and Hogan," *Studies in American Indian Literature,* 6 (Spring 1994): 83–98;

Studies in American Indian Literature, special issue on Hogan, edited by Betty Louise Bell, 6 (Fall 1994);

Terry P. Wilson, *The Underground Reservation: Osage Oil* (Lincoln: University of Nebraska Press, 1985).

E. Pauline Johnson (Tekahionwake)

(10 March 1861 - 7 March 1913)

A. LaVonne Brown Ruoff
University of Illinois at Chicago

See also the Johnson entry in *DLB 92: Canadian Writers, 1890-1920.*

BOOKS: *The White Wampum* (London: John Lane / Boston: Lamson, Wolffe, 1895);
Canadian Born (Toronto: Morang, 1903);
Legends of Vancouver (Vancouver, B.C.: Privately printed, 1911);
Flint and Feather (Toronto: Musson, 1912); republished, with introduction by Theodore Watts-Dunton (Toronto: Musson, 1913; London: Hodder & Stoughton, 1913);
The Moccasin Maker (Vancouver, B.C.: Briggs, 1913);
The Shagganappi (Toronto: Briggs, 1913).
Editions: *Pauline Johnson: Her Life and Work,* edited by Marcus Van Steen (Toronto: Musson, 1965);
Flint and Feather: The Complete Poems of E. Pauline Johnson (Tekahionwake) (Markam, Ont.: PaperJacks, 1972);
The Moccasin Maker, edited by A. LaVonne Brown Ruoff (Tucson: University of Arizona Press, 1987).

SELECTED PERIODICAL PUBLICATIONS – UNCOLLECTED: "Indian Medicine Men and Their Magic," *Dominion Illustrated,* 1 (April 1892): 140-143;
"Forty-Five Miles on the Grand," *Brantford Expositor* (December 1892): 19-20;
"The Iroquois of the Grand River," *Harper's Weekly,* 38 (23 June 1894): 587-589;
"The Six Nations," *Brantford Expositor,* Souvenir Number, 1895;
"A'bram," *Brantford Expositor,* December 1901, pp. 13, 16;
"The Cariboo Trail," *Toronto Saturday Night* (13 October 1906): revised as "Coaching on the Cariboo Trail," *Canadian Magazine,* 42 (February 1914): 399-400;

E. Pauline Johnson

"Mothers of a Great Red Race," *Mother's Magazine,* 3 (January 1908): 5, 14; revised as "Iroquois Women of Canada," *Halifax Herald,* 1909;
"Duke of Connaught as Chief of the Iroquois Indians," *Daily Province Magazine,* 2 July 1910, p. 4;
"The Great New Year White Dog: Sacrifice of the Onondagas," *Daily Province Magazine,* weekly supplement, 14 January 1911, p. 16.

The Mohawk writer and performer E[mily] Pauline Johnson (Tekahionwake) was born on 10 March 1861 at Chiefswood, the impressive house built by her father on the Grand River Reservation of the Six Nations near Brantford, Ontario. She was the daughter of George Henry Martin Johnson, also known as the Mohawk chief Teyonnhehkewea, and Emily Susanna Howells Johnson, the English-born cousin of William Dean Howells. A strong influence on Johnson was her paternal grandfather, John "Smoke" Johnson (Sakayengwaraton), a hero of the War of 1812 and a renowned orator in the Iroquois councils. A gifted speaker in his own right, her father frequently made speeches on behalf of his people and served as a liaison between them and the whites.

Johnson was primarily educated at home by her mother, who stimulated a love of literature in Pauline and her sister and two brothers by reading to them works by the English Romantics. Johnson's father was severely beaten in 1865 for trying to eradicate illegal alcohol and timber traffic on the reservation. Eight years later another gang beat and shot him and left him for dead; he survived but never fully recovered from his injuries. Despite these attacks, and another in 1878, George Johnson redoubled his efforts to curb lawlessness on the reservation.

At fourteen Pauline Johnson enrolled at the Brantford Collegiate Institute, where she particularly enjoyed performing in plays and pageants. After leaving school in 1877 she returned to Chiefswood and led the kind of life typical of young middle-class women of the time as they waited to be married: attending social activities, entertaining potential suitors, visiting friends and relatives and hosting them in return. She also wrote poetry, little of which has survived.

After George Johnson's death in 1884 the family could no longer afford to live at Chiefswood. In 1885 Pauline Johnson, her mother, and her sister moved to nearby Brantford. Johnson returned to writing poems, several of which were published in *The Week,* a Toronto magazine. Her career as a performer began in 1892 when her recitation of her poem "A Cry from an Indian Wife" at a Toronto literary evening electrified her audience. To earn money to go to Great Britain to arrange for the publication of her poetry, Johnson toured for the next two years, reciting her works to enthusiastic audiences in Ontario and along the East Coast of the United States. Billed as "The Mohawk Princess," Johnson performed the Indian portion of her program in a fringed buckskin dress of her own design and the remainder in an evening gown.

In April 1894 Johnson traveled to London, where she performed or was a guest in the homes of such prominent members of society as Sir Charles Tupper, the Canadian high commissioner to London; George Frederick Samuel Robinson, first marquis and second earl of Ripon, the former viceroy of India and Britain's colonial secretary; Lady Helen Munroe-Ferguson, duchess of Montrose; and Lady Constance Villiers Stanley, countess of Derby.

Johnson's first volume of poetry, *The White Wampum* (1895), comprising thirty-six poems, established Johnson as an Indian writer of talent and sensibility. *The Week* praised her "power of lucid, picturesque, forcible expression." The destructiveness of intertribal warfare is the theme of several of the eight poems that are devoted to Indian subjects. "As Red Men Die," a tribute to an ancestor of the author's, describes the bravery of a Mohawk captive who defies his Huron torturers. "Dawadine" recounts the legend of an Indian maid's love for an enemy warrior. "Ojistoh," a melodramatic monologue with complex sexual overtones, depicts a Mohawk wife's struggle to outwit the Hurons who kidnap her: riding behind one of her captors, Ojistoh seduces her enemy into loosening her bonds and then kills him with his own knife. In "Cattle Thief" a Cree woman's powerful speech about how whites have destroyed the Indians dissuades white vigilantes from mutilating the body of the fearless Brave Eagle, whom they have just murdered for stealing cattle to feed his people. In "A Cry from an Indian Wife" a woman alternates between grief at the knowledge that her husband will probably die if he goes to war against whites and her courageous commitment to resisting white depredations against her people.

"Wolverine," a dramatic monologue told in dialect by a white narrator, chronicles whites' unjust treatment of an Indian brave who tries to help them, while tragic love between a white man and an Indian woman is the focus of "The Pilot of the Plains." Some of Johnson's Indian poems lament the inevitability of the displacement of traditional Indian life by white migration. "The Happy Hunting Grounds" celebrates the beauty of the western prairies and mourns the demise of the Plains Indians' traditional way of life. This displacement is also the subject of "Joe," a portrait of a nine-year-old "semi-savage" son of white settlers who husks Indian corn before shambling home to the backwoods, where forests await the pioneer's ax and the settler's plow.

Most of the poems in the volume are lyrical evocations of nature; especially popular were those on canoeing. Johnson's best-known poem is "The Song My Paddle Sings," which was memorized by generations of Canadian schoolchildren. The author, an accomplished canoeist, describes drifting dreamily along a river and then plunging through the boiling rapids to arrive at a silent pool. Another favorite is the descriptive-reflective "Shadow River (Muskoka)," a delicate lyric in which the author depicts her reactions as she floats on the river. "In the Shadows," which recalls Alfred Tennyson's "Soft and Low," captures the author's sensuous response to nature while canoeing languorously on the river:

On the water's idle pillow
Sleeps the overhanging willow,
Green and cool;
Where the rushes lift their burnished
Oval heads from out the tarnished
Emerald pool.

Her nature lyrics also reflect her reading of the poetry of James Thomson, Percy Bysshe Shelley, and A. C. Swinburne.

For most of Johnson's adult life, performing was her major source of income. Following her return to Canada in July 1894, she expanded her tours to western Ontario, northern Michigan, Manitoba, and British Columbia. After her mother died in 1898 Johnson moved to Winnipeg. That year she became engaged to Charles Robert Lumley Drayton, whose parents opposed their son's marriage to a mixed-blood stage performer who was older than he. Drayton broke the engagement in 1900 to marry someone else. Vulnerable after her broken engagement and the loss of her mother, Johnson may have been romantically involved in 1900–1901 with her unscrupulous manager, Charles Wuerz (in *Pauline: A Biography of Pauline Johnson* [1981] Betty Keller incorrectly gives his name as Wurz). The theme of the betrayal of Indian women by white men runs through many of her works, both before and after her relationships with Drayton and Wuerz. In 1909 Walter McRaye, with whom she had toured briefly in 1897, became her partner and manager.

Johnson's second poetry collection, *Canadian Born* (1903), disappointed critics because it included many poems written years earlier and because the new ones lacked the fresh voice of the earlier volume. *Canadian Born* comprises thirty-one poems; especially poignant is "The Corn Husker," in which an old Indian woman, "Age in her fingers, hunger in her face, / Her shoulders stooped with weight of work and years," remembers the days before injustice banished her people, who are unheeded like "the dead husks that rustle through her hands," from their land. Johnson also pays tribute to Indian women in "The Quill Worker," about the daughter of a Sioux chief. "The Legend of Qu' Apelle Valley" describes a young brave's journey to his beloved, only to find her dead. The best of the other poems focus on nature; one of these, "Crows' Nest Pass," was undoubtedly influenced by Shelley's "Mont Blanc."

Poster advertising Johnson's first book

Johnson received rave reviews for her performances in London in 1906. In 1907 she and McRaye toured the midwestern United States, Colorado, and Massachusetts. That year she began contributing stories and articles to *The Mother's Magazine* and *Boys' World,* both of which were published by the David C. Cook Company of Elgin, Illinois. In 1908 she retired from performing and settled in Vancouver. She continued writing for the two magazines until 1912.

Legends of Vancouver (1911), which Johnson wanted to call "Legends of the Capilanos," gathers together her imaginative and dramatic interpretations of stories from the Northwest Coast Indians, many of which she learned from Chief Joe Capilano, an old Squamish chief she had met in London in 1906. Johnson also incorporates some Iroquois stories. The stories, many of which originally appeared in the *Vancouver Province* in 1910 and 1911, include some of her best writing. "Deep Waters" includes both Squamish and Iroquois flood myths. "A Royal Mohawk Chief" recounts the 1869 ceremony in which Queen Victoria's son Arthur, duke of Connaught, was made a chief of the Six Nations Indians; the author's Mohawk grandfather and father participated in the event. Most of the Northwest Coast stories are associated with specific places, which Johnson describes in poetic detail. She frames the Indian stories with a description of the circumstances of the storytelling, such as conversations she had with Capilano during a walk or family picnic or a chance meeting with an old Salish woman friend. Johnson concludes each story with a return to the setting, the storyteller, and the listener. She achieves a far more conversational style in this volume than in her original fiction or her poetry.

From the beginning of her career Johnson took on the role of serving as a mediator between the Indian, particularly the Iroquois, and white worlds. She explained Iroquois history, culture, and customs in such articles as "Indian Medicine Men and Their Magic" (1892); "The Iroquois of the Grand River" (1894); "The Six Nations" (1895); "A'bram" (1901); "Mothers of a Great Red Race" (1908), revised as "Iroquois Women of Canada" (1909); and "The Great New Year White Dog: Sacrifice of the Onondagas" (1911). In "A Strong Race Opinion on the Indian Girl in Modern Fiction" (1892), most of which is reprinted in Keller's book, Johnson criticizes the portrayals of Indian women by non-Indian writers. She strongly attacks white authors for denying Indian girls' spontaneity, originality, and specific tribal backgrounds while depicting them as suicidal and as victims of doomed love affairs. Keller, however, argues that Johnson's own later articles and comments sometimes seem condescending and reflect a loss of faith in the Indians' adaptability. Johnson's skill as a travel writer is exemplified in "Forty-Five Miles on the Grand" (1892) and especially in "Coaching on the Cariboo Trail" (1914), a revised and expanded version of "The Cariboo Trail" (1906).

In 1912 Johnson published *Flint and Feather,* including poems from her two earlier volumes as well as additional work. During the final stages of her struggle with cancer her supporters published *The Shagganappi* (1913), a collection of twenty-one stories and an essay on how the Iroquois raised their sons. Dedicated to the Boy Scouts, the volume includes a tribute to Johnson by Ernest Thompson Seton. The stories, which are designed to provide boys with suitable role models, recount the exploits of Indian and non-Indian boys courageously facing danger and doing good deeds. The Indians are uniformly generous, honest, and loyal to the whites they befriend. Johnson's concern with the theme of the mixed-blood is reflected in the title story, which depicts the prejudice encountered by young Fire Flint Larocque, who is part French but mostly Cree. The stories provide ethnographic information on such groups as the Iroquois, Blackfoot, and Salish. Some are fictionalized versions of actual events, such as "The Delaware Idol," an account of how her father destroyed a Delaware religious artifact when he was sixteen. Johnson died on 7 March 1913.

Johnson's finest lyrics are "Morrow Land," written at Easter 1900; "Heidelburgh" (originally titled "To C. W."); and "Song," all unpublished in her lifetime. Keller and Carole Gerson conjecture that these poems reflect Johnson's relationship with Wuerz. *Canadian Magazine* published "Song" in October 1913 and "Heidelburgh" – here spelled "Heidelberg" – in November 1913. Mrs. W. Garland Foster published "Morrow Land" in *The Mohawk Princess* (1931). "Heidelburgh" reveals powerful and bitter personal emotions not present in Johnson's earlier work. Her mature lyricism is exemplified in "Song":

> The night-long shadows faded into gray,
> Then silvered into glad and gold sunlight,
> Because you came to me, like a new day
> Born of the beauty of an autumn night.

The author's supporters collected her stories about women and her essay "A Pagan in St. Paul's Cathedral" as *The Moccasin Maker,* which was published posthumously in 1913. Like the heroines in most women's nineteenth-century fiction, the female protagonists of Johnson's stories inevitably triumph over great difficulty. They and their lovers recognize that genuine love between men and women reflects shared values. Johnson combines the domestic romance with protest literature, expressing her anger at the injustices experienced by women and Indians in "Red Girl's Reasoning" and "As It Was in the Beginning," two of the best stories in the collection. In both, she combines the plot of the mixed-blood woman betrayed by a weak white lover with a forceful attack on white religious hypocrisy. "The Legend of Lillooet Falls," "Tenas Klootchman," and "Catherine of the 'Crow's Nest' " depict the deep love Indian women feel for their natural and adopted children, as well as the roles they play as guardians of tribal traditions. Mother love is also a powerful force in Johnson's stories about white frontier women, such as "My Mother," a fictionalized account of her parents' courtship and marriage. In "A Pagan in St. Paul's Cathedral" Johnson draws parallels between Indian and white religions and concludes that the differences are unimportant.

Critics have had mixed reactions to Johnson's work. Although they have praised the lyricism of some of her poems, they also have noted her tendency to sentimentalism in her verse and her fiction. Many focused on the extent to which her Indian poetry was or was not authentic. Charles Mair, a Canadian poet and a friend of Johnson's, acclaimed her as one " 'who spoke loud and bold,' not for the Iroquois alone, but for the whole red race, and sang of its glories and its wrongs in strains of poetic fire." The British critic Theodore Watts-Dunton saw her as representing an authentic Indian voice and predicted in his introduction to the 1913 edition of *Flint and Feather* that Johnson would hold a "memorable place among poets in virtue of her descent and also in virtue of the work she has left behind, small as the quantity of that work is." Johnson's reputation reached its zenith in the 1920s, when Canadian critics focused new attention on her generation of writers. The reaction against her poetry is voiced most forcefully by A. J. M. Smith, who argues that critics and journalists played up her Indian birth, which "has been accepted as convincing proof that she spoke with the authentic voice of the Red Man." Smith is unaware, however, that the poetry of many nineteenth- and turn-of-the-century Indian writers was strongly influenced by English and American romanticism.

The 1960s and 1970s saw a renewed interest in Johnson's poetry. Ray Daniels, a Canadian literary scholar, ascribes her popularity to the fact that she wrote at the beginning of Canadian literature and "satisfied a felt need. Like [Robert] Service and [William Wilfrid] Campbell, she associates a broadly Romantic view of life with the elements of the vast natural landscape." Norman Shrive says that Johnson was "one of the few people who saw through the new popular image of the Indian and said so in writing" but that her work reflects the "flabby Victorian romanticism so familiar" in the art of the period.

Elizabeth Loosely emphasizes the Indian-white dualism in Johnson's work. Loosely and Marcus Van Steen suggest that Johnson's need to perform and write to support herself and her mother may have prevented her from reaching her full potential. George W. Lyon notes that Johnson does not create characters or actions in her Indian poems that are "culturally representative of any tribe." Like Loosely, he finds Johnson both attracted to and repulsed by Christianity. A. LaVonne Brown Ruoff has focused new attention on *The Moccasin Maker;* in her introduction to the 1987 edition of that work and in her article "Justice for Indians and Women: The Protest Fiction of Alice Callahan and Pauline Johnson" (1992) she examines Johnson's use of the domestic romance and the traditions of sentimentalism popular in nineteenth- and turn-of-the-century women's fiction as a vehicle for protesting injustices to Native American women.

With the rise of interest in Native American and women's literature Johnson has gained new readers. In the United States there is greater interest in her prose than in her poetry. The first Indian woman to publish books of poetry and a collection of short fiction, Johnson was also one of the first to explore the theme of the search for identity of those with mixed ancestry and to focus on issues affecting Indian women.

Biographies:

Mrs. W. Garland Foster, *The Mohawk Princess, Being Some Account of the Life of Takahion-wake (E. Pauline Johnson)* (Vancouver, B.C.: Lions Gate, 1931);

Walter McRaye, *Pauline Johnson and Her Friends* (Toronto: Ryerson, 1947);

Betty Keller, *Pauline: A Biography of Pauline Johnson* (Vancouver, B.C.: Douglas & McIntyre, 1981).

References:

Ray Daniels, "Minor Poets 1880–1920," in *Literary History of Canada: Canadian Literature in English,* volume 1, edited by Carl F. Klinck, second edition (Toronto: University of Toronto Press, 1976), pp. 438–446;

Carole Gerson,"Some Notes Concerning Pauline Johnson," *Canadian Notes & Queries,* 34 (1985): 16–19;

Elizabeth Loosely, "Pauline Johnson," in *The Clear Spirit: Twenty Canadian Women and Their Times,* edited by Mary Quayle Innes (Toronto: University of Toronto Press, 1966), pp. 74–90;

George W. Lyon, "Pauline Johnson: A Reconsideration," *Studies in Canadian Literature,* 15, no. 2 (1990): 136–159;

Charles Mair, "Johnson: An Appreciation," *Canadian Magazine,* 41 (July 1913): 281–283;

Walter McRaye, *Town Hall To-Night* (Toronto: Ryerson, 1929);

A. LaVonne Brown Ruoff, "Justice for Indians and Women: The Protest Fiction of Alice Callahan and Pauline Johnson," *World Literature Today, from This World,* issue on Contemporary American Indian Literature, 6, no. 2 (1992): 249–255;

Norman Shrive, "What Happened to Pauline?," *Canadian Literature,* 13 (Summer 1962): 25–38;

A. J. M. Smith, " 'Our Poets': A Sketch of Canadian Poetry in the Nineteenth-Century," *University of Toronto Quarterly,* 12 (1942): 75–94.

Papers:

The Johnson family papers are in the Brant Historical Society and Museum, Brantford, Ontario. The Mills Memorial Library, McMaster University, Hamilton, Ontario, has the largest collection of materials about Johnson in its Emily Pauline Johnson and Walter McRaye Collections. Additional artifacts and materials are in the Museum and the Archives of the City of Vancouver. The North York Public Library in North York, Ontario, has letters about Johnson from McRaye and Charles Mair to Newton McFaul MacTavish in the MacTavish papers. Other papers can be found in libraries of the University of Toronto, Queens University, and the University of Western Ontario.

Maurice Kenny

(16 August 1929 -   )

Michael D. Wilson
University of Wisconsin – Milwaukee

BOOKS: *Dead Letters Sent, and Other Poems* (New York: Troubador, 1958);

With Love to Lesbia: A Sheaf of Poems (New York: Aardvark, 1958);

And Grieve, Lesbia: Poems (New York: Aardvark, 1960);

North: Poems of Home (Marvin, S.Dak.: Blue Cloud Quarterly, 1977);

Dancing Back Strong the Nation: Poems, introduction by Paula Gunn Allen (Marvin, S.Dak.: Blue Cloud Quarterly, 1979; revised and enlarged edition, Buffalo, N.Y.: White Pine, 1981);

I Am the Sun (Buffalo, N.Y.: White Pine, 1979);

Only as Far as Brooklyn (Boston: Good Gay Poets, 1979);

Kneading the Blood (New York: Strawberry, 1981);

Boston Tea Party (San Francisco: Soup, 1982);

Blackrobe: Isaac Jogues, b. March 11, 1604, d. October 18, 1646: Poems (Saranac Lake, N.Y.: North Country Community College Press, 1982);

The Smell of Slaughter (Marvin, S.Dak.: Blue Cloud Quarterly, 1982);

The Mama Poems (Buffalo, N.Y.: White Pine, 1984);

Is Summer This Bear (Saranac Lake, N.Y.: Chauncey, 1985);

Rain and Other Fictions (Marvin, S.Dak.: Blue Cloud Quarterly, 1985; revised edition, Buffalo, N.Y.: White Pine, 1990);

Between Two Rivers: Selected Poems 1956–1984 (Fredonia, N.Y.: White Pine, 1987);

Humors and/or Not So Humorous (Buffalo, N.Y.: Swift Kick, 1987);

Greyhounding This America: Poems and Dialog (Chico, Cal.: Heidelberg Graphics, 1988);

The Short and Long of It (Little Rock: University of Arkansas Native Studies Program, 1990);

Last Mornings in Brooklyn (Norman, Okla.: Renegade, 1991);

Tekonwatonti, Molly Brant, 1735–1795: Poems of War (Fredonia, N.Y.: White Pine, 1992);

On Second Thought: A Compilation (Norman: University of Oklahoma Press, 1995);

Backward to Forward: Essays (Buffalo, N.Y.: White Pine, 1997).

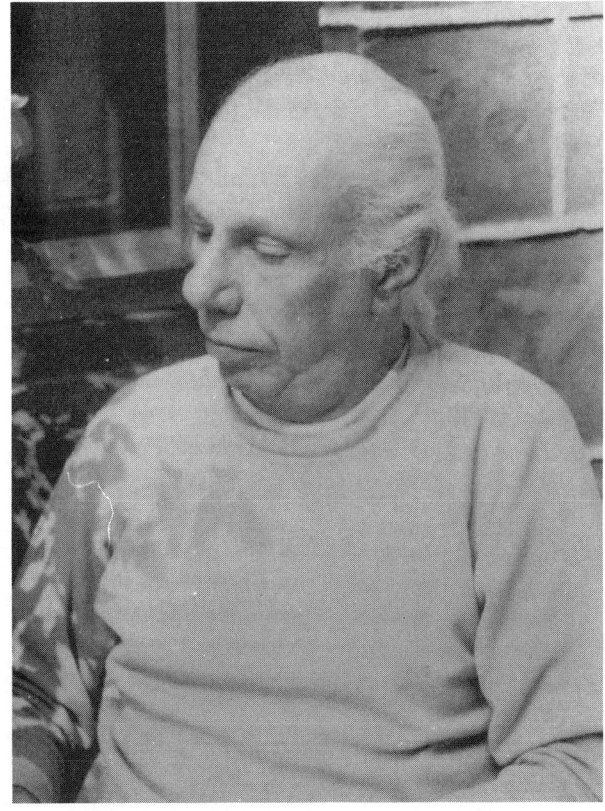

Maurice Kenny (courtesy of White Pine Press)

OTHER: "Adowe: We Return Thanks," in *The Remembered Earth: An Anthology of Contemporary Native American Literature,* edited by Geary Hobson (Albuquerque: University of New Mexico Press, 1981), pp. 13–16;

Wounds beneath the Flesh, edited by Kenny (Marvin, S.Dak.: Blue Cloud Quarterly, 1983);

Michael Castro, *Interpreting the Indian: Twentieth-Century Poets and the Native American,* introduction by Kenny (Albuquerque: University of New Mexico Press, 1983);

"Yaikni," in *Earth Power Coming: Short Fiction in Native American Literature,* edited by Simon J. Ortiz

(Tsaile, Ariz.: Navajo Community College Press, 1983), pp. 103–115;

"Waiting at the Edge: Words toward a Life," in *I Tell You Now: Autobiographical Essays by Native American Writers,* edited by Brian Swann and Arnold Krupat (Lincoln: University of Nebraska Press, 1987), pp. 37–54;

New Voices from the Longhouse: An Anthology of Contemporary Iroquois Writing, edited by Joseph Bruchac; consulting editors, Kenny and Karoniaktatie (Greenfield Center, N.Y.: Greenfield Review, 1989);

"Wet Moccasins," in *Talking Leaves: Contemporary Native American Short Stories,* edited by Craig Lesley (New York: Dell, 1991), pp. 173–183;

"Fear and Recourse," in *Earth Song, Sky Spirit: Short Stories of the Contemporary Native American Experience,* edited by Clifford E. Trafzer (Garden City, N.Y.: Doubleday, 1992), pp. 163–188;

"Sky Woman" and "Now it seems there were brothers . . . ,' " in *Returning the Gift: Poetry and Prose from the First North American Native Writers' Festival,* edited by Bruchac (Tucson: University of Arizona Press, 1994), pp. 178–181;

"Legacy" and "They Tell Me I Am Lost," in *Smoke Rising: The Native North American Literary Companion,* edited by Janet Witalec (Detroit: Visible Ink, 1995), pp. 269–275.

SELECTED PERIODICAL PUBLICATIONS – UNCOLLECTED: "The Creative Process: Wild Strawberry," *Wicazo Sa Review,* 1 (Spring 1985): 40–44;

"Blackening the Robe," *Studies in American Indian Literature,* 4 (Fall 1985): 153–158.

Twice nominated for the Pulitzer Prize, and a recipient of the American Book Award for *The Mama Poems* in 1984, Maurice Kenny is one of the most innovative and influential poets to emerge from the renaissance of American Indian literature during the 1970s. Prolific and versatile, Kenny experiments with voice and verse structures to approximate Indian songs, dance, and nature philosophy, especially those of his Mohawk ancestors. In addition to being an innovative and award-winning poet, Kenny is a former editor of the influential journal *Contact II* and was the founder in 1976 of the Strawberry Press, which is dedicated to the publication of works by Indian authors. He frequently travels across the country, giving readings and enthusiastic encouragement to younger Indian poets. In both his personal and professional life Kenny has been a major contributor to the growth and health of the field of Native American literature.

Much of the power of Kenny's poetry derives from his Iroquois heritage; his mother was Seneca and his father Mohawk. Born on 16 August 1929 in Watertown, New York, to Andrew Anthony and Doris Marie Parker Herrick Kenny, Maurice Francis Kenny grew up, he says in "Waiting at the Edge: Words toward a Life" (1987), in the foothills of the Adirondack Mountains with his parents and sisters. His childhood was not an especially pleasant one, for he frequently found himself alone because of his natural shyness. When he was thirteen Kenny, one of his sisters, and their mother, who had separated from their father, moved to Bayonne, New Jersey; but after about a year Kenny got into trouble at school and was "rescued" by his father, who took him back to Watertown.

Kenny remained in New York until his late teens, after which he spent several years in Saint Louis, Missouri, with his sister's family before enrolling at Butler College in Indianapolis in 1952. There Werner Beyer, a John Keats scholar, and Roy Marz, a religious poet, steered him away from poetry toward prose. During this time Kenny corresponded with the poet John Crowe Ransom, who, like Marz, thought that Kenny lacked the intuitive sense of rhythm required for poetry. Kenny, recalling this period, says in "Waiting at the Edge": "Little did either poets or teachers ever suspect that European classical poetry might not be my forte."

In 1956 Kenny left Butler for Saint Lawrence University in Canton, New York, near the Akwesasne reservation, the home of his father. There Douglas Angus, a novelist, encouraged him to go back to poetry, a suggestion for which Kenny says in the introduction to *Between Two Rivers: Selected Poems 1956–1984* (1987) that he "will always be thankful." At his father's request, Kenny took and passed the entrance examination for Columbia University, but he decided instead to work in a bookstore. In 1957–1958 he attended New York University, where he studied under the poet Louise Bogan. Bogan taught him the value of a heightened sense of detail in poetry, a lesson of critical importance since it showed him how to create strong moments of identification between poet and reader. He says in *Between Two Rivers:* "To her, a tree was not a tree but an elm, a white pine, a birch; a bird was not a bird but a hawk, a titmouse; a river was not a river but the St. Lawrence or Mohawk. You establish communication by identification."

This idea of establishing communication by identification is fundamental to Kenny's poetry, which derives much of its power by establishing a unique language of place, an intense offering of detail that is peculiar to a region or to a tribal community. It is perhaps this moment of identification that Kenny refers to as "home," which exists anywhere that one finds an acute sense of linguistic identification. Kenny writes in "Waiting at the Edge": " 'Place' is an extremely important theme in my poetry, and I have been questioned many times where that 'place,' that 'home' is. Is it northern New York with mountains and rivers, woods and fields; is it the reservation, the town in which I grew up; or is it Brooklyn, where I currently live? . . . It is all these places and things. It is even, yes, even the poems themselves."

Working out this relationship to his home has been an issue for Kenny since his earliest work, written while he was under the tutelage of Bogan. In "Dead Letters Sent," included in his first collection, *Dead Letters Sent, and Other Poems* (1958), for example, the narrator contemplates his uneasy relationship to his home, for he lacks a close relationship to his love, who is gone, and to the land, which is difficult to farm:

> Now there are long
> Moments to think of you before the dust
> Drives the fields to weeds and the corn leans
> In the heat of the sun.

The narrator has "fought the muscled earth, / The bugs and even God to get a crop," and he derives a sense of strength and purpose from farming. Still, the prevailing mood of the poem is one of loss:

> Home is a house of ghosts and shadows, sounds
> which are restless throughout the long dark night,
> Dark even when the moon lies asleep on the pillow.
> A man can't take the moonlight in his arms.

The poem is a necessary but perhaps futile attempt to recover a connection, to establish a moment of communication with both the land and the lost love.

After *Dead Letters Sent* and *With Love to Lesbia: A Sheaf of Poems* (1958) – the latter, Kenny says, is highly imitative of Catullus – Kenny did not publish poetry for more than a decade. During this period he held various jobs, including waiting tables and writing obituaries for the *Chicago Sun.* His next major publication, "I Am the Sun," appeared in the Indian newspaper *Akwesasne Notes* in 1973 and signaled Kenny's turn toward American Indian themes and traditions. But even as early as 1969 or 1970, Kenny said in a 1987 interview with Joseph Bruchac, he was writing poems, such as "First Rule," that defined a philosophical position with respect to Indian traditions, nature, and writing.

"First Rule" is the opening poem in *North: Poems of Home* (1977), a collection that consists mostly of reflections about Kenny's relationships to the land and people of northern New York – poems such as "Black River," "In North Country Graveyards," "Home," "North (In Memory of My Father)," and "Land." Unlike *Dead Letters Sent,* Kenny's later poetry usually establishes strong connections with nature; indeed, in many of the poems, as James Ruppert notes, "the narrative voice speaks from the point of view of the natural object." The poems in *North* display the power a detailed identification with the landscape has to create a sense of community and belonging.

In "First Rule" – which, Kenny said in his interview with Bruchac, would be the "frontispiece if my autobiography is ever published" – the central image is that of expanding circles of ripples in a pool. Alongside this natural image Kenny places the image of a man-made circle of stones that mirrors nature, as does his poetry:

> stones must form a circle first not a wall
> open so that it may expand
> to take in new grass and hills
> tall pines and a river
> expand as sun on weeds, an elm, robins.

This expanding circle of stones is solid yet permeable, stable yet changing, indicating a valuing both of tradition and of innovation. The poem demonstrates the importance of finding and securing a sense of home, along with an understanding that the concept of home is constantly changing. Furthermore, the poem suggests not only the value of the traditional circles of value but also their necessity: "words cannot be spoken first" – that is, actions must dominate. Without this sense of home, this preexisting community of language and traditions, one is unable to speak or to be heard. Kenny said in the Bruchac interview: "It was probably that poem which led me back into the oral tradition."

I Am the Sun, which was published separately in 1979, relies heavily on the oral tradition of the Lakota people. Kenny says that he wrote the poem in 1973 during the confrontation of members of the American Indian Movement and federal agents at Wounded Knee, South Dakota, because a heart attack prevented him from participating in any way except to "sing it out of me." *I Am the Sun* is based on a chant from the Ghost Dance religion, a movement among many tribes in the late 1800s that attempted to resurrect the past spiritually and even

Cover for the collection of poems in which Kenny tries to reunify his family

physically through songs and dances. The poem consists of chanting refrains:

> Chankpe Opi Wakpala!
> Chankpe Opi Wakpala!
> Chankpe Opi Wakpala!
> Father, give us no more graves;
> Father, give us back our arrows!
> We have learned to hold them sacred.

A note at the end of the poem says that "This chant is based upon a Lakota-Sioux Ghost Dance Song. *Chankpe Opi Wakpala* is Lakota-Sioux meaning Wounded Knee."

The metaphor of the Ghost Dance reflects the beginning of Kenny's desire to reaffirm the power of the past, as he does in *Dancing Back Strong the Nation* (1979) and in his two volumes of historical poetry, *Blackrobe: Isaac Jogues, b. March 11, 1604, d. October 18, 1646: Poems* (1982) and *Tekonwatonti, Molly Brant, 1735–1795: Poems of War* (1992). In each of these works Kenny establishes a language that draws him, his tribal past, and the reader together. In the Bruchac interview he described "home" as a "way of drawing a reader's very rich imagination into my imagination." These moments of identification among history, reader, and author establish circles within which identification and communication can occur. The past, then, is another language of home, a language Kenny recharges and enlivens for others to see, to understand, and to embrace.

In *Blackrobe,* for which he received a Pulitzer Prize nomination, Kenny presents poetic perspectives on the Jesuit priest Isaac Jogues's life among the Mohawk people. Although it is principally about Jogues, the book begins with the story of the bringing together of five tribes by the Peacemaker to form the Iroquois Confederacy in the fifteenth century. The book also ends with poems about the Peacemaker, suggesting an abiding tradition that existed before, and will continue to exist long after, the coming of other religious and political forces. Within this frame – this "home" – Kenny chronicles the life of Jogues to his death at the hands of the Mohawks. Kenny draws from historical records and the oral tradition to provide a montage of voices describing Jogues's commitment, foolhardiness, and arrogance in his relationship with the Mohawk people. He allows these voices to give different, sometimes inconsistent interpretations of events: among those who speak are Jogues's "aunt," who adopts Jogues and tries to keep him alive; a French report that calls Jogues a fool and expresses outrage at his willingness to anger a possible ally in the Mohawks; and Jogues himself, who ignores and devalues Haudenosaunee stories, medicines, and customs. In the poem "People of the Flint," Jogues says:

> I openly refute their foolish tales
> that the world was built on a turtle's back.
> I try to reason that the sun possesses no intelligence,
> and that the sun is no god to man nor moose.

Blackrobe shows that a vital, unified Native community existed prior to and after the coming of non-Indian people and that no single voice is capable of telling the complete history of Iroquois-Jesuit relations, whether it be Jogues's, Kenny's, or the voice of divine providence.

In *Tekonwatonti, Molly Brant, 1735–1795* Kenny follows Brant's life from her birth, showing her lifelong devotion to the British loyalist William Johnson and her willingness to lead men into battle, and ending with her exile, death, and burial away from Mohawk country. Kenny writes in the preface that he is completing a circle not only for Brant but also for himself: "Two Mohawks, Molly and her poet, return to home country having left, I hope, some mark on the western country." Brant's story, Kenny points out, has been long neglected, partly because she was a woman and partly because she lived in the shadow of her famous brother, Joseph Brant (Theyendanegea). Both Kenny and Brant leave their homes and widen their circle of influence, later to return to their homes – Kenny physically, Brant as a chapter in the story of the Iroquois people.

As he did *Blackrobe,* Kenny begins *Tekonwatonti* with a poem about the Peacemaker, thus establishing the context of the drama within Iroquois traditions and thought. Also similar to the method of *Blackrobe* is the way Kenny puts together a montage of voices about Brant's life, including those of Johnson; Aroniateka, the Mohawk leader also known as Chief Hendrick; Brant herself; and such recent writers as E. Pauline Johnson and Jennie Sanford, who provide a vital link between the past and the present. The words are Kenny's, but the facts are drawn from many sources. Each voice, old or new, provides a dramatic and personal perspective on the events of Molly's life and the lives of other Haudenosaunee people before, during, and after the Revolutionary War. Kenny's method shows the significance of these events not only as important moments in history but also as defining moments for present-day Native American people.

In *The Mama Poems,* which won an American Book Award, Kenny again demonstrates the complexity of his conception of "home." As he did *Blackrobe* and *Tekonwatonti,* he places this book of poems within the context of Iroquoian traditions. In the first piece, "1911," he writes about his mother's difficult childhood, when she cleaned her father's house and picked berries until she "bled profusely on the fruit." The stain of these berries remained on her face for the rest of her life: "And it stayed on your cheek. It was there last month in the coffin. Brilliant in its / birthmark. Not even my kiss washed it away."

In the next piece, "Little Voices," Kenny recounts the traditional story of the gift from the "little people" of strawberries and stories to a starving family, which ensures the continued physical and cultural health of the Iroquois. By emphasizing his mother's connection with the berries and by telling the stories of his family in *The Mama Poems* Kenny establishes thematic links among his family, his poetry, and Iroquois oral traditions. His approach suggests the healing power, both for individual families and for communities of Native American people, of stories and poetry that emerge from their traditions.

Kenny in 1982 (photography by Paul Rosado)

Establishing these connections, however, is often a painful process, for "home" in *The Mama Poems* is a complex site of conflict, rage, devotion, and love. Because of his parents' separation the family left its home in the Adirondacks and scattered. The book attempts to counter this dispersal, bringing the family back together through memory, desire, and art. The dedication reads: "For my Mother Doris (d. 2/22/82), my sisters, Agnes and Mary, and in memory of my father, Andrew . . . we are together again." The final two poems in the book show the tensions in this project of recovery. The penultimate poem, "Place," which begins, "Come home," presents positive recollections of home that include berry pie, old movies, and chocolate walnut fudge. But the final poem, "1982," which begins "Home," questions the possibility of such easy resolutions to and recollections of history. It questions the validity of photographs and memorabilia that the poet and his mother possess, showing that these icons are "facades" for the complexity that they seem to represent. His mother, the poet says, not only believed these facades but was herself an example of such a facade. "Withered age was merely a mask" on his mother, he says, for she was essentially a "girl" and a "flirt." The poems suggest that making a vital connection with home is not a simple act of affirmation and closure but a constant and changing relationship to memories, emotions, and stories from the past: "We're still reaching for an understanding. Of so many things."

Because of the honesty and depth of Kenny's poetry, his reputation has grown steadily, especially since the publication of award-winning works such as *Blackrobe* and *The Mama Poems.* In 1987 *Between Two Rivers* was nominated for the Pulitzer Prize. This important collection shows Kenny's development from his early poems, written under Bogan's tutelage, to recent works inspired by his Iroquoian culture and history.

Although principally known as a poet, Kenny has published many essays, some of which are collected in *Backward to Forward* (1997). He has also written drama and short fiction, a sampling of which is collected in *Rain and Other Fictions* (1985). His short fiction has also appeared in several anthologies, including *Earth Power Coming* (1983), *Talking Leaves* (1991), *Earth Song, Sky Spirit* (1992), *Returning the Gift* (1994), and *Smoke Rising* (1995).

Interview:

Joseph Bruchac, "Our Own Pasts: An Interview with Maurice Kenny," in his *Survival This Way: Interviews with American Indian Poets* (Tucson: University of Arizona Press, 1987).

Bibliography:

"ASAIL Bibliography 4," *Studies in American Indian Literature,* 7 (Winter 1983): 1–13.

References:

Joseph Bruchac, "New Voices from the Longhouse: Some Contemporary Iroquois Writers and Their Relationship to the Tradition of the Ho-de-no-sau-nee," in *Coyote Was Here: Essays on Contemporary Native American Literary and Political Mobilization,* edited by Bo Schöler (Århus, Denmark: Seklos, 1984), pp. 147–161;

James Ruppert, "The Uses of the Oral Tradition in Six Contemporary Native American Poets," *American Indian Cultural and Research Journal,* 4, no. 4 (1980): 87–110;

Carolyn Scott, "Baskets of Sweetgrass: Maurice Kenny's *Dancing Back the Strong Nation* and *I Am the Sun,*" *Studies in American Indian Literature,* 7 (Winter 1983): 8–13;

Andrew Wiget, *Native American Literature* (Boston: Twayne, 1985), p. 112.

Thomas King

(24 April 1943 -)

James Ruppert
University of Alaska – Fairbanks

BOOKS: *Medicine River* (Markam, Ont. & New York: Viking, 1990);

A Coyote Columbus Story (Toronto: Groundwood, 1992);

Green Grass, Running Water (Boston: Houghton Mifflin, 1993);

One Good Story, That One: Stories (Toronto: HarperPerennial, 1993).

OTHER: *The Native in Literature,* edited by King, Cheryl Calver, and Helen Hoy (Toronto: ECW, 1987);

An Anthology of Short Fiction by Native Writers in Canada, edited by King (Toronto: Canadian Fiction Magazine, 1988);

All My Relations: An Anthology of Contemporary Canadian Native Fiction, edited by King (Toronto: McClelland & Stewart, 1990) – includes "The One about Coyote Going West," by King, pp. 95–106;

"A Seat in the Garden," in *Talking Leaves: Contemporary Native American Short Stories,* edited by Craig Lesley (New York: Dell, 1991), pp. 184–194;

"Traplines," in *Something to Declare: Selections from International Literature,* edited by Christine McClymont and others (Toronto: Oxford University Press, 1994), pp. 42–51;

"Native Literature in Canada," in *Dictionary of Native American Literature,* edited by Andrew Wiget (New York: Garland, 1994), pp. 353–369.

TELEVISION: *Medicine River,* screenplay by King and Ann McNaughton, Canadian Broadcasting Corporation and Medicine River Productions, 1993;

"Animals," teleplay by King, *North of Sixty,* Canadian Broadcasting Corporation, 1994;

"Border," teleplay by King, *Four Directions Anthology,* Canadian Broadcasting Corporation, November 1996;

Thomas King

"Simple Suffering," teleplay by King, *North of Sixty,* Canadian Broadcasting Corporation, November 1996.

RADIO: *The One about Coyote Going West,* script by King, Canadian Broadcasting Corporation, 1993;

Borders, script by King, Canadian Broadcasting Corporation, 1993;

Medicine River, script by King, Canadian Broadcasting Corporation, 1993;

Traplines, script by King, Canadian Broadcasting Corporation, 1994;

The Dead Dog Café Comedy Hour, six untitled scripts by King, Canadian Broadcasting Corporation, October–December 1996.

SELECTED PERIODICAL PUBLICATIONS – UNCOLLECTED:

FICTION

"Not Counting the Indian, There Were Six," *Malahat Review,* 80 (Fall 1987): 76–81;

"Bingo Bigbear and the Tie-and-Choker Bone Game," *Canadian Fiction Magazine,* 60 (1987): 89–98;

"One Good Story, That One," *Malahat Review,* 82 (Spring 1988): 38–43.

NONFICTION

"N. Scott Momaday: Literature and the Native Writer, an Interview," *MELUS: Journal of Multi-Ethnic Literatures of the United States,* 10 (Winter 1983): 66–72;

"Godzilla vs. Post Colonialism," *World Literature Written in English,* 30 (Autumn 1990): 10–16.

Thomas King's work has been influential in the Native American literary community of Canada for some years, and he has won some impressive awards. Now he is beginning to find an audience in the United States. His mixture of close human observation, popular-culture satire, and historical perception make his work both entertaining and penetrating.

King was born in Sacramento, California, on 24 April 1943 to Robert Elvin King, a Cherokee from Oklahoma, and Katheryn Konsonlas King, who was of Greek ancestry. He and his brother, Christopher, were raised in Roseville, California, by their mother after their father left the family when Thomas was about five. After graduation from high school in Roseville, King worked at several jobs, including ambulance driver and craps croupier. He attended Sacramento State University in 1961–1962 and Sierra Junior College from 1962 to 1964. In 1964 he worked his way to Australia and New Zealand on a tramp steamer. He found employment as a photojournalist in Australia, working mostly for *Everybody's Magazine.* On his return to the United States in 1967, he became a draftsman for Boeing Aircraft in Seattle.

He decided to go to California State University at Chico because his mother had attended the institution and because of its reputation for an "exciting" social life. He enrolled in 1968 and received his B.A. in English in 1970. That year he married Kristine Adams; they had a son, Christian, in 1971. From 1971 to 1973 King worked at the University of Utah, first as a counselor for Native American students and then as the director of the newly established Native studies department. He completed his M.A. in English at Chico in 1972 and entered the doctoral program at the University of Utah. In 1973 he became associate dean for student services at Humboldt State University in Arcata, California.

In 1977 he took a position as coordinator of the history of the Indians of the Americas program at the University of Utah. He taught Native studies there in 1978–1979. He became assistant professor of Native studies at the University of Lethbridge, Alberta, in 1980. His marriage ended in 1981. He taught at Lethbridge for ten years, serving as chair of the Native studies department from 1985 to 1987. While at Lethbridge he was able to work with Native people from the reservations, especially Cree and Blackfoot (Canadian relatives of the Montana Blackfeet). King received his Ph.D. in English and American studies from the University of Utah in 1986 with the dissertation "Inventing the Indian: White Images, Native Oral Traditions and Contemporary Native Writers." In 1989 he became associate professor of American and Native studies at the University of Minnesota. He took a leave of absence for the academic year 1993–1994 to work as a story editor for the Canadian Broadcasting Corporation (CBC) in Toronto.

In 1995 he moved back to Canada with his partner, Helen Hoy, and their two children: Benjamin Hoy, born in 1985, and Elizabeth King, born in 1988. He teaches at the University of Guelph in Ontario.

King's work is characterized by his determined use of contemporary Native characters to burst romantic stereotypes of Native Americans. His characters are complex; often they are outsiders or are returning home after a long absence. He depicts a variety of Indians and Indian viewpoints, avoiding the purist dichotomy that would define as inauthentic any Indian living in the city or in the twentieth century. For King, holding such an outlook is as dangerous as believing in romantic stereotypes about Indians.

Humor is one of King's chief tools. Any aspect of a story is open to his satiric touch, from names to religion. King shies away from the label of comic writer, preferring to be seen as a serious author who makes his points with irony and satire. Yet many of King's characters are in the process of defining and remaking themselves, and such an optimistic task suits comic fiction. A participant in the activism of

Dust jacket for the novel in which King blends myth and realism

the 1960s, King carries his political and historical awareness into a new kind of confrontation with the establishment. He wants to counter the defeatist and victimizing pictures of nineteenth-century Indians, but he also wants to expose the social forces that have created so much repression and death. While he shares this goal with many other Native writers, a distinctive strategy is King's use of popular white culture to point up the limited perspective of that culture. For example, in the novel *Green Grass, Running Water* (1993) some old Indians step into a John Wayne movie and change the ending so that the Indians win. This action alternately confuses and inspires the other Indian characters, who then take small steps toward breaking out of the victim roles assigned them. King carries on the ancient storyteller's conviction that stories create the world, that all that people know about themselves comes from their stories. This belief in the ability of narrative to create reality unites King with many other postmodern writers.

King began to publish short fiction in 1987 in small magazines such as *Whetstone* and the *Malahat Review,* but his stories were quickly selected for inclusion in anthologies. His first published story, "Joe the Painter and the Deer Island Massacre," has been reprinted three times; Margaret Atwood calls it and "One Good Story, That One" perfect, commenting on his exquisite timing, subversive humor, and inventive narrative twists.

King's first novel, *Medicine River* (1990), is set in the fictional Alberta town of Medicine River, next to the Blackfoot reservation. The protagonist is a mild-mannered, fortyish mixed-blood who has drifted through life; with intentional irony, King names him Will. A successful commercial photographer who lives with a white woman in Toronto, Will is not committed to his profession, his relationship, or anything else. Perhaps his detachment stems from the absence of his father, who had abandoned his wife and two sons to join the rodeo. When Will goes back to Medicine River for the funeral of his Blackfoot mother, he assumes that no one will remember or care about him.

In Medicine River he falls into the clutches of Harlan Bigbear, a compassionate trickster who knows what is best for everyone. But Harlan is no mere busybody: his humor, empathy, and belief in the bonds of community and kinship allow him to penetrate to the heart of people's real needs. Harlan decides to bring Will back to Medicine River permanently. He tries to persuade Will to set up a studio in town so that the Indians will not have to go to whites for their portrait photographs. Harlan is also convinced that Will is the perfect match for Louise Heavyman, a competent businesswoman who has no desire to get married but wants to have a child. Harlan tricks Will into a closer connection to the community by getting him to join the Native Friendship Centre's basketball team. Then he involves Will in a moneymaking scheme to shoot photographs for the center's calendar.

An important turning point for Will is the birth of Louise's daughter: when Will arrives at the hospital, the staff mistakes him for the father and asks him what the girl's name is to be; he looks above their heads, sees a sign, and immediately names her South Wing. While this parody of Indian naming traditions delights the reader, it also cements an intimate connection between Will and the child as well as between Will and Louise: he has become a father, if only a surrogate one. At this point Will decides to stay in Medicine River.

Photography is, emotionally, the perfect occupation for Will: he can remain out of the picture, observant and detached. But when he tries to take a portrait of Joyce Blue Horn's family, everyone is crowded into the photograph – including Will, who now knows that he belongs in the community.

King's subtle efforts to counter stereotypes generate much of the humor in the book. Gone are the nineteenth-century clichés about Indians not wanting to have their photographs taken. King's modern Indians may be successful photographers and accountants, or they may be traveling in Australia. Certainly there are those who are disadvantaged and cannot stay out of jail, but his Indian characters are capable and human – not alienated Natives wrapped up in victimist history.

Part of the appeal of *Medicine River* comes from its interweaving into the main action of many humorous, touching, maddening, and sad stories of the Native community of Medicine River – especially the stories that Will's mother told and did not tell her children. As Will is pulled back into the community, the reader cannot help but follow. The book won the best novel award from the Writers' Guild of Alberta and the P.E.N./Josephine Miles Award, and it was a runner-up for the Commonwealth Writer's Prize. King adapted the novel for a

Cover for a collection of King's short stories

1993 CBC television movie starring Graham Greene.

The title of King's second novel, *Green Grass, Running Water,* is a reference to the language found in many treaties, which promised the Indians that the land would be theirs "as long as the grass is green and the water runs." The work, which was on the short list for the Governor General's Award, builds on the strengths of King's first novel: the interweaving of several story lines, the humor, the political insights, and the emphasis on contemporary and accomplished Native characters are continued, but here they take a more experimental form. The novel is full of puns, humorous reversals of history, and satire of the images of Indians created by European Americans. Three narratives that are separate at the beginning of the novel are slowly woven together until the mythic and realistic worlds unite. First the narrator and a talking coyote discuss storytelling and creation myths. Mixing creation stories from the Blackfoot, the Iroquois, the Ojibwa, and the Navajo, King robs the Christian account of its cultural hegemony but does not set up any account as the official one. As the narrator says, "There are no truths, Coyote. Only stories." Creation stories are told repeatedly throughout the text, and each is altered by characters who seem to be out of the control of the storyteller. Often the story must start again. "How many times do we have to do this?" asks Coyote. "Until we get it right," replies the narrator. The first and last lines of the novel are identical, and the same words are frequently repeated in the text: "And here's how it happened." King thus shows that the invention of stories by which people define themselves is a never-ending process.

The second narrative level consists of the stories of contemporary Blackfoot people in the town of Blossom, Alberta, near the Blackfoot reservation. Professor Alberta Frank wants to have a child but does not want to marry either of her suitors, Lionel Red Dog and Charlie Looking Bear. Eli Stands Alone, a retired literature professor, has taken up residence in his mother's cabin and is holding up a dam project with a steady stream of legal briefs. Latisha Red Dog tries to make a success of her Dead Dog Café by selling tourists dishes such as Old Agency Puppy Stew and Saint Bernard Swiss Melts. Working their way between the other two levels are four old Indians who have escaped from an insane asylum and who call themselves Ishmael, Hawkeye, Robinson Crusoe, and the Lone Ranger. While present in Blossom, they also show up in the mythic narrative, where they argue about storytelling and wander through time. All of the stories converge on the Blackfoot Sun Dance and the dam project.

King's other works include a children's book, *A Coyote Columbus Story* (1992), and a collection of short fiction, *One Good Story, That One* (1993). *The Native in Literature* (1987), edited by King, Hoy, and Cheryl Calver, is a collection of papers presented at a conference held in Lethbridge.

While King is not yet as well known as some other Native American writers, his work is receiving ever-widening notice. His writing becomes more innovative and entertaining with each publication, and he is destined to become an important figure in contemporary American and Canadian literature.

Interviews:

Constance Rooke, "Interview with Tom King," *World Literature Written in English,* 30 (Autumn 1990): 10–16;

Clark Munsell, "An Interview with Thomas King," *The World & I,* 8 (June 1993): 306–309.

References:

Margaret Atwood, "A Double-Bladed Knife: Subversive Laughter in Two Stories by Thomas King," *Canadian Literature,* 124/125 (Summer–Spring 1990): 243–250;

Elizabeth Blair, "Setting the Story Straight," *The World & I,* 8 (June 1993): 284–295;

Laura Donaldson, "Noah Meets Old Coyote; Or, Singing in the Rain: Intertextuality in Thomas King's *Green Grass, Running Water,*" *SAIL: Studies in American Indian Literature,* 7 (Summer 1995): 27–43;

Thomas Matchie and Brett Larson, "Coyote Fixes the World: The Power of Myth in Thomas King's *Green Grass, Running Water,*" 63 (Spring 1996): 153–168;

James Ruppert, "When Coyote Dreams," *The World & I,* 8 (June 1993): 297–305;

Percy Walton, " 'Tell Our Own Stories': Politics and the Fiction of Thomas King," *World Literature Written in English,* 30 (Autumn 1990): 62–76.

Francis La Flesche

(25 December 1857 – 5 September 1932)

Jarold Ramsey
University of Rochester

BOOKS: *The Middle Five: Indian Boys at School* (Boston: Small, Maynard, 1900);

The Omaha Tribe, by La Flesche and Alice Fletcher, U.S. Bureau of American Ethnology, Twenty-seventh Annual Report, 1905–1906 (Washington, D.C., 1911);

The Osage Tribe: Rite of the Chiefs; Sayings of the Ancient Men, U.S. Bureau of American Ethnology: Thirty-sixth Annual Report, 1914–1915 (Washington, D.C., 1921);

The Osage Tribe: The Rite of Vigil, U.S. Bureau of American Ethnology: Thirty-ninth Annual Report, 1917–1918 (Washington, D.C., 1925);

The Osage Tribe: Two Versions of the Child-naming Rite, U.S. Bureau of American Ethnology: Forty-third Annual Report, 1925–1926 (Washington, D.C., 1928);

The Osage Tribe: Rite of the Wa-xo'-be, U.S. Bureau of American Ethnology: Forty-fifth Annual Report, 1927–1928 (Washington, D.C., 1930);

A Dictionary of the Osage Language, Smithsonian Institution: Bureau of American Ethnology, Bulletin 109 (Washington, D.C.: U.S. Government Printing Office, 1932);

War Ceremony and Peace Ceremony of the Osage Indians, Smithsonian Institution: Bureau of American Ethnology, Bulletin 101 (Washington, D.C.: U.S. Government Printing Office, 1939);

Ke-ma-ha: The Omaha Stories of Francis La Flesche, edited by Daniel Littlefield and James W. Parins (Lincoln: University of Nebraska Press, 1995);

The Osage and the Invisible World: From the Works of Francis La Flesche, edited by Garrich A. Bailey (Norman: University of Oklahoma Press, 1995).

Editions: *The Omaha Tribe* (Lincoln: University of Nebraska Press, 1967);

The Middle Five: Indian Boys at School (Lincoln: University of Nebraska Press, 1978).

OTHER: "The Story of a Vision," in *The Singing Spirit: Early Short Stories by Native American Indians,* edited by Bernd Peyer (Tucson: University of Arizona Press, 1989), pp. 69–73.

Francis La Flesche (Smithsonian Institution National Anthropological Archives, Bureau of American Ethnology Collection)

SELECTED PERIODICAL PUBLICATIONS – UNCOLLECTED: "A Study of Omaha Indian Music," by La Flesche, Alice Fletcher, and John Comfort Fillmore, *Archæological and Ethnological Papers of the Peabody Museum,* 1, no. 5 (1893): 1–152;

"One Touch of Nature," *Southern Workman* (August 1913): 427–428;

"The Symbolic Man of the Osage Tribe," *Art and Archaeology,* 9, no. 2 (1920): 68–75.

Francis La Flesche, "Zhogaxe" (Woodworker), the first American Indian to become a professional ethnologist, published few literary works in the course of his long and productive scholarly career; but his literary interests and talents ran deep and gave his ethnographic work on the Omaha and Osage tribes a verbal and imaginative dimension unique in his time, the "golden age" of American anthropology. His acute renderings of Plains-culture ceremonial songs have significantly influenced the understanding of traditional Native American poetry through most of the twentieth century. As interest in transcultural studies and ethnographic literary theory grows, La Flesche's remarkable sensitivity to his position between the Indian and Anglo worlds seems increasingly important and worthy of study.

La Flesche was born on 25 December 1857 on the Omaha Reservation in eastern Nebraska, the oldest son of the last principal chief of the Omahas, Joseph La Flesche, or Iron Eye, and his wife, Tainne, or "Lizzie." Francis had four half sisters, a sister, and a brother. Joseph La Flesche, the son of a French trader and a Ponca mother, had been adopted by the Omaha chief Big Elk and had become a progressive leader who urged his people to master the advantages of white society while preserving their essential Indian identity. Accordingly, Iron Eye established a village for his progressive followers (his conservative enemies derided it as "the village of make-believe white men"); and, while Francis and his brother and sisters were properly trained in Omaha religion and ceremony, they were also sent to the local Presbyterian mission school. By fifteen La Flesche had taken the crucial part of "the Sacred Child" in the *Wa-wan,* or Pipe Ceremony, and had served as a runner/scout in one of his tribe's last buffalo hunts. He had also acquired the reservation-school education he would later describe in *The Middle Five: Indian Boys at School* (1900).

In June 1877 La Flesche married Alice Mitchell; she died the following year. He married Alice Cline in August 1879. In 1879–1880 he accompanied his sister, Susette ("Bright-Eyes"), and the Ponca chief Standing Bear on a political speaking tour to Washington, Boston, and other eastern cities. It was on this trip that Susette (and presumably her brother) met Henry Wadsworth Longfellow, who effused that Susette *was* Minnehaha – thus helping to launch her own remarkable career as a writer, speaker, and champion of Indian rights. In Washington, Francis La Flesche encountered two scholars who would shape the direction of his life: James Owen Dorsey and Alice Fletcher. (He may already have met and worked as a translator with Dorsey in Nebraska.)

La Flesche's father, Joseph, or Iron Eye (Nebraska State Historical Society)

In 1881 La Flesche accepted an appointment as a clerk and translator in the Office of Indian Affairs in Washington. There he worked closely with Dorsey on the latter's study of Omaha society, in the process acquiring extensive training in linguistics. He also began part-time studies at National University that would lead to two law degrees.

When Fletcher commenced her freelance efforts to save the Omaha's lands in 1882 by setting up a land-allotment program (anticipating the Dawes Act of 1887), La Flesche became her indispensable assistant. When she began ethnological research on the Omahas in 1883, their working relationship became one of collaboration. Furthering her pioneering interest in Native American music, he made extensive graphophone recordings of Omaha songs in the 1890s, and he devoted himself increasingly to the task of recording the tribal ceremonies in which he had participated as a boy. The great monument to this work and to his collaboration with Fletcher is *The Omaha Tribe* (1911), a classic of American ethnography.

By the turn of the century La Flesche was well established in Washington social and intellectual circles, living in Fletcher's house and often escorting her to events in the city – occasioning some gos-

The Presbyterian mission school on the Omaha reservation, where La Flesche received his early education (Smithsonian Institution National Anthropological Archives)

sip, despite their difference in age of nearly twenty years. (His second marriage had ended in divorce in 1884.) The relationship seems to have been that of idealized mother and son, perhaps reflecting La Flesche's early loss of contact with his own mother following her estrangement from his father. His marriage in 1906 to Rosa Borassa, an Ojibwa and a fellow employee in the Indian Service, ended in divorce in 1908, but La Flesche's filial devotion to Fletcher continued until her death in 1923.

Meanwhile, his career was finding its own independent path between the Indian and Anglo domains. From his earliest years in Washington he returned to the Omaha Reservation for a month or so each summer, providing opportunities for field research on the Omaha and their neighbors. In 1900 he published *The Middle Five: Indian Boys at School,* a poignant memoir of his years at the Presbyterian mission school. This delightful book – which has never been out of print since its first appearance – quickly became a classic of Native American childhood biography, alongside Charles Eastman's contemporaneous *Indian Boyhood* (1902).

The title of La Flesche's work refers to a "gang" of five preadolescent boys, including La Flesche, who stood in age and social status between the oldest boys, who called themselves "The Big Seven," and the school's youngest pupils. La Flesche's account of life and learning at an agency boarding school in the 1870s is unblinking: he and his Omaha schoolmates were denied the use of their native language, and on entry were given such inappropriate Anglo names as Phil Sheridan, Ulysses S. Grant, and Edwin Stanton; discipline was both harsh and capricious, and in most ways the school seems to have followed Richard Henry Pratt's infamous dictum that to educate Indian children it was necessary to "kill the Indian" in them.

Although La Flesche's account of his school days is unsentimental, it is also richly evocative of cherished memories of escapades and schoolboy pranks and of intense friendships – the narrative ends with the tragic illness and death of his best friend, "Brush," an orphan for whom the school was home. Of special importance for La Flesche's scholarly and literary career are episodes of forbidden after-hours traditional storytelling and singing of Anglo hymns and tunes and Omaha songs. The latter were, of course, forbidden, but when a visiting official asked for an "Indian song," La Flesche and his schoolmates burst spontaneously into a rousing Omaha victory song. The official's response – "That's savage, savage! They must be taught music" – led to the introduction of musical study and singing in the school curriculum and no doubt contributed to La Flesche's lifelong scholarly interest in music, both European American and Indian.

In 1910 La Flesche accepted an appointment as ethnologist with the Bureau of American Ethnology (BAE). By then his research interests had shifted from the Omaha to their linguistic and social kin the Osage, and between 1921 and 1930 his four volumes on Osage ceremonies appeared in the annual reports of the BAE – constituting, as Hartley P. Alexander would write in an obituary notice in the *American Anthropologist* in 1933, "the most complete single record of the ceremonies of a North American Indian people."

Throughout his career La Flesche communicated with prominent ethnologists and anthropologists, especially those with a literary inclination such as Alexander, Daniel Brinton, Washington Matthews, Franz Boas, and Paul Radin. In 1922 he was elected president of the Anthropological Society of Washington, and in 1926 he was awarded an honorary doctorate of letters by the University of Nebraska. On retiring from the BAE in 1929, he returned home to the Omaha community in Nebraska. He died at the home of his brother, Carey, near Macy, on 5 September 1932. At his funeral he was given Presbyterian, Masonic, and traditional Omaha rites.

By all accounts, Francis La Flesche was a genial, intelligent, sophisticated man, in whom Anglo and Indian traits maintained a harmonious balance. Something of his good-humored poise is expressed in his remark, recorded in Norma Kidd Green's *Iron Eye's Family: The Children of Joseph La Flesche* (1969), on the occasion of receiving the honorary degree from the University of Nebraska, that "as a lad he had planned to become a great buffalo hunter, but the white people came and ate up the buffalo, so he turned to writing." In appearance he was burly, even bearlike, an impression accentuated by photographs of him in middle age wearing an Indian buffalo robe; on the other hand, there are accounts of him as a Victorian/Edwardian gentleman in his Washington social outings as Fletcher's escort. La Flesche was a kind of obverse of Ishi, the "last wild Indian," who came out of the California wilderness in 1911 and lived with anthropologists in San Francisco until his death in 1916. Ishi's and La Flesche's lives define each other by contrast, and yet they seem to have had much in common: most notably, an affable self-knowledge and self-possession and – allowing for the drastic differences in their circumstances – mind-and-heart dedication to the task of recording and preserving the vanishing traditional ways of their people.

La Flesche and his sister, Susette, in Washington, D.C., during their 1879–1880 lecture tour (Nebraska State Historical Society)

From his earliest collaborations with Fletcher, La Flesche seems to have been driven, in Margot Liberty's words in *American Indian Intellectuals* (1978), by "a sense of almost unbearable urgency" to record the Plains Indian legacy in the face of rapid acculturation. His zeal to do so in the case of the Omaha was intensified by initial resistance on the part of many tribal elders, who had decided that since the buffalo were gone the ceremonies and songs of the buffalo cult should die with them and not be uselessly handed on. La Flesche's feelings, as an Omaha tribesman, about the prospect of such loss must have brought him into frequent conflict with the standards of the day that called for "objective" ethnographic writing; and from time to time the impersonal prose of *The Omaha Tribe,* mostly written by Fletcher, gives way to something personal and evocative from La Flesche:

> As I listened to the old priest [Yellow Smoke, who had at first refused to perform the songs of the Sacred Pole] his voice seemed as full and resonant as when I had heard him years ago, in the days when the singing of these very songs in the Holy Tent meant so much to each gens and to every man, woman, and child in the tribe. Now the old man sang with his eyes closed, and watching him there was like watching the last embers of the religious rites of a vanishing people.

Such a passage, at once scholarly and yet richly personal and participatory, is characteristic of La Flesche's ethnography at its best and explains the special appeal his writings have always had for readers who want the *feel* of Native American rites and customs as well as the dry generalizations of ethnological reports. La Flesche clearly lavished much attention in his translations and commentaries on matters of literary presentation, symbolism, and dramatic setting, making him one of the true predecessors of ethnopoetics. It is unfortunate that his astute renderings of songs and ritual scenarios – one of his practices was to include all repetitions, rather than eliding them in the fashion of Anglo anthropologists – were not more widely copied by later researchers. That his work has contributed substantially to the understanding of Native American song and ceremony is demonstrated by the inclusion of examples of his Omaha and Osage texts in virtually every serious anthology of Indian poetry, from Natalie Curtis's pioneering *The Indians' Book* (1911) and George Cronyn's *The Path on the Rainbow* (1918) to later collections edited by A. Grove Day, Margot Astrov, William Brandon, John Bierhorst, and Jerome Rothenberg.

One Osage song text and commentary – which has, oddly, been ignored by later anthologists – illustrates La Flesche's skillful care in bringing his "artifacts" to verbal and imaginative life. In *The Osage Tribe: Rite of the Chiefs; Sayings of the Ancient Men* (1921) a ritual planting song is sung by female relatives of the men who are being raised to the status of chief. La Flesche first sets the scene, then presents the song, which is beautiful in itself but more beautiful in the setting provided.

> (The [priest] puts into the hands of each of the women a woven bag and a planting pole. Each woman throws upon her back the bag, drawing the carrying strap around her shoulder, and stands with the pole in her right hand. The woman is the planter, the cultivator, the harvester of the corn, and this little scene is meant to portray the important part she plays in the drama of life. In the song, she is made to speak of her own actions as she plants the grains that are to spring into life and bear the fruit that will feed her people.)

> I have made a footprint, a sacred one.
> I have made a footprint, through it the blades spring upward.
> I have made a footprint, over it the blades float in the wind.
> I have made a footprint, over it the ears lean forward to one another.
> I have made a footprint, over it I pluck the ears.
> I have made a footprint, over it I bend the stalks to pluck the ears.
> I have made a footprint, over it the blossoms lie gray.
> I have made a footprint, smoke arises from my house.
> I have made a footprint, there is cheer in my house.
> I have made a footprint, I live in the light of day.

Like many ethnographers and anthropologists then as now, La Flesche had literary aspirations beyond what his scholarly work permitted him: besides *The Middle Five,* which was rejected by several publishers because its clear-eyed view of the experience of Indian boys in an Anglo school did not square with prevailing stereotypes, he wrote the libretto for an opera, *Da-o-ma,* that was never published and apparently was never performed, and published two "ethnographic" short stories in the *Southern Workman* magazine: "The Story of a Vision" in February 1901 and "One Touch of Nature" in August 1913. Among his manuscripts in the Fletcher/La Flesche file in the National Anthropological Archives are many stories and story fragments and what appears to be the beginning of a novel; all of them have lovingly detailed Indian settings, and some are autobiographical accounts of young Indians trying to find their ways between the Indian and Anglo worlds. These pieces have been published in *Ke-ma-ha: The Omaha Stories of Francis La Flesche* (1995), edited by Daniel Littlefield and James W. Parins. One can only regret that the buffalo-hunter-turned-writer, lacking the precedents and encouragements available to today's Native American writers, did not further pursue his inclination toward fiction and the informal personal essay.

References:

Hartley P. Alexander, "Francis La Flesche," *American Anthropologist,* new series 35 (1933): 328–331;

Norma Kidd Green, *Iron Eye's Family: The Children of Joseph La Flesche* (Lincoln, Neb.: Johnson, 1969);

Margot Liberty, "Francis La Flesche: The Osage Odyssey," in *American Indian Intellectuals,* edited by Liberty (Saint Paul, Minn.: West, 1978);

Joan Mark, *A Stranger in Her Native Land* (Lincoln: University of Nebraska Press, 1988);

Jarold Ramsey, "Francis La Flesche's 'The Song of Flying Crow' and the Limits of Ethnography," in *American Indian Persistence and Resurgence,* edited by Karl Kroeber (Durham & London: Duke University Press, 1994), pp. 181–196;

Robin Ridington, *Blessing for a Long Time* (Lincoln: University of Nebraska Press, forthcoming 1997);

Jerome Rothenberg, *Shaking the Pumpkin: Traditional Poetry of the Indian North Americans,* revised edition (New York: Alfred van der March Editions, 1986), pp. 392–394, 497–510;

Dorothy Clarke Wilson, *Bright Eyes: The Story of Susette La Flesche* (New York: McGraw-Hill, 1974).

Papers:

The Alice Fletcher and Francis La Flesche papers are in the National Anthropological Archives of the Smithsonian Institution, Washington, D.C. The La Flesche Family Collection, in the Nebraska State Historical Society, Lincoln, includes La Flesche's diary.

John Joseph Mathews

(16 November 1894 - 11 June 1979)

Terry P. Wilson
University of California, Berkeley

BOOKS: *Wah'Kon-Tah: The Osage and the White Man's Road* (Norman: University of Oklahoma Press, 1932);

Sundown (New York: Longmans, Green, 1934); republished, with an introduction by Virginia H. Mathews (Norman: University of Oklahoma Press, 1988);

Talking to the Moon (Chicago: University of Chicago Press, 1945);

Life and Death of an Oilman: The Career of E. W. Marland (Norman: University of Oklahoma Press, 1952);

The Osages: Children of the Middle Waters (Norman: University of Oklahoma Press, 1961).

SELECTED PERIODICAL PUBLICATIONS – UNCOLLECTED: "Hunting the Red Deer of Scotland," *Sooner Magazine*, 1 (April 1929): 213–214, 246;

"Hunting in the Rockies," *Sooner Magazine*, 1 (May 1929): 263, 278–280;

"Passing of Red Eagle," *Sooner Magazine*, 2 (February 1930): 160, 176;

"Admirable Outlaw," *Sooner Magazine*, 2 (April 1930): 241, 264;

"Hunger on the Prairie," *Sooner Magazine*, 2 (June 1930): 328–329;

"The Trapper's Dog," *Sooner Magazine*, 3 (January 1931): 133, 141;

"Beauty's Votary," *Sooner Magazine*, 3 (February 1931): 171, 181–182;

"Ea Sa Rah N'eah's Story," *Sooner Magazine*, 3 (June 1931): 328–329;

"Ole Bob," *Sooner Magazine*, 5 (April 1933): 206–207.

John Joseph Mathews (courtesy of Garrick Bailey)

Most scholars cite John Joseph Mathews's *Sundown* (1934), with its mixed-blood protagonist and its emphasis on the problems of being Native in a largely non-Native world, as the first modern Native American novel. The Osage writer's nonfiction books have, however, received more critical acclaim and a wider readership than his single novel. All five volumes of his prose exhibit two notable characteristics: an elegant and erudite style and a respect and affection for the author's tribal people and their twentieth-century home, Oklahoma.

The eldest of five children, Mathews was born on 16 November 1894 in Pawhuska, Indian Territory. His father, William Shirley Mathews, was a quarter-blood Osage married to a non-Native woman when he arrived in 1874 at the tribe's last reservation, located in the northeastern part of what became the state of Oklahoma in 1907. The family occupied a large stone house perched on Agency Hill overlooking the burgeoning frontier community of Pawhuska. In a 1972 interview with Guy

Logsdon, Mathews recalled his initial impressions of his tribespeople: sleeping alone, he listened to "a long drawn-out chant broken by weeping. . . . It filled my little boy's soul with fear and bittersweetness, and exotic yearning. . . . I hoped fervently that there would be more of it, and yet was afraid that there might be."

Although the ethos of traditional Osage culture permeated the life of the Mathews family, the racially mixed household stood apart. Mathews learned to speak haltingly the tribal language his father spoke fluently. Osage families came to trade at his father's mercantile business and later at the bank that he founded. Mathews was of the fifth generation of his family to live among the Osages, yet he invariably referred to the tribal full-bloods as "they" and "them" in conversation as well as in his writings. Because he lived in a nuclear family arrangement, attended Pawhuska's public and private schools rather than a government or missionary Indian institution, and was left out of much of the quotidian affairs of the Osage community, Mathews always placed himself on the fringe of its culture, vitally affected by and interactive with "them" but ultimately a step removed from full community involvement.

Mathews was elected to the tribal council in 1934; however, the short distance leading from his family residence to the council hall required forty years and a circuitous route to arrive there. His journeys took him beyond the reservation boundaries, out of Oklahoma, and eventually across the Atlantic to England, the European mainland, Africa, and finally California. After attending a privately run elementary school and spending two years at a parochial school Mathews enrolled in the largely white-populated public high school in Pawhuska. He captained the football and basketball teams while showing early promise as a writer by helping write and edit the school's first yearbook.

Outside the classroom and organized activities, Mathews was exposed daily to nature and tribal custom. Recalling his boyhood years, he told Logsdon, "I rode all over the northern part of this reservation on my horse and with my dog and camped and just had a wonderful time." His earliest ambition was to be an ornithologist. He also visited the lodges of encamped Osages at irregular intervals, unconsciously and unsystematically soaking up an awareness of kindred spirit that would eventually lure him back to Oklahoma from his intercontinental travels.

After high-school graduation in 1914 Mathews chose the University of Oklahoma to pursue a degree in geology. His education was interrupted for three years when Mathews joined the army after the United States entered World War I. The athletic patriot sought and received a cavalry assignment, but he soon transferred to the aviation section of the Signal Corps. Part of his enlistment was spent in Europe, where he became a flight instructor after it was discovered he possessed exceptional night vision.

Returning to the university, Mathews received course credit in aerodynamics in recognition of his military service and graduated in 1920 with the uneasy feeling that his degree did not represent a finished education. A chance to remedy any imagined academic disadvantage appeared when he was offered a Rhodes scholarship to Oxford. Mathews turned down the scholarship as "too restrictive" but spent three years at the English university, reading natural science and earning a B.A. From there Mathews traveled to Switzerland, where he enrolled at the University of Geneva's School of International Relations. The *Philadelphia Ledger* hired him as a temporary correspondent to cover the activities of the League of Nations.

After a year of class work and watching league delegates futilely wrangling over postwar problems, Mathews vacationed in Europe and North Africa. During a hunting expedition his party was rushed by Arab tribesmen brandishing Winchesters and sabers. Exuberance rather than hostility had prompted their display, and the horsemen dismounted and joined the hunters for dinner. It reminded Mathews of an incident that had occurred years before on the Oklahoma prairies when he had encountered a band of Osage warriors "joy shooting." He confessed to Logsdon that the episode left him homesick, and he left Africa soon thereafter.

Mathews made only a brief visit to Pawhuska, however, before moving westward to California. He married a woman he had met in Geneva – nothing is known about her except that she was a member of the Singer family of sewing-machine fame – and settled down in Los Angeles to sell real estate. During a year on the West Coast, Mathews left his wife and business several times for extended hunting trips in the northern Rocky Mountains. Following a divorce in late 1929 he returned to his family's ranch in Osage County, Oklahoma. Local hunting expeditions with his fellow tribesmen provided the raw material for his first publications beyond his Geneva news dispatches: a series of adventure sketches appearing in *The Sooner Magazine,* the University of Oklahoma's alumni news journal. As a contributing editor Mathews published nine short pieces between April 1929 and April 1933.

None longer than four thousand words, the articles and stories reveal as much about the author as his characters. All feature outdoors themes, and the first three exhibit an overly ornate prose style, redolent of a cultured Oxonian's notion of literature. Their titles are burdened with lengthy subtitles, including the wildly alliterative "The Wary Bull Wapiti Worthy Foe of Hunter's Skill." He soon discarded such literary conceits as prefacing a red deer hunting sketch with a quotation from Sir Walter Scott's *The Lady of the Lake* (1810) in favor of straightforward outdoor narratives that successfully juxtapose philosophical ponderings about man and nature with the dialectical dialogues of Indian and rural white hunters. After a few stories Mathews hit his descriptive stride in "Hunger on the Prairie" (1930), with passages such as: "It was an iron-bound world. There had been snow and sleet for several days. . . . The crackling trees in the ravines sounded like rifle shots. The air was metallic as struck steel."

The Sooner Magazine not only published Mathews's maiden literary efforts but also heralded the success of his first book, *Wah'Kon-Tah: The Osage and the White Man's Road* (1932). The book represented the benefits of the young author's friendship with two men, Joseph Brandt, the editor of the University of Oklahoma Press, and Laban J. Miles, the Quaker agent for the Osages from 1878 to 1884 and again from 1889 to 1892. Diaries and notes Miles kept of his reservation experiences were willed to Mathews when the retired agent died in April 1931. This legacy provided the primary research base for *Wah'Kon-Tah.*

It was Brandt who first urged Mathews to use Miles's records to write a book. Excited by the suggestion, Mathews rented an abandoned house located in an isolated area twenty miles from Pawhuska. Beginning on 4 July 1931, he finished the manuscript shortly before Thanksgiving. He lived a spartan existence while engaged in writing. Sleeping on a screened-in porch facing east, he awoke, catching the early sunlight, and readied himself for work by showering with cold water draining through holes punched in the bottom of a bucket that he had hoisted up a tree. He played Indian music on a portable phonograph or hunted and fished in the surrounding forest and nearby streams when restless after lengthy stints at a folding typewriter placed on a card table. His only social distractions were occasional visits by Osages who, hearing of their fellow tribesman's project, stopped by to offer tidbits of information about early days on the reservation.

The result of this intense effort was published as the third volume in Brandt's Civilization of the American Indian series. The Oklahoma editor sent proofs of Mathews's manuscript to the Book of the Month Club with a biographical sketch of the author. Brandt and Mathews were invited to the club's offices to meet with Christopher Morley, the juror most enthusiastic about *Wah'Kon-Tah.* Replicating the "old boy" network of England's public schools, Morley, an Oxonian of a generation before Mathews, shook the new author's hand and immediately launched into a gossipy reminiscence of old school days.

Wah'Kon-Tah was the first university press book chosen by the club and was its November 1932 selection. Even at a Depression Era price of $2.50 the book proved a strong commercial success, selling fifty thousand copies through the club and a few thousand more at retail bookstores. Mathews recalled his exhilaration in the Logsdon interview with characteristic aplomb: "I didn't know I was a writer until the Book-of-the-Month Club told me. I wrote that book just as a wood thrush would sing. He's not conscious of how he sings; he just sings because he feels it." Mathews insistently stressed the casual nature of the writing: "I just wrote it because I had to write it – suddenly. Having lived more or less a whimsical life from boyhood, this was my whim of the moment. If I hadn't finished it when I did, I might have gone deer hunting and forgotten about it."

Wah'Kon-Tah achieved critical success as well as commercial profit. Henry Seidel Canby in a *New York Times* review (18 December 1932) compared it stylistically to Willa Cather's *Death Comes to the Archbishop* (1927), suggesting that Cather's work "had in it more conscious literary quality and a less intimate acquaintance with the subject." He praised Mathews's portrayal of the Osages as "neither opinionated nor over-romantic – he motivates his Indians so that their dignity, their bewilderment and their poetry are placed in proper perspective." Canby concluded that it was the combined white and Indian strains within Mathews that produced a unique perspective, "naturally and realistically without any signs of clash."

Mathews's chronicle of federal policies aimed at acculturation and Osage responses to the "civilizers" – teachers, missionaries, and government agents – benefited from his mixed-blood perspective. Bilingual and bicultural, Mathews effectively meshed Miles's written documents with Osage oral remembrances to create an informal history of early reservation events. His ties to tribal place and people and the added unexpected triumph of *Wah'Kon-Tah* compelled the cosmopolitan traveler to stay in Osage County and make the Osages his life's work. Cultural associations belied his Caucasian features and minuscule one-eighth blood quantum.

The heritage of prior interracial encounters on the Osage people is noted in *Wah'Kon-Tah.* In 1874 when political and demographic pressures forced the tribe to sell its huge reservation in Kansas and accept a smaller one in Indian Territory, mixed-bloods numbered 280 among the nearly 3,000 total Osage population. Most of them, unlike the Mathews family, were of French and Indian descent, and as a group they exerted considerable influence on tribal affairs. Miles, the tribe's second Quaker agent on their new reservation, used some of their number as interpreters, linguistically and culturally, in dealing with the larger full-blood contingent.

Mathews's *Wah'Kon-Tah* easily balances government policy that sought an Indian acceptance of the white man's road with Osage tenacity in clinging to tradition, reserving for the tribe decision making power over issues of partial sovereignty and limited acculturation. With a leavening of good humor, and without sentimentalizing or condemning either group's views, Mathews relates the mutual frustrations of whites and Native Americans as cultural perspectives clashed. Scholars trained in ethnohistorical methodology since the 1970s might criticize a too willing presumption of goodwill on the part of government bureaucrats while approving the inclusion of Native American motivations and thought processes.

Mathews was not attempting a scholarly history – indeed by his own admission, he was not especially cognizant of a potential readership. His narrative is thoughtful and well crafted but almost devoid of strong feeling beyond a simple desire to capture on paper the essence of the recent past. As informal history it succeeds: those who enjoy the anecdotal and the picturesque find plenty to excite the imagination in *Wah'Kon-Tah,* skimming over the mundane accounts of agency affairs. More-serious readers grow impatient with trivial meanderings into local mythology but savor the "insider" viewpoints of the Osages. Contemporary readers, particularly easterners, were probably most surprised to discover that the western reservation scene was less remote from "civilization" than imagined: the acculturationists and Osages did not interact in isolation, as interlopers of all kinds from cowboys and outlaws to merchants and lawmen impinged upon tribal and agency life.

Another review of *Wah'Kon-Tah,* appearing in Pawhuska's *Osage County News* (14 October 1932), praised Mathews's accomplishment and unwittingly provided a key to the writer's future life and choice of theme for his book. The reviewer condemned the conduct of most Osages, whose "enormous incomes from oil that made the tribe the richest in the world, lolled in luxury, built palaces on the plains, and bought purple automobiles with the money that rolled in." He exempted Mathews from his caustic characterization: "one of the younger tribesmen has plodded along the rough road that leads to scholarly attainment and literary recognition."

The Osages had grown rich from royalties on natural gas and petroleum, first drilled on their reservation in 1897 and extracted in quantity after World War I. The likely reason Mathews refused the Rhodes scholarship was lack of financial need, as he drew a full share, or headright, of his tribe's underground reservation: when the surface rights were individually allotted in 1906, bowing to political pressure for statehood, the Osages retained their mineral estate in communal ownership. The surety of wealth contributed to Mathews's indulgence in his "whimsies" and near embarrassment over unearned monetary ease. The white majority in Osage County, although benefiting from their honest and dishonest exploitation of their Native American neighbors, sneered at Osage excesses, coming as they did without labor, thus being "unearned" according to their Protestant ethic. The favorable review of *Wah'Kon-Tah* probably heightened Mathews's ambivalence toward the oil largesse and ruefulness at his own aimlessness.

Sundown, written in response to a publisher's invitation in 1934, clearly constituted for Mathews a psychological self-probing. The novel's Osage mixed-blood protagonist, Challenge Windzer, is obviously modeled on the author. Mathews told Logsdon that he only reluctantly yielded to pressure for another book after *Wah'Kon-Tah* and that he never read the novel after its publication. Writing *Sundown* may have exorcised some of Mathews's personal devils, but the book failed to achieve the success of his first volume.

Literary scholars agree that *Sundown* is an early prime example of a mixed-blood Native American author drawing on his own life experience to express the alienation of the partially assimilated in the divided world of Indian and white. Beginning with his birth when "the god of the great Osages was still dominant over the wild prairie and the blackjack hills," the novel traces Chal Windzer's early years on the reservation at the time when oil royalties enriched the tribe, through his attendance at a state university, service in the army air corps, and return to the reservation in the 1920s. The last portion of the novel deals with Chal's disillusion-

Major Laban J. Miles

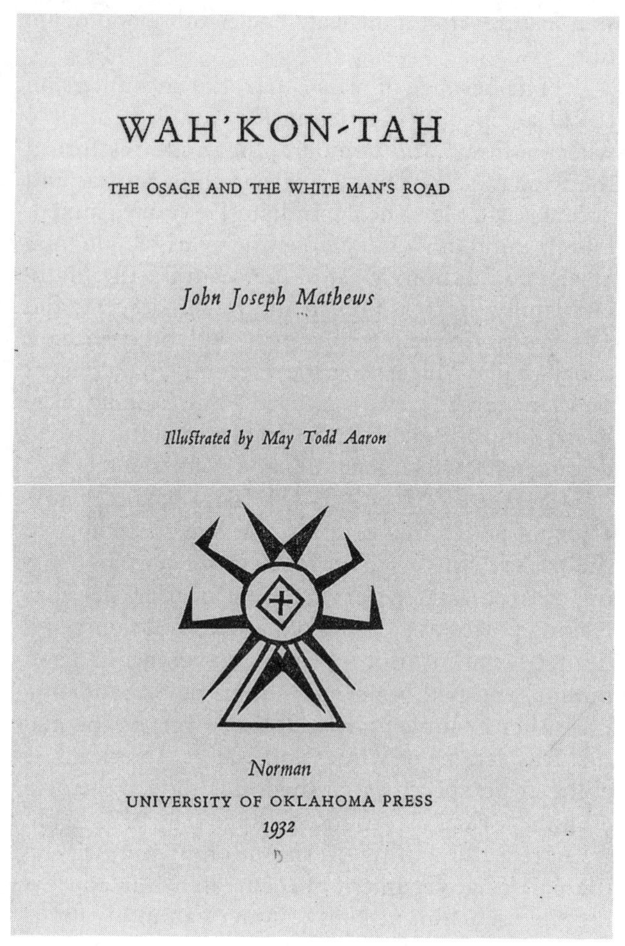

Frontispiece and title page for Mathews's study of government policy toward the Osages and the Indians' responses

ment and confusion over his search for a viable identity: he "learned long ago to have a purpose and that a practical one, to hide his purposelessness."

The notion of mixed-bloods rendered lost between traditional tribal life and the surrounding white world is key to the novel's plot. Chal's father is portrayed as a prototypical "progressive" mixed-blood, forever railing against the "conservative" and "backward" full-bloods who are slow to walk the white man's road to oil riches. Ironically, the father, politically influential, works for allotment of the reservation – Congress had made the dissolution of all tribally held lands, reservations, a condition for Indian Territory to become a state – which tragically diminishes the condition of mixed-blood and full-blood alike. Ultimately he is the instrument of his own death as his faith in white civilization causes him to leave his pistol behind on a trip, despite his wife's urging that he carry it for protection as had been his custom, and he dies at the hand of bandits who steal his new car.

Throughout the novel Chal vacillates between traditional life and progressive new ways. At the university he agonizes over his proper position in the campus community, a dilemma made acute by the accompanying presence of two boyhood friends, full-bloods named Sun-on-His-Wings and Running Elk. When the three Osages arrive for their freshman year with three white boys from Pawhuska, Chal feels "a little annoyed with them for acting like Indians"; the two full-bloods sit "like wooden images, replying 'yes' or 'no' to attempted conversation" by upperclassmen. Chal fears that they will be misunderstood by their white classmates, and he wants them to be liked and appreciated.

As the three Osage friends try desperately to adjust to college social life, they pledge fraternities. Chal finds himself as ill-equipped to converse casually as the others and is more readily accepted only because of his lighter skin and more assimilable name. Yet it is the full-bloods who pledge readily and Chal who obstinately holds out until the last moment. The three prepare to attend their first "pledge court," and Chal worries that Running Elk and Sun-on-His-Wings will not grasp the innocence of mock trials and punishments. He wants to tell the white brothers that the Osages "would not understand this sort of thing – that to touch an Indian's body constituted an insult" but realizes that the brothers would only laugh at him. The two full-bloods refuse to submit to the paddling that Chal endures, and the next day they leave the campus. "In a way, he was glad they were going; their going would relieve him of much responsibility, and the fear which seemed to be with him always, the fear that they would do something wrong."

After the war Chal returns to the reservation and discovers that Running Elk has become an alcoholic, caring only for drunken revels and reckless driving in expensive automobiles purchased with oil revenues. In contrast, Sun-on-His-Wings has adopted a syncretized spiritual life by joining the Osage peyote church. Chal samples both of his friends' choices and finds some solace among the "blanket Indians." The conversion proves short-lived as Chal cannot overcome feelings of alienation as a mixed-blood among full-bloods, destined never to penetrate the spiritual mysteries of the tribe. The novel ends on a note of ambivalence as Chal is left uncertain about his and his tribe's eventual future, but there is a presentiment of optimism that an acculturated mixed-blood with traditional sensibilities might well represent an alternative to unadulterated cultural loss and biological extinction.

Mathews employs descriptions of nature throughout the novel to connote traditionalism and tribal survivals. As a child Chal is depicted as an integral part of his natural surroundings, content in the old ways. He grows older, and his homeland undergoes changes emanating from "civilization's progress." That Mathews viewed the discovery of fossil fuels and the subsequent intertwining of Osages and oil with a decidedly jaundiced eye can be discerned in his description of the transformation of the reservation: "Slowly from the east the black oil derricks crept toward the west, rising above the blackjacks [scrub oaks], like some unnatural growth from the diseased tissues of the Earth."

Mathews seemed not to care that *Sundown* found only a tiny audience, and he stopped writing for nearly a decade. On 4 June 1934 he was elected to the Osage tribal council for the first of two successive four-year terms. The eight-man council was headed by an elected principal chief and an assistant principal chief. Although common usage held the council to be a tribal government, its mandate, beginning in 1908 through the authority of the 1906 Osage Allotment Act, provided for a business council, which was meant to function similarly to a board of directors. To hold office or even vote for council members required that an Osage be male, older than twenty-one, and an original allottee (born before 1 July 1907 and registered). Until the hard times of the 1930s Depression the council was almost wholly concerned with pleasant decisions, such as how many 160-acre parcels to offer at the periodic auctions for petroleum companies to bid on for drilling rights or how large a royalty to charge for each new producing gas well.

The price of energy fuels dropped dramatically in the early 1930s, and many Osages, previously insulated from earning a living, were faced with all the exigencies of the Depression. The Osage council's deliberations changed from discussing the maximizing of profits to minimizing the effects of the continuing sharp decline of royalty payments. By the time of the 1934 election a majority of the Osage electorate – 485 mixed-bloods and 165 full-bloods – voted for a council that included several mixed-bloods such as Mathews in the expectation that these acculturated office seekers could protect the tribe's interests. Following established custom, the principal chief's position was filled by a full-blood, Fred Lookout. Terry P. Wilson relates that when conservative full-bloods grumbled about the mixed-blood majority's power, Lookout challenged the mixed-blood council majority: "You have the thoughts of white men, but you have the interests of your people in your hearts. Do what you think is best. . . . If you let your white man tongues say what is in your Indian hearts you will do great things for your people."

Mathews not infrequently found himself cast in the role of tribal spokesman while he served two consecutive terms on the council. He was invariably the first to speak when visiting dignitaries or technocrats from Washington visited the tribal leaders. His formal education in geology aided him in dealing with the technical aspects of natural resource development. Partially on the strength of his personal competency, Mathews successfully enlisted Assistant Indian Commissioner William Zimmerman in keeping a degree of control over the Osage agency's minerals division in the hands of the council.

Fortunately for Mathews and the Osages, local tribal autonomy was encouraged for a time in the 1930s. President Franklin Roosevelt appointed John Collier to be commissioner of Indian affairs, and, although Oklahoma's Native Americans were excluded from the 1934 Indian Reorganization Act

(IRA) because of opposition from some acculturated tribes, the impact of the deepening Depression on the state's Native peoples convinced some to rethink their position. During the meetings held across the state over Oklahoma Indian participation in the IRA, Mathews, ardently supporting the New Deal from the beginning, debated Sen. Elmer Thomas, who opposed the new legislation. While the IRA was enacted without the inclusion of the state's tribes Mathews saw his arguments vindicated in 1935 when Congress passed the Oklahoma Indian Welfare Act, which essentially extended the IRA provisions to the state's Native population.

Mathews discovered that his tribe's past reputation as wealthy spendthrifts worked against his petitions for relief and recovery aid from the federal government. He led several council delegations to Washington and persuasively argued that his tribespeople's past profligacy was no different from that of their white neighbors during the preceding decade of prosperity. The council pushed hard to ensure the Osages a share of loans for agricultural development, participation in the Indian Civilian Conservation Corps, and education grants.

Mathews headed the tribal committee that made educational loans, but he saved his primary energy to facilitate a pet project: the funding and establishment of a tribal museum. Mathews pitched the idea to Collier when the commissioner visited Pawhuska, outlining the need for "a meeting place for the interchange of ideas . . . to carry on tribal traditions . . . someplace to store [dance] costumes, a museum." Collier surprised the council with an immediate and enthusiastic endorsement for the funding request from the Works Progress Administration (WPA). Construction began in summer 1936, prompting Mathews to begin a series of projects to enhance the museum's development that so preoccupied him that he wrote about one of them in his 1945 work, *Talking to the Moon.*

His public record as an effective, concerned councilman during the 1930s and early 1940s belies Mathews's personal life, which during these years was exceptionally private. After *Wah'Kon-Tah* was published he looked for a permanent residence, eventually choosing his own surface-land allotment – located eight miles from Pawhuska – as a building site. Atop a forest-covered ridge amid the hilly countryside that characterized the eastern half of Osage County, Mathews's red and yellow stone house resembled a hunting lodge, with its large fireplace (the principal source of heat), mounted deer's head, and stuffed birds, the products of Mathews's own taxidermy. Adorning the fireplace was a marble mantel with a Latin inscription that Mathews had read in North Africa over the entrance of an excavated Roman bathhouse: "Venari Lavari Ludere Ridere, Occast Vivere" (To Hunt, To Bathe, To Play, To Laugh, That is to Live).

Bearskin rugs were strewn over a concrete floor between the fireplace and some overflowing bookshelves. Mathews wrote at either a portable typewriter on a rolltop desk or a standard machine affixed to a metal stand. A large studio couch and a few metal chairs upholstered in green and red leather completed the furnishings. Attached to the cabin was a spacious screened-in porch, and a smaller screened room served as a kitchen. Surrounding the lodge was a low ornamental iron fence.

Mathews's life on the ridge is well chronicled in *Talking to the Moon.* This unusual work that some scholars have termed an "Osage *Walden*" is a casual but carefully crafted account of a decade at The Blackjacks, Mathews's home, named for its location in the forest. His travels, rather than making him restless, left Mathews anxious to escape an urbanizing world. He shared reminiscences about his return to Osage country with Logsdon: "I have an empathy with individuals, but groups – crowds – Tom Wolfe called them the 'man swarm.' . . . I never could get adjusted to the 'man swarm.'" Mathews explains in his third book that his coming back was "dramatic in a way; a weight on the sensitive scales of nature, which I knew would eventually be adjusted if I lived as I had planned to live; to become a part of the balance."

He failed to fulfill that goal. With a gentle irony and self-deprecatory wit characteristic of much Native American humor, he writes about that failure. The first year on the ridge he contented himself with observing wildlife, striving not to disturb their comings and goings. During the following years, however, he "brought conflict" in the form of guineas, chickens, and pheasants. "Perhaps," he opined, "my position was unnatural, living as I did, not from the ridge, but feeding myself artificially from cans. . . . I was not a part of the economic struggle of the ridge . . . and therefore I was really an anomaly."

At first, intent on not upsetting the natural flow of things, Mathews marked for building materials only those blackjacks "that ought to be cut . . . diseased, with black tree blood running from their sores." But as time passed the hunter in him was aroused and gunfire echoed across the ridge country with increasing frequency. This disclosure undoubtedly discountenances some nature enthusiasts reveling in the lyrical and learned descriptions of flora and fauna in *Talking to the Moon,* but Mathews thought differently. He discussed the feelings of respect for his "predacious neighbors," achieving "a greater harmony with my environment. . . . I realized for the first time that with responsibility come enemies." In his writing as in his life Mathews never succumbs to the facile sentimentalization of Indians as "natural ecologists." The Osages had always been hunters from necessity, while Mathews continued the tradition from choice. That he used the meat and skin of the deer whose antlers graced his lodge wall scarcely requires noting; he did not seek trophies but continued to hunt until physically unable, exhilarated by the chase, admitting that it was "a feeling that is very hard to understand; but it is life."

Talking to the Moon suggests a solitary life, and the arrangement of his narrative to the Osage lunar calendar – "the moon of popping trees" (winters so cold the trees snap and crack audibly) – conjures a picture of a near hermit; yet Mathews was not alone. Besides the regular trips to Pawhuska for provisions, council meetings, and to check on the construction of the museum, he hosted frequent visitors. These activities, too, are chronicled – descriptions of hale and hearty gatherings of hunters cooking the meat they had slain and quaffing large quantities of beer. These passages might have lended *Talking to the Moon* an Ernest Hemingway aura were they not interspersed with respect for nature and the enduring traditional Osages.

Mathews writes humorously about the results of one of his museum-related projects that left a valuable legacy to the tribe. The energetic councilman pried a second grant from the WPA in 1936 to commission a Chicago artist, Todros Geller, to paint a series of oil portraits of Osages to hang on the as-yet-unfinished museum walls. During the exceptionally hot, dusty summer, Mathews drove the diminutive Geller around the county in his station wagon, introducing the artist to his subjects, mostly older full-bloods of imposing height and bulk. The minor frustrations and triumphs the pair experienced as Mathews cajoled the generally reluctant and often haughty Osages to sit for the preliminary ink sketches offer as quintessential a portrayal of Indian humor as can be found in print. The finished portraits decorate the walls of the museum and draw the eye with their essence of powerful dignity.

Perhaps Mathews possessed too little of Hemingway's masculine prose style to appeal to a nation engaged in a world war. *Talking to the Moon* gained few readers and slight, albeit polite, response from literary critics at the time. The book went out of print, then was republished in 1981 when more-recent Native American literature created a vogue for earlier works. It is still not widely known, though specialists in the field often pick it as their favorite among Mathews's books.

Despite his distaste for close juxtaposition to "the man swarm," Mathews remained active beyond the environs of Osage County. In 1935 he accepted an appointment from Oklahoma governor E. W. Marland to the state board of education. Four years later he was awarded a Guggenheim Fellowship, which took him to Mexico for a year to study the history of European and Native conflict in preparation for a comparative study with the confrontation of the races in Oklahoma – a study he never wrote. Indian Commissioner John Collier chose him as a representative to the 1940 Indians of Americas Conference at Lake Patzcuaro in Michoacán, Mexico.

Governor Marland, a lifelong friend, was the subject of Mathews's fourth book, *Life and Death of an Oilman: The Career of E. W. Marland* (1952). The Osage writer expressed grave doubts about this venture while it was still in manuscript form. There were some difficulties with the University of Chicago Press over requests for additional information, and Mathews canceled the publication, thinking to "novelize the story, believing that it would make a first rate novel . . . that would be preferable to a second rate biography." Corresponding with Savoie Lottinville, an editor at the University of Oklahoma Press, Mathews admitted to a change of heart after rereading the manuscript.

Lottinville published the biography, which is described by Mathews as highly personal and impressionistic rather than scholarly. Despite the author's misgivings, reviewers praised the work, especially J. Frank Dobie in a *New York Times* review (21 October 1951), who called it "mature both in style and wisdom, in perspective, compass and interpretative power." The volume's strengths lay in superbly described natural settings and imaginative comparisons such as "cars were being spawned like salmon by Henry Ford." The sales of the biography were about average for a university press offering and prompted a New York literary agent to contact Mathews about a possible movie deal, but the negotiations did not go far.

Mathews married Elizabeth Palmour in 1945. She served as collaborator and typist for the biography and his last publication, *The Osages: Children of the Middle Waters* (1961). The two worked for several years, culling reams of manuscript materials for a comprehensive tribal history. Professional historians had difficulties with the final result, nearly eight hundred pages of narrative beginning with Osage creation accounts and stretching to a mid-nineteenth-century conclusion. The historian William T. Hagan reviewed *The Osages* for the *Mississippi Valley Historical Review* (Winter 1962), questioning Mathews's dependence on "mouth-to-ear history" and use of "instinctive knowledge" to reconstruct undocumented events. Mary E. Young, writing for the *American Historical Review* (July 1962), correctly surmised that "the intended result is . . . epic rather than monographic," with its complete lack of footnotes and reliance on oral tradition. The increasing popularity and acceptance of ethnohistorical methodology, like oral tradition, has caused the tribal history to be considered in a more positive light by scholars since the 1970s.

Eighteen years passed between the release of *The Osages* and Mathews's death on 11 June 1979. He had moved with his wife into a house on Agency Hill to Pawhuska, until illnesses required closer access to doctors and hospitals. Until the end he remained concerned about the tribal museum, visiting frequently and, after thieves broke into the building in the early 1970s, telephoning the curator's office near closing time each day to ensure that all doors and windows were locked. He continued writing until his death, leaving behind two unpublished manuscripts: a novel completed in 1952 and titled "Within Your Dream" and a massive autobiography completed in 1974 with the working title "Twenty Thousand Mornings." Still "polishing" the manuscript in 1978, Mathews commented in the Logsdon interview that publishers had expressed dismay about its length. Mathews's reaction characterizes his literary efforts and much of his life: "Well, you see I'm writing it anyhow; I'm not writing it for publishers."

Mathews's work continues to be read primarily by Oklahomans, historians, and scholarly specialists in Native American culture. Generally scholars, historical and literary, have rehabilitated Mathews's stature from the artifactual – as one of the earliest American Indian writers – to critical appreciation, especially for *Sundown, Talking to the Moon,* and *The Osages.* Literary styles have changed too drastically from Mathews's ornate phrasings, and his historical scope was too narrowly focused on the Osages for wider acclaim or a much expanded readership. Nonetheless, despite his self-admitted near dilettantish attitude toward his writing, Mathews's reputation as a significant pioneer of now classic Native American literary themes and ethnohistorical methodology will probably endure and grow.

Interview:

Guy Logsdon, "John Joseph Mathews – A Conversation," *Nimrod,* 16 (April 1972): 70–75.

References:

Garrick Bailey, "John Joseph Mathews," in *American Indian Intellectuals,* edited by Margot Liberty (Saint Paul: West, 1978), pp. 205–216;

Carol Hunter, "The Protagonist as a Mixed-Blood in John Joseph Mathews' Novel Sundown," *American Indian Quarterly,* 6 (1982): 319–337;

Hunter, "The Protagonist as a Mixed Blood in John Joseph Mathews' Sundown," *MELUS,* 9 (1982): 61–72;

Charles R. Larson, *American Indian Fiction* (Albuquerque: University of New Mexico Press, 1978), pp. 55–65;

Louis Owens, *Other Destinies: Understanding the American Indian Novel* (Norman: University of Oklahoma Press, 1992), pp. 49–60;

Robert Allen Warrior, *Tribal Secrets: Recovering American Indian Intellectual Traditions* (Minneapolis: University of Minnesota Press, 1995);

Terry P. Wilson, "Osage Oxonian: The Heritage of John Joseph Mathews," *Chronicles of Oklahoma,* 59 (Fall 1981): 264–293.

D'Arcy McNickle

(18 January 1904 – 18 October 1977)

Birgit Hans
University of North Dakota

BOOKS: *The Surrounded* (New York: Dodd, Mead, 1936);

They Came Here First: The Epic of the American Indian (Philadelphia: Lippincott, 1949; revised edition, New York: Harper & Row, 1975);

Runner in the Sun: A Story of Indian Maize (New York: Holt, Rinehart & Winston, 1954);

Indians and Other Americans: Two Ways of Life Meet, by McNickle and Harold E. Fey (New York: Harper, 1959; revised edition, New York: Harper & Row, 1970);

The Indian Tribes of the United States: Ethnic and Cultural Survival (London & New York: Oxford University Press, 1962); republished as *Native American Tribalism: Indian Survivals and Renewals* (New York: Published for the Institute of Race Relations by Oxford University Press, 1973);

Indian Man: A Life of Oliver La Farge (Bloomington: Indiana University Press, 1971);

Wind from an Enemy Sky (San Francisco: Harper & Row, 1978);

The Hawk Is Hungry and Other Stories, edited by Birgit Hans (Tucson: University of Arizona Press, 1992).

Editions: *The Surrounded* (Albuquerque: University of New Mexico Press, 1978);

Runner in the Sun: A Story of Indian Maize (Albuquerque: University of New Mexico Press, 1987);

Wind from an Enemy Sky (Albuquerque: University of New Mexico Press, 1988).

SELECTED PERIODICAL PUBLICATIONS – UNCOLLECTED: "Four Years of Indian Reorganization," *Indians at Work,* 5 (July 1938): 4–11;

"A U.S. Indian Speaks," *Americas,* 6 (1954): 8–11, 27;

"The Indian in American Society," *Social Welfare Forum* (1955): 68–77;

"The Healing Vision," *Tomorrow* (1956): 25–31;

"Indian and European: Indian-White Relations from Discovery to 1887," *Annals of the American Academy of Political and Social Science,* 311 (May 1957): 1–17;

D'Arcy McNickle (The Newberry Library)

"It's Almost Never Too Late," *Christian Century,* 74 (1957): 227–229;

"The Indian Tests the Mainstream," *Nation* (26 September 1966): 275–279;

"A Record of the Vanishing West," *Nation* (25 December 1967): 693–694;

"American Indians Who Never Were," *Indian Historian,* 3 (1970): 4–7.

In 1936 D'Arcy McNickle's *The Surrounded* joined two other novels by Native Americans that dealt with contemporary Native American life:

Mourning Dove's *Cogewea* (1927) and John Joseph Mathews's *Sundown* (1934). McNickle's work was the last such novel to be published until N. Scott Momaday's *House Made of Dawn* (1968) was added to the short list, which grew rapidly thereafter. McNickle's novel is unusual in that it rejects assimilation of Native peoples into mainstream Euro-American culture; neither *Cogewea* nor *Sundown* go beyond questioning the exploitative actions of the federal government. The disappearance of Native cultures is lamented, but the underlying philosophical tenets of westward expansion are never really questioned by Mourning Dove or Mathews. In an earlier manuscript version of *The Surrounded,* however, McNickle expresses the same convictions as Mourning Dove and Mathews: Native cultures, locked in their primitive though picturesque state, must disappear in the interest of progress. This version is a Western romance like *Cogewea,* and its publication would have aligned it with Mourning Dove's and Mathews's assimilationist novels. McNickle moved away from the basic assumptions shared by the Euro-American reading public and early Native writers and reinterpreted the history of westward expansion, thereby anticipating the novels of Momaday, Leslie Marmon Silko, James Welsh, and a host of others by thirty years.

Over the years there have been many discussions of the "Indianness" of various Native American writers. McNickle has not escaped this controversy, and critics have tried to prove that he was not really the quarter-blood that his enrollment record in the Flathead tribe claims. Such discussions are, ultimately, unproductive. It is the prerogative of federally recognized tribes to make enrollment decisions; also, though the circumstances of McNickle's growing up and his involvement in national Indian policy may have kept him away from the Flathead reservation, he never ceased to see himself as a Native American. Instead of belonging to a tribal community, McNickle chose to be part of the national Native community. His choice is in keeping with traditional practices of Native American tribal cultures, wherein individuals were able to negotiate memberships in various groups. It is not for the literary critic to determine whether McNickle was a Flathead or even a Native American; it is more useful to look in his work for those themes that have been identified as peculiar to Native American fiction and to examine the ways he deals with those themes.

William D'Arcy McNickle was born on 18 January 1904 in Saint Ignatius, Montana. He was the youngest of three children of Philomene Parenteau McNickle, a Métis whose father had had to flee Canada because of his participation in the Louis Riel rebellion of 1885, and William McNickle, a white man from Pennsylvania who tried his hand at several occupations, such as working on the railroad and teaching in an industrial school. Philomene and her children were adopted into the Flathead tribe in 1905 and received allotments of land on the reservation under the provisions of the General Allotment Act of 1887 (Dawes Act). McNickle and his sisters grew up on and near the Flathead Reservation until 1914, when their parents were divorced. William McNickle maintained control over the children's allotments after the divorce. There is no evidence that D'Arcy McNickle had any contact with his father after that time.

In a letter written to the commissioner of Indian affairs during the divorce proceedings, McNickle's mother said that she intended to raise her son as a Euro-American, which would ensure a better life for him than that of unassimilated Indian. In the spirit of the time, however, Philomene, as an Indian, was considered an unfit mother by the superintendent of the Flathead Reservation, and ten-year-old D'Arcy, thirteen-year-old Florence, and fourteen-year-old Ruth were removed from her custody and sent to the Indian boarding school in Chemawa, Oregon. In *Indians and Other Americans* (1959), co-authored with Harold E. Fey, McNickle discusses the destructive nature of government boarding schools, whose goals were to teach Native children the evil of their ancestral traditions, strip them of their Native languages, and assimilate them as completely as possible into Euro-American culture. In the manuscript version of *The Surrounded,* however, the main character, Archilde, believes that the harsh treatment of Native children is justifiable, since it enables them to participate in Euro-American culture, and he insists that his nephews attend the boarding school in Oregon where he had been a student. McNickle's attitude toward boarding schools would change considerably by the time he published *The Surrounded:* one of Archilde's nephews is so psychologically crippled by his boarding-school experience that only participation in a traditional Flathead dance ceremony can restore his emotional balance.

McNickle left Chemawa in 1917 and joined his mother and her new white husband, Gus Dahlberg. After attending high schools in Montana and Washington State, depending on where the family was living at the time, he became a student at the University of Montana in 1921 – he was probably the first Native American to attend the school –

to study literature and history. McNickle was on the staff of the university's literary journal, *The Frontier,* in which he published some poems and two short stories. Both stories reflect the literary conventions of the time. "The Silver Locket" (1923) is a "rags-to-riches" tale that shows that material success cannot replace human relationships. "Going to School," published in the 1928–1929 issue of *The Frontier,* is an account of a day in the lives of three teenagers in a western settlement. Since McNickle is writing here from personal experience, there is a more authoritative voice in "Going to School" than in the earlier story, and something of his brilliance in writing descriptive passages can already be seen here.

In 1925 McNickle sold his allotment of reservation land and used the money to go to England to study at Oxford, but his funds ran out before he could finish his degree requirements. He settled in New York City after his return from Oxford in 1926 and married Joran Birkeland, whom he had met at the University of Montana. He worked as a manuscript reader and editor for various publishing houses and trade journals in New York and, for a short time, in Philadelphia. He spent the summer of 1931 studying at the University of Grenoble.

During his years in New York, McNickle collected – as he put it – a drawerful of rejection slips from publishers for versions of the novel that was to become *The Surrounded.* The writers of the rejection slips encouraged him to keep revising the manuscript, and he did so. How many versions of the novel actually existed is not clear, but he used at least two working titles – "The Hungry Generations" and "Dead Grass" – before finally settling on *The Surrounded.* The manuscript in The Newberry Library does not have a title page, but internal evidence suggests that it must be one of the versions written under the title "The Hungry Generations."

The first part of the manuscript version is similar to that of the published novel. Archilde, the youngest son of a Spanish father, Max, and a Flathead mother, returns to his father's ranch after some years of playing the violin in urban centers in the western states. He plans to say good-bye to his mother and move on; but he reluctantly becomes involved in the harvesting of Max's fields and takes his mother on a hunting trip that results in the deaths of his brother Louis and a game warden. He is arrested in connection with the game warden's disappearance but released for lack of evidence. Finally, he is reconciled with his father. The middle part of the manuscript version is entirely absent from *The Surrounded:* after his father's death Archilde journeys to Paris to educate himself; walks around the city or practices on his violin; strikes up friendships with some American music students; meets the young American Claudia Burness; remembers his experiences at the boarding school in Chemawa; and, after learning of his mother's death, departs for Montana to manage his father's ranch. The final part of the manuscript version also has no counterpart in the published novel: it includes Archilde's attempt to turn his nephews into Euro-American farmers, his troubled relationship with the storekeeper Moser, his arrest for the murder of the game warden, his weeks in jail, his trial and acquittal, and Claudia's letter announcing her imminent arrival. The manuscript version includes lengthy passages of interior monologue that give the reader an insight into Archilde's increasing self-assurance but otherwise tend to be tedious.

McNickle's depiction of Flathead culture in the unpublished manuscript version of his novel is in tune with the public taste of his time. There is not a single strong Native character in this version. Archilde's mother even remains nameless throughout. Blind Michel, a Flathead elder whom Archilde encounters on his way home after the trial, is described somewhat sympathetically, but he is dirty and smelly. Archilde's brothers are alcoholics or are demented as a result of sexually transmitted diseases caught from Indian women. His nephews, though they are finally persuaded by their mother to testify on their uncle's behalf, are portrayed as ingrates for the shabby way they repay Archilde's attempts to assimilate them into white culture. The General Allotment Act of 1887 is mentioned repeatedly; the act attempted to make Native peoples individual instead of collective landowners, as Euro-Americans believed that all "civilized" people should value private property. McNickle's description of Archilde's brother's farm, with its unused agricultural tools and air of general neglect, makes it clear that the policy is not working, that the Flathead have no understanding of civilization as Euro-Americans define it and are incapable of "bettering" themselves. Archilde is an exception, as his defense attorney points out at the trial.

Archilde sees only one way to join Euro-American culture: he must remove himself from Flathead territory and become civilized by attending an eastern college and traveling to Paris. McNickle followed a well-established tradition in sending Archilde east, but his pilgrimage teaches Archilde that ambition can be destructive – Claudia's mother's boundless ambition for her sons'

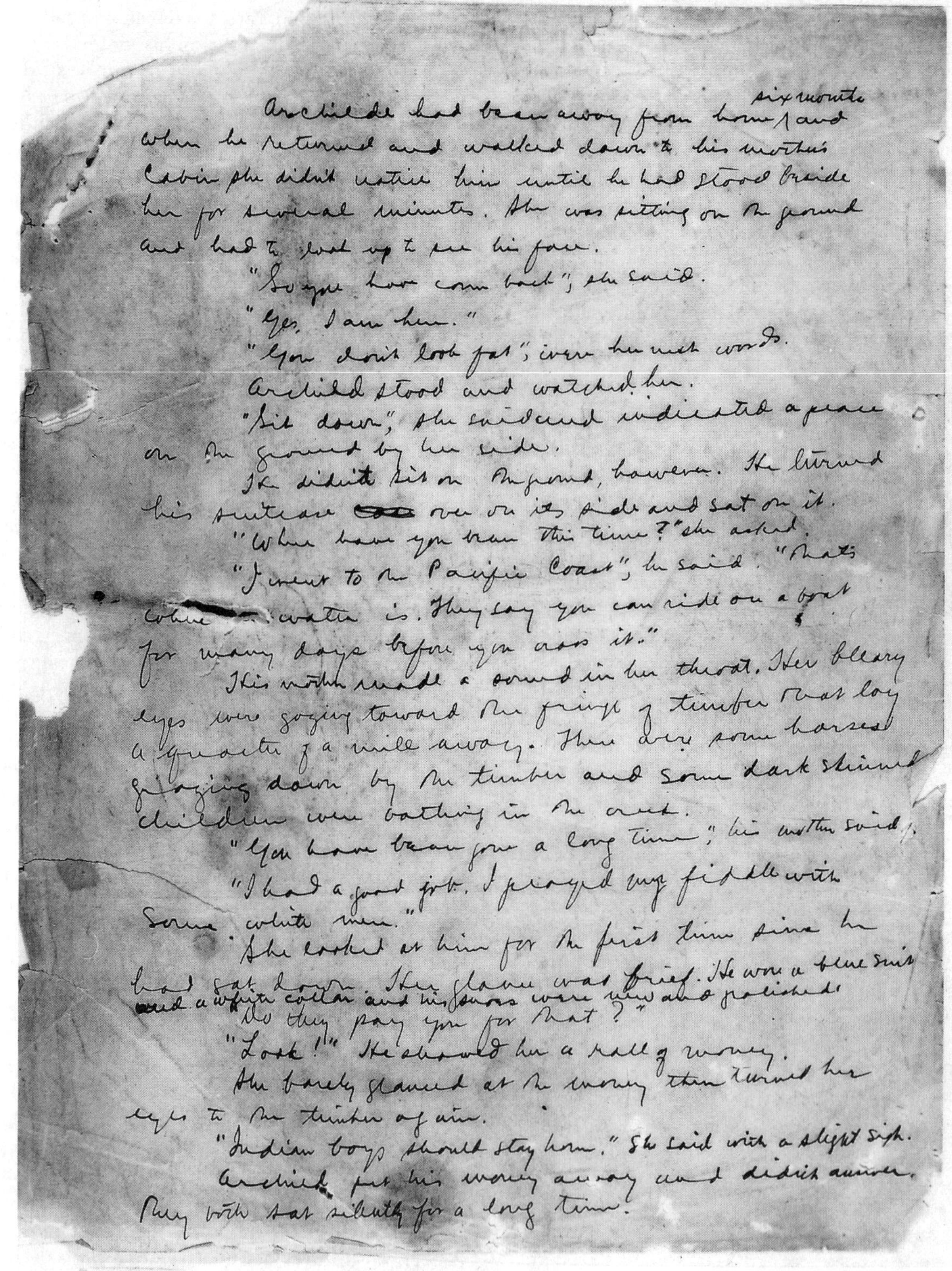
Archilde had been away from home six months and when he returned and walked down to his mother's cabin she didn't notice him until he had stood beside her for several minutes. She was sitting on the ground and had to look up to see his face.

"So you have come back," she said.

"Yes, I am here."

"You don't look fat," were her next words.

Archilde stood and watched her.

"Sit down," she said and indicated a place on the ground by her side.

He didn't sit on the ground, however. He turned his suitcase over on its side and sat on it.

"Where have you been this time?" she asked.

"I went to the Pacific Coast," he said. "That's where [illegible] water is. They say you can ride on a boat for many days before you cross it."

His mother made a sound in her throat. Her bleary eyes were gazing toward the fringe of timber that lay a quarter of a mile away. There were some horses grazing down by the timber and some dark skinned children were bathing in the creek.

"You have been gone a long time," his mother said.

"I had a good job. I played my fiddle with some white men."

She looked at him for the first time since he had sat down. Her glance was brief. He wore a blue suit and a white collar and his shoes were new and polished.

"Do they pay you for that?"

"Look!" He showed her a roll of money.

She barely glanced at the money then turned her eyes to the timber again.

"Indian boys should stay home." She said with a slight sigh.

Archilde put his money away and didn't answer. They both sat silently for a long time.

Page from the manuscript for one of the unpublished versions of McNickle's novel The Surrounded *(1936) (The Newberry Library)* musical careers destroys her and could have destroyed her sons, as well. Although McNickle deleted this middle part of the manuscript version, he rewrote it later as a short story, "In the Alien Corn." The desire to be part of civilized culture is the focus of another short story, "Six Beautiful in Paris," in which a professor of Romance literature is mortally embarrassed by a surprise encounter with his rough-edged but wealthy brother. Etiquette and form have replaced human feelings in the professor, and prejudice against his nephew's Jewish girlfriend is part of the "most civilized" life he is leading. Both stories were published in *The Hawk Is Hungry and Other Stories* (1992).

The official view of westward expansion is given by the prosecuting attorney at Archilde's trial at the end of the unpublished manuscript version of *The Surrounded.* There is no need, he says, to justify the displacement of Native peoples; the Euro-Americans represent a higher order of existence. Native peoples must be forced to participate on a lower level of that superior order, but any attempt on their part, such as Archilde's, to become respected members of Euro-American society should be discouraged. Louis's death is not even an issue; the game warden who killed him is regarded as the victim of a form of violence that is irrational to a thinking Euro-American but a natural attribute of Indians. The defense attorney, as well, makes it clear to the court that the respect he feels for Archilde does not extend to the Flathead community in general; he reaffirms the prosecutor's ethnocentric attitudes toward Native peoples by emphasizing Archilde's uniqueness. The judge's final words are addressed to the exceptional individual Archilde, who will henceforth be counted as a member of Euro-American society in Montana.

Mathews used a similar structure in *Sundown.* His young Osage character, Chal, is also searching for his place in Euro-American culture. Like Archilde, Chal never doubts the value of assimilation, even though he feels respect for some of the strong Native American characters in the novel. His search also leads him away from the reservation, first to college and then into the air force. But, unlike Archilde, Chal has no clear vision of what his role in the dominant culture should be. His inability to understand the underlying assumptions of the alien culture and to see Euro-Americans as individuals dooms his attempt to assimilate from the beginning. Archilde, on the other hand, recognizes that he can be successful in his assimilation only if he understands the dominant culture; therefore, the reader finds him sitting in the lounge of his Paris hotel, reading a history book. Mathews also brings up the problems caused by the Allotment Act; but, whereas in McNickle's manuscript the failure of the policy is blamed on the Flatheads' inability to elevate themselves, Mathews's Osages are betrayed by the government. The belief that the basic policy is sound permits Chal to remain steadfast in his advocacy of assimilation. Both McNickle and Mathews thus subscribe, though in different ways, to the official Euro-American version of history.

A theme that is dominant in the manuscript version of *The Surrounded* but plays a much less important role in the published novel is the mixed-bloodedness of the main character. Archilde's father's reflections on the issue take up considerable space in the manuscript, and, again, McNickle chooses not to dispute the dominant ideas of his time. One belief was that the mixing of "inferior" Native with "superior" Euro-American stocks led to a deterioration of the superior one; another belief was that the mixed-blood inherited the worst traits of both parents. It is in this context that Max's attitude toward his sons can be understood: he calls them "ugly" and "black" and regards them as irredeemably lost. But if Archilde marries Claudia, a white girl, Archilde's inferior Indian blood will be diluted in their offspring and further degeneration will be prevented. Certainly, one of the greatest achievements of the published version of *The Surrounded* is that it deals with the mixed-blood issue in a way that rejects popular beliefs. Mourning Dove and Mathews also use mixed-bloods as main characters; but, while Cogewea comments on the unjust treatment of the mixed-bloods by the Euro-American and Native communities, Chal feels superior to the backward full-blood community and is ashamed when he views the full-bloods' actions through Euro-American eyes.

McNickle's manuscript version, the published version of *The Surrounded,* Mourning Dove's *Cogewea,* and Mathews's *Sundown* are alike in their vivid descriptions of Western life and landscape. *The Surrounded,* because of the absolute control of language that McNickle had attained at this point in his literary career, is even more powerful than the manuscript version in this respect. McNickle's writing style is spare; everything unnecessary has been trimmed away. His remarkable command of the English language, he himself felt, was in large measure because of his training at Oxford. Mathews, who attended Oxford as well, also makes every word count.

The manuscript version of *The Surrounded* reflects McNickle's cultural beliefs during the early years of his residence in New York City; after he had started to rethink the white ethnocentric attitudes he had been taught, he reflected in his journal that he had bought into the "salesman's dream" and had suppressed his instincts so as to make a place for himself in modern urban America. The turning point for McNickle seems to have been the birth of his daughter Antoinette in 1933. Since leaving the boarding school in Chemawa in 1917 McNickle had used his stepfather's name, Dahlberg; even his passport listed both names. Antoinette's birth forced him to make a decision about which name to perpetuate, and he chose McNickle – even though the name must have reminded him of those difficult years growing up on and near the Flatland Reservation as well as of the years in the boarding school in Chemawa. He also reestablished contact with his mother. On an economic level, the Great Depression forced him to reexamine the Euro-American materialistic definition of success.

His journals written in 1934 manifest a growing frustration with publishers. He had followed their suggestions carefully in revising the manuscript, but they continued to reject it. That year he began his most thorough revision of "The Hungry Generations"; everything, except for the first forty pages, was completely rewritten, and the new version was given the working title "Dead Grass." No version of "Dead Grass" seems to have survived, but a reader's report indicates that everything superfluous had been trimmed away and a major rethinking of cultural assumptions had taken place. By the time he completed the final revision of *The Surrounded* he had lost his earlier confidence that he could be economically successful as a writer. McNickle says in his journal that publishing has little to do with promoting art or exploring new ideas; publishers are interested in profits and are unwilling to support a novel that does not fit into the public taste, especially one by an unknown author.

Desperate for a source of income to support his family, McNickle looked for employment opportunities outside the publishing world. The Indian Reorganization Act of 1934 rejected the assimilationist policies of earlier years, and Indian Commissioner John Collier's promise of preferential hiring of Native Americans indicated that Native peoples were finally to have a say in their own future. McNickle applied for a position with the Bureau of Indian Affairs in 1934; but when he moved to Washington, D.C., in 1935 it was to participate in the Federal Writers' Project, a New Deal program. His application to the Bureau of Indian Affairs was still pending, however, and in 1936 McNickle finally joined the bureau.

The Surrounded was published by Dodd, Mead in 1936. It is the first Native American novel with a nonassimilationist voice. While the manuscript version portrays the General Allotment Act of 1887 as well-intentioned and attributes its failure to the Flatheads' inability to rise above their savage state, *The Surrounded* shows the negative economic and social impact of the act. The hopelessness of the Native people who have lost their ancestral land is contrasted with the temporary worries about the drought on the part of the white farmers who are using the land. McNickle paints a powerful picture of the abject poverty on the reservation in his description of an old woman bringing home from the slaughterhouse, in a child's wobbly wagon, the bloody entrails that will serve as a meal for her family. Even the old missionary, Father Grepilloux, comments on the physical decline the Flatheads have experienced; of course, for him this loss is balanced by their conversion to Christianity.

Max, Archilde's father, is ambivalent about what the loss of their land has done to the Flatheads. Having come from Spain and a tradition that also values land more than money, he feels a spiritual connection to the Flathead Valley at his first sight of it, but his greatest joy comes when he sees the cross planted in the valley. He sees himself as rooting his family as firmly in this soil as he had been anchored in the Spanish soil. In his eagerness to accomplish this goal he alienates his sons, and he has no understanding, at least initially, that the Native culture might value the land in different ways. He expects his wife, Catherine, who has been introduced to Euro-American ways and, of course, has been converted, to share his vision of an agrarian paradise; when his values clash with Catherine's Flathead ones, he rejects her. When he finally reconciles with his youngest son, Archilde, however, he suggests that the latter go off to study music; his relationship with Archilde no longer depends on the son's willingness to take care of his father's land.

The mixed-blood theme is given much less prominence in *The Surrounded* than in the manuscript version, and social theories are not discussed. In the published novel Euro-Americans automatically consider mixed-bloods to belong to the Native community. McNickle portrays the Flatheads in much more sympathetic terms here than in the manuscript version; there are strong male and female Flathead characters, Archilde's mother and her uncle Modeste among them, whose dignified behavior and wisdom contrasts favorably with the greed of the storekeeper Moser, the prejudice of the sheriff, the indifference of the white farmers, and the bureaucratic attitude of the Indian agent. Archilde's fate is left open at the end of the novel; but, whether or not he is convicted of the game warden's murder, he has gained something much more important than freedom: his connectedness to the community and the beginning of an understanding of his mother and her people.

Other themes introduced in *The Surrounded* that are not found in the manuscript version include the importance of Flathead oral tradition and the destructive role of the Catholic Church. McNickle uses stories from the oral tradition of Catherine's people not only to move the plot of the novel along but also to explain to the reader the way in which the Flatheads organize their universe. The stories are presented without disclaimer or apology; they are an important part of Flathead life and give a hint of the rich culture that is being destroyed. That the oral tradition is alive despite the pressures of Christianity is demonstrated by the story that Father Grepilloux tells Max about "Big Paul," a Christianized Flathead from a distinguished family who is destroyed by the conflict between tribal law and Christian beliefs. Father Grepilloux says that he has heard several versions of the story; it has been incorporated into the oral tradition and is perhaps the contemporary version of a much older tale. The Flathead oral tradition, then, is an enduring one, and the story of Archilde and his mother will become part of that tradition, as well.

In contrast to McNickle, neither Mourning Dove nor Mathews addresses the Catholic Church's role in the assimilation effort; the church would, however, assume a prominent place in later Native American fiction – for instance, in Momaday's *House Made of Dawn,* Silko's *Ceremony* (1977), and Louise Erdrich's *Love Medicine* (1984). McNickle juxtaposes two priests in *The Surrounded.* The old priest, Father Grepilloux, is described in sympathetic terms as a man whose life has been devoted to the conversion of Native peoples. He has a fond indulgence for some Native rituals and expresses doubts about the policy of assimilation – but, of course, not about the Christianization of Native peoples. The young priest, Father Jerome, lacks the commitment of Father Grepilloux; there is no indulgence or questioning in his attitude. He simply demands assimilation as a prerequisite to Christianization, and he cherishes the form of Christian worship rather than spiritual commitment to it. The reader's final view of the church is an ambivalent one; there seems to be no place for Catholicism among the Flatheads, and Father Jerome's attitude precludes any adjustment on the part of the church.

Neither *Cogewea* nor *Sundown* has such striking Native women characters as Catherine and Elise in *The Surrounded.* In *Cogewea* the Stemteema is a keeper of traditions and helps Cogewea to find her own way with the help of the buffalo skull, but she is a presence rather than a participant in the action; in *Sundown* Chal's mother occasionally gives her son a nudge in the right direction. Neither is a fully developed character, though. Catherine, on the other hand, not only determines her son's life but is a full participant in the plot and undergoes major character development. The high esteem in which she is held by the Flathead people surprises Archilde, whose Euro-American education has taught him to regard Native women as inferior; in traditional cultures relationships of men and women were built on reciprocity, and women held honored positions within the tribe. Catherine's acceptance of civilization is superficial, but her adherence to Christianity is so staunch that she is called "Faithful" Catherine. The murder of her son Louis and her killing of the game warden in the mountains provide a turning point; she now sees that the church has caused disunity and lawlessness. In their night council the Flathead elders acknowledge the damage wrought, punish Catherine's guilt in the traditional way – by whipping her – and determine to return to their ancestral beliefs and assume responsibility for their spiritual well-being once more. Catherine's refusal to see the priest before her death shows that her rejection of Christianity is complete.

Archilde's girlfriend, Elise La Rose, on the other hand, is an example of what the Euro-American educational system can do to Native girls. While Catherine accepted her education outwardly without internalizing its teachings, Elise rebels against it; but she does not have Catherine's strong traditional culture to fall back on. Like Catherine, however, she is not the meek, subservient Indian woman of Euro-American stereotype; she takes charge when Archilde is too stunned to make decisions, and she kills the sheriff to keep Archilde from being rearrested and prosecuted for the game warden's murder. The parallels to Catherine are obvious; if her traditional culture had not been educated out of her, Elise could have become another strong female elder.

Mourning Dove, Mathews, and McNickle all use a dance scene to contrast Native American and

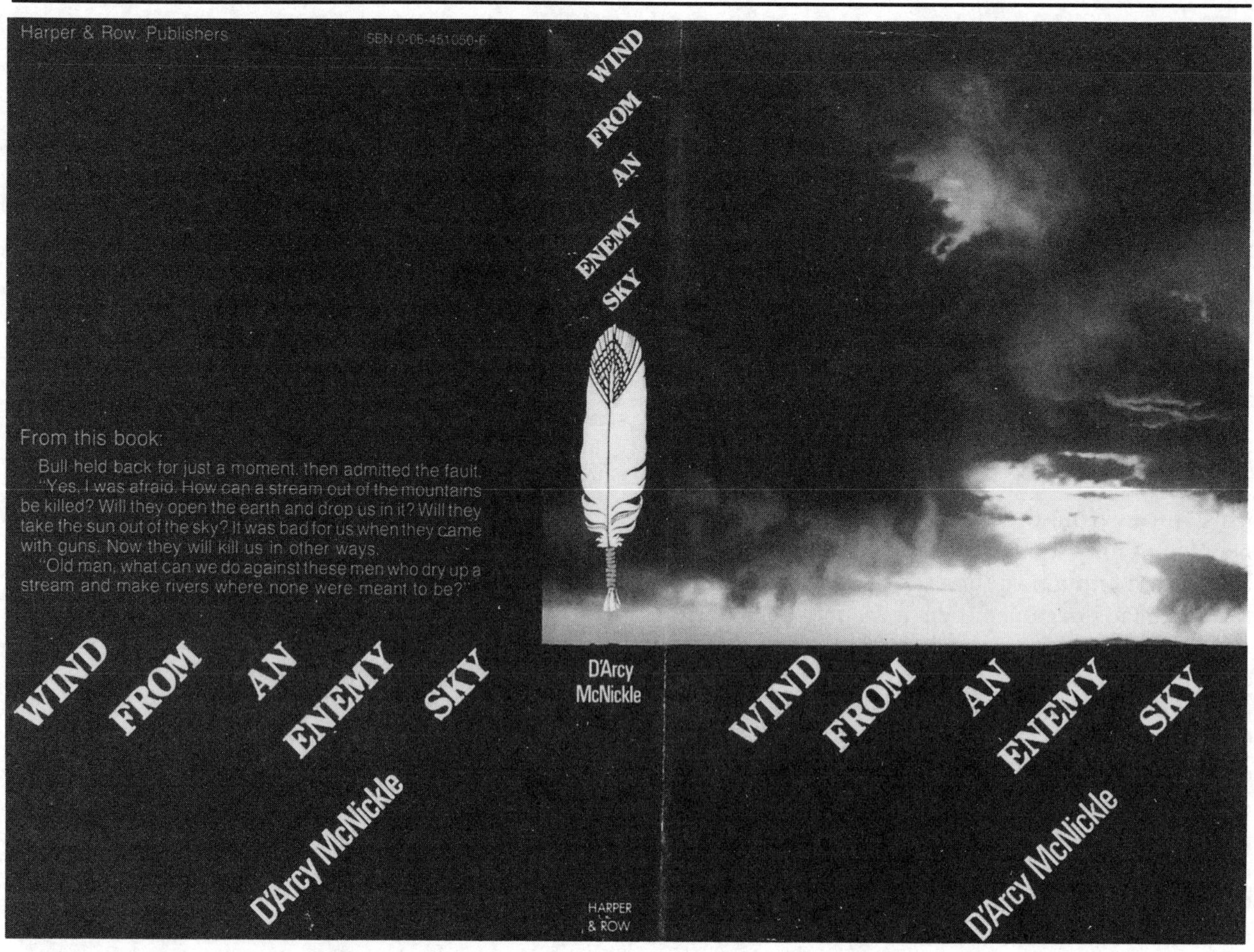

Dust jacket for McNickle's posthumously published novel about the Little Elk people, a fictional tribe meant to represent Native Americans in general

Euro-American values. In all three novels Euro-American spectators have no understanding of what they are seeing; if anything, they consider the dance's monotony boring. Mourning Dove explains what the dance means; her heroine, Cogewea, shows respect for the traditions of the Native peoples and laments the ignorance of the Euro-American spectators but does not become emotionally involved in the dance. Chal's reaction in *Sundown* is much more complex: embarrassed by the tourists and truly affected by the dance, he nevertheless cannot forget what is expected of someone "civilized." Later, while drunk, he desecrates the spiritual nature of the dance. Mourning Dove and Mathews then use the dance scenes to express their main characters' disconnectedness from their tribal heritages. In *The Surrounded,* however, Archilde keenly feels the desecration of the dance that is caused by the presence of the Euro-American observers, to whom it is a spectacle similar to rodeo events and barn dances, and he removes himself from the scene. The spiritual connectedness with his people that he feels at the dance proves the turning point for Archilde.

The reviews of *The Surrounded* were generally favorable, especially mentioning McNickle's fine descriptions of western life and landscape. None of the reviewers, however, except Oliver La Farge in *The Saturday Review of Literature* (14 March 1936), did more than mention the Indian themes of the novel; none of them discussed Archilde's growing respect for the Flathead culture. Some of the reviewers thought that the novel's plot could have been stronger and more convincing.

McNickle and Joran were divorced shortly after the move to Washington; Antoinette remained with McNickle. On 13 September 1939 McNickle married Roma Kauffman; their daughter, Kathleen, was born in 1940.

While McNickle was still living in New York City he had started writing a second novel. Like *The*

Surrounded, this work, posthumously published in 1978 as *Wind from an Enemy Sky,* also went through many revisions and distinct versions. Also as in the case of the earlier novel, there is one extant manuscript of an early version, titled "How Anger Died," at The Newberry Library. The main theme of "How Anger Died" and *Wind from an Enemy Sky* is the same: the repatriation of a sacred medicine bundle named Feather Boy to the tribe. There all similarity ends. "How Anger Died" is a romance, and Feather Boy is returned intact in a spectacular scene involving the landing of an airplane on a meadow. The commissioner of Indian affairs, who fired the Indian agent because of the latter's role in the repatriation effort and his opposition to the exploitation of the tribal people under his care, is forced to reinstate him under media pressure. The future of the tribal people is bright, and the agent will help them to incorporate the best of Euro-American traditions without damaging their cultural integrity. Like all of McNickle's fiction, "How Anger Died" includes excellent descriptions; among them is the encounter between the commissioner of Indian affairs and the traditional chief, Bull, in Washington, D.C. The plot of "How Anger Died" is more loosely structured, and the prose is not as compact, as in the published novel. Like *The Surrounded,* this novel gained by being rewritten many times.

While McNickle continued to revise his second novel and occasionally wrote short stories, fiction took up less and less of his time during his Washington years. He published a history of Indian-white relations from a Native American viewpoint, *They Came Here First: The Epic of the American Indian* (1949), and contributed articles on a wide range of Native American issues to scholarly journals and popular magazines.

McNickle was involved in the founding of the National Congress of American Indians in 1944. He moved up through the ranks of the Bureau of Indian Affairs until 1952; he left the service that year because he could not support the federal policy of termination, which sought to end all moral and legal obligations toward Native peoples. After his resignation McNickle moved to Denver and became executive director of American Indian Development, a nonprofit organization funded by the Field Foundation. Roma eventually returned to Washington; their marriage, however, would not be dissolved until 1967. McNickle returned to fiction in 1954 with a juvenile novel, *Runner in the Sun,* which has a pre-Columbian setting. In 1959 he and Fey published *Indians and Other Americans: Two Ways of Life Meet.* McNickle participated in the all-Indian conference in Chicago in 1961 that drafted the Declaration of Indian Purpose; the document would influence federal policy for years to come. His *Native American Tribalism: Indian Survivals and Renewals* (1973), though somewhat dated, has become a classic and is used in college classrooms throughout the nation.

In 1966 McNickle received an honorary doctor of science degree from the University of Colorado. That same year he accepted an invitation to establish and become chairman of the anthropology department at the University of Saskatchewan's Regina campus. He married his third wife, Viola Pfrommer, in 1967; she had been his field assistant in his community work for American Indian Development in Colorado. McNickle remained chairman of the anthropology department until his retirement to Albuquerque, New Mexico, in 1971. His biography of La Farge, *Indian Man,* was published that year. In 1972 the board of The Newberry Library appointed him program director of its prestigious Center for the History of the American Indians, which was renamed for him after his death. Viola McNickle, who had developed Alzheimer's disease shortly after their marriage, died a few months before her husband's death of a massive coronary at his home in Albuquerque on 18 October 1977.

Wind from an Enemy Sky was published the following year. It is set among the Little Elk people, a fictional tribe that, as McNickle pointed out in a letter of 6 July 1976, was meant to represent Native Americans in general. In addition to commenting on federal Indian policy, McNickle is concerned here with the lack of respect among Euro-Americans for Native American spirituality. When the novel opens, the Little Elk chief, Bull, is angry about the dam that has flooded an area sacred to his tribe. Henry Jim, Bull's older brother, who chose to assimilate and now holds a respected position among the Euro-American ranchers of the area, attempts to heal the thirty-year-old breach between himself and his brother by asking for the return of the Feather Boy medicine bundle, the spiritual center of the tribe, that he had given to the missionary. The support of Rafferty, the superintendent of the Little Elk Reservation, is won for the plan, despite the objections of the missionary and the commissioner. Henry Jim dies before the goal can be accomplished, but before his death he rejects all symbols and teachings of Euro-American culture. Bull and his band bury him in the traditional way, shooting his horse so that it can accompany him into the afterlife. Adam Pell, whose museum acquired the sacred bundle, agrees to return it. Preparations progress smoothly until Pell reveals that carelessness has destroyed the bundle. Deprived of hope for the spiritual healing of his people, Bull shoots Rafferty and Pell and is, in turn, shot by an Indian policeman. By killing Pell, Bull has avenged the destruction of his tribe's spiritual center and has assumed, for the final time, the responsibility of chief; but Rafferty's death deprives the Little Elk of their only protection from the greedy Euro-Americans. The novel thus closes on a pessimistic note.

When *Wind from an Enemy Sky* was submitted to Harper and Row, the strongest criticism of the publisher's reader was that there was not enough "Indian" in it. Much of the novel deals with Superintendent Rafferty's growing understanding of and respect for the Little Elk people. He recognizes that there is a spiritual quality in the Native peoples' lives that is absent from his own. Rafferty also understands what the loss of Feather Boy means to the Little Elk, and he advises Pell, in strong language, not to offer Bull a magnificent gold statue as a replacement for the medicine bundle: it is impossible to substitute one people's spiritual symbols for another's. Rafferty's encounters with other representatives of Euro-American culture, including his own staff, the U.S. marshal, and the white ranchers who lease land on the Little Elk Reservation, have taught him that the Natives are pawns in his own people's greedy pursuit of more and more land. The General Allotment Act, which was supposed to benefit the Natives, has instead been used to deprive them of what little land they had left; Rafferty is shocked when his research shows that there is not enough land for every person living on the Little Elk Reservation to become a farmer, even if he or she wished to do so. His attempts to repatriate for the Little Elk some of the land that has been leased to Euro-American ranchers meet with no encouragement from the Bureau of Indian Affairs; in fact, Rafferty finds the bureau helping Euro-Americans to take over even more land. While the reader of *The Surrounded* sees the poverty and despair caused by the Allotment Act through the eyes of Archilde, who is part of the Native community, the reader of *Wind from an Enemy Sky* hears the final indictment of the bureaucracy that is supposed to serve the Native peoples from the representative of the bureaucracy itself. Rafferty experiences a growing affinity for the land – McNickle's descriptions of the mountain landscape are as masterful here as in his earlier novel – that ultimately leads him to renounce a basic tenet of "civilization," as Euro-Americans define it, that only farmers can "own" the land. Alienated from his own culture and having lost the trust of the Native community because of Pell's actions, he has nowhere to turn; thus, his death at Bull's hands is not a tragedy but a deliverance.

The church, such a prominent theme in *The Surrounded,* is given little space in *Wind from an Enemy Sky,* though its disapproving and malevolent presence is often felt. The missionary sees himself as a martyr, with little to show for his life among the Little Elk people. In his opinion the Natives will never be counted among the civilized people of the world; their ultimate disappearance is inevitable and not to be regretted. He is devoid of sympathy and even of basic human compassion; religion for him has become a mere formula. McNickle had hinted at this possibility in his description of the young priest in *The Surrounded.* The Indian Reorganization Act of 1934 had guaranteed Native peoples freedom of religion, but in *Wind from an Enemy Sky* the Bureau of Indian Affairs does not acknowledge the Little Elk people's right to the center of their spirituality: it fears that the return of the Feather Boy bundle will prevent their complete assimilation. The church, not surprisingly, supports the federal government in this position. Although Pell has some sensitivity to the cultural rights of other peoples, he only understands the problems in the abstract. His final action devalues Native cultures and their spiritual expressions; one sacred object, he seems to think, is as good as any other. Like many other Euro-Americans, he thinks of Native peoples as "Indians" rather than as distinct cultures. It was not until 1978, the year that *Wind from an Enemy Sky* was published, that the American Indian Religious Freedom Act was passed by Congress; long before the act became a political reality, McNickle had recognized that the strong, vital spirituality of Native cultures was entitled to the protection of the law.

D'Arcy McNickle was a persuasive writer as well as an outstanding craftsman. His reputation, among both literary scholars and historians, is secure, and his work continues to be read by Native Americans and Euro-Americans alike. Literary critics consider his first novel to have been his masterpiece.

Biography:

Dorothy R. Parker, *Singing and Indian Song: A Biography of D'Arcy McNickle* (Lincoln: University of Nebraska Press, 1992).

References:

Birgit Hans, "Re-Visions: An Early Version of *The Surrounded*," *Studies in American Indian Literatures,* 4 (Summer/Fall 1992): 181–195;

Louis Owens, "Maps of the Mind: John Joseph Mathews and D'Arcy McNickle," in his *Other Destinies: Understanding the American Indian Novel* (Norman: University of Oklahoma Press, 1992), pp. 49–89;

Owens, "The Red Road to Nowhere: D'Arcy McNickle's *The Surrounded* and 'The Hungry Generations,' " *American Indian Quarterly,* 13 (1989): 239–248;

John Lloyd Purdy, *Word Ways: The Novels of D'Arcy McNickle* (Tucson: University of Arizona Press, 1990);

Purdy, ed., *The Legacy of D'Arcy McNickle: Writer, Historian, Activist,* American Indian Literature and Critical Studies Series, volume 21 (Norman: University of Oklahoma Press, 1996);

James Ruppert, *D'Arcy McNickle,* Western Writers Series, no. 38 (Boise, Idaho: Boise State University Press, 1988);

Ruppert, "Textual Perspectives and the Reader in *The Surrounded*," in *Narrative Chance: Postmodern Discourses on Native American Indian Literatures,* edited by Gerald Vizenor (Albuquerque: University of New Mexico Press, 1989), pp. 101–120.

Papers:

D'Arcy McNickle's letters, journals, and published and unpublished manuscripts are at The Newberry Library, Chicago.

N. Scott Momaday

(27 February 1934 –)

Matthias Schubnell
University of the Incarnate Word

See also the Momaday entry in *DLB 143: American Novelists Since World War II, Third Series.*

BOOKS: *The Journey of Tai-me* (Santa Barbara, Cal.: Privately printed, 1967);

House Made of Dawn (New York: Harper & Row, 1968; London: Gollancz, 1969);

The Way to Rainy Mountain (Albuquerque: University of New Mexico Press, 1969);

Colorado: Summer, Fall, Winter, Spring, with photographs by David Muench (New York: Rand McNally, 1973);

Angle of Geese and Other Poems (Boston: Godine, 1974);

The Colors of Night (San Francisco: Arion, 1976);

The Gourd Dancer (New York & London: Harper & Row, 1976);

The Names: A Memoir (New York: Harper & Row, 1976);

The Ancient Child (New York: Doubleday, 1989);

In the Presence of the Sun: A Gathering of Shields (Santa Fe, N.Mex.: Rydal, 1992);

In the Presence of the Sun: Stories and Poems, 1961–1991 (New York: St. Martin's Press, 1992);

Circle of Wonder: A Native American Christmas Story (Santa Fe, N.Mex.: Clear Light, 1994).

Editions: *The Way to Rainy Mountain* (Albuquerque: University of New Mexico Press, 1976);

The Gourd Dancer (Tucson: University of Arizona Press, 1976);

The Names: A Memoir (Tucson: University of Arizona Press, 1976);

The House Made of Dawn (Tucson: University of Arizona Press, 1996);

The Names (Tucson: University of Arizona Press, 1996);

The Way to Rainy Mountain (Tucson: University of Arizona Press, 1996).

PLAY PRODUCTION: *The Indolent Boys,* Syracuse, New York, Syracuse Stage, 8 February 1994.

N. Scott Momaday

OTHER: *The Complete Poems of Frederick Goddard Tuckerman,* edited by Momaday (New York: Oxford University Press, 1965);

"An American Land Ethnic," in *Ecotactics: The Sierra Club Handbook for Environmental Activists,* edited by John G. Mitchell and Constance L. Stalling (New York: Trident Press, 1970), pp. 97–105;

"The Man Made of Words," in *Indian Voice: The First Convocation of American Indian Scholars,* edited by Rupert Costo (San Francisco: Indian Historian Press, 1970), pp. 49–84; reprinted in *Literature of the American Indian,* edited by Abraham Chapman (New York: New American Library, 1975), pp. 96–110; reprinted in *The Remembered Earth,* edited by Geary Hobson (Albuquerque: University of New Mexico Press, 1981), pp. 162–173;

"I Am Alive," in *The World of the American Indian,* edited by Jules B. Billard (Washington, D.C.: National Geographic Society, 1975), pp. 11–26;

"Native American Attitudes toward the Environment," in *Seeing With a Native Eye,* edited by Walter Holden Capps (New York: Harper & Row, 1976), pp. 79–85;

"To Save a Great Vision," in *A Sender of Words: Essays in Memory of John G. Neihardt,* edited by Vine Deloria Jr. (Salt Lake City: Howe, 1984), pp. 30–38;

"Landscape with Words in the Foreground," in *Old Southwest, New Southwest: Essays on a Region and Its Literature,* edited by Judy Nolte Lensink (Tucson: Tucson Public Library, 1987), pp. 1–5;

"The Native Voice," in *Columbia Literary History of the United States,* edited by Emory Elliott (New York: Columbia University Press, 1988), pp. 5–15;

"Sacred Places," in *Sacred Places: Native American Sites* (San Francisco: Sierra Club Special Edition Calendar, 1993).

SELECTED PERIODICAL PUBLICATIONS – UNCOLLECTED: "Eve My Mother, No," *Sequoia,* 5 (Autumn 1959): 37;

"Los Alamos," *New Mexico Quarterly,* 29 (Fall 1959): 306;

"The Well," *Ramparts,* 2 (May 1963): 41–43;

"The Morality of Indian Hating," *Ramparts,* 3 (Summer 1964): 29–40;

"Learning from the Indian," *Viva: Northern New Mexico's Sunday Magazine* (9 July 1972): 2;

"Figments of Sancho Panza's Imagination," *Viva: Northern New Mexico's Sunday Magazine* (31 December 1972): 2;

"Finding a Need for Nature," *Viva: Northern New Mexico's Sunday Magazine* (13 May 1973): 2;

"A First American Views His Land," *National Geographic Magazine,* 105 (July 1976): 13–18;

"A Vision beyond Time and Place," *Life* (July 1976): 67.

When N. Scott Momaday received the 1969 Pulitzer Prize for fiction for his first novel, *House Made of Dawn* (1968), the literary community recognized the arrival of a major contemporary Native American writer; the event marked the beginning of what Kenneth Lincoln would later describe as the Native American Renaissance. Since then Momaday has told his story and the stories of his people, the Kiowa, in such works as *The Way to Rainy Mountain* (1969), *The Gourd Dancer* (1976), *The Names: A Memoir* (1976), *The Ancient Child* (1989), and *In the Presence of the Sun: A Gathering of Shields* (1992). By drawing attention to the high quality and cultural richness of Native American writing, his success has prepared the way for a whole generation of indigenous writers whose works expand and enrich the canon of American literature. Many Native American writers, among them the Acoma poet Simon Ortiz and the Laguna poet and critic Paula Gunn Allen, have acknowledged their literary debt to Momaday, and Momaday's use of mythic subtexts in *House Made of Dawn* may have influenced Leslie Marmon Silko and Louise Erdrich, who used and developed this technique in *Ceremony* (1977) and *Tracks* (1988), respectively. Silko's memoir, *Storyteller* (1981), also bears some similarities to Momaday's *The Names.* In a more general sense, Momaday's work is important because it is grounded in aboriginal oral traditions, sacred landscapes, and ancient ritual. It speaks to the reader in ancestral voices, simultaneously remote and immediate, and it is informed with the rhythms of magic formulas and the mysterious power of images originating in prehistoric petroglyphs and ancient cave paintings.

Momaday's work, however, reflects the multiple cultural contexts and traditions into which he was born or that he explored later as a student of literature and painting. It thus poses particular challenges, for Momaday writes out of the tension between these ethnic worlds, assimilating and synthesizing a wide variety of elements from Native American, European American, and European oral, literary, and artistic traditions. It is only against this complex background that the full significance of Momaday's contribution to American letters becomes apparent. Thus, it is imperative that the critic transcend any narrow notion of Momaday's identity as a modern Kiowa and approach him as a sophisticated, multicultural writer.

This critical principle applies equally to Momaday's paintings and drawings, for besides being a major literary figure he has received recognition as an artist. As the son of a well-known painter, Momaday was exposed to the visual arts as a child; but it was not until 1974, when he took art classes from Leonard Baskin, that he began to pursue this talent seriously. Since then, his drawings and paintings have become an integral part of his creative work. Visual and literary expression merge in some of Momaday's earliest paintings of Kiowa shields, on whose images calligraphic poems are superimposed, and *The Names* includes many drawings by the author. Momaday's latest works reflect his growing integration of art and literary expression: his watercolor portrait of a bear on the dust jacket of *The Ancient Child* represents the novel's unifying symbol, while the work itself offers Momaday's definition of a Native American version of Expressionism; his suite of sixteen shield drawings and sixteen stories in *In the Presence of the Sun: A Gathering of Shields* and the extensively illustrated *In the Presence of the Sun: Stories and Poems, 1961–1991* also testify to Momaday's remarkable dual talent. In the latter work Momaday acknowledges Emil Nolde, Francis Bacon, Pablo Picasso, and George Baselitz as major influences on his art. In 1993 a twenty-year retrospective exhibition of Momaday's work at the Wheelwright Museum in Santa Fe acknowledged his stature as a significant contemporary Indian artist.

Navarro Scott Mammedaty was born in Lawton, Oklahoma, on 27 February 1934 to Alfred Morris Mammedaty, a full-blood Kiowa, and Mayme Natachee Scott Mammedaty, who is of Scottish, French, and Cherokee descent. Later his father changed the spelling of the family name to Momaday. When Scott was six months old, Pohd-lohk, a Kiowa elder, named him Tsoai-talee (Rock Tree Boy), thus linking the child to one of the ancient stories in Kiowa mythology: to account for the origin of Devils Tower, the strange landmark in what is now northeastern Wyoming that they had come upon on their journey south from the Yellowstone area, the Kiowa created a story about a boy who was transformed into a bear and chased his seven sisters up a tree; the tree became Devils Tower and the sisters became the Big Dipper. To reinforce this mythic connection, his parents took him to Devils Tower. The myth has become so much a part of Momaday's identity that his writings gravitate to it again and again; it provides the unifying subtext for *The Ancient Child.*

When Momaday was two his parents left Kiowa country for a series of teaching positions: on the Navajo reservation at Shiprock, New Mexico; at Tuba City and Chinle, Arizona; and, in 1946, at a two-teacher day school at Jemez Pueblo, New Mexico. As a Kiowa among Navajo and Pueblo people who was also being guided by his parents toward success in the larger society beyond Jemez, Momaday inhabited a complex world of intersecting cultures. The need to accommodate himself to these circumstances prepared him for the perceptive treatment of encounters with various cultures that characterizes his literary work.

Momaday's formal education took place at the Franciscan Mission School in Jemez; the Indian School in Santa Fe; high schools in Bernalillo, New Mexico; and the Augustus Military Academy in Fort Defiance, Virginia. In 1952 he entered the University of New Mexico at Albuquerque as a political science major with minors in English and speech. He spent 1956–1957 in the law program at the University of Virginia, where he met William Faulkner; the encounter helped to shape Momaday's early prose and is most clearly reflected in the evocation of Faulkner's story "The Bear" (1942) in Momaday's poem of that title (collected in *Angle of Geese and Other Poems,* 1974). Returning to the University of New Mexico, Momaday graduated in 1958 and took a teaching position on the Jicarilla Apache reservation at Dulce, New Mexico. There he met and, on 5 September 1959, married Gaye Mangold. They have three daughters: Cael, Jill, and Brit.

Content with his new career, Momaday had no plans for further academic training; but in 1959, on the urging of a friend, he applied for and received a Wallace Stegner Creative Writing Fellowship to Stanford University. There the poet and critic Yvor Winters became his mentor, his friend, and the single most important influence on his early career. Winters persuaded Momaday to pursue a doctorate in American literature and proposed and supervised his thesis, an edition of the works of the nineteenth-century poet Frederick Goddard Tuckerman that was published by Oxford University Press in 1965. In a letter to the editor published in the 23 February 1967 issue of *The Reporter* Winters predicted Momaday's impending literary acclaim. And he critiqued the drafts of *House Made of Dawn,* which, to him, provided further evidence of Momaday's immense talent. Winters's untimely death in 1968, a year before Momaday's Pulitzer award, prevented him from seeing his pronouncements on his student's literary potential validated.

After receiving his Ph.D. in 1963 Momaday taught at the University of California, Santa Barbara. The origin of *House Made of Dawn* can be traced to the early 1960s, when Momaday was working on his doctorate at Stanford. Having initially conceived the work as a cycle of poems, Momaday had turned to prose and, in 1963, had published a short story, "The Well," that anticipates the themes of culture clash, witchcraft, and identity conflict that he develops in depth in the novel. While the story is set on the Jicarilla Apache reservation, where he had taught in 1958, as the settings for *House Made of Dawn* Momaday chose Jemez, which is called Walatowa in the novel, and – as the urban counterpoint to the Pueblo world – Los Angeles.

Abel, the protagonist of *House Made of Dawn,* is a composite of individuals Momaday knew in

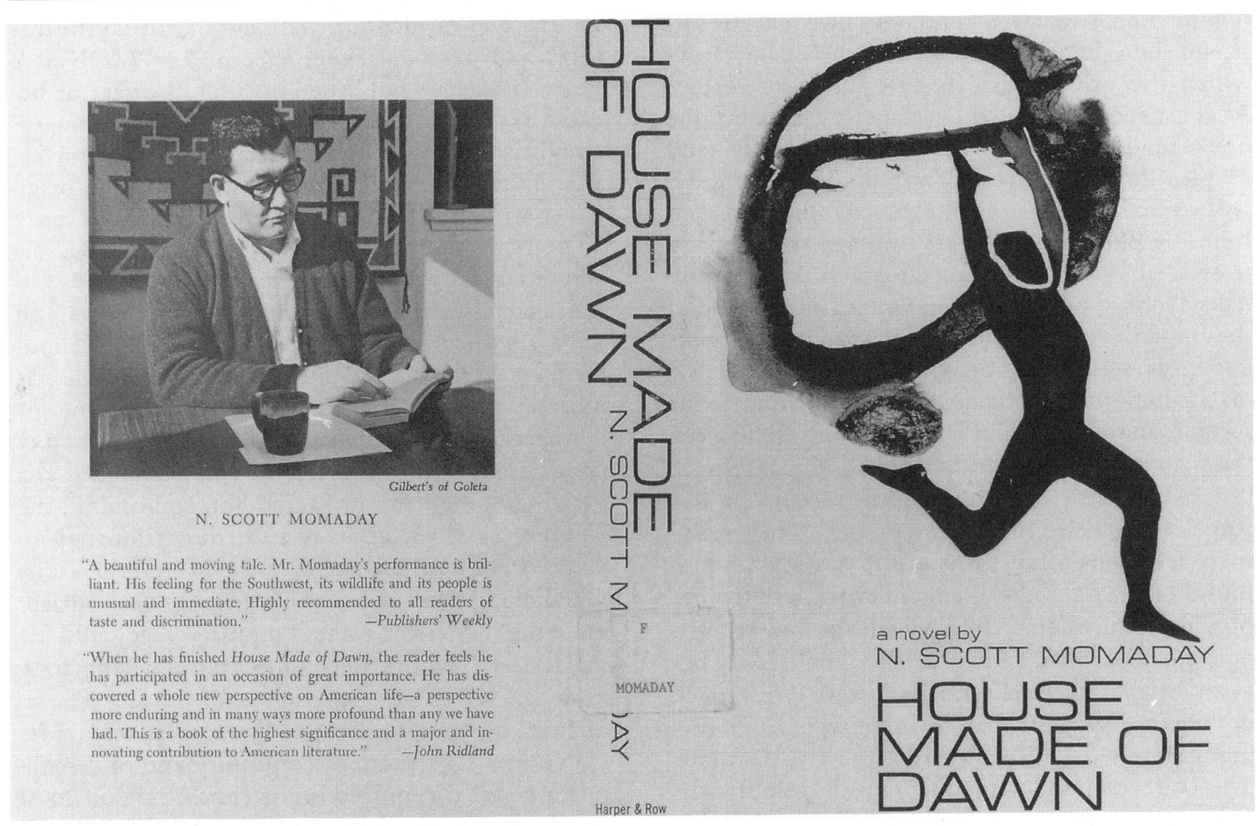

Dust jacket for N. Scott Momaday's first novel, which won the Pulitzer Prize in 1969

Jemez: young men whose inability to cope with conflicting cultural patterns led them into alcoholism, violence, and death; and veterans who failed to reintegrate themselves into their tribal community after fighting in World War II. Abel's troubles, however, are not caused by his exposure to the world beyond the Indian village; his war experiences and the alien milieu of the modern American city only deepen an identity crisis that already troubles Abel as a young man. Isolated within the tribe – his father was an outsider who left the family – and further set apart by the deaths of his mother and brother, Abel grows up with his grandfather, Francisco, who tries, with little success, to teach him the old ways. Abel's killing of an eagle he has captured shows his ignorance of the traditional hunting code. His distance from his people's ceremonial life results in a generational conflict with Francisco: "You ought to do this and that, his grandfather said. But the old man had not understood, would not understand, only wept, and Abel left him alone. It was time to go, and the old man was away in the fields."

Abel's quest for identity leads him first into World War II and then back to his village, where he tries to attune himself to the land and his people's traditions. Failing to resolve his inner conflict by ceremonial means, he seeks solace in a sexual encounter with Angela St. John, who initially exploits Abel but will later become instrumental in his healing process; finally, he kills a mysterious albino whom he identifies as a witch. In disposing of the "evil spirit" Abel, for the first time, acts in accordance with tribal law, signaling his return to his tribe. But he is convicted of murder and sent to jail, a world in which he is ill equipped to survive.

The remainder of the novel traces Abel's struggle to escape the conflicting cultural forces that threaten to tear him apart after his release from eight years in prison and his relocation to Los Angeles. The disjointed structure of the work, particularly in the chapter "The Priest of the Sun," owes much to Faulkner's narrative technique and reflects the protagonist's confusion, gradual disintegration, and near death. Yet it also holds the seed of Abel's restoration to his homeland and its ancient ceremonies. Abel's vision of the runners after evil, following his nearly fatal beating by an evil policeman, "Culebra" Martinez, reveals to him the possibility of dealing with witchcraft ceremonially rather than through violence. This experience lays the foundation for Abel's renewed faith in his own culture. His friend Ben Benally's Navajo night chant, from which the novel takes its title, helps to restore Abel's psychic balance by centering him in "the house made of dawn" – the Navajo universe – and by pleading for the restoration of his mind, body, and voice. Ben and another character, the Reverend John Big Bluff Tosamah, are foils for Abel. Benally tries to live the American Dream and constantly talks about it, but his imagination is still centered in the Indian world. Tosamah, an urban Indian, lacks any understanding of or sympathy for Abel. Tosamah is important in the novel for articulating, in his sermon on the Gospel of John, the contrast between the written word and the oral tradition.

Abel's visit with Angela as he recovers in Los Angeles also helps his healing process. Their seemingly frivolous affair turns out to have had a profound effect on Angela, engendering love for her previously unwanted child, which she now regards not as her husband's but as Abel's, and leading her to an insight into Abel's tribal heritage. While much in the novel suggests that the bridging of cultures is impossible – the difficulty that the two Catholic priests have in understanding their Pueblo flock is an example – the conclusion of Abel's and Angela's relationship offers hope for cultural synthesis.

Abel's final encounter with the dying Francisco further prepares him for his reintegration into his culture. Francisco's last utterances – fragmented lessons on the importance of the land, the solar calendar, and hunting ceremonies (Francisco's account of his successful bear hunt contrasts directly with Abel's failure to act appropriately on his eagle hunt) – prompt Abel to prepare Francisco's body for burial in the traditional manner. Abel's subsequent joining of the race of the dawn runners confirms the restoration of his body, and his singing of "House Made of Dawn" as he runs affirms that he has left inarticulateness and alienation behind and is running toward a new day both for himself and his tribe.

Not all critics have interpreted the novel's conclusion so positively; Charles Larson, for example, views the ending as a run toward death. This reading, however, fails to acknowledge not only the dawn imagery that permeates the novel but also the significance of the healing ceremony and the mythic subtexts that Susan Scarberry-García explains in her *Landmarks of Healing: A Study of* House Made of Dawn (1990).

House Made of Dawn dramatizes the difficulties Native Americans face in reconciling the conflicting demands of different cultures; Momaday's next work delineates his own construction of a contemporary Kiowa identity. Its blending of myth, history, and personal experience makes *The Way to Rainy Mountain* – published in 1969, the year he became associate professor of English and comparative literature at the Berkeley campus of the University of California – perhaps Momaday's most original contribution to American literature. In his essay "The Man Made of Words" (1970) Momaday asserts that "we are what we imagine. Our very existence consists in our imagination of ourselves." In his early thirties Momaday began to wonder about his place in the history of the Kiowa; the result was a deeply personal, spiritual, and artistic groping for connections to a tribal world that, as Momaday soon discovered, remained only in fragments. His viewing of the Kiowa's sacred Sun Dance doll, the Tai-me, in 1963, and his subsequent journey to Rainy Mountain Cemetery, near Mountain View, Oklahoma, where many of his ancestors are buried, were the first critical stages on his journey into his tribal past. The first encounter afforded Momaday a deeply religious experience of lasting consequence; his presence among his dead ancestors resulted in a sense both of continuity and of disconnection that is captured in the concluding poem of the book, "Rainy Mountain Cemetery." While the poem portrays the geographical end point of the Kiowa's migration, it also conveys the state of mind that led Momaday to embark on his own actual and imaginative retracing of their journey.

A problem Momaday faced in delving into the oral tradition of his people was that he could not speak Kiowa. His father helped him to collect and translate the material from Kiowa storytellers that was privately printed in 1967 in an edition of one hundred copies as *The Journey of Tai-me*. As he reworked this collection he added two framing poems – "Headwaters," dealing with the emergence of the Kiowa through the hollow log, and "Rainy Mountain Cemetery," about the final destination of his ancestors – a prologue, an introductory essay, and an epilogue. The prologue and introductory essay contain, as Winters put it in his letter to the editor of *The Reporter,* where the introductory essay first appeared on 26 January, "the history of a people (the Kiowas) and the pathos of their combined grandeur and triviality; the biography of a Kiowa (Aho), in which the history is summed up; a commentary on both by the grandson and author." The prologue and the introductory essay reveal Momaday's connection to his past through Aho and provide a historical framework that helps the reader to place the twenty-four triads that make up the three sections of the book: "The Setting Out," "The Going On," and "The Closing In." Each triad consists of a mythical, a historical or anthropological, and a personal rendering of Kiowa experience and documents a moment in the rise and fall of Kiowa culture as it moved from the Yellowstone area to the Great Plains, Oklahoma, and the Staked Plains of Texas, with occasional expeditions as far as Mexico. The journey lasted from the late 1600s to 1887, when the last sun dance was held on the Washita River. In *The Way to Rainy Mountain* the landscape is both the common denominator of the Kiowa's evolution as a tribe and a formative influence on their perception of the world and of themselves as a people. Momaday's emphasis on the sacredness of a "remembered earth" is an early expression of the concern for nature and sacred places that places him in the forefront of contemporary environmental thinkers.

"The Setting Out" emphasizes the mystery of creation and the vulnerability of the Kiowa as they struggled to establish themselves as a community. While many triads center on the theme of separation, others teach the sacredness of language as the principal means of dealing with reality. Some triads relate the adventures of the mythical Hero Twins and convey the emerging veneration of the sun as a deity. The arrival of the Tai-me religion, which came later, is the focus of a separate triad. While this first section of the book describes the gradual physical and spiritual consolidation of the Kiowa people, "The Going On" portrays them in firm control of their environment and their destiny. Through their mastery of word magic they direct natural and supernatural forces; expert horsemen, they excel as hunters, warriors, and explorers; and their tribal laws assure communal harmony by severely sanctioning antisocial behavior. "The Closing In" traces the demise of the Kiowa through disease, military defeat, and the loss of their horses, courage, and moral values. The falling of the Tai-me bundle from its ceremonial stand signals an impending spiritual crisis, just as the falling of the stars in 1833, described in the epilogue, had heralded the collapse of the Kiowa world.

The tone of *The Way to Rainy Mountain* is formal, often grave. It relates the journey of a people with pathos and respect, yet without regret or bitterness for the horrors that accompanied the final stage of traditional Kiowa culture. Far from dwelling on the losses, the work celebrates the continuity of the tribal spirit as it prevails in the imagination and artistic expression of a contemporary heir to a proud tradition.

The Way to Rainy Mountain has been widely anthologized and may well be the principal work for which Momaday will be remembered. The publication in 1988 of the seventeen essays in *Approaches to Teaching Momaday's* The Way to Rainy Mountain, edited by Kenneth M. Roemer, in the Modern Language Association's prestigious Approaches to World Literature series, has ensured the work's presence in the American classroom, where it serves not only as a nontraditional expression of American cultural history but also as a model for students in articulating their own personal histories.

Momaday returned to Stanford as a professor of English in 1973. He wrote a column for *Viva: Northern New Mexico's Sunday Magazine* from April 1972 to December 1973; he also wrote many articles dealing with environmental issues from an Indian perspective, including "An American Land Ethic" (1970), "Learning from the Indian" (1972), "Finding a Need for Nature" (1973), "I Am Alive" (1975), "Native American Attitudes toward the Environment" (1976), and "A Vision beyond Time and Place" (1976). "A First American Views His Land" (1976) appeared in the U.S. bicentennial issue of *National Geographic Magazine*. Momaday also communicates his native perception of the natural world in two poems from this period, "The Delight Song of Tsoai-talee" and "New World."

Colorado: Summer, Fall, Winter, Spring (1973), Momaday's most sustained piece of nature writing, follows logically from his precise descriptions of nature and evocations of the southwestern landscape's spiritual and mythic significance in *House Made of Dawn* and *The Way to Rainy Mountain*. In the novel Momaday emphasizes that Abel's reawakening to the rhythms of his ancestral land is a prerequisite for the restoration of his physical and psychic health, and one of the most frequently quoted passages from *The Way to Rainy Mountain* anticipates Momaday's concern for an appropriate relationship of humanity to the earth:

> Once in his life man ought to concentrate his mind upon the remembered earth, I believe. He ought to give himself up to a particular landscape in his experience, to look at it from as many angles as he can, to wonder about it, to dwell upon it. He ought to imagine that he touches it with his hands at every season and listens to the sounds that are made upon it. He ought to imagine the creatures there and all the faintest motions of the wind. He ought to recollect the glare of the noon and all the colors of the dawn and dusk.

His 1970 essay "The Man Made of Words" addresses the destructive influence of technology and modernity in eroding one's sense of place: "We have suffered a kind of psychic dislocation of ourselves in time and space. . . . I doubt that any of us knows where he is in relation to the stars and the solstices. Our sense of natural order has become dull and unreliable." Momaday then shows how people can

Dust jacket for Momaday's complex novel about an artist and a young woman who rediscover their Indian identities

overcome their detachment from the land by sharpening their vision of nature and formulating a new land ethic.

Colorado, a collaboration with the photographer David Muench, follows in the tradition of Mary Austin and Ansel Adams's *Taos Pueblo* (1930), which sought to evoke a specific place through the juxtaposition of images and words. Momaday paints and sketches the changing landscape of the Rocky Mountains through the seasonal cycle with a subtle verbal palette, anticipating his branching out into the visual arts the following year. His surfaces are alive with textures and hues, colors and shadows; yet Momaday is not content with capturing nature's surface. His vignettes conjure up the geologic processes at work below the ground and delineate the minute and incremental changes in the Colorado landscape. This evocation of geologic time not only puts into perspective the human presence in the land but also instills a sense of awe at nature's creative energy at work across the ages.

Perhaps the most memorable passages in *Colorado* are those in which Momaday reminds the reader that the earth is alive and vital, and that human beings ought to incorporate this vitality into their lives. When he is infused by the "keen sense of the original earth, of its deep, definitive life," or when the impulse of life emanating from a glorious landscape takes hold of him, Momaday's mysticism is reminiscent of Loren Eiseley's. When he finds his participation "in the irresistible continuum of life" confirmed in the bristlecone trees, "the thorns of the ancient earth," he contemplates his own immortality within the cosmic design. Momaday's nature writings call for a greater spiritual and emotional involvement in the physical world. They seek to break down the anthropocentric, detached view of nature and restore the wonder, enchantment, and sense of the sacred that have been lost as nature has become the domain of science and technology.

In 1974 Momaday taught for a year at the University of Moscow. His poetry first appeared in book form that year in a handsomely published chapbook, *Angle of Geese and Other Poems,* and then in 1976 in *The Gourd Dancer.* All the poems from *Angle of Geese* are republished in *The Gourd Dancer,* along with two dozen additional pieces. These small collections represent almost twenty years of poetic expression, suggesting that Momaday heeded the advice he received from Winters in a letter dated 15 July 1964: "any poet with a critical conscience will publish a small body of work."

Momaday had begun his career as a poet, and his first published works were two poems that appeared in 1959: "Eve My Mother, No" in *Sequoia* and "Los Alamos" in the *New Mexico Quarterly*. Winters's influence is reflected in Momaday's syllabic, postsymbolist poetry: Winters urged his students to organize poetic lines by the number of syllables, regardless of how they went together metrically, and to avoid the obscurity of symbolist poetry by first conceptualizing an abstract idea within a rational framework and then conveying the idea through a cluster of sharp sensory details. Typical of this method among Momaday's earlier poems are "The Bear," for which he received the 1962 Academy of American poets prize, "Angle of Geese," "Comparatives," "New World," and "Buteo Regalis." Many of his other poems, however, might be called prose poetry; among these are "The Stalker," "The Colors of Night" sequence, and "The Fear of Bo-talee," all of which are reminiscent of the pieces in *The Way to Rainy Mountain*. Still others, including "Plainview: 2" and "The Delight Song of Tsoai-talee," imitate the traditional poetic forms of Native American prayers and chants.

Among the themes Momaday examines in *The Gourd Dancer* is the spirit of the wilderness in "The Bear," a poetic reexpression of Ike McCaslin's encounter with Old Ben in Faulkner's short story. The mystery of death is probed in "Angle of Geese," which contrasts human death with a death in nature; in "Comparatives," which views death against the backdrop of geological time; and in "Before an Old Painting of the Crucifixion," which resembles Wallace Stevens's "Sunday Morning" (1915) in its questioning of Christ's resurrection. "The Gourd Dancer" is a moving tribute to Mammedaty, Momaday's grandfather. "Earth and I Gave You Turquoise," "New World," "Carriers of the Dream Wheel," "The Eagle Feathered Fan," and "The Delight Song of Tsoai-talee" celebrate the natural beauty of America and the spiritual power of its indigenous people.

Among the poems dealing with significant figures and places in Momaday's experience is "Forms of the Earth at Abiqui," a tribute to his friendship with Georgia O'Keeffe and to their mutual regard for the New Mexican landscape. "Krasno-presnenskaya Station" and "Abstract: Old Woman in a Room" reflect his 1974 visit to Moscow. In "Long Shadows at Dulce" he recalls the change from fall to winter on the Jicarilla Apache reservation, and "To a Child Running with Outstretched Arms in Canyon de Chelly" may be a flashback to his own childhood. The poems in *The Gourd Dancer* are testimony to Momaday's precision and depth of vision, his poetic control, and his ability to fuse philosophical themes and vibrant images.

Momaday's other major publication of 1976, *The Names: A Memoir,* is best described as an extension of *The Way to Rainy Mountain:* while the earlier work conveys the mythic and historical precedents to Momaday's personal experiences in story fragments within an associative structure, *The Names* is a chronological account of his childhood and adolescence. Mick McAllister described the book in *Southern Review* (1978) as "a portrait of the artist as a young Indian." As in *House Made of Dawn,* Momaday employs modern narrative techniques, ranging from the long, unpunctuated stream-of-consciousness passage in part 3 to the presentation of individual scenes from multiple narrative perspectives. Writing in a middle ground between fiction and history, Momaday imagines conversations with ancestors and Kiowa elders he never actually met. The book is enriched with photographs and drawings by the author; dialogue fragments and vignettes evoking the landscapes of Kentucky, Oklahoma, and New Mexico; poems; and a short story. The book's structure is designed to adapt the Western literary genre of autobiography to his purpose of describing his emerging tribal self, thus accommodating the dual aspects of his personal and communal identities. Momaday achieves this end by prefacing his own story in part 1, which comprises a quarter of the memoir, with accounts of his racial and familial past, extending back four generations into his Kiowa, French, Cherokee, and Scottish ancestry. By framing the four parts of the memoir (*4* is a sacred number for many Native American tribes) with a prologue and an epilogue, he also reconciles the Western idea of linear, chronological time with the Native American concept of cyclical, mythic time.

The four parts follow, chronologically and geographically, Momaday's childhood and adolescence from his birth in Oklahoma to his late teens in New Mexico. The prologue conjures up the moment of tribal origin, relating the Kiowa's emergence from a hollow log into the world; the epilogue describes Momaday's personal encounter with a hollow log as he retraces the Kiowa migration route. This passage illustrates the author's imaginative participation in the daily lives of his ancestors as he makes his way back to the tribe's place of origin. His linear journey through personal and historical time and geography intersects with the mythic world of the Kiowa.

Apart from the autobiographical information *The Names* provides, the work's main interest lies in the way it illustrates Momaday's contention in "The Man Made of Words" that one creates oneself through an act of the imagination. His own Kiowa name is of particular significance in this context, for the act of naming is equivalent to the act of creation: the text opens with the assertion, "My name is Tsoai-talee, I am, therefore, Tsoai-talee; therefore I am." Momaday further elaborates this idea, which is the philosophical underpinning of the whole work: "The storyteller Pohd-lohk gave me the name Tsoai-talee. He believed that a man's life proceeds from his name, in the way that a river proceeds from its source." Names, language, stories, and myths, Momaday argues, engender a sense of personal identity through a necessary and continuing process of the imagination.

To underscore the centrality of this concept, Momaday concludes part 4 on the same note as that on which he opened the book. In a highly symbolic scene, he relates his fall from innocence to experience as he loses his footing while descending the red mesa near Jemez on the day before his departure to the military academy in Virginia. With the benefit of hindsight, the mature Momaday articulates the significance of this event: "I should never again see the world as I saw it on the other side of that moment, in the bright reflection of time lost. There are such reflections, and for some of them I have the names." The fall symbolically marks the transition from history into myth – the beginning of Momaday's mythopoetic journey between his present and the Kiowa's tribal past. Having been cast off from the rock of youth, Momaday enters the world at large. He carries with him the names that hold the essence of his ancestors and the seeds of stories, providing him with the framework and the material for telling his own story. After all, Momaday explains, "life . . . is simply the construction of an idea of having existence, place in the scheme of things." This definition equally applies to Momaday's idea of art, for his writings simply express the continuing story of his place in the collective stories of his people.

On 21 July 1978 Momaday married Regina Heitzer, whom he had met while he was a visiting professor at the University of Regensburg in Germany; they have a daughter, Lore. In 1981 Momaday moved to the University of Arizona in Tucson, where he is Regents Professor of English.

In the thirteen years between *The Names* and *The Ancient Child* Momaday's published output was minimal. Literary critics were, however, busy analyzing his previous writings, producing a quickly growing body of scholarship that included the first book-length studies devoted exclusively or in part to his work. Three chapters in Alan R. Velie's *Four American Indian Literary Masters* (1982) focus on Momaday, while Lincoln's *Native American Renaissance* (1983) dedicates one chapter to a discussion of Black Elk and Momaday as "word senders." In 1985 Matthias Schubnell's critical biography, *N. Scott Momaday: The Cultural and Literary Background,* placed Momaday in the larger cultural and intellectual context that has shaped his work. Roemer's *Approaches to Teaching Momaday's* The Way to Rainy Mountain reinforced Momaday's reputation as not only the leading Native American writer of his generation but also as a major literary figure in America.

The Ancient Child was greeted with mixed reviews; most critics, however, agreed that it was a novel of extraordinary complexity. The similarities between *The Ancient Child* and *House Made of Dawn* are obvious: the protagonists embark on journeys to recover their tribal sense of self, guided by initiation helpers who lead them to a new understanding of names, myths, and rituals; both awaken to the spiritual significance of their ancestral land and restore their voices in the context of an oral culture. In *The Ancient Child* this process of healing and self-discovery is facilitated through art, specifically painting. The novel probes the sources of human creativity in what may best be described as a Kiowa version of Expressionism.

No other work by Momaday demands as broad a cultural and literary approach as *The Ancient Child.* One can appreciate *House Made of Dawn* without reference to Faulkner or D. H. Lawrence, and *The Names* works without an awareness of Isak Dinesen's influence; but Momaday's references to George Bizet, Jacques Brel, Katsushika Hokusai, Franz Kafka, and particularly to Emi Nolde and his painting *Wanderer among the Stars* demand that these leads be followed to do the novel justice. This is a task that awaits critical attention.

The novel traces the respective transformations of Locke "Loki" Setman, a successful but disingenuous Kiowa painter, and Grey, a young woman of Navajo and Kiowa descent. Set, as he is called, has sold out his art for commercial success. Approaching midlife, he recognizes that he is about to lose his soul. A mysterious telegram that calls him back to his native Oklahoma to visit an old woman named Kopemah, who is on her deathbed, sets in motion a series of events that lead him to reclaim his lost tribal identity. Under the guidance of Grey, Set confronts "the ancient child" within him and accepts his destiny as the modern incarnation of the bear whose origin is told in the ancient Kiowa myth about Devils Tower.

In her encounter with Set, Grey, too, undergoes a transformation: she evolves from an immature, narcissistic girl with a fantasy crush on Billy the Kid to a medicine woman who carries out the traditional responsibilities associated with this role. While Momaday's treatment of Billy the Kid expands the mythic dimension of the novel by bringing to life the exploits of this semilegendary figure of the American frontier, it tends to get in the way of the main plot. Another problem is that Grey's relinquishing of her imaginary allegiance to Billy implies that to be true to her Indian identity she must leave behind the immature myths of the American West. In a novel that affirms the universality of myth this is a troubling feature, and it contradicts the author's own experience of reconciling myths of various cultural origins.

An illustration of Momaday's virtuosity in synthesizing multiple cultural, philosophical, mythical, and literary borrowings is his choice of the protagonist's name. Combining Kiowa culture, John Locke's philosophy, Latin etymology, Norse mythology, and a 1926 children's book about Navajo and Pueblo life in the Southwest by Grace Moon, the name signifies the protagonist's inner divisions and provides a chart of his quest for vision and transformation. The significance of one's name in Indian cultures is far-reaching: it reflects the individual's essence, changes, accomplishments, and, as Momaday explains in "Figments of Sancho Panza's Imagination" (1972), his or her origin and destiny: "The name was that of the seed, from which the man issued into the world as well as that of the memory into which the man dissolves." Set's first name, the name of his mother, reflects his biological and cultural ties to the modern, Western world that has obliterated his tribal consciousness. For the seventeenth-century empiricist philosopher Locke, the mind at birth is a tabula rasa, a blank slate on which ideas are inscribed by experience; he vehemently attacks the Rationalist notion of innate ideas. This position precludes any concept of a racial or tribal memory.

When Set first visits Oklahoma his modern, empirical consciousness initially denies and then evades the intuitive pull to his tribal homeland, the geographical center of the bear myth to which he is tied by his last name, which (according to James Mooney's *Calendar History of the Kiowa Indians,* 1898) means "Bear Man" or "Bear Above." Set's task is to reconnect himself through visions and dreams to his tribal collective memory, thereby to encounter the ancient child and affirm his "bearness." Thus, his first and last names mark the boundaries of the field of tension between his modern, empirical mindset and his primal, tribal mentality.

Set's nickname, Loki, offers other clues to the situation in which he finds himself. *Loci* is Latin for "of place" or "belonging to a place," and in the context of Set's repressed tribal allegiance it becomes apparent that he must surrender to the genius loci, the spirit of his tribal homeland, before he can escape his limiting modern mentality and find his true personal and artistic identity. His journey culminates in his visit to Tsoai, or Devils Tower, the geographic embodiment of the myth about the seven sisters and their brother who were transformed into the Big Dipper and the bear. To become the bear man, the embodiment of the powerful bear medicine, Set must venture to the place of his name's mythic origin.

On his first arrival in Oklahoma, Set senses that he is approaching a personal revelation:

> The bare ground of the path was saturated with softest sanguine light. He could not remember having seen earth of that color; it was red: earlier a flat brick red, now deeper, like that particular conte crayon that is red and brown, like old blood, at the same time – or catlinite, the color of his father's name.

His intuitive acknowledgment that he is nearing the place where his native earth, bloodline, and bear identity converge foreshadows the process of awakening he is about to experience under the influence of the spirit of place. At the novel's close Set reenacts the bear-transformation myth in the shadow of Devils Tower: "Shapes and shadows shifted upon the great green igneous columns, upon the huge granite planes, across the long black vertical fissures." Momaday thus not only unifies the titles of the novel's four books – "Planes," "Lines," "Shapes," and "Shadows" – into a sketch of Tsoai but he also indicates that Set has finally placed the fragments of his Kiowa identity into a cohesive whole, that his self has merged with the mythic place that held his destiny.

While Kiowa mythology is the guiding force in Set's quest for identity, Momaday ties his story into a larger mythic context that suggests the universal power of myth to shape human lives. Loki is one of the major figures in Nordic mythology, a

Dust jacket for a collection of Momaday's short stories, poems, and shield drawings (courtesy of the Lilly Library, Indiana University)

trickster god. His name is associated with Ansuz, the third of twenty-five Viking runes and one of the thirteen runes in the cycle of initiation. Ralph Blum notes in *The Book of Runes* (1993) that Ansuz represents "Signals, the Messenger Rune, The God Loki," and he points out that it heralds a new stage in life, initiated by sacred knowledge and unexpected new connections that emerge as unconscious motives become integrated with conscious intentions. The strength that results from this exploration of life's foundation empowers the individual to support his family and community. In this context, the relevance of Set's nickname becomes readily apparent: sacred knowledge, initiation, new connections, and pathways leading to new stages in life link him to Kopemah, Grey, and the bear medicine bundle; the unconscious is the individual's basis of selfhood and the origin of the visions Set transforms into painted canvases; and the final acquisition of community manifests itself in Set's foundation of a family with Grey and his return to his tribe's mythic world. The nickname Loki, then, stands for the formative process Set undergoes once he has fallen under the influence of Grey and the spirit of his tribal homeland.

There is yet another revealing context for the nickname of Momaday's protagonist: Moon's 1926 juvenile novel *Chi-weé and Loki in the Desert.* Moon's text chronicles the adventures of a Pueblo boy and a Navajo girl, ranging from horse racing and hunting to being kidnapped in the desert; pertinent to Momaday's novel is an episode in which Loki, after killing a rabbit, gets his foot caught under a large rock. As the boy ponders his fate of dying alone in the desert, he hears something: "Nearer and nearer came the sound, and I felt very sure now what it was, and in a very little I could see him coming through the sage – it was a bear – a great one!" Like Locke Setman in his dream encounter with the bear in Momaday's novel, Loki tries to speak out, but he cannot. Both remain speechless as the bears confront them, but eventually they are liberated by the bears – literally so in Moon's book, as the bear lifts the rock to get at the rabbit. Set's liberation is figurative, for the confrontation with the bear finally restores him to his aboriginal identity and strips from him the false modern sense of self that had held him captive.

Analyzing the name of his protagonist brings to light not only Momaday's economy as a writer – the central issues of the novel are compressed in a single name – but also his interest in broadening the cultural context of his work. Momaday's writings hold many delightful surprises for those who approach him not simply as a Native American or Kiowa writer but as a borrower and synthesizer of all of the cultural resources at his disposal.

Momaday's reference to the German Expressionist painter Nolde serves as another example of his artistic inclusiveness and points to a significant subtext in the novel. Set's lover Lola Bourne's likening of Set's painting *Night Window Man* to Nolde's *Wanderer among the Stars* introduces an intricate web of connections between Set's groping for his inner self through his painting and Nolde's Expressionist theory. Moreover, as Set distances himself from the dictates of the art market he begins to share the Expressionist belief that art must take its origin in a particular geographical location whose influence is channeled through the artist's unconscious. Other tenets of Expressionist art expounded in the novel include the use of myths and tribal expression as models for modern painting, the spontaneous expression of a subjective vision of reality through a vocabulary of colors, and the yearning to retrieve a childlike, uncorrupted view of the world.

Thus, in his search for a primal, mythic mentality through which he may retrieve his true identity and reinvigorate his artistic power, Set follows many Expressionist artists, Nolde among them, who turned away from modern civilization to restore the power of myths and affirm the role of place and the unconscious in the genesis of artistic expression.

The same creative forces gave rise to Momaday's next work, *In the Presence of the Sun: A Gathering of Shields*. This collection of sixteen drawings of shields and sixteen accompanying stories was published in 1992 in a limited edition of 140 copies, 26 of which were hand colored, by Rydal Press of Santa Fe. This edition was followed by a separate edition, limited to forty-eight copies, of the drawings alone. While the full visual effect and the exceptional bookmaker's craft of the Rydal Press edition are lacking in the St. Martin's Press trade edition, *In the Presence of the Sun: Stories and Poems, 1961–1991* – also published in 1992 – the magic of the text is not.

In his introduction to *In the Presence of the Sun: A Gathering of Shields,* "A Word on the Plains Shields," Momaday describes the shields as artifacts, weapons, objects of beauty, and symbols of the bearer's essence. The vision that leads to the design and construction of the shield is sacred and providential. The story on each shield is taken from the oral tradition, and the text's power is reinforced by its structure, which revolves around the magic number *4*. To purify the spirit through the encounter with the shields, Momaday recommends that "the stories ought to be told in the early morning or late afternoon, when the sun is close to the horizon, and always in the presence of the sun."

Reminiscent of Momaday's best writing in *The Way to Rainy Mountain,* each story captures some quintessential moment in the shield bearer's life and relates how the shield shapes his destiny. Some stories tell of triumph through the strength, courage, and perseverance that emanated from the vision, while others relate decline and loss. Some of the shields symbolize the tie to the land, others the bond between generations, while yet others affirm the communion between mortals and supernatural powers. *In the Presence of the Sun: A Gathering of Shields* functions in much the same way as the secular, pictorial calendar histories of the Kiowa, which aimed to preserve memorable personages and events in the collective tribal mind; but Momaday's intent is to bring the reader into the presence of the sacred.

In addition to reprinting the text and the shield drawings, the trade edition, *In the Presence of the Sun: Stories and Poems, 1961–1991,* includes fifty-four paintings and drawings in a variety of media, twenty-nine poems of the original forty-three in *The Gourd Dancer,* the poems and stories about Billy the Kid that were interspersed in *The Ancient Child,* and twenty-seven new poems. The Billy the Kid material explores the split in this figure's personality between the sensitive, considerate, polite young man loved by women of all ages and the sharklike instinctual death force capable of the cold-blooded murders on which his legendary reputation rests. Of the new poems, "The Great Fillmore Street Buffalo Drive," a moving evocation of an urban Indian's vision of the Kiowa's glory days, stands out, as do "December 29, 1890 – Wounded Knee Creek" and "Fort Sill – Set-angia," which preserve, in Momaday's precise diction and haunting images, the memory of Indians dying. The final poem, "At Risk," is a major addition to Momaday's poetic canon. Its persona's descent into the remote past not only provides a poetic commentary on the novel *The Ancient Child* but also reveals Momaday's artistic struggle as he traverses existential crises and the realms of ancient myths and ritual in search of authentic expression. It delineates the risk the writer must accept as he or she, like a shaman or medicine woman, conjures up the irresistible power of words to shape reality.

While many of Momaday's comments on the environment date from the 1970s, he has recently returned to these concerns. In "Sacred Places" (1993) he calls for the preservation of natural sites not only on ecological but also on spiritual grounds. Published by Sierra Club Books, this essay shows Momaday in a more overtly activist role, a stance he has eschewed in the past. To his other accomplishments Momaday has added a delightful Christmas story for children, *Circle of Wonder* (1994).

N. Scott Momaday is steeped in both Native and European-American traditions, and his synthesis of these sources is a hallmark of his work. In drawing on the most ancient and sacred traditions of his and other Native people, who have called America home for at least thirty thousand years, he has actualized what William Carlos Williams, in *In the American Grain* (1925), identified as the crucial step toward creating truly American art: descending into the American earth, touching its aboriginal spirit, and allowing it to inform one's artistic creation. He conceives his writings and paintings with the spirit of a cave painter, a maker of masks, a shaman, an ancient storyteller, a night chanter, and a shield maker. As he puts it in "The Native Voice," the opening chapter of the *Columbia Literary History of the United States* (1988), the American Indian oral tradition "is so deeply rooted in the landscape of the New World that it cannot be denied. And it is so distinguished an expression that we cannot afford to lose it." As one listens to Momaday's native voice, one's sense of American literature is enlarged and newly defined.

Interviews:

"The Magic of Words," in *Survival This Way,* edited by Joseph Bruchac (Tucson: University of Arizona Press, 1987), pp. 173-191;

Charles L. Woodard, *Ancestral Voice: Conversations with N. Scott Momaday* (Lincoln: University of Nebraska Press, 1989);

Laura Coltelli, *Winged Words: American Indian Writers Speak* (Lincoln & London: University of Nebraska Press, 1990), pp. 88–100;

"Interview by Louis Owens," in *This Is about Vision: Interviews with Southwestern Writers,* edited by William Balessi, John F. Crawford, and Annie O. Eysturoy (Albuquerque: University of New Mexico Press, 1990), pp. 59-69;

Daniele Fiorentino, "The American Indian Writer as Cultural Broker: An Interview with N. Scott Momaday," *Studies in American Indian Literatures,* 8 (Winter 1996): 61–72.

Biographies:

Martha Scott Trimble, *N. Scott Momaday,* Boise State Western Writers Series, no. 9 (Boise: Boise State University Press, 1973);

Matthias Schubnell, *N. Scott Momaday: The Cultural and Literary Background* (Norman: University of Oklahoma Press, 1985).

References:

Peter G. Beidler, "Animals and Human Development in the Contemporary American Indian Novel," *Western American Literature,* 14 (Summer 1979): 133–148;

Roger Dickinson-Brown, "The Art and Importance of N. Scott Momaday," *Southern Review,* new series 14 (January 1978): 30–45;

Lawrence J. Evers, "Words and Place: A Reading of *House Made of Dawn,*" in *Critical Essays on American Indian Literature,* edited by Andrew Wiget (Boston: G. K. Hall, 1985), pp. 211–227;

Marion Willard Hilton, "On a Trail of Pollen: Momaday's *House Made of Dawn,*" *Critique,* 14, no. 2 (1972): 60–69;

Bernard Hirsch, "Self-Hatred and Spiritual Corruption in *House Made of Dawn,*" *Western American Literature,* 17 (Winter 1983): 307–320;

Linda Hogan, "Who Puts Together," *Denver Quarterly,* 14, no. 4 (1980): 103–111;

Charles Larson, *American Indian Fiction* (Albuquerque: University of New Mexico Press, 1978), pp. 78–96;

Kenneth Lincoln, *Native American Renaissance* (Berkeley: University of California Press, 1983), pp. 95–121;

Lincoln, "Tai-Me to Rainy Mountain: The Making of American Indian Literature," *American Indian Quarterly,* 10 (Spring 1986): 101–117;

Harold S. McAllister, "Be a Man, Be a Woman: Androgyny in *House Made of Dawn,*" *American Indian Quarterly,* 2 (Spring 1975): 14–22;

McAllister, "Incarnate Grace and the Paths of Salvation in *House Made of Dawn,*" *South Dakota Review,* 12, no. 4 (1974): 115–125;

Mick McAllister, "The Topology of Remembrance in *The Way to Rainy Mountain,*" *Denver Quarterly,* 12, no. 4 (1980): 19–31;

Carol Oleson, "The Remembered Earth: Momaday's *House Made of Dawn,*" *South Dakota Review,* 11, no. 1 (1973): 59–78;

Louis Owens, *Other Destinies: Reading the American Indian Novel* (Norman: University of Oklahoma Press, 1992), pp. 90–127;

Paintbrush: A Journal of Contemporary Multicultural Literature, special issue, "The World of N. Scott Momaday," edited by Richard F. Fleck, 21 (Autumn 1994);

Kenneth M. Roemer, "Ancient Children At Play – Lyric, Petroglyphic, and Ceremonial," in *Critical Perspectives on Native American Fiction,* edited by Fleck (Washington, D.C.: Three Continents, 1993), pp. 99–113;

Roemer, "Survey Courses, Indian Literature, and *The Way to Rainy Mountain,*" *College English,* 37 (February 1976): 619–624;

Roemer, ed., *Approaches to Teaching Momaday's* The Way to Rainy Mountain (New York: Modern Language Association, 1988);

Susan Scarberry-García, *Landmarks of Healing: A Study of* House Made of Dawn (Albuquerque: University of New Mexico Press, 1990);

Matthias Schubnell, "Locke Setman, Emil Nolde and the Search for Expression in N. Scott Momaday's *The Ancient Child,*" *American Indian Quarterly,* 18 (Fall 1994): 468–480;

Alan R. Velie, "*House Made of Dawn:* Nobody's Protest Novel," in his *Four American Indian Literary Masters* (Norman: University of Oklahoma Press, 1982), pp. 51–64.

Mourning Dove (Humishuma)

(between April 1882? and 1888? – 8 August 1936)

Alanna Kathleen Brown
Montana State University

BOOKS: *Cogewea, the Half-Blood: A Depiction of the Great Montana Cattle Range, by Hum-ishu-ma, "Mourning Dove" . . . Given through Sho-pow-tan, with Notes and Biographical Sketch by Lucullus Virgil McWhorter* (Boston: Four Seas, 1927);

Coyote Stories, edited by Heister Dean Guie (Idaho: Caxton Printers, 1933);

Tales of the Okanogans, edited by Donald M. Hines (Fairfax, Wash.: Ye Galleon, 1976);

Mourning Dove: A Salishan Autobiography, edited by Jay Miller (Lincoln: University of Nebraska Press, 1990);

Mourning Dove's Stories, edited by Clifford E. Trafzer and Richard D. Scheuerman (San Diego: San Diego State University Press, 1991).

Editions: *Cogewea, the Half-Blood: A Depiction of the Great Montana Cattle Range,* edited by Dexter Fisher (Lincoln: University of Nebraska Press, 1981);

Coyote Stories, edited by Jay Miller (Lincoln: University of Nebraska Press, 1990).

OTHER: "The Story of Green-Blanket Feet," in *Spider Woman's Granddaughters,* edited by Paula Gunn Allen (Boston: Beacon, 1989), pp. 117–125;

"Coyote Juggles His Eyes," in *Voice of the Turtle: American Indian Literature, 1900–1970,* edited by Allen (New York: One World/Ballantine, 1994), pp. 72–77.

SELECTED PERIODICAL PUBLICATIONS – UNCOLLECTED: "Learning Love Medicine," edited by Clifford E. Trafzer and Richard D. Scheuerman, *Fiction International,* 20 (Fall 1991): 142–156;

"Mourning Dove's 'The House of Little Men,' " edited by Alanna Kathleen Brown, *Canadian Literature,* 144 (Spring 1995): 49–60.

The works of Mourning Dove (Humishuma) are vital to an understanding of the settlement/assimilation period (1880s–1930s) on Native peoples, and they are also a crucial link in the evolution of Native American literature. As a novelist Mourning Dove focused on the difficult issues of mixed-blood heritage and the vulnerability of Indians to white exploitation, as well as the incorporation of Indian storytelling into the Western romance, making *Cogewea, the Half-Blood: A Depiction of the Great Montana Cattle Range* (1927) the first truly bicultural novel to convey an Indian worldview. Her reflections on her life in what would be titled *Mourning Dove: A Salishan Autobiography* (1990) provide the

Mourning Dove (Historical Photograph Collections, Washington State University Libraries)

Mourning Dove, circa 1916. In her younger years she was also known as Christine or Christal Haines (Historical Photograph Collections, Washington State University Libraries).

most thorough revelation of assimilation pressures on a collapsing Indian culture now in print. In the face of that potential annihilation, *Coyote Stories* (1933) demonstrates the choice to keep the Salish oral heritage alive by utilizing the literary forms of the conquering culture.

The year of Mourning Dove's birth is in question. A 1908 marriage license states April 1882; a family anecdote suggests 1884; various tribal enrollment and allotment records list both 1886 and 1887; and Mourning Dove always asserted that her birth date was April 1888. Whatever the actual year, she was born in the decade when federal policies turned toward assimilation. Throughout her lifetime it was assumed that distinct Indian cultures would die out by the end of the twentieth century. At her birth she was given the Christian name Christine. Her Indian birth name may have been Humishuma (Mourning Dove), but no verifying records survive. Her mother, Lucy Stuikin, was either a full-blooded Colville or of Colville and Arrow Lakes descent. Her father, Joseph Quintasket, was of Nicola and Okanogan descent on his mother's side, and there is reference to his father's being an Irishman named Haines or Haynes who worked for the Hudson Bay Company. The family history becomes more confusing and complex, however, as the same Haines/Haynes is listed as Mourning Dove's father on allotment records. Mourning Dove grew up in the family of Lucy and Joseph Quintasket near what is today Kettle Falls, Washington, on the west side of the Columbia River, on the Colville Reservation.

Mourning Dove was the oldest child; her sisters Julia and Mary Margaret were born in 1891 and 1892, respectively. Mourning Dove was placed in the Goodwin Mission School of the Sacred Heart Convent at Ward, Washington, in 1895. Punished for speaking Salish and locked in a stairwell closet for misbehaving, she returned home ill within months. Nonetheless, she went back to the mission and was enrolled there, on and off, for four years. When federal funding for religious instruction for Native students was cut in 1899, she continued her education at the newly formed Bureau of Indian Affairs–sponsored Fort Spokane School for Indians in 1899–1900. The school was composed of converted military barracks at the confluence of the Columbia and Spokane Rivers.

Mourning Dove's baby sister, Marie, fell ill and died on 29 April 1900. Her mother died at age thirty on 8 May 1901, and Mourning Dove's brother, Johnny, who was four or five, died on 8 July 1902. When Joseph Quintasket married a twenty-five-year-old woman, Cecelia Williams, Mourning Dove, who was then the primary female caretaker, traveled on horseback to Jennings, Montana, with thirteen-year-old Julia and twelve-year-old Mary Margaret to visit their maternal grandmother; a brother, Louis, remained with their father. Then the girls were separated. Julia stayed with her grandmother and eventually married a rancher; Margaret was sent to an aunt in Curlew, Washington; and Mourning Dove arranged to work as a matron in exchange for room and board and the privilege of attending classes at the Fort Shaw Indian School outside Great Falls, Montana.

Mourning Dove had traveled as far east as she would ever go, and she had chosen to pursue a white education. While at Fort Shaw she signed her name as Christine Haines, and she spent four years not only assimilating herself but also helping other Indian children assimilate. On 31 July 1908, having adopted the nickname "Christal," Mourning Dove married Hector McLeod, a mixed-blood who was one-eighth or one-fourth Flathead

Indian, in Kalispell, Montana. While they lived in Ronan, the newlywed couple established a livery-stable business in Polson, Montana. As Christal McLeod, Mourning Dove was as close to an assimilated white identity as she would ever come.

Her marriage was not easy: Hector was an alcoholic and was also abusive. Mourning Dove was hospitalized after one of his violent outbreaks, and, whether through damage inflicted by her husband or sterilization by a doctor, she would never be able to bear children. In 1912 she left her husband and moved to Portland, Oregon.

Probably in late 1912 she traveled to Calgary, Alberta, where she attended two years of business school to learn typing, shorthand, and composition skills. By 1914 she had a typed draft of *Cogewea* and twenty-two Okanogan legends in transcription. At that juncture, Mourning Dove met Lucullus Virgil McWhorter at the Walla Walla Frontier Days Celebration; she was in a singing and drumming group McWhorter had hired. As McWhorter was transcribing Yakima legends at the time, Mourning Dove was urged by a mutual acquaintance to draw on McWhorter's expertise to edit and help publish her collection. She was between twenty-six and thirty-two, and McWhorter was fifty-four. The letters from their nineteen-year collaboration and twenty-two-year friendship provide extensive information about the tensions she experienced in finding her voice as an author and about the process of working with collaborators.

The earliest years of their correspondence, from 1914 to 1920, show that for her family Mourning Dove was an unattached experienced worker and was needed by everyone. She was constantly pressed with invitations to visit, which were always requests for help. Her writing was considered a hobby by her family, and none of them believed that her desire to write was more important than their needs. For McWhorter, on the other hand, there was no question that Mourning Dove's writing should be of primary importance.

J. P. MacLean, McWhorter's elder mentor, had even higher expectations for Mourning Dove. He urged McWhorter and Mourning Dove to write their Yakima and Okanogan legends both in English and in the appropriate Indian dialect, although no lexicons of such dialects existed at the time. Moreover, MacLean wanted to arrange a speaking tour for Mourning Dove in the East, beginning in Ohio and going on to Philadelphia and Boston. McWhorter and MacLean wanted Mourning Dove to address the wrongs done to Native Americans; they wanted her to transform the racial biases of the day through her personal presentations as well as her writing.

Mourning Dove's response was to try to meet the needs of everyone. In 1915 she helped her sister Mary Margaret in Canada and her father in Napoleon, Washington. She then stayed with McWhorter in the winter of 1915–1916 to create a publishable manuscript of her novel. Immediately afterward she took care of Julia's family in Jennings, Montana, while her sister recovered from an operation and the children suffered from measles. She then went to Spokane to care for the family of a cousin who had suffered a hemorrhage. While visiting her best friend, Jenny Lewis, in Polson, Montana, she learned of an opportunity to publish *Cogewea,* and she contracted to take care of a widower's six children to earn her share of the sixty-five dollars in publication costs. It is not surprising that exhaustion overwhelmed her. By the winter of 1916–1917 Mourning Dove was deathly ill from inflammatory rheumatism and pneumonia. She nearly died that January.

To recover, Mourning Dove went to live with Mary Margaret and her family on the Inkameep Reserve in British Columbia. Continuing chest and shoulder pain as well as fainting spells were compounded by a severe toothache in 1917. Then in early 1918 an eye problem prevented Mourning Dove from reading or sewing. In April a quack doctor suggested that a tonsillectomy would cure her rheumatism, and she had the operation in August. Within months she was bedridden with the killer flu of 1918–1919. Mourning Dove survived these two years of medical crises and pain. They stimulated in her a deepening commitment to writing and caused her to consider marriage for a second time. In February 1918 she bought an Oliver typewriter, and on 14 August 1919 she married Fred Galler, a half-blood Wenatchee, in Okanogan County, Washington.

An important literary theme in *Cogewea* reveals itself in Mourning Dove's 1917–1918 letters. As she wrote of life in Canada, the split consciousness of being a partially assimilated Indian came to the fore. While she believed that the healing powers of a medicine-woman aunt had helped her recover from inflammatory rheumatism and pneumonia, when her traditionally educated sister asked her to cleanse the house and grounds by burning whatever a late stepson had touched and to wash the buggy and milk cow with rose bushes to drive away evil spirits, Mourning Dove obeyed; but she described her sister's requests as superstitions and considered such beliefs comically odd. She was also an outsider in regard to the Indian community's Christian faith: "The people are so loyal and true to their church in their simple untrained mind" (18 March 1918). Her education and experiences had led her to doubt religion, yet she envied her Canadian family and their neighbors and believed that she would be happier if she were like them.

Ironically, having chosen to write about Indian issues deepened the dilemma of Indian identity for Mourning Dove. She was being called upon to look at her culture anthropologically, to disassociate herself from it while at the same time becoming a representative voice of her tribe and her generation. Once called to that path, she did not shrink from the tensions or responsibilities such a role demanded.

The letters demonstrate that from 1921 to 1928 the collaboration between Mourning Dove and McWhorter intensified. While Mourning Dove managed a house with fourteen boarders or joined her husband in harvesting fruit in their orchard, she also worked on transcribing more Salishan legends and editing the ones she had already recorded. Late in 1921 she sent McWhorter the thirty-seven legends that he would reorganize into the thirty-eight tales of the original manuscript, titled "The Okanogan Sweat House." The title page ascribed the work to "HUM-IS HU-MA: 'MOURNING DOVE.' "

In the last two months of 1921 and throughout the following year McWhorter focused on getting both the novel and the collection of Okanogan tales ready for publication. This second period of intense collaboration was carried out by mail, and their correspondence reveals a great deal about McWhorter's concern for accuracy, his desire to write a work that would receive an ethnographer's approval. Mourning Dove responded to his commitment by answering his queries quickly and by working to see the tales from his perspective, which required that she develop some skill as a linguist and lexicographer. McWhorter asked her to work with others to develop an English spelling for Salish words. He also wanted to know word derivations, and he assumed that Mourning Dove would have such knowledge or would know whom to ask.

But assimilation was moving swiftly: languages that could have explained the derivation of certain words had died out, and some assumptions about traditional Indian ways already included European influences. Mourning Dove would write to McWhorter that Indians had no fingered gloves before their interaction with whites, so she would have to contrive a word for "hand cover"; or that because an entire tribe had been wiped out, it was no longer possible to trace the meaning of a particular word.

Cogewea had been accepted for publication in 1916 and 1918, but the cost of materials and labor during World War I had led the publishers to withdraw their offers. McWhorter submitted the manuscript several times afterward but always received polite refusals. He apparently believed that if more political and moral substance were added to the novel, it would have a better chance of success, and in 1922 his frustration over the difficulties in publishing *Cogewea* overwhelmed his better judgment. He took upon himself the reworking of *Cogewea* and did not share his editing of and additions to the novel with Mourning Dove. Initially, ethnographic annotations, notes, and the insertion of poetic lead-ins for the chapters were to be his contributions to the novel. He also helped Mourning Dove make her sentences grammatically correct and helped her think through the development of the plot. But in 1922 McWhorter added diatribes against Christian hypocrisy and government corruption. He also chose to elevate the language of the heroine to such a rarefied air that her words ceased to be believable speech. *Cogewea* became a mouthpiece for McWhorter's rage against white hypocrisy and injustices.

McWhorter solicited Upton Sinclair's support in his attempt to get the novel published, but the book agent Sinclair recommended turned *Cogewea* down in 1924. In 1925 the Four Seas Company of Boston agreed to publish the book. Mourning Dove arranged to have a lunch stand set up at a large Indian camp during the harvesting season to raise the $200 needed to subsidize the publication. McWhorter created circulars, and early orders were solicited for the book. The galley proofs for the novel, excluding notes, did not arrive until June 1926, and then the work languished again. In Mourning Dove and McWhorter's correspondence the Four Seas Company became the Four Puddles, and then the Four Liars; in February 1927 McWhorter gave notice to the company that he would report it to the U.S. Postal Service for fraudulent use of the mail. The company agreed to publish *Cogewea* soon, but still no book appeared; most people asked for their money back, and Mourning Dove and McWhorter were humiliated.

Although 1927 is given as its copyright date, *Cogewea* appears not to have been printed and in circulation until June 1928. By then the expected advance sales of almost 1,250 copies had dropped to 250, and the first edition never sold out. Mourning Dove did not receive even twenty-five dollars in cash (the equivalent of the pay for four or five days of apple picking) for the publication, and in a final settlement with the publisher the authors received copies of the unsold novel.

Two problems arose when *Cogewea* finally came to print. The more significant was that Mourning Dove saw the changes to the novel for the first time: "I have just got through going over the book Cogeawea, and am surprised at the changes that you made. . . . I felt like it was some one elses book and not mine at all. In fact the finishing touches are put there by you, and I have never seen it. . . . Oh my Big Foot, you surely roasted the Shoapees. strong. I think a little too strong to get their sympathy" (4 June 1928). Her criticisms of McWhorter's additions were critically insightful and are at the core of the interpretive debate about the novel today. The other issue was that McWhorter inadvertently signed away the copyright to the novel; thus, when Harl J. Cook approached Mourning Dove and McWhorter about writing a script for a movie adaptation of *Cogewea* in November 1928, the copyright was in the hands of the Four Seas Company. Nonetheless, the publication of *Cogewea* allowed Mourning Dove to pursue the social and political activism that marked the final eight years of her life.

That activism began with her founding in 1928 of the Eagle Feather Club, an organization to mentor, educate, and meet the social needs of Indian women in Omak. With Mourning Dove as spokeswoman, the club addressed government commissions on the corruption of business practices and government ineptitude on the reservation. In 1930 she became a spokeswoman for the Colville Indian Association. In 1934 she offered to help Commissioner John Collier secure adoption of the Indian Reorganization Act, and although reorganization was voted down in 1935 by the Colville Indians, Mourning Dove was elected to the Tribal Council in that same year, the first woman to win such an office.

Mourning Dove and McWhorter entered into their third and final period of intense collaboration in 1929. This time they were joined by Heister Dean Guie, a young newspaperman who wanted to expand into freelance writing and editorial work. McWhorter and Mourning Dove had just begun editing McWhorter's 1921–1922 manuscript for "Okanogan Sweat House" when McWhorter's wife died in August 1929. McWhorter lost interest in the project; Mourning Dove presented him with increasingly complex linguistic and cultural questions in an attempt to take his mind off his loss. Guie had

Lucullus Virgil McWhorter, Mourning Dove's collaborator (Historical Photograph Collections, Washington State University Libraries)

more energy than either of them, and they gratefully let him take charge. His first significant change was to reformulate the tales to meet the standards for the juvenile literature of the day by speeding up the action, avoiding repetition, and using simpler words.

Yet Guie also wanted to be sure that the legends were made accurate, that they did not contradict other ethnographic accounts, even while he modified the stories so that they would not shock white 1930s sensibilities – for example, the tales' references to excrement or incest. Mourning Dove considered Guie a demanding taskmaster, a "severe teacher" (19 May 1930), and she believed his attention to detail would strengthen the work. She wanted to see the tales published to honor the storytellers, many of whom had died, and she wanted to preserve some of her culture for future generations of Indians.

Mourning Dove became involved with the Seventh-Day Adventists and then with the Jehovah's Witnesses in her final years, but her movement to Euro-American religions was balanced by

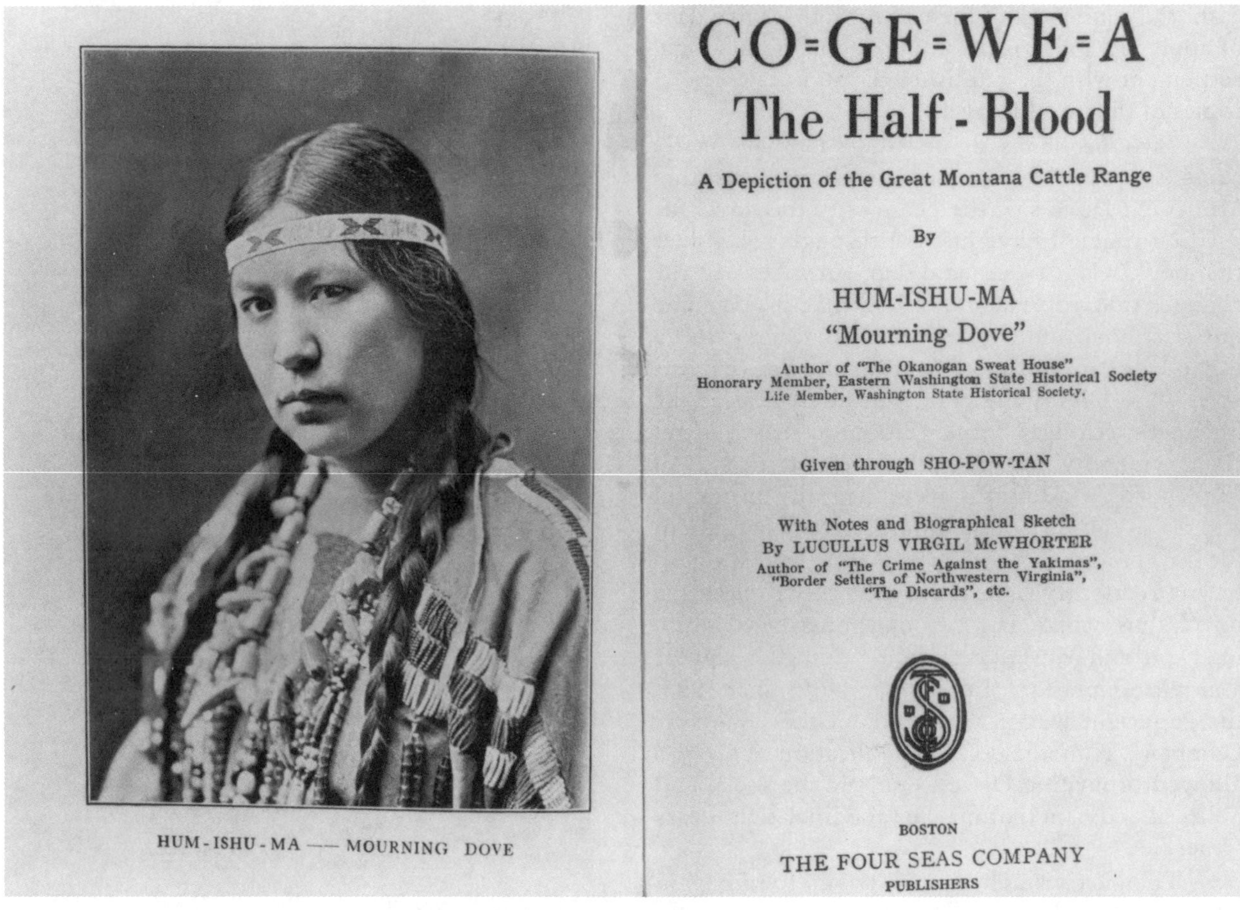
HUM-ISHU-MA —— MOURNING DOVE

CO=GE=WE=A
The Half - Blood

A Depiction of the Great Montana Cattle Range

By

HUM-ISHU-MA
"Mourning Dove"

Author of "The Okanogan Sweat House"
Honorary Member, Eastern Washington State Historical Society
Life Member, Washington State Historical Society.

Given through SHO-POW-TAN

With Notes and Biographical Sketch
By LUCULLUS VIRGIL McWHORTER
Author of "The Crime Against the Yakimas",
"Border Settlers of Northwestern Virginia",
"The Discards", etc.

BOSTON
THE FOUR SEAS COMPANY
PUBLISHERS

Frontispiece and title page for Mourning Dove's novel (courtesy of the Lilly Library, Indiana University)

her affirmation of traditional Indian beliefs. She frequently returned to her sister Mary Margaret's home in Canada, where she would meditate, gather healing herbs, greet the sunrise, and center herself in her Indian identity. Assimilated Native Americans had to hold within themselves many paradoxes. Mourning Dove's growing consciousness of those paradoxes, as well as her realization that younger Indians did not know what life had been like for her generation, led her to work on three final manuscripts: a novel, "Son of the Squaw"; and two nonfiction collections, "Tepee Life" and "Educating the Indian." She also wanted the dominant culture to understand the disruptions through which her people had struggled; she wanted them to see the settlement period through Indian eyes.

She worked on these manuscripts while she, Guie, and McWhorter were transforming "Okanogan Sweat House" into *Coyote Stories,* as well as in following years. But her commitment to her work had to be maintained in the face of poor health, difficult physical work, financial difficulties, family tragedies, and an eroding marriage. Her beloved half sister, Milly, died in April 1931, and Mary Margaret's husband, who had been severely burned in a firestorm in August 1931, also died. Finally, her second husband, like her first, had turned out to be an alcoholic. He gambled away their car in May 1930 and spent a month's pay partying in November 1933; the Gallers were always in debt. At times they had physical fights. They kept the marriage together, crisis after crisis, and Mourning Dove was still willing to move with him in 1934 to a tent while he worked on the Grand Coulee Dam project; but her trust in him was gone.

Mourning Dove was disappointed with "Son of the Squaw," and though she wrote of recasting it in 1930, no surviving draft has been found. "Tepee Life" and "Educating the Indian" were never finished, because on 30 July 1936 she was admitted to the hospital at Medical Lake, Washington, in extreme mental distress, with abrasion marks and bruises on her chest, shins, and buttocks. On 8 August the family was told that she had died of a brain hemorrhage. The death certificate, however, says that Christine Galler died of "exhaustion from manic depressive psychosis." She was buried in the Omak, Washington, cemetery. A pauper's cinder block engraved "Mrs. F. Galler" marked the grave until 1991, when Jay Miller, the editor of her final manuscripts – at the request of her half brother, Charlie Quintasket – paid for a more appropriate gravestone to mark the site.

The fundamental problem that confronts critics of *Cogewea* is how to read a novel that is a work of collaboration in some sections, a highly edited piece in others, and the product of the editor in still others. Mourning Dove and McWhorter worked collaboratively on the revision and completion of the original 1912 manuscript in the winter of 1915–1916; the most moving parts of the published novel, including Stemteema's stories and the Fourth of July races, were honed during this collaborative period. McWhorter would have helped with the grammar and spelling, and mutual discussions may have helped Mourning Dove flesh out certain sections of the novel, including the ending. The text was hers; the revisions were theirs. When she left to rejoin her family McWhorter worked on the notes, the dedication, small revisions, and poetry headings for the chapters. He shared all of these additions with Mourning Dove, but the process was no longer strictly collaborative. The problem came in 1922, when McWhorter added the sections of social and political commentary and elevated the language of the heroine, without sending the revisions to Mourning Dove for her review. His additions, substitutions, and dialogue changes created serious disjunctures in the text; those disjunctures, however, add to readers' understanding of the settlement/assimilation period. The only way to read *Cogewea* successfully is to listen for both voices.

Mourning Dove's narrative describes a place and time she knew well, the Flathead Reservation of Montana in the early 1900s, when Polson was a town of about five hundred and "Missourians," or settlers, were moving in and wanted to fence and farm the open ranges needed for cowherding. What makes Mourning Dove's story particularly poignant is her focus on being a mixed-blood, and it is the character Stemteema who brings that issue into clearest focus. In telling the Green-Blanket Feet story she suggests that the Great Spirit is displeased by racial intermarriage. In "The Second Coming of the Shoyahpee" she expresses shock at having mixed-blood grandchildren and warns about the white man: "His words are poison! his touch is death." Yet, if she wishes the knowledge of her people to be passed on, she must share her stored wisdom about the cataclysmic coming of the whites with her grandchildren, who may be offended by the telling since their mixed-blood is a clear indication of the loss to the physical and cultural integrity of the tribe.

Mourning Dove's presentation of the complexities of being a mixed-blood on the frontier, as well as her incorporation into her work of Indian rituals and daily practices, stretched the Western romance into new realms of subject matter. The inclusion of Salishan oral traditions made Mourning Dove's romance the first bicultural Indian/white novel. Family tales, tribal accounts, and creation stories reinforce Indian community values and promote self-understanding. The tribal story of Green-Blanket Feet, the recounting of the chief's grief over the coming of Meriwether Lewis and William Clark, the medicine man's vision of a catastrophic future for his people, and the references to Thunderbird and Frog Woman enable Cogewea to come to an understanding of her world and to an understanding that her experiences are part of a larger, continuing story.

From his first reading of Mourning Dove's original manuscript, McWhorter recognized the significance of using a novel to portray "the social status of the Indian," and he was delighted by the inclusion of oral narratives (letter of 3 January 1916). Yet from the start, McWhorter's premises differed from Mourning Dove's in two crucial ways. First, McWhorter assumed, as did the majority of Euro-Americans, that Indian cultures would die out by the end of the twentieth century. McWhorter's poetic headings for each chapter were meant to evoke sympathy and understanding for the vanishing Indian. He did not believe, however, that this genocide was a by-product of Manifest Destiny. McWhorter perceived the destruction of the Indian to be a product of callousness and greed, sanctified by notions of racial and religious superiority. He was affronted by the cultural elitism of the conquering culture and the exploitation of indigenous peoples. It was for that reason that he created high-flown language for Cogewea so that the heroine would sound better-educated than the average white person. He wanted to shame white readers for their indifference to the abuses that were going on all around him. The second premise dividing Mourning Dove and McWhorter is equally sharp. Mourning Dove trusted her readers. She believed that the storyteller's craft is to stimulate the imaginative comprehension of the listener-reader creating a dialogue from which meaning emerges. McWhorter distrusted his readers and created monologue rather than dialogue in order to instruct or to reprimand.

Cogewea is a splintered text, but that splintering is revelatory. Mourning Dove's presentation of Indian spiritual and cultural values, as well as the problem of being a half-breed on the frontier, brought new and substantive subject matter to what was already clichéd, formulaic Western romance. Her adaptation of the novel to incorporate indigenous oral forms makes it a forerunner of late-twentieth-century Native American writing. On the other hand, McWhorter's impassioned defense of Native peoples is one of the few firsthand accounts by a white of the degree of white corruption and Indian degradation that Euro-American settlement brought to Indian country. *Cogewea* is a rough-hewn gem in which two people from divergent backgrounds insightfully comment on their times.

The Salishan stories Mourning Dove transcribed exist in four versions. First there are the 1921 transcriptions for "Okanogan Sweat House" that Mourning Dove typed, including her own handwritten corrections and some of McWhorter's, preserved at Holland Library of Washington State University in Pullman. The second is *Coyote Stories,* a highly edited version of twenty-four of the original thirty-seven tales. The third version is the most thoughtful transcription of "Okanogan Sweat House": *Tales of the Okanogans* (1976), edited by Donald M. Hines. All thirty-seven stories are included, and the illustrations convey the mythic power of a period when beings could be human and animal. Finally, Clifford E. Trafzer and Richard D. Scheuerman's edition of *Mourning Dove's Stories* (1991) combines eleven tales from "Okanogan Sweat House" with five stories Mourning Dove transcribed late in life. The "Okanogan Sweat House" pieces show Guie's revisions to stories that he ultimately decided not to include in *Coyote Stories* because of their risqué or taboo subject matter; for example, "Coyote the Medicine-Man" alters "Coyote Takes His Daughter as a Wife" to avoid the incest theme. "The Ant," "The Rivals' Last Stand," "The Legend of Omak Lake," "One Who Follows," and "The Blind Dog Monster" are later compositions, and they include more explanatory history and Christian references than does Mourning Dove's earlier work.

Coyote Stories came out in 1933 and was in a second printing by 1934. While some reviewers put Mourning Dove into a passive listener-recorder role, others, among them A. B. Guthrie in the *Lexington Leader* (17 December 1933), recognized her storytelling ability and complimented "her fine simplicity of expression" that "makes less impossible the impossible events she recounts." The collection

Mourning Dove in 1933 (Historical Photograph Collections, Washington State University Libraries)

not only introduced the reading public to Native American legends but also made them consider the devastating effects of assimilationist policies. The reviewer for the *Daily Oklahoman* (14 January 1934) wrote that *Coyote Stories* made him realize that no such collection of tales existed for the tribes in his own state, and he cautioned that the failure to collect such stories would mean "the loss of a spiritual heritage which [could] never be replaced."

The thirty-seven narratives Mourning Dove had transcribed by 1921 are genesis stories that explain physical phenomena, the temperament of animals, the relationships between animal groups, and behaviors appropriate or inappropriate to community survival. They explain how various northwest mountain ranges came to be and where the waterfalls are along the Big River (Columbia) tributaries ("The Camas Woman"), and where one can find salmon ("Coyote Breaks the Salmon Dam"). They also explain the intimate relationship between the Earth and the Sun and the Moon ("The Moon and Sun Gods"). Many stories include plot elements that explain natural phenomena – for example, where tree moss comes from ("Coyote Eats His Children"), how chipmunk got those finger marks down her back and how Meadow Lark got her necklace and yellow vest ("Owlwoman and Coyote"). Such stories teach children to observe the physical world, but they have an even more important purpose: they teach and reinforce thoughtful relationships among people. No character in Salishan legends is more important in that respect than Coyote.

Coyote is an ambivalent hero. He is irresponsible, irrepressible, subject to swift mood swings, self-important, self-indulgent, lazy, and vain. He is a liar who must constantly interpret events so that he always seems to be in control. But Coyote is also the consummate fool. When he is self-aggrandizing, and when he thoughtlessly violates taboos (for example, in "Coyote Eats His Children" and "Coyote Takes His Daughter as a Wife"), he becomes a ridiculous figure. The audience for the tales, as well as the characters in the stories, know that such behaviors are demeaning and destructive. Nonetheless, there is an innocence about Coyote, and an energy for acting and creating that makes him fearless, tenacious, and innovative. When these qualities are combined with a sense of heroism and adventure and even a perverse sense of slapstick humor, Coyote can change the world.

The reconfiguration of a narrative such as "Owlwoman and Coyote" into *Cogewea* also shows the sustaining power of the stories. In the novel Cogewea is intelligent, curious, impulsive, carefree, and warmhearted; these also are the traits of Chipmunk in the traditional Owl Woman story. Cogewea – her name is the Salish word for chipmunk – needs guidance and direction. Cogewea's guidance is provided by the wise grandmother, who sees through the wily ways of the white villain, Densmore, the counterpart to the child-eating Owl Woman of legend. The cowboy Celluloid Bill, based on Tattler or Meadow Lark from the Salishan tales, leads Densmore to Cogewea through tall tales of Cogewea's wealth, and another cowboy, Silent Bob – representing the other side of Tattler – rides to tell Jim of Cogewea's trouble. The abilities to refer to and to adapt such legends to the stresses of assimilation have been crucial to Indian survival.

When she died, Mourning Dove's written works seemed to die with her. From the 1940s to the 1970s there was almost no reference to her books or manuscripts. Then Charles R. Larson included a critique on the problems of dual authorship in *Cogewea* in the appendix of *American Indian Fiction* (1978), and Alice Poindexter Fisher completed a sympathetic and insightful dissertation on Zitkala-Ša and Mourning Dove in 1979. By that time Gerry Guie, Heister Dean Guie's widow, had discovered the unfinished manuscripts "Tepee Life" and "Educating the Indian," which Mourning Dove had asked her husband to edit in the 1930s. Erna Gunther, an anthropologist, began to revise and edit the materials; she was later joined by Jay Miller. In 1981 the University of Nebraska Press reprinted *Cogewea,* and in the early 1980s short pieces of critical commentary began to appear in overviews of Native American literature. Mary Dearborn's *Pocahontas's Daughters: Gender and Ethnicity in American Culture* (1986) was the first book to devote a major chapter to an analysis of Mourning

Coyote Stories

By Mourning Dove *(Hu-mis'-hu-ma)*

Edited and illustrated by Heister Dean Guie with notes by L. V. McWhorter *(Old Wolf)* and a foreword by Chief Standing Bear, Oglala Sioux

The CAXTON PRINTERS, Ltd.
CALDWELL, IDAHO
1934

Title page for the second printing of Mourning Dove's collection of Salishan tales

Dove's novel. Since then, two scholars have been particularly important in recovering Mourning Dove's works. Alanna Kathleen Brown has worked extensively with Mourning Dove's letters to bring an understanding of oral traditions, assimilation pressures, and collaboration into the discussion of her works. Miller edited the republication of *Coyote Stories* (1990) and the first publication of *Mourning Dove: A Salishan Autobiography.*

Mourning Dove: A Salishan Autobiography is the most extensive reflection on the period of assimilation by a Northwest Indian in print. Caution is necessary in reading the text, however: readers must understand that the organization of the subject matter is that of Gunther and Miller and that Miller has corrected Mourning Dove's Indian English, thus obscuring her tone, humor, and dramatic emphasis. He also annotated her work in a manner that undermines her purpose and her authority.

Miller uses three sources to test Mourning Dove's accounts of tribal experience and her own life: the ethnographic record, the Euro-American historical record, and contemporary informants, primarily male. Three notes in chapter 4, "The Dutiful Wife," illustrate how Miller uses ethnographic material. In note 1 Miller expands on Mourning Dove's text, although the shaman dress he discusses may or may not be in Mourning Dove's experience or appropriate to her tribe. Note 3 corrects the text by pointing out that balsam root "was more than just a 'famine food' " – quoting appropriate white male authorities – and note 6 assures the reader that Mourning Dove is accurate about which pandemic diseases devastated her people. Miller also uses the observations of white explorers and public officials to correct Mourning Dove's accounts of past events, as when he draws on David Thompson's journals to refute the tribal recollection of generosity to the first white explorers in Kettle Falls. Most surprising, Miller uses Mourning Dove's half-brother, Charlie Quintasket, born in 1909, to ridicule Mourning Dove's memory of her mother struggling to protect her children from near starvation in the severe winter of 1892-1893. Why does Miller represent Charlie Quintasket's word as being more reliable than Mourning Dove's? Is Mourning Dove wrong when she describes or recounts what she has experienced or heard if it does not verify white scholarship or Euro-American historical accounts? What is the source of ethnographic authority? With early Native American texts a reader must always be aware of the complexities involved in collaboration.

Interest in Mourning Dove is no longer the purview only of Native American scholars. Her texts have found a place in the larger discussion of American literature that is reformulating the literary canon. Issues of finding one's voice as a Native American woman writer at the turn of the last century, of understanding the settlement of the West from an Indian perspective, and of learning how to read collaborative texts have heightened the importance of Mourning Dove's texts. The Smithsonian Institution Press plans to publish *Mourning Dove's Letters and Salish Narratives,* thus making most of Mourning Dove's writing available to the reading public it so richly deserves.

Letters:

Mourning Dove's Letters and Salish Narratives, edited by Alanna Kathleen Brown (Washington, D.C.: Smithsonian Institution Press, forthcoming 1998).

Interviews:

"Colville Indian Girl Blazes Trail to New Conception of Redmen in Her Novel, 'Cogewea,' Soon to Be Published," *Spokane Review,* 19 April 1916;

"Indians Do Not Fish for Sport, Says Learned Leader," *Wenatchee Daily World,* 11 April 1930, p. 19.

References:

Paula Gunn Allen, *The Sacred Hoop: Recovering the Feminine in American Indian Traditions* (Boston: Beacon, 1986), pp. 81–84, 151;

Elizabeth Ammons, *Conflicting Stories, American Women Writers at the Turn into the Twentieth Century* (New York: Oxford University Press, 1991), pp. 121–122, 136–138, 197–199;

Susan Bernardin, "Mixed Messages: Authority and Authorship in Mourning Dove's *Cogewea, the Half-Blood: A Depiction of the Great Montana Cattle Range,*" *American Literature,* 67 (September 1995): 487–509;

Peter Biedler, "Literary Criticism in *Cogewea:* Mourning Dove's Protagonist Reads *The Brand,*" *American Indian Culture and Research Journal,* 19, no. 2 (1995): 45–65;

Alanna Kathleen Brown, "The Choice to Write: Mourning Dove's Search for Survival," in *Old West–New West: Centennial Essays,* edited by Barbara H. Meldrum (Moscow: University of Idaho Press, 1993), pp. 261–271;

Brown, "The Evolution of Mourning Dove's *Coyote Stories,*" *Studies in American Indian Literatures,* 4 (Summer/Fall 1992): 161–180;

Brown, "Looking through the Glass Darkly: The Editorialized Mourning Dove," in *New Voices in Native American Literary Criticism,* edited by Arnold Krupat (Washington, D.C. & London: Smithsonian Institution Press, 1993), pp. 274–290;

Brown, "Mourning Dove, an Indian Novelist," *Plainswoman,* 11 (January 1988): 3–4;

Brown, "Mourning Dove, Trickster Energy, and Assimilation Period Native American Texts," in *Tricksterism in Turn-of-the-Century American Literature: A Multicultural Perspective,* edited by Elizabeth Ammons and Annette White-Parks (Hanover & London: University Press of New England, 1994), pp. 126–136;

Brown, "Mourning Dove's Canadian Recovery Years, 1917–1919," *Canadian Literature,* 124 (Spring/Summer 1990): 113–122;

Brown, "Mourning Dove's Voice in Cogewea," *Wicazo Sa Review,* 4 (Fall 1988): 215;

Brown, "Profile: Mourning Dove (Humishuma) 1888–1936," *Legacy: A Journal of Nineteenth-Century American Women Writers,* 6 (Spring 1989): 51–58;

Mary Dearborn, *Pocahontas's Daughters: Gender and Ethnicity in American Culture* (New York: Oxford University Press, 1986), pp. 12–30;

Alice Poindexter Fisher, "The Transformation of Tradition: A Study of Zitkala Sa and Mourning Dove, Two Transitional American Indian Writers," in *Critical Essays on Native American Literature,* edited by Andrew Wiget (Boston: G. K. Hall, 1985), pp. 202–211;

Linda Karell, " 'The Story I Am Telling You Is True': Collaboration and Literary Authority in Mourning Dove's *Cogewea,*" *American Indian Quarterly,* 19 (Fall 1995): 451–465;

Charles R. Larson, *American Indian Fiction* (Albuquerque: University of New Mexico Press, 1978), pp. 173–180;

Jay Miller, "Mourning Dove: The Author as Cultural Mediator," in *Being and Becoming Indian, Biographical Studies of North American Frontiers,* edited by James A. Clifton (Chicago: Dorsey, 1989), pp. 160–182;

Louis Owens, "Origin Mists: John Rollin Ridge's Masquerade and Mourning Dove's Mixed-bloods," in his *Other Destinies: Understanding the American Indian Novel* (Norman: University of Oklahoma Press, 1992), pp. 32–48;

Andrew Wiget, *Native American Literature* (Boston: Twayne, 1985), pp. 71–72.

Papers:

Correspondence, the "Okanogan Sweat House" manuscripts, and the photographs of Mourning Dove taken by McWhorter are in the Lucullus Virgil McWhorter Collection, Holland Library, Manuscripts, Archives and Special Collections Division, Washington State University, Pullman. Some of the manuscript material for "Tepee Life" and "Educating the Indian" are in the Erna Gunther Collection, Manuscripts, Archives and Special Collections Division, University of Washington, Seattle. Clifford E. Trafzer, Richard D. Scheuerman, and Jay Miller have copies of the final two manuscripts found by Gerry Guie. Sealed medical records about Mourning Dove's death are at Medical Lake, Washington; permission for their review must be granted through the Superior Court of the State of Washington, Spokane County, Mental Health Department.

Duane Niatum

(13 February 1938 -)

Jarold Ramsey
University of Rochester

BOOKS: *After the Death of an Elder Klallam, and Other Poems,* as Duane McGinnis (Phoenix: Baleen, 1970);
A Cycle for the Women in the Field (Baltimore: Laughing Man, 1973);
Taos Pueblo and Other Poems (Greenfield Center, N.Y.: Greenfield Review, 1973);
Ascending Red Cedar Moon (New York: Harper & Row, 1974);
Turning to the Rhythm of Her Song (Seattle: Jawbone, 1977);
Digging out the Roots: Poems (New York: Harper & Row, 1977);
Songs for the Harvester of Dreams: Poems (Seattle: University of Washington Press, 1981);
Pieces (New York: Strawberry, 1981);
Raven and the Fear of Growing White (Amsterdam: Bridge, 1983);
Stories of the Moons (Marvin, S.Dak.: Blue Cloud Quarterly, 1987);
Drawings of the Song Animals: New and Selected Poems (Duluth: Holy Cow!, 1991).

OTHER: *Carriers of the Dream Wheel: Contemporary Native American Poetry,* edited by Niatum (New York: Harper & Row, 1975);
"Crow's Song," in *The Remembered Earth: An Anthology of Contemporary Native American Literature,* edited by Geary Hobson (Albuquerque: Red Earth Press, 1979), pp. 395-399;
"History in the Colors of Song: A Few Words Here on Contemporary Native American Poetry," in *Coyote Was Here: Essays on Contemporary Native American Literary and Political Mobilization,* edited by Bo Schöler (Århus, Denmark: Seklos, 1984), pp. 25-34;
"On Stereotypes," in *Recovering the Word: Essays on Native American Literature,* edited by Brian Swann and Arnold Krupat (Berkeley & Los Angeles: University of California Press, 1987), pp. 555-562;

Duane Niatum at the time of Carriers of the Dream Wheel

"Autobiographical Sketch," in *I Tell You Now: Autobiographical Essays by Native American Writers,* edited by Swann and Krupat (Lincoln: University of Nebraska Press, 1987), pp. 127-139;
Harper's Anthology of 20th Century Native American Poetry, edited by Niatum (San Francisco: Harper & Row, 1988);

Dust jacket for Niatum's groundbreaking poetry anthology, which played a major role in stimulating the Native American literary renaissance of the 1970s and 1980s

"Crow's Sun," in *Talking Leaves: Contemporary Native American Short Stories,* edited by Craig Lesley (New York: Dell/Laurel, 1991), pp. 208–216;

"North American Native Writers Journey to a Place Where the Air Is a Gift of Promise," in *Returning the Gift,* edited by Joseph Bruchac (Tucson: University of Arizona Press, 1994), pp. 201–202;

"Transforming the Ruins: Voices Finding the Way Home," introduction to *Durable Breath: Contemporary Native American Poetry,* edited by John E. Smelcer and D. L. Birchfield (Anchorage, Alaska: Salmon Run, 1994), pp. 1–6.

SELECTED PERIODICAL PUBLICATIONS – UNCOLLECTED: "Niatum on Niatum," *Niagara Magazine,* 5 (Summer 1976): 5–6;

"On Stereotypes," *Parnassus,* 7 (Fall/Winter 1978): 160–166;

"My Aim as a Writer," *Greenfield Review,* 11 (Winter/Spring 1984): 1–4;

"Net-picking," *Greenfield Review,* 11 (Winter/Spring 1984): 8–13;

"The Mistress of the House," *North Dakota Quarterly,* 53 (Spring 1985): 110–118;

"Traveling the Road That Once Was You," *North Dakota Review,* 59, no. 4 (1991): 55–60.

The accomplished poet and influential editor Duane Niatum was born in Seattle on 13 February 1938. His mother, Dorothy Patsy, was of Klallam (Salish) extraction; his father was an Italian-American merchant seaman. His mother's subsequent marriage to Howard McGinnis, an Anglo commercial fisherman, gave the future poet the surname he would carry into young manhood, though the marriage broke up after a few years. Niatum has described his growing up as troubled and confused; he was insecure about whether he belonged to the Indian or the Anglo branch of his family, and he rebelled against his status as a mixed-blood. After several stints in reform schools he enlisted in the navy at seventeen. Further troubles led to a month in a marine brig, vividly fictionalized in his short story "Crow's Sun"(1991). He spent some of his naval duty in Japan, where his interest in the artistic relations between cultures was awakened.

After his discharge in 1959 McGinnis lived briefly in New York City but mainly in and around Seattle. He was married for a time and has a grown son, Marc, from this marriage. Eventually he entered the University of Washington, from which he graduated with a B.A. in English in 1970. A boyhood passion for jazz and the alto saxophone had already been replaced by a more durable passion for

Dust jacket for Niatum's second anthology. Like the first, it is part of Harper and Row's Native American Authors Program, of which Niatum served as general editor in 1973–1974

writing; and in the excitement and camaraderie of Washington's creative-writing program at this time, with such authors as Theodore Roethke, David Wagoner, Nelson Bentley, Elizabeth Bishop, Louise Bogan, and Stanley Kunitz at least briefly on the faculty and with fellow students such as Tess Gallagher, McGinnis laid down solid literary and technical foundations for his career. By the time he received an M.A. in creative writing from Johns Hopkins University in 1972, he had already published his first poetry collection, *After the Death of an Elder Klallam* (1970).

This book, one of the first to bring Northwest Indian myth and tradition into modern poetry, appeared under the name Duane McGinnis; but in the spring of 1971 the poet's growing sense of allegiance to his mother's Klallam ancestry, nurtured over the years by his maternal grandfather, Francis Patsy, and other relatives in the Klallam village of Hadlock, Washington, was formalized in the gift from his great-aunt Anna Patsy Duncan of his great-great-grandfather's name, Niatum. The name was subsequently legalized, and in *I Tell You Now* (1987) he emphasizes its importance: "because I feel this is a sacred trust, I have reason to suspect that if I live long enough, this name will turn out to be what ultimately changed the character of my life."

Although he has held short-term appointments at the University of Washington, Evergreen State College, Eastern Washington University, and Seattle Central Community College, Niatum has not followed the academic path common among writers today. Instead, he has made a strenuous literary living through readings, consultantships, and freelance editing, and, in 1973–1974, as the general editor of Harper and Row's ambitious and controversial Native American Authors Program. Under Niatum's direction Harper and Row published important books by such writers as N. Scott Momaday, Ray Young Bear, Simon Ortiz, and James Welch, and Niatum's own *Ascending Red Cedar Moon* (1974); later Niatum's *Digging out the Roots* (1977) appeared in the series. This series, which also included the groundbreaking poetry anthology *Carriers of the Dream Wheel* (1975), edited by Niatum, was a major stimulus to the Native American literary renaissance of the 1970s and 1980s.

Since 1980 Niatum has traveled extensively in Europe, pursuing both a poet's and a scholar's interest in nineteenth- and twentieth-century painting. Of this long-standing predilection, he has written in *I Tell You Now* that

> it was the work and lives of the Impressionist and post-Impressionist painters that inspired me to try very hard at writing poetry. I couldn't see or read enough about these artists.... Several lives and selves later, these wonderful painters still illuminate the world and my life. Yes, I learned a great deal about poetry and music and drama from them and have found that collective vision has been extremely helpful to my art.

In the mid 1980s his fascination with painting and aesthetics led him to begin graduate study in the Program in American Culture at the University of Michigan, in preparation for a doctoral thesis on North Coast Indian pictorial art. He expects to complete the degree in 1997 or 1998.

Meanwhile, Niatum worked steadily at his craft, and his reputation as a poet advanced as his work appeared in little magazines and in poetry anthologies. In 1981 the University of Washington Press published his *Songs for the Harvester of Dreams;* his most ambitious gathering of poems to date, the volume won wide critical acclaim and the 1982 American Book Award from the Before Columbus Foundation. *Harper's Anthology of 20th Century Native American Poetry,* a greatly enlarged successor to *Carriers of the Dream Wheel,* appeared in 1988. In 1991, twenty-one years after the publication of his first book of poems, a "new and selected" collection was published as *Drawings of the Song Animals.* In 1994 Niatum was a featured participant in the second "Returning the Gift" National Native American Writers Conference at Neah Bay, Washington, the homeland of the Klallams' Salish cousins, the Makahs. Along with work on his first collection of short stories, he was readying a new collection of poems, "The Crooked Beak of Love," for publication.

Although he says that he has no theory of the arts, Niatum's work has shown a striking consistency from the beginning, and his extensive critical comments over the years, as well as his persistent revision of his work, give the impression of a body of poetry steadily and self-consciously unfolding from a coherent set of ideas rather than developing in a haphazard fashion. From the beginning of his career Niatum has attempted to mediate between the urban Anglo world in which he mainly grew up, and where he still mostly lives, on the one hand, and the traditional world of his Klallam ancestors, on the other. His devotion to the latter realm is profound, but, unlike other poets who have "dug out their roots," he rarely sentimentalizes his recovered tribal heritage; and although his poems often expose the crassness and waste of modern Anglo life, Niatum is too self-consciously and honestly a part of that life for him to allow his critiques to degenerate into mere diatribes. He identifies, as the ground of his being, the Pacific Northwest – meaning both the mythic maritime region of his Indian forebears on Puget Sound and the Olympic Peninsula and, superimposed thereon, the modern geopolitical region that includes Seattle, Port Angeles, Boeing Aircraft, Pioneer Square, and so on. The value for Niatum's writing of this complex sense of place is that it provides solid ground for his imaginative endeavor to hold all of the disparate elements of his being in mind at once. The result is a poetry that is at once intensely local and also urbane.

In terms of style and literary models, this urbanity is especially conspicuous in his poetry from *Songs for the Harvester of Dreams* onward. Part 1 of that book, "Voices from the World and the People," consists of brief poems, in the form and manner of traditional Salish songs and chants, that are dense with allusions to mythic figures such as Raven, Eagle, Salmon, Old Man, Owl, and Cougar. Yet in "Cougar" the poet's imagination seems to have conjured up Rainer Maria Rilke's Panther alongside the American mountain lion; the juxtaposition is eerie and characteristic of Niatum:

His solitude warms our blood
As he runs from our eyes
Following him into the brush.
What strength we have left
In our hearts goes back to him.

In part 2 of the collection, "Spinning the Dream Wheel," the stylistic and formal range widens markedly to include intimations of the work of W. S. Merwin, Ted Hughes, and especially Roethke: "The Art of Clay" is a villanelle in the manner of Roethke's "I Wake to Sleep" (1953). More recently, in *Drawings of the Song Animals,* Niatum pays his old master the ultimate technical compliment of a sonnet sequence, "Lines for Roethke Twenty Years after His Death."

Niatum's range and versatility as a poet, and his extensive knowledge of modernist literature and art, probably underlie the controversial position he takes in his essay "On Stereotypes" in *Recovering the Word: Essays on Native American Literature* (1987). There he expresses his "resentment at being categorized, boxed and sealed: 'Indian writer' " by reviewers and critics, even when such stereotyping is laudatory; he goes further, arguing against Leslie Marmon Silko that "there is not a Native American aesthetic today that we can recognize as having separate principles from the standards of artists from Western European and American cultures. And anyone who claims there is encourages a conventional and prescriptive response from both Native Americans and those from other cultures." Niatum acknowledges the inescapable primacy of American English, with its freight of forms and traditions, for modern Indian writers as well as for members of all other ethnic and racial groups who use it. He admits that Indian poetry and fiction have features that differentiate them, at least in degree, from mainstream Anglo writing – most notably, the high valuation Native American writers place on the spiritual power of words that are formed and used properly. But Niatum rejects the proposition that such differences constitute a pan-Indian aesthetic or poetics. An Indian writer must be able to use the full range of available literary resources, Anglo as well as Indian; he or she must not be limited to a special category of "pan-Indian" resources and measures that are understood to be somehow derived from all the tribal literary traditions but transcend them.

Near the end of part 1 of *Songs for the Harvester of Dreams* Niatum places a short poem of one sentence in eight lines, titled "Raven and the Fear of Growing White," that is paradigmatic of his outlook and style:

When the legends cannot feed the village fire,
When mother spruce answers no child in the dark,
When hawk fails to reach his shadow on the river,
When First Woman beats hummingbird to the earth,
And salmon eats the rapids until his bones shatter,
When otter steals the long-awaited promises of stars,
And blue jay stops naming each new storm,
It will end its fear of growing white.

In its allusions to Raven, First Woman, Salmon, and so on, the poem employs the distinctive "mythological grammar," at once traditional Salish and intensely personal, that has been evolving in Niatum's poetry from the beginning. But here the imaginative mediation between Indian foreground and Anglo surroundings takes on a special urgency. The poem brings mordantly into view the prospect of utter deracination, the loss of personal connection with a storied collective past. Its ironic form is that of the Fool's prophecy in William Shakespeare's *King Lear* (circa 1605–1606), act 3, scene 2, "foretelling" the abuses of the present, or the bitter "retroactive prophecies" that appear to have been added to traditional myth narratives in the early contact era, "predicting" disastrous consequences of the coming of the whites – consequences that were already at hand. As the *When* clauses hammer out the poem's form, the sense of inexorable dislocation and loss grows until, at last, Raven is foreseen as ending "its fear of growing white" because now it *is* white – that is, utterly bereft of what should make it Indian.

The fear of deracination is a central theme in Niatum's poetry and in Native American writing generally; but it can hardly be labeled merely an "Indian theme." One measure of the power of this poem is that, paradoxically, through its localized Klallam details it seems to speak to a general modern fear of "growing white," that is, of drifting irretrievably out of touch with one's origins. Rarely has Niatum posed the issue of cultural loss so harshly. His more recent poems, such as the "New Poems" in *Drawings of the Song Animals,* suggest more confidence in the Native American roots of his identity.

Since the mid 1980s Niatum, always a skilled prosodist, has been writing his most lyrical work to date. The evidence of late poems such as "Round Dance," in *Drawings of the Song Animals,* suggests that this gifted poet has attained an "elder's" status in the patient mastery of his art:

Fox woman, come dance with me,
let's find earth's beach, unravel yourself and tide,
let grass burn ocher, your hands be blue camas,
we'll turn as mischievous as Raven stealing light.
O I am best welcoming a friend.
So let's mingle with guest and ancestor,
Duckabush river and tamahnous, release the abalone
    yearnings, the eyeless flights.

(The Duckabush is a river on the Olympic Peninsula in Washington; tamahnous is a spirit guardian.)

Roethke used to tell his students, rather intimidatingly, that "the important thing is to get your real work done." Niatum has clearly been following his mentor's advice.

Interviews:

Survival This Way, edited by Joseph Bruchac (Tucson: University of Arizona Press, 1987), pp. 193–210;

Gaetano Prampolini, "The Heart's the Actor: A Conversation with Duane Niatum," in *Native American Literatures: A Forum,* 4–5 (1992–1993): 81–103.

References:

Anne Bromley, "The Reality of Dreamtime in Some Contemporary Native American Poetry," *Greenfield Review,* 11 (Winter/Spring 1984): 18–28;

Andrea Lerner, "Duane Niatum," in *Dictionary of Native American Literature,* edited by Andrew Wiget (New York: Garland, 1994), pp. 479–482;

Jarold Ramsey, "On Niatum's *Songs for the Harvester of Dreams,*" *Studies in American Indian Literature,* 6 (Fall 1982): 6–13;

Ramsey, "Tradition and Individual Talents in Modern Indian Writing," in his *Reading the Fire: Essays in the Traditional Indian Literatures of the Far West* (Lincoln: University of Nebraska Press, 1983), pp. 180–194;

Ramsey, "Word-Magic," *Parnassus,* 5 (Fall/Winter 1975): 165–175;

A. LaVonne Brown Ruoff, *American Indian Literatures* (New York: Modern Language Association, 1990), pp. 103–104;

Eugene Smith, "A Spinner of Dreams," *Greenfield Review,* 11 (Winter/Spring 1984): 14–17;

Andrew Wiget, *Native American Literature* (Boston: Twayne, 1985), pp. 106–107.

Samson Occom

(1723 - 14 July 1792)

Ruth Rosenberg
Brooklyn College

BOOK: *A Sermon Preached at the Execution of Moses Paul, an Indian; Who Was Executed at New-Haven, on the Second of September, 1772; for the Murder of Mr. Moses Cook, Late of Waterbury, on the 7th of December, 1771. Preached at the Desire of Said Paul* (New Haven: Printed & sold by Thomas & Samuel Green, 1772); republished as *A Sermon at the Execution of Moses Paul, an Indian, Who Had Been Guilty of Murder, Preached at New Haven in America* (London: Reprinted & sold by Buckland, 1788).

OTHER: *A Choice Collection of Hymns and Spiritual Songs: Intended for the Edification of Sincere Christians, of All Denominations,* edited, with contributions, by Occom (New London, Conn.: Printed & sold by Timothy Green, 1774);

"An Account of the Montauk Indians, on Long Island," in *Collections of the Massachusetts Historical Society,* volume 9 (Boston: Hall & Hiller, 1804), pp. 105–110; reprinted in *The History and Archeology of the Montauk,* pp. 151–153;

"Sam Occom's Diary," edited by Julia Clark, in *The History and Archeology of the Montauk,* edited by Gaynell Stone (Stony Brook, N.Y.: Amereon, 1993), pp. 223–283;

"A Short Narrative of My Life," in *The Heath Anthology of American Literature,* volume 1, edited by Paul Lauter (Lexington, Mass.: Heath, 1994), pp. 942–947.

SELECTED PERIODICAL PUBLICATION – UNCOLLECTED: "An Account of the Montauk Indians on Long Island," *Collections of the Massachusetts Historical Society,* 10 (1809): 105–111.

Samson Occom; mezzotint by J. Spilsbury after an oil painting by Mason Chamberlin

Samson Occom's *A Sermon Preached at the Execution of Moses Paul, an Indian* (1772) and *A Choice Collection of Hymns and Spiritual Songs: Intended for the Edification of Sincere Christians, of All Denominations* (1774) are believed to be the first two books published in English by a Native American. A. LaVonne Brown Ruoff, noting that the sermon has appeared in at least nineteen editions, calls it "the first Indian best-seller." Occom's account of his own life, dated 17 September 1768 (published in 1994), is probably the earliest autobiography written by a Native American. As an educator, Occom taught his students literacy in a second language through singing and through games he invented using cedar chips and verses on cardboard. Julia Clark's publication in 1993 of Occom's diaries makes available a forty-six-

Eleazar Wheelock, whose charity school in Lebanon, Connecticut, Occom attended. Later Occom recruited students and raised money for the school, which was moved in 1769 to Hanover, New Hampshire, and ultimately became Dartmouth College. Portrait by Joseph Steward (courtesy of Dartmouth College).

year record of observations about "Indian ways of everyday life, housing, travel, communication, legal status, politics, and dress."

Occom, a Mohegan, was born in 1723 in a wigwam on the west side of the Thames River between New London and Norwich, Connecticut, to Joshua and Sarah Ockham. By midcentury the Mohegans were impoverished by colonial encroachment, having been denied access to fishing sites and hunting grounds that had extended in the time of Uncas – from whom Occom was said to claim matrilineal descent – to the Rhode Island and Massachusetts borders. The evangelistic preachers seemed to offer a mode of survival, and at seventeen Occom responded to James Davenport's call to the "Great Awakening" and was converted. On 6 December 1743 he was admitted to a school kept in Lebanon in the home of Eleazar Wheelock, Davenport's Yale classmate and brother-in-law. During his four years there Occom learned to read and write English and studied Greek, Latin, and Hebrew, but he was prevented by poor health and severe eyestrain from going on to college. On 5 November 1766 Wheelock wrote of his gifted student: "Mr. Occum had been long confined by Sore Sickness before he came to me, and was then, and all the time he was with me, [in] a low State of health."

Occom taught in New London in the fall of 1747; in 1749 he sought a position as schoolmaster. A group of about thirty-two families of Montauk living at the tip of Long Island invited him to instruct them; unable to offer a salary, they promised to take turns feeding him. Occom wrote to the Boston Board of Correpondents for Propagating Christian Knowledge for permission, thinking that the board would provide financial support for him; but it was not until 1751, after his marriage to one of his students, Mary Fowler, that he was paid the inadequate sum of fifteen pounds a year. The retirement of the local minister, Azariah Horton, in 1757 meant that Occom had to add pastoral duties to his teaching responsibilities, but he was not paid for the extra work. As his family grew, his debts accumulated, so he resorted to farming, fishing, hunting, selling objects he made of cedar (such as churns, buckets, mortars and pestles, and ladles), and rebinding the books in the library of Samuel Buell of Easthampton.

On 12 November 1756 Occom was ordained by the New Light Calvinist sect of Connecticut. He passed the rigorous examination for ordination by the Presbytery of Suffolk, Long Island, on 13 July 1757 and was ordained on 29 August 1759. He was to be sent to minister to the Cherokee under the auspices of the Scotch Society of Missions at the substantial salary of seventy pounds a year. Occom was prevented from carrying out the proposed venture by fighting between the Cherokee and settlers who were trying to take over their land; instead, he was sent west to recruit Oneida students for Wheelock's school. With his brother-in-law, David Fowler, he left Connecticut on 10 June 1760 to teach the Oneida in what is now New York and to bring back promising youths. The Oneida chiefs gave Occom and Fowler a wampum belt to bind their friendship when they departed on 19 September 1760. That winter Occom taught himself to speak Oneida so that he would not need an interpreter when he returned in 1762. His third mission was aborted by the Pontiac war of 1763.

On 3 April 1764 Occom moved his family to the village of his birth, which by then was called Mohegan; they lost their household goods in a storm during their crossing of Long Island Sound. On the ancestral land where his mother, his sister Lucy, and his brother Jonathan still lived he constructed a two-story house that later became a historic landmark. By this time he and his wife had had seven children: Mary, born in 1752; Aaron, born in 1753; Tabitha, born in 1754; Olive, born in 1755; Christiana, born in 1757; Talitha, born in 1761; and Benoni, born in 1763.

In the spring of 1765, after Occom had accompanied him on his sixth tour of the colonies, George Whitefield, the greatest preacher and missionary of his age, considered taking Occom back to England with him; later he suggested that Wheelock bring Occom. On 23 December 1765 Occom and another clergyman, Nathaniel Whitaker, set sail from Boston to raise funds for Wheelock's Indian Charity School; they arrived in England on 3 February 1766. Occom's charismatic preaching elicited donations far in excess of those given to any other colonial institution: he raised £9,497 from 2,169 people in 305 churches in England; and in Scotland, where he displayed the Oneida wampum belt, he raised an additional £2,529. Occom's charm transcended sectarian rivalries, making him a truly ecumenical figure; his tact and diplomacy earned him esteem wherever he spoke. London's leading Baptist, Andrew Gifford, became a friend, and William Warburton, bishop of Gloucester, made "overtures of Episcopal ordination" to him. He was the guest of John Newton, the composer of the hymn "Amazing Grace," at Olney. In Edinburgh Occom modestly declined an honorary doctorate.

Occom returned to Mohegan in the fall of 1768 and soon became bitter about his treatment at the hands of whites. He found his wife and children living in poverty, even though Wheelock had promised that they would be cared for while he was in Britain. Also, because Occom had spoken out in favor of a lawsuit to regain Mohegan land that had been fraudulently taken by white colonists (the suit had been decided in the colonists' favor in 1766), a rumor campaign had been started against him. It was to correct these misrepresentations – that he was not really a Mohegan, that he had not been converted until just before his trip to Britain, and that he was an alcoholic – that he wrote his ten-page autobiography of 17 September 1768. Furthermore, Wheelock's school, for which Occom had raised so much money, was moved in 1769, over Occom's objections, to Hanover, New Hampshire; as Occom had feared, it ceased to be an Indian school and later became Dartmouth College. Finally, Occom was left without income after a rupture with the Boston board. In his biography, *Samson Occom* (1935), Harold Blodgett says that rumors that "he had fallen into intemperance" were started because Occom was dizzy from "having been all day without food." According to Leon Burr Richardson, who edited Occom's letters (1933), Occom was so poor that he "drank only cold water."

A daughter, Theodosia, was born in 1769, and a son, Lemuel, in 1771. On 2 September 1772 Occom preached a temperance sermon at the execution of Moses Paul, a Christianized Indian who had committed murder while intoxicated and had been sentenced to hang. The sermon attracted a massive audience of people who had heard of the charismatic preacher. It was published the same year.

In 1773 Occom and his former pupil Joseph Johnson, who had married Occom's daughter Tabitha, began to plan a migration of the converted New England Indians to land in New York offered to them by the Oneida. Occom's final child, Andrew Gifford, was born in 1774. That same year his collection of hymns, an interdenominational compilation Occom had put together during and after his trip to England, was published. Johnson left for New York first – the project had really been his idea – but was killed in the Revolutionary War in 1776.

Occom left his family in Connecticut and traveled back and forth to the new settlement in Brothertown, New York, acting as an itinerant preacher along the way. In 1784 he toured New England to raise funds for the settlement, and he collected donations for it for six years. He moved his family to Brothertown in 1789. The migration was impeded by war, by lack of funds, and by extensive litigation over the land, which the Oneida ceded to New York. Occom had befriended legislators in Albany on his many fund-raising trips, and they finally deeded the land to him – one of the few instances of whites living up to an agreement with Indians. About 250 Indians migrated to Brothertown in 1791. Occom established the first Indian Presbyterian church in Brothertown in 1792; shortly thereafter, on 14 July, he died suddenly while gathering cedar wood with which to complete a churn.

Much of the scholarship on Occom has focused on the execution sermon, but the diary he kept from 1743 to 1790 deserves at least equal attention. Among the educational innovations he describes are sets of cards containing Bible verses that he would deal out to children; he would then comment on how each card was appropriate to the child who had drawn it. He also describes how, carrying a copy of his own hymnal in his pocket on his travels, he would lead the singing in the frontier cabins he visited. From his patrons he requested only songbooks. In the introduction to her edition of the diary, Clark says that the work shows the process of

Occom; portrait by Nathaniel Smibert (Bowdoin College Museum of Art)

Occom's acquisition of English: the early entries are "short, clumsy, inexpressive," while later ones show an expanded vocabulary and improved phrasing. Abbreviated though the entries are, they offer many insights into the narrative gift that made Occom's sermons so memorable; he was noted for his compelling stories. Blodgett quotes one anecdote that remained vivid even after the lapse of seventy-seven years: "An old Indian, he said, had a knife which he kept till he wore the blade out; and then his son took it and put a new blade to the handle, and kept it till he had worn the handle out"; but it remained the same knife. The story serves as an analogy for the resiliency of Indian culture.

Occom could wring every possible nuance out of a repeated phrase, as is evident in a letter to Robert Cleveland that is quoted by Blodgett: "You turned yourself out of our School, and You turn'd yourself out of the Church, and you are turning yourself out of the Favour of every Body . . . take Care that you don't turn your Self out of Heaven." Though Blodgett asserts that "there is not a hint of lightheartedness in all his writings, Occom's first biographer, William DeLoss Love, claims that "there was a dry humor in his sayings, at which he never laughed himself, but which must have amused his listeners."

Today various groups of indigenous people are basing claims for federal recognition of tribal status on Occom's writings. Among the communities that have cited him in court are the Mohegans of southeastern Connecticut; the Narraganset of Charlestown, Rhode Island; the Pequots of Stonington and Groton, Connecticut; the Niatic of Lyme, Connecticut; the Tunxis, Quinnipiacs, and Wangunks of Farmington, Connecticut; and the Montauks of Long Island, New York. The Mohegan Tribal Council, under the leadership of Courtland Fowler, a descendent of Occom, petitioned for federal recognition in 1984 on the basis of the "Sociocultural Authority" of Occom. Citing the fifty-two roots with healing properties Occom learned of from Ocus, a tribal herbalist and medicine man, in 1761, the Montauk invoke Occom as one who inspired them to preserve their cultural heritage, including their "green medicine," or ethnobotanical knowledge. Thus, more than two hundred years after his death, Samson Occom continues to help his people.

Letters:

An Indian Preacher in England, edited by Leon Burr Richardson (Hanover, N.H.: Dartmouth College Publications, 1933).

Biographies:

William DeLoss Love, *Samson Occom and the Christian Indians of New England* (Boston: Pilgrim, 1899);

Harold Blodgett, *Samson Occom* (Hanover, N.H.: Dartmouth College Publications, 1935).

References:

James Axtell, *The Invasion Within: The Contest of Cultures in Colonial North America* (New York: Oxford University Press, 1985), pp. 204–217;

Henry Warner Bowden, *American Indians and Christian Missions: Studies in Cultural Conflict* (Chicago: University of Chicago Press, 1981);

Richard L. Bushman, *From Puritan to Yankee: Character and the Social Order in Connecticut, 1690–1765* (Cambridge, Mass.: Harvard University Press, 1967);

John W. DeForest, *History of the Indians of Connecticut from the Earliest Known Period to 1850* (Hartford, Conn.: Humersley, 1851), pp. 454–477;

Michael Elliott, " 'This Indian Bait': Samson Occom and the Voice of Liminality," *Early American Literature,* 29, no. 3 (1994): 233–253;

Melissa Fawcett-Sayet, "Sociocultural Authority: The Mohegan Case," in *Rooted like the Ash Trees: New England Indians and the Land,* edited by Richard G. Carlson (Naugatuck, Conn.: Eagle Way, 1987), pp. 52-53;

David Murray, "Christian Indians: Samson Occom," in his *Forked Tongues: Speech, Writing and Representation in North American Indian Texts* (Bloomington: Indiana University Press, 1991), pp. 49-57;

Bernd Peyer, "Samson Occom: Mohegan Missionary and Writer of the Eighteenth Century," *American Indian Quarterly,* 6 (Fall/Winter 1982): 208-217;

A. LaVonne Brown Ruoff, "Introduction: Samson Occom's *Sermon Preached . . . at the Execution of Moses Paul,*" *Studies in American Indian Literatures,* 4 (Summer/Fall 1992): 75-81;

William S. Simmons, *Spirit of the New England Tribes: Indian History and Folklore 1620-1984* (Hanover, N.H.: University Press of New England, 1986), pp. 30-36, 46-48;

Gaynell Stone, ed., *The History and Archeology of the Montauk: Readings in Long Island Archaeology and Ethnohistory* (Stony Brook, N.Y.: Suffolk County Archeological Association, 1993);

Margaret Connell Szasz, *Indian Education in the American Colonies, 1607-1783* (Albuquerque: University of New Mexico Press, 1988), pp. 232-257;

Laurie Weinstein, "Samson Occom: A Charismatic Eighteenth-Century Mohegan Leader," in *Enduring Traditions: The Native Peoples of New England,* edited by Weinstein (Westport, Conn.: Bergin & Garvey, 1994), pp. 91-101.

Papers:

The papers of Samson Occom are on microfilm in the Connecticut Historical Society. The Mohegan Documents Collection is at the Huntington Free Library in the Bronx, New York City. Manuscripts for Occom's early sermons, his diary, and three hymns in his handwriting are in the archives of the Dartmouth College Library. Occom's medicinal remedies, dated 1754, are at the New London County Historical Society. The history of the Mohegan Land Controversy is in the holdings of the New Haven Historical Society. Other papers are in the Massachusetts Historical Society Collections: Series I, 9, 10; Series IV, 4; Series V, 9. Records of the Society for Propagating the Gospel are in the New England Historical Society, Boston. Occom's letter of 19 October 1772 to the Reverend Andrew Gifford of London is in the Yale University Library.

Simon J. Ortiz

(27 May 1941 -)

Susan Scarberry-García
Navajo Preparatory School

See also the Ortiz entry in *DLB 120: American Poets Since World War II, Third Series.*

BOOKS: *Naked in the Wind* (Pembroke, N.C.: Quetzal-Vihio, 1971);

Going for the Rain (New York: Harper & Row, 1976);

A Good Journey (Berkeley, Cal.: Turtle Island, 1977);

Howbah Indians (Tucson, Ariz.: Blue Moon, 1978);

The People Shall Continue (San Francisco: Children's Book Press, 1978; revised, 1988);

Song, Poetry and Language: Expression and Perception (Tsaile, Ariz.: Navajo Community College Press, 1978);

Fight Back: For the Sake of the People, for the Sake of the Land (Albuquerque: University of New Mexico Press, 1980);

From Sand Creek (New York: Thunder's Mouth, 1981);

A Poem Is a Journey (Bourbonnais, Ill: Pteranodon, 1981);

Blue and Red (Acoma, N.Mex.: Acoma Childhood Development Program, 1982);

The Importance of Childhood (Acoma, N.Mex.: Acoma Childhood Development Program, 1982);

Fightin': New and Collected Stories (New York: Thunder's Mouth, 1983);

Woven Stone (Tucson: University of Arizona Press, 1991);

After and Before the Lightning, Sun Tracks, volume 28 (Tucson: University of Arizona Press, 1994).

Edition: *A Good Journey* (Tucson: University of Arizona Press, 1984).

VIDEO: *Surviving Columbus: The Story of the Pueblo People,* script by Ortiz, PBS Home Video, KNME Albuquerque, and the Institute of American Indian Arts, 1992.

OTHER: "The San Francisco Indians," "Kaiser and the War," "A Story of Rios and Juan Jesús," "The Killing of a State Cop," and "The End of Old Horse," in *The Man to Send Rain Clouds: Contemporary Stories by American Indians,* edited by Kenneth Rosen (New York: Vintage, 1974), pp. 9-13, 47-60, 79-81, 101-108, 145-148;

Simon J. Ortiz at the time of Going for the Rain *(photograph by Hilary Langhorst)*

Carriers of the Dream Wheel: Contemporary Native American Poetry, edited by Duane Niatum, contributions by Ortiz (New York: Harper & Row, 1975), pp. 141-159;

The Remembered Earth: An Anthology of Contemporary Native American Literature, edited by Geary

Hobson, contributions by Ortiz (Albuquerque: Red Earth Press, 1979; reprinted, Albuquerque: University of New Mexico Press, 1980), pp. 257–297;

A Ceremony of Brotherhood, edited by Ortiz and Rudolfo Anaya (Albuquerque: Academia, 1981);

Earth Power Coming: Short Fiction in Native American Literature, edited by Ortiz (Tsaile, Ariz.: Navajo Community College Press, 1983);

"Always the Stories: A Brief History and Thoughts on My Writing," in *Coyote Was Here: Essays on Contemporary Native American Literary and Political Mobilization,* edited by Bo Schöler, *Dolphin,* 9 (Århus, Denmark: Seklos, 1984), pp. 57–69;

"The Language We Know," in *I Tell You Now: Autobiographical Essays by Native American Writers,* edited by Brian Swann and Arnold Krupat (Lincoln: University of Nebraska Press, 1987): 187–194;

Harper's Anthology of 20th Century Native American Poetry, edited by Niatum, contributions by Ortiz (New York: Harper & Row, 1988), pp. 139–151;

"What We See: A Perspective on Chaco Canyon and Pueblo Ancestry," in *Chaco Canyon: A Center and Its World,* edited by Mary Peck (Santa Fe: Museum of New Mexico Press, 1994).

SELECTED PERIODICAL PUBLICATIONS – UNCOLLECTED: "Towards a National Indian Literature: Cultural Authenticity in Nationalism," *MELUS,* 8 (Summer 1981): 7–12;

"The Creative Process ['That's the Place Indians Talk About']," *Wicazo Sa Review: A Journal of Indian Studies,* 1 (Spring 1985): 45–49;

"Our Image of Ourselves," *Akwe:kon Journal,* 10 (Spring 1993): 38–39;

"Believing the Story," *Winds of Change,* 10 (Autumn 1995): 114–119;

"Meeting Our Elders," *Winds of Change,* 10 (Autumn 1995): 117, 119.

One of the most significant Native American writers of the latter part of the twentieth century, Simon J. Ortiz is known for his insistence that the oral tradition of his Acoma Pueblo people is the guiding spirit behind all of his work. In 1993 the Returning the Gift Festival of Native Writers recognized Ortiz with a Lifetime Achievement Award for literature, and in the mid 1990s Ortiz was one of the most visible poet-storytellers on the lecture circuit in the United States. The author of more than a dozen books of poetry, short fiction, and essays, Ortiz is known for the strong sociopolitical comments on Southwestern history and American culture embedded in his stories and poems about the struggles and joys of everyday life.

Born on 27 May 1941 in Albuquerque, Simon Joseph Ortiz was raised in the small outlying Acoma Pueblo community of McCartys, New Mexico (Deetziyamah in his people's Keresan language). Ortiz's mother, Mamie Toribio Ortiz, was a member of the Eagle clan; his father, Joe L. Ortiz, belonged to the Antelope clan. From a large family, Ortiz grew up in dry country spotted with sage, juniper, and the rough basalt terrain known as El Malpais. Inhabitants of Acoma's mother pueblo on a great mesa nearby – the oldest continuously inhabited settlement in North America – have prayed for rain in this area for at least a thousand years, and Ortiz is heir to and carrier of this tradition.

In 1948 Ortiz began attending the Bureau of Indian Affairs day school in the village, where he learned English as a second language. After sixth grade he transferred to Saint Catherine's Indian School in Santa Fe, where the library opened a new world to him; he also experienced a profound homesickness. Later he attended Albuquerque Indian School and, in 1961–1962, Fort Lewis College in Durango, Colorado. After serving in the army from 1963 to 1966, he returned to Albuquerque and enrolled at the University of New Mexico. While there he encountered the Kiowa writer N. Scott Momaday's influential novel *House Made of Dawn* (1968); Momaday's tightly crafted poetry and luminous prose became an inspiration to the young Ortiz, who was looking for life stories that paralleled his own and for models of writing that could articulate complex spiritual realities. He received a master of fine arts degree from the University of Iowa in 1969. That same year Ortiz was recognized for his skills in journalism with a Discovery Award from the National Endowment for the Arts. He worked as public-relations director at Rough Rock Demonstration School on the Navajo Reservation in 1969–1970 and as a newspaper editor for the National Indian Youth Council in Albuquerque from 1970 to 1973. He was an instructor in creative writing and Native American literature at San Diego State University and at the Institute of American Indian Arts in Santa Fe in 1974; at Navajo Community College in Tsaile, Arizona, from 1975 to 1977; at the College of Marin in Kentfield, California, from 1976 to 1979; and at the University of New Mexico in Albuquerque from 1979 to 1981. In 1982–1983 he was consulting editor for the

Pueblo of Acoma Press. He taught at Sinte Gleska College, Rosebud, South Dakota, in 1985–1986. In 1989, after acting as tribal interpreter for a year, Ortiz served as lieutenant governor of Acoma Pueblo. He taught at Lewis and Clark College in Portland, Oregon, in 1990. He married Marlene Foster in December 1981; they were divorced in September 1984, after the birth of their daughter, Sara.

After publishing a chapbook, *Naked in the Wind,* in 1971, Ortiz attempted to publish a four-hundred-page book of poetry. When advised that this was much too large a project for a new author, Ortiz rewrote some of the poems and published them as two books, *Going for the Rain* (1976) and *A Good Journey* (1977). Along with the Blackfeet/Gros Ventre writer James Welch's *Winter in the Blood* (1974) and *Riding the Earthboy 40* (1976), *Going for the Rain* was one of the most significant Native American works to reach the general reading public after Momaday's *House Made of Dawn* won the Pulitzer Prize for fiction in 1969. *A Good Journey* was published in the same year as the Laguna Pueblo writer Leslie Marmon Silko's extraordinary first novel, *Ceremony.* These six works laid the groundwork for a flourishing of contemporary Native American literature during the next two decades.

Going for the Rain springs from the oral tradition of Ortiz's people and brings Ortiz's personal voice surprisingly near the reader's ear. Ortiz writes of the beauty of the natural world and of the pains and pleasures of continually traveling to and from home on a high desert plateau in western New Mexico. It is a carefully composed book of inner and outer journeying that conveys the colors of Ortiz's newborn daughter's skin and the scent of piñon after a recent rainfall.

Going for the Rain consists of four parts – "Preparation," "Leaving," "Returning," and "The Rain Falls" – preceded by a prologue. The prologue establishes an attitude of prayer and prepares the reader to understand that the speaker is ready to depart on a sacred journey that will result in his maturation as a human being. The song summons the *Shiwana* (rainmakers), who return from the other world to bring blessings to the land and the people. Ortiz is actively participating in the experience of renewal and of finding the good in life, of "going for the rain." Themes that emerge here center around home, the Acoma people, children, language, and self. Ortiz writes: "A man leaves; he encounters all manners of things. He has adventures, meets people, acquires knowledge, goes different places; he is always looking. . . . His travelling is a prayer as well, and he must keep on."

The first poem in "Preparation," "The Creation, According to Coyote," recounts the origin of the Keresan Pueblo people and their journey upward through successive worlds until they emerge through a small *sipapu* (hole in the ground) onto the earth's surface. The Keresan War Twins – Uyuyayeh (Younger Brother) and Masaweh (Elder Brother) – have many adventures as they learn what life is about. Ortiz is using parallelism, one of the earmarks of oral tradition, when he implicitly compares his own life journey to the journeys of the Twins and the migrations of the people who came before him. Coyote the trickster, while not totally reliable, is a storyteller, like Ortiz himself. This identification of Coyote with Ortiz will persist through much of Ortiz's work.

This section of *Going for the Rain* includes several poems for Ortiz's son, Raho Nez, and his daughter Rainy Dawn. "Forming Child" and "To Insure Survival" are for Rainy Dawn. In the first he wishes that the unborn child will grow up with a sense of respect, appreciation, and thoughtfulness, thereby honoring her mother, Joy Harjo, the Creek poet. In the second poem he uses land and flesh imagery to describe the beauty of his newborn daughter, who is of the earth:

You come forth
the color of a stone cliff
at dawn,
changing colors,
blue to red
to all the colors of the earth.

Rainy Dawn is blessed by Grandmother Spider, a cocreator of the universe with her sisters, according to Keresan mythology. In "Two Women" the poet compares a Navajo woman weaver to Grandmother Spider, the originator of weaving in the Southwest, thus strengthening the correspondences between past and present and between humans and nonhumans. Grandmother Spider brought to humans the gifts of language and fine-tuned thought as well as the gift of corn in the form of her Corn Sisters' bodies; honoring these qualities and substances enables one to maintain good health. At the end of "Buck Nez" the writer prays: "What I want is a full life / for my son, / for myself, / for my Mother, / the Earth." This yearning for wholeness and realized possibilities characterizes Ortiz's work.

In "Leaving" the poet's concerns broaden out to encompass his varied experiences as he travels across America. Ortiz exhibits a wry sense of humor in "Many Farms Notes" as he imagines a sheep saying, " 'You don't see many Acoma poets passing through here.' " In the same poem the poet responds to a Navajo's question with utter seriousness:

"What would you say that the main theme
of your poetry is?"
"To put it as simply as possible,
I say it this way: to recognize
the relationships I share with everything."

In "Travels in the South" Ortiz takes heart when other Indian people show him kindness and lend support: "Once, in a story, I wrote that Indians are everywhere. Goddamn right." In this same poem he recalls pulling off the road to hug a tree when he heard about the killing of four students by National Guardsmen at Kent State University in Ohio on 4 May 1970: such is the depth of his pain and compassion for a nation that had turned against itself.

Other poems in "Leaving" express sorrow for the loss of Indian land and life in Florida and the unspeakable losses of Indians forcibly relocated to the cities by the U.S. government in the 1950s: "I am lonely for hills. I am lonely for myself." Once the poet lost some of his poems, his airplane ticket, and nearly himself: "New York City almost got me / last night at Kennedy Airport. / So messed up." The poet's situation is reminiscent of the Pueblo and Navajo myths in which young men wander into dangerous territory, ultimately to offer their lives to the great Gambler in exchange for dazzling possessions or the thrill of playing for high stakes. There are poems of loss, recovery, and disorientation, such as "Today, the A-Train, 168th to 14th," and poems of longing to return to health, such as "Hunger in New York City." Back home in western New Mexico, Ortiz sees urban life taking a toll in "For Those Sisters & Brothers in Gallup," about a reservation border town where lives are often wasted by alcoholism. Ortiz links the exploitation of the Native population by white shopkeepers to the relentless cycle of oppression that encourages people to drink and to die walking the long road home.

"Evening Beach Walk" affirms the poet's need to keep searching, to keep living in spite of the hardships, to maintain a positive attitude:

It's a duty with me,
I know, to find the horizons,
and I keep on walking on the ocean's edge,
looking for things in the dim light.

Frustrated by not seeing the horizon clearly, the speaker is determined to seek clarification. Here Ortiz anticipates the imagery that he will use in *After and Before the Lightning* (1994), a book of poems set in the endless-horizon country of South Dakota.

"Returning," the third part of *Going for the Rain,* includes some poems of hope. "Washyuma Motor Hotel" describes a vision from underground, as "the ancient spirits of the people conspire sacred tricks" against the mainstream Americans who are sleeping upstairs, ignorant of the natural forces that are undermining the artificially contrived foundations of the motel. There is a sense that corrupt America will be undone by powerful original forces that will regenerate the land; if Indians are patient, they will outlast this wave of invaders. Ortiz writes in "Crossing the Colorado River into Yuma": "Neon is weak. / Concrete will soon return to desert." In proclaiming this vigilant outwaiting Ortiz joins Momaday, who says about Pueblo Tanoan speakers in *House Made of Dawn:* "They have assumed the names and gestures of their enemies, but have held on to their own, secret souls; and in this there is a resistance and an overcoming, a long outwaiting."

Ortiz mentions that he is a veteran, but he expands the definition of the term to include one who has survived millennia of struggles: "I am a veteran of at least 30,000 years / when I travelled with the monumental yearning / of glaciers." Here, as elsewhere in *Going for the Rain,* the poet acknowledges his ancestry in northern Asia and his kinship with the plants and peoples of that place. In "Fragment" the speaker is consoled in a difficult moment by a small stone he holds in his hand; this "fragment / of the earth center" gives him strength and reassurance. The poet is also heartened by a long bus ride that is bringing him back home to Albuquerque. In "East Of Tucumcari" crevices along the road are sensually described as womanly, as taking him in. This long journey home is "overwhelming" for the traveler, who can "even smell / the northern mountains / in the water."

"The Rain Falls," the last part of the book, brings together many of the dominant themes and concerns of the volume. Written in common, everyday language, the poems here reiterate a vision of harmony and of integration with the natural world. In "Spreading Wings on Wind" the poet tells himself:

I must remember
that I am only one part
among many parts,
not a singular eagle
or one mountain. I am
a transparent breathing.

"Four Dheetsiyama Poems" includes the remark that "when loneliness / for myself has overcome me, /

Dust jacket for Ortiz's collection of poems about his travels across America

the Mountain has occurred." Mount Taylor, or Kaweshtima (Snowed Peak), is willing to share its centering presence with the poet.

In "For Nanao" a Japanese poet friend is honored for his joyous discovery that he and a Navajo woman who lives on the rim of Canyon de Chelly share a common language that dates back to the Ice Age. In "Juanita, Wife of Manuelito" Ortiz looks at a hundred-year-old photograph of another Navajo woman and imagines what she looked like when she was a child, "driving her sheep." Her demeanor would have darkened when, as a mature woman, she endured the several-hundred-mile Long Walk in 1864 to Fort Sumner, New Mexico, when nine thousand Navajos were forcibly removed from their homelands by federal troops under Kit Carson and Gen. James Carleton and their crops and livestock were destroyed. Ortiz learns patience and survival from Juanita's story as he teaches this history lesson to his son.

Ortiz strives for keen perception in several poems about animals. In "Hawk" he recognizes the hawk as "this man, he knows what he is doing." In "Buzzard" the bird of the title is valued for his role in the circle of life and for his powers of sight, inspiring the poet to meditate on the "quality of regenerating visions." In "A Deer Dinner" an old clan mother is honored by being offered the eyes of the deer, the gateway to its spirit. Sight imagery also occurs in "Morning Star," with its description of Pueblo sacred space:

> The space before dawn
> holds morning star
> in its true eye,
> the center of all places
> looking out
> and always in

The Morning Star is associated in Pueblo mythology and ritual practice with Masaweh of the Twin War Gods, who, like the star, is a guide.

Going for the Rain deepens in intensity as Ortiz eloquently struggles toward a more finely honed perception and a greater sensitivity than he has ever known. Like his father, who, as a mason, enjoys repairing "stone woven together" in a four-hundred-year-old wall, Ortiz has created a book that will last. But as the poet modestly reminds the reader in "Curly Mustache, 101-Year Old Navajo Man," "I got the story from someone way back."

The poems in *A Good Journey* deal with themes similar to those in *Going for the Rain:* the struggles of personal growth, fatherhood, traveling the country searching for oneself, Coyote, the violence that permeates America. Ortiz prefaces the book with comments from an interview. In response to the questions "Why do you write?" and "Who do you write for?" he says:

> Because Indians always tell a story. The only way to continue is to tell a story and that's what Coyote says. The only way to continue is to tell a story and there is no other way. Your children will not survive unless you tell something about them – how they were born, how they came to this certain place, how they continued.

Dedicated to his children Raho Nez and Rainy Dawn, the volume is prefaced with the lines

> The stories and poems come forth
> and I am only the voice telling them.

They are the true source themselves.
The words are the vision
by which we see out and in and around.

Stories come from a sacred source, a center of being that has a life of its own. To live one's life consciously within a story is to center oneself in the flow of generations, to find one's place in the vast scheme of things. The poet impresses upon his children, largely through repetition, that "the only way to continue" is to speak one's story. The story contains a "map" of the place from which his family has come and the places that he has visited. Ortiz is self-deprecating but honest when he tells his children that he is just the vehicle for the stories, which have their own integrity and their own ways of becoming known to human beings.

A Good Journey is divided into five sections, each successive one adding to the momentum of the whole – much as an old pickup truck going down the road gains speed with each shift of the gears. The poet's journey here is a continuation of his transcontinental travels in *Going for the Rain*. It is, indeed, a "good journey," even though there are moments of pain and temporary dislocation along the way.

Like *Going for the Rain,* this book opens with a tribute to Coyote, one of the prime movers of the created universe. The poet-critic Patricia Clark Smith points out that Ortiz identifies with this wily creature in part because of Coyote's contradictory nature: Coyote exhibits the powers both of creation and of destruction, and he is, above all, unpredictable in his buffoonish antics. Walking the tightrope between the sacred and profane worlds, Coyote sometimes falls to certain death yet manages to pick himself up and travel on. So, too, does Ortiz see himself as living for a time in limbo between the dangers of overindulgence in alcohol and the blessings of corn food, between the draw of the city and the pull of home.

In "Telling about Coyote" Ortiz retells a traditional Pueblo narrative. On his way to Zuni, Coyote "lost / everything. Everything. / and that included his skin, his fur." It is not hard to see the parallels between this poignant story of loss and the poet's experience in the autobiographical poem "Grants to Gallup, New Mexico," in part 4 of the volume: "Once, I been to California. / Got Lost in L.A., got laid / in Fresno, got jailed in Oakland, / got fired in Barstow, and came home." On another level Ortiz may be suggesting that Coyote's being stripped to the bone is a parallel to the genocide and cultural destruction inflicted on Indians in the Southwest during the past 450 years.

In another retelling of a Pueblo Coyote story the poet graphically describes an encounter between Coyote Lady (*Tsuushki* in Keresan) and Spider Grandmother (*Kahmaasquu Baba*). Spider Grandmother, a powerful deity who created the world, helps the stranded Coyote Lady down from a pinnacle, but the latter disobeys a promise not to look back up from the swinging basket. As a result of her irresponsibility, Coyote Lady plunges to the earth and is dashed to pieces. But the ever-curious Skeleton Fixer (*Shuuwimuu Guiguikuutchah*) sings and dances over her, bringing her shattered body back to life. (This symbolic healing pattern of fragmentation and reassemblage through ritual action is also found in Navajo culture.) Coyote Lady jumps up and runs away, and Skeleton Fixer exclaims: "Oh, it's just you Coyote – I thought / it was someone else." The reader recognizes that Ortiz is talking to himself when he asks: "Coyote, old man, wanderer, / where you going, man?"

The good feelings displayed in the Coyote stories are also prevalent in such poems as "How to make a good chili stew," "Earth and Rain, The Plants & Sun," "A Birthday Kid Poem," and "Apache Love." In the last poem Ortiz stresses in repetitive lines that "It is how you feel / about the land . . . about the children . . . about the women . . . about all things." When the feeling is right, *Hozhoni* (a Navajo term for a sense of beauty and balance) pervades everything. Ortiz values intuition and right living, which come from maintaining respect and balanced energies. "How to make a good chili stew" is the story of a recipe transformed into a supper in the La Plata Mountains near Durango, Colorado. Enacting an age-old drama of Pueblo-style campsite cooking with natural ingredients, the poet teaches the listener that a proper attitude of "good thoughts" and thinking "of a song to go along with it" will produce a stew that nourishes both body and spirit. "Look all around you once in a while," Ortiz advises. "Pay the utmost attention to everything, and that means the earth, clouds, sounds, the wind. All these go into the cooking." The stew, stirred into being in the big iron kettle over an open fire, is part of the place where it is made. Although cooking over a campfire may be a commonplace activity, Ortiz is writing from a culture in which multiple significances are associated with daily events. As Antonio G. Idini has observed in an unpublished 1993 paper, "the symbol of food in this tribe works as a means of keeping the world in balance, or restoring the balance when it is broken." In regard to this poem Idini, following Leslie White, says that "the preparation of food has important ceremonial and religious implications," because male assistants to the war chiefs "do the ceremonial cooking, and supply them with deer meat." Ortiz would undoubtedly be aware of this traditional male role that is an extension of hunting ritual. In his poem, then, Ortiz celebrates both an everyday activity and the performance of a ritualistic process that is reminiscent of a sacred social act.

The second section of the book, "Notes for My Child," includes several elemental poems that celebrate the poet's son's connection with the earth, his new home. "Grand Canyon Christmas Eve 1969" describes a camping trip on which the boy awakens crying and then "snuggle[s] down / like he was back / on Siberian ice, / the winds howling." The poem closes with images of eternity:

> I lie down on my earth bed.
> Here it is possible
> to believe legend,
> heros praying on mountains,
> making winter chants,
> the child being born Coyote,
> his name to be the Christ.
>
> Here it is possible
> to believe eternity.

In this sacred place the natural world convinces people that mythological events still hold sway over the destinies of mortal men and women. In "Canyon de Chelly" little Raho puts a stone in his mouth, and his father thinks: "The taste of stone. / What is it but stone, / the earth in your mouth. / You, son, are tasting forever." The act of incorporating the stone into his body links the child to eternity, to the land of mythology.

Announcing that "Today the Katzina come," the pueblo village crier celebrates the renewal of creative energies in the central dance plaza. Arriving "dancing prayers," the *Katzina* (masked spirit beings) mediate between the human side and the realm of the deities. Because of "the fragile cycle of the universe," people must "learn how to recognize sadness, the small and large tragedies" of life, so that they may better cope with them. For the Pueblos, the Katzina provide strength that signals that life will go on. "Endure . . . be enduring" is the appropriate attitude, and this act of enduring is accomplished by right thinking: "Think of all the things you love. think peace and humility / and certainty and strength" so "it shall continue well."

"How Much He Remembered," part 3 of *A Good Journey,* focuses on traveling and aching for home. When the poet is queried at the end of "Places We Have Been" about "*How Much Coyote Remembered,*" he responds, "O, not too much. / And a whole lot. / Enough" – suggesting that Ortiz has traveled to the edge of oblivion and back again into ordinary consciousness.

The fourth section of *A Good Journey,* "Will Come Forth in Tongues and Fury," is filled with sadness and bitterness. In "Grants to Gallup, New Mexico" the racist attitudes of shopkeepers and authorities in Gallup, where "the cops wear riot helmets . . . and you better / not be Indian," are cause for feeling "like / going on. / West into the sun at evening." While replete with well-placed anger, this section of the book is also rich with compassion. In the poignant "For Our Brothers: Blue Jay, Gold Finch, Flicker, Squirrel" Ortiz touches the twisted, crushed bodies of the roadkill casualties of fast-paced industrialized society and speaks to them in an apologetic voice. He tells Gold Finch, "I sorrowed for you." To "Flicker, my proud brother," he says: "Your ochre wings were meant / for the prayer sticks." These birds embody the sacred colors blue, yellow, and red, which are symbolically associated by the Acoma with the cardinal directions; thus, Ortiz must also lament the loss of their intact feathers, which could have carried the people's prayers upward to the spirit world, the land of the kachinas. Ultimately, his best response to the animals' unnecessary deaths is to tell their story, hoping to make amends: "You tell the stories of their struggles. . . . That is the only way."

Part 5 of *A Good Journey,* "I Tell You Now," is introduced by a line drawing of a great bird by the Navajo-Pueblo artist Aaron Yava. Opening with images of dawn breaking and his father singing or weaving stone walls, it conveys a healthy feeling, as if the bitterness and sense of loss of the previous poems has dissipated. One sign that hope has returned is the presence of old men: Uncle Jose, Touching Man, and Amado Quintana, known as Old Man Humped Back. The blind Amado "can see in his mind, / and he tells his grandson" to recognize the living history in places:

> "You can see that canal that runs
> from that gathering of cottonwoods
> and then turns to the south
> by Faustin's field, that canal
> was dug by the first people
> who came down from the Old Place.
> It was dug then."

Gathering is always a positive image in Ortiz's work, since it is an act of wholeness. In this passage the grandfather expresses crucial local knowledge through oral tradition as he tells the boy about the hand-maintained irrigation ditch. It was the ancestors, or "first people," probably the Anasazi, who, a millennium ago, brought the life-giving water downstream into the desert plain at the base of Enchanted Mesa and the Pueblo of Acoma.

A long way from Acoma is the Veterans Hospital in Fort Lyons, Colorado, where Ortiz was treated for alcoholism in the 1970s. One of the "Poems from the Veterans Hospital" is "Travelling," a paean to intellectual curiosity, restless energy, and life on the road. Ortiz sketches himself in the hospital library, "looking at the maps, the atlas, and the globe, / finding places," hungry for knowledge and experience of the world. From moment to moment "He is Gaugin, he is Coyote, he is who he is, / travelling the known and unknown places, / travelling, travelling." Charting his life by the stars and paper grids, the poet, in various personae, imagines where the winds of destiny will take him.

An elegiac farewell is offered "For a Taos Man Heading South." As the thunder sounds, the poet anticipates rain and speaks in Keresan, his Acoma language:

> Qow kutsdhe neh chah dhyuuh.
> Hah uh, qow kutsdhe nehchah dhyuuh.
>
> Let it rain.
> Peh eh chah.

After a warning to "stay out of those deadly bars," the poet invites the man, whose name is Mondragon, to come to Acoma for the summer dances and feasting:

> "You be good and strong now, good buddy.
> Come up to Acu. The people are having dances
> in July, four days, when the katzina come.
> Come visit. Bring your family."

As these words are said, thunder sounds, creating a "travelling prayer" of moisture, a blessing on Mondragon's journey back to New Mexico. This storm foreshadows the storms on the northern Plains that will resound in *After and Before the Lightning*.

"I Tell You Now" is written in the form of an imaginary conversation with a woman from Isleta Pueblo whom he saw on a street in downtown Albuquerque, the ancestral homeland of the Isleta. Ortiz apologizes for the limitations of his words; he wishes that he could convey the depth of his feeling for her people's sorrows and the tenacity of their long struggle against colonialism. He mentions the Isleta resistance to the Catholic priest who "had the earth of your church cemented over" – a reference to the kiva (traditional underground ceremonial chamber of Pueblo religious activity). Old attitudes toward Native people persist, as is shown by a fatal train accident involving an Indian family: "the AT&SFRY railroad never bothered to protect you when they laid their tracks through your land." The Isletas are actively resisting further encroachment on their land and further harm to their people: "The fight the Isleta people put up against the State when the State wanted to use your land for an Interstate was really something." *A Good Journey* ends on a hopeful note with the poet's recollection of meeting a family years before in El Paso. The family was apparently from Ysleta del Sur, the Tigua-speaking pueblo that splintered off from the mother pueblo during the Pueblo Revolt more than three hundred years ago: "the man said they had relatives up north on the river and said some day they were going to visit because it had been a long time since they had come south." This family would eventually reclaim a portion of its identity by traveling north along the Rio Grande to home.

In 1980 Ortiz published *Fight Back: For the Sake of the People, for the Sake of the Land.* This spirited book commemorates "the Pueblo Revolt of 1680 and our warrior Grandmothers and Grandfathers." *Fight Back* consists of poems and story narratives that tell both a panoramic and a personal history of the region where Ortiz grew up. Spanning the time from before the arrival of the Spanish in the Southwest in 1539–1540 to the 1980s, the book emotionally chronicles the history of encounters in the troubled region now known as New Mexico. It primarily concerns Pueblo interaction with the Spanish and later with the Anglos, but others, such as the Navajos and Chicanos, have their places in the story, too.

While on the surface this history is that of a tug-of-war over landownership and use, it is also a battle over cultural values – in particular, concepts of obligation versus possession. At the crux of *Fight Back* is a presentation of the contrasting spiritual and epistemological systems that demarcate different cultures' worldviews. Ortiz makes it clear that the underlying assumptions of the conquerors were that land was a commodity to be stolen, sold, or bartered for and that indigenous claims to place, based on continual habitation and sacred obligation, could be dismissed. With the new inhabitants of the Southwest came new philosophies and apparatuses, often designed to stake irrefutable claims to recently acquired plots of land. Out of this struggle over land base arose, over time, an uncomfortable and wary accommodation of each culture with the values and ways of life of the other. (This story is also told, from a Pueblo perspective, in the videotape *Surviving Columbus: The Story of the Pueblo People* [1992], written by Ortiz and narrated by his nephew Conroy Chino, a well-known newscaster who is also from Acoma Pueblo.) The main theme of *Fight Back* is that in spite of their domination by foreign powers for five hundred years, the Pueblo people continue to survive and to maintain their old ways. Pueblos are noted for their resiliency, which is, in part, because of their remaining rooted in their ancestral lands. Whereas other tribes, such as the Cherokees and Creeks, were forcibly relocated by the government in the early 1800s, the relative isolation of the Southwestern tribes allowed them to remain at home.

"Mid-America Prayer" opens the volume with a call for unity among all generations of the poet's people. He wants to join them "in a relationship that is responsible / and proper, that is loving and compassionate, / for the sake of the land and all people." Just as the hand-carved wooden Zuni war gods must all reside in Zuni Pueblo country to ensure abundant rainfall worldwide, so, too, must there be a genuine spirit of cooperation among the Pueblos if they are to continue.

Fight Back continues with a recent economic history of the Grants, New Mexico, area, to the north of Acoma. When he was a boy the atomic bomb was tested at White Sands missile range in southeastern New Mexico. Elders among the Pueblos still remember "the false dawn" of that day in 1945 and have lived to cry alarm. Ironically, the radioactive materials employed in the detonation of that prototype bomb, and in the subsequent bombs used by the United States government against the Japanese, came from the Laguna-Acoma area, home to people with essentially peaceful agrarian values that promote life. The world's largest open-pit uranium mine – the Anaconda Jackpile – was located on Laguna Pueblo land adjacent to Acoma; this source of employment was also a source of grave illness and death. Before the health hazards were well known, Ortiz had worked as a uranium miner. The Grants, New Mexico, farming belt that used to call itself "The Carrot Capitol of the World" has contaminated its own soil. In "Final Solution: Jobs, Leaving" the poet shows how colonization has made for dependency: "We had to buy groceries, / had to have clothes, homes, roofs, / windows. Surrounded by the United States, / we had come to need money." All of this newly created reliance on standard material goods contrasts with the self-sustaining communities that the Pueblos maintained before the American period began with the Treaty of Guadalupe Hidalgo that ended the Mexican-American War in 1848.

One of Ortiz's most frequently cited poems, "That's the Place Indians Talk About," appears in *Fight Back.* Contrasting Indian and white concepts of land use, Ortiz juxtaposes the U.S. Navy's fenced enclosure of the Coso Hot Springs, within the China Lake Naval Station, to the Paiute tribe's traditional use of this sacred place for healing purposes. Indians can hear "the stones in the earth rattling together" and the voice of the earth "talking to" them. Acknowledging the power of the hot springs is crucial for becoming identified with the potent life forces that heal.

Several poems in the central section of *Fight Back* are concerned with essential truth and knowledge, with ultimate life-giving values. In "We Have Been Told Many Things But We Know This To Be True," the poet voices his Puebloan philosophy that there has always been a reciprocal relationship between the land and the people: "the land has given us our life, / and we must give life back to it." This comment is echoed in "Mama's and Daddy's Words," where the poet's parents say: "You have to fight / by working for the land and the People." It becomes evident, then, that what Ortiz means by fighting is assuming a peaceful warrior's stance against cultural exploitation and destruction of the environment. The last two poems in this section, "Returning It Back, You Will Go On" and "It Will Come; It Will Come," resonate with the rhythms of chant; the reader hears the poet's father's heart beating: "Life beating / Earth beating / All beating." All of existence pulsates when things are planted, cared for, and given a chance to grow: "Thundering, the coming Rain . . . will come," blessing the people with new energy for continuance.

The last third of *Fight Back* is a long mixed-form narrative titled "No More Sacrifices." Interweaving personal reflections from a poetic journal and a prose narrative history of his people, Ortiz balances intimate scenes with grandiose vistas. Ortiz declares that there will be "no more sacrifices" of his ancestral land. Native sovereignty will prevail.

The poetic journal threaded throughout "No More Sacrifices" is structured around a journey to the top of Srhakaiya, the Acoma sacred mountain to the west. The poet approaches the mountain, climbs it, gathers perspective on his life, and then starts back home. Parched by thirst on his way down, he unknowingly drinks from a polluted spring and becomes ill. This sickness is associated with a strong sense of "otherness," a feeling of alienation caused by loss:

> I had drunk some water the evening before
> on the northside of Srhakaiya.
> The spring was scummed over.
> A Garden Deluxe wine empty lay nearby.

The poisoned water is thus compared to alcohol; both foul the beautiful primeval land. The sour water reminds him of stories he heard when he was a child:

> My mother said the people
> drank
> from the nearby river
> when she was a girl
> But when I was a boy,
> we used it only for washing clothes.
> We could not drink it.

The contrast between pure water and polluted, foul-smelling water is a metaphor for the progressive decline of Native culture since the first contact with Europeans. Even though "there are songs / about the rain," the poet is thirsty and is briefly full of despair, with "no hope at all." The dryness reminds him of the Felipe brothers' act of desperation in the 1950s, when they killed a witch in the guise of a state policeman near the base of Srhakaiya. (This incident is fictionalized in Momaday's *House Made of Dawn,* Ortiz's "The Killing of a State Cop" [1974], and Silko's "Tony's Story" [1974].) Significantly, the poet looks northwest of the mountain, the side ritually associated with the direction of death, and sees "clouds . . . towards Ambrosia Lake," which is home to dangerous "underground mines." By the time Ortiz has hiked back to the base of Srhakaiya, his "feeling / of 'otherness' " has passed. He is able to see beauty again as he watches a pair of Indian horses gallop into a canyon as the last light of sunset is fading.

Intermingled with this personal story, "No More Sacrifices" is a historical narrative that has been transmitted to Ortiz through the oral tradition. Ortiz says that his ancestors came from the northwest, in the vicinity of Mesa Verde and Chaco Canyon, former homes of the Anasazi. A millennium ago the *Aacqumeh hanoh* (Acoma people) settled at their present location, amid "red and orange cliffs" south of Kaweshtima. *Aacqu* means "Which Is Prepared"; the name, bestowed by the ancient leaders at the end of a long migration journey, signifies that this place is his people's rightful spot on earth.

When the Spanish arrived at Acoma, Capt. Hernando de Alvarado, traveling under orders from Francisco Vásquez Coronado, was impressed by the people who lived in this "strange place":

> When the Spaniard came in 1540, he found Aacqu very wealthy in its material security, social well-being, and spiritual integrity. . . . The streets of the city, as he called it, were very clean and orderly, and he was impressed by its location on a magnificent rock. . . . The Aacqumeh hanoh welcomed him, fed him, and gave him many gifts.

In spite of the hospitality and generosity shown them, the Spaniards' demands for tribute escalated over the years until, in 1598, the Acomas attacked and killed a contingent of soldiers under the command of Juan de Zaldívar. In retaliation Zaldívar's brother Vicente and his men attacked the mesa-top village on 21 January 1599, killing at least eight hundred Acomas; of the survivors, each male who was twenty-five or older had one foot amputated, and the young women were enslaved. These atrocities led the Acomas to join the other unified Pueblos in the successful Pueblo Revolt:

> In August of 1680 when the Pueblo people rose against the ruling Spaniard oppressor, they were joined in the revolt by the mestizo and genizaro, ancestors of the Chicano people, and the Athapascan-speaking peoples whose descendants are the peoples of the Navajo and Apache nations, and descendants of Africans . . . [who] were all commonly impoverished.

Twelve years later, the Spanish under Diego de Vargas reconquered the region. American rule was even worse than that of the Spanish: Ortiz says that his tribe "had never seen thieves like the Mericano before." Consequently, he advocates a continuation of "that courageous liberation struggle" begun by his ancestors four centuries earlier.

"No More Sacrifices" can be read as a guide to right living through traditional Pueblo ways. Ortiz says that his ancestors possessed

> a system of life which spelled out exactly how to deal with the realities they knew. The people had developed a system of knowledge which made it possible for them to work at solutions. And they had the capabilities of developing further knowledge to deal with new realities.

These flexible ways of thinking, rooted in nature, can continue to provide direction and hope in the modern world.

Ortiz writes of corn's sacred role in Pueblo spiritual life: "It is a food, gift, seed, symbol, and it is the very essence of humankind's tending and nurturing of life, land, and product of physical, mental, and emotional work." In Pueblo conceptions, human misbehavior causes drought; conversely, respectfulness and cooperation encourage rainfall. "The hanoh anxiously watch the springs at Ghoomi and Gaanipah" as signs or indicators of the health of the land. As long as fresh water seeps out, there is the certainty that prayer and ritual remain efficacious means of blessing the home. As an antidote to American society's self-destructive tendencies, Ortiz offers the Pueblo ideal of self-reliance.

From Sand Creek (1981), one of Ortiz's most overtly political works, won the 1981 Pushcart Prize for poetry. The book takes its point of departure from the 29–30 November 1864 massacre of 133 Cheyenne and Arapaho at Sand Creek, Colorado, by cavalry troops under the command of Col. John Chivington. Ortiz declares in the preface that this volume of poetry, a bittersweet lament for lost ones, is also "an analysis of myself as an American, which is hemispheric, a U.S. citizen, which is national, and as an Indian, which is spiritual and human." Thus, Ortiz intertwines the narrative of his own life with the greater narratives of the western Indian nations and of the United States as a whole. The poems were written at the Fort Lyons Veterans Administration Hospital, where Ortiz was being treated for alcoholism, and his perspective is shaped by these bleak circumstances. In *From Sand Creek* Ortiz explains that "*Europe was hungry for raw material, and America was abundant forest, rivers, land.*" Since colonial times there has been an onslaught of greedy settlers, blind to life-giving values, who have pushed westward without "regret / for the slaughter / of their future." Coming generations of American children will suffer from this reduced inheritance.

Ironically, the poet, whose people have had their land stolen, is himself suspected of being dishonest. A clerk follows him around in a Salvation Army store, expecting him to steal some recycled goods: "She caught me; / Carson caught Indians." Although he "couldn't have stolen anything," the poet feels that he should have done so as a means of avenging past wrongs: "my life was stolen already."

One of the causes of the shrinking of the land base of Native peoples was the arrival in 1879 of the railroad in the region that would become New Mexico, giving Anglos from the East Coast and the Midwest easy access to Indian country. Ortiz writes of the unnatural sounds that originate from the tracks a mile north of his Acoma Pueblo home: "*Thunder rolling across the plains is a beautiful valorous noise, but the train that became America roars and cries.*" The train is a metaphor for America, which is on a long journey to find and define itself. (Yet in a 1992 interview with David King Dunaway [published in 1995], Ortiz recalled fondly how his father, who worked for the Santa Fe Railroad, would sing Jimmie Rodgers songs, such as "Waiting for a Train." In that interview Ortiz also remembered growing up listening, with his brother, to "battery-powered radios in the late 1940s and early 1950s" that brought them music. For Ortiz, radio was "a voice from another world. It was the connection that really indicated the changes that were taking place.")

In addition to treating temporal themes in *From Sand Creek,* Ortiz also reminds the reader of the manifestations of spirit in the Pueblo world: "In this hemisphere, corn is ancient and young; it is the seed, food, and symbol of a constantly developing and revolutionary people." Corn is life-giving, as are the stars: "Indian astronomers studied the stars and set them in their memory so their people would not ever forget their place in all creation." Ortiz writes of the value of dreams as guiding forces: "Dreams are so important because they are lifelines and roadways, and nobody should ever self-righteously demean or misuse them." It is with strength born of awareness of these stabilizing forces that Ortiz summons the hope and compassion to love America, in spite of everything: "I have always loved America; it is something precious in the memory in blood and cells which insists on story, poetry, song, life, life."

Although Ortiz is primarily known as a poet, he also writes fiction. Two collections of his short stories have appeared: *Howbah Indians* (1978) and *Fightin': New and Collected Stories* (1983). *Fightin'* includes nearly twenty stories, a handful of which magnificently illustrate the complex dynamics of conflicting white and Indian worldviews. Contrasting the materialistic values and narrow-mindedness of the dominant society to the respectfulness and generosity of the Pueblo nations, Ortiz suggests that a peaceful resolution of cultural conflict requires serious accommodation on both sides. Ortiz's most admirable non-Indian characters, such as Bill and Ida in "To Change in a Good Way," the nameless narrator in "Hiding, West of Here," and the Swedish family in "Pennstuwehniyaahtsi: Quuti's Story," transcend the limitations of their backgrounds and share a willingness to be imaginative, think beyond ethnic stereotypes, and feel deeply for others.

"To Change in a Good Way" appeared in poetic form in *Fight Back*. The prose version allows Ortiz to expand the details and develop a slow buildup to Slick's death, which brings about a broadening of perspectives for his older brother Bill and Bill's wife, Ida. At the beginning of the story the lifestyle of Bill and Ida is contrasted to that of their newfound Pueblo friends, Pete and Mary. The Okie newcomers Bill and Ida struggle to water Ida's small garden with a plastic hose hooked to an ever-diminishing town water supply, and Ida's corn comes up "kind of stunted and wilty looking." Meanwhile, Pete and Mary's garden flourishes with water from the runoff of the Rio de San Jose. The couples become friends, and the Pueblos share their gardening skills with the whites. When Bill and Ida are notified that Slick, a soldier serving in Vietnam, has accidentally been killed by stepping on an American land mine, Pete and Mary and their children wrap a cornhusk bundle with feathers and cedar, enclosing the sacred substances cotton, beads, and tobacco. This gift is, Pete tells Bill,

> "for Slick, for his travel from this life among us to another place of being. You and Ida are not Indian, but it doesn't make any difference. It's for all of us.... You take these sticks and feathers and you put them somewhere you think you should, someplace important that you think might be good, maybe to change life in a good way, that you think Slick would be helping us with."

Accompanying the bundle is a dry ear of white corn – *Kasheshi* in Keresan – that is meant to show Bill and Ida that "life will keep on, your life will keep on. . . . Slick will be planted again. He'll be like that, like seed planted, like corn seed, the Indian corn.... You and Ida, your life will grow on." The Kasheshi is placed, lovingly, next to Slick's photograph; eventually it will be planted in Ida's flourishing garden.

Realizing that the mining company for which he and Pete work is indifferent to the safety of miners, Bill decides to place the cornhusk bundle in the mine shaft, "down behind a slab of rock," where it will spiritually help to hold up the support timbers. As Bill secures the bundle he offers a prayer for Slick, who is now identified eternally with the bundle, to help all of them from the other side. Even though Slick, like Ida's garden, has failed to thrive and mature, Slick still has the power as a spirit helper to warn and protect his extended human family on earth. The gift of the corn bundle is reminiscent of the offerings that Fly and Hummingbird made to Corn Mother long ago. The mining company has profaned sacred space in the underworld, and when the men emerge on the earth's surface they are seemingly "re-creating" an episode in the Keresan origin story.

Dust jacket for one of Ortiz's two collections of short stories

"Men on the Moon," another short story in *Fightin',* contrasts Indian and white ways of thinking about technology. In 1969 an old Pueblo man, Faustin, watches the first manned lunar landing on television. He decides that the space program is senseless and futile: "Faustin wondered if the men had run out of places to look for knowledge on the earth." Ortiz characteristically parallels a story from oral tradition to the contemporary story: Faustin dreams about a threatening *Skquuyuh mahkina* that frightens *Anaweh* (Flintwing Boy, a Pueblo culture hero) and *Tshuski* (Coyote). But they repel the destructive mahkina with corn and arrows. On the basis of this dream, Faustin's family takes heart against the forces of technology that threaten to destroy the integrity and sanctity of the solar system.

"Kaiser and the War" takes place in Acoma country during the 1940s or 1950s. The story is rife with ambiguity and dark humor. To avoid being inducted into the army, Kaiser hides out in the hills at sheep camp. The tenderfeet lawmen pursue him, but Kaiser holds out with assistance from Grandfather Faustin. He finally comes in when he realizes that the government will not give up on him. Kaiser is put in jail, where he is reduced to a shadow of his former self. Eventually returning home, Kaiser dies at sheep camp after asking his sister to return to the government a gray suit he had worn continuously. This cryptic ending to the story, which is told by a boy whose father had been a good friend of Kaiser's, suggests that the old gray suit that has come to symbolize Kaiser's identity also represents the disintegration of the American dream.

"Hiding West of Here" is narrated by a nameless Anglo miner. Stumbling upon two Pueblo men performing a ritual at a rock shrine in the mountains, he is unsure what to look at, what to avoid, or what to think: "I never seen anything like that." But because he is sensitive to the natural world and open-minded, he is allowed to witness their chants and prayers at the rock: "it felt like I was part of that prayer that was going on." He is brought into the circle because of his respectful attitude.

"Pennstuwehniyaahtsi: Quuti's Story" is a story within a story. As Santiago and his twelve-year-old grandson, Cholly, walk from the sheep camp back down to the pueblo, Santiago is reminded of a long walk that his friend Quuti had taken many years before. Quuti's story is an important lesson for the boy about values, language, and education. The story shifts into first-person narration as Quuti describes how whites forcibly took him away from home in a wagon and put him on a train bound for the Carlisle Indian School in Pennsylvania: "They just simply took me. They had a piece of paper on which was written something that would take me. My grandmother and my father and mother protested but it was of no avail." Quuti is given food and cornmeal for protection as he leaves home, but he is expected to eat foreign food using alien utensils. He intuitively resists the government's attempt to assimilate him, to make him "a good Indian" speaking "Mericano." Forbidden to speak his Pueblo language, Quuti resorts to talking to cows in the school barn. On turning fifteen Quuti runs away from the school to return home. As he departs, an Apache friend teaches him a traveling song to ensure a "good journey" home.

On his long walk from Pennsylvania back to New Mexico, Quuti takes cover in a barn during a snowstorm. Worried about his stranded cows, the Swedish immigrant farmer tunnels through the snowdrifts into the barn. "And he was so glad to see they were alright he started to kiss them and hug them and rub their hides to warm them up. And [he was] talking to them in this strange language." The farmer discovers Quuti, and the family boards him until spring. Although they do not speak English, Quuti "learned to speak their language a little, and they learned to speak a little of ours." Later Quuti names his son Yoonson to honor the Swedish family who had shown him such kindness on his journey home. As the story closes, Santiago remarks that his grandson is a strong walker and would have been a good companion for Quuti on his walk.

The more than two hundred poems and short narratives in *After and Before the Lightning* take the form of journal entries written down during Ortiz's stay on the Lakota Sioux Rosebud Reservation in South Dakota from November 1985 through March 1986. Two black pages, located after one poem about lightning and before another, represent storms bringing life-giving rain and blessings; for many Native American cultures, storytelling time occurs in these sacred intervals. The book is divided into four sections: "The Landscape: Prairie, Time and Galaxy," "Common Trials: Every Day," "Buffalo Dawn Coming," and "Near and Evident Signs of Spring."

In "Destination, Seeking," in the first section, the poet observes: "Early this morning, the moon glides / into the galaxy that is my soul. / Everything is huge, dimensions so vast / there is no need to seek significance." He offers a prayer to the Creator Spirit: "Thank you, Creator Spirit in the trees, in the snowy prairie hills, in today's cloudless sky, in all the little items of life, and in all the large things. These things are ourselves. Thank you for us every day, every moment, in all beginnings and endings." Even box elder bugs, who "wander here and there, mapping journeys as they make them," are beautiful and interesting to Ortiz, who identifies "with their wanderings." They, like he, "never rest" but are "always fervent with seeking destiny, always urgent to keep on their journey. . . . I thank them, their awareness and endurance."

The book ends at the vernal equinox with "Our Eagerness Blooms," which closes:

How completely we feel the tremoring
and shuddering pulse of the land now

as we welcome the rain-heart-lightning
into our trembling yearning selves.

This image is reminiscent of the deer, with arrow lifelines arching from mouth to heart, that is traditionally painted in outline on Acoma pottery.

In 1994 Ortiz successfully defended the title he had won the year before in the Heavyweight Poetry Championship of the World in Taos, New Mexico. Asked by Lewis MacAdams about the title, Ortiz modestly replied: "The attention the championship gives to poetry is very important, but poetry as individualism is a waste of time. I think the real winner should always be the people and the people's voice." In the fall of that year he joined a dozen other authors at the Native American Writers Forum, sponsored by the Telluride Institute in Colorado. In 1995 Ortiz participated in the Seeds of Change Festival, devoted to the role of the artist in creating community in New Mexico; he also offered a summer workshop, "Mapping the Cosmos: A Native American Perspective," for the Omega Institute for Holistic Studies in Rhinebeck, New York.

As a grandfather in the 1990s, aware of global concerns, Ortiz has a sense of urgency about supporting indigenous peoples' causes. And as he contributes toward redefining an image of Pueblo people that will lead them to a positive identity in the future, no doubt the *Shiwana* are returning.

Interviews:

Jane Katz, *This Song Remembers: Self Portraits of Native Americans in the Arts* (Boston: Houghton Mifflin, 1980), pp. 178–185;

Joseph Bruchac, *Survival This Way: Interviews with American Indian Poets* (Tucson: University of Arizona Press, 1987), pp. 214–229;

Kathleen Manley and Paul W. Rea, "An Interview with Simon Ortiz," *Journal of the Southwest,* 31 (Autumn 1989): 362–377;

Laura Coltelli, *Winged Words: American Indian Writers Speak* (Lincoln: University of Nebraska Press, 1990), pp. 103–119;

David King Dunaway, *Writing the Southwest* (New York: Plume, 1995), pp. 151–154.

References:

Lawrence J. Evers, "The Killing of a New Mexican State Trooper: Ways of Telling an Historical Event," *Wicazo Sa Review: A Journal of Indian Studies,* 1 (Spring 1985): 17–25;

Willard Gingerich, " 'The Old Voices of Acoma': Simon Ortiz's Mythic Indigenism," *Southwest Review,* 64 (Winter 1979): 18–30;

Gingerich, "Simon Ortiz," *fiction international,* 15 (1984): 208–212;

Arnold Krupat, "Sectarian and Secular Criticism: Simon Ortiz's *Fightin',*" *New Scholar: Voices of the First America: Text and Context in the New World,* 10, no. 1–2 (1986): 385–391;

Kenneth Lincoln, "The Now Day Indi'ns / Common Walls: The Poetry of Simon Ortiz," in his *Native American Renaissance* (Berkeley: University of California Press, 1983), pp. 189–201;

Lewis MacAdams, "Let's R-u-m-b-l-e!!!," *Los Angeles Times Magazine,* 24 July 1994, pp. 21–22, 32–33;

Robert M. Nelson, "Simon J. Ortiz," in *Dictionary of Native American Literature,* edited by Andrew Wiget (New York: Garland, 1994), pp. 483–489;

William Oandasan, "Simon Ortiz: The Poet and His Landscape," *Studies in American Indian Literature,* 11 (1987): 26–37;

Patricia Clark Smith, "Coyote Ortiz: '*Canis latrans latrans*' in the Poetry of Simon Ortiz," in *Studies in American Indian Literature: Critical Essays and Course Designs,* edited by Paula Gunn Allen (New York: Modern Language Association of America, 1983), pp. 192–210;

Smith, "Simon J. Ortiz," in *American Writers: A Collection of Literary Biographies,* supplement 4, part 2, edited by A. W. Litz and Molly Weigel (New York: Scribners, 1996), pp. 497–515;

Studies in American Indian Literature, special issue on Ortiz, 8 (Summer–Fall 1984);

Andrew Wiget, *Native American Literature* (Boston: Twayne, 1985), pp. 108–111;

Wiget, *Simon Ortiz,* Western Writers Series, volume 74 (Boise, Idaho: Boise State University Press, 1986).

John Milton Oskison

(21 September 1874 – 25 February 1947)

Gretchen Ronnow
Wayne State College

BOOKS: *Wild Harvest: A Novel of Transition Days in Oklahoma* (New York: Appleton, 1925);
Black Jack Davy (New York: Appleton, 1926);
A Texas Titan: The Story of Sam Houston (New York: Doubleday, 1929);
Brothers Three (New York: Macmillan, 1935);
Tecumseh and His Times: The Story of a Great Indian (New York: Putnam, 1938);
Cherokee Tales, by Oskison and Rennard Strickland (Muskogee, Okla.: Indian Heritage Association, 1974).

OTHER: *American Indian Spirit Tales: Redbirds, Ravens, and Coyotes,* collected by Oskison, edited by Rennard Strickland and Jack Gregory (Muskogee, Okla.: Indian Heritage Association, 1974);
Cherokee Spirit Tales and Indian Women Spirit Tales, collected by Oskison, edited by Gregory and Strickland (Muskogee, Okla.: Indian Heritage Association, 1974).

SELECTED PERIODICAL PUBLICATIONS – UNCOLLECTED:

FICTION

"I Match You: You Match Me," *Indian Chieftain* (27 May 1897): 1;
"Tookh Steh's Mistake," *Indian Chieftain* (22 July 1897): 1;
"A Schoolmaster's Dissipation," *Indian Chieftain* (23 December 1897): 1;
"Only the Master Shall Praise," *Century Magazine,* 59 (January 1900): 327–335;
"When the Grass Grew Long," *Century Magazine,* 62 (June 1901): 247–250;
"To Younger's Bend," *Frank Leslie's Monthly,* 56 (June 1903): 182–188;
"Working for Fame," *Frank Leslie's Monthly,* 56 (August 1903): 372–382;
"The Fall of King Chris," *Frank Leslie's Monthly,* 56 (October 1903): 586–593;

John Milton Oskison

"The Quality of Mercy: A Story of the Indian Territory," *Century Magazine,* 68 (June 1904): 178–181;
"The Problem of Old Harjo," *Southern Workman,* 36 (April 1907): 235–241;
"Young Henry and the Old Man," *McClure's,* 31 (June 1908): 237;

"Koenig's Discovery," *Collier's,* 45 (28 May 1910): 20–21;
"Out of the Night That Covers," *Delineator,* 78 (August 1911): 80;
"Walla-Tenaka-Creek," *Collier's,* 51 (12 July 1913): 16–17, 32;
"An Indian Animal Story," *Indian School Journal,* 14 (January 1914): 213;
"Apples of the Hesprides, Kansas," *Forum,* 51 (March 1914): 391–408;
"The Man Who Interfered," *Southern Workman,* 44 (October 1915): 557–567;
"Other Partner," *Collier's,* 74 (6 December 1924): 14–15;
"The Singing Bird," *Sunset,* 54 (March 1925): 5–8, 87–89.

NONFICTION

"Trip to Yosemite Valley," *Indian Chieftain* (8 August 1895): 1;
"John Oskison Writes of His Visit in Europe," *Indian Chieftain* (9 August 1900): 1;
"Biologist's Quest," *Overland,* new series 38 (July 1901): 52–57;
"Cherokee Migration," *Tahlequah Arrow* (31 May 1902): 1;
"The President and the Indian: Rich Opportunity for the Red Man," *Vinita Weekly Chieftain* (25 December 1902): 1;
"The Outlook for the Indian," *Southern Workman,* 32 (June 1903): 270–273;
"Lake Mohonk Conference," *Native American* (4 November 1905): 1;
"Remaining Causes of Indian Discontent," *North American Review,* 184 (1 March 1907): 486–493;
"Making an Individual of the Indian," *Everybody's Magazine,* 16 (June 1907): 723–733;
"John Smith Borrows $20," *Collier's,* 43 (4 September 1909): 14;
"Exploiters of the Needy," *Collier's,* 44 (2 October 1909): 17–18;
"Case of the Western Slope," *Collier's,* 44 (15 January 1910): 19;
"Competing with the Sharks," *Collier's,* 44 (5 February 1910): 19–20;
"Lung-Mender for the Lord," *Collier's,* 44 (19 February 1910): 24;
"Institute and Treatment Frauds," *Collier's,* 44 (5 March 1910): 23;
"Carlisle Commencement," *Collier's,* 45 (4 June 1910): 21–22;
"Carlisle Commencement as Seen by Collier's Weekly," *Red Man,* 3 (September 1910): 18–22;
"Diverse Tongues: A Sketch," *Current Literature,* 49 (September 1910): 343–344;
"Round-up of the Financial Swindlers," *Collier's,* 46 (31 December 1910): 19–20;
"Spider and the Fly," *Woman's Home Companion,* 38 (October 1911): 9;
"The Indian in the Professions," *Red Man,* 4 (January 1912): 201–204;
"Cooperative Cost of Living," *Collier's,* 48 (27 January 1912): 48;
"Address by J. M. Oskison," *Red Man,* 4 (May 1912): 397–398;
"Little Mother of the Pueblos," *Delineator,* 81 (March 1913): 170;
"An Apache Problem," *Quarterly Journal of the Society of American Indians,* 1 (April 1913): 25–29;
"Farming on a Business Basis," *System,* 23 (April 1913): 379–384;
"$1,000 on the Farm," *Collier's,* 51 (26 April 1913): 24, 51; (3 May 1913): 26;
"Farm, the Thousand, and the Ifs," *Collier's,* 51 (24 May 1913): 24, 51; (7 June 1913): 24;
"New Way to Finance the Vacation," *Delineator,* 83 (August 1913): 10;
"New Farm Pioneers," *Collier's,* 51 (2 August 1913): 27;
"Hired Man's Chance," *Collier's,* 51 (9 August 1913): 24–25;
"Acquiring a Standard of Value," *Quarterly Journal of the Society of American Indians,* 2 (January–March 1914): 47–50;
"Arizona and Forty Thousand Indians," *Southern Workman,* 43 (March 1914): 148–156;
"Boosting the Thrift Idea," *Collier's,* 53 (4 April 1914): 22;
"With Apache Deer Hunters in Arizona," *Outing,* 64 (April/May 1914): 65–73, 150–163;
"The Closing Chapter: Passing of the Old Indian," *Indian Leader,* 17 (May 1914): 6–9;
"Less Known Edison," *World's Work,* 28 (June 1914): 180–185;
"Chemist Who Became King of an Industry," *World's Work,* 28 (July 1914): 310–315;
"Road to Betatakin," *Outing,* 64 (July–August 1914): 392–409, 606–623;
"American Creator of the Aluminum Age," *World's Work,* 28 (August 1914): 438–445;
"What a Modern Sea Fight Is Like," *World's Work,* 29 (November 1914): 87–91;
"Why Am I an American?," *World's Work,* 29 (December 1914): 209–213;
"How You Can Help Feed and Clothe the Belgians," *World's Work,* 29 (January 1915): 275–277;

"Indian Kicking Races," *Outing*, 65 (January 1915): 441–447;

"The Record of the Naval Conflicts," *World's Work*, 29 (January 1915): 345–350;

"From John Paul Jones to Dewey," *World's Work*, 29 (February 1915): 447–469;

"In Governing the Indian, Use the Indian," *American Indian Magazine*, 5 (January–March 1917): 36–41;

"The New Indian Leadership," *American Indian Magazine*, 5 (April–June 1917): 93–100;

"Back-Firing against Bolshevism," *Outlook*, 122 (30 July 1919): 510–515;

"Herbert Hoover: Engineer – Economist – Organizer," *Industrial Management*, 61 (1 January 1921): 2–6;

"Hoover Message to Export Manufacturers," *Industrial Management*, 65 (March 1923): 131–135;

"Favorite Novelist of State in the Second Tribune Radio Interview Over KVOO Phone," *Tulsa Tribune*, 10 January 1930, pp. 1–2;

"A Letter by John Milton Oskison (1874–1947), Cherokee Journalist," *Native Press Research Journal*, 6 (Fall 1987): 1–7.

John Milton Oskison was one of the first major Native American writers to grapple with the issues of being a highly educated mixed-blood trying to defend a tribal heritage while at the same time writing as a serious journalist, editor, and contributor to the country's leading periodicals and major newspapers in some of the nation's largest cities. This struggle is readily apparent in his fiction, especially his short stories, and in his articles concerned with non-Indian issues, and it deserves critical assessment. In light of the current interest in authors from diverse ethnic backgrounds, readers and critics are looking for early Native American authors who pioneered genres and influenced publishers to become more interested in Native American materials. Readers and critics who have mentioned Oskison's stories in their analyses have tended to claim him as a Native American author but to dismiss his work as sentimental and, ironically, lacking a Native American focus. However, closer readings of Oskison's fiction show a strong Native American point of view reflecting his Cherokee background, his years spent in Indian Territory and, later, Oklahoma, and his experiences with other Native American tribes he encountered in his travels. His Native American point of view and sympathy are often overtly evident or strongly encoded in the text, embedded in narrative complexities and rhetorical and stylistic peculiarities.

In his unpublished autobiography, written in 1947, Oskison calls himself a "replica in temperament" of his "restless, nervous, short-tempered father." That restlessness brought Oskison's father from England to Indian Territory, where he married Rachel Crittenden, whose parents' name in Cherokee meant "buzzard." She was a widow with a four-year-old daughter, Sarah. Oskison writes that "her Indian blood had been mixed with white until she was only a quarter Cherokee." Thus, Oskison would have been one-eighth Cherokee, although he is listed on the Cherokee Nation Census and the Dawes Commission Rolls of 1904 as "Race, Indian; Degree of blood 1-4." His brother Richard is listed on the Census Roll as "Degree of blood 1-8," and his brother William (Bert) is listed as "Degree of blood 1-16." The discrepancy speaks to the difficulty of being Indian in Indian Territory at the turn of the century and perhaps to the desirability of claiming to have a lesser quantity of Indian blood. When Oskison's mother and father married, his father became by Cherokee law "an adopted citizen of the Nation, with all the rights and privileges of any fullblood."

John Milton Oskison was born in Indian Territory on 21 September 1874. The family soon headed for Oregon to homestead, but his mother became seriously ill in Oregon and desired to return to her home in Indian Territory, so the family moved back to Oklahoma. After his mother died the family began to farm on land near Pryor Creek, Oklahoma, where Oskison and his brothers experienced the hardships and glories of ranching in Indian Territory – activities that would provide recurring themes for Oskison's fiction. Oskison's early education suffered because his father demanded he miss school to work on the ranch. He writes in his autobiography that "looking back, I have thought of our life at that time as a bleak, pagan existence. It was unbroken by children's parties, Thanksgiving and Christmas celebrations, and church going. One thing only dominated our minds, father's iron determination to make our cattle venture succeed." Oskison finally graduated from Willie Halsell College in Oklahoma in 1894. He narrowed his choice of universities to Vanderbilt and Stanford University; but he writes in his autobiography that his father made the decision for him, sending him to Stanford to study law. Stanford was a "new and different" university, experimental for its time. Oskison describes his surprise at seeing a "negro" among the seniors who planned to attend a San Francisco law school.

Dust jacket for Oskison's novel about frontier life in Vinita, Oklahoma (courtesy of the Lilly Library, Indiana University)

Oskison earned his law degree from Stanford in 1898. The longest section of his autobiography is devoted to detailed and enthusiastic descriptions of his classes and experiences at Stanford.

Ultimately, with his father's blessing, Oskison enrolled at Harvard to study English, Spanish, literature, and psychology; but when he had a short story published in 1900 in *Century Magazine,* he embarked on a literary and journalistic career. He married Florence Ballard Day, a relative of the railroad magnate Jay Gould, in New York City on 21 October 1903. They had two children, Helen and Oliver, but divorced in Paris in 1920. He later married Hildegard Hawthorne, the granddaughter of Nathaniel Hawthorne, on 16 July 1920. She was also a writer, and they enjoyed traveling together; but eventually they, too, drifted apart and later divorced.

While at Harvard Oskison was notified that a story he had submitted to a fiction-writing contest at *Century Magazine* had won first prize. This event gave him the confidence to choose professional writing as a career. He became a writer and editor for *Collier's Weekly* and the *New York Evening Post,* as well as a contributor of stories and articles to most of the other leading magazines of the time. By 1917 almost every major magazine in the country had published his articles. Throughout this time he was also writing essays for Native American journals and newspapers. During World War I he enlisted in the army and was sent to France as a first lieutenant in the 77th Division of the American Expeditionary Force.

After the war Oskison begin to write novels set in Oklahoma and peopled with character types he had known or heard about in his ranching days. He spent much of his life in New York City and Paris rather than Oklahoma, although he served in Oklahoma as one of the supervisors of the Works Progress Administration's Oklahoma writers project, and later he returned often to keep viable his ties to his homeland and to research materials for his fiction writing. He also traveled to Hawaii, Bermuda, and Palestine, as well as extensively in the American Southwest and Europe.

Oskison's short works fall roughly into three categories. From 1897 to 1917 he wrote letters and articles about "Indian-problem" issues, mostly for

Indian Territory newspapers and Indian school journals, but he also found a national audience with "Remaining Causes of Indian Discontent" (1 March 1907), in the *North American Review,* "Making an Individual of the Indian" (June 1907), in *Everybody's Magazine,* and "Arizona and Forty Thousand Indians" (March 1914), in *Southern Workman.* Oskison made no secret of his Indian blood. He belonged to the Society of American Indians, and in 1911 his name appears on the letterhead of the American Indian Association (which also declares that active memberships apply to "Persons of Indian Blood Only"), which lists him as a member of the "Temporary Executive Committee." At this time he was writing articles for Native American journals such as *Red Man,* the *Indian School Journal,* the *Tahlequah Arrow,* the *Indian Leader,* and the *Quarterly Journal of the Society of American Indians.*

American Indian authors, Oskison included, writing in the first half of the twentieth century are often credited (or accused) by critics with being assimilationists, those who believed that the "Indian problem" would be eliminated by urging Indians to join the mainstream of American institutionalism and society. At first glance Oskison's articles on Indian topics may justify such a label, but a closer look at his rhetorical technique belies it. He often juxtaposes issues without indicating his own opinion about them: traditional values versus mainstream values, formal education versus the teachings of Native American elders, intermarriage versus separatism, and ingenuous Native Americans versus the sophistication of tribal legal scholars. It is not clear which side of these issues he supports. In articles about Indian issues, Oskison often quotes politicians or scholars without affirmation or comment of his own. His articles seem to demonstrate a belief in the power of big institutions, big cities, and big government, but there is often an ironic tone in the writing, produced by droll metaphors and a certain distance sensed between Oskison the man and Oskison the author. For example, in "The President and the Indian: Rich Opportunity for the Red Man," a *Vinita Weekly Chieftain* (25 December 1902) essay, Oskison writes: " 'In portions of the Indian Territory,' says President Roosevelt, 'the mixture of blood has gone on at the same time with progress in wealth and education, so that there are plenty of men with varying degrees of purity of Indian blood who are absolutely indistinguishable in point of social, political, and economic ability from their white associates.' " Oskison remains neutral in his reportage; he cites the effort but does not endorse the results. Oskison hoped to enable individuals, especially those already in his audience, to make their own choices as individuals confronting discrete issues, present and future, and not be pushed aside by the powerful machinery of "progress."

In "The Indian in the Professions," published in the January 1912 *Red Man,* Oskison declares his allegiance to the struggle of Native Americans in the modern world: "In my small way, I've tried to make myself an interpreter to the world, of the modern, progressive Indian." For Native American spokespeople from Samson Occom and William Apess to the present it has been a thankless and almost impossible task to interpret the Indian – especially, perhaps, the modern, "progressive" Indian – to the world. Oskison's early articles reveal his determination to portray Indians as contemporary, forward-thinking individuals, and not to see as "Indian" only the romanticized, noble "red man" – an image perhaps more imprisoning than openly negative stereotypes. Oskison wanted to expand the repertoire of images of the Indian to include the dignified traditional, the hardworking farmer and laborer, and the well-educated professional. In this effort Oskison was ahead of his time: he was in the difficult position of having to report on the loss of specific and unique tribal cultures and on the tribal person as a shadow or sometimes poor second of his or her potential counterpart in white society.

In his writings Oskison was earnestly engaged in trying to find a rhetorical or discoursive middle ground, especially since he saw firsthand the consequences of trying to maintain an absolute distance and difference between tribal and Anglo cultures. He was troubled by the dilemma, and he realized that the boundaries were blurred. At first glance it may appear that he advocated assimilation indiscriminately. His journalistic tone is apparently confident and brightly optimistic, his spirit naively bright. But if his corpus is taken as a whole, the reader will begin to notice darker tones of irony, reservation, and doubt about progress and assimilation. Oskison was aware of the differences in tribal cultures – from the Cherokee's long tradition of acceptance of progress and intercultural mixing to the long tradition of isolation and aloofness of some of the tribes of the Southwest and every possible combination in between. His cosmopolitan overview is thus apparent in his essays.

In his short stories, published between 1897 and 1925, Oskison tries to capture the ruggedness of frontier life in the Indian Territory, a life in which he had participated. In stories such as "Only the Master Shall Praise" (*Century Magazine,* January 1900), "The Quality of Mercy" *(Century Magazine,* June 1904), "Out of the Night That Covers" (*Delineator,* August 1911), "The Man Who Interfered" (*Southern Workmen,* October 1915), and "Other Partner" (*Collier's,* 6 December 1924), for instance, the characters are drawn from the people he knew at home. The heroes and main characters are inevitably mixed-bloods, women, or members of other marginalized groups. These stories often follow a coyote-tale format with compassionate trickster protagonists. A substantial number of Oskison's short stories have a main character who stands on the sidelines to observe and record the event. It seems to be an Oskison-like character – an insider-outsider – in these stories who is interested in the possibilities of texts within texts within texts. The character-author's fascination with embedded textuality reveals a sophisticated modernist's awareness. For Oskison to write himself into each story is also inherently to assert a Native American point of view that questions the easy assumptions some readers have made about what being Indian means or what Native American writing is.

Oskison's stories are "Westerns" of a type: they are tales of the frontier, but they differ diametrically from the popular Western genre of the time in major ways. The then-prevailing Western formula presented a strong and attractive hero, a hero's quest, a rejection ultimately of the wilderness and wilderness values, and an acceptance of civilization and its cultural sensitivities. Almost every Oskison story has mixed-blood or full-blood main characters or characters modeled on the author or his mixed-blood brothers, and his stories are permeated by a substructure of Cherokee myth and mythological worldview. His heroes are almost never young, strong, handsome defenders of American manifest destiny – in fact they are characters who would be considered villains in most pulp fiction. They are not obsessed with masculinity and rarely use a gun or even have a horse. The moral geography of his stories is ambiguous, and the action is often incompletely resolved or the story concludes with a troubled suspension of judgment.

The quester-conqueror motif is not the governing theme as much as is the Cherokee mythos, concerned with wise or humble souls who seek balance, synthesis, and harmony. The traditional Cherokee story world is populated with invisible spirits and invisible little people who are for the most part benevolent and helpful toward humans but who insist that the person who is helped never speak of his encounters with the invisible ones. Many of Oskison's stories feature a character who is a "little person" in some sense of the word. The role of such characters in Oskison's stories is to help the downtrodden or erring characters of the story and then fade away, sometimes even die, or return to invisibility without proper acknowledgment or thanks. These almost nondescript characters in Oskison's stories perform the "heroic" deeds, but they are not heroic in the sense of conventional Westerns, which emphasized physical strength and prowess.

Between 1909 and 1921 Oskison also submitted a series of articles on topics of national interest to popular mainstream American magazines. In "John Smith Borrows $20" (*Collier's,* 4 September 1909), "Exploiters of the Needy" (*Collier's,* 2 October 1909), "Competing with the Sharks" (*Collier's,* 5 February 1910), "Cooperative Cost of Living" (*Collier's,* 29 January 1912), "Farming on a Business Basis" (*System,* April 1913), and "Boosting the Thrift Idea" (*Collier's,* 4 April 1914), he discusses money – how to earn it, how to save it, and how not to be swindled out of it. He wrote of ingenuity and creativity, lauding inventors, scientists, industrialists, and politicians. He wrote of modern military might; World War I was immediately imminent, and he was impressed by its machinery as seen in articles such as "What a Modern Sea Fight Is Like" (*World's Work,* November 1914), "Why Am I an American? " (*World's Work,* December 1914), "How You Can Help Feed and Clothe the Belgians" (*World's Work,* January 1915), and "Back-Firing against Bolshevism" (*Outlook,* 30 July 1919). He also contributed an occasional letter or article for the armchair adventurers among his readers about his trips to Yosemite or Europe or about deer hunting and hiking among the ruins in the Southwest, as in "Trip to Yosemite Valley" (*Indian Chieftan,* 8 August 1895), "Little Mother of the Pueblos" (*Delineator,* March 1913), "Road to Betatakin" (*Outing,* July–August 1914), and "Indian Kicking Races" (*Outing,* January 1915). These articles are of importance mainly to show the vast range of Oskison's interests, of his travels both abroad and domestically, and of his desire to experience personally the events of his era.

After 1925 Oskison chose to devote all of his efforts to writing novels and book-length biographies. He felt he still had not done justice in his short stories to the intensity and color of life in Indian Territory, so he decided to try longer, more sustained narratives. In *Wild Harvest: A Novel of Transition Days in Oklahoma* (1925) Oskison creates

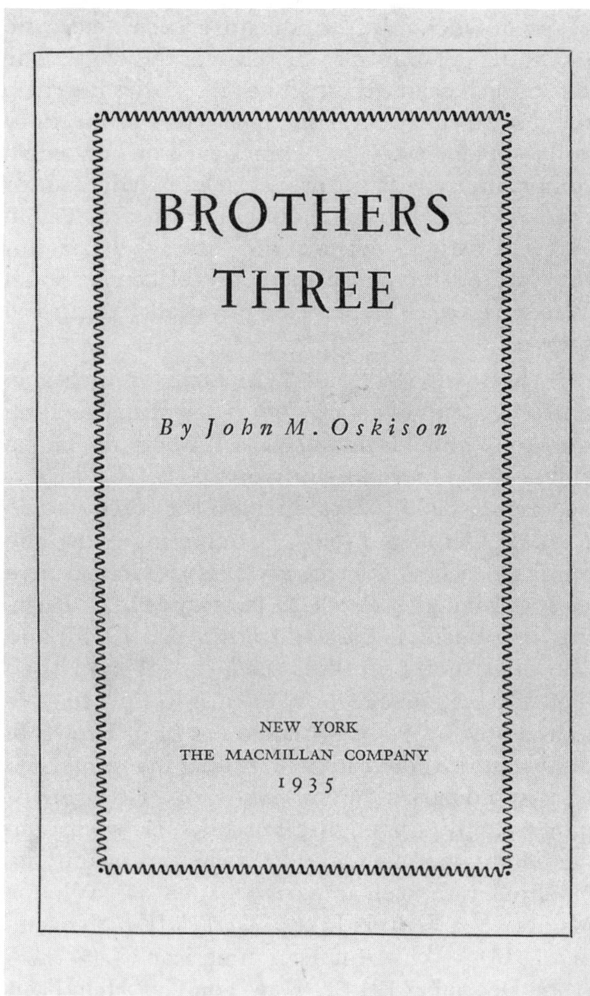
BROTHERS THREE
By John M. Oskison
NEW YORK
THE MACMILLAN COMPANY
1935

Title page for the novel in which Oskison based the main characters on himself and his brothers, Richard and Bert

the character of Nan Forest, a young woman living in Indian Territory with her father. She finds that her soul responds to the magic of the prairie, to its rich soil and windswept vistas. She comes to love the struggle of ranching and of the various humans of diverse cultures learning to interact and intermingle. She becomes involved in the Indians' efforts to quarantine Texas cattle against disease and is forced to appreciate the ancient endurance and adaptibility of the indigenous prairie peoples. The hero, Tom Winger, is a cowboy, although not a genre-typical one, and there is enough shooting and killing to qualify the novel as a vivid Western.

A reviewer writing in *The New York Times Book Review* (20 September 1925) says that the novel might have "ranked as a very good tenth-rate stock Western story if the author had not been ambitious to introduce some intelligence into the substance and background of his yarn." *Wild Harvest* reiterates the standard themes of the conventional Western in that it applauds the necessity of law and order. The narrator proclaims that "against the Hayes family and what Ruby Engel represented stood the forces of order and decency. . . . Here were [the heroes] instantly and willingly taking up the defense of . . . law and order that must be established if life was to become secure." But Nan also gets to lecture another character, Gabe, on the sophistication, intelligence, and institutionalized power of the Native American Indian characters. Gabe then summarizes the prevailing white point of view – that they are "oncivilized [*sic*] . . . like Geronimo" – before repeating her catechism: "Here they've got a regular government: chief, second chief, a senate, a council, courts, schools, asylums, churches an' preachers. They've got plenty of educated men an' women; they've got lawyers an' doctors an' traders; they've got their political parties an' tribal newspapers an' public men that have growed up thinkin' and talkin' about their own problems till they can hold their own with Congress when they go to Washington as delegates." Such a statement about Indians is extremely rare if not unique in Westerns of the day. It is clearly the voice of John Oskison appealing to the readers to be more open-minded about the political realities of Indian Territory.

Many of the same characters appear in Oskison's next novel about frontier life in Vinita, Oklahoma: *Black Jack Davy* (1926). The frontier characters assist the teenage Davy and his elderly adoptive parents in working a farm they have rented in Indian Territory from Ned Warrior, a full-blood Cherokee. A string of violent clashes between them and a cruel neighbor culminates in the death of Davy's adoptive father, but the experience and Davy's love affair with Mirabelle redefine families and redraw the boundaries of interpersonal and intercultural relationships. Here, too, are wisps of some of the lyrical prose occasionally to be found in Oskison's writings: "Mirabelle loved to read aloud sometimes . . . romantic bits, colorful with words like roses and moonlight, honey dew, murmuring brooks, nightingales, fragrance and gallantry."

Richard Mansfield Dickinson, then the director of the Tulsa Little Theatre, wrote a stage adaptation of the novel, and the play was performed in Tulsa, in Norman, and in Oskison's hometown, Vinita, Oklahoma. It also won the

Playhouse Prize of the University of Oklahoma for the best play by an Oklahoman, and it won the second prize in the national Drama League competition in New York City in 1930.

Oskison's longest novel is *Brothers Three* (1935), an intensely autobiographical novel fictionalizing his brother Richard as Timmy, nicknamed "Bud"; his brother Bert as Roger, nicknamed "Bunny"; and himself as the main character, Henry, nicknamed "Mister." This book remained the longest novel written by a Native American author until the publication of Leslie Marmon Silko's *Almanac of the Dead* (1991). It is an epic of generations of people upon the land much in the tradition of O. E. Rölvaag's *Giants in the Earth* (1927). Readers and reviewers have noticed autobiographical details in this novel; in fact it is almost totally autobiographical. Even tiny details, most of the minutiae, and much of the phrasing of *Brothers Three* and Oskison's autobiography are identical. In the novel Francis Odell, after prolonged wandering, finally homesteads in Indian Territory with a part-Cherokee wife and baby son. They expand their ranching endeavors into mercantile investments, but it is a second generation's wife's love of, and dedication to, the land that saves the family from complete ruin after the patriarch's death and the crash of the stock market.

Francis Odell is described physically in the same way as Oskison describes his own father, and much of the family dialogue in the novel echoes that recorded in the autobiography. The three brothers of the novel parallel Oskison and his brothers, although characteristics of the actual brothers are rearranged in composite to form the fictional brothers. The first section of the novel is called "Timmy," after the oldest son, who is dependable, capable, serene, and quick to learn the ways of the prairie and of his sometimes ferocious father. Timmy is always the peacemaker, soothing the hired hands and watching out for his soon-to-be-invalided mother. Oskison describes here much of the same sexual inexperience and coming-of-age experimentation he describes in his autobiography. He the reader see and feel the life and the land as he had. He writes of Francis's desire to have his wife "see it all as he did," and then includes pages and pages of Thomas Wolfe–like lists of details, touches, smells, places, and objects. The reader is convinced that Oskison has been bitten by "pale scorpions that hurt almost intolerably when the stingers in the ends of their upcurled tails sank into the flesh of careless hands" and that he has seen spring seasons that are "long unfoldings of beauty, broken by snatches of premature summer, days of snow flurries and wind-driven sleet, and by deafening, flooding thunder storms."

As Timmy matures he becomes conscious of the "change that was being wrought by the invaders of this Indian land, turning it from Indian serenity to white man turbulence. More and more alien families, unlike the first settlers on Bee Creek and Redbud Creek who were proud of a Cherokee strain on at least one side of the house, these newer comers were all white, living on land leased from Indians." These newcomers are shiftless drifters, "contemptuous of the Indians, and [they] promised to hasten the movement for making the Indian Territory into a 'white man's state.' They carried on, in grotesque caricature, the tradition that the 'savage red man' must, because of his incompetence, give way to the white. Their dirtiest tow-headed moron child of fifteen was taught to feel superior to such boys as Timmy – to any child however slightly 'tainted' by Indian blood."

The next section of the novel, "The Herdsman," describes Roger, who is constantly at odds with his stern disciplinarian father, to the point that the son leaves home as soon as he can to lead the rugged life of a cattleman. The last section, "Mister," is about Henry, the youngest boy, who goes off to Stanford to become a writer and ultimately chooses to live in New York City to enjoy its power, commodities, and lifestyle. Henry speaks enthusiastically of his days at Stanford, also mentioning a Negro classmate, and claiming to have had "a number of friends of the race." He then pointedly remarks that "if it had been known in California that [he] was part Indian it would have been worse for [him] than being part negro. . . . Race pride, and prejudice – absurd." But Oskison is right in remarking that being Indian in nineteenth-century, even late-nineteenth-century, California, was a discomforting, even dangerous, situation.

When Oskison describes Henry, he is describing himself: "Henry experienced the old transformation; out of sight of Manhattan's towers, his mind leaped toward the Farm, recovering an eagerness to record and interpret that which had always seemed vital. It was absurd, of course, to think that life in New York was less significant and absorbing than in that Oklahoma backwater. . . . But he could not help feeling the unreality of New York, and the solid worth of the Odell background as the framework of his stories." The character Henry then asks the questions that seemed to plague or perhaps please Oskison for most of his life: "Aside from my writing, who am I, and of what importance to anybody? If there's substance to Henry Odell, it's ex-

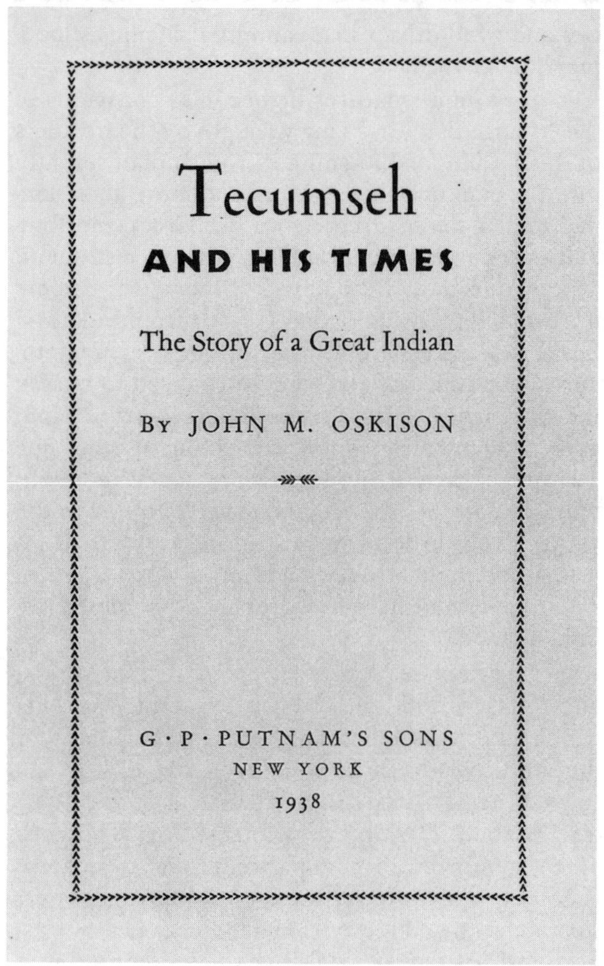

Tecumseh AND HIS TIMES The Story of a Great Indian By JOHN M. OSKISON G·P·PUTNAM'S SONS NEW YORK 1938

Title page for Oskison's fictionalized biography of the great Shawnee chief

pressed in his writing. . . . He does it honestly, with all the talent he has. Compared to other writers, he may not be significant, but what he does is his own; and he thinks it's grand." By that measure, Oskison's works, too, can be judged successful. Oskison even includes some of the remarks or observations of his contemporary critics when he has a character, Ann, in the novel critique Henry's literary attempts. Ann says, "You love your people, and presented them as they seem to you, seen through the veil of 'prairie dust.' They're not real, naturally – even your country girl prostitute must have fine qualities, reform, marry, and rear children." Oskison was obviously not unaware of what critics saw as weaknesses in his writings, but he chose, nonetheless, to remain true to his vision of his own experience: to the prairie dust on the "impermanent people [he] knew, the renters and drifters, against the solidity of the Farm that [had] always seemed so permanent to [him]." It is this kind of integrity that endears Oskison and *Brothers Three* to the reader.

Oskison also wrote *A Texas Titan: The Story of Sam Houston* (1929) and *Tecumseh and His Times: The Story of a Great Indian* (1938), both fictionalized biographies written with careful attention to the details of Indian life and thought. On the title page Oskison dedicates *Tecumseh and His Times* "to all dreamers and strivers for the Integrity of the Indian race, some of whose blood flows in my veins; and especially to the Oklahoma Shawnee friends of my boyhood." The text draws on dozens of journals, testimonies, treaties, descriptions of military strategies, and eyewitness and historical accounts. He writes: "When the split-off from the Delaware occurred in the white man's reckoning of years, can only be guessed. To the Indians it was a matter of indifference, this fixing of events by definite dates. Only the accurate succession of chiefs, battles, removals, and other memorable happenings was passed along. Time was relative – as it always is to historians with perspective." "Men like George Croghan, who penetrated the Ohio country when it was exclusively Indian, marveled at the towering sycamores along the streams, at the giant bur oaks and hickories, the incredible abundance of migratory birds, the black loam soil 'a mile deep,' and the scents of flowering plum, hawthorn, wild grape, and honeysuckle. To imagine that the Indians were insensible to that land's richness and beauty is stupid." He stresses that Tecumseh "grew up in all ways an Indian – in dress, in habit of thought, in the love of the land where existence meant freedom to enjoy life as it unrolled from day to day."

The last two passages might constitute Oskison's rebuttal to prevalent criticisms of Indians and their habits; it was apparently important to him to make these statements even though he had chosen city life and world travel over "Indian life." He admits that "of course the Indians were ruthless" – though not as ruthless as the stories portrayed them as being. "They were fighting for their homes. They were as ruthless as the Ethiopian tribesmen who fought Mussolini's soldiers . . . or the civil war combatants in Spain." Here is an early and balanced multiculturalism.

The Tecumseh narrative picks up speed and energy toward the end, as Oskison reminds readers of the scope and depth of sorrows, betrayals, and outright atrocities committed against the Indians by their Christian statesmen counterparts. He describes the politics and lives of Dekanawida, the Huron idealist; Pontiac; Cornstalk; Logan; Osceola; the Seminole Frances the Prophet; the Seneca Red Jacket; Kanakuk of the Kickapoos; Black Hawk of the Sacs; Captain Jack of the Modocs; Chief Joseph, Sitting Bull, Cochise, Nache; Geronimo; and Tedyuskung, a chief of the Delawares. Oskison writes that Tecumseh belongs "with Metacomet, known to the New Englanders as King Philip, second son of that Massasoit who had welcomed the Pilgrims at Plymouth Rock. As the victorious Kentuckians were said to have flayed Tecumseh's body and made razor strops of his skin, so the truculent saints of Massachusetts cut up Metacomet's body, and, as recorded by the Rev. Increase Mather, hung up his quarters 'as a monument of revenging justice.' " Readers who complain that Oskison avoids writing of Indian characters, topics, or issues should note the intensity of emotion and detailed knowledge of the complete history of Indians in all of North America in *Tecumseh and His Times*.

Oskison also defends in some detail the peyote church – claiming that it preserves that which is distinctively Indian – and Tecumseh's relation to it. He then writes that

> probably twenty-five tribes maintain peyote lodges. There are missionaries, usually educated mixed bloods, who move secretly from tribe to tribe extending the cult. So far, no individual has emerged as a leader strong enough to fuse the movement into one of active protest against a rubber-stamp Christian civilization. It is unlikely that any one will, for the leaders are well enough read in Indian history to know that the sure way to extinction for the peyote religion is to bring it into the open.

Oskison speaks here with the voice of a trusted insider, trusted and "Indian" enough to know the leaders and the secrets of the cult, and jaded enough by Christian civilization to criticize its influence. He concludes the biography by writing that "what stirred Tecumseh to attempt the formation of an Indian confederation was a hope as old as the races of man: that it might be possible in a changing and turbulent world to find permanent peace and plenty. Because we understand that longing, and because in all of us burns some spark of resentment at encroachment on our liberties, we know why Tecumseh has become, in the minds and memories of three peoples [Britain, white America, Indian America], a knightly symbol and an enduring legend." Some sources credit Oskison with writing the novels *Vision Victorious* (1931) and *Lone Rider* (1933), but Hildegarde Hawthorne is the author of *Lone Rider* and is sometimes credited with being the author of *Vision Victorious*.

Oskison suffered poor health during the last few years of his life but was working on a new novel about missionaries from New England sent to the Indian Territory in the first half of the nineteenth century. He had also contracted with a New York firm to publish his autobiography. He was staying with an Oklahoman friend, Richard Mansfield Dickinson, in Tulsa when he died of a heart ailment on 25 February 1947.

Oskison's complexities and interests are evident. In his essays he describes the manifestations of national and international power structures and their modes of deployment; but he was also drawn to the romance and history of his experiences in the Oklahoma Indian Territory, not the least of which romances were the roles and heritages of its Indian populations and their struggles and achievements. The position of Native Americans in Oskison's America was not a monolithic situation but varied from state to state, city to countryside, and tribe to tribe, and Oskison was well aware of its difficulties. This awareness is evident in his writings. He was also familiar with the national world of commerce and journalism, even the international world of wars, travel, and logistics. These diversities were explicit in his own biological and personal background. What he wrote could only be mandated by his own experiences and perceptions. For that reason, what he wrote is far more complex than seems at first apparent. What seems to be popular discourse in Oskison's writings is, in fact, filled with contradictions and ambiguities hiding both the "truth" of his message and the exact thinking of the man himself.

Bibliographies:

Angeline Jacobson, *Contemporary Native American Literature: A Selected and Partially Annotated Bibliography* (Metuchen, N.J.: Scarecrow Press, 1977), pp. 181–182;

Daniel F. Littlefield Jr. and James W. Parins, *A Biobibliography of Native American Writers, 1772–1924* (Metuchen, N.J.: Scarecrow Press, 1981), pp. 114–116;

Tom Colonese and Louis Owens, *American Indian Novelists: An Annotated Critical Bibliography* (New York: Garland, 1985), pp. 65–73.

References:

O. B. Campbell, *Vinita, Indian Territory: The Story of a Frontier Town of the Cherokee Nation, 1871–1907* (Oklahoma City: Metro Press, 1969);

Agnes Morley Cleveland, "Three Musketeers of Southwestern Fiction," *Overland Monthly,* 87 (December 1929): 385;

Charles Larson, *American Indian Fiction* (Albuquerque: University of New Mexico Press, 1978), pp. 34–37, 46–55, 63–65;

Priscilla Oaks, "The First Generation of Native American Novelists," *MELUS,* 5 (Spring 1978): 57–65;

Louis Owens, *Other Destinies: Understanding the American Indian Novel* (Norman: University of Oklahoma Press, 1992), p. 24;

Gretchen Ronnow, "John Milton Oskison, Cherokee Journalist: A Singer of the Semiotics of Power," *Native Press Research Journal,* 4 (Spring 1987): 1–15;

A. LaVonne Brown Ruoff, *American Indian Literatures: An Introduction, Bibliographic Review, and Selected Bibliography* (New York: Modern Language Association, 1990), pp. 71, 132, 141;

Arney L. Strickland, "John Milton Oskison: A Writer of the Transitional Period of the Oklahoma Indian Territory," *Southwestern American Literature,* 2 (Winter 1972): 125–134;

Andrew Wiget, *Native American Literature* (New York: Twayne, 1984), pp. 65–66, 73–74.

Papers:

The John Milton Oskison Collection at the University of Oklahoma includes the manuscript for Oskison's unpublished autobiography.

Alexander Posey

(3 August 1873 - 27 May 1908)

Betty Booth Donohue
University of California, Los Angeles

BOOKS: *The Poems of Alexander Lawrence Posey,* edited by Minnie H. Posey, with a memoir by William Elsey Connelley (Topeka, Kans.: Crane, 1910);

The Fus Fixico Letters, edited by Daniel F. Littlefield and Carol Hunter (Lincoln: University of Nebraska Press, 1993).

SELECTED PERIODICAL PUBLICATIONS – UNCOLLECTED: "Sequoyah," *Red Man,* 12 (July-August 1893): 8;

"An Indian on the Problems of His Race," *Review of Reviews,* 12 (December 1895): 694–695;

"The Indian's Past Olympic," *Muskogee Phoenix,* 17 December 1896, p. 5;

"Two Famous Prophets," *Twin Territories,* 2 (September 1900): 180–182;

"A Creek Fable," *Twin Territories,* 2 (October 1900): 213;

"The Fall of the Redskin (with Apologies to Edwin Markham)," *Indian Journal,* 18 January 1901;

"Where the Rivers Meet," *Twin Territories,* 3 (February 1901): 24;

"Fable of the Foolish Young Bear," *Indian Journal,* 22 March 1901;

"The Devil's Parodies," *Indian Journal,* 10 January 1902;

"Journal of Alexander Lawrence Posey," edited by Edward Everett Dale, *Chronicles of Oklahoma,* 45 (1967–1968): 393–432; 46 (1968): 2–19.

Alexander Posey in 1908 (courtesy of Daniel F. Littlefield Jr.)

The educator, journalist, poet, and political satirist Alexander Lawrence Posey was one of the Creek Nation's most prominent writers and political activists. Living at a crucial time in Creek history, Posey saw the dissolution of his tribe's land base and the creation of the state of Oklahoma, and he played a role in the events surrounding the termination of tribal status for Oklahoma's native people. Educational institutions serving Indian youth at the end of the nineteenth century had strict acculturationist policies: Native languages and customs were considered unworthy of perpetuation, and Indian students were encouraged to accommodate themselves to Euro-American thought systems and to emulate Euro-American styles. Thus, in Posey's early writing, especially his poetry, Native themes are expressed in European forms, using European rhetorical devices. His later work, however, is written in a style Posey developed, one that uses Indian compositional principles, language patterns, and metaphors. The conventions he employed are

Posey around the age of seven (Archives and Manuscripts Division of the Oklahoma Historical Society)

used today by such Indian writers as N. Scott Momaday, Leslie Marmon Silko, James Welch, Paula Gunn Allen, and Louise Erdrich.

Posey was born in the Creek Nation near Eufaula, Indian Territory (now Oklahoma), on 3 August 1873. His mother, Nancy Harjo Posey, a full-blood, was a member of Tuskegee town and belonged to the Wind clan. His father, Lewis Henderson Posey, a farmer, was an orphan who had been raised by a Creek woman near Fort Gibson. Lewis Posey's ancestry is obscure: the name Posey is French, while local tradition indicates that he was of Indian-Scotch-Irish extraction. The elder Posey was a fluent Creek speaker who frequently acted as an interpreter. Alexander Posey grew up in a bicultural, bilingual environment: he was exposed to Creek customs and traditions, yet his education, which included the services of a tutor who lived in the Posey home, several years at the Eufaula Indian School, and three years at Bacone Indian University in Muskogee, was comparable to that of any non-Indian of the time and place.

While a student at Bacone, Posey attracted notice through his oratory. In the spring of 1892 he gave a commencement address, "The Indian: What of Him?," which was later printed in the *Indian Journal,* a newspaper published in Eufaula. The following year he spoke to another commencement audience on Sequoya, the originator of the Cherokee writing system. This speech was also carried in newspapers, including the *Cherokee Advocate,* the Cherokees' official tribal news publication, and the *Red Man,* the organ of Carlisle Industrial School, a training school for Indian youth in Pennsylvania.

While at Bacone, Posey wrote some poetry, including a curious piece titled "Death of a Window Plant," which ostensibly relates the death by frostbite of a houseplant but metaphorically laments the passing of a race of people – a theme that figures prominently in Posey's later works. Many Indian groups, when transplanted to a "foreign," inimical soil, failed to prosper and died: "I'll dig thy grave, / Inter thee grandly . . . Should all thy race / Thus disappear, / In death forsake the / Soil in which you / Grew, the world would / Then be sad as I." The poem has a dignified tone and an epic quality: "The air was chill, / The leaves were hushed, / The moon in grandeur / Climbed the spangled / Wall of heaven, / When the angel came / That whispers death."

After leaving college in 1895, Posey won a seat in the House of Warriors, the lower chamber of the Creek National Council. He was appointed superintendent of the Creek Orphan Asylum near Okmulgee, the capitol of the Creek Nation, that same year. Thus began a career of public service that was to last until 1902, during which he served as superintendent of education for the Creek Nation, superintendent of Eufaula Boarding School, and superintendent of the Wetumka National School. Posey married Minnie Harris, a young teacher working in Creek schools, on 9 May 1896. They had three children: a son, Yahola, born in 1897; Pachina, another son, who died fifteen months after his birth in 1899; and a daughter, Wynema, born in 1902. It was while he was administering tribal schools that Posey wrote most of his poetry.

The influence of the dominant culture is most obvious in the fixed forms and rhetorical devices of Posey's poetry, elements he could never move beyond the level of clichés. Posey's biographer, Daniel F. Littlefield, thinks that Posey was too much influenced by "American and British romantic poets of the early nineteenth century and their imitators in later decades, such as Bret Harte, Thomas Bailey Aldrich, Joaquin Miller, and James Whitcomb Riley." Like the Romantics, Posey emphasizes the superiority of the natural to the artificial and claims that all things, animate and inanimate, have indestructible spirits. There is nevertheless an impulse in his poems that is distinctly Indian; in fact, the early Romantic writers drew some of their theories from their understanding of the metaphysics of "primitive" people. Posey is sensitive to the same subject matter that appealed to writers such as William Wordsworth, Percy Bysshe Shelley, and John Keats, and his handling of that subject matter is imitative of those poets: among his works one finds verse dedicated to daffodils, robins, morning warblers, and idle breezes. But at the same time there are poems about coyotes, Indian meadowlarks, and crows, as well as odes to Husse Lotka Enhotulle (the West Wind) and Wahilla Enhotulle (the South Wind). Juxtaposed to references to Pan are allusions to Stechupco, the mythological Creek figure who inhabits the forests of America and plays a reed instrument. In a Keatsian manner Posey describes "Night pin[ning] on her dark / Robe with a large bright star"; yet he positions her above the Tulledegas, the mountains near his home at Bald Hill. He writes encomiums to the Creek headmen Crazy Snake and Daniel McIntosh, but he also composes a reflection on a marble medallion of Dante. Crazy Snake is "the noble red man still"; McIntosh is an "Indian brother, true"; while Dante's physiognomy is "such as is not stamped / upon a human face / Once in a thousand years." American Indians respect their outstanding political and religious leaders, so Posey's admiration of what he considers great men is consistent with the Indian tradition from which he comes.

Motifs in Posey's poems that seem atypical for an American Indian writer are world-weariness and a desire for solitude. Lines similar to Alfred Tennyson's "I am aweary, aweary" occur with surprising frequency in the work of so young a poet. In "Twilight" the poet begs: "O Twilight, fold me, let me rest within / Thy dusky wings; / For I am weary, weary." In "The Call of the Wild" he confesses: "I'm tired of the life / In the ways of strife; / Heart-weary, I long / For the river's song." "What I Ask of Life" pleads for no more than a "cottage hid in songbird's neighborhood . . . A spot where coarse souls enter not." This petition seems strange coming from a man who wrote gossip columns in college and later relished attacking the chicanery of politicians, but it is typical of the bifurcation between his public actions and the private sentiments he revealed in his writings.

Posey's early verse expresses his deep feelings for his wife, his children, and his best friend, George Riley Hall. Some of his most tender poetry is for his wife, whom he called Lowena. In "To My Wife" she is the "love, the beauty, and the dreams" that stand "true at my side, silent at my neglect." His children gave meaning to his life: a "house is but a pile of brick or lumber, / Till baby feet have pattered thro' the hall." Hall, a fellow poet, inspired "sweet memories" of shared "joys and griefs." Posey's later works are less sentimental; in them men and women elicit piercingly satiric comments.

Nature is the theme that most often emerges in Posey's poetry. His best lines describe natural phenomena in metaphorical language that allows the reader to make associations with the human world. In "Sunset" one finds: "By coward clouds forgot, / By yonder's sunset glow, / The Day, in battle shot, / Lies bleeding, weak, and low." In "To the Indian Meadow Lark" Posey writes: "Oh! golden-breasted bird of dawn / Through all the bleak days singing on, / Till winter, wooed a captive by thy strain, / Breaks into smiles, and spring is come again." In these examples Posey's use of personification intensifies the Indian concept of the interrelation of all things: clouds take on human characteristics; day becomes a warrior; winter is charmed by the song of the meadowlark.

More often, however, Posey writes at length about the restorative power of nature and its beneficence to man. This theme has Romantic overtones, but it is also in harmony with American Indian assumptions. "A Vision of June" affirms that with the coming of summer the poet's "spirit in . . . largeness grows, / And every thorn is hidden by the rose," while "Song of the Oktahutchee" attests to "the good" the river does. "Trees lean over, glad to hear me flow. / Thro' field and valley, green because of me." Posey's readers would later find those lines quite poignant: Oktahutchee is the Creek name for the North Canadian River, in which the poet drowned.

As Posey matured, his nature descriptions became less contrived. In a passage from an unpublished journal titled "Notes Afield," written on 5 April 1902 while Posey was rowing on the Wewoka River with a friend, he notes seeing "a swamp rabbit sitting shoulder deep in water among the knarled [*sic*] roots of a beech tree as if it were his house. . . . Perhaps he was hiding from dogs or feeding on the tender bark of the beech roots." This passage is certainly more at ease with itself than is "I laid amid the hum of bumblebees, / And O, and O, / Above me, to and fro, / The clover-heads were tossing in the breeze!," which is found in the poem "Trysting in Clover." The change is indicative of his willingness to cast aside the lessons of his youth and proceed according to his own inclinations and judgments.

Posey's wife, Minnie, and their sons, Pachina and Yohola (courtesy of Daniel F. Littlefield Jr.)

A generally accepted belief among American Indians is that there is no sharp division between the material and spiritual realms, and Posey advances this concept in several of his poems. For him, all things are imbued with spirits. "Brook Song" insists that "If you'll but pause and / Listen, listen long, / There're far-off voices / In a wee brook's song." "Flowers" rhetorically asks, "When flowers fade, why does / Their fragrance linger still? / Have they a spirit, too, / That Death can never kill?"

Posey's poetry consistently affirms the bond between human beings and objects of the natural world. In "To a Daffodil" the poet says that "When Death has shut the blue skies out from me, / Sweet Daffodil, / And years roll on without my memory, / Thou'll reach thy tender figures down to mine / of clay, / A true friend still / Although I'll never know thee till the Judgment / Day." The connectedness between humanity and nature is expressed more explicitly in "To Wahilla Enhotulle," where the poet sees the South Wind as both friend and teacher: "Oh, take me, Wind into / Thy confidence, and tell / Me, whispering soft and low, / The secrets of the dell." He petitions Wahilla Enhotulle to give him cosmic understanding and let him join in the "mystic brotherhood" of all natural things. This sentiment, apparently Romantic, is also reflective of the Indian tradition that all things in the universe are connected to, and dependent on, each other; at one time they even shared a common language. Posey's nature poems stress the affinity between humanity and nature and nature's beneficence to human beings, which includes the communication of essential information to them.

Some of the strongest links to the Romantics are Posey's reveries on the poet's function, the ephemeral nature of poetic inspiration, and the futility of human ambition. Posey conceptualizes the poet as one who interprets the mysteries of nature for his fellows and attempts to maintain a state of balance through his knowledge. "What My Soul Would Be" explains that the poet's "soul would be / To harmony [what] woodland valleys are / To echoes." "At the Sirens' Call" depicts a musing poet: "I fancy that I sit beside / The shore of slumbers' phantom sea / And see sweet visions die, and hear / The siren voices calling me. / Am I a shell cast on the shore / . . . To hear and whisper evermore / The music of Eternity?" The poet is marked for an unkind destiny: he "sings but fragments," is designated an "outcast," and is marked by a "blood-stained leaf " to render truth.

Among Posey's best poems are those written in commemoration of notable Indians. "Ode to Sequoyah," perhaps the most rich of Posey's works in its melding of classical and American Indian allusions, was composed in 1899, toward the end of Posey's poetry-writing career. He had first written about Sequoya when he was a student at Bacone, and his interest in the man and his syllabary, which gave the Cherokees the means to preserve their language and, to some extent, their customs and their past, persisted through the years. Like many legendary heroes, Sequoya simply disappeared; he is reported to have died en route to Mexico, where he had gone in search of Cherokees thought to be living there, and to have been buried in an unmarked grave in Mexico. Posey eulogizes him: "Thy genius shaped a dream into a deed. / By cloud-capped summits in the boundless west, / or mighty river rolling to the sea, / Where'er thy footsteps led thee on that quest, / Unknown, rest thee, illustrious Cherokee!"

In 1902 Posey bought and made himself the editor of the *Indian Journal.* Between 1902 and 1908 he wrote the Fus Fixico letters, a series of seventy-three short satiric pieces; most of them were first published in the *Indian Journal,* and they were often picked up by mainstream newspapers, such as the *Saint Louis Republic* and the *Kansas City Star.* The Fus Fixico letters are among the most brilliant of the humorous dialect columns that were published around the turn of the century by many newspapers of the period, both Indian and non-Indian, commenting on national, local, or tribal social and political issues. The Fus Fixico letters anticipate the work of the Cherokee satirist Will Rogers, but their literary merit derives largely from their adherence to American Indian compositional principles.

The Fus Fixico letters revolve around the conversations in Creek dialect of four men: the medicine man Choela, who is replaced in the thirteenth letter by another medicine man, Hotgun Harjo; Tookpafka Micco, a *busk* (ceremonial) ground leader, a kind of informal religious leader; and Kono Harjo and Wolf Warrior, warriors of the Skunk and Wolf clans, respectively. These men represent the holy medicine, the power that heals, balances humanity with nature, and orders the universe. The holy medicine works by means of special words, but the efficacy of the words is enhanced by the use of fire, water (sometimes saliva), and tobacco. The narrator, Fus Fixico, whose name means either "Warrior Bird" or "Heartless Bird," does not participate in the dialogue but assumes the role of a *yohola* (echo), the person in Creek society who traditionally circulates important information to the citizenry. Like a bird, he flits from place to place, relating the words of others; like a heartless warrior, he defends his occupation, although in a humorous, parodic way. In the letters Indian and non-Indian politicians are judged according to traditional Indian standards and are found wanting. The meretricious and the transitory pass in rapid succession in front of an Indian panel that represents the enduring dignity, power, and truth of the old ways. The "grafters" and the "pie eaters" have their day in court. They give their "own excuse for being" but eventually fall short in the presence of integrity and the eternal verities.

Choela and Hotgun are modeled on medicine men of the same names who were acquaintances of Posey's. Choela means "dying deer"; his name suggests his own demise as well as the extinction of the Creeks' traditional meat and leather supply. Hotgun takes Choela's place and becomes the principal character in the letters. *Hotgun* is the disguised Creek word *hvtke,* which means "white" and is pronounced *hutcun.* Thus, Hotgun's name points to his holy function as a man of purity and peace, symbolized by the color white. While Choela practices medicine in the ancient way, Hotgun is depicted primarily as a speaker and moralizer; his shamanistic function is referred to only obliquely. The replacement of Choela by Hotgun reflects the decline of medicine men as practicing shamans and their acquisition of more modern roles as religious leaders.

Tookpafka Micco is also based on a real person, a man who was prominent in the Creek National Council. *Micco* is a Muskogean word designating a leader; *Tookpafka* means "foxfire," the fungus that produces a glow in rotten logs. Tookpafka Micco's name, therefore, is emblematic of the council fire of a busk ground, a kind of holy fire around which stomp dances are performed. Kono Harjo's name literally means "outstanding skunk warrior." He and Wolf Warrior, both fictitious characters, are the defenders of the old ways. They rarely speak; they "was pay close attention" or "grunt an spit behin' the backlog."

The four men "drink sofky . . . an' talk long time over they pipes by the fireside." *Sofky* is a Creek staple made from corn. Boiled, it is soup; fermented, it is an intoxicant. Corn is more than sustenance to southeastern Indians: it is symbolic of the earth and annual rejuvenation. The annual Green Corn Ceremony is the most significant celebration of the year for members of the Five Tribes: it is a time for spiritual and physical cleansing, for retelling the histories of the nations, and for honoring renewed existence. The names of the four men featured in the Fus Fixico letters are all busk ground, or ritual, names and indicate that ritual meanings are being evoked. The constant presence of corn, tobacco, and saliva around the men reinforces the concept of medicine, or ritual ceremony, and their participation in it. As the two holy men and two warriors talk, eat corn, smoke, and ritually make offerings to the fire by spitting into it – thus acknowledging their gratefulness to the sun, the giver of life – they compare personages of the day to people venerated by the Creeks. Invariably, the former are found wanting: "Well, so Hotgun and Tookpafka Micco and Wolf Warrior and Kono Harjo was all happened to meet up together last Sunday at the Weogufky stomp ground and was weighed Bony Parts in the balance and found him whitewashing." ("Bony Parts" refers to Charles J. Bonaparte, a federal investigator searching for graft in the operations of the Dawes Commission.)

Early in the nineteenth century the U.S. government had set aside the area that is now Oklahoma as a vast reservation and had moved many tribes there from other parts of the country. By the later part of the century non-Indians were clamoring for access to the land, and pressure was put on Congress to open it for settlement by whites. The formal leasing of the Cherokee Outlet to Texas cattle ranchers in 1883 had been followed in 1887 by the General Allotment Act, which broke up tribally owned land in nearly all parts of the United States except Indian Territory. In 1898 the Curtis Act had extended the General Allotment Act to Indian Territory. The law reassigned tribal lands to individual Indians, who could then sell their portions. The allotment acts were seen as a triumph for assimilationists, who believed that if Indians abandoned their

Posey in 1905 with the pipe of the Creek statesman Yadeka Harjo, whose death the following year was the subject of one of Posey's best poems (Archives and Manuscripts Division of the Oklahoma Historical Society)

practice of communal ownership of land, their systems of tribal government, and their native religions and languages, they would begin to act like members of the dominant society: they would be "civilized." The allotment acts plunged Indians into a period of cultural dissolution that did not begin to turn around until the late 1960s, when tribes started to reclaim their languages and sociopolitical systems.

The ownership of land in severalty became a subject of great debate among members of the Five Tribes, and it is one of the main topics of discussion in the Fus Fixico letters. Sentiment was divided along progressive and conservative lines. Indian progressives believed that it was impossible to maintain the ancient ways in the face of modern advancements and that Indians should be accorded the same privileges enjoyed by others in the United States. Often educated in the Euro-American tradition, they found it humiliating to live in their own country as second-class citizens who could not vote, buy alcoholic beverages, own property, or conduct business on par with non-Indians. Conservatives, on the other hand, wanted the federal government to honor the treaties under which the tribes had been removed to Indian Territory and allow Indians to live with the social, political, and religious systems they had created there; the conservatives thought enough concessions had been made to "progress."

The first letter, published in the *Indian Journal* on 24 October 1902, opens with a greeting in the Creek language: "Un Hesse Mahhe, Mr. Editor, Toyets Kat" (You are my real friend, Mr. Editor). The use of Creek instead of English clues the reader that what follows will be serious: Creek is the language of the ritual ground and the practice of medicine. Fus goes on to note that he is ill. He had taken his dogs out 'possum hunting and caught "nothing but bad cold"; he feels as though he has been in the "calaboose all night in Eufaula." The writer is, thus, out of balance with the universe. His head "is almost busted," and he "can't breathe." The next paragraph spells out the political problem, which is analogous to the cold in his head: his failure to receive his allotment deed. When all eligible Creeks received the deeds mandated by the Dawes Commission, they could then "shut up that old council house" and "rent it to some mens like the Dawes commission that's got lots a time and money from Washington." When all the land had been divided, the Creek Nation would cease to exist as a sovereign body. In this letter Posey sets up the tension that will characterize all the letters: the old ways versus the new, the holy versus the profane.

In the second letter Fus has been to Choela, a medicine man, and Choela has cured him. "Old Choela was sure good doctor. He was just take his grubbing hoe and go out in the woods and dig up lots medicine anywhere. Then he was take his cane and blow in the medicine pot long time and sing little song with it, too, like at busk ground. . . . he make you so well you just want whole lot sofky." The medicine that Choela makes tastes good and does not "stink like white man medicine." Choela's medicine not only makes the patient well, but it also makes him want to return to the native traditions symbolized by the sofky. The second letter ends with Fus noting that Tookpafka Micco "was stay all night with me when he get back from council. . . . He got heap influence too and make them other Injins vote like he say all time nearly." As his name implies, Tookpafka represents the council fire, the central element of the Creek religion, social organization, and government. Without the fire, Creek traditional life cannot proceed. The fire must be tended and cared for in a ritual manner, and the spot on which the ritual deliberations are performed cannot be changed at will. The bond between the fire and the earth must not be severed until another system has been chosen and is in place.

Tookpafka is the presence around which the others group. He rarely speaks, and when he does it is usually to ask questions that keep the medicine man's conversation going. Occasionally he summarizes an argument, and he always gets to the unvarnished truth. For example, his humorous comment on the infamous ink-bottle throwing, fisticuffs, and general mayhem of the first Oklahoma legislative sessions, described by Hotgun as a "prize ring," is classic irony: "I don't think my long experience in Creek council was train me for strenuous work like that. In the Creek council all I had to do was smoke an' spit an' hol' up my han' to vote if I was awake."

The issue most often discussed in the Fus Fixico letters is the impending creation of the state of Oklahoma. When it became evident that statehood was inevitable, the next pressing question was whether Oklahoma would be admitted to the Union as one state or two. In 1889 the central part of Indian Territory, known as the Unassigned Lands, had been opened to non-Indian settlement, and that area, together with land assigned to tribes other than the Five Tribes, became known as the Oklahoma Territory. Generally, those who resided in Oklahoma Territory wanted to be admitted to the Union along with the Five Tribes' reservations; but, to preserve some measure of self-determination, the residents of those reservations petitioned Congress to come into the Union as the separate state of Sequoyah. Posey, a progressive, at first favored single statehood. In 1903 he sold his newspaper and accepted a position with the Dawes Commission registering Creeks for tribal rolls and allotment portions. As he registered the recalcitrant Snakes, he became convinced that dual statehood was necessary. Six of the seven Fus Fixico letters published in 1905 advocate dual statehood; in one of them Posey writes that Oklahoma and Indian Territory "didn't had nothing in common, unless, maybe so, it was a weakness for firewater."

The Fus Fixico letters do not always correspond to Posey's own political positions; Posey was more progressive than any of his characters and was convinced that Indians had to "advance." Although he admired the tenacity of the Snake faction and described their leader, Chitto Harjo, as "a noble red man" who should be exalted, he believed that it was futile to cling to the old ways and that it was to the Indians' advantage to gain political leverage and deal with the existing system on its own terms, no matter how distasteful it might be to do so. At no time, however, was Posey ever misled about the nature of the new order. Hotgun describes the quarrels in the Oklahoma Constitutional Convention over which name to choose for the deity in the document's preamble:

> Hotgun says, Well, so, they couldn't decide what name to give the Great Spirit, an' that bring up lots o' talk an' extra expense. Look like the Great Spirit was a stranger in the convention, an' non o' the delegates could remember His name. Boss Haskell he think it was God, but no one was second his motion. An' Henry Asp he think it was the Supreme Ruler o' the Universe, but no one was agreed with him. An' Alfalfa Bill he say he believe it was Divine Providence, but there was no second to his motion neither. Tookpafka Micco he smoke . . . an' say, "Well so, Alfalfa Bill an' Boss Haskell an' Henry Asp could settled their differences an' saved lots o' work for the printer an' give general satisfaction if they had recognized Confucius for the Chinaman, an' Budda for the Hindu, an' Mohamet for the Turk, an' Saint Patrick for the Irishman, an' the totem pole for the Eskimo, an' the almighty dollar for the American."

Here Posey represents the Great Spirit, the Indian God, as the norm opposing the white man's fictions and uncertainties. The passage also demonstrates the non-Indian's factionalism, lack of cohesion, and, in the case of the Americans, greed.

Posey's satire is hard-hitting. One of his favorite targets is the congressmen and Washington bureaucrats who occasionally toured Oklahoma to assess the condition of the natives. These visits were incredibly superficial: on one trip through Oklahoma, en route to the Far West for a hunting expedition, President Theodore Roosevelt made stops of two to ten minutes at several towns located on railroads; at other towns his train merely slowed down. In reference to an eight-minute stop Roosevelt made in Muskogee, one of the largest cities in the territory, Hotgun paraphrases Matthew 19:14: "Well, so 'cause the Great White Father from Washington was suffered 'em to come unto 'im on the grand stand, while he was showing his teeth and shaking the Big Stick before the multitude up to Muskogee." By turning biblical phrasing against Roosevelt, this passage shows the resentment that Indians felt toward Washington for such condescension. The allusion to a biblical text, even in a parodic way, also underlines the seriousness of the work. It is a subtle way of equating the Indian canon with wisdom literature or "truth."

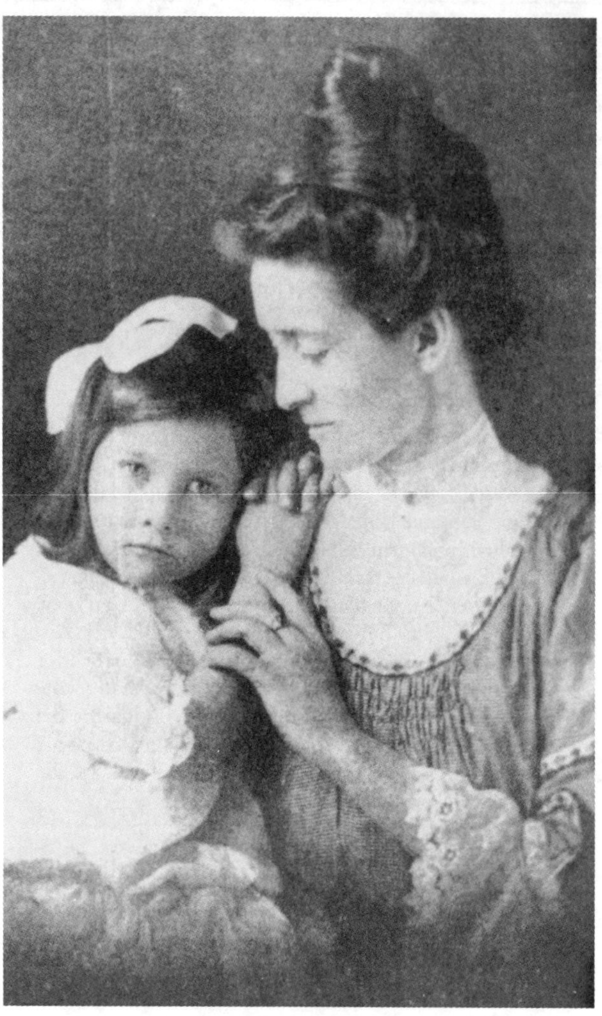

Minnie Posey with her daughter, Wynema, in 1910

There are times, however, when the letters are not bitingly satiric but lyrical: "The old squirrel dog he wag his tail and peep in the kitchen and the bees grumble in the flowers and the south wind was blow over the hills from Kialegee and make it cool under the catapa [*sic*] tree" (letter 50); " . . . while the locusts was singing in the blackjack trees . . . [and] the women folks was pounding sofky corn" (letter 55). Some passages in the letters are whimsical; others are witty. Cotton is the "fleecy staple"; home brew is "the home-made"; and Christians are those who will "eat chicken in Zion." Spring is the "time to go barefooted and quote poetry and spark some widow woman that was had a good family history on the Loyal Creek roll." In the United States "Everybody was created free and equal – subject to later developments. . . . We [are] the cream a civilization – if you don't mind the whey." After a conference called by the principal chiefs of the Five Tribes to discuss dual statehood, Hotgun declares that "the Injin has spoken. Long time ago he give a war whoop and go on the warpath; this time he call a convention and go on record."

Posey's punning with names is one of the most amusing and telling features of the Fus Fixico letters. In a kind of warrior strategy, this wordplay intensifies the seriousness of the letters while at the same time diverting attention away from it. For the most part, it is the names of non-Indian characters that are parodied. Their appellations are "earned names," sobriquets conferred on the basis of their actions. Conversely, the names of Indians that are mentioned are primarily busk ground or powerful ritual names – Yaha Tustanugga, Nocose Yahola, Effa Ematha, Woxie Harjochee. By corrupting English names, Posey minimizes their power. Roosevelt is President Rooster Feather; Secretary of the Interior Ethan Allen Hitchcock is Secretary Itscocked; Tams Bixby, chairman of the Dawes Commission, is Tams Big Pie; J. Blair Shoenfelt, Indian agent at Muskogee, is Shoamfat; W. F. Rampendahl, the Muskogee city attorney, is Ram-it-in-all. Some Indian politicians' names are satirized, but the humor here is kind: Choctaw chief Green McCurtain is Chief Make Certain; Cherokee chief Thomas M. Buffington is Chief Puffingtown; and Chickasaw chief Palmer Mosely is Chief Mostly.

Modern readers will be disturbed by the racial slurs directed at African Americans in the letters; Creek freedmen and tribal members of African descent are often subjects of Posey's ire. The white person who comes off best is Cornelius Foley of Eufaula, referred to as "Connie" in the letters. Foley was a delegate to Congress from Indian Territory and enjoyed a good reputation among his native constituents; when he ran for mayor of Eufaula, only one vote was cast for his opponent. As Hotgun explains, "We Injins was kind a raise Connie and maybe so he do what's right." His name is the only non-Indian one that is never parodied, in sharp contrast with those of other local non-Indians such as Pliny Soper (Plenty So Far) or Clarence B. Douglas (Clarence Bee Dug Last). White women, particularly Alice Robertson, a missionary, and the unnamed trollops whose cologne wafts through the various constitutional conventions, are objects of criticism. Indian women silently pound corn and stay out of view.

Rich in biblical and classical allusions, the letters represent the demise of one world and the emergence of another. They remain surprisingly current: many of the persons named in the letters are the ancestors of individuals now living in Oklahoma and functioning in the new world Posey so aptly described. Although the old council house of the Creeks is now a museum, their council fires are still burning, and the old ways have been preserved in the hearts of a few. Descendants of Crazy Snake still meet at Hickory Ground and Weogufky; they talk, smoke, spit in the fire, and let the politicians in Muskogee carry on as usual.

Posey's best poem, "Hotgun on the Death of Yadeka Harjo," was written in 1908, the year Posey himself died. The poem captures the deep feelings occasioned in Posey by Harjo's death in 1906, and it reflects the technical confidence of the writer's developed style. Harjo's father, who had fought with Andrew Jackson during the War of 1812, had lived to see Jackson force the Creeks into ceding twenty-five million acres of land in the Treaty of Fort Jackson in 1814, following the Battle of Horseshoe Bend. Yadeka Harjo had come into Oklahoma during the removal, had served in the Union army during the Civil War, and had spent his final days as a Creek statesman; he had lived to see the Creek Nation transplanted and then dissolved. His death is related by Hotgun to Tookpafka Micco, Wolf Warrior, and Kono Harjo. The solemn tone of the poem, the extensive use of assonance, and the slow rhythm created by the dialect create a measure of dignity and stark beauty rarely found in American Indian poetry:

"Well so," Hotgun he say,
    "My ol'-time frien', Yadeka Harjo, he
Was died the other day,
An' they was no ol'-timer left but me."

"Hotulk Emathla he
    Was go to be good Injin long time 'go,
An' Woxie Harjochee
    Been dead ten years or twenty, maybe so.
All had to die at las',
    I live long time, but now my days are few;
'Fore long poke-weeds an' grass
    Be growin' all aroun' my grave-house, too."

Wolf Warrior he listen close,
    An' Kono Harjo pay close 'tention, too;
Tookpafka Micco he almos'
    Let his pipe go out a time or two.

Themes of death and intimations of death are significant features of Posey's work. In "A Vision of Rest" he beholds "ashen branches tossing to and fro" and knows that "the wind is rude and cold." Presumably to his wife he writes, "Upon Love's sea, our barques shall sail / No more together . . . The cruel Fates, at last, sweetheart, / Our love must sever, / Must furl our sails, drift us apart / For aye and ever." In "To Our Baby, Laughing," he says: "If I were dead, sweet one . . . I know you'd laugh the same . . . And pat my pallid face / With chubby hands and fair." In an ironic coincidence, the English poet Posey chose to emulate and to eulogize was Shelley, whose boat went down in the Bay of Lerici in 1822 in much the same way that Posey's boat capsized in the North Canadian River on 27 May 1908. Posey hung onto a young tree for several hours; when he tried to grab a rope thrown to him by rescuers, he lost his grip and drowned. His poem "My Fancy" has struck many readers as eerily premonitory: "Why do trees along the river / Lean so far out o'er the tide? / Very wise men tell me why, but / I am never satisfied; / And so I keep my fancy still, / That trees lean out to save / The drowning from the clutches of / The cold, remorseless wave." Posey's widow published his collected poems in 1910; the Fus Fixico letters were published in book form by Littlefield and Carol Hunter in 1993.

Bibliographies:

Daniel F. Littlefield and James W. Parins, *A Biobibliography of Native American Writers, 1772–1924* (Metuchen, N.J.: Scarecrow Press, 1981), pp. 135–140;

Donald DeWitt, ed., *American Indian Resource Materials in the Western History Collections, University of Oklahoma* (Norman: University of Oklahoma Press, 1990), items 165, 326, 335, 379.

Biography:

Daniel F. Littlefield, *Alex Posey: Creek Poet, Journalist, and Humorist* (Lincoln: University of Nebraska Press, 1992).

Papers:

Posey's papers are in the Alexander Posey Collection at the Thomas Gilcrease Institute of American History and Art, Tulsa, Oklahoma.

John Rollin Ridge

(19 March 1827 – 5 October 1867)

James W. Parins
University of Arkansas at Little Rock

BOOKS: *The Life and Adventures of Joaquín Murieta, the Celebrated California Bandit,* as Yellow Bird (San Francisco: W. B. Cooke, 1854; revised and enlarged, San Francisco: F. MacCrellish, 1871);

Poems (San Francisco: Henry Payot, 1868).

SELECTED PERIODICAL PUBLICATIONS – UNCOLLECTED: "North American Indians," *Hesperian,* 8 (March 1862): 1–18; 8 (April 1862): 51–60; 8 (May 1862): 99–109.

John Rollin Ridge's literary work has been regarded as a prime example of early Native American writing in English. His novel and poetry are widely studied in literature courses and American Indian studies programs. His journalistic writing, especially his pieces on American Indians, is less widely known but is important because of its perspective. Ridge's *The Life and Adventures of Joaquín Murieta, the Celebrated California Bandit* (1854) is considered to be the first novel written in California, as well as the first written by an American Indian. *The Life and Adventures of Joaquín Murieta* was extremely popular and was widely pirated. Versions appeared as books, were serialized in periodicals, and were translated into foreign languages. Adaptations appeared in verse, and at least one motion picture was based on Ridge's story. Although many versions were produced in the nineteenth century, others have appeared more recently, including Pablo Neruda's 1967 drama *Fulgor y Muerta de Joaquín Murieta.*

In 1827, the year Ridge was born on 19 March to John and Sarah Bird Northrup Ridge, the Cherokee Nation was in a state of turmoil. Earlier in the century some Cherokees had deserted their ancestral homelands in eastern Tennessee, western North Carolina, and northern Georgia to immigrate to western Arkansas and later to Indian Territory. The majority, however, were determined to remain, despite the pressure of white settlers and the federal

John Rollin Ridge (courtesy of the Western History Collections, University of Oklahoma Library)

government, who wanted the Cherokees to leave their lands and immigrate to territories in the West that had not been reached by the advancing frontier. Ridge was born into an important Cherokee family; both his father and his grandfather, Major Ridge, were leaders in the tribe, and they, like the majority of the Cherokee Nation, at first opposed leaving their lands and moving to the wilds of the West. As time went on, however, they and other educated Cherokees began to regard such resistance as futile. They negotiated with the federal government, made the best bargain they thought they could, and in 1835 signed a treaty that ceded their lands in the East for land in what is now Oklahoma. This began the time in Cherokee history known as the Trail of Tears (1838–1839), during which U.S. troops forcibly removed the majority of the tribe, most of whom did not agree with the treaty the Ridges had signed. In 1839 Ridge's father was dragged from his bed and brutally assassinated in front of his family. Ridge's grandfather and his uncle Elias Boudinot, the first editor of the *Cherokee Phoenix,* were killed on the same day.

Ridge's family fled to Arkansas and later moved to Massachusetts. Ridge's education was a rich one, especially in literature and history. He began writing poetry and essays as a young man, even as he settled down to a life as a farmer and rancher first on the border of Arkansas, then in Missouri, and later in the Cherokee Nation. He married a white woman, Elizabeth Wilson, and looked forward to a life in which he would rebuild the social and economic prominence his family had lost since his father's death. In 1849, however, Cherokee affairs again intruded. Ridge was involved in a fight over a horse with a man from the Cherokee faction still hostile to his family. Ridge shot and killed his adversary and was forced to flee. Early the next year he joined a wagon train for the California gold fields, never to return to the Cherokee Nation.

He tried gold mining in California, but finding the work hard and unprofitable, he soon found employment as a writer. He was first a reporter from the gold rush towns, then editor of several of the newspapers springing up in northern California. At the same time, he was writing poetry and publishing it in newspapers and in San Francisco literary journals. His reputation as a writer grew, and it was greatly enhanced when he published *The Life and Adventures of Joaquín Murieta, the Celebrated California Bandit.* This romance was widely read and even cited as historical data later in the century. In the years immediately preceding and during the Civil War, Ridge edited several California newspapers, allying himself with the anti-Abolitionist Democrats, and he editorialized in his party's favor. He wrote and published articles on Native Americans in his later years, as well as some poetry.

Most of Ridge's poetry, however, was written in Arkansas and during his early years in California. The early work is romantic, often autobiographical and personal. Much of it deals with nature and the poet's reaction to the natural environment. Ridge's experiences with the environment often take on the spiritual or transcendental qualities seen in the works of other writers of the time. These special or enlightening encounters with nature are most often the result of the poet's imaginative powers.

An example is "To a Star Seen at Twilight," which is important for its assertion of the power of the imagination. It is also a declaration of Ridge's public persona. The poem's structure is tripartite. In the first section, lines 1–16, the persona describes a solitary star in the twilight sky, "companionless in light," peerless and aloof. Separate from earth, the star is part of another reality; it seems to have an eternality and immutability not found in mortal realism. After the speaker describes the star, he begins to meditate on the similarity between his own spirit and the distant object. Both are isolated, far from the rest of their kind. But there the similarity ends. The spirit of the persona, anchored by his own mortality, cannot match the pureness and nobility of the star. Although his spirit can partake of the transcendental experience, it cannot as yet enter the eternal world permanently as the star does.

At this point Ridge makes a statement about his own poetic vision and, by implication, the ability of all poets. He wishes "all people could their bosoms drink / Thy loveliness and light like me." Poets are able to make their mystical perceptions visible to common people. The poet's role, for Ridge, is to use his power to translate his own experiences – transcendental or otherwise – to his readers. The poet is to re-create, as far as possible, his own insights into the universe surrounding us all. Thus Ridge establishes himself as one of the seers, one of the priests of nature. In the third section the personal exults in the star's isolation: "Thou are the throne / Of thy own spirit, star! / . . . 'Tis great to be alone!"

Many of Ridge's poetic works echo those by other writers of the nineteenth century. An example is "A Night Scene," reminiscent of the odes of John Keats. It follows the structure of the Keatsian ode and contains some rather standard romantic metaphors found throughout the poetry of William Wordsworth, Percy Bysshe Shelley, and George Gordon, Lord Byron.

As the poem opens, the persona waits for that Wordsworthian "impulse from the vernal wood":

> I sit
> And muse alone – the time and the place are fit –
> And summon spirits from the blue profound.
> That answer me and through my vision flit.

At this point his vision has not yet come, but in the next stanza it appears in the guise of a maiden, "a beauteous being" "with hair night-hued, and brow

Ridge's parents, John and Sarah Ridge (courtesy of the Western History Collections, University of Oklahoma Library)

and bosom white." She seems to float in the soft light and shadows of evening, and for the moment all is still. Then he hears a heavenly sound whose "tones are filling up the air, / That brings them, with the star-light blended now, / And wavelet murmuring from below." The maiden's voice and harp are making this nightingale song, and the music lures him to her. He knows there is an abyss between them, yet still he reaches out for the momentary glimpse, that fleeting perception of immortality: "But o'er that gulf my spirit loves to lean," he says. With his "spirit bride" he senses a connection with the divine, if only in promise; but the tryst if futile, and it is not long before he is called back to his own reality. The poem ends on a plaintive note:

Fair words, like ripples o'er the watery deep
When breezes softly o'er the surface play,
In circles one by one ye stretch away,
Till, lost to human vision's wildest sweep
Our souls are left to darkness and dismay.

The poem follows a familiar romantic three-part movement. It opens with the persona outside the vision, isolated in his own humanity, but clearly reaching beyond himself. In the second part comes the connection of the persona and the object of his imagination. But the coming together is temporary, and in the third part the persona finds himself alone again, musing on the experience. Ridge's diction and imagery are typically romantic as well. Obvious examples are his use of the "watery deep" to convey the vast immutability of eternity and the references to the breezes that play on both the surface of the water and on the human soul. The form the vision takes, too, is important, and recalls the ghostly maidens of poems by Edgar Allan Poe, Shelley, and Keats.

Ridge's best-known poem, "Mount Shasta," closely resembles Shelley's "Mont Blanc" (1853) in its theme, use of natural description, diction, and even meter. Both poems are written in blank verse with indiscriminate rhyme. The diction in many cases is strikingly similar. For example, Ridge's "vast Reflector in / The dome of heaven" resembles Shelley's "infinite dome / Of Heaven." Shasta as a "monarch mountain" and "Imperial midst the less heights" compares with Mont Blanc towering about "Its subject mountains." Both poems deal with the perception of eternity in the face of the all-consuming flux of time. The mountain peaks in both cases symbolize the ultimate reality that stands behind and occasionally intrudes into the transient and mortal world. Mount Shasta is seen as "the great material symbol of eternal / Things!" in much the same way as the Alpine pinnacle is depicted as the immutable in a changing universe.

Many of Ridge's early poems deal with love. Some are conventional, describing unspecified women, but others are clearly autobiographical and personal. An example of the latter is a poem addressed to his wife, written on his trek across the plains to California. "To Lizzie" shows that Ridge recognized, valued, and missed her calming influence, especially after he was forced to leave her behind in Arkansas. The poem also expresses his image of himself as a Cain figure, a defiant exile who roams the world far from home.

His self-image is revealed in another poem that is perhaps a romanticized version of his and Lizzie's courtship. "The Stolen White Girl" tells of a "wild half-breed" who takes a beautiful white girl captive, not by means of the usual weapons and bonds, but by his own attractiveness. If the poem does present the self-portrait it seems to, Ridge saw himself as a romantic hero – a dashing, passionate adventurer.

In "The Harp of Broken Strings" several themes emerge, the chief one being isolation. Written shortly after Ridge's arrival in California, the poem's narrator describes himself as "a stranger in a stranger land," following again the romantic-exile motif. He recognizes his own psychic instability when he says he takes a perverse delight in his misery. His only solace seems to be his ability to conjure up the image of his beloved, thus bringing him some "delight," although it often is of the perverse variety. But implied here, too, is the threat of losing this power, since his harp bears broken strings, implying the loss of youth, potential, and opportunity. This threat of loss is often seen in the work of other romantic poets.

"The Still Small Voice" is another poem written in the romantic tradition, in which he assesses his situation as an outcast. Here he comments on the twin forces of fate and history that he believes govern his life. The narrator asserts that wherever he goes, whatever he does, he hears a voice within him saying, "Too late! too late! the doom is set, the die is cast." His every action, he believes, has been ordained in the past; his present and future are ruled by his history. Applied to Ridge's own life, this theory is correct. His preoccupation with revenge, his ambition to become a successful man, and his chronic financial instability all had their genesis in two key events in Ridge's past: the assassinations of John and Major Ridge and the related killing of David Kell. In this poem, as in "The Harp of Broken Strings," the narrator seems to relish his despondency and the hopelessness of his situation; perhaps like a Byronic hero he considers that he is being given special attention by Fate.

"A Cherokee Love Song" and "Song – Sweet Indian Maid" are traditional invitational poems in which the speaker urges his love to escape with him into a bower of bliss. In "Song – Sweet Indian Maid" an Indian woman is asked to accompany the narrator on a journey on the river to an island he knows where they will be alone and may do as they please. A similar situation exists in "A Cherokee Love Song," but this time the woman invited on the canoe trip is white. As in the other poem, Nature is cooperative, even, as the narrator points out, approving of the tryst. It is interesting to note that in the posthumous volume of his poetry – edited by his wife – "A Cherokee Love Song" with its white heroine is included, while "Song – Sweet Indian Maid" is not. As he does in the other love verse, in the invitational poems Ridge uses traditional language, imagery, conceits and exaggeration, and structure.

While Ridge was able to establish his literary reputation in California through the publication of poems in newspapers and San Francisco literary journals, it was his novel that spread his fame. Shortly after he arrived in California, the newspapers were full of reports of Mexican bandits stealing livestock, holding up businesses, and waylaying travelers. Some of the bandits organized into large bands and became well known; one, however, surpassed all the others in the popular imagination, Joaquín Murieta, whom Ridge called the "Rinaldo Rinaldini of California." Murieta became the scourge of the state, according to newspaper accounts. Such was his reported prowess that he seemed able to be in two places at once, robbing a saloon in one town as he terrorized miners in another. He robbed both whites and Asians but refrained from molesting Mexicans or other Spanish Americans. In return he was protected by members of the Spanish-speaking population, who provided him with hideouts and refused to cooperate with the authorities trying to catch him.

Murieta's career spanned three years, from 1851 through 1853. Newspaper accounts and purported interviews with the bandit provide a sketchy account of his life and the events that led him into banditry. He reportedly had fought in the Mexican War as one of the Jurate guerrillas. He moved to Los Angeles in 1846 and fell in love with Rosita Felix, whose father opposed Murieta's display of affection. The couple consequently eloped and moved to Shaw's Flat, where Murieta mined for gold. Soon a group of Americans told him that Mexicans were not allowed to mine in the area. When Murieta protested, he was beaten and his wife was insulted – in some versions Rosita was raped in front of her husband. Murieta started mining in another spot but was forced off that claim, as well. According to the tradition, he tried gambling for a living, setting up a monte game at Murphy's Flat. But there, too, he ran into trouble with Americans who tried to run him out of the camp. Finally, Murieta was unjustly accused of stealing by a mob who probably seized upon the first Mexican they could find. He was summarily judged guilty, tied to a tree, and flogged. In one version of the story, Murieta's half-brother was hanged by the American mob. After this episode Murieta, who said he had liked Americans until he moved to California, vowed to retaliate. He organized his outlaw band, drawing on desperadoes such as the notorious Manuel García, or Three-Finger Jack, and began his campaign of revenge. It was not long before Murieta became well known as a bandit and killer.

In response to Murieta's activities the citizens of California hired Capt. Harry Love, a Texan who had been a deputy sheriff in Los Angeles County, to bring the bandit down. Love easily recruited twenty men at Quartzburgh in Mariposa County and set out armed with pistols, rifles, and Bowie knives to capture or kill the bandits. For two months these men, known as the California Rangers, traveled around the area chasing bandits, recovering stolen livestock, and keeping the peace. In July 1853 they came across a group of Mexicans camped on a creek and recognized a man they thought to be Murieta. A fight ensued and four bandits were killed. Among the fallen were Murieta and Three-Finger Jack. Two of the band were captured and others escaped, but the rangers had done their job.

To authenticate their victory they decapitated Murieta and García. García's mutilated hand was included for good measure. Two of the rangers were dispatched to Millerton carrying their grisly cargo in a flour sack; their orders were to find a preservative for the heads and hand. On the way, García's head began to deteriorate in the summer sun and was discarded. When the rangers reached Millerton, they deposited their trophies in a keg of whiskey; later, the head and hand were transferred into a large glass jar of spirits. The rangers brought the jar back to Sacramento after obtaining affidavits at Quartzburgh and Stockton that the head was, indeed, Murieta's. They collected their reward and ninety days' pay; later the legislature rewarded them with an extra $5,000.

Ridge lived and traveled in the region where Murieta had operated. According to a report, Murieta had a sister in Marysville whom he visited frequently in 1850 and 1851, when Ridge was in the area. It is likely that Ridge heard the stories of Murieta's exploits and read about him in the newspapers, especially when the sensational details of the Love expedition were published. Ridge had already launched his writing career, having had both poetry and prose published in various periodicals. Murieta's tale was a ready subject, since by this time Ridge was thoroughly familiar with the background of the disputes between the "Americans" and "foreigners"; he could provide a good sense of the setting from his travels in the area; and he knew people upon whom he could model his characters. As for the plot, it had already been supplied by the bandits and Love's rangers. Ridge knew a good story when he saw it.

Another major factor in his decision to write the story was a problem that he had grappled with before and that would haunt him in the future: a shortage of money. With much of California buzzing about Murieta's exploits as reported in often-conflicting newspaper accounts, the possibility of offering the whole story to an audience hungry for it must have seemed a financial opportunity too good to pass up. Finally, Murieta himself must have fascinated Ridge. Here was a man who had tried to live peacefully despite wrongs inflicted on his family and friends. Murieta's only crime at first was that he did not belong to the faction in power. Driven to the brink by his enemies, he reacted violently. This action forced him into exile, where his intelligence and courage let him revenge himself on his persecutors. He was admired by his own people and feared by his enemies. In many ways Murieta's early history resembled that of the writer who was to immortalize him; his later career had to appeal to Ridge's deep thirst for revenge. More important, in Murieta, Ridge had found a kindred soul with a similar personality and motivation.

The Life and Adventures of Joaquín Murieta, the Celebrated California Bandit is not pure history, but it is not pure fiction, either. It is more like modern-day novels such as Truman Capote's *In Cold Blood* (1966), productions based on fact but liberally sprinkled with embellishments to titillate the audience. There is no doubt that Murieta's story was meant to be sensational. That Ridge wanted a best-seller is clear; money was a prime motivation, and his quest for literary fame was a close second.

As for the historical part of the tale, Ridge gathered his basic information from newspaper stories of the day. The major episodes in the book had been reported, reprinted, and rehashed in the local press. The accuracy of the press accounts is questionable, however. It seems unlikely that one man with twenty followers could have committed all the crimes with which Murieta was charged. More likely, he got the blame for what other bandits were doing as well. Since Ridge relied to a large extent on contemporary newspaper accounts, it is likely that some of his details were inaccurate, no matter how conscientious he had been in his research or how dedicated he was to historical accuracy.

That Ridge embellished the basic story is beyond doubt. For example, he records conversations he never could have heard. In one instance Murieta and his men come across a party of young American hunters. Although the Americans have not threatened the bandits, Murieta suspects they have recognized him and feels his only recourse is to kill them to prevent their reporting his presence in the area. When he tells the hunters what is in store, one of them, a young man from Arkansas, comes forth and bravely addresses the bandit captain. He promises not to reveal the group's encounter with Murieta and furthermore vows to shoot any of his companions who attempt to do so. The outlaw, taken with the man's bravery, allows the hunters to leave unharmed. Ridge comments: "I have never learned that the young man, or any of his party, broke their singular compact" – without addressing the problem of how the author learned of the episode. Even if one gives credence to Ridge's claim that he interviewed people acquainted with Murieta, the verbatim reports of whole conversations smack of artistic license.

As Ridge describes his hero, Murieta bears a strong physical resemblance to his biographer. The author's portrayal of Murieta's situation before his troubles with the Americans show him as having built a comfortable residence for his wife and himself and as ready to settle down to a life of marital bliss. This happy scene is broken up by hostile forces. Murieta and Rosita's early life is analogous to that of Ridge and his wife before the 1849 shooting incident. It is hard to tell whether Ridge discovered similarities between himself and Murieta in his research for the book or created the bandit character in his own image.

Ridge's book was popular with the public and the literati of the time. In addition, important nineteenth-century historians, such as Hubert Howe Bancroft and Theodore H. Hittell, apparently believing Ridge's claim of authenticity for his work, extracted information on Murieta from Ridge's book and cited it in footnotes. Ridge's story, then, passed not only into the popular imagination but also into the history books. Ridge finally received the respect for which he yearned, but not until decades after his death. The profit he expected from the book never developed in his lifetime.

Ridge's wife, Elizabeth Wilson Ridge (courtesy of The Bancroft Library)

In his later years, up to his death on 5 October 1867, Ridge wrote little other than journalistic pieces in his role as newspaper editor. The verse he did write was decidedly different from his early work. His significant later works include "Poem," "The Atlantic Cable," and "California." All deal with Ridge's view of history and his belief in the nineteenth-century view that societies, races, and nations are evolving toward higher and higher levels, but at different rates.

The hunter-gatherer societies, in this view, had barely begun the climb of progress. The Western nations, on the other hand, had reached the highest levels and were at the cutting edge of the evolutionary process. The theory could be supported empirically: one could see the advances being made every day in developed countries – the laying of the telegraph cable across the Atlantic was a notable example – and compare this activity with the stagnation of less advanced societies.

Among the implications of such a theory is the premise that the "advanced" nations are morally obligated to spread their ideas and methods to the benighted peoples of the world, who should accept these offerings and learn to live like their more civilized counterparts. The message for American Indians is obvious. By the time Ridge wrote these poems, he believed that his family had made the transition in only three generations from a primitive aboriginal existence to a modern civilized one. His own experience and success as a writer helped to encourage this view.

John Rollin Ridge was one of the earliest Native Americans to earn his living primarily from his writing. As a poet Ridge probably fits somewhere in the middle ranks of nineteenth-century American writers. His work conformed to many of the romantic conventions of the period, but some of it carried Ridge's special stamp. Many of the poems set in California – "Mount Shasta," for example – demonstrate a well-developed sense of place. He often waxes lyrical or plaintive in his autobiographical poems, in the best tradition of romantic expressionism. As a poet he seems to have had the almost universal, if sometimes grudging, admiration of his contemporaries.

The Life and Adventures of Joaquín Murieta, one of the first examples of prose fiction by an American Indian writer, treated a topic that continues to be popular, especially among Latinos. Although the work is based to some extent on contemporaneous accounts, Ridge's imagination furnished much of its content. The influence of the book goes beyond fiction and romance and even colors California history. It is a tribute to Ridge's substantial narrative talent and his ability to synthesize information from several sources.

Biography:

James W. Parins, *John Rollin Ridge: His Life and Works* (Lincoln: University of Nebraska Press, 1991).

References:

Angie Debo, "John Rollin Ridge," *Southwest Review,* 17 (1931): 59–71;

Carolyn Thomas Foreman, "Edward W. Bushyhead and John Rollin Ridge," *Chronicles of Oklahoma,* 14 (September 1936): 295–311;

Remi Nadeau, *The Real Joaquin Murieta: Robin Hood Hero or Gold Rush Gangster?* (San Francisco: Trans-Anglo Books, 1974);

Louis Owens, *Other Destinies: Understanding the American Indian Novel* (Norman: University of Oklahoma Press, 1992), pp. 32–40;

M. A. Ranck, "John Rollin Ridge in California," *Chronicles of Oklahoma,* 10 (December 1932): 560–569;

Franklin Walker, "Yellow Bird," *Westways,* 30 (November 1938): 18–19;

Thurman Wilkins, *Cherokee Tragedy: The Story of the Ridge Family and the Decimation of a People* (New York: Macmillan, 1970).

Lynn Riggs

(31 August 1899 - 30 June 1954)

Phyllis Cole Braunlich

BOOKS: *Big Lake: A Tragedy in Two Parts, as Performed by the American Laboratory Theater, New York City* (New York: French, 1927);

Sump'n Like Wings and A Lantern to See By: Two Oklahoma Plays (New York: French, 1928);

Knives from Syria (New York: French, 1928);

Roadside: A Comedy (New York: French, 1930);

The Iron Dish (Garden City, N.Y.: Doubleday, Doran, 1930);

Green Grow the Lilacs: A Play (New York, Los Angeles & London: French, 1931);

Russet Mantle, and The Cherokee Night: Two Plays (New York, Los Angeles & London: French, 1936);

Four Plays (New York: French, 1947) – comprises *A World Elsewhere, The Year of Pilar, The Cream in the Well,* and *The Dark Encounter*;

Hang on to Love: A Play in Two Acts (New York: French, 1948);

Toward the Western Sky: A Music Play, by Riggs and Nathan Kroll (Cleveland: Press of Western Reserve University, 1951);

This Book, This Hill, These People: Poems by Lynn Riggs, with introductions by Phyllis Cole Braunlich (Tulsa, Okla: Lynn Chase, 1982).

Lynn Riggs in 1949

PLAY PRODUCTIONS: *Knives from Syria,* Santa Fe, N.Mex., Santa Fe Players, 1925;

Big Lake, New York, American Laboratory Theatre, 8 April 1927;

The Domino Parlor, Broad Street Theater, Newark, N.J., 18 June 1928;

Rancor, Moylan-Rose Valley, Pa., Hedgerow Theatre, 12 July 1928;

Roadside, New York, Longacre Theater, 27 September 1930;

A Lantern to See By, Detroit, Detroit Playhouse, September 1930;

Green Grow the Lilacs, New York, Theatre Guild, 26 January 1931;

Sump'n Like Wings, Detroit, Detroit Playhouse, 1931;

The Cherokee Night, Moylan-Rose Valley, Pa., Hedgerow Theatre, June 1932;

The Lonesome West, Ames, Iowa State University, 15 November 1932;

The Son of Perdition, Moylan-Rose Valley, Pa., Hedgerow Theatre, 25 February 1933;

More Sky, Evanston, Ill., Northwestern University, July 1934;

Russet Mantle, New York, Masque Theatre, 16 January 1936;

A World Elsewhere, San Diego, Globe Theater, 8 April 1940;

The Cream in the Well, Washington, D.C., National Theater, 14 January 1941;

Laughter from a Cloud, Falmouth, Mass., Tanglewood Theater, August 1947;

All the Way Home, Ridgefield, Conn., Summer Theater, 8 August 1948;

Out of Dust, Westport, Conn., Westport Country Playhouse, 9 August 1949;

Toward the Western Sky, by Riggs and Nathan Kroll, Cleveland, Western Reserve University, 11 June 1951.

MOTION PICTURES: *Beyond Victory,* screenplay by Riggs, Pathé, 1930;

Siren Song, screenplay by Riggs, Pathé, 1930;

Laughing Boy, screenplay and scenario by Riggs, M-G-M, 1933;

Stingaree, screenplay by Riggs, RKO, 1933;

Andrew's Harvest, screenplay by Riggs, Paramount, 1934;

Family Man, screenplay by Riggs, RKO, 1934;

Wicked Woman, screenplay by Riggs, M-G-M, 1934;

Delay in the Sun, screenplay by Riggs, Universal, 1935;

The Garden of Allah, screenplay by Riggs and W. P. Lipscomb, Selznick, 1936;

The Plainsman, screenplay by Riggs, Harold Lamb, and Waldsmar Young, Paramount, 1936.

TELEVISION: *Song in the A.M.,* Philco-Goodyear Playhouse, 1953.

OTHER: *Reckless,* in *One-Act Plays for Stage and Study: Fourth Series* (New York: French, 1928), pp. 103–115;

Cowboy Songs, Folk Songs, and Ballads from "Green Grow the Lilacs," edited by Riggs (New York: French, 1932);

A World Elsewhere, in *The Best One-Act Plays of 1939,* edited by Margaret Mayorga (New York: French, 1940), pp. 801–838;

The Hunger I Got, in *One-Act Plays for Stage and Study, Tenth Series* (New York: French, 1949), pp. 117–132;

"Spring Morning – Santa Fe," in *Here and There: 100 Poems about Places,* edited by Elinor Parker (New York: Crowell, 1967), p. 57;

The Cherokee Night, Scene 6, "The Arid Land," "Always the Gulls," and "Santo Domingo Corn Dance," in *Heath Anthology of American Literature,* volume 2, edited by Paul Lauter and others (Lexington, Mass.: Heath, 1990), pp. 1446–1455.

SELECTED PERIODICAL PUBLICATIONS – UNCOLLECTED:

FICTION

"We Moved to Pomona," *Laughing Horse,* 20 (Summer 1938), n.p.;

"Eben, the Hound, and the Hare," *Gentry,* 7 (Summer 1953): 92–98.

NONFICTION

"When People Say 'Folk Drama,' " *Carolina Play-Book,* 4 (June 1931): 39–41;

"High, Wide and Handsome," *Nation,* 16 (16 December 1931): 674;

"A Credo for the Tributary Theatre," *Theatre Arts,* 25 (February 1941): 16;

"We Speak for Ourselves: A Dance Poem," *Theatre Arts,* 27 (December 1943): 752–757.

Lynn Riggs is the premier playwright from Oklahoma and wrote most of his plays about that state. Most of his twenty-five full-length plays saw production, and many were published. In addition to writing plays and motion-picture scripts, throughout his adult life he published poems in magazines. Although his poems, which were collected in two volumes, have received little critical attention, they constitute a significant body of work, with colorful imagery, a strong sense of place, and metaphors that reflect his Cherokee roots. He is best known for his play *Green Grow the Lilacs,* which was produced on Broadway in 1931 by the Theatre Guild. In 1943 the same company produced a musical version of the play, with music by Richard Rodgers and lyrics by Oscar Hammerstein II; the phenomenal success of *Oklahoma!,* which closely follows Riggs's plot and dialogue, would alone be sufficient to establish Riggs's reputation as an outstanding writer. *Green Grow the Lilacs* also continues in frequent amateur performances throughout the United States.

Riggs was born on 31 August 1899 near Claremore in northeast Indian Territory, which became the state of Oklahoma in 1907, to William Grant Riggs, a non-Indian rancher who became president of the Farmer's Bank and Trust Company in Claremore, and Rose Ella Buster Gillis Riggs, who was one-eighth Cherokee. Cherokee rolls and court records list Riggs's first name as Rollie, although some references call him Rolla; he used R. Lynn, or simply Lynn, from young adulthood. Two of Riggs's four siblings lived past infancy: Mary Martha (Mattie) born in 1896, and William Edgar, born in 1898. Rose Ella Riggs died of typhoid fever in 1901. As enrolled Cherokee citizens, her children each received an allotment of Indian Territory land at her death. Six months later William Grant Riggs married Juliette Chambers, who was one-fourth Cherokee.

Riggs graduated from Claremore's Eastern University Preparatory School in 1917 and signed

Riggs on a 1928 trip to Spain and France (Barrett H. Clark Papers, Beinecke Library, Yale University)

up as a cowpuncher on a cattle train bound for Chicago. From there he went to New York, where his jobs included reading proof for the *Wall Street Journal* and playing bit parts in cowboy movies that were produced in the rural areas of Astoria and the Bronx. In 1919 he went to Hollywood, where he worked again as a film extra. In 1920 he enrolled as a fine-arts major at the University of Oklahoma, with special interests in music and drama, and became a teaching assistant in English. In 1922 H. L. Mencken and George Jean Nathan published a short story and the first of many poems by Riggs in their magazine, *Smart Set*. In the summer of that year Riggs went on a Chautauqua tour of the Midwest with the university's Sooner Quartet. He had become friends with Witter Bynner, a poet in residence at the university; ill and depressed in the fall of 1923, Riggs followed Bynner to Santa Fe. After a few weeks in Sunmount Sanatorium Riggs recovered his strength and threw himself into the free-living ambience of the ancient city, home to many impoverished but talented writers and artists. Gaining confidence, Riggs moved back to New York and began writing plays. He frequently directed college productions of his plays, and he taught drama for a semester at Baylor University in 1941. His home for most of his life was an apartment in Greenwich Village, but he often returned to Santa Fe.

Although he was proud of his Cherokee ancestry, Riggs was torn between white and Indian worldviews. His feelings of alienation and struggle for synthesis influenced his plays and poems in demonstrable ways. He was most interested in portraying the unusual personalities he had known in Oklahoma, and he often used their actual names. Yet, he said in a 14 August 1928 letter to his agent, the theater historian Barrett H. Clark, "The range of life there is not to be indicated, much less its meaning laid bare, by a few people in a few plays." He hoped that a "kind of truth" about early Oklahoma would emerge from his plays. Although he said that he did not set out to create a historical record of Oklahoma life, he includes in his plays details about home furnishings, clothing, food, transportation, and cattle ranching, showing how people kept milk and cream cold by putting the containers in their water wells and how they considered the horse-drawn surrey the most elegant means of transportation across prairie roads – especially if it was made of genuine leather, with side lanterns, curtains, and silk fringe around the canopy. He portrays activities that are gone from the American scene, such as the cattle drives to the railhead in Kansas, the "play-party" frolics, and the "wagon yard" hostelries in the towns. Riggs also wanted to preserve the many folk songs he knew from his early years. To this end, he included old songs in many of his plays, and he published an anthology, *Cowboy Songs, Folk Songs, and Ballads from "Green Grow the Lilacs,"* in 1932. He described his play *Green Grow the Lilacs* as "an old song" and thought that it was like one of the long ballads he had sung on the hotel front porch with transient railroad workers.

Riggs celebrates the freedom that the West represented, even as that freedom was being lost as the range was being enclosed for farming. This outward change was, for Riggs, a metaphor for the spiritual change that was being forced on Native Americans, who believed that the land was a gift to all people from the Great Spirit, as they were forced into confinement and eventually into landowning by the federal government. Some Indians demonstrated their displeasure by refusing to enroll as tribal citizens in the 1890s, thereby depriving themselves and their descendants of benefits such as land allotments, mineral rights, and credentials as Indian artists. Riggs presents the modern Native American condition in his one specifically Indian play, *The Cherokee Night* (1932).

Because of his emphasis on character and relationships, critics sometimes found Riggs weak in plotting, but they agree that he had an unerring ear for the language that characterized conversations in the Oklahoma of his youth. In an interview in the *New York Evening Post* (24 January 1931) Riggs said that, far from idealizing the poetic quality of that speech, he had not even equaled it; his aunt, he said,

> naturally speaks a much more highly charged poetic language than I can contrive to write in their vein. To listen to her is a delight. From morning until night she will comment on the affairs of the household, on the state of the weather, on the goings-on of the neighbors, in a language which would gladden the heart of any poet who loves apt and spontaneous word-images. And this was generally true of the Oklahoma folk of thirty years ago.

Off-Broadway and college theaters produced many Riggs plays. He supported the community theater movement as it developed across the country, and he spoke out for the artistic independence of indigenous American drama – independence from Broadway, as well as from European influence. His lifelong friend and mentor was Ida Rauh Eastman, a free-spirited actress and sculptor who had organized the innovative Provincetown Players with Eugene O'Neill and others. It was she who encouraged Riggs to write his one-act play *Knives from Syria,* which she produced and directed with the Santa Fe Players in 1925.

Riggs's work first went to Broadway on 8 April 1927, when the American Laboratory Theatre produced *Big Lake,* a tragedy about the vulnerability of adolescents in a world of evil adults and malicious gossipers. *Big Lake* was long popular with community theater groups, although its action is slow. It was offered for production in the Samuel French catalogue for decades, along with Riggs's *Green Grow the Lilacs, Roadside* (1930), *Russet Mantle* (1936), and *Hang on to Love* (1948). Although critics praised the poetic quality and evocation of mood of *Big Lake,* some called it an amateurish first attempt. In his introduction to the published version of the play (1927) Clark said that he saw a new *winged lightness* in Riggs's dialogue; he also wrote: "I am sure that in Lynn Riggs our American theatre has found a poet who can bring to it an authentic note of ecstasy and passion, expressed in terms of drama. He is one of the few native dramatists who can take the material of our everyday life and mould it into forms of stirring beauty."

Sump'n Like Wings, published in 1928, was performed at the Detroit Playhouse in 1931 and in Belgium in 1932. The heroine exhibits the ambitious and hardworking spirit that transformed many poor, uneducated pioneers into the builders of a new civilization in the wilderness, in Oklahoma as elsewhere. Riggs wrote *A Lantern to See By* in 1926; it was published together with *Sump'n Like Wings* in 1928. The critic David Russel wrote in the *Dallas Morning News* (28 December 1928), "Here is tragedy and realism caught in a form of haunting and moving beauty. No one who wishes to follow the best that is being written in the theater today can afford to miss reading these plays." The leading characters in both plays are young adults eager for a better life and struggling against an impoverished environment. When *A Lantern To See By* was produced at the historic Hedgerow Theatre in Moylan-Rose Valley, outside Philadelphia, a critic wrote in the *Philadelphia Ledger* (13 July 1931), "It shows Lynn Riggs gifted with a flair for bringing out touches of character, for molding earthy native types, making them human, virile and alive yet escaping coarseness; building scenes of intense dramatic value and filling them with words that need no battery to galvanize them to pulsating power." A tragedy of domestic incompatibility, *Rancor,* played at the Hedgerow Theatre in 1928 and later at four universities but was never produced on Broadway.

It was his comedies that brought Riggs his greatest popular success. The picaresque *Roadside,* a

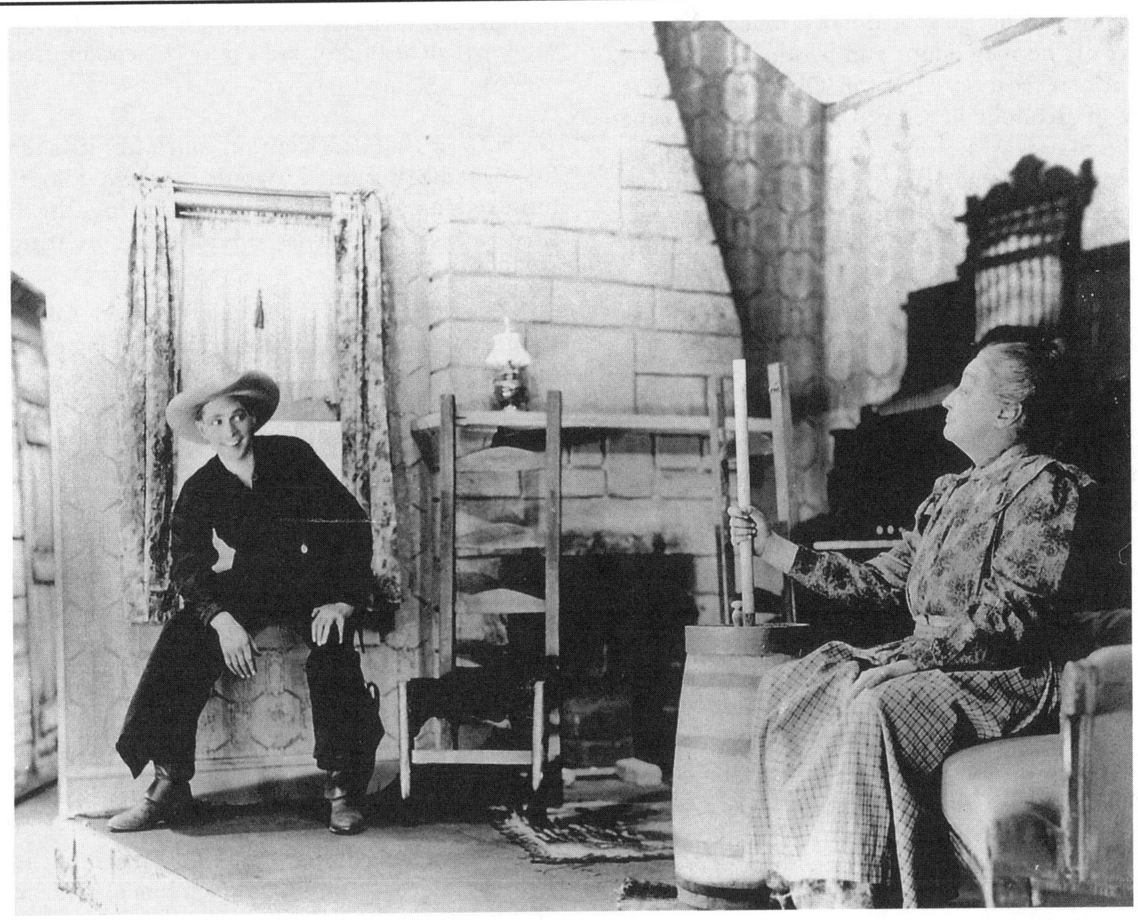

Franchot Tone as Curly and Helen Westley as Aunt Eller in the opening scene of the 1931 Theatre Guild production of Riggs's Green Grow the Lilacs

country version of William Shakespeare's *The Taming of the Shrew* (1594), had a brief run at New York's Longacre Theater in 1930 and at the Hedgerow in 1931. It continued to be popular in community theater productions for decades. The pretty and unruly Hannah, who has left her ineffectual husband, Buzzey, and their farm near Verdigris, wanders the country roads with her rascally father, Pap Rader, in an early version of a recreational vehicle. They meet the wild and reckless Texas, who is just the "world-slingin', star-traipsin' son-of-a-gun" that Hannah has been waiting for, one who is able to match her restless spirit and to eschew roots and regulations. Since no jail can hold Texas, a comic courtroom scene ends with the larger-than-life couple happily hitting the road. In the foreword to the book version Arthur Hopkins called *Roadside* "the first American dramatic classic." In *Twenty-Five Modern Plays* (1953) the drama historian Alan S. Downer says that *Roadside* is "rich in speech and feeling. . . . And its theme, the conflict between the farmer and the cowhand, the settler and the vagabond, organized society and the individual, is part of the 'life of poetry' in which everyman can see himself." An example of the play's richness of speech is Hannah's explanation to her former husband of how she came to marry him in the first place:

> All I c'n recollect was once about two year ago it was Spring, and Pap and me stopped by that little branch that run th'ough yore cow pasture. And you come down to set the dogs on us. When you seen me – you didn't. So I fell in a daze er sump'n – and when I come to, it seemed like I was kinda married to you – All on account of it bein' Spring, and you not settin' the dogs on us – and one other thing. I was all set to marry someone along about then – and I never thought to be picky and choosy.

In *The Domino Parlor* (1928) men gather at the Mission Club, joke and curse, drink alcoholic beverages, gamble at dominoes, and witness two fights, a shooting, two murders, and the return of a hardened blues singer who attempts to rekindle an old love. When the play premiered on 18 June 1928 in Newark, the critic in the *Newark News* (19 June) expressed shock at the low language and moral tone and at the amounts of "bootleg liquor and bootleg love" to be found in a recreation parlor in Oklahoma, where the sale of alcoholic beverages was still against the law. The play was, however, based on a real place in Claremore, real characters, and events that would not have surprised anyone who lived there at the time. Riggs thought that the producers, the Shuberts, misunderstood the intention of the play, and he refused to make changes during the tryouts. Clark wrote in *An Hour of American Drama* (1930) that it was badly miscast. Revised in 1948 as *Hang on to Love,* the play continues in amateur productions.

Folkways and folk songs are preserved in Riggs's best play, *Green Grow the Lilacs,* written while Riggs was in France on a Guggenheim Fellowship in 1929–1930. When the Theatre Guild delayed production of the work, Riggs went to Hollywood to accept an offer to write screenplays for Pathé Studios, beginning with *Beyond Victory* (1930) and *Siren Song* (1930). He wrote many screenplays over the years and made many close friends in Hollywood, including Sidney Howard, Bette Davis, Gloria Swanson, Joan Crawford, and Franchot Tone. Tone played Curly in *Green Grow the Lilacs* when it opened on Broadway on 26 January 1931. The play centers around the love story of the flirtatious Laurie and the dashing but conceited cowboy Curly; it closes with declarations of the exciting future in the new state of Oklahoma that awaits those who are "hearty" and willing to work hard. The critic Robert Littell wrote in the *New York Morning World* (27 January 1931), "it is one of the most thoroughly satisfying evenings that the Guild has given us in a long time – full of rich, free humor, salty poetry, and some reckless tenderness that was America's before she was tamed and civilized by fences and mortgages and chain grocery stores." John Mason Brown wrote in the *New York Evening Post* (27 January 1931), "It has a racy vigor that is undeniable and a swing to many of its finely cadenced lines which indicates that it is a poet who has fashioned them . . . a refreshing and authentic sense of having sprung from the earth, and of belonging to it." Critics generally praised the play as a breath of fresh air with a lighter, cleaner, more American style than Broadway had seen theretofore. In his introduction to a 1954 Limited Editions reprint of the play, Brooks Atkinson recalled the opening night:

> Mr. Riggs's rolling, cadenced dialogue and his robust story conveyed a joyous mood. In the program *Green Grow the Lilacs* was described as a folk-play. It was more than that; it was the uncalculated poetry of a middlewestern troubadour and a piece of individual literature.

Green Grow the Lilacs went on tour after its successful Broadway run. It would receive about six hundred amateur productions during the next fifty years, with gross royalties amounting to about $40,000.

The Hedgerow Theatre premiered *The Cherokee Night* in June 1932. It played at the University of Iowa later that year, at Syracuse University in 1934, and at the Federal Theatre in New York in 1936. Critics were divided on the play's merits and puzzled by its unchronological scenes, but few could deny that something important had been presented in it. Literature about Native Americans, up to this point, either idealized them as children of nature or focused on the wars between Indians and whites in the West; neither of these themes is found in Riggs's play. His main characters are mixed-breed Cherokees who are bereft of the culture of their past yet unable to fit comfortably into the white culture of the present. Riggs wrote to Clark on 10 March 1929, "An absorbed race has its curiously irreconcilable inheritance." Riggs's production notes say that the play is a study of certain Cherokee qualities – "bravery, sense of ritual, independence, pride, cunning, fierceness, aesthetic sense, in sum their authentic glory" – and the "present perversion of these qualities." A drumbeat that varies in tempo and loudness introduces and concludes each scene; the drum recalls traditional ceremonial dances. Unlike some of his other plays, this one has become more contemporary with the passage of time; it illustrates the failure of the assimilation policy, the loss of tribal and individual identity, and the need for Cherokee pride. Published with *Russet Mantle* in 1936, *Cherokee Night* makes haunting reading.

Riggs's adaptation of James Gould Cozzens's 1929 novel, *The Son of Perdition,* set in Cuba, had only a short run at the Hedgerow Theatre in 1933. A spectacular mythological play set in the lost city of Atlantis, *More Sky* played only at Northwestern University in July 1934. *A World Elsewhere,* set in Mexico in 1939, was produced in San Diego in 1940 and published in Riggs's *Four Plays* in 1947, along with *The Year of Pilar, The Dark Encounter,* and *The Cream in the Well.*

Meanwhile, Riggs worked on two of his better-known screenplays, *The Garden of Allah* (1936), with Marlene Dietrich and Charles Boyer, and *The Plainsman* (1936), starring Gary Cooper as Wild Bill Hickock and Jean Arthur as Calamity Jane and based on stories by Courtney Ryley Cooper and Frank J. Wilstach. According to Mary Hunter Wolf, who directed some of Riggs's plays, his films brought a more realistic depiction of cowboy life to American Western films.

Riggs's comedy *Russet Mantle* opened on Broadway at the Masque Theatre on 16 January 1936 and ran for 117 performances. Critics praised this comic story of wealthy Anglos who retire to a New Mexican chicken ranch, their rebellious daughter, poor and earthy New Mexican Hispanics, and a revolutionary young poet. Riggs's next Oklahoma play, *The Cream in the Well* (1941), however, was received with shock and disgust by Broadway critics. Riggs was stunned by the response to his story of frustrated incestuous desire. The play closed after twenty-four performances in New York. In the *Nation* (1 February 1941) Joseph Wood Krutch praised Riggs for his attempt, noting that tragedy is a more difficult genre than comedy.

Oklahoma! opened on Broadway on 31 March 1943 and ran for a record-breaking five years and nine months. It received the first Pulitzer Prize ever awarded to a musical. A perennial favorite in many countries, it has been revived in New York several times. In 1955, after Riggs's death, it became a popular movie. Critics paid tribute to its freshness, gaiety, poetic language, humor, and optimism. Those who saw it only as a country love story missed the background theme of the courage and strength required of pioneers in a new land as they built a more civilized and secure future. Hammerstein said in a letter to *The New York Times* (5 September 1943), "Mr. Riggs' play is the well-spring of almost all that is good in 'Oklahoma!' I kept most of the lines of the original play without making any changes in them for the simple reason that they could not be improved upon – at least not by me. . . . Lynn Riggs and 'Green Grow the Lilacs' are the very soul of 'Oklahoma!' "

Riggs wrote another series of promising plays that failed to reach Broadway: *Laughter from a Cloud,* a comedy set in New Mexico, tried out in Falmouth, Massachusetts, in 1947. *All the Way Home,* set in "Tulsey-town" (Tulsa) in 1910, based on Riggs's Aunt Mary and her daughters and incorporating a mysterious love story, a night in a storm cellar, and much folk material, was performed in summer theaters in 1948 in New Jersey and Connecticut. *Out of Dust,* a powerful drama set on a cattle drive on the Shawnee Trail from Oklahoma to the railroad at Baxter Springs, Kansas, played for a week in Westport, Connecticut, in August 1949. The unrelenting hardships of the trail form a fitting background for the story of a cruel father who despises his sons' weakness as he keeps them weak, torments them with their bondage to him, and taunts them by threatening to withhold their inheritance. An Iago-like character, King, the subboss, incites the sons to murder the father.

Riggs's final Oklahoma comedy, *Some Sweet Day,* written in 1950 and never performed on stage, concerns the odyssey of eight-year-old Duncan, who runs away from his stepmother's cruelty in 1910. As he waits for the train in Claremore to go to his "Granmaw's house" in Sapulpa, he makes new friends in the wagon yard, a rustic hostelry provided in many Oklahoma towns for those who were visiting overnight, seeking shelter from a snowstorm, or waiting for trains. People lived in their wagons, cooked over a campfire, cared for their animals and children, and took refuge when necessary inside a crude building warmed by a woodstove. Riggs revised a portion of this musical play as *Song in the A.M.* for an hour-long television production in 1953.

In Riggs's plays one finds the language and ambience of early Oklahoma life, but his poems use highly literate diction without colloquialisms. The metaphors in his poems are, however, reminiscent of a Native American worldview. Riggs first gained attention when his poetry appeared in magazines during his college years. *Poetry* magazine frequently published his work and devoted the entire Summer 1923 issue to him. Riggs gathered forty-eight of his poems in the critically successful volume *The Iron Dish* (1930). Many of the poems had been previously published in *Poetry,* the *Nation,* the *New York Herald Tribune, Harper's,* the *New Republic,* the *Bookman,* and the *Laughing Horse,* an experimental literary journal in Santa Fe. Harold A. Ehrensperger of Northwestern University said in the *Evanston Review* (June 1932) that *The Iron Dish* is "a source for discovering a new poet whom Carl Sandburg, John Farrar and William Rose Benét have already marked for success." *The Iron Dish* poems take the reader through the sights, sounds, and colors of old Santa Fe. "Spring Morning – Santa Fe" begins,

> The first hour was a word the color of dawn.
> The second came, and gorgeous poppies stood
> Backs to a wall.
> . . . .
> At ten, black shawls of women bowed along
> The Alameda. Sleepy burros lay
> In the heat and lifted up their ears. A song
> Wavered upon the wind and died away.

"Acequia Madre" (Mother Ditch) evokes the colors seen in Santa Fe's uniquely clear light:

Riggs, circa 1951, in his New York City apartment

I walk along the acequia
Over patches of red, over squares of magenta earth.
The low fence turns, dips,
Goes this way for a ditch,
That way for a corner of yellow roses.

In "A Letter" the poet finds color again as, from his sunny patio, he watches his neighbor, Lucinda, wash her shining black hair; chickens are like snow in the yard; a pink dress and a blue wagon play in the road. "Here in a black bowl are [yellow] calendulas, in my neighbor's garden, sun."

There are also notes of sadness, loneliness, and bitterness. "Santo Domingo Corn Dance" yearns with the rhythm of the Indian pueblo rain dance. "As we bring now / Our gift of dance and song / to You – who dance not, nor sing – Bring rain!" In the final verse a dry and exhausted dancer pleads, "One drum-note more, one voice, / One slant of bodies, / And my tears will fall like rain upon this ground."

Riggs's images, usually of inanimate objects, create a haunting mood and make an elusive personal statement. Light is benevolent, signifying peace and blessing. Among the pervasive mission bells, religious processionals, and rituals common in Santa Fe's culture, Riggs evokes ambiguous images that may be read as either religious or personal. In "The Cross," a lyric in tightly rhymed four-line stanzas, the bearer makes a cross a thing of winged, feathery lightness, composed of "tatters of joy": "This burden burdened him: / To love this sapless limb / Because he hated those / Which blossomed while he froze." While "The Cross" finds beauty in pain, "Wonder," written in loosely rhymed, long/short rhythms, finds pain in beauty:

This is the wonder of wonders:
To be assailed
By this sharp incredible beauty,
To be nailed
By such arrowy barbs to a cross
Of my own making,
While the chants rise from the harsh hills,
And from under
The near crags dawn is breaking!

The poems Riggs wrote from 1930 to 1948 tend to deal more with inner than with external spaces. In 1952 he gathered many of his later poems into a manuscript that he called "Hamlet Not the Only. . . . " He did not find a publisher for the collection, but it appeared in 1982, many years after his death, as *This Book, This Hill, These People,* with introductions by Phyllis Cole Braunlich and illustrations by the late Oklahoma artist Ray Piercey. Most of the poems had been published in periodicals, including *Poetry, The New Republic, Harper's, Lyric, Theatre Arts,* the *New York World,* and the *New York Herald Tribune,* during Riggs's lifetime. Riggs's poetic style in these poems is generally a classic one; he preferred the sonnet but worked in other lyric forms and in free verse. One can discern Native American influences in his images and metaphors; for example, in "Of Oak and Innocence" (at one time the title poem of his manuscript) he warns poets against being "precious" and adds:

> We must go backward to a timeless wood
> of soft-dropping light and green moss underfoot,
> and sit in the sun that idles where we stood
> centuries ago and long: back to the root
> of oak and innocence – back to the year
> when the young sun soaked the amazing earth
> and crashed through fibrous stem and stone to be
> wombed in the darkest cell of soil and tree –
> when the simplest leafy motion was a birth,
> and the quiet word a thundering in the ear.

In his later poems one hears echoes of Native American legends, sung out by a storyteller around a campfire in a starlit forest alive with spirits – not ghosts, but the life force they saw in everything in nature: animals, plants, mountains, rocks, earth, and stars. For example, in "The True Seducers" Riggs sees trees not as fixtures in a landscape but as wise elders, "like every oak in any wood or year, spacious with leaves and rooted majesty." He acknowledges fierce anger in nature, as well as beneficence. For example, in "But Momentary," a "lightning flare springs in the dark and harries like a hound the fleeing shadow in that bowl of air." He sees people, too, as both organic and inorganic, surprisingly pairing "writhing blinded cells" or "ventricle of heaving heart" with clods of earth, "vapor and ocean, rock and farthest star."

In "You'd Think . . . " a "lonely watcher" allies himself with "all liquidity, dissolving, as the clods disintegrate / in the soft compulsion of the a watery weight, the crag and furrow that he seems to be." Then, "erased in line and contour," he "would flow as waters run / down among fibrous root and cellular / organic waste and worm to be as one / with wider reaches of identity: / vapor and ocean, rock, and farthest star." He speaks of "wren and root," "follicle of air," and "cavity of sky." An August day is lit "floodlight to zenith – and the speaking land one giant bird call is, when bodies flit / feathered or otherwise, enraptured."

An eerie Gothic poem, "All Hallow's Eve," typically juxtaposes organic and inorganic images: "Root, maple, thigh and all things tender / wither the way the cell is bent." Again, in "The Awakening," "Alarm I feel in every flooded cell; / That is the goal, the beach of stimuli, / if there is harbor in the ventricle / of heaving heart." "Securely Radiant Never Dream" compares the human being to the sea on a "stony earth set in its fluid air . . . man's body being a swift resilience / with multitudinous writhing blinded cells / burning and burning in their little shells."

Most of Riggs's poems evoke loneliness, a continual farewell, and the feeling of being, as he once said, "outside the rush of light" from the campfire. Such is the description of a warm adobe house with a "not lyrical inner lair" in "The Shaped Room": "Alone you must be in the end; / the inner room appends unto / whatever wood or mud you bend / to shape of room whose shape is you." His search for meaning in the wisdom of natural and legendary creatures and his images of abandonment create a persona feeling deserted, like a young brave suffering deprivation to encounter his initiatory vision: the tribe cannot help him. The "battle" that love is, the bowl of air, the speaking land, the call of the giant bird, and the "message speaking in the flowering brain" all mark the lifetime journey toward a safe haven – which, on approach, recedes with the horizon. His "hopeful nightmares" turn him back to the land he fled, with orders to look there for that friendlier place. With their psychological insights into a person mentally divided against the strains within and the judgments without, echoing the inner conflict of a person part Cherokee and part pioneer, part conformist and part rebel, Riggs's later poems offer rich rewards to the perceptive reader.

Although in failing health during the winter of 1952–1953, Riggs published "Eben, the Hound, and the Hare" (1953), a wry but profound autobiographical short story set at his country home on Shelter Island, New York, and worked on what would have been his first novel. He died of cancer on 30 June 1954 in Memorial Hospital, New York, with his sister Mattie, Eastman, and two other friends at his bedside. His work brought him little recognition or recompense during his lifetime. When the Pulitzer Prize for drama eluded *Green Grow the Lilacs* and was awarded to Susan Glaspell for *Alison's House,* which was only performed twenty-five times over a five-month period, Riggs had commented generously in the *Tulsa World* (8 May 1931): "I am very glad for Susan, for it will mean that her interest in the American theater will receive a stimulant." In fact, it was her last play. Riggs received modest $250 weekly royalties during performance runs of *Oklahoma!* – nothing like the more than $50,000 earned by each of the ten investors who had gambled $1,500 on the production. With typical wry humor, Riggs told a friend in 1953 that *Oklahoma!* "has kept me in bourbon all these years."

Riggs never had much money, but his pockets were always open to a friend in need of a loan. Having the Native American spirit of generosity, he viewed possessions as transient. He was mystical, superstitious, a graceful dancer, a music lover. Echoes of drum rhythms and stomp dances remained with him, as well as folk songs from many sources. He was firm in drawing his unusual characters as he saw them, rather than bowing to conventions of drama. In *The New York Times* (1 February 1931) Isaac Goldberg called Riggs a person who had "the courage of his exaltations." He described Riggs as tall, fair, soft-spoken yet confident, with a dreamy look in the eyes behind his horn-rimmed glasses – "unmistakably the poet." The comedies *Green Grow the Lilacs* and *Russet Mantle* brought Riggs the most applause, but students of his plays as literature most admire his serious dramas, especially *Out of Dust* and *All the Way Home,* in which he lamented the plight of the "unassimilated" Native American and the hard lives of the pioneers. Although Riggs is a "regional" writer, reflecting life in Oklahoma and New Mexico, his themes are universal. His expressions of alienation complement those of other Lost Generation writers who felt "not quite at home" in American society during the early twentieth century.

Interviews:

"Dialect in Folk Plays; Lynn Riggs, Author of the Guild's Green Grow the Lilacs, Has Not Tried to Idealize the Speech of His Oklahomans," *New York Evening Post,* 24 January 1931;

Isaac Goldberg, "And Now Lynn Riggs," *New York Times,* 1 February 1931, section 8, p. 3;

Frank Dennis, "An Oklahoman in Santa Fe Leads Enviable Existence," *Daily Oklahoman,* 19 September 1936.

Biographies:

Eloise Wilson, "Lynn Riggs, Oklahoma Dramatist," dissertation, University of Pennsylvania, 1957;

Phyllis Cole Braunlich, *Haunted by Home: The Life and Letters of Lynn Riggs* (Norman: University of Oklahoma Press, 1988).

References:

Charles Aughtry, "Lynn Riggs, Dramatist: A Critical Biography," dissertation, Brown University, 1959;

Phyllis Cole Braunlich, "The Cherokee Night of R. Lynn Riggs," *Midwest Quarterly,* 30 (Autumn 1988): 45-59;

Braunlich, "The Oklahoma Plays of R. Lynn Riggs," *World Literature Today,* 64 (Summer 1990): 390-394;

Barrett H. Clark, *An Hour of American Drama* (Philadelphia: Lippincott, 1930), pp. 152-159;

Clark, *Intimate Portraits* (Bristol, Conn.: Hildreth, 1951), pp. 213, 215-217, 220-223;

Clark and George Freedley, eds., *A History of Modern Drama* (New York: Appleton-Century, 1947), pp. 693-712, 722, 731;

John Gassner, "Our Lost Playwrights," *Theatre Arts,* 38 (August 1954): 19-21;

Horace Gregory, "Lynn Riggs as Poet," *Nation* (17 January 1931): 22;

Frederick Koch, "Playboy of Oklahoma," *Carolina Play-Book,* 4 (June 1931): 62;

Joseph Wood Krutch, "Tragedy Is Not Easy," *Nation* (1 February 1941): 137;

Burns Mantle, ed., *Best Plays: Yearbook of the Drama in America* (New York: Dodd, Mead, 1931), pp. 375-410;

Ilse L. Nesbitt, "Study of Dialect in Oklahoma in the Plays of Lynn Riggs," thesis, University of Tulsa, 1948;

Henry Roth, "Lynn Riggs and the Individual," in *Folk-Say: A Regional Miscellany,* edited by Ben A. Botkin (Norman: University of Oklahoma Press, 1930), pp. 386-395;

Stanley Vestal, "Lynn Riggs, Poet and Dramatist," *Southwest Review,* 15 (Autumn 1929): 64-71.

Papers:

Lynn Riggs's former agent, Lucy Kroll, donated some of Riggs's manuscripts and correspondence to the Beinecke Library at Yale University. The Barrett H. Clark Papers at the Beinecke Library have some correspondence and photographs, as do the Witter Bynner Papers at Houghton Library, Harvard University. The University of Oklahoma's Western History Collection has many Riggs letters and photographs as well as memoirs of Riggs by friends such as faculty members Walter S. Campbell and Joseph Benton. Some papers are at the McFarlin Library at the University of Tulsa. Uncatalogued manuscripts, photographs, and memorabilia are stored at Rogers State College, Claremore, Oklahoma.

Wendy Rose

(7 May 1948 –)

Helen Jaskoski
California State University, Fullerton

BOOKS: *Hopi Roadrunner Dancing* (Greenfield Center, N.Y.: Greenfield Review Press, 1973);
Long Division: A Tribal History (New York: Strawberry Press, 1976; enlarged, 1981);
Academic Squaw: Reports to the World from the Ivory Tower (Marvin, S.Dak.: Blue Cloud Press, 1977);
Builder Kachina: A Home-Going Cycle (Marvin, S.Dak.: Blue Cloud Press, 1979);
Aboriginal Tattooing in California (Berkeley: Archaeological Research Facility, University of California, 1979);
Lost Copper (Banning, Cal.: Malki Museum Press, Morongo Indian Reservation, 1980);
What Happened When the Hopi Hit New York (New York: Contact II Publications, 1982);
The Halfbreed Chronicles & Other Poems (Los Angeles: West End Press, 1985);
Going To War With All My Relations (Flagstaff, Ariz.: Northland Publishers, 1993);
Now Poof She Is Gone (Ithaca, N.Y.: Firebrand, 1994);
Bone Dance: New and Selected Poems, 1965–1992 (Tucson: University of Arizona Press, 1994).

OTHER: "Just What's All This Fuss about Whiteshamanism, Anyway?," in *Coyote Was Here,* edited by Bo Schöler (Århus, Denmark: University of Århus, 1984), pp. 13–24;
"Neon Scars," in *I Tell You Now,* edited by Brian Swann and Arnold Krupat (Lincoln: University of Nebraska Press, 1987) pp. 251–261;
"The Great Pretenders: Further Reflections on Whiteshamanism" in *The State of Native America: Genocide, Colonization and Resistance,* edited by M. Annette Jaimes (Boston: South End Press, 1992), pp. 403–424;
"For Some It's a Time of Mourning," in *Without Discovery,* edited by Ray Gonzalez (Seattle: Broken Moon Press, 1992), pp. 3–7.

SELECTED PERIODICAL PUBLICATIONS – UNCOLLECTED: "In Search of a Native American Aesthetic," *Margins,* no. 8 (1973): 4–5;

Wendy Rose

"American Indian Poets of California," *Poetryflash,* no. 91 (October 1980);
"American Indian Poets and Publishing," *Book Forum,* 5, no. 3 (1981): 400–402.

Wendy Rose has made important contributions to American poetry in the second half of the twentieth century. Her poems are strong and often angry or satiric, and they frequently are indictments of historical injustice. The circumstances of her life have compelled her to create an independent identity, and the record of that journey is embedded in her poems. She takes her place with other postmodern artists and thinkers who have embraced marginalization as a condition of insight, flexibility, and compassion.

Rose was born Bronwen Elizabeth Edwards on 7 May 1948 in Oakland, California, and grew up in the San Francisco area. Her father was Hopi, and her mother can trace descent from Miwok as well as European ancestors. Rose's own efforts have forged the identity she claims, however, and many of her poems speak powerfully for her sense of that struggle. Her childhood during the 1950s and 1960s was tumultuous; she dropped out of high school and, as a teenager on her own, became connected with some of the bohemian artistic circles in San Francisco. She also made the first of two important pilgrimages to her father's birthplace in Arizona. Her earliest poems date to this period, although some were not published for many years. From 1966 through 1980 Rose was enrolled in Cabrillo and Contra Costa Junior Colleges and the University of California, Berkeley, where, in 1978, she received a master of arts degree in cultural anthropology and went on to complete course work for the Ph.D. in anthropology. During this period she published five volumes of poetry.

The 1960s and 1970s saw major political movements among Native Americans. One of the most visible actions was the protracted occupation of Alcatraz Island, once the site of a federal penitentiary, by Indians from many tribes seeking to create a new community and awaken the consciousness of fellow citizens. Rose's first collection, *Hopi Roadrunner Dancing* (1973), includes several poems alluding to this event. "Oh My People I Remember," for instance, describes the gathering on the island as the fulfillment of a sacred dream vision. Other poems in this volume reflect Rose's ongoing search for personal, cultural, and ethnic identity. "Oh Father" is dedicated to her father and ends with the question "oh father, who am I?" Another poem, "Newborn Woman, May 7, 1948," re-creates the birth experience of a strong, vocal girl child into an "already alien world."

These early poems articulate the pervasive theme of the quest for, and creation of, an identity that is reimagined and made whole from the shards of a shattered, withheld heritage. One element of this self-creation has been Rose's adoption of names she has devised for herself. Some of her earliest poems, published in anthologies, were printed under the name Chiron Khanshendel; she adopted Chiron as an expression of her love of horses and fascination with the mythical centaur and Khanshendel as a name purely of her own invention. Yet another element in her life as a young adult was a short-lived relationship with a man whose last name, Rose, she adopted for the sake of convention. She has continued using this name, together with the diminutive of her birth name, both personally and professionally.

Long Division: A Tribal History (1976), Rose's second volume of poems, is dedicated to Arthur Murata, a magician and judo expert, whom she married in 1976. The subject matter in this brief collection marks an important transition in the poet's maturing work: from the contained descriptive mode or emotional self-absorption that characterized the previous volume to social criticism, irony, and moral witness. Rose's research and teaching have emphasized cultural anthropology, and early in her career she developed a sense of dual vision as both scientist and the object of the scientist's study. In "The Anthropology Convention," for example, the speaker appropriates the authoritative position on behalf of the "object of investigation" by reminding the reader "O we are / the Natives." Another poem, "Mission Bells," introduces a characteristic structure of Rose's poems. Two epigraphs taken from accounts of early California missions open the work; one of these passages makes a racist statement about California Indians. The body of the poem then speaks for others who refuse to be silenced: "we poets . . . sing here / in the Mission" despite persecution and misunderstanding.

The title of Rose's third book, *Academic Squaw: Reports to the World from the Ivory Tower* (1977), announces the duality of scholar and subject as a major theme. One of the poems frequently reprinted from the collection is an untitled piece that begins "I expected my skin and my blood to ripen." A brief epigraph opens the poem; the note is taken from an auction catalogue and gives the prices of items stolen from the bodies of Lakota men, women, and children massacred in 1890 at Wounded Knee, South Dakota. The speaker of the poetic text that follows is one of the murdered women, who recalls with chilling understatement what it was like to see her infant taken away and bayoneted and then for herself to be killed, stripped, and dismembered. This poem continues the method introduced in "Mission Bells" and complicates the dialogue with the introduction of the specific persona whose response to the voice of authority forms the body of the poem.

"Three Thousand Dollar Death Song," another early example of this format, offers an initial amorphous voice responding to a valuation of American Indian skeletons. The speaker begins by addressing the invoicer: "You: who have / priced us." The ending of the poem, however, moves beyond the particular dialogue to a vision of resurrection and reanimation in which the collections of bones, artifacts, and even horses awaken and reconstitute the vanished world. The ultimate price for all this purloined universe will finally be paid in "woodpecker scalp, turquoise / and copper, blood and oil, coal / and uranium." The poem is reminiscent of the visionary prophecies in the old Ghost Dance religion. The idea of creation through dreaming recurs in many of Rose's poems, both in the sense of a whole universe dreamed into being and as the work of an individual's envisioning-creating herself through the dream story.

While publishing her poems and illustrating her own books and those of others, Rose was also committed to academic course work and research. One project was a monograph titled *Aboriginal Tattooing in California* (1979), published by the University of California, Berkeley. Another major scholarly endeavor undertaken at this time was a bibliography of works written by indigenous authors of the Americas. This massive compilation has not been published in its entirety, although Rose has generously shared parts of it with other researchers working on bibliographical projects in Native American studies.

With publication of *Lost Copper* (1980), Rose's first retrospective collection, it became possible to identify important themes that pervade all of her work. One of these major themes is identification with the earth, strongly evoked by the "Frontispoem" to the volume. The persona tells of tending fields with a bone-handled spade and remarks how the dust remains on her hands. Eventually the persona describes rolling like a horse on the earth, seeking to "grow from the ground that bears me." Such communion with the earth is actually a rite undertaken by some tribal peoples to emphasize and reconstitute their relationship to the earth through the specific site of their birth; in Rose's poem the persona verbally performs the rite that is physically enacted in traditional settings. Many poems in *Lost Copper* include such expressions of oneness with, and love of, the earth.

Other poems in the collection honor individuals who have inspired or made an impact on the poet. Four poems addressed to poet Ron Tanaka dwell on the poet's integrity in the face of adverse reception; two of them compare Tanaka's poems with netsuke, a traditional Japanese art form of exquisite miniature carvings. "Magic Arthur," a lyrical love poem, addresses the poet's husband. The magic of the encounter collapses time and eases sharp memories that are figured as an "Iron Maiden," the sharp edges of which the magician is able "to patiently file . . . down"; a note further explains that the iron maiden is really a stage device, suggesting the power of love to create a new reality that can neutralize old pain. "For Mabel: Pomo basketmaster and doctor" is a brief song dedicated to Mabel McKay, a Pomo healer and artist. The poem celebrates Mabel's powers in the natural world and alludes to the artistry of Pomo baskets woven with the finest of stitches and incorporating "tiny feathers, / tan and red."

Lost Copper also continues the negotiation between conflicting worlds that is so crucial to the poet's self-identification. Another variant on the dialogue form is "Apology and Flight," in which the persona speaks as an archaeologist who has seen machinery dig up a woman's bones. Sorrow at disturbing the woman's final rest mingles with outrage at the destruction of the landscape. Ultimately the persona identifies with the skeletal woman – "it was I found by you" – and asks a blessing. "Dancing with the New Kachina: Worm Song" demonstrates Rose's approach to her Hopi connections. Kachinas are supernatural beings associated with elements of the Hopi universe such as ancestors, clouds, animals, and birds; they are embodied by dancers during certain ceremonies and are figured in carved wooden statuettes prized by art collectors. Rose's invention of a new kachina bespeaks a felt need for spiritual power and guidance in a condition for which the tradition does not explicitly provide. The persona asks for "a kachina / for people like me / whose songs are too late / to be kiva-whipped, / too wild yet to be Ph.D.'d." The feeling of marginalization is acute, yet the self-described "semi-squaw" affirms tradition while offering the possibility of creative reshaping of tradition to embrace new conditions in a changing world.

Builder Kachina: A Home-Going Cycle (1979), a twelve-page chapbook comprising four poems, is included in its entirety in *Lost Copper*. This short series of poems explores another pervasive theme in Rose's poetry: her search for ancestry, roots, and family connection. The trip commemorated in these verses was Rose's second pilgrimage to her father's Hopi village, as the title page proclaims: "Journey from the land of my mother in California to the land of my father in Arizona, August, 1977"; each poem is identified with a point on the itinerary from the San Joaquin Valley, California, to the Hopi village of Hotevilla, Arizona. The builder kachina of the title is Rose's creation, a figure that appears to be one possible answer to the need expressed in "Dancing with the New Kachina." A builder kachina will embody life-affirming creative potential; such a figure suggests the spirit guides sought by many tribal peoples in visionary experience. In the last poem of the series, "Builder Kachina: Going Home," the persona bears witness to the presence of the kachina, "invisible / yet touching me all over."

In 1983 Rose took a permanent position with the American Indian Studies Program at Fresno City College in Fresno, California; she is director of the program, in which she initiates and teaches a broad range of courses relating to American Indian life and culture. She lives with her husband in the foothills of the Sierra Nevada, near Yosemite National Park and overlooking the San Joaquin Valley. The location of her home, neither mountain nor valley but part of both, echoes Rose's ongoing preoccupation with existence between worlds, between cultures, between established definitions. It is important to her to live in a rural area, in close connection with the natural cycle of the seasons. Another expression of her identification with the earth is in her plant and reptile collections. As early as her first publication Rose described herself as an "amateur herpetologist," and her home includes a garage converted into a greenhouse that contains her extensive collection of euphorbias, cacti, and other tropical plants as well as several rare lizards. In her ongoing negotiation of her multifaceted identity Rose consciously invokes closeness to the earth in both personal and cultural terms. She recalls as an important moment her father's telling her that she must find and set down her roots not in institutions but in the earth itself; this advice had come in answer to Rose's questioning of her anomalous relation to matrilineal Hopi society. After her move to the San Joaquin Valley, she sought counsel from tribal elders and healers in the *rancherias* of the area: identity and character, healing and growth, in her view, spring from the land and the spirituality that evolves within a given place, as well as from generational ties.

Four volumes of poems have been published since Rose's move to the San Joaquin Valley. *What Happened When the Hopi Hit New York* (1982) can be seen as part of an ongoing conversation with Maurice Kenny, a Mohawk poet based in rural New York. The unique character of various landscapes is a strong theme throughout the collection. Several poems describe landscapes as seen from airplanes or on brief stopovers – Alaska, Denver, Iowa City, New Orleans – and other poems center on the urban scene of Brooklyn. "Subway Graffiti, An Anthropologist's Impressions" incorporates the cryptic messages scrawled on subway surfaces and offers a personal view of the speaker's responses and speculations about the origins and interpretations of the anonymous messages. As in many of Rose's poems inspired by western archaeological sites, the persona of "Subway Graffiti" both identifies with the object under study and attempts to enter into the subjectivity of the creators of the graffiti, to understand their messages from their perspectives.

The poems in *What Happened When the Hopi Hit New York* are often permeated with a wry humor, an element of Rose's character and writing often overlooked by critics focusing on her poems as political statements or expressions of personal confrontation with pain and conflict (Andrew Wiget, who mentions the wit he sees in many of her pieces, is an exception). "Cemetery, Stratford, Connecticut" presents a bemused view from a West Coast perspective of a New England cemetery as "horizontal tenement / like the South Bronx." The speaker views the scene with eyes accustomed to the extremes of the western part of the country, which range from "the very ancient" to "things new enough / to smell like carpet glue"; she locates her own point of view as balanced "between the petroglyph / and the mobile home." Another poem encapsulating a moment in transition is "Chicago," in which "the foodless corridors / of O'Hare Airport" can offer little but "what is hoped / is a real coffee pot."

Two subsequent books, *The Halfbreed Chronicles & Other Poems* (1985) and *Going To War With All My Relations* (1993), include some of Rose's strongest poems. The poems of the former, among Rose's best, are dialogues similar to "Mission Bells." They reach out to embrace individuals from many places, historical eras, and backgrounds who have suffered injustice and misunderstanding: Truganinny, a Tasmanian woman whose body is displayed in museums; Julia Pastrana, a woman exhibited in a freak show; and an anonymous Salvadoran mother describing a massacre.

In "Julia" the voice that speaks Julia Pastrana's feelings shatters the silencing glass of the display coffin housing her body and that of her infant child and rescues her from disappearing into the consuming gaze of the freak-show audience. The historical Julia Pastrana had a genetic condition that caused hair to grow over most of her body, and this was the pretext for her designation as a freak. In the poem she remakes her identity in reverie before a mirror, where she sees herself "reflected / as the burnished bronze woman / skin smooth and tender" that she feels herself to be. Yet she also realizes in an expression of nonbeing as fundamental as the assertion of her self-created identity that "I was there in the mirror / and I was not." The poem begins with an address to her husband, "Tell me it was just a dream, / my husband," and returns to the exhortation in the last section as the speaker apparently seeks to transpose dream and reality. A crucial transformation occurs in the poem's last lines. Julia's "stage name," as noted in the epigraph to this poem, was "Lion Lady," referring to her hirsute condition; she appropriates the label and its power in the last lines of the poem when she describes herself as "with child, / lioness / with cub." "Julia," like the other poems of *The Halfbreed Chronicles,* is a complex and powerful statement, fusing compassion for the disinherited with outrage at the public commodification of private tragedy.

Other poems in *The Halfbreed Chronicles* appear within sections titled "Sipapu," "Haliksa'ii!," and "If I Am Too Brown or Too White For You." Many of the poems in the first two sections set out to recover specifically Hopi identity. "Haliksa'ii!" is the traditional Hopi formula for opening a story, and "Sipapu" is a word signifying the small round entryway in the earth through which, according to the Hopi creation story, the first people emerged onto the surface of this world. The refrain "we emerge / we emerge" repeats through the poem; the repetition of this chorus suggests sacred song and renders immediate and vivid the continuing act of creation-emergence that defines the Hopi people and links them to the Anasazi, their ancient forebears.

"Sipapu" is a joyful, celebratory poem – a recurrent mode in Rose's work. Although her ironic or satiric poems have received more critical attention, a significant portion of her poetry is lyrical, even ecstatic. One such poem is "Throat Song: The Whirling Earth," which takes its inspiration from a note in an Eskimo publication, *Inuktitut Magazine,* explaining that "Eskimo throat singers imitate the sounds the women hear . . . when they learned the world was turning, they made a throat-singing song about it." The concept of imitating the sound of the turning earth motivates the persona of the poem to address the earth: "I always knew you were singing!" The persona, who is also poet, singer, and creator, identifies with the earth, "the mud of me," which in turn resonates within her as "tiny drums . . . flutes and reeds"; the poem ends with a recapitulation of the ecstatic opening line.

The Halfbreed Chronicles also develops a concept of pan-Indian identity, as in the poem titled "Wounded Knee: 1890–1973," which commemorates two significant events at Wounded Knee on the Sioux reservation. The first of these was the massacre of hundreds of women, children, and men by U.S. Army troops in 1890. Later, in 1973, Indians associated with the American Indian Movement recovered and reoccupied the Wounded Knee site, demanding long-neglected treaty and legal rights and creating a cooperative, self-determined community. The persona of the poem identifies with all the people within the compound during the 1973 siege, asserting a common vulnerability: "they shoot / at me / at all / my relations." The phrase "all my relations" reemphasizes Rose's insistence on the relational aspect of self-definition and emerges in the resonant and ambiguous title of her next book.

Going To War With All My Relations, which offers a more overtly political statement than most of her preceding works, is dedicated "to the memory of Charles Loloma." Rose notes in the preface that the poems are "a memoir of sorts," documenting "thirty years of observation and activity within the Fourth World (Indigenous Peoples) Movement." Some of these poems spring from observations of academic activities: excavation of a mission church where human bones were discovered embedded in the walls, conferences of scholars reporting on research among so-called primitive peoples, and the insensitivity of educational bureaucracies. Other poems reflect isolated moments of personal insight. "Men Talking in the Donut Shop," for instance, relates the conversation of several workmen discussing a husband who has shot his wife. It is the ordinariness of the scene, the casual "chitchat / over coffee" that endows this brief poem with its chilling power.

Rose has indicated that *Going To War With All My Relations* expresses directly some of her most deeply held convictions. The poem "Comment on Ethnopoetics and Literacy" confronts another issue Rose has addressed in her essays – the phenomenon that she and fellow poet and critic Geary Hobson call "whiteshamanism." The "whiteshaman" is a poet or other cultural worker who seeks to appropriate native literary forms, arts, culture, and customs to lay claim to a spurious "Indian" identity. Gary Snyder is one poet whom Rose has identified as having whiteshaman aspirations; Jerome Roth-

Frontispiece by Rose for Duane Niatum's anthology Carriers of the Dream Wheel *(1975)*

enberg, to whom the poem is addressed, is another. In some of his publications Rothenberg has attempted to rework translated texts (without knowing the original languages) into versions he deems more attuned to a "tribal spirit," a practice he calls ethnopoetics; Rothenberg also performs readings of these reworked texts. Rose's poem figures "ethnopoetics" as a kind of literary taxidermy: the agent first kills, then dismembers, guts, reassembles, and stuffs the prey – in this case, poem texts analogized as the hunter's catch. The final step is construction of a diorama in which the creature-text is exhibited, analagous again to the hunter-translator's performance or to publication in an anthology of similar worked-over texts. Read in the context of such poems as "Truganinny" and "Julia," which denounce the exhibition of human remains for entertainment, "Comment on Ethnopoetics and Literacy" is a stinging indictment of cultural appropriation, ventriloquism, and exploitation.

Bone Dance: New and Selected Poems, 1965–1992 (1994) is Rose's second major retrospective collection. It contains poems from all her previous books as well as from a collection of new poems, titled *Now Poof She Is Gone* (1994). Rose's introduction to *Bone Dance* offers her retrospective view of her poetic career, including changes in her quest for cultural identity and influences such as that of Maurice Kenny on her work. She concludes with an affirmation of art – and especially poetry – that is accessible to everyone, not just the property of highly trained specialists. She also affirms the validity of personal expression, especially the expression of women and marginalized persons, in texts that have not been accorded a place in what she calls "Literature (capital L)."

The poems in *Now Poof She Is Gone* represent another type of retrospective vision. Rose mentions in her introduction that this collection includes poems written throughout her poetic career, including some of her early work not previously published. Many of these texts explore perceptions of feminism and identity as woman. Rose had declined to publish much of this material, she explains, because of its deeply personal subject matter, in deference to her sense that "the world is not interested in the private pain of women." When she determined to publish the collection Rose, a committed feminist, sought out Firebrand Press, a publishing house founded by and for women. Even the early and most personal of these poems express Rose's perception of individual identity as embedded in relationships with others. An example is "What Debris-Woman Needs," written in 1967, which figures the persona's inner struggle as "the colonial thrust / and the native resistance." Another poem, "Urban Breed, Go Get Your Gun," dated 1971, in the lines "you are too white / for the red, too red for the white" anticipates "If I Am Too Brown or Too White For You" from *The Halfbreed Chronicles.*

The poem "Naming Power" dates to the journey commemorated in *Builder Kachina.* A recurrent refrain, "There has to be / someone / to name you," both continues Rose's characteristic dialogic mode and suggests the incantatory nature of many tribal songs. The voice of the marginalized persona, in dialogue with the tribal mandate that has left her "standing / in the beat / of my silence," eventually affirms her self in connection with the earth, "rust that roots in this place / with my mothers before me." The assertion of selfhood and integrity in these poems counters the other sense, also pervasive in Rose's work, of incipient dissolution and erasure. "Is It Crazy To Want To Unravel," for instance, expresses the sensations and emotions of a woman who feels her identity and sense of selfhood dissolving into nothing; the possibility of vanishing "sideways / before a funhouse mirror" recalls the mirror of Julia Pastrana, in which the persona finds "I was there in the mirror / and I was not." This negative aspect of identity, a recognition of nonbeing, is a necessary correlate of the kind of self-determination carefully worked out in many of Rose's poems: the self-created self is at every moment subject to erasure by that same creative force.

Another theme that has engaged Rose's attention since her earliest creative efforts in the Bay Area is that of the fantastic and mythological. *Academic Squaw* is dedicated to Chelsea Quinn Yarbro, a writer of fantasy and science fiction who gave early encouragement to Rose's work. Themes associated with the fantastic, in particular dreamlike images of women and centaurs, appear in many of Rose's color pen drawings. Many of her poems also honor the knowledge derived from dreams – an important aspect of American Indian traditions – and *Now Poof She Is Gone* celebrates dreams and fantasies as elements in the process of self-creation. "April, a Dream" depicts a dream vision of a woman dreaming, bringing herself into being through a series of metamorphoses: "a knife that is changing / into a butterfly that is the woman."

The intensely personal, confessional mode of these poems links Rose with other women poets of the present century who have challenged conventional dicta regarding appropriateness or importance of poetic subject matter. As early as 1967, in "Child Held, Child Broken," Rose introduced the phrase "neon scars," which became the title for her most explicit autobiographical statement. The essay "Neon Scars" was commissioned for a volume of autobiographical pieces and appeared at the same time as "These Bones Are Alive" (1987), an interview with poet and publisher Joseph Bruchac. Both of these prose pieces continue the dialogic mode of many of Rose's poems. Whereas the interview is a conventional dialogue between Rose and Bruchac, "Neon Scars" offers an intense, acutely rendered set of alternating passages in which interlocking voices question, comment on, and critique each other in attempting to come to terms with a history of pain, rejection, and conflict that has nevertheless been part of a significant creative achievement. "I live with ghosts," Rose's narrator asserts; and this essay – like many of her poems – both exorcises and transforms those ghosts in a ritual of acknowledgment, naming, and incorporation: by making the ghosts part of her story, the persona of the essay seizes authority-authorship and transcends manipulation.

Rose's other prose writings have emphasized her aesthetic principles and her views of poetry and poets who have adopted or been given the designation "American Indian." She consistently opposes the patronizing view of American Indian artists (especially writers of fiction and poetry) as producers of ethnic curios or works of mainly anthropological interest. She has criticized the placement of fiction by American Indian authors in the anthropology sections of libraries and bookstores and has pointed out repeatedly that Native American writers are like all other writers in drawing upon their own experience and context in creating their works of art. Rose has also been generous in bringing to readers' attention the work of little-known and underappreciated authors, as in her articles on American Indian writers of California and the Southwest. Another theme in her essays as well as her poems is the attack on "whiteshamanism." Her prose in general continues the critique that runs throughout her poetry of the worst aspects of the powerful of the world: exploitation of the weak by the strong, commodification of the personal for material gain, and cruelty and injustice everywhere.

Critical reception of Rose's work has frequently touched on the theme of creating an identity through art. In his essay "Blue Stones, Bones and Troubled Silver: The Poetic Craft of Wendy Rose" (1993), Wiget regards this motif as central to her poems; noting the recurring imagery of bones in her poems, he links the image both with her experience in anthropology and archaeology and with her consciousness of "body as resource and body as residuum." Wiget also notes Rose's technical virtuosity in manipulating accent, rhythm, repetition, and consonance. Both Wiget and James R. Saucerman, in "Wendy Rose: Searching through Shards, Creating Life" (1989), focus on Rose's dual consciousness as anthropologist and Indian, both studier and studied. Saucerman emphasizes the ordering power of poetry, which can make sense of chaotic and painful reality for the "frustrated anthropologist and healing artist." In "The Uses of Oral Tradition in Six Contemporary Native American Poets" (1980) James Ruppert also traces a process of personal growth in Rose's poetry of the 1970s; he links her expression of deepening understanding to affinity for traditional oral poetic forms. Fellow poets N. Scott Momaday and Paula Gunn Allen have commended Rose's work, in particular its spiritual dimensions. In his preface to *Lost Copper* Momaday praises the musicality of Rose's poems, noting their emphasis on voice and singing as well as their own musicality. In *The Sacred Hoop: Recovering the Feminine in American Indian Traditions* (1986) Allen places Rose's poems in a context of feminine spirituality, regarding them primarily as texts in which "personal images and statements . . . become metaphors for spirit-infused consciousness."

In addition to writing, drawing and painting, teaching, and research, Rose has been consultant, editor, panelist, and adviser for community and academic projects. She is a member of the American Federation of Teachers and has served on the local executive council of that organization; she has been consultant-bibliographer for a federal recognition project, seeking formal recognition of the status of the North Fork Mono Tribe; and she has served as facilitator for the Association of Non-Federally Recognized California Tribes. Rose is in demand for poetry readings, which have taken her to all parts of the country on trips that have also inspired new poems. Her art has been exhibited in the western states and on the East Coast. She has served on various editorial boards and has granted many interviews. An important indication of Rose's distinguished reputation is the number of anthologies of American and contemporary literature that include her work. More than sixty anthologies, poetry collections, and prize volumes contain one or more of her poems; these include feminist collections such as *In Her Own Image* (1980), small regional publications such as *Dreaming of the Dawn* (1980) and comprehensive anthologies of American literature, American Indian literature, and literature by women, including *The Heath Anthology of American Literature* (1990), *The Sound of Rattles and Clappers* (1994) and *Women Poets of the World* (1983). Her work has been translated into French, German, and Danish.

Wendy Rose's poetry will stand with the work of other poets of the last half of the century, notably among those artists who have brought new material to poetry. With poets such as Ann Sexton, Sylvia Plath, and Adrienne Rich, Rose has made the elements of her life as a woman a rich source for her work, and like poets such as Ntozake Shange, Mitsuye Yamada, and Gloria Anzaldúa, she has offered the special feminist perspective of a woman of color. Rose's work has shown the connections between the personal and the political, addressing issues of justice, equity, and probity as they create and destroy in the lives of ordinary people.

Interviews:

Carol Hunter, "A *MELUS* Interview: Wendy Rose," *MELUS,* 10 (Fall 1983): 67–87;

Hunter, "An Interview with Wendy Rose," in *Coyote Was Here,* edited by Bo Schöler (Århus, Denmark: University of Århus, 1984), pp. 40–56;

Lynn Gray, "The Power of Words: An Interview with Poet/Artist/Teacher Wendy Rose," *Akwesasne Notes,* 17 (Winter 1985);

Joseph Bruchac, "These Bones Are Alive: An Interview with Wendy Rose," in *Survival This Way: Interviews with American Indian Poets,* edited by Bruchac (Tucson: University of Arizona, 1987), pp. 249–269;

Laura Coltelli, *Winged Words* (Lincoln: University of Nebraska Press, 1990), pp. 121–133.

References:

Paula Gunn Allen, *The Sacred Hoop: Recovering the Feminine in American Indian Traditions* (Boston: Beacon, 1986);

Christoph Irmscher, "Anthropological Roles: The Self and Its Others in T. S. Eliot, William Carlos Williams and Wendy Rose," *Soundings,* 75 (Winter 1992): 587–603;

Linda Koolish, "The Bones of This Body Say, Dance: Self-Empowerment in Contemporary Poetry of Women of Color," in *A Gift of Tongues: American Poetry Reconsidered,* edited by Marie Harris and Kathleen Aguero (Athens: University of Georgia Press, 1987), pp. 1–56;

Kenneth Lincoln, "A Contemporary Tribe of Poets," *American Indian Culture and Research Journal,* 6, no. 1 (1982): 79–101;

Lincoln, "Finding the Loss," *Parnassus,* 10 (Spring–Summer 1982): 285–296;

N. Scott Momaday, Introduction to Rose's *Lost Copper* (Banning, Cal.: Malki Museum Press, Morongo Indian Reservation, 1980), pp. ix–x;

James Ruppert, "The Uses of Oral Tradition in Six Contemporary Native American Poets," *American Indian Culture and Research Journal,* 4, no. 4 (1980): 87–110;

James R. Saucerman, "Wendy Rose: Searching through Shards, Creating Life," *Wicazo-Sa Review,* 5 (Fall 1989): 26–29;

Andrew Wiget, "Blue Stones, Bones and Troubled Silver: The Poetic Craft of Wendy Rose," *Studies in American Indian Literatures,* series 2, 5 (Summer 1993): 29–33.

Greg Sarris

(12 February 1952 -)

Kenneth Lincoln
University of California, Los Angeles

BOOKS: *Keeping Slug Woman Alive: A Holistic Approach to American Indian Texts* (Berkeley: University of California Press, 1993);

Mabel McKay: Weaving the Dream (Berkeley: University of California Press, 1994);

Grand Avenue (New York: Hyperion, 1994).

TELEVISION: *Grand Avenue,* screenplay by Sarris, produced by Sarris, Robert Redford, Paul Aaron, and Rachel Pfeffer, Home Box Office, June 1996.

OTHER: "Battling Illegitimacy: Some Words against the Darkness," in *Multitude: A Selection of Cross Cultural Readings,* edited by Chitra B. Divakaruni (New York: McGraw-Hill, 1992), pp. 194–211;

"Waiting for the Green Frog," in *Looking Glass,* edited by Clifford E. Trafzer (San Diego: San Diego State University Press, 1992), pp. 26–42;

"What I'm Talking about When I'm Talking about My Baskets," in *De/Colonizing the Subject: Politics and Gender in Women's Autobiographical Practice,* edited by Sidonie A. Smith and Julia Watson (Minneapolis: University of Minnesota Press, 1992), pp. 20–33;

"Rosie Jarvis," "Mabel McKay," "Essie Parrish," and "Tsupu," in *Native American Women: A Biographical Dictionary,* edited by Gretchen M. Bataille (New York: Garland, 1993), pp. 123, 169–170, 197–198, 265–266;

"Keeping Slug Woman Alive: The Challenge of Reading in a Reservation Classroom," in *Ethnography of Reading,* edited by Jonathan Boyarin (Berkeley: University of California Press, 1993), pp. 238–269;

"Hearing the Old Ones Talk: Reading Narrated Indian Lives in Elizabeth Colson's *Autobiographies of Three Pomo Women,*" in *New Voices in Native American Literary Criticism,* edited by Arnold Krupat (Washington, D.C.: Smithsonian Institution Press, 1993), pp. 419–452;

Greg Sarris at the time of Mabel McKay: Weaving the Dream *(photograph by Jerry Bauer)*

"American Indian Lives and Others' Selves: Invention of Indian Selves in Narrated Autobiography," in *Thinking Bodies,* edited by Juliet Flower MacCannell (Palo Alto, Cal.: Stanford University Press, 1994);

"Living with Miracles: The Politics and Poetics of Writing Kashaya Pomo/Coastal Miwok Identity," in *Displacement, Diaspora, and Geographical Identities,* edited by Smadar Lavie and Ted Swedenburg (Durham, N.C.: Duke University Press, 1994);

"Storytelling in the Classroom: Crossing Vexed Chasms," in *Norton Anthology of Writing* (New York: Norton, 1994);

The Sound of Rattles and Clappers: A Collection of New California Indian Writing, edited by Sarris (Tucson: University of Arizona Press, 1994);

Dust jacket for Sarris's book about his "Pomo granny"

"Critical Approaches to Native American Literature," special issue of *Studies in American Indian Literature,* edited by Sarris (Fall 1994);

Beyond the Ivory Tower: Essays on the New Writing of Scholarship, edited by Sarris (Berkeley: University of California Press, forthcoming).

SELECTED PERIODICAL PUBLICATIONS – UNCOLLECTED: "A Culture under Glass: The Pomo Basket," *In Writing* (Spring 1987): 44–53;

"On the Road to Lolsel," *News from Native California* (Summer 1988): 3–6;

"Stanford University at Kashaya: A Mutual Aid Pact," *News from Native California* (Fall 1989): 53–57;

"The Verbal Art of Mabel McKay: Talk as Culture Contact and Cultural Critique," *MELUS,* 16 (Spring 1990): 95–112;

"Encountering the Native Dialogue: Critical Theory and American Indian Oral Literatures," *College Literature,* 18 (October 1991): 126–131;

"Telling Dreams and Keeping Secrets: The Bole Maru as American Indian Religious Resistance," *American Indian Culture and Research Journal,* 16 (1992): 71–85.

Greg Sarris has gone from college athlete to creative writer, from street tough to academic, from undergraduate English major to professor of American Indian studies. He is generating some of the most talked-about interdisciplinary and cross-cultural scholarship in the country. He has written a classic biography of a California Indian woman, the last Cache Creek Pomo Basket Maker and healing dreamer; he is writing fiction about growing up with off-reservation Indians and turning that fiction into screenplays for television and film. Along with Sherman Alexie, Gordon Henry, and Debra Earling, Sarris is in the advance guard of a second wave of multifaceted Indian artists and intellectuals who are carrying on a Native American renaissance.

Sarris was born on 12 February 1952 in Santa Rosa, California. His Miwok-Pomo-Filipino father, Emilio "Meatloaf" Hilario, who had played football for the University of Southern California, eventually drank himself to death; his mother, Bunny Hartman, who was German Jewish and Irish, died in childbirth. Sarris, in his own words, grew up in

"Northern California, around Santa Rosa and west to Stewart's Point, with Indian and Hispanic mixed-bloods, street gangs. I was an adopted orphan, in and out of different families. Mabel McKay, the last Cache Creek Pomo Basket Maker, became kind of a guardian to me." He attended the University of California, Los Angeles, where he played defensive secondary on the football team and received a bachelor's degree in English in 1978. He then went to Stanford, where he completed a master's degree in creative writing in 1981. He worked as a lecturer in writing and American studies at the University of California, Santa Cruz, then returned to Stanford. After receiving a doctorate in modern thought and literature in 1989, he joined the UCLA English Department, where he teaches contemporary American fiction, creative writing workshops, American ethnic minority autobiography, a graduate seminar in cultural worldviews of Native America, and lower-division introductions to American Indian literature. From 1989 through 1991 he held the prestigious University of California President's Postdoctoral Fellowship. In 1990 he was elected to the executive committee of the Discussion Group on American Indian Literatures of the Modern Language Association, and in 1992 he was appointed to the MLA Committee on the Literatures and Languages of America. He was associate director of the UCLA American Indian Studies Center in 1991–1992. He is a consultant for Turner Broadcasting System on California Indians and was coexecutive producer of a 1996 Home Box Office miniseries he adapted from his short-story collection *Grand Avenue* (1994). He serves on the advisory boards of the Sundance Film Institute and the California Indian Radio Project. He has received several distinguished teaching awards and has presented more than seventy public lectures.

Sarris has worked with Foothill College in Los Altos Hills, California, to design a program for teaching multicultural literatures and has advised the California Kashaya Pomo Reservation School on cross-cultural education. He has been a guest lecturer and visiting scholar at the American Indian Language Institute at the University of Arizona and writer in residence with the American Indian Studies Program at the University of California, Riverside. He has designed programs for the California Rural Indian Health Board. He was elected in 1992 and reelected in 1993 and 1994 as chairman (or chief) of the Federated Coast Miwok Tribes, some three thousand Native Americans who are trying to gain federal recognition and recover tribal lands in northern California.

Sarris's first book, *Keeping Slug Woman Alive: A Holistic Approach to American Indian Texts* (1993), is a collection of his essays on such topics as Pomo basketry, oral tradition, Indian autobiography, classroom cultural diversity, and reading contemporary fiction. Against the "objective" methodologies of traditional anthropologists and literary critics, Sarris advocates dialogic interaction between authority and audience, students "talking back" to texts and teachers. Against treating Indian art and literature as artifact, Sarris recommends a holistic approach that takes into consideration how oral or written texts are produced and how different readers bring different assumptions to bear on the texts. Sarris makes use of the insights of such social scientists as Stephen Tyler, Renato Rosaldo, George E. Marcus, and Michael M. J. Fischer and of such literary theorists as Stanley Fish and David Bleich. Fusing autobiography with ethnography, he mixes storytelling and literary criticism. Storytelling – as a topic of analysis, as a mode of criticism, and as a pedagogical method – pervades the book. Sarris is interested in a kind of talk that leads to what he calls "generative understanding" between peoples. For literary critics and teachers he advocates "a dialogue that interrupts and disrupts preconceived notions" about fixed texts and closed interpretations.

"Born so-called illegitimate," as he says, not knowing his mother or father, Sarris sees himself as "a mixed blood caught in the middle" of cultural skirmishes, as an adopted orphan looking for family, home, culture, and history. Talk about the problems of reading things up front, he advises repeatedly; critical thinking sparks an interpersonal, cross-cultural exchange that validates everyone. Social scientists today agree, he points out, that there is no such thing as an "Indian," no representative summary of the more than three hundred tribal cultures that exist in the United States alone. Current ethnological methodologies, espoused by such scholars as James Clifford and Vincent Crapanzano, encourage individual portraits of particular people at a given moment. "What is pure or authentic," Sarris argues, "is that which is complex and dynamic" in experience. Instead of deploying the "us-them" rhetoric that has too long governed minority discourse, Sarris demonstrates that "all of us can and should talk to one another" cross-culturally. He exposes the biases and frustrates the expectations of various interpreters (including himself) concerning things "Indian." This elimination of clichés and racial stereotypes clears a path for more-immediate, more-honest intercultural exchanges.

Essie Parrish, Pomo healer and friend of Mabel McKay

"Open this collection of essays and find yourself irresistibly drawn into it," said *Publishers Weekly* (November 1993) about *Keeping Slug Woman Alive.* "Although a work of scholarship, the text is written with the style and flair of fiction. . . . this is a good read." *Choice* (November 1993) said, "Pointedly, but without arrogance, Sarris (UCLA) challenges lingering academic and non-Indian presumptions about meanings and functions of Native American narrators. This text is as close to a hands-on discussion of Native American narratives as can be achieved." In his reader's report on *Keeping Slug Woman Alive* for the University of California Press, Fischer calls the collection an "outstanding" book that "should become a classic exercise in any anthropology, linguistics, or folklore class." He continues:

> One of the pleasures of Sarris' text is the rhythm of weaving: beginning with a (usually first person) story that needs unpacking, moving into a more discursive topic, introducing a (usually puzzlingly decontextualized) myth or traditional story, and eventually returning to the opening story as a way of making a puzzle fall into coherence. A second pleasure of the text is the simplicity of its prose: even academic debates are presented conversationally without losing any of their rigor, thereby making them potentially accessible to a wide range of readerships. In both these ways, Sarris' exquisitely literate presentation mimics oral storytelling. It both demonstrates and explains how oral story telling operates. And it shows the patient wisdom of Mabel McKay's only seemingly enigmatic, "Don't ask me what it means, the story. Life will teach you about it, like the way it teaches you about life." The third pleasure of Sarris' text is that its material illustrates how classroom and other discussion settings can be made to come alive for children and adults in reading back and forth across cultural boundaries, between one's own experiences and various kinds of knowledge bases. The lovely insistence that the narrator is also only one with partial knowledge, and that the point is not to get the story or explication of a tale right (there is no one right way or single authoritative version or interpretation), but rather to encourage others to add to the story telling, to add on insights from their positions of partial knowledge and experience to make the communication come alive – is a lesson both for the classroom and for crossing emotional boundaries.

Of the some six hundred published "autobiographies" by American Indians, 83 percent are not written by the Indians themselves but are told to non-Indians, who often have silently erased the contexts of fieldwork and interviewing. Sarris advocates emphasizing individual circumstances, field data, interpersonal dynamics, and subjective reflections. These are the methods he uses in his book about his "Pomo granny," *Mabel McKay: Weaving the Dream* (1994). When Mabel Boone was born in 1907 the indigenous California Indian population had been decimated by more than 97 percent in half a century; when she was four Ishi, the last of four thousand Yana exterminated in late-nineteenth-century California, staggered into the Oroville slaughteryard. Yet California was – and still is – the most densely populated corridor of Native America, even though it has few reservations or tribal councils with federal recognition. Los Angeles is home to the largest population of urban Indians – some 120,000 – and California, with 242,164 in the 1990 census, vies with Oklahoma for the largest state figures. Americans hear of Navajo in Arizona and Sioux in the Dakotas, but few know about the Yokuts, Wappo, Yuki, Konkow, or Costanoan nations of northern California; the Indians there hid themselves away in cultural pockets of buried history and underground tradition. Thus, many California Indians live as strangers among themselves, as mixed-bloods questioning both sides of their lineage and wondering who they are, where they fit in, and when they can come home. Infighting, bickering, gossiping, and suspicions of hexing go hand in hand with chronic unemployment, poor education, ill health, malnutrition, substance abuse, cultural loss, homelessness, and historical displacement.

Mabel was given up by her mother and raised by her grandmother, did not bear the children she herself raised, healed strangers with her dream songs, wove baskets all her life, and died as the last of the Cache Creek Pomo. "Now listen to me. This is what I'm saying, what Essie was talking to you about. This has rules. It's your life," Mabel tells the young doctoral candidate Sarris: he will not only be telling her story but also hearing his own. To university students who spend a "long time studying," Mabel says: "You have to know me. How what I say, it turns out. And that's a long time. That's knowing me." The book is a patiently woven narrative of everyday detail; embedded in it is the spiritual power to bind up and heal the people.

Mabel's life is that of a twentieth-century off-reservation Indian who gathers roots and dreams, cans apples, weaves baskets, washes lettuce, and dances the Charleston for fifty cents in a traveling carnival. She survives as a dish scrubber, housecleaner, caretaker, clothes washer, cattle herder, storyteller, dream dancer, university lecturer, basket weaver, and "sucking doctor." Her attention to daily detail is an attending to the world realizing itself. All are included, "white people and strangers," natives and immigrants. With the young narrator the reader listens to the old ones talk and hears himself or herself woven into the fabric of community, included in a story woven against loneliness, estrangement, and the isolating despair of mortality. In fear of dying alone, people fail to live together; such futility poisons modern life. If people listen, the spirits of the old ways will bring them back to the tribe, where each is one among many, never alone, ever going on collectively.

"Greg, you're part of the gang," Essie Parrish's daughter Violet tells him, as she stands in the open door of her house trailer in pink curlers with a cigarette in her hand. "Get in here and quit acting like a stranger." A generation earlier, Violet's mother, a medicine woman, had taken Mabel in across Pomo-Wintun tribal boundaries, saying, "You don't have a people. You will be the last of your people. But you will have a people. You know who I am, and I know who you are. You'll be part of me, my people."

"Watch how it turns out," the spirits told Mabel, a troubled child who heard voices. Later, Essie and Mabel "sat down with their handpicks and garden trowels and began working. They worked a long time, digging and cutting, piling wet soggy roots on newspapers and gunnysacks." When the two women break for coffee, Essie says that a dam will soon flood this area; the nonnative world will encroach on the centuries-old marsh where willow rod, sedge, and redbud are gathered for sacred basketry. There is heartbreaking loss here, but no apocalypse: "sitting there in that afternoon spring sun, Mabel felt something timeless, endless, something familiar and forever about digging roots by the water with another woman" – a Native America that keeps on going on, binding itself up with talk, gossiping to keep the people in line, weaving small baskets of sedge and bird feathers to keep the spirits listening. Mabel's plastic Kmart shopping bag is filled with ceremonial objects, Sarris notes. Her heart stays strong with compassion for lost children, her mind sharp with native humor, her soul as clear as the sedge-root stream. A deft native wit keeps her resilient and resourceful as she jokes about lunch at the Happy Steak in Woodland with Pope John Paul II, who requested a meeting with her, or discusses calamine lotion as a cure for poison oak. Mabel's humor is simple and direct, if elliptically coy. Her baskets, stories, and dreams weave the estranged Sarris into tribal patterns that bring him home.

Mabel's presence makes the reader aware of the reality of Native Americans, not as exotic shamans or visionary medicine men, not as tragic warriors or hapless princesses, but as human beings who question their past and hope for a promising future as they struggle between cultures. Finally, we are "all related," the narrator discovers at his graduation party, diploma in hand; we all have "Lots of family. Jews. Catholics. Filipinos. Mexicans. Indians. . . . While trying to help her, while trying to trace her story, I traced my own. . . . Her story, the story, our story." Why was he asked to stay and listen, and finally invited to come in and add his story to the others? The old woman has the last word: " 'Because you kept coming back.' "

Sarris's *The Sound of Rattles and Clappers: A Collection of New California Indian Writing* (1994) brings together poetry and prose by ten contemporary writers; the volume includes Sarris's own short stories "Slaughterhouse" and "Strawberry Festival." Sarris's introduction sets a compelling call to readers: "From this place called California, then, you have the voices of many California Indians. They are singing, telling stories, their voices echoing on the pages so you will know. Listen. This place, these rolling, oak-dotted hills, redwood forests, deserts and ocean shores are sounding." *The Sound of Rattles and Clappers* is culturally diverse and expertly

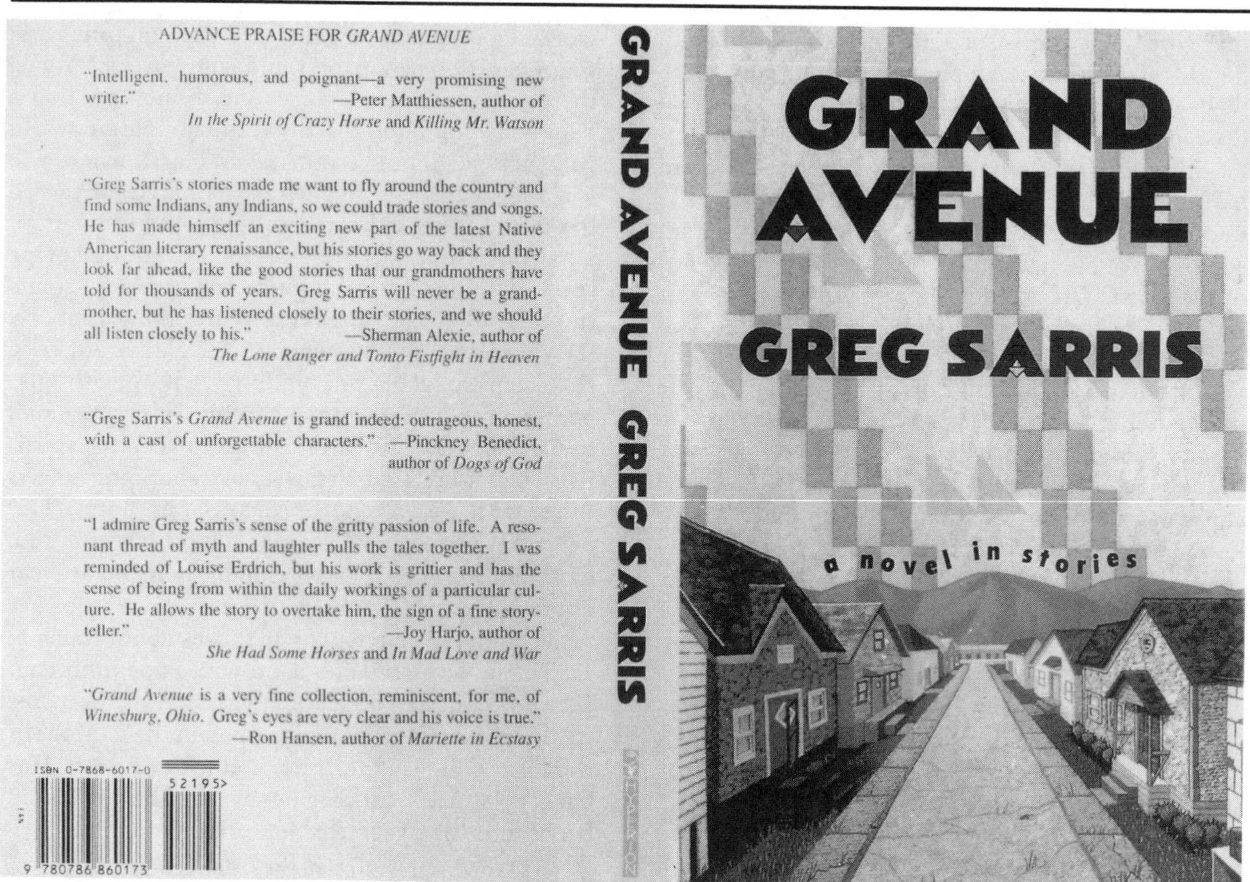

Dust jacket for Sarris's collection of stories set in Santa Rosa, California

crafted, up to date and rich with talent. A review in *Native California* (Spring–Summer 1994) called it "beautiful, lively, and fresh, rich and generous in literary style and scope."

Kirkus Reviews (1 July 1994) calls *Grand Avenue,* a collection of ten of Sarris's short stories, a "touching, often poignant, debut collection. Without being mawkish or sentimental, he creates a variety of voices – male and female – who tell the struggles of a people and their determination to survive." The story "How I Got to Be Queen" was originally published in Craig Lesley's anthology of Native American writing, *Talking Leaves* (1991). Written with a fine edge of humor despite the pathos and loss it depicts, it is a story about modern off-reservation Indians who are struggling to regain personal dignity and cultural integrity in the face of overwhelming social and economic odds. "Slaughterhouse" was republished in the anthology *Best in the West Short Fiction* (1993) and has been included in three other anthologies. The story portrays a mixed-blood's initiation into manhood at a slaughterhouse used as a brothel.

The stories are set in squalid Santa Rosa, where off-reservation Indians are, as Sarris observes, half dislocated from themselves. All are interrelated; everybody's lineage is suspect; fathers are missing, mothers are talked about. A Pomo mailman, married to an Apache, has an illegitimate son by his half-sister, who was raised across town. "Reality is like the sun on a summer morning," a frustrated mother says. "It burns right through the fog. As I always think in looking back, Vietnam got Joaquin James and Albert Silva got me. Two kids becomes eight, and a husband's earnings become a welfare check. I peel apples at the cannery when there's work, and Mama's burdened caring for my kids. Half the Indians in town live up the street or around the corner, and of those too many are on the front porch asking for Uncle." The stories counter cultural romanticism, check racial stereotypes, and seek to understand and purge nationalist xenophobia. Everyone here is all mixed up with everyone else. "That boy's your third third cousin," Mama warns in the opening story, and her daughter replies, "We're tangled up with everybody." This tangle complicates the traditional Indian call to "all my relatives." A rancorous Portuguese father calls Indians "worse than niggers." A hundred-year-old conjurer calls an Indian grandmother "God-damn white man whore." A woman calls her daughter "Damned black-neck squaw" for dating an Afro-American. This caustic name-calling hexes language, as it poisons relatives into festering isolation.

The old ones – the healers and tellers and singers, the carriers of children and culture – know the trouble and also know how to work through the poison. Old spirits are mixed up with new things to reconnect people: a mail-order Plains pipe is added to the traditional Pomo basket, flint, and cocoon rattle for conjuring. Grandma Nellie goes to her sedge sloughs on a four-legged aluminum walker and has a stroke in McGill's cow pasture, but she still gets down to the water for roots. Passing on her green-frog songs and sedge root basketry to the next generation, Auntie insists in the final story: "Talk. It's important to talk. Us Indians here are all family. That's the trouble, no one talks. Stories, the true stories, that's what we need to hear. We got to get it out. The true stories can help us. Old-time people, they told stories, Alice. They talked." This elder, surely a cousin of Mabel McKay, ends *Grand Avenue* on a note of promise: "I'm not too old for miracles."

The talk is real and has a simple storyteller's eloquence: "And when the moment came Mama couldn't coax another breath out of Marie, Mama sighed and looked as if she'd just lost a hand of cards, her eyes searching the bed, the still body, for a sign she'd been cheated. She pulled the shades over the window, looked back once at Marie, propped up in her bed and staring blankly, then left the house forever." Common voices are raised slightly, to a level of revelation: "You dream and plan, plan and dream," an Indian mailman says. "It's like ivy. It looks pretty at first, the way it climbs a tree. Then it takes the life right out of the tree, strangles it."

The stories are realistically fleshed out with the everyday details of working-class life. Grandmothers make tuna casserole; mothers cook macaroni and cheese; sisters set out Wonder Bread and peanut butter. Metaphors are down to earth: "I'd like to throw her like a stone out of my sight," a shamed husband says of his young Indian temptress. "I picture her as a small hard rock in my hand, and I'm tossing her with all my might, like when I was chucking rocks with my brothers at an old barn, when I didn't know any better." A half-breed woman, who dates a Portuguese boy and has a daughter dying of cancer, opens a confrontational scene: "One night while I was punching down fry dough as if I were killing a wild dog, Mama took my arm." In the next story a young narrator, taken in by extended kin and faced with yet another stepfather in a house of half-related strays, says, "My stomach slid like a tire on an icy road." These are likenesses invented by real people from their everyday lives.

A compelling collection, *Grand Avenue* shows Sarris to be one of his generation's finest Native writers. In the *Los Angeles Times* (4 September 1994) Michael Dorris calls it "a gritty, power-filled book, unsparing and unapologetic. . . . It is a book to read once for story, a second time to better understand how the pieces perfectly fit together and illuminate each other, a third time for the sheer pleasure of fine writing. . . . not only one of the very best works of fiction by and about Native Americans, it's one of the most important imaginative books of the year, period."

References:

William Bright, "*Slug Woman,*" *San Francisco Review of Books* (April–May 1993): 34–35;

Helen Jaskoski, "California Renaissance," *College English,* 56 (April 1994): 461–470;

Michael Kowalewski, "Coming into Knowledge," *Hungry Mind Review* (Summer 1994): 1–2;

Kenneth M. Roemer, "Indian Lives: The Defining, the Telling," *American Quarterly,* 46 (March 1994): 81–91;

Alison Schneider, "Words as Medicine: Professor Writes of Urban Indians from the Heart," *Chronicle of Higher Education,* 42 (19 July 1996): B4–B5.

Jane Johnston Schoolcraft

(1800 - 22 May 1841)

James W. Parins
University of Arkansas at Little Rock

BOOK: *The Literary Voyager or Muzzeniegun,* by Schoolcraft and others, edited by Philip P. Mason (Lansing: Michigan State University Press, 1962).

Jane Johnston Schoolcraft was respected by her contemporaries as a woman of intelligence, literary talent, and wit, and writers such as Anna Jameson, Harriet Martineau, and Thomas McKenney admired her work and traveled from afar to visit her. She earned this reputation even though all of her writing appeared in one magazine, *The Literary Voyager or Muzzeniegun,* published by Jane and her husband, Henry Rowe Schoolcraft, the noted documenter of Native American life and customs. The magazine was an outgrowth of a reading society established by the Schoolcrafts among the American and Canadian citizens of Sault Sainte Marie, Michigan, who met weekly to discuss books and scholarly subjects. The society and the magazine provided a welcome literary diversion for the snow- and ice-bound inhabitants of the border region near Lake Superior. While the magazine was largely for the residents of the Sault, as the settlement on both sides of the Saint Mary's River was called, it was circulated in Detroit and New York City, as well. Its contents included articles on Ojibwe history, legends, lore, and customs; linguistic studies; and biographies of and speeches by contemporary Native Americans. In addition, *The Literary Voyager or Muzzeniegun* carried original poems and retellings of traditional tales, many of which were written by Jane Schoolcraft under the pen names Rosa and Leelinau.

Jane Johnston, whose Ojibwe name, Bame-wa-wa-ge-zhik-a-quay, means "Woman of the Stars Rushing through the Skies," was born in 1800 in Sault Sainte Marie to John Johnston, an Irish fur trader, and Ozha-guscoday-way-quay, or Susan Johnston, daughter of the Ojibwe chief and storyteller Waub Ojeeg. The Johnstons had met at a Lake Superior trading post near La Pointe, Wisconsin; after their marriage they had relocated to the Sault, where they ran a trading post and raised seven children.

As Sault Sainte Marie had no schools, Jane and her siblings were educated at home by John Johnston, who taught them European literature, history, and the classics using his extensive library. Jane read widely on her own, as well. Susan Johnston taught her children the Ojibwe language and educated them in the customs, traditions, myths, and legends of the native people. She also taught them family history, especially the exploits of her father and his father, Ma Mongazida. As she grew older Jane added to her knowledge of the world by traveling with her father to Detroit, Quebec City, and Montreal. In 1809 her parents sent her to Ireland to complete her education.

In 1822 the twenty-nine-year-old Henry Rowe Schoolcraft arrived at the Sault to take the post of Upper Great Lakes Indian agent, serving the tribes in the northern areas of Michigan, Wisconsin, and Minnesota. As part of his duties Schoolcraft sought answers to a series of questions about Native American history, traditions, languages, customs, and religion raised by the governor of Michigan, Lewis Cass. Schoolcraft enlisted the Johnston family to help in this research, and Jane became one of his primary sources of information. A year after his arrival at the Sault, Schoolcraft and Jane Johnston were married. Schoolcraft's interest in Native American culture did not flag after he had answered Cass's queries; he would go on to write more than twenty books and hundreds of articles on the subject.

The first issue of *The Literary Voyager or Muzzeniegun* appeared in December 1826 with a letter of introduction written by Jane under the pen name Leelinau. Here she invents the persona of a traditional Native American woman who, through her father, has descended from "one of the most ancient and respected leaders of the Ojibway bands." Leelinau promises to contribute articles that will acquaint readers with the ancient traditions and customs of her people. The editor, Henry Schoolcraft, comments that he looks forward to those contributions, as well as to the poems that she will write under the name Rosa.

The first tale she relates, "The Origin of the Robin. An Oral Allegory" (January 1827), is about an old man who directs his only son to undertake the traditional practice of fasting to secure a guardian spirit on whom his future will depend. The father instructs the son in how to prepare himself in the sweat lodge and bath, then takes him to a special lodge where he is to fast and wait for the arrival of his spirit helper. Because the father has great ambitions for his son to surpass all others in the tribe, he tells the young man to fast for twelve days, an unusually long time. After nine days the son tells his father that he has been dreaming of evil things and that he wishes to end the fast. The old man denies permission. After the eleventh day the son repeats his request but is told to go on with his ordeal. On the twelfth day the father sees his son painting his chest with vermilion stain. Before his father's eyes the son is changed into a robin, who explains that although he cannot bring his father the glory the old man desires, he will always live near people and will spread peace and joy through his song. The message of this allegory seems to be that overweening ambition leads to disaster.

"Moowis, the Indian Coquette" (12 January 1827) is an allegory about an Ojibwe flirt who is punished by spiritual powers for her misdeeds. "Mishosha, or the Magician and His Daughters" (January 1827) is a less didactic story about orphan brothers who thwart a magician and rescue his two daughters. "Origin of the Miscodeed, or the Maid of Taquimenon" (February 1827) is a traditional tale that recounts the mythical origin of a species of northern violet: the flower is the spirit of an Indian maid who was killed in an act of revenge.

Schoolcraft's poetry uses metrics that were conventional in her time, mostly couplets in iambic tetrameter or pentameter. Her topics are historical, inspirational, or personal. Two historical poems, both published in the 10 March 1827 issue of *The Literary Voyager* and both dealing with Waub Ojeeg, especially stand out. "Otagamiad" recounts a council at which the question of whether the band should take up arms against its enemies is discussed. Waub Ojeeg surveys the situation and sees enemies on every side. He declares that the choice is between war and slavery, and he urges war: "Thick crowding arrows, bristled o'er the plain, / And joyous warriors rais'd the battle strain." Other chiefs raise their voices as well, and in the end the decision is made to fight. "Invocation on My Maternal Grandfather on Hearing His Descent from Chippewa Ancestors Misrepresented" refutes a rumor that the revered Chippewa chief was in reality a Sioux who was taken from the mortal enemies of the Ojibwe when he was a child. Schoolcraft emotionally points out that one so valiant, one who rose in battle "Like a star in the west," must be Ojibwe.

Schoolcraft was ill for long periods, and two inspirational poems published in February 1827 show how she tried to cope with such adversity. "Lines Written under Affliction" says that difficulties are an essential part of life: "How could a landscape please, if it showed us no feature but light? / Tis the dark shades alone that give pleasure & ease / Tis the union of sombre and bright." In "Lines Written Under Severe Pain and Sickness" she turns to God for solace: "Oh! then on Thee, my Savior, I will trust . . . In Thee, with my whole heart I will confide, / And hope with Thee, forever to abide." In "To Sisters on a Walk in the Garden, after a Shower" (December 1826) and "Resignation" (December 1826) her theme is that life is hard but that one must face difficulties with faith and resignation.

The fourteenth and last issue of *The Literary Voyager,* dated 28 March 1827, begins with a notice of the death in February of William Henry Schoolcraft, the Schoolcrafts' son, at the age of two years, eight months. The parents expressed their grief in poems: Henry's "Lines of a Father on the Death of His Son" and Jane's "Sonnett" and "To My Ever Beloved and Lamented Son William Henry." "Sonnett" is not really written in sonnet form; it is a ten-line poem on the loss of her child and her turn for solace to "Faith – pleading the merits of the Cross, / And Him, whose promise gives a sure relief." "To My Ever Beloved and Lamented Son William Henry" is one of her few metrical experiments; it consists of tercets, each followed by the alternating refrain "Sweet Willy" or "My Willy." The Schoolcrafts later had a daughter and another son.

Jane Johnston Schoolcraft's style and diction are those of contemporary writers in the eastern United States, and many of her personal and inspirational verses are conventional. Her main value as a writer is her ability to use her considerable literary skills in English to depict with accuracy and empathy the traditions and history of her people. She died on 22 May 1841.

Leslie Marmon Silko

(5 March 1948 –)

William M. Clements
Arkansas State University

and

Kenneth M. Roemer
University of Texas at Arlington

See also the Silko entry in *DLB 143: American Novelists Since World War II, Third Series.*

BOOKS: *Laguna Woman: Poems by Leslie Silko* (Greenfield Center, N.Y.: Greenfield Review Press, 1974);

Ceremony (New York: Viking, 1977);

Storyteller (New York: Seaver, 1981);

Almanac of the Dead: A Novel (New York & London: Simon & Schuster, 1991);

Sacred Water (Tucson: Flood Plain Press, 1993);

Yellow Woman and a Beauty of the Spirit: Essays on Native American Life Today (New York: Simon & Schuster, 1996).

OTHER: *The Man to Send Rain Clouds: Contemporary Stories by American Indians,* edited by Kenneth Rosen (New York: Viking, 1974) – includes Silko's "The Man to Send Rain Clouds," "Yellow Woman," "Tony's Story," "Uncle Tony's Goat," "A Geronimo Story," "Bravura," and "From Humaweepi the Warrior Priest";

Carriers of the Dream Wheel: Contemporary Native American Poetry, edited by Duane Niatum (New York: Harper & Row, 1975) – includes Silko's "Toe'osh: A Laguna Coyote Story," "Prayer to the Pacific," "Poem for Ben Barney," and "Indian Song Survival";

Voices of the Rainbow: Contemporary Poetry by American Indians, edited by Rosen (New York: Viking, 1975) – includes Silko's "When Mountain Lion Lay Down With Deer," "When Sun Came to Riverwoman," "Love Poem," "Poem for Myself and Mei: Abortion," "Deer Song," "Toe'osh: A Laguna Coyote Story," "Alaskan Mountain Poem #1," "Poem for Ben Barney," "Four Mountain Wolves," "Slim Man Canyon," "Prayer to the Pacific," "Indian Song: Survival," "In Cold Storm Light," "Sun Children," "Hawk and Snake," "The Time We Climbed Snake Mountain," "Horses at Valley Store," and "Preparations";

Leslie Marmon Silko

"Language and Literature from a Pueblo Indian Perspective," in *English Literature: Opening Up the Canon,* edited by Leslie A. Fiedler and Houston A. Baker Jr. (Baltimore: Johns Hopkins University Press, 1981), pp. 54–72.

SELECTED PERIODICAL PUBLICATION – UNCOLLECTED: "An Old-Time Indian Attack in Two Parts," *Yardbird Reader,* 5 (1976): 77–84.

During the early 1970s – the emergent years of what Kenneth Lincoln has called the "Native American Renaissance" – Leslie Marmon Silko was perhaps the movement's preeminent writer of short fiction. She had also published a collection of highly regarded poems, *Laguna Woman* (1974). Yet it was the publication of her novel *Ceremony* (1977) that confirmed her position among American Indian writers of the late twentieth century. Subsequent books – including *Storyteller* (1981), stories and poetry unified around her interest in the continuity of verbal art at her native Laguna Pueblo; *Almanac of the Dead* (1991), a novel; the self-published *Sacred Water* (1993), a collection of prose pieces dealing with the role of water in the arid Southwest; and *Yellow Woman and a Beauty of the Spirit* (1996), a collection of nonfiction – have continued to develop the themes that Silko introduced into her earliest fiction and poetry.

Leslie Marmon Silko was born on 5 March 1948 in Albuquerque, New Mexico, and grew up in Old Laguna, a pueblo some forty miles to the west. Her mixed-blood heritage mirrors the tensions and the strengths that have characterized life at this Native American community at least since the late nineteenth century. In 1869 Walter Marmon came from Ohio to Laguna to survey the pueblo boundary. He remained in New Mexico, becoming a government schoolteacher at Laguna in 1871. The following year his brother, Robert G. Marmon, Silko's great-grandfather, settled at Laguna as a surveyor and trader. His second wife was Marie Anaya, a Laguna who had attended the Indian boarding school in Carlisle, Pennsylvania. While Silko was a child, Marie Marmon – whom she called "Grandma A'mooh" – lived next door and provided the future novelist with a significant link to traditional Laguna ways.

Walter and Robert Marmon both served terms as pueblo governors during the 1870s. At that time the synthesis of Laguna spirituality and Roman Catholicism that had endured for three centuries was facing challenges from Protestant missionaries. As Protestants, the Marmons were agents of change and bore at least some of the responsibility for the destruction of the largest kivas at Laguna and for the undermining of Catholic influences. Some Laguna traditionalists even abandoned the community at this time, creating a spiritual vacuum that was not filled until the mid twentieth century when some Native American ceremonies began to be revived.

The ability of the Marmons – recent Euro-American arrivals who quickly rose to political power in the pueblo – to affect community affairs, religious as well as secular, reflected the general adaptability of Laguna culture. The pueblo's location on a major route west – one that later became U.S. Highway 66 (now I-40) – probably influenced its receptivity to external influences, including that of the Marmons. The presence of Anglo ranchers in the area beginning in the mid nineteenth century and the discovery of uranium on pueblo lands a hundred years later also guaranteed that contact with the mainstreams of Euro-American culture would be felt in Laguna life.

Traditional ways have also continued, however, and despite her ancestors' negative impact on some aspects of Laguna tradition, Silko was made well aware of the Indian side of her heritage during her childhood. In addition to Grandma A'mooh, an important source of Laguna cultural knowledge for Silko was Susie Reyes Marmon, the wife of her grandfather's brother. Having attended both Carlisle Indian School and Dickinson College, Aunt Susie taught school at Laguna in the 1920s, while maintaining her commitment to the community's oral tradition. She handed that commitment on to Silko.

Among other family members who contributed to Silko's early development were her grandfather Henry Marmon, whose aspirations to design automobiles were stifled by early-twentieth-century preconceptions about the career possibilities suitable for Native Americans; Francesca Stagner Marmon (Grandma Lillie, Henry Marmon's wife), who had been reared by a Navajo woman; and Silko's father, Lee H. Marmon, a highly regarded photographer whose work appears in *Storyteller.* The most important lessons they taught Silko reflected the emphasis on the forces of continuity and adaptability in Laguna traditional culture – forces that their position in Laguna society and that of their Marmon ancestors had demonstrated, and which appear in Silko's poetry and fiction.

Silko began her formal education at the local Bureau of Indian Affairs school. After completing the fifth grade she moved to Catholic schools in Albuquerque, where she also later attended the University of New Mexico. There she received a B.A.

Silko on her cradle board, where, according to tribal custom, she spent the first twelve months of her life (photograph by Lee H. Marmon)

in English in 1969. She then began law school in a program designed to provide Native Americans with Indian lawyers. Silko taught two years at Navajo Community College in Tsaile, Arizona, and spent another two years in Ketchikan, Alaska, where she wrote *Ceremony*. She then taught at the University of New Mexico and the University of Arizona. In 1981 Silko received a five-year MacArthur Foundation Grant, which gave her the opportunity to write most of *Almanac of the Dead*. She also received a National Endowment for the Humanities Grant to make films based on Laguna oral traditions. Silko has been divorced twice and has two sons, Robert William Chapman and Cazimir Silko.

The principal themes in Silko's writing derive to some degree from her family background and from her ancestors' participation in community affairs. They also reflect the continuing interaction between Laguna and mainstream Euro-American cultures. For while Silko has drawn consistently upon Laguna tradition, especially storytelling, she recognizes that the adaptability of her community heritage is an essential component of its strength. Instead of focusing nostalgically on a static past before Euro-American contact had influenced Laguna ways – a situation that has not existed at the pueblo for several centuries – Silko shows how Laguna tradition can and must adapt to the twentieth century. While Laguna culture remains distinct and viable, it does so through flexibility and an ability to incorporate and shape outside influences. Just as Laguna society had incorporated the Marmon family, so the rituals, customs, patterns of storytelling, and other aspects of culture have survived by adapting to and exploiting the modern world.

Silko's first important publication was the short story "The Man to Send Rain Clouds," written while she was a student at the University of New Mexico and published in the *New Mexico Quarterly* in 1969. Stemming – as does much of her work – from an actual incident at Laguna, the story treats the tensions between the Catholic Church and the local religious tradition. Though they depend primarily on traditional approaches in their funeral preparations, relatives of a deceased Laguna elder manage to involve the parish priest in the ceremony. While he realizes that sprinkling holy water on the old man's grave does not have the significance for the mourners that he would wish, the priest goes through with the ritual anyway. According to Laguna belief the act encourages the dead man's spirit to return in the form of rain clouds to refresh the parched New Mexico landscape.

The integration of Native American and Euro-American religious beliefs and actions that colors this story parallels the sociocultural context in which Silko grew up. Her first published work, the story also anticipates one of the important themes that has dominated her poetry and fiction: the necessity of cultural flexibility when faced with the dynamism engendered by culture contact. Her most successful works have continued to show how people from Laguna, and occasionally from other American Indian communities, are able to retain the values associated with their heritages while incorporating, manipulating, and exploiting a Euro-American culture whose dominance may be only superficial.

When Kenneth Rosen put together an anthology of short fiction by Native American writers in 1974, he used Silko's story as the main title for his collection. *The Man to Send Rain Clouds,* the first such anthology to emerge from the Native American Renaissance, includes six other pieces by Silko; her stories, in fact, comprise about a third of the volume. The best known of these is "Yellow Woman," which updates a motif from Laguna oral tradition, the abduction of mortal women by spiritual beings. Silko's story represents the continuation of the community's storytelling heritage as it develops from oral to written presentation. The first-person narrative voice transforms the old Laguna stories into immediate experiences, as immediate and tactile as the opening lines: "My thigh clung to his with dampness, and I watched the sun rising up through the tamaracks and willows. The small brown water birds came to the river and hopped across the mud, leaving brown scratches in the alkali-white crust."

The reader follows the perceptions and thoughts of the narrator as she awakens after spending the night away from her family with a handsome stranger she knows only as Silva. She rises and begins her journey back home, but changes her mind and stays. Her actions suggest more than romantic or sexual attraction. Prompted by Silva's habit of calling her Yellow Woman (the only name readers know her by), she begins to identify with the mythical woman abducted in her "old grandpa's" stories: "I was wondering if Yellow Woman had known who she was – if she knew that she would become part of the stories." The narrator is not completely sure what to believe. She assumes that Silva is using the Yellow Woman stories as a means of enticing her to stay with him. Still, her experience with Silva transcends her everyday sense of a romantic encounter and puts her in touch with the experiential origins of her storytelling traditions. Near the end of the story it becomes obvious that Silva is a cattle rustler; he may even shoot a fat rancher beyond the narrator's range of vision. As she hears the shots, she knows it is time to return to her everyday life. When she arrives at her home, her husband, Al, is playing with their baby, and her mother is teaching grandma how to make Jell-O. As she forms her explanation for her absence ("some Navajo kidnapped me"), she wishes her grandfather were alive because he loved to tell Yellow Woman stories. The narrator of "Yellow Woman" invites modern readers to experience vicariously a magical landscape between the daily and the mythic. It is one of Silko's most powerful expressions of the continuity of storytelling traditions.

Besides "The Man to Send Rain Clouds" and "Yellow Woman," several other notable Silko stories appeared in Rosen's collection. "Uncle Tony's Goat" is a delightful account of the misadventures of a misanthropic barnyard animal. The story recalls tales Silko heard from family members as she grew up at Laguna. "Tony's Story" has much darker origins. As Lawrence J. Evers explains in "Killing of a New Mexican State Trooper" in the Spring 1985 issue of *Wicazo Sa,* on "Good Friday in 1952 New Mexico State Trooper Nash Garcia was killed and burned in his patrol car twenty miles from McCartys, New Mexico." Silko and several other Native American writers, notably Simon Ortiz, have transformed the stories they heard about the trooper and his killers (two brothers from Acoma Pueblo) into fiction.

Once again Silko uses an effective first-person narrator, Tony, a traditionalist. Much of the story focuses on his friend Leon, who has come "back from the army" with new drinking habits and new ideas about Indian rights. Through most of the story the narrator invites the reader to believe that Leon will be the one to have a violent and possibly fatal encounter with a state trooper who seems to enjoy harassing Indians in general and Leon in particular. To the surprise of both reader and Leon, it is Tony who shoots the trooper. Leon is appalled: " 'My God, Tony. What's wrong with you? That's a state cop you killed.' " From Leon's viewpoint Tony has committed an insanely extreme act. From Tony's viewpoint he has committed a logical and necessary act based upon careful observations of the trooper's behavior and appearance that have convinced him that this witch must be destroyed. He reassures Leon: " 'Don't worry, everything is O.K. now, Leon. It's killed. They sometimes take on strange forms.' " Silko has given readers another moving expression of her belief that traditional stories and worldviews continue to shape perception in the twentieth century.

The time setting of "A Geronimo Story" is the nineteenth century. But once again this story exemplifies the relationship between Silko's written art and Laguna storytelling traditions. A coming-of-age narrative, "A Geronimo Story" tells of a youth's accompanying the Laguna Regulars – a group of scouts who assist a contingent of U.S. Cavalry – in pursuit of an Apache warrior. The Lagunas turn what they know will be a futile quest into a holiday, but the young man also learns something about the racism of the cavalry leaders. In each of these stories, Silko's ties to her cultural heritage are foregrounded, but she clearly recognizes – in fact, celebrates – the ways in which that heritage has successfully adjusted to the nineteenth and twentieth centuries. Her own stories, which she perceives as a continuation of the culture's literary tradition, exemplify this successful adjustment.

Rosen's *The Man to Send Rain Clouds* brought Silko's short fiction to the attention of mainstream readers in 1974. This anthology was only one of three important events in Silko's career that year. Another was the publication of *Laguna Woman,* a poetry collection. *Laguna Woman,* which Silko's Flood Plain Press reprinted in 1994, was published by a small press (Greenfield Review) and had a limited readership. Most readers were introduced to poems from her collection and several poems not included in *Laguna Woman* in two anthologies published in 1975 by large commercial publishers: Kenneth Rosen's *Voices of the Rainbow: Contemporary Poetry by American Indians* (Viking) and Duane Niatum's *Carriers of the Dream Wheel: Contemporary Native American Poetry* (Harper and Row). The latter was the fifth volume in Harper and Row's Native American Publishing Program; it had a wide distribution.

At first glance the form of many of Silko's poems reflects little of her Laguna heritage. The brevity of the poems, the visual effects of short stanzas and indentations of individual words or short phrases that often trail across the page, and the avoidance of conventional stanza length, meter, and rhyme all suggest the influences of the modern lyric poem expressed in free verse. Silko does, however, use repetition occasionally in combination with indentation and separation of words and phrases to create a chantlike drive and urgency in her poems. For example, in the second half of "In Cold Storm Light" (which first appeared as "Snow Elk" in the 1972 Southwest Poets Conference publication *Quetzal*), Silko combines both the imaginative use of indentation/separation and one key instance of repetition to capture the power of winter storms and majestic animals:

> Out of the thick ice sky
>   running swiftly
>   pounding
>   swirling above the treetops
> The snow elk come,
> Moving, moving
>   white song
>   storm wind in the branches.
> And when the elk have passed
>   behind them
>   a crystal train of snowflakes
>   strands of mist
>   tangles in rocks
>   and leaves.

As this poem suggests, another reflection of Silko's Laguna background in her poetry is her fascination with the animals and landscape of the Southwest (although even in her early poetry she did not limit her settings rigidly, as indicated by her poems "Alaskan Mountain Poem #1" and "Prayer to the Pacific"). Her love of her region is expressed in the titles of most of the eighteen poems by Silko included in *Voices of the Rainbow,* for example, "Where Mountain Lion Lay Down With Deer," "Deer Song," "Four Mountain Wolves," "Slim Man Canyon," "The Time We Climbed Snake Mountain," and "Horses at Valley Store." Her roots in the Southwest are defined in strong sensual imagery. Utilizing repetition with variation, indentation, and an appeal to the senses, Silko's persona describes the approaching storm in "In Cold Storm Light":

> The wind is wet
>   with the smell of piñon.
> The wind is cold
>   with the sound of juniper.

In "When Sun Came to River Woman" Silko uses sense imagery to dramatize the intimate relations that connect landscape and people:

> The muddy fast water
>   warm around my feet
>   you move in to the current slowly
>
>   brown skin   thighs
>   deep   intensity
>   flowing water
> Your warm penetrates
>   yellow sand and sky.

The language and situation of these lines – which parallel the opening of Silko's "Yellow Woman" short story – indicate another connection between Silko's poetry and Laguna Pueblo: her belief in the power of storytelling as a means of preserving tradition and of adapting and surviving in a changing world. A delightful and penetrating expression of this belief is found in "Toe'osh: A Laguna Coyote Story," which is probably the most frequently anthologized poem from *Laguna Woman.* The poem juxtaposes eight brief poetic vignettes. Three concisely present traditional Laguna, Acoma, or Navajo trickster episodes. The rest reveal how Coyote survives in the twentieth century. He lives in the ambitions of Charlie Coyote, who, if elected governor of Laguna, wants to run all "the other men off / the reservation / and keep all the women for himself." He lives in the tactics of Laguna who invite a "Trans-Western pipeline vice president . . . to discuss right-of-way," "let him wait" the whole day, and tell him to return tomorrow because "he is a busy and important man." And he lives in the barroom protests of poet Simon Ortiz (to whom the poem is dedicated), who asks "white people" to say " 'Excuse me,' / And the way Simon meant it / was for 300 or maybe 400 years."

In "Indian Song: Survival," which first appeared in 1973 in *Chicago Review,* Silko's creative use of indentation and separation, her love of the landscape and animals of the Southwest, and her belief in the preservation and survival power of storytelling combine in one of her best poems. The journey motif unifies the ten sections of the poem, which evoke the landscape, many traditional myths (hero journey, romantic escape and abduction, and animal spirits who help humans survive – especially Mountain Lion), and the history of Indian/white relationships. The poem is full of ironies ("We went north / to escape winter") and toughness ("It is only a matter of time, Indian/you can't sleep with the river forever. / Smell winter and know."). Still, the poem concludes with a beautiful image of survival:

Mountain forest wind travels east and I answer:
taste me,
I am the wind
touch me,
I am the lean gray deer
running on the edge of the rainbow.

Besides the publication of *Laguna Woman* and the appearance of *The Man to Send Rain Clouds,* another important literary event for Silko in 1974 was the publication of one of her most highly respected short stories, "Lullaby," which appeared in both *Chicago Review* and *Yardbird Reader.* The story examines the conflicts between an elderly Navajo couple who live near Laguna and Euro-American authority. However, instead of absolutely condemning the latter, Silko shows that the tensions arise from differences in cultural values, which neither the Navajos nor the Euro-Americans fully appreciate. Though the story ends with the old man's death, it also reaffirms life and the power of tradition as his widow sings a lullaby she had learned from her grandmother. "Lullaby" was selected for inclusion in *The Best American Short Stories of 1975.*

In 1976 Silko published a brief essay in *Yardbird Reader* that has created controversy and perhaps discomfort among some Euro-American writers who have used Native American materials in their work. In "An Old-Time Indian Attack Conducted in Two Parts," she expresses the frustration that many Native Americans had been feeling over what they viewed as the appropriation of their traditions by non-Indian artists. Silko singles out literary works such as *Laughing Boy* (the 1929 Pulitzer Prize–winning novel about Navajo life by New Englander Oliver La Farge), the novels of William Eastlake, and the poetry of Jerome Rothenberg and Gary Snyder. Snyder's *Turtle Island* (1974), which won the Pulitzer Prize for poetry, merits the entirety of the second part of Silko's attack. She focuses on two implicitly imperialist assumptions that permit these and similar works to be produced. One of these assumptions holds that Euro-American cultural superiority allows writers to master the essence of Native American worldviews so expeditiously that they can write from an Indian point of view. The other imperialist assumption singled out by Silko holds that oral materials gathered from Native American storytellers and singers and published by ethnologists in sources such as the bulletins and annual reports of the Bureau of American Ethnology have become public property, which Euro-American writers can revise and present as they choose. Essentially a critique of what Geary Hobson calls "white shamanism," Silko's piece served as a timely reminder that imperialism remained vital, even if its target had become American Indian art and ideology instead of land and economic resources.

Silko's early poems and particularly her short stories have received considerable attention, mostly because one of the stories, "Yellow Woman," is the focus of Melody Graulich's casebook, *Leslie Marmon Silko, "Yellow Woman"* (1993), and because several of the poems and stories ("The Man to Send Rain Clouds," "Lullaby," and "Yellow Woman" especially) have appeared in anthologies of contemporary American literature and of women's writing as well as in collections focusing exclusively on the work of American Indian authors. But an important milestone for Silko and for the Native American Renassiance was the publication of *Ceremony. Ceremony* has been republished in paperback several times and is one of the most widely read works by a Native American writer. Silko's narrative concerns the attempts by a Laguna veteran of the Pacific theater in World War II to come to terms with a variety of conflicts rooted in his mixed-blood background, his wartime experiences, and the changing culture of Laguna in the 1940s and 1950s.

Written during a two-year residence in Alaska, *Ceremony* demonstrates effectively the ways the oral storytelling tradition can inform the work of Native American novelists. Silko skillfully interweaves poetic renderings of Laguna mythology with the story of Tayo, the novel's protagonist, to show the influence of her tribal heritage in a highly acculturated pueblo of the mid twentieth century. Tayo comes to terms with his sense of alienation and guilt by recognizing how values that have been central in Laguna life for generations continue – albeit with necessary changes and adaptations – to provide a way of defining his place in the world. Tayo's alienation stems originally from his mixed-blood status, a condition that isolates him from both mainstream Euro-American and Laguna cultures.

Born of a Laguna mother who during her brief life had survived as a prostitute in Gallup, New

Dust jacket for a collection of Silko's essays on contemporary Native American culture

Mexico, and an absent Euro-American father, he has grown up in the family of his mother's sister Thelma ("Auntie," as Tayo calls her). Auntie is a self-righteous woman who will not let her charge forget his mixed-blood genealogy. Others in the household include Tayo's grandmother, who still adheres to traditional Laguna ways; Josiah, his uncle and Auntie's brother, whose skills as a storyteller and dreams of wealth from raising range cattle reflect continuing commitments to tradition; and Rocky, his cousin and Auntie's son, who has become devoted to mainstream Euro-American values during his schooling in nearby Albuquerque. From Auntie's perspective Rocky represents the family's future, and she consistently stresses Tayo's subservient status to her own son. For example, she allows Tayo to become involved with Josiah's cattle-raising scheme, an old-fashioned pursuit that she would deem inappropriate for the progressive Rocky.

In spite of Auntie, Tayo and Rocky are devoted friends who join the military together and are ultimately sent to the Philippines. There Rocky dies. Tayo returns to Laguna after the war with a burden of guilt that stems from several sources: his failure to protect Rocky, whom Auntie had made his responsibility; the death of Josiah, which occurs while Tayo is away; the loss of his cattle herd, which has wandered away; the sins of his mother, whom Auntie will not let him forget; and the drought plaguing the New Mexico desert, a situation Tayo feels he has caused by trying to pray away the downpours of the Philippine rain forest. Moreover, Tayo suffers from his awareness of the loss of traditional values at Laguna.

Tayo's many layers of guilt suggest the complexity of contextual factors that inform the novel. Besides a "survivor guilt," Tayo's condition is shaped by traditional Laguna beliefs about the interrelatedness of all life and nature. Silko also portrays some of the ways that American Indians have frequently dealt with guilt arising from such sources and with the alienation brought on by the loss of their traditional cultures. Tayo's contemporaries, other Lagunas who have returned from military service, react to these problems with rounds of heavy drinking, violence, sexual promiscuity, and boasting about their martial and sexual conquests while in uniform. Though Tayo is tempted to join them in using these means to escape his guilt and alienation, he does not fully yield to them.

Yet he has not received much help from conventional approaches to healing, either from veterans' hospitals or from the ceremony performed by Ku'oosh, a traditional Laguna medicine man. Significant healing begins for Tayo only when he encounters Betonie, a part-Navajo healer who lives near Gallup in a dwelling furnished with materials from both Native American and Euro-American cultures. Like Tayo, who has experienced life outside the tribal environment, Betonie understands the necessity for change. But he stresses that change means adaptation, not rejection of the past. Betonie combines parts of a traditional Navajo Red Antway ceremony with modern counseling techniques. He also encourages Tayo to take responsibility for his own healing, a process that for Tayo takes the form of a quest – with mythic overtones – to find Josiah's spotted cattle.

Betonie's emphasis on ceremony and myth reinforces another important theme in *Ceremony* and Silko's other works: the importance of stories and storytelling. The account of Tayo's healing, which comprises the book's second half, involves his enacting parts of traditional sacred stories that Silko interweaves in poetic passages throughout the novel. Tayo returns to sacred time, the setting for myth, by ascending Mount Taylor, a landmark of spiritual significance for Lagunas and most other Native peoples of western New Mexico. There he finds Josiah's lost cattle and encounters Ts'eh, a woman whose love for Tayo and obvious ties to the sacredness of nature contribute to his restoration. Renewed and reharmonized with the cosmos – the goal of many Native American healing traditions including Laguna and Navajo – Tayo descends from the holy mountain with the fundamentals of spiritual health restored.

The novel's climactic scene occurs at an abandoned uranium mine where Tayo has hidden to escape his former friends, the other Laguna war veterans, who are now bent upon killing him. As Tayo watches in horror, they torture one of their number, and he feels compelled to try to stop them. But he senses that such an act would be self-destructive, that the witchery embodied in others actually lurks within himself waiting for an opportunity to emerge, and that the recommitment to holiness that he had made on Mount Taylor through living within myth requires that he not participate in their violence. As the novel ends, Tayo is invited to reveal the story of his healing to Laguna elders. They obviously believe that his story is part of a mythic pattern begun long ago. So does Tayo's grandmother. She is no longer "excited" by "these goings-on around Laguna" because " 'It seems like I already heard these stories before . . . only thing is the names sound different.' "

The achievement of *Ceremony* in stressing the enduring powers of restoration in an American Indian heritage, especially the role of storytelling that artists such as Silko are continuing to practice, brought the novel generally favorable reviews. Though reviewers complained about the book's occasional verbosity and loss of precise focus, comparing it disadvantageously to Silko's tightly structured short stories, even these critics, for the most part, admired the novel's narrative power and its dramatization of the continuing vitality of Native culture. *Ceremony* also clearly established Silko as one of the most important figures in the Native American Renaissance, second only perhaps to Momaday, whose *House Made of Dawn* won the Pulitzer Prize for fiction in 1969. A significant body of critical scholarship on *Ceremony* has appeared since 1977, most of which has placed it within the traditions of Native American narrative art, of which Silko views her work as an extension.

Silko's growing prominence received a further boost from the publication of *Storyteller*. Impossible to categorize in terms of standard Euro-American literary genres, this book affirms the role of the storyteller as preserver of cultural values, as contributor to communal and individual spiritual health, and as definer of the cosmos. Though rooted clearly in Silko's Laguna experience (some critics, in fact, have considered autobiography to be the most apt generic designation for *Storyteller*), the themes of the book transcend any particulars of time and place. In fact, she dedicates it to "the storytellers as far back as memory goes and to the telling which continues and through which they all live and we with them." One of Silko's purposes in *Storyteller* is to stress the continuity of her literary work with the oral tradition that she had absorbed from Grandma Am'ooh, Aunt Susie, and others at Laguna during the 1950s. Verbal and photographic portraits of these ancestors – and of many other members of Silko's family – appear in the book, for it is a work that focuses specifically on her family heritage and on the Laguna oral literary heritage as well as more generally on the processes of storytelling across a variety of media.

Storyteller brings together much of Silko's previously published work, both short fiction from Rosen's anthology and elsewhere and poems from *Laguna Woman*. The book also includes nonfictional vignettes of her life at Laguna and some poems and short stories written since *The Man to Send Rain Clouds, Voices of the Rainbow,* and *Laguna Woman.* The title story, originally published in *Puerto de Sol* (Fall 1975), reflects the themes of the entire work – those already well known to readers of Silko's poetry and fiction.

Set in Alaska – and consequently Silko's only major work of published fiction not set at least partially in the Southwest – "Storyteller" deals with an orphaned Inuit girl who lives with an elderly couple. After the old woman dies, Euro-American oil drillers living in a nearby community sexually exploit the girl, but she eventually lures the village storekeeper, who is responsible for her parents' deaths, onto the ice of a frozen river, where he breaks through and drowns. Meanwhile, the old man with whom she continues to live is telling a story about a polar bear's relentless stalking of a hunter in the snow- and ice-covered wilderness. Concurrently, the implacable cold of the Arctic winter is gradually overpowering the futile attempts of civilization to deal with the harsh environment. Clearly, the girl's revenge reverberates with mythic and legendary overtones as it parallels the actions of the bear in the old man's story. Though it is a product of a seemingly moribund culture, his story continues to exert a force on the present. And that story is founded in the seasonal cycle, the pol[illegible] bear's destruction of the hunter being just as inev[illegible]table as the coming of winter cold.

Though it gathers together pieces, many of which were published separately in their original incarnations, *Storyteller* is far more than a "collected works" volume. As she does with traditional myth and her own narrative in *Ceremony,* Silko creates an integrated whole in *Storyteller* by interweaving retellings of stories from the Laguna oral heritage with family stories, photographs, and her poetry and fiction. She has cited John Cage's *A Year from Monday* (1967) as a precedent for her arrangement. All the material in *Storyteller* works conjointly to demonstrate the dialectic of continuity and change.

Silko juxtaposes her short story "Yellow Woman," for example, with retellings of traditional legends about abductions of women by spiritual entities, thus showing how these legends have retained their vitality. Her short story "Uncle Tony's Goat" parallels accounts of legendary roosters which figured into her family's trove of tales and consequently becomes an extension of the heritage of family storytelling with which Silko grew up. The trickster figure Coyote, a character in Laguna and other Native American traditions, has modern relatives who appear in Silko's poetry as well as in the Laguna womanizer who tricks some Hopi women into letting him feel their thighs in the short story "Coyote Holds a Full House in His Hand."

While the theme of continuity and change may be evident in the individual pieces, it emerges with most clarity through the ways in which Silko forges interconnections among various forms, genres, and media. Moreover, she clearly sees herself as a representative of the archetypal figure of the book's title. Like Grandma A'mooh and Aunt Susie, like the generations of verbal artists who have performed Coyote myths and abduction legends, like her father (whose photographs appear in the volume), Silko herself is a tribal storyteller who extends an oral tradition into a modern medium – written English. She reinforces this point in "Language and Literature from a Pueblo Indian Perspective," a talk she delivered to the English Institute in 1979 and which was published in 1981.

While not as widely read as *Ceremony, Storyteller* received an equally positive response from reviewers, many of whom, though, were unsure what to [illegible] the book. Generic categorization has [illegible] a concern of some commentators, [illegible] addressed such matters as how the [illegible] structure and its successful use of various [illegible] contribute to Silko's celebration of the con[illegible]g role of storytelling in Laguna life and in [illegible] contexts.

A useful companion piece to both *Ceremony* and *Storyteller* is Silko's essay "Landscape, History, and the Pueblo Imagination," which appeared in *Antaeus* in 1986. An overview of some important components of Pueblo thought, the essay provides essential information on storytelling and on the way in which place figures into oral tradition. Silko stresses the centrality of story to Pueblo experience, relating how people at Laguna and other pueblos perceive themselves as part of a continuing story that begins with their primordial ancestors' emergence from the fourth world into this world. Acknowledging this perception is what restores Tayo to health in *Ceremony.* In the essay Silko also shows how specific features of the terrain inform storytelling. Knowledge of the landscape and the communal processes of oral narration, which her work especially in *Storyteller* continues, reinforce one another.

The visual dimension that figures into the content and structure of *Storyteller,* her father's profession as a photographer, and some academic training in film were among the factors that turned Silko's attention to filmmaking during the late 1970s and early 1980s. In a lecture delivered at the University of Texas at Arlington on 17 April 1985, Silko explained that the immediate inspiration for her film work was her experience with a twenty-eight-minute film, *Running on the Edge of the Rainbow: Laguna Stories and Poems* (1978), which was part of the *Words & Place: Native Literature from the American Southwest* video series produced by Evers and directed by Dennis W. Carr. In the film she reads from her poetry collection *Laguna Woman* and discusses the importance of storytelling. In particular she stresses continuity. Traditional stories were still vital elements of Laguna culture because they continued to be reenacted in the present. Silko had already expressed this viewpoint in powerful stories such as "Yellow Woman" and in *Ceremony*. Now she hoped to express this message in film. In her Arlington lecture she recalled that she hoped to achieve a "total translation," one that would allow viewers to "see" the continuity and to see and hear the people and the landscape.

After an unsuccessful attempt to gain funding from the Columbia University Translation Center, Silko received a grant from the National Endowment for the Humanities in 1981. According to the Arlington lecture, part of her Laguna Film Project would be "Stolen Rain," a three-part series designed for the Public Broadcasting System. The first two parts would introduce information about Laguna life, philosophy, land, and history. The last segment was to be filmed on land near Laguna that had been in her family's care for several generations. It would be a dramatization of one of the Pueblo Estoy-eh-muut (Arrowboy) stories. "Stolen Rain" was never made, but in 1982 Silko did complete a sixty-minute work print of a motion picture titled "Arrowboy and the Witches." Many of the lines in "Arrowboy and the Witches" are taken directly from her narrative poem "Estoy-eh-muut and the Kunideeyahs [destroyers or witches]," which appeared in *Storyteller*.

Silko's film version of Arrowboy's discovery that his wife Kochinako (Yellow Woman) was a member of the witch clan follows the basic plotline of her poem and of many other versions of this Pueblo narrative: Arrowboy suspects his wife, follows her at night to her meeting with other witches, and is detected by the witches who magically transport him to a high narrow ledge from which there is no apparent escape. With the help of Spider Woman, small creatures (usually squirrels), and rapidly growing trees, Arrowboy frees himself and takes revenge on his wife, who dies or disappears by the end of the narrative. To adapt this story for filming and for a PBS audience, Silko made numerous changes. For example, she obviously thought that the witches' "excrement bundle" mentioned in her poem was inappropriate for PBS, and, to facilitate filming, Spider Woman appeared in human (grandmother) form. Also, Silko repositioned Arrowboy at the bottom of an encircling, narrow cliff and used a lizard who blazed a trail up the canyon instead of talking squirrels and magical trees. The most important change – the one that makes the film a significant expression of Silko's belief in narrative continuity – is the multilayered time line. As in *Ceremony,* Silko set the action in the 1950s, when the Jackpile uranium mine near Laguna was in a high production phase and the Laguna experienced a severe drought. The primary narrative frames are set in the present, as a Laguna grandmother sits at the head of a dining table telling the Arrowboy story. The words she speaks are out of "time immemorial," as Tayo's grandmother in *Ceremony* would say. To make sure that the audience knows that time immemorial has a long reach, Silko closes the film in the present with a shot of a black car rounding the curve outside the grandmother's home. It is the same car as the one driven by the witches in the 1950s dramatization. Silko has not been able to raise the funds for the final editing, so viewing of the film has been limited mainly to conference and university presentations.

Anne Wright's *The Delicacy and Strength of Lace* (1986) is a collection of letters from 1978 to 1980 between the poet James Wright, Anne's husband, and Silko. The collection presents an epistolary friendship that began when James Wright, who had met Silko briefly when she gave a reading in Michigan, wrote to express his appreciation for *Ceremony*. Silko responded to his gracious letter, and for the next couple of years they wrote one another regularly. Silko was putting *Storyteller* together at the time, so some insights into what lies behind this book emerge from the correspondence. But she also treats personal concerns – her life in the Tucson Mountains and the loss of a child-custody case, for example – and the older Wright served somewhat as a mentor, both professionally and personally. The correspondence ends with Wright's death in March 1980, a couple of months after Silko visited him in a New York City hospital, only the second time the two met face-to-face. The letters, some of which contain material that Silko also uses in *Storyteller,* document mutual warmth and respect between two artists who forged a personal relationship based initially on their shared artistry.

Some of Silko's readers expressed disappointment with *Almanac of the Dead,* written partially under the auspices of the five-year MacArthur Foundation Grant she received in 1981 but not pub-

Silko in the Tucson Mountains, Arizona (photograph by Denny Carr)

lished until a decade later. A sprawling novel of more than seven hundred pages, *Almanac of the Dead* provided Silko with challenges she had not dealt with previously: particularly the management of dozens of characters and the projection of strident ethnic militancy without losing a sense of aesthetic purpose. Though she may not have been totally successful in meeting these challenges, the book has many interesting, compelling features, especially its delineation of individual characters and the scenes and episodes set in Tucson, where Silko lived during most of the book's composition.

The title *Almanac of the Dead* refers to a set of notebooks bequeathed in the nineteenth century to Yoeme, a Yaqui Indian. One of her granddaughters, Lecha, a television talk-show psychic now living in a heavily guarded compound near Tucson, wants to decipher these notebooks, which contain traditional Native American history and apocalyptic prophecies of a unified movement of tribal peoples designed to reassume their control of North America. She attempts to do so with the help of Seese, who has come to Tucson from San Diego, California, in hopes that Lecha's psychic powers can locate her kidnapped child.

The scenes in the Tucson compound, which also affords a base for drug- and gun-smuggling operations, provide only one setting for the action in this complex novel. Another major center of plot development in the book is Tuxtla Gutierrez, in Chiapas, the southernmost and most Indian state in Mexico, where Menardo Panson, a mestizo who has made a fortune through the drug and gun trades, lives in lavish, repressive splendor. Menardo serves as foil to a revolutionary army that is being organized in central Mexico to march northward to reclaim tribal lands, part of the apocalypse foretold in Yoeme's notebooks.

These principal narrative threads – the deciphering of Yoeme's notebooks and the preparations of the revolutionary army – take place against a panorama of other plotlines and imagery that stresses a recurrent point: North America as dominated by Euro-Americans has become a place of consummate corruption, but it will ultimately be retaken by the tribal peoples from whom it was stolen. Consequently, Silko presents an encyclopedic portrayal of perversions, mostly sexual and violent in nature, to illustrate what Euro-American hegemony has produced: child pornography, bestiality, and drug abuse, to name only a few. Even those Native American characters who have been corrupted by Euro-American influences commit these sins. But it is all to end soon as the age-old prophecies in the Almanac of the Dead work themselves out so that tribal values may be reasserted.

Both the bleakness and the radical hope depicted in the novel find expression in Sterling, the principal Laguna character. When the reader first encounters him, Sterling is working as a gardener at Lecha's compound after being exiled from Laguna. Sterling had been assigned the responsibility of supervising a film crew working in the community, and when they came across esoteric religious knowledge at the pueblo, he was accused of revealing sacred secrets. He has consequently experienced and suffered from the corrupting influence of Euro-American values. Before the novel has ended, though, Sterling becomes reintegrated with the sacred forces of his ancestral heritage. His sense of traditional values is restored as he awaits the inevitable apocalypse, but this restoration comes only with his rejection of the influences that have tainted him.

Despite the obvious differences in scope, tone, and message between *Almanac of the Dead* and Silko's earlier fiction, there is still an emphasis on traditional story as a paradigm for contemporary and future behavior. The Indians in Mexico and the Southwest who are setting the stage for tribal recovery of the North American continent are, like Tayo in *Ceremony,* following the patterns of mythology, particularly as sacred stories have been preserved in Yoeme's notebooks. Traditional patterns and motifs involving heroic twinship and serpent power, for instance, inform the impending resurgence of tribal peoples.

Some critics probably responded negatively to *Almanac of the Dead* because of its graphic brutality and bitter tone. Others suggested that, while the book has many scenes, episodes, characterizations, and descriptions of real power, they often become buried in many less-successful sections. But Silko's reason for including so much in the novel may be to reinforce the imagery of Euro-American perversity. For many readers the result, though, is loss of focus. While *Almanac of the Dead* has been reviewed in many major periodicals, it has received less attention from scholarly commentators, a situation that will surely change as they begin to assess this novel's place in the body of Silko's work.

Recently Silko has returned to an art she enjoyed as a child: bookmaking. *Sacred Water* is a collection of autobiographical vignettes relating to experience (her own, her family's, Laguna society's, Native Americans') with water in the arid Southwest, which appeared first in 1993 and in a second edition the following year. Like *Storyteller,* this book exploits visual as well as written images; Silko juxtaposes on facing pages verbal pictures with graphic designs. Moreover, she has assumed control of the physical production of this book, which is published under her own imprint, Flood Plain Press. She assembles, numbers, and binds every copy by hand. Silko has also produced a new edition of *Laguna Woman* through Flood Plain Press.

The most recent book-length addition to Silko's bibliography is a collection of essays on contemporary Native American life titled *Yellow Woman and a Beauty of the Spirit* (1996). Appearing in various periodicals or anthologies between 1981 and 1994, the pieces deal with such topics as the importance of landscape for Laguna oral tradition, Silko's experiences growing up in the community, and the role of the visual, especially the expressive power of photography, in her own work and in Native American aesthetics generally. Many of the essays, which were composed while she was writing *Almanac of the Dead,* assume the novel's apocalyptic tone, and several deal specifically with injustices of federal and state Indian policy and with the insensitivity of government agencies such as the Border Patrol. The collection stresses themes that have begun to emerge more overtly in Silko's work since the publication of *Storyteller,* but that have continually figured into her writing since her first publications.

It is too early fully to assess the general impact of her recent work – *Yellow Woman and a Beauty of the Spirit, Sacred Water,* or even *Almanac of the Dead* – on the direction that Silko's art is taking. In addition to the forcefully political direction that her work has assumed, it remains obvious that her poetry and prose – both fiction and nonfiction – represent some of the most stimulating and influential writing to come out of the Native American Renaissance. Even without its ethnic label, Silko's work deserves the attention of readers who wish to examine ways in which a literary tradition originating in an orally performed verbal art has maintained its ties to that art while utilizing many of the devices of written literature. Silko's principal achievement thus far is the novel *Ceremony,* but to single out that or any of her other works dilutes the thematic and methodological continuities that color all of her poetry, short fiction, nonfiction, and novels.

Letters:

The Delicacy and Strength of Lace: Letters Between Leslie Marmon Silko and James Wright, edited by Anne Wright (Saint Paul, Minn.: Graywolf Press, 1986).

Interviews:

Lawrence J. Evers and Dennis W. Carr, "A Conversation with Leslie Marmon Silko," *Sun Tracks: An American Indian Literary Magazine,* 3 (Fall 1976): 28–33;

James Fitzgerald and John Hudak, "Leslie Silko: Storyteller," *Persona* (1980): 21–38;

Dexter Fisher, "Stories and Their Tellers: A Conversation with Leslie Marmon Silko," in *The Third Woman: Minority Women Writers of the United States* (Boston: Houghton Mifflin, 1980), pp. 18–23;

Elaine Jahner, "The Novel and Oral Tradition: An Interview with Leslie Marmon Silko," *Book Forum,* 5, no. 3 (1981): 383–388;

Per Seyersted, "Two Interviews with Leslie Marmon Silko," *American Studies in Scandinavia,* 13 (1981): 17–33;

Kim Barnes, "A Leslie Marmon Silko Interview," *Journal of Ethnic Studies,* 13, no. 4 (1986): 83–105;

Laura Coltelli, "Leslie Marmon Silko," in *Winged Words: American Indian Writers Speak* (Lincoln: University of Nebraska Press, 1990), pp. 135–153;

Coltelli, "*Almanac of the Dead:* An Interview with Leslie Marmon Silko," in *Native American Literatures,* edited by Coltelli (Pisa: Servizo Editoriale Universtaro, 1994), pp. 65–80.

References:

Paula Gunn Allen, "The Feminine Landscape of Leslie Marmon Silko's *Ceremony,*" in *Studies in American Indian Literature,* edited by Allen (New York: Modern Language Association, 1983), pp. 127–133;

Judith A. Antell, "Momaday, Welch, and Silko: Expressing the Feminine Principle through Male Alienation," *American Indian Quarterly,* 12, no. 3 (1988): 213–220;

Peter G. Beidler, "Animals and Theme in *Ceremony,*" *American Indian Quarterly,* 5, no. 1 (1979): 13–18;

Robert C. Bell, "Circular Design in *Ceremony,*" *American Indian Quarterly,* 5, no. 1 (1979): 47–62;

Edith Blicksilver, "Traditionalism vs. Modernity: Leslie Silko on American Indian Women," *Southwest Review,* 64, no. 2 (1979): 149–160;

Susan Blumenthal, "Spotted Cattle and Deer: Spirit Guides and Symbols of Endurance and Healing in *Ceremony,*" *American Indian Quarterly,* 14, no. 4 (1990): 367–377;

Alanna Kathleen Brown, "Pulling Silko's Threads Through Time: An Exploration of Storytelling," *American Indian Quarterly,* 19, no. 2 (Spring 1995): 171–179;

Laura Coltelli, "Leslie Marmon Silko's *Sacred Water,*" *Studies in American Indian Literatures,* 8, no. 4 (1996): 21–29;

Coltelli, "Re-Enacting Myths and Stories: Tradition and Renewal in *Ceremony,*" in *Native American Literatures,* edited by Coltelli (Pisa: Servizo Editoriale Universtaro, 1989), pp. 171–183;

Linda Danielson, "*Storyteller:* Grandmother's Spider Web," *Journal of the Southwest,* 30, no. 3 (1988): 325–355;

Danielson, "The Storytellers in *Storyteller,*" *Studies in American Indian Literatures,* 1, no. 2 (1989): 21–31;

Elizabeth N. Evasdaughter, "Leslie Marmon Silko's *Ceremony*: Healing Ethnic Hatred by Mixed Breed Laughter," *MELUS,* 15, no. 1 (1988): 83–95;

Lawrence J. Evers, "The Killing of a New Mexico State Trooper: Ways of Telling a Historic Event," *Wicazo Sa Review,* 1 (Spring 1985): 17–25;

Reyes Garcia, "Senses of Place in *Ceremony,*" *MELUS,* 10, no. 4 (1983): 37–48;

Nancy Gilderhus, "The Art of Storytelling in Leslie Silko's *Ceremony,*" *English Journal,* 83, no. 2 (1994): 70–72;

Melody Graulich, ed., *Leslie Marmon Silko: "Yellow Woman"* (New Brunswick, N.J.: Rutgers University Press, 1993);

David E. Hailey Jr., "The Visual Elegance of Ts'its'tsi'nako and the Other Invisible Characters in *Ceremony,*" *Wicazo Sa Review,* 6, no. 2 (1990): 1–6;

Bernard A. Hirsch, "'The Telling Which Continues': Oral Tradition and the Written Word in Leslie Marmon Silko's *Storyteller,*" *American Indian Quarterly,* 12, no. 1 (1988): 1–26;

Michael Hobbs, "Living in Between: Tayo as Radical Reader in Leslie Marmon Silko's *Ceremony,*" *Western American Literature,* 28, no. 4 (1994): 301–312;

Geary Hobson, "The Rise of the White Shaman as a New Version of Cultural Imperialism," in *The Remembered Earth: An Anthology of Contemporary Native American Literature,* edited by Hobson (Albuquerque: University of New Mexico Press, 1980), pp. 100–108;

Dennis Hoilman, "'A World Made of Stories': An Interpretation of Leslie Silko's *Ceremony,*" *South Dakota Review,* 17, no. 4 (1979): 54–66;

Elaine Jahner, "An Act of Attention: Event Structure in *Ceremony,*" *American Indian Quarterly,* 5, no. 1 (1979): 37–46;

Helen Jaskoski, "Thinking Woman's Children and the Bomb," *Explorations in Ethnic Studies,* 13, no. 2 (1990): 1–24;

Linda J. Krumholz, "'To understand this world differently': Reading and Subversion in Leslie Marmon Silko's 'Storyteller,'" *Ariel,* 25 (1994): 89–113;

Arnold Krupat, "The Dialogic of Silko's *Storyteller,*" in *Narrative Chance: Postmodern Discourse on Native American Indian Literatures,* edited by Gerald A. Vizenor (Albuquerque: University of New Mexico Press, 1989), pp. 69–90;

Toby C. S. Langen, "*Storyteller* as Hopi Basket," *Studies in American Indian Literatures,* 5, no. 1 (1993): 7–24;

Charles A. Larson, *American Indian Fiction* (Albuquerque: University of New Mexico Press, 1978), pp. 150–161;

Kenneth Lincoln, *Native American Renaissance* (Berkeley: University of California Press, 1983), pp. 222–250;

Paul H. Lorenz, "The Other Story of Leslie Marmon Silko's 'Storyteller,'" *South Central Review,* 8, no. 4 (1991): 59–75;

Ambrose Lucero, "For the People: Leslie Silko's *Storyteller,*" *Minority Voices,* 5, nos. 1–2 (1981): 1–10;

Kathleen Manley, "Leslie Marmon Silko's Use of Color in *Ceremony,*" *Southern Folklore,* 46, no. 2 (1989): 133–146;

Mary McBride, "Shelter of Refuge: The Art of Mimesis in Leslie Marmon Silko's 'Lullaby,'" *Wicazo Sa Review,* 3, no. 2 (1987): 15–17;

Carol Mitchell, "*Ceremony* as Ritual," *American Indian Quarterly,* 5 (1979): 27–35;

David L. Moore, "Myth, History, and Identity in Silko and Young Bear: Postcolonial Praxis," in *New Voices in Native American Literary Criticism,* edited by Krupat (Washington: Smithsonian Institution Press, 1993), pp. 370–395;

Robert M. Nelson, "He Said/She Said: Writing Oral Tradition in John Gunn's 'Ko-pot Ka-nat' and Leslie Silko's *Storyteller,*" *Studies in American Indian Literatures,* 5, no. 1 (1993): 31–50;

Nelson, *Place and Vision: The Function of Landscape in Native American Fiction* (New York: Peter Lang, 1993), pp. 11–39;

William Oandasan, "A Familiar Love Component of Love in *Ceremony,*" in *Critical Perspectives on Native American Fiction,* edited by Richard F. Fleck (Washington: Three Continents Press, 1993), pp. 240–245;

Lisa Orr, "Theorizing the Earth: Feminist Approaches to Nature and Leslie Marmon Silko's *Ceremony,*" *American Indian Culture and Research Journal,* 18 (1994): 145–157;

Louis Owens, *Other Destinies: Understanding the American Indian Novel* (Norman: University of Oklahoma Press, 1992), pp. 167–191;

Gretchen Ronnow, "Tayo, Death, and Desire: A Lacanian Reading of *Ceremony,*" in *Narrative Chance: Postmodern Discourse on Native American Literatures,* edited by Vizenor (Albuquerque: University of New Mexico Press, 1989), pp. 55–68;

A. LaVonne Ruoff, "Ritual and Renewal: Keres Traditions in the Short Fiction of Leslie Silko," *MELUS,* 5, no. 4 (1978): 2–17;

James Ruppert, "Dialogism and Meditation in Leslie Silko's *Ceremony,*" *Explicator,* 51 (1993): 129–134;

Ruppert, *Mediation in Contemporary Native American Fiction* (Norman: University of Oklahoma Press, 1995), pp. 74–91;

Ruppert, "The Reader's Lessons in *Ceremony,*" *Arizona Quarterly,* 44, no. 1 (1988): 78–85;

B. A. St. Andrews, "Healing the Witchery: Medicine in Silko's *Ceremony,*" *Arizona Quarterly,* 44, no. 1 (1988): 86–94;

Janet St. Clair, "Uneasy Ethnocentrism: Recent Works of Allen, Silko, and Hogan," *Studies in American Indian Literatures,* 6 (1994): 83–98;

Susan J. Scarberry, "Memory as Medicine: The Power of Recollection in *Ceremony,*" *American Indian Quarterly,* 5, no. 1 (1979): 19–26;

Lee Schweninger, "Writing Nature: Silko and Native Americans as Nature Writers," *MELUS,* 18 (1993): 47–60;

Per Seyersted, *Leslie Marmon Silko* (Boise, Idaho: Boise State University Press, 1980);

Mary Slowik, "Henry James, Meet Spider Woman: A Study of Narrative Form in Leslie Silko's *Ceremony,*" *North Dakota Quarterly,* 57, no. 2 (1989): 104–120;

Edith Swan, "Healing Via the Sunwise Cycle in *Ceremony,*" *American Indian Quarterly,* 12, no. 4 (1988): 313–328;

Swan, "Laguna Symbolic Geography and Silko's *Ceremony,*" *American Indian Quarterly,* 12, no. 3 (1988): 229–249;

Joan Thompson, "Yellow Woman, Old and New: Oral Tradition and Leslie Marmon Silko's *Ceremony,*" *Wicazo Sa Review,* 5, no. 2 (1989): 22–25;

Jude Todd, "Knotted Bellies and Fragile Webs: Untangling and Re-spinning in Tayo's Healing Journey," *American Indian Quarterly,* 19, no. 2 (Spring 1995): 155–170;

C. W. Truesdale, "Tradition and Ceremony: Leslie Marmon Silko as an American Novelist," *North Dakota Quarterly,* 59, no. 4 (1991): 200–208;

Alan R. Velie, *Four American Indian Literary Masters: N. Scott Momaday, James Welch, Leslie Marmon Silko, and Gerald Vizenor* (Norman: University of Oklahoma Press, 1982), pp. 105–122;

Norma Wilson, "Outlook for Survival," *Denver Quarterly,* 14, no. 4 (1980): 22–30;

Hertha Dawn Wong, *Sending My Heart Back Across the Years: Tradition and Innovation in Native American Autobiography* (New York: Oxford University Press, 1992), pp. 186–196;

Shamoon Zamir, "Literature in a 'National Sacrifice Area': Leslie Silko's *Ceremony,*" in *New Voices in Native American Literary Criticism,* edited by Krupat (Washington: Smithsonian Institution Press, 1993), pp. 386–415.

Luci Tapahonso

(8 November 1953 –)

Gretchen M. Bataille
University of California, Santa Barbara

BOOKS: *One More Shiprock Night: Poems* (San Antonio: Tejas Art Press, 1981);

Seasonal Woman (Santa Fe: Tooth of Time, 1981);

A Breeze Swept Through (Albuquerque: West End, 1987);

Sáanii Dahataał: The Women Are Singing, Sun Tracks, volume 23 (Tucson: University of Arizona Press, 1993);

Bah's Baby Brother Is Born (Washington, D.C.: National Organization on Fetal Alcohol Syndrome, 1994);

Navajo ABC (New York: Macmillan, 1995).

OTHER: "The Way It Is," in *Sign Language: Contemporary Southwest Native America* (New York: Aperture, 1989), pp. 37–45;

"The Kaw River Rushes Eastward," in *A Circle of Nations: Voices and Visions of American Indians,* edited by John Gattuso (Hillsboro, N.Mex.: Beyond Words, 1993), pp. 106–110;

"Come into the Shade," in *Open Places, City Spaces: Contemporary Writers on the Changing Southwest,* edited by Judy Nolte Temple (Tucson: University of Arizona Press, 1994), pp. 73–85.

SELECTED PERIODICAL PUBLICATION – UNCOLLECTED: "Singing in Navajo, Writing in English: The Poetics of Four Navajo Writers," *Culturefront,* 2 (Summer 1993): 36–41, 74.

Luci Tapahonso at the time of A Breeze Swept Through
(photograph by Armando De Aguero)

With the publication of her fourth book of poetry, *Sáanii Dahataał: The Women Are Singing* (1993), Luci Tapahonso joined such writers as Joy Harjo, Louise Erdrich, and Leslie Marmon Silko as an important female voice in the American Indian literary landscape. The book demonstrates her versatility and maturity as a writer and brings together the elements of landscape, tradition, and humor that were evident in earlier works. In this volume Tapahonso combines poetry and fiction and places herself in the "foreign" landscape of Kansas, so different from the arid New Mexico where she grew up and where the San Juan and Rio Grande rivers are quiet compared to the wide, brown waters of the Kaw River in her new midwestern home.

Tapahonso was born on 8 November 1953 in Shiprock, New Mexico, on the largest Indian reservation in the United States in both area and population, to Eugene Tapahonso Sr., of the Bitter Water clan – one of the four original Navajo clans – and Lucille Deschenne Tapahonso, of the Salt Water clan. (Ironically, for one born in a land of little rain, she bears a surname that in Navajo means "Edge of Big Water.") Navajo is her first language. She was educated at Navajo Methodist School in Farming-

Cover for Tapahonso's third poetry collection

ton, New Mexico, and Shiprock High School. The mesquite, tamarack, sagebrush, greasewood, and chaparral of the arroyos and buttes of Arizona and New Mexico still inform Tapahonso's poetry and short fiction even as she lives in the flat terrain of Kansas. She writes in *Saanii Dahataał,* "the place of my birth is the source of the writing."

Tapahonso attended the University of New Mexico, where she was influenced and inspired by Silko, who was then a faculty member there. It was then that she began to take her writing seriously. She graduated with a B.A. in English in 1980, taught briefly at San Felipe Elementary School at San Felipe Pueblo, and earned an M.A. in creative writing and English from the University of New Mexico in 1982. She taught at the University of New Mexico from 1982 to 1989, except for 1983, when she taught at Southwestern Indian Polytechnic Institute in Albuquerque. Since 1990 she has been an associate professor of English at the University of Kansas. Her husband, Bob G. Martin, a Cherokee, is president of Haskell Indian Nations University in Lawrence, Kansas. They have two daughters, Lori and Misty Dawn. Tapahonso is a commissioner on the Kansas Arts Commission and serves on the board of directors of the American Indian Law Resource Center and the Telluride Institute Writers Forum Advisory Board. In 1989 the New Mexico Commission of Higher Education named her a New Mexico Eminent Scholar.

For Tapahonso, her identity includes her family, clan, and nation. As she acknowledges in *Sáanii Datahaał,* "This writing, then, is not 'mine,' but a collection of many voices that range from centuries ago and continue into the future." In the autobiographical essay "Just Past Shiprock," in the same volume, she says: "This land that may seem arid and forlorn to the newcomer is full of stories which hold the spirits of the people, those who live here today and those who lived centuries and other worlds ago." Just as her poetry is contemporary but rooted in Navajo tradition, her sense of identity includes shopping malls as well as velvet skirts and turquoise necklaces. In a 1991 interview with Sylvie Moulin, Tapahonso commented, "When I was growing up they used to say that nobody is an orphan, that everybody has a mother and that your mother is the Earth and your father is the Sky." In the poems "It Has Always Been This Way" and "Sháá Áko Dahjiníleh Remember the Things They Told Us," in *Sáanii Datahaał,* she writes of the importance of remembering the advice of the *yeis* (Holy People) about how to rear children and of being sure not to break taboos during pregnancy. She remembers to place pollen on her own child's tongue and knows where to bury an infant's umbilical cord.

Tapahonso uses both English and Navajo in her poetry. In interviews she has said that one of her most popular poems, "Hills Brothers Coffee," is a direct translation from the Navajo. Phrases such as "the store is where I'm going to" and "It does it good for me" mirror Navajo syntax. Tradition appears in her work in the form of important figures such as the yeis or simply through her retelling of the familiar stories. She says in *Sáanii Dahataał,* "To know stories, remember stories, and to retell them well is to have been 'raised right.' " As Tapahonso says in her article "Singing in Navajo, Writing in English: The Poetics of Four Navajo Writers" (1993), it is by the knowledge of the stories that "an individual is directly linked to the history of the entire group."

Tapahonso often alludes to the traditional power of women in Navajo society. The "seasonal woman" of the title poem in her 1981 collection is a "woman of fierce seasons and gentle mornings." She begins *Seasonal Woman* (1981) with "Misty Dawn at Feeding Time," a poem about nursing her daughter. For Tapahonso the sustenance she is providing is more than milk; it is the passing on of stories and traditions to her own children, to other Navajo children, and to the public that reads her words. The last line of the poem, "and i will live and live and live," is a testament to the continuance of these traditions.

In "A Breeze Swept Through," the title poem of her next collection, published in 1987, she writes of birth and of the relationship between the mythical past and the spiritual present:

The first born of dawn woman slid out amid
crimson fluid streaked with stratus clouds
her body glistening August sunset pink
light steam rising from her like rain on warm rocks[.]

The poem connects the birth of her first daughter, in August, with the unusual cool breeze that alerted the child's grandfather that the birth had occurred. Tapahonso's second daughter was born in the middle of November:

She is born of damp mist and early sun.
She is born again woman of dawn.
She is born knowing the warm smoothness of rock.
She is born knowing her own morning strength.

The first poem of *Sáanii Dahataał* is also about birth. In "Blue Horses Rush In" white, yellow, blue, and black horses – one from each of the four directions – accompany the birth of Chamisa Bah Edmo, blessing it with the balance and wholeness of the Navajo world: "You will grow strong like the horses of your past. / You will grow strong like the horses of your birth."

In some poems the character Leona Grey speaks for all women in their various guises. She represents the oral tradition, telling both traditional stories and contemporary gossip about women who are too wild or who drink too much. Leona Grey appears in four poems in *Seasonal Woman.* In "Time Flies" Leona has a baby. "Her Daughter's Eyes" deals with the themes of motherhood and generations:

Leona looked into her daughter's face
knowing they breathe the same memories, the same blood –
dark and wet circulating
forever into time and others[.]

In "Time Flies" Leona Grey's baby is born, and in "No Particular Reason" Leona's husband kills her with a beer mug, "ending her nightlife / and life, in

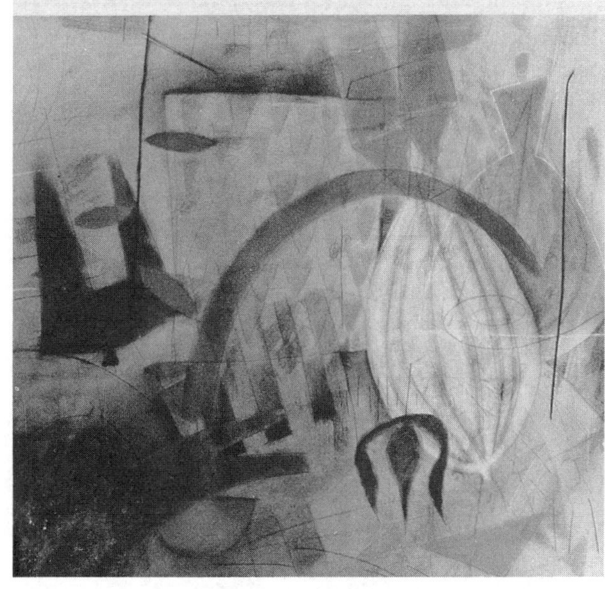

Cover for the poetry collection that established Tapahonso as an important American Indian woman writer

general." In "Light a Candle" Tapahonso asks that a candle be lighted in Leona's memory.

Tapahonso's grandmother, mother, and daughters all appear in her poetry, representing the continuance of the female line that is traced back to First Woman. Indian women are depicted as life givers, but also as carriers of traditions and knowledge to be passed on to their children. In her poetry collection *One More Shiprock Night* (1981) she says, "A lot of my writing has to do with my children, about my daughters who are growing up in a totally different way. . . . So my writing has a circular form – it comes back to me through the children and together it becomes a prayer of sorts back to the land, the people, and the families from whence we came originally."

Some of Tapahonso's poems are humorous. In "How She Was Given Her Name" in *Sáanii Dahataał,* a child is given the name " 'Beep-beep' / because she liked to be a roadrunner / and she liked having people try to catch her." Naming is a serious subject for Indians, but Tapahonso recognizes that even important traditions can evoke laughter. Other poems, however, deal with the racism that permeates the Southwest and is especially virulent in towns close to the reservations. She knows of deaths for no reason, of alcoholism bred by despair, and of children who suffer. In "Hard to Take," in *Seasonal Woman,* the cashier at Foodway and saleswomen at Merle Norman insult or ignore Navajo customers; "Pay Up or Else," in the same volume, tells of an Indian who was murdered in a robbery that netted the killer only ninety-seven cents. In "Uncle's Journey" and "The Snakeman," both in *Sáanii Dahataal,* children learn about the "other worlds" of the dead: Uncle becomes a star, and a little girl visits her parents at the cemetery and talks to her mother every night.

Tony Lamas, pickups, country and western clothing and music, and strong black Hills Brothers coffee all appear in Tapahonso's poetry and stories. These elements of contemporary Navajo life represent changes occurring within the strong traditions of her people. "Raisin Eyes," published first in *Seasonal Woman,* has often been reprinted and is one of the most frequently requested poems at Tapahonso's readings. It tells of the modern Navajo woman trapped by her attraction to Navajo cowboys:

> These Navajo cowboys with raisin eyes
> and pointed boots are just bad news
> but it's so hard to remember that
> all the time.

In "The Way It Is" (1989) Tapahonso discusses the superimposition of new traditions of roadside vendors, video games, and carnivals on traditional Navajo life. Ice cubes and portable toilets exist side by side with feast days and frybread. Pickup trucks and motorbikes have replaced horses for many families, but amid these differences some things never change. When she leaves the reservation to return to Kansas in "The Weekend is Over," in *Sáanii Dahataal,* she stops to buy strong coffee, mutton, green chilies, and sweet blue-corn Navajo cake so that she can take the taste of home with her.

In "What I Am," in *Sáanii Dahataal,* the main character carries pollen to Paris and watches it drift from the top of the Eiffel Tower to the plaza below: "It was while I stood on top of the Eiffel Tower that I understood that who I am is my mother, her mother, and my great-grandmother." This strong matrilineal line gives Tapahonso strength and identifies her place among her people. She knows her heritage and will pass that knowledge on to her daughters to give them the accumulated strength of generations of Navajo women. She often writes of *hózhó,* a state of harmony with all things, both living and nonliving. By adhering to the old stories and songs, by transforming them so that a new generation continues the beliefs, and by chanting her poems as prayers, Tapahonso maintains that harmony in her own life.

Interviews:

Joseph Bruchac, "A *MELUS* Interview: Luci Tapahonso," *MELUS,* 11 (Winter 1984): 85–91;

Jennifer Skeet, "Interview," *Maazo* (Spring 1985): 35;

Bruchac, "For What It Is: An Interview with Luci Tapahonso," in *Survival This Way: Interviews with American Indian Poets,* edited by Bruchac (Tucson: University of Arizona Press, 1987), pp. 271–285;

William Balassi, John F. Crawford, and Annie O. Eysturoy, eds., *This Is about Vision: Interviews with Southwestern Writers* (Albuquerque: University of New Mexico Press, 1990), pp. 195–202;

Sylvie Moulin, "Nobody Is an Orphan: Interview with Luci Tapahonso," *Studies in American Indian Literatures,* 3, no. 3 (1991): 14–18;

Heimbrecht Breinig and Klaus Losch, "Interview," in *Facing America,* edited by Breinig and Wolfgang Binder (Middletown, Conn.: Wesleyan University Press, 1994), pp. 114–130, 333–346;

Andrea M. Penner, "The Moon Is So Far Away: An Interview with Luci Tapahonso," *Studies in American Indian Literatures,* 8 (Fall 1996): 1–12.

References:

Floyce Alexander, "A New Voice Among the Navajo," *Greenfield Review,* 11, no. 1 (1983): 191–193;

Jo Ann Baldinger, "Navajo Poet: Tapahonso Holds Home in Her Heart," *New Mexico Magazine,* 70 (August 1992): 31–35;

Andrea Millenson Penner, "At Once, Gentle and Powerful: Voices of the Landscape in the Poetry of Luci Tapahonso," M.A. thesis, Northern Arizona University, 1993.

Gerald Vizenor

(22 October 1934 -)

Kimberly M. Blaeser
University of Wisconsin – Milwaukee

BOOKS: *Poems: Born in the Wind* (Minneapolis: Privately printed, 1960);

The Old Park Sleepers: A Poem (Minneapolis: Privately printed, 1961);

Two Wings the Butterfly: Haiku Poems in English (Saint Cloud: Minnesota State Reformatory, 1962);

South of the Painted Stones: Poems (Minneapolis: Privately printed, 1963);

Raising the Moon Vines: Original Haiku in English (Minneapolis: Callimachus, 1964);

Seventeen Chirps: Haiku in English (Minneapolis: Nodin, 1964);

Summer in the Spring: Lyric Poems of the Ojibway, Interpreted and Reexpressed (Minneapolis: Nodin, 1965); republished as *anishinabe nagamon* (Minneapolis: Nodin, 1970); revised as *Summer in the Spring: Ojibwe Lyric Poems and Tribal Stories* (Minneapolis: Nodin, 1981); republished as *Summer in the Spring: Anishinaabe Lyric Poems and Stories, New Edition,* American Indian Literature and Critical Studies, volume 6 (Norman: University of Oklahoma Press, 1993);

Slight Abrasions: A Dialogue in Haiku, by Vizenor and Jerome Downes (Minneapolis: Nodin, 1966);

Empty Swings: Haiku in English (Minneapolis: Nodin, 1967);

Thomas James White Hawk (Mound, Minn.: Four Winds, 1968);

anishinabe adisokan: Tales of the People (Minneapolis: Nodin, 1970);

The Everlasting Sky: New Voices from the People Named the Chippewa (New York: Crowell-Collier, 1972);

Tribal Scenes and Ceremonies (Minneapolis: Nodin, 1976); enlarged as *Crossbloods: Bone Courts, Bingo, and Other Reports* (Minneapolis: University of Minnesota Press, 1990);

Darkness in Saint Louis Bearheart (Saint Paul: Truck, 1978); republished as *Bearheart: The Heirship Chronicles* (Minneapolis: University of Minnesota Press, 1990);

Gerald Vizenor at the time of The Heirs of Columbus

Wordarrows: Indians and Whites in the New Fur Trade (Minneapolis: University of Minnesota Press, 1978);

Earthdivers: Tribal Narratives on Mixed Descent (Minneapolis: University of Minnesota Press, 1981);

Beaulieu and Vizenor Families: Genealogies (Minneapolis: Privately printed, 1983);

Matsushima: Pine Islands (Minneapolis: Nodin, 1984);

The People Named the Chippewa: Narrative Histories (Minneapolis: University of Minnesota Press, 1984);

Griever: An American Monkey King in China (Normal: Illinois State University Press / New York: Fiction Collective, 1987);

The Trickster of Liberty: Tribal Heirs to a Wild Baronage (Minneapolis: University of Minnesota Press, 1988);

Interior Landscapes: Autobiographical Myths and Metaphors (Minneapolis: University of Minnesota Press, 1990);

The Heirs of Columbus (Hanover, N.H.: Published for Wesleyan University Press by University Press of New England, 1991);

Landfill Meditation: Crossblood Stories (Hanover, N.H.: Published for Wesleyan University Press by University Press of New England, 1991);

Dead Voices: Natural Agonies in the New World, American Indian Literature and Critical Studies, volume 2 (Norman: University of Oklahoma Press, 1992);

Manifest Manners: Postindian Warriors of Survivance (Hanover, N.H.: Published for Wesleyan University Press by University Press of New England, 1994);

Shadow Distance: A Gerald Vizenor Reader (Hanover, N.H.: Published for Wesleyan University Press by University Press of New England, 1994);

Hotline Healers: An Almost Browne Novel (Hanover, N.H.: Published for Wesleyan University Press by University Press of New England, forthcoming 1997).

PLAY PRODUCTION: *Ishi and the Wood Ducks: Postindian Trickster Comedies,* Chicago, Red Path Theatre, 27 March 1996.

MOTION PICTURE: *Harold of Orange,* screenplay by Vizenor, Minnesota Film-in-the-Cities, 1983.

OTHER: *Escorts to White Earth, 1868–1968: 100 Years on a Reservation,* compiled and edited by Vizenor (Minneapolis: Four Winds, 1968);

Louis Untermeyer, ed., *The Pursuit of Poetry,* contributions by Vizenor (New York: Simon & Schuster, 1970), pp. 205–206;

"Long after the Rivers Change," "The Moon upon a Face Again," "Fathers of My Breath," and "An Old Spider Web," in *An American Indian Anthology,* edited by Benet Tvedten (Marvin, N.Dak.: Blue Cloud Abbey, 1971), pp. 45–48;

"Tribal People and the Poetic Image: Visions of Eyes and Hands," in *American Indian Art: Form and Tradition* (Minneapolis: Walker Art Center, 1972), pp. 15–22;

"Haiku," in *From the Belly of the Shark,* edited by Walter Lowenfels (New York: Vintage, 1973), pp. 69–70;

Cor van den Hevel, ed., *The Haiku Anthology,* contributions by Vizenor (Garden City, N.Y.: Doubleday, 1974), pp. 200–203;

"Indians of the Guthrie," "Tribal Stumps," "Unhappy Diary Days," "February Park," "Tropisms on John Berryman," "Tyranny of Moths," "Thumbing Old Magazines," "Family Photograph," and "Haiku," in *Voices of the Rainbow,* edited by Kenneth Rosen (New York: Viking, 1975), pp. 31–45;

"I Know What You Mean, Erdupps MacChurbb," in *Growing Up in Minnesota: Ten Writers Remember Their Childhoods,* edited by Chester Anderson (Minneapolis: University of Minnesota Press, 1976), pp. 79–111;

"The Psychotaxidermist," in *The Minnesota Experience,* edited by Jean Ervin (Minneapolis: Adams, 1979), pp. 220–228;

"Gerald Vizenor, Ojibway Chippewa Writer," in *This Song Remembers: Self-Portraits of Native Americans in the Arts,* edited by Jane B. Katz (Boston: Houghton Mifflin, 1980), pp. 163–169;

"Winter Camp at Berkeley," "Creation Fires," and "Museum Bound," in *The Clouds Threw This Light: Contemporary Native American Poetry,* edited by Phillip Foss, contributions by Vizenor (Santa Fe, N.Mex.: Institute of American Indian Arts, 1983), pp. 317–320;

"Reservation Cafe: The Origins of American Indian Instant Coffee," in *Earth Power Coming: Short Fiction in Native American Literature,* edited by Simon J. Ortiz (Tsaile, Ariz.: Navajo Community College Press, 1983), pp. 31–36;

"White Earth Reservation 1980," "Indians of the Guthrie," "Minnesota Camp Grounds," "Auras on the Interstates," and "Holiday Inn at Bemidji," in *Songs from This Earth on Turtle's Back: Contemporary American Indian Poetry,* edited by Joseph Bruchac, contributions by Vizenor (Greenfield Center, N.Y.: Greenfield Review, 1983), pp. 261–266;

"White Noise," in *White Noise, The Fellin Sisters, The Man of Sorrows,* by Vizenor, Lon Otto, and Jonis Agee (Saint Paul: Fodder, 1983), pp. 1–13;

"Land Fill Meditation," in *Words in the Blood: Contemporary Indian Writers of North and South America,* edited by Jamake Highwater (New York: New American Library, 1984), pp. 136–147;

"Episodes in Mythic Verism, from Monsignor Missalwait's Interstate," in *The New Native American Novel: Works in Progress,* edited by Mary Dougherty Bartlett (Albuquerque: University of New Mexico Press, 1986), pp. 109–126;

"Crows Written on the Poplars: Autocritical Autobiographies," in *I Tell You Now: Autobiographical Essays by Native American Writers,* edited by Arnold Krupat and Brian Swann (Lincoln: University of Nebraska Press, 1987), pp. 99–110;

"Socioacupuncture: Mythic Reversals and the Striptease in Four Scenes," in *The American Indian and the Problem of History,* edited by Calvin Martin (New York: Oxford University Press, 1987), pp. 180–191;

Touchwood: A Collection of Ojibway Prose, edited by Vizenor (Saint Paul: New Rivers, 1987);

"Wampum to Pictures of Presidents," in *Different Shores: Perspectives on Race and Ethnicity in America,* edited by Ronald Takaki (New York: Oxford University Press, 1987), pp. 126–128;

"White Earth: Images and Agonies," "March in North Dakota," "Shaman Breaks," "Surrendered Names," and "Seasons in Santa Fe: Four Haiku," in *Harpers Anthology of 20th Century Native American Poetry,* edited by Duane Niatum, contributions by Vizenor (New York: Harper & Row, 1988), pp. 71–74;

Narrative Chance: Postmodern Discourse on Native American Indian Literatures, edited by Vizenor (Albuquerque: University of New Mexico Press, 1989) – includes Vizenor's "Trickster Discourse: Comic Holotropes and Language Games," pp. 187–211;

"Almost a Whole Trickster," in *A Gathering of Flowers,* edited by Joyce Carol Thomas (New York: Harper & Row, 1990), pp. 3–20;

"Bone Courts: The Natural Rights of Tribal Remains," in *The Interrupted Life,* edited by Jan Heller Levi (New York: Museum of Contemporary Art, 1991), pp. 58–67;

"Confrontation or Negotiation," in *Native American Testimony,* edited by Peter Nabokov (New York: Viking Penguin, 1991), pp. 376–380;

"Heirs of Columbus," in *Looking Glass,* edited by Clifford E. Trafzer (San Diego: San Diego State University Press, 1991), pp. 182–192;

"The Last Lecture," in *American Indian Literature,* edited by Alan Velie (Norman: University of Oklahoma Press, 1991), pp. 339–347;

"Luminous Thighs," in *The Lightning Within,* edited by Velie (Norman: University of Oklahoma Press, 1991), pp. 67–89;

"Moccasin Games," in *Without Discovery,* edited by Ray Gonzales (Seattle: Broken Moon, 1992), pp. 73–89;

"Ishi Bares His Chest: Tribal Simulations and Survivance," in *Partial Recall: Photographs of Native North Americans,* edited by Lucy R. Lippard (New York: New Press, 1992), pp. 65–71;

"The Moccasin Game," in *Earth Song, Sky Spirit: Short Stories of the Contemporary Native American Experience,* edited by Trafzer (Garden City, N.Y.: Doubleday, 1992), pp. 37–62;

"July 1947: Many Point Camp," in *Inheriting the Land,* edited by Mark Vinz and Thom Tammaro (Minneapolis: University of Minnesota Press, 1993), pp. 313–318;

"The Tragic Wisdom of Salamanders," in *Sacred Trusts: Essays on Stewardship and Responsibility,* edited by Michael Katakis (San Francisco: Mercury House, 1993), pp. 161–176;

"Trickster Discourse: Comic and Tragic Themes in Native American Literature," in *"Buried Roots & Indestructible Seeds": The Survival of American Indian Life in Story, History and Spirit,* edited by Mark Lindquist and Martin Zanger (Madison: Wisconsin Humanities Council, 1993), pp. 33–41;

"Wings on the Santa Maria," in *Avante-Pop: Fiction for a Daydream Nation,* edited by Larry McCaffery (Boulder, Colo.: Black Ice, 1993), pp. 199–206;

"The Ruins of Representations: Shadow Survivance and the Literature of Dominance," in *An Other Tongue,* edited by Alfred Arteaga (Durham, N.C.: Duke University Press, 1994), pp. 139–167;

"Almost Browne: The Twice Told Tribal Trickster," in *Listening to Ourselves: More Stories from "The Sound of Writing,"* edited by Alan Cheuse and Caroline Marshall (Garden City, N.Y.: Doubleday, 1994), pp. 233–241;

Native American Literature: A Brief Introduction and Anthology, edited by Vizenor (New York: HarperCollins, 1995) – includes Vizenor's "Measuring My Blood," pp. 68–70; "Heartlines," pp. 142–157; and *Ishi and the Wood Ducks,* pp. 299–336.

SELECTED PERIODICAL PUBLICATIONS – UNCOLLECTED:

POETRY

"An Introduction to Haiku," *Neeuropa* (Spring–Summer 1991–1992): 63–67;

"Our Land: Anishinaabe," *Native Peoples Magazine* (Spring 1993): 32–35.

FICTION

"Migration Tricks from Tribalness: Five Sorties," *Minnesota Monthly* (January 1978): 8–9;

Dust jacket for Vizenor's volume of "reexpressions" of traditional tribal songs

"Smallpox and the River Are Dead," *Minneapolis Tribune Sunday Picture Magazine,* 30 December 1979, p. 12;

"Tribal Trickster Dissolves: White 'Word' Piles with a Red Man's Brew," *Minneapolis Star,* 31 August 1981, p. A4;

"Feral Lasers," *Caliban,* 6 (Fall 1989): 16–23;

"Stone Trickster," *Northeast Indian Quarterly,* 8 (Fall 1991): 26–27;

"Trickster Photography: Simulations in the Ethnographic Present," *Exposure,* 29 (Fall 1993): 4–5;

"Monte Cassino Curiosa: Heart Dancers at the Headwaters," *Caliban,* 14 (1994): 60–70.

NONFICTION

"The Ojibway," *Twin Citian,* 8 (May 1966): 18–19;

"The Urban Indian," *Twin Citian,* 8 (June 1966): 13;

"Job Corps Center at Lydick Lake: For Some a Wager – For Others a Chance," *Twin Citian,* 9 (August 1966): 15–21;

"1966: Plymouth Avenue Is Going to Burn," *Twin Citian,* 9 (October 1966): 20–21;

"How Sly Davis Sees It," *Twin Citian,* 10 (October 1967): 60–62;

"We Rarely Turn Anyone Down," *Twin Citian,* 6 (October 1969): 35–38;

"Preserving Trivial Tattle in California," *Minneapolis Tribune,* 5 February 1978, p. A13;

"Dennis Banks: What Sort of Hero?," *Minneapolis Tribune,* 22 July 1978, p. A4;

"Indian Manikins with a Few References," *Minneapolis Tribune,* 5 September 1981, p. A10;

"Buffalo Bill: An Emblem of Ersatz History," *Minneapolis Tribune,* 29 November 1981, p. A19;

"Brixton: A New Circus of Proud People," *Minneapolis Tribune,* 31 January 1982, p. A15;

"Indian Alcoholics Are Individuals, Not White Mice," *Minneapolis Tribune,* 23 April 1982, p. A15;

"Mystic Warrior Speaks with Tongue Forked and a Vision Flawed," *Minneapolis Star and Tribune,* 18 May 1984, p. C16;

"Trickster Discourse," *Wicazo Sa Review,* 5 (Spring 1989): 2- 7;

"Native American Dissolve," *Oshkaabewis Native Journal,* 1, no. 1 (1990): 63–65;

"Introduction," *Genre,* 25 (Winter 1992): 315–319;

"Native American Indian Literature: Critical Metaphors of the Ghost Dance," *World Literature Today,* 66 (Spring 1992): 223–227;

"Gambling on Sovereignty," *American Indian Quarterly,* 16 (Summer 1992): 411–413;

"Christopher Columbus: Lost Havens in the Ruins of Representations," *American Indian Quarterly,* 16 (Fall 1992): 521–532;

"Manifest Manners: The Long Gaze of Christopher Columbus," *boundary 2,* 19 (Fall 1992): 223–235;

"Native American Indian Identities: Autoinscriptions and the Cultures of Names," *Genre,* 25 (Winter 1992): 431–440;

"The Envoy to Haiku," *Chicago Review,* 39, no. 3 (1993): 55–62;

"The Power of Names," *News from Native California,* 7 (Summer 1993): 38–41.

The author of more than twenty-five books and a scholar of international reputation, Gerald Vizenor is one of the most prolific and versatile of contemporary Native American writers. His works, which include poetry, fiction, autobiography, a screenplay, narrative history, journalism, essays, and critical theory, display his eclectic knowledge and intellectual sophistication. Revolutionary in style and vision, Vizenor's works have broken new ground in the field of Native American literature. Particularly notable are his celebratory representations of mixed-blood identity, his use of a trickster dynamic, and his blending of the postmodern with the tribal. An inveterate coiner of words, Vizenor consistently challenges the limits of written language and tries in his works to privilege the oral aesthetic. He received the American Book Award and the Fiction Collective Award for his novel *Griever: An American Monkey King in China* (1987) and the PEN Oakland Book Award for his autobiography, *Interior Landscapes: Autobiographical Myths and Metaphors* (1990). N. Scott Momaday, in the *Columbia Literary History of the United States* (1988), calls him "the supreme ironist among American Indian writers of the twentieth century." The subjects on which Vizenor has wielded his satire include historical and literary representations of Native Americans, contemporary identity politics, repatriation of tribal remains, reservation gaming, American Indian Movement leaders, and Christopher Columbus. His fearsome challenges to romantic Indian fallacies often situate the author and his literary works in the center of controversy, and he thrives there.

Throughout his life Vizenor has found ways to thrive in circumstances that might have destroyed a less hardy individual. Born on 22 October 1934 to twenty-four-year-old Clement William Vizenor, a house painter of French and Anishinaabe (Chippewa) ancestry, and LaVerne Lydia Peterson, a white teenage school dropout, Gerald Robert Vizenor was to receive little parental nurturing from either. Vizenor's father had moved from the White Earth Reservation in northwestern Minnesota to Minneapolis to find work; there he had met and married Vizenor's mother, but their union lasted less than a year. Clement Vizenor took Gerald and moved in with his mother and brothers and sisters. In late June 1936 Vizenor's father was murdered by a mugger; the crime remains unsolved. In the ensuing years Vizenor would live in a tenement with his paternal relatives, be reclaimed by his mother and endure loneliness and desperate poverty, and be abandoned by her to foster homes. Finally, LaVerne Vizenor remarried in 1943 and brought Gerald to live with her and her new husband, Elmer Petesch. Eight years later she abandoned both of them. Petesch died in an accidental fall down an elevator shaft on Christmas Eve, 1951.

Family, ancestors, and a sense of place have figured largely in Vizenor's artistic vision despite the harsh circumstances of his childhood and the absence of a stable family setting. In the first chapter of his autobiography, *Interior Landscapes,* he traces his connection to the Crane Clan and to the White Earth Reservation and offers brief sketches of several of his ancestors. Among those whose influence is felt most strongly in Vizenor's work is Theodore Hudon Beaulieu, editor of *The Progress,* the first newspaper to be published on the White Earth Reservation. Vizenor has retold in several of his works the government challenge to the paper's existence. He celebrates his connection to the tribal orators of the crane clan and to those who first claimed the right to publish Native American perspectives, and in his own work Vizenor marries this dual heritage of storytelling and rebellion.

In one of his earliest rebellions Vizenor dropped out of high school at eighteen to join the army. A routine army intelligence test gave him his first vision of himself as intellectually gifted, and during his time in the service he began to read seriously and to contemplate the possibility of a college education and a writer's life. Stationed for a time on the island of Matsushima in Japan, Vizenor was exposed to the Asian literature and culture that would fuel his early writing and would continue to be an important influence on later works.

Discharged from the army in 1955, Vizenor enrolled at the University of Minnesota. There he received encouragement from a professor of Asian literature, Edward Copeland, to pursue his interest in haiku poetry. He married Judith Horns in 1959, and their only child, Robert, was born in 1960. Vizenor earned a bachelor's degree in child development in 1960. From 1960 to 1962 he was a social worker at the Minnesota State Reformatory. In 1962 *Two Wings the Butterfly,* his first collection of haiku, was privately printed. He took graduate courses in anthropology, library science, and Asian studies at the University of Minnesota from 1962 to 1964. *Two Wings the Butterfly* was followed by five more haiku collections: *Raising the Moon Vines* and *Seventeen Chirps* in 1964, *Slight Abrasions* with Jerome Downes in 1966, *Empty Swings* in 1967, and *Matsushima: Pine Islands* in 1984.

Vizenor's fascination with haiku derives, first, from its use of nature and, second, from the restraint of the form – the absence that leaves space for reader response. In the introduction to *Matsushima* he sketches his understanding of the form, referring to haiku scholars and practitioners such as Donald Keene, R. H. Blyth, and Daisetz Suzuki. Through haiku, Vizenor claims, one arrives at a "dreamscape," a moment of transformation or

Dust jacket for Vizenor's futuristic satire

natural harmony. He quotes Blyth's comment that "Haiku is the expression of a temporary enlightenment, in which we see into the life of things" and goes on to explain: "Words are turned back to nature, set free in the mythic dreamscapes of a haiku." For Vizenor, the power of haiku stems from its ability to liberate one from language, to reconnect one to experience:

> The printed words in haiku are rendered; nothing remains but dreams, oral traditions, the light around our hands, petals, the rain. A haiku is not a narrative scheme; no sense riots, confusions at the verb, no sound of a book closed at the end of a proper narrative, no death in printed words. The angles of the whole moon shed our grammars in the red pine.

Vizenor has been recognized as one of the finest American haiku practitioners; his poems have been used as examples of the form in Louis Untermeyer's *The Pursuit of Poetry* (1970) and have been anthologized in such collections as *The Haiku Anthology* (1974). A poem from the autumn haiku section of *Matsushima* is representative of Vizenor's style:

> morning mist
> squirrels in the eucalyptus
> cones resound[.]

Like many of his haiku, this work describes the visual aspect of a natural setting, then attempts to awaken a multidimensional experience – here, by following the visual with the auditory. Other haiku by Vizenor embody the voice he calls in *Matsushima* the "street dancer . . . the trickster, the picaresque survivor in the wordwars." These haiku often jar the reader with unusual perspectives. The title poem in *Seventeen Chirps* is a case in point:

> It took seventeen chirps
> For a sparrow to hop across
> My city garden[.]

This "trickster" haiku calls attention to the modern preoccupation with enumerative measurement and, by showing its inappropriate application in this instance, playfully suggests that one live life rather than count and record each moment. Vizenor's haiku have many subjects and perspectives, yet the poems all strive, as Vizenor quotes Roland Barthes in *Matsushima,* to "halt language" and to arouse in the reader the experience of enlightenment.

In their desire both to reflect and to awaken a visionary experience, haiku are, for Vizenor, kindred to Ojibwa dream songs. "There is a visual dreamscape in haiku," he says in *Matsushima,* "which is similar to the sense of natural human connections to the earth found in tribal music, dream songs." In an unpublished 1987 interview Vizenor claimed that Ojibwa dream songs "are sort of the Ojibway haiku – in song." The similarity between the two extends to form as well as content: both are brief, tightly constructed works offering succinct images that frequently arise out of experience of nature. It is understandable, then, that during the time Vizenor was writing his early haiku he also undertook the translation of traditional Ojibwa songs. His "reexpressions," which make significant use of Frances Densmore's recordings and translations of songs in her two-volume *Chippewa Music* (1910), were published as *Summer in the Spring: Lyric Poems of the Ojibway* in 1965. This song, of fairly typical form, illustrates the singer's engagement with nature:

overhanging clouds
echoing my words
with a pleasing sound[.]

Vizenor followed his work on dream songs with reexpressions of Ojibwa stories in *anishinabe adisokan: Tales of the People* (1970). The two books were combined in 1981 under the title *Summer in the Spring: Ojibwe Lyric Poems and Tribal Stories,* and this collection was republished in 1993 as *Summer in the Spring: Anishinaabe Lyric Poems and Stories, New Edition.*

At the same time Vizenor was writing and publishing his haiku and his Ojibwa translations, his political interests began to lead him toward journalism. From 1964 to 1968 he was a community organizer, holding posts as a social worker for the Waite Settlement House in Minneapolis in 1965 and executive director of the American Indian Employment and Guidance Center in 1966, and much of his energy was given to earning Bureau of Indian Affairs (BIA) support for Indians who had relocated to the cities. He began to write articles for the *Twin Citian* magazine and the *Minneapolis Tribune;* many of the pieces were collected in his *Tribal Scenes and Ceremonies* (1976) and reprinted in an expanded collection, *Crossbloods: Bone Courts, Bingo, and Other Reports* (1990). Vizenor's freelance work led to a job as a general-assignment reporter for the *Tribune* in 1968–1969; he was an editorial writer for the paper in 1974 and a contributing editor from 1974 to 1976.

Vizenor's reporting on a Lakota premedical student, Thomas White Hawk, who was convicted of murder helped establish his reputation as a journalist. He wrote a long essay in which he identified in White Hawk a condition he labeled "cultural schizophrenia" and saw the young man's case as symbolic of the situation of many Native American people living in a "white-dominated society." The essay, which first appeared in the *Twin Citian,* was republished as a book, *Thomas James White Hawk* (1968); it was included in *Tribal Scenes and Ceremonies* and reworked in two of Vizenor's later books.

Vizenor's journalistic pieces covered topics ranging from Indian education and treaty rights to Indian child welfare, but a series of editorials he wrote on the American Indian Movement (AIM) in 1973 attracted the most attention. At a time when AIM was at the height of its popularity, Vizenor questioned the "confrontation idiom" of the radical organization and suggested that its leaders capitalized on romantic images of Indians, were mainly interested in publicity, and failed to stay around to work out the changes that would improve conditions for Native American people. A series of sketches Vizenor published as *The Everlasting Sky: New Voices from the People Named the Chippewa* (1972) could be seen as a counterpoint to the AIM editorials. Here Vizenor positively characterizes those he calls the "oshki anishinabe" ("new people of the woodland") and outlines some of their survival strategies and dreams. With this book Vizenor began the deromanticizing of the Indian that continues to preoccupy him today.

The seventeen pieces in *Wordarrows: Indians and Whites in the New Fur Trade* (1978) recognize the displacement of the white/Indian conflict from the literal battlefield to what Vizenor calls "cultural word wars." He illustrates his thesis that "language determines culture and the dimensions of consciousness" through accounts such as that of White Hawk's cultural schizophrenia and that of Marlene American Horse, an alcoholic whose true problem Vizenor sees as "internal word wars" fed by the guilt she has been taught to feel by white society. In several places Vizenor quotes from Momaday's *House Made of Dawn* (1968) and "The Man Made of Words" (1970); the title of the col-

Dust jacket for Vizenor's second novel, in which he links the Native American trickster and Chinese Monkey King traditions

lection refers to Momaday's story of an arrow maker whose survival depended on language. In this book and in later works Vizenor builds on Momaday's ideas about language, imagination, and storytelling.

Several of the pieces in *Wordarrows* are said to be taken from "an unpublished novel by Saint Louis Bearheart," which is described as "a strange book about tribal pilgrims and their grave reports from the word wars." The novel, *Darkness in Saint Louis Bearheart,* was actually by Vizenor, and it appeared in the same year as *Wordarrows.* A futuristic satire, it is the story of an odd assortment of pilgrims who, when an oil shortage closes down America's consumer culture, travel from a rural Minnesota reservation to New Mexico in search of the "vision window" to the "fourth world." Vizenor weaves together themes that he has continued to develop in his later works; among the most important of these themes is the notion of "terminal creeds," or static beliefs. In the novel the "terminal believers" die, while those who are able to adapt and change survive. The terminal beliefs exposed by Vizenor center around the romanticized stance of the "invented Indian."

As Vizenor has related in interviews, and as Louis Owens notes in his afterword to the 1990 edition, *Bearheart: The Heirship Chronicles,* the novel has generated strong reactions. Purposely "lost" by several publishers and rejected as pornography by one typesetter, it has been criticized for its irreverence toward the popular myth of the Indian and for the sex and violence it depicts. But, Owens contends, the real source of the negative response is "the novel's outrageous challenge to all preconceived definitions, what *Bearheart* calls 'terminal creeds.'" In trickster fashion, Vizenor dares to challenge his readers' most dearly held beliefs.

The style and tone of *Bearheart* also create a challenge for readers, establishing a pattern that has come to be associated with Vizenor's work. Vizenor incorporates thinly disguised people, places, and events from history, current affairs, and his personal experience. The plot, which incorporates elements of tribal myth – including the "evil gambler," the tribal trickster, dream visions, and transformations – is episodic and resists closure. Alan Velie, one of the first scholars to explore Vizenor's work, recognized in the book the joining of the postmodern novel with the trickster tradition that has become Vizenor's trademark.

While Vizenor was making the transition from poetry to journalism and fiction, he was also making the transition to the college classroom. He served as a summer instructor in a special program on tribal cultures at Bemidji State University in Minnesota in 1966 and took a one-year teaching job at Lake Forest College in Illinois in 1970. In the 1971–1972 academic year he was back at Bemidji State as director of Indian studies. Later he taught at several Twin Cities campuses, including Augsburg, Macalester, Hamline, and the University of Minnesota. In 1976 he accepted an appointment as lecturer in Native American studies at the University of California, Berkeley, and for several years he split his teaching duties between Berkeley and the University of Minnesota. In 1978 he was named the James J. Hill Visiting Professor in American Indian Studies at the University of Minnesota; in 1989 he was provost of Kresge College at the University of California, Santa Cruz; and in 1990 he held the David Burr Chair at the University of Oklahoma. Although Vizenor's writing continued to draw from his work in the Indian community, it began to reflect more academic and theoretical concerns.

Vizenor situates several of the stories in *Earthdivers: Tribal Narratives on Mixed Descent* (1981) in a university setting. "The Chair of Tears," for example, is a zany account of a university where the Department of Indian Studies is put up for sale to the highest bidder and a dip is used to adjust the skin of Indian mixed-bloods to a more politically advantageous color. Vizenor emphasizes the mixed-blood – what he later calls "crossblood" – condition in this collection of fiction and literary journalism, aligning that ambiguous state with that of the trickster and identifying the role of both as "earthdivers." While the traditional earthdivers dove underwater to bring back the sand from which the earth was built, the "mixedblood earthdiver," Vizenor writes in his preface, must "dive into unknown urban places now" searching for "a few honest words upon which to build a new urban turtle island" with which "to create a new consciousness of coexistence." Vizenor's preface also explores his use of the trickster as a metaphor for the mixed-blood, the theory behind his unusual use of language, some ideas about autobiography, and a critique of several anthropological trickster theories. Since he continues to develop all of these topics in his later works, this preface is an important statement of Vizenor's purpose and method and an early example of his growing concern with literary and cultural theory.

Vizenor's depiction of "earthdivers" continues with his screenplay for the motion picture *Harold of Orange,* which won the Film-in-the-Cities Award in 1983. The characters Vizenor calls "trickster founders of this new earth" are the "Warriors of Orange," a group of Indians who trick a charitable foundation into funding a miniature orange grove on their reservation and then a pinch bean coffee scam. The film makes it clear that both sides are playing a game in which each gets what it wants: the foundation receives "a good name," the Indians "a little money." In this delightful comedy Vizenor comments on Indian stereotypes, repatriation of tribal remains, and the distortions of history. In one memorable scene Harold Sinseer, the leader of the Warriors of Orange, suggests that some bones that are on display may actually be not Native American but those of an anthropologist who was lost in a snowstorm. Vizenor proves in this film, as he says in *The Heirs of Columbus* (1991), that "humor has political significance."

The issue of historical distortion raised in *Harold of Orange* gets much fuller treatment in *The People Named the Chippewa: Narrative Histories* (1984), in which Vizenor uses a storytelling method to discuss the problem of imposed histories and offer alternative accounts of historical events. Vizenor not only challenges the alleged facts but also questions the motives and methods of historiography: "The cultural and political histories of the Anishinaabe were written in colonial language by those who invented the Indian, renamed the tribes, allotted the land, divided ancestries by geometric degrees of blood, and categorized identities on federal reservations." Vizenor creates a collage of voices – historical, contemporary, mythic, and fictional – that converge and overlap to offer a more complete account of events and ideas.

In a similar vein, Vizenor's second novel, *Griever: An American Monkey King in China,* mixes mythical, historical, and fictional characters and events to critique the political scene of contemporary China. Vizenor had been divorced from his first wife in 1968 and in 1981 had married Laura Jane Hall, who was of British and Chinese-Guyanese background. The two taught for several months in 1983 at Tianjin University of China,

Dust jacket for Vizenor's novel in which Christopher Columbus's DNA is found to have healing properties

where Vizenor was struck by the similarity between the mythical Chinese Monkey King and the Native American trickster figure. He links the two traditions in *Griever,* in which the reservation trickster Griever de Hocus becomes a teacher at Zhou Enlai University. In typical trickster fashion, Griever works for liberation from Chinese strictures at every turn, freeing birds and prisoners, challenging the one-child rule, and ultimately flying away in an ultralight airplane.

More trickster fiction followed as Vizenor published a novel, *The Trickster of Liberty: Tribal Heirs to a Wild Baronage* (1988); a collection of short fiction, *Landfill Meditation* (1991); and two more novels, *The Heirs of Columbus* and *Dead Voices: Natural Agonies in the New World* (1992). Vizenor's trickster is, as he says in *Earthdivers,* a "compassionate tribal trickster," an "imaginative trickster, the one who cares to balance the world between terminal creeds and humor with unusual manners and ecstatic strategies." In an unpublished interview Vizenor has said: "The thing I want to emphasize about him in my experience and in my writing is that he is liberator."

That key quality is evident in *The Trickster of Liberty,* an account of a family of Anishinaabe tricksters from Vizenor's reservation, White Earth. Marked throughout with reappearances of characters from previous works, the novel presents perhaps Vizenor's most cutting indictment of the "invented Indian." In the chapter "The Last Lecture at the Edge" a group of "mixedblood educators, tribal radicals, writers, painters, a geneticist, a psychotaxidermist, and various pretenders to the tribe" deliver one last account of themselves before they take on new names and identities. Through these confessions Vizenor seeks to liberate his readers from their stereotypes about Indians.

Landfill Meditation brings together revised versions of previously published short stories and such new works as "Almost Browne" and "Ice Tricksters." "Almost Browne" offers one of Vizenor's most playful renditions of the trickster character. Almost, who symbolizes the mixed-blood state, describes his origin: "I was born in the back seat of a beatup reservation car, almost white, almost on the reservation, and almost a real person." The story plays on the trickster role of mediation as Almost attends a reservation school and then a white school and interprets the world for his white friend Drain. It emphasizes the role of imagination in literature as the protagonist learns to read "almost" books, whose pages were burned at the edges in a fire at the reservation library, and finds that the imagined stories are more real than the words on the page.

The Heirs of Columbus, written in connection with the quincentenary of Columbus's arrival in America, tells the story of Stone Columbus, supposed descendant of the great explorer, who discovers healing genes in Christopher Columbus's DNA. Thus, the symbol of Native American's demise becomes a means of their survival. Vizenor overturns the enshrined historical accounts, questioning Christopher Columbus's religious and racial identity, rewriting the romantic accounts of Pocahontas, and deconstructing the explorers' declarations of discovery.

Dead Voices is organized around a *wanaki* game, Vizenor's fictional version of an Ojibwa game, in which a player draws a card that pictures an animal of some sort and must then, through imagination and meditation, experience the life of that creature for a day and tell stories from its viewpoint. The novel restates and advances many of Vizenor's early concerns about language. The emphasis in *Dead Voices* is on the living quality of words that link one, through imagination, to experience; words as mere concepts, on the other hand, are "dead." Vizenor also draws a distinction between written and oral language and gives clear preference to the oral because of its dialogic quality and immediacy.

In 1989 Vizenor edited *Narrative Chance: Postmodern Discourse on Native American Indian Literatures,* which includes his "A Postmodern Introduction" and his essay "Trickster Discourse: Comic Holotropes and Language Games." He began to publish theoretical essays and mixed-genre works in journals such as *boundary 2* and *World Literature Today,* and in 1994 he brought many of his essays together in the collection *Manifest Manners: Postindian Warriors of Survivance.* This challenging book explores contemporary Indian identity politics, revisits and puts new twists on the notion of "cultural word wars," and finds a source of tribal survival in the "literature of liberation" of "tribal poets and novelists." Employing the terminology and ideas of

Dust jacket for the novel in which Vizenor restates and develops many of his early ideas about language

scholars and theorists such as Jean Baudrillard, Michel Foucault, Mikhail Bakhtin, and Larzer Ziff, Vizenor claims that "Indians" never existed because "the word has no referent in tribal languages or cultures."

Prior to the publication of his autobiography, *Interior Landscapes,* in 1990, Vizenor had published several shorter pieces showing an increasing concern with the form. In *Interior Landscapes* he uses both the first and the third person, writing about his own production of his account of his life and including theoretical comments by scholars such as Paul John Eakin and Avrom Fleishman. He quotes Eakin's assertion that in the "autobiographical act . . . the materials of the past are shaped by memory and imagination to serve the needs of present consciousness." Vizenor's telling of his life incorporates myths such as that of the evil gambler, and he weaves a trickster presence throughout his story. He comments on the various interpretations he made of the incidents of his life and the stories he created about those incidents. His autobiography does not emphasize dates and details but imaginative meanings. It is, as the title suggests, as much a rendering and interpretation of myth and metaphor as it is a biographical account.

The publication of *Shadow Distance: A Gerald Vizenor Reader* (1994), which includes fiction, autobiography, essays, and the screenplay for *Harold of Orange,* attests to the importance and the sheer volume of his work. Known internationally, with works translated into French, Italian, and German, Vizenor has blazed a path for a new generation of Native American writers and scholars whose work reflects links to national and international literature, theory, and politics, as well as to tribal traditions and concerns. Called the "most radically intellectual of American Indian authors" by Owens, Vizenor continues his campaign to upset the social and literary status quo.

Returning to Berkeley in 1991 after holding appointments at other institutions, Vizenor continued his campaign to have a campus building named after Ishi, the last Yahi Indian, whose bones had been displayed in the Museum of Anthropology at the university since 1911. Vizenor repeatedly petitioned the campus officials and criticized the university regents in essays. Finally, Vizenor succeeded in having an interior court named after Ishi, who had come to symbolize for him both the "museumized" Indian "specimen" and the tribal survivor. His play, *Ishi and the Wood Ducks,* was published in *Native American Literature: A Brief Introduction and Anthology,* a collection Vizenor edited in 1995, and was performed by the Red Path Theatre in Chicago in 1996.

Vizenor's recent literary efforts include *Hotline Healers: An Almost Browne Novel,* to be released in 1997. Here, as in most of his trickster writing, Vizenor seeks to achieve liberation, survival, and healing through the use of humor. As he told Joseph Bruchac, "The tricksters in all my work, everywhere, and, in one character or another, disrupt the ambitions of people, contradict, unsettle, and unglue the creeds. . . . My imagined tricksters are compassionate and comic." Vizenor's works invite their readers to abandon static beliefs and become comic survivors.

Interviews:

Neal Bowers and Charles L. P. Silet, "An Interview with Gerald Vizenor," *MELUS,* 8, no. 1 (1981): 41–49;

Joseph Bruchac, "Follow the Trickroutes: An Interview with Gerald Vizenor," in his *Survival This Way: Interviews with American Indian Poets* (Tucson: University of Arizona Press, 1987), pp. 287–310;

Laura Coltelli, *Winged Words: American Indian Writers Speak* (Lincoln: University of Nebraska Press, 1990), pp. 154–182.

References:

Linda Ainsworth, "History and Imagination: Gerald Vizenor's *The People Named the Chippewa,*" *American Indian Quarterly,* 9 (Winter 1985): 52–53;

Franchot Ballinger, "Sacred Reversals: Trickster in Gerald Vizenor's Earthdivers: Tribal Narratives on Mixed Descent," *American Indian Quarterly,* 9 (Winter 1985): 55–59;

Betty Louise Bell, "Almost the Whole Truth: Gerald Vizenor's Shadow Working and Native American Autobiography," *A/B Auto/Biography,* 7 (Fall 1992): 180–195;

Kimberly M. Blaeser, *Gerald Vizenor: Writing in the Oral Tradition* (Norman: University of Oklahoma Press, 1996);

Jonathan Boyarin, "Europe's Indian, American's Jew: Modiano and Vizenor," in his *Storm from Paradise: The Politics of Jewish Memory* (Minneapolis: University of Minnesota Press, 1992), pp. 9–31;

Patricia Haseltine, "The Voices of Gerald Vizenor: Survival through Transformation," *American Indian Quarterly,* 9 (Winter 1985): 31–47;

Elaine Jahner, "Allies in the Word Wars: Vizenor's Uses of Contemporary Critical Theory," *Studies in American Indian Literature,* 9 (1985): 64–69;

Maureen Keady, "Walking Backwards into the Fourth World: Survival of the Fittest in Bearheart," *American Indian Quarterly,* 9 (Winter 1985): 61–65;

N. Scott Momaday, "The Native Voice," in *The Columbia Literary History of the United States,* edited by Emory Elliott (New York: Columbia University Press, 1988), pp. 5–15;

Louis Owens, "Acts of Recovery: The American Indian Novel in the 80's," *Western American Literature,* 22 (1987): 53–57;

Owens, "Ecstatic Strategies: Gerald Vizenor's Trickster Narratives," in his *Other Destinies: Understanding the American Indian Novel* (Norman: University of Oklahoma Press, 1992), pp. 225–254;

Bernadette Rigal-Cellard, "Vizenor's Griever: A Post-Maodernist Little Red Book of Cocks, Tricksters, and Colonists," in *New Voices in Native American Literary Criticism,* edited by Arnold

Krupat (Washington, D.C.: Smithsonian Institution Press, 1993), pp. 317–343;

A. LaVonne Brown Ruoff, "Gerald Vizenor: Compassionate Trickster," *American Indian Quarterly,* 9 (Winter 1985): 67–73; (Spring 1985): 52–63;

Ruoff, "Woodland Word Warrior: An Introduction to the Works of Gerald Vizenor," *MELUS,* 13 (Spring–Summer 1986): 13–43;

James Ruppert, *Mediation in Contemporary Native American Literature* (Norman: University of Oklahoma Press, 1995), pp. 92–108;

Cecilia Sims, "The Rebirth of Indian and Chinese Mythology in Gerald Vizenor's *Griever: An American Monkey King in China,*" in *Critical Perspectives on Native American Fiction,* edited by Richard F. Fleck (Washington, D.C.: Three Continents, 1993), pp. 171–177;

Alan Velie, *Four American Literary Masters: N. Scott Momaday, James Welch, Leslie Marmon Silko, and Gerald Vizenor* (Norman: University of Oklahoma Press, 1982), pp. 123–148;

Velie, "Gerald Vizenor," in *Dictionary of Native American Literature,* edited by Andrew Wiget (New York: Garland, 1994), pp. 519–525;

Velie, "The Trickster Novel," in *Narrative Chance: Postmodern Discourse on Native American Indian Literature,* edited by Vizenor (Albuquerque: University of New Mexico Press, 1989), pp. 121–140.

James Welch

(18 November 1940 –)

Sidner J. Larson
University of Oregon

BOOKS: *Riding the Earthboy 40* (New York: World, 1971; revised edition, New York: Harper & Row, 1976);

Winter in the Blood (New York: Harper & Row, 1974);

The Death of Jim Loney (New York: Harper & Row, 1979);

Fools Crow (New York: Viking, 1986);

The Indian Lawyer (New York: Norton, 1990);

Killing Custer, by Welch and Paul Stekler (New York: Norton, 1994).

TELEVISION: "The American Experience: Last Stand at Little Big Horn," script by Welch and Paul Stekler, WGBH/Boston, 20 November 1995.

James Welch at the time of The Indian Lawyer *(photograph by Marc A. Hefty)*

It is generally accepted that the Native American Renaissance in literature started with N. Scott Momaday's *House Made of Dawn* in 1968. James Welch's *Winter in the Blood* (1974) is the second major work of the renaissance, placing Welch as one of the early writers of the modern American Indian literary movement. Welch remains a major writer in the field of Native American literature, as evidenced by his most recent book, *Killing Custer* (1994).

James Welch was born on 18 November 1940 in Browning, Montana, located on the east slope of the Rocky Mountains, almost directly east of Glacier National Park. The tribal headquarters of the Blackfeet Indian Nation are located in Browning, where Welch is enrolled as a member of the Blackfeet tribe. He is also Gros Ventre on his mother's side. Welch attended schools on the Blackfeet and Fort Belknap reservations before graduating from Washburn High School in Minneapolis, Minnesota. He attended the University of Minnesota, Northern Montana College, and the University of Montana, graduating from Montana in 1965. After graduation he entered the M.F.A. program at Montana, studying with Richard Hugo and Madeline DeFrees.

Welch's work has been the subject of much attention since his collection of poems, *Riding the Earthboy 40* (1971), first appeared. Indian attitudes of relationship to the land imply that the health of a person demands a horizon, and that horizon is the land, or "place." It has been said the drone in Indian music is known as the horizon note; this is similar to the way painters utilize a focal point around which to arrange their compositions. So it goes with people as well; life is conducted in counterpoint to the places where it is lived – place is the steady, walking base to which the events of a life are syncopated.

In Welch's poem "Birth on Range 18" the reader moves from the beginning to the end with the sense that something has happened, although no event is specifically described. The poem signifies life cycles – of land, cattle, people – lived out on the semiarid grazing land that compromises most of the Fort Belknap Indian reservation. Its title has to do with organization of land in a literal sense. At the

EARLY PRAISE

"Jim Welch writes beautifully and knows things that aren't in the other books. A true book is one you think you needed; I read *Winter in the Blood* with that kind of relief."
TOM McGUANE

"This book is a very strong, simple, natural statement. Welch tells his story with the ease of an Indian talking. If you want to know what it's like to be an original American, to suffer and enjoy, to experience a life in Indian country, then read *Winter in the Blood*."
WILLIAM EASTLAKE

"In *Winter in the Blood*, James Welch has brought together prose and poetry. It is a triumphant reminder that all of the force of the Christian proselytizers' Long Knives failed to undo an indigenous peoples' spirit. Our ancient medicine men are still among us; James Welch is one."
ISHMAEL REED

"James Welch has captured the remote ugly west where the space between people, like the enormous, empty land, sours finally into void and all relationships become marginal and desperate and, because the void cannot be safely endured forever, beautifully vital."
RICHARD HUGO

"A superior novel. It deals with contemporary American Indians with brilliance and authenticity."
VINE DELORIA

"*Winter in the Blood* is a wonderful novel. The dialog is marvelously apt, and the contrast between traditional and contemporary qualities very powerful. As an 'Indian' novel, it doesn't bow to any other sort of novel. It is deeply and strangely 'American' in a way that very few of our novels are."
JIM HARRISON

06-452500-7

Dust jacket for Welch's first novel

time of allotment, land along the Milk River was divided into small parcels of forty acres, which were designated with the names of their original owners combined with numbers for purposes of reference; "Earthboy 40" refers to such a parcel. Prairie land south of the river, practically useful only for summer grazing, was divided into larger portions of up to 360 acres. The government organized this area into what are known as range units, some larger than others according to the quality of the land, and put up fences around them to facilitate use by individual cattle operators. The units were numbered, and "Range 18" refers to a grazing area south of Welch's family ranch.

Many of Welch's poems are skillful descriptions of particular scenes. An example is "Day After Chasing Porcupines":

Rain Came. Fog out of the slough and horses
asleep in the barn. In the fields, sparrow hawks
glittered through the morning clouds.

No dreamers knew the rain. Wind ruffled quills
in the mongrel's nose. He sighed cautiously,
kicked further beneath the weathered shed and
slept.

Timid chickens watched chickens in the puddles.
Watching the chickens, yellow eyes harsh
below the wind-drifting clouds, sparrow hawks.

Horses stamped in the barn. The mongrel whimpered
in his dream, wind ruffled his mongrel tail,
the lazy cattails and the rain.

The poem relies heavily on repetition: it begins and ends with the word *rain*; chickens watch chickens, even as sparrow hawks watch the chickens from the clouds; the word *mongrel* is repeated three times. Such repetition produces language that is soothing and hypnotic.

"Magic Fox," the first poem in the surrealistic "Knives" section of *Riding the Earthboy 40,* describes a different scene:

They shook the green leaves down,
those men that rattled
in their sleep. Truth became
a nightmare to their fox.
He turned their horses into fish,
or was it horses strung

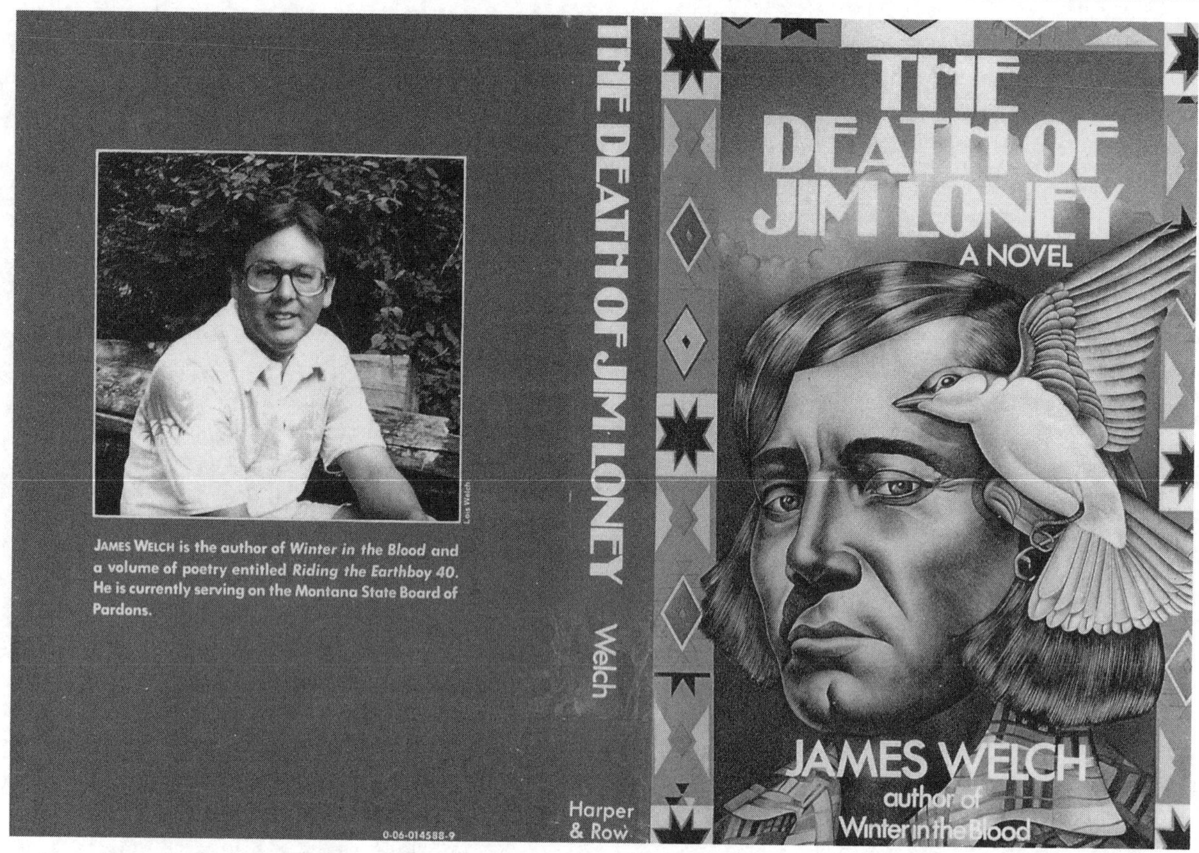

Dust jacket for Welch's novel about a man who orchestrates his own death at the hands of a tribal policeman

like fish, or fish like fish,
hung naked in the wind?

Stars fell upon their catch.
A girl, not yet twenty-four
but blonde as morning birds, began
a dance that drew the men in
green around her skirts.
In dust her music jangled memories
of dawn, till fox and grief
turned nightmare in their sleep.

And this: fish not fish but stars
that fell into their dreams.

Welch communicates extensively in an abstract manner, and even the straightforward "Day After Chasing Porcupines" urges the reader to see beyond the eyes, to associate wind and birds with spirits communicating through dreams. The contrast in Welch's writing – simplistic accessibility on one hand and extreme levels of complexity on the other – is characteristic.

Welch's poetry shows the influence of Surrealism; critics have cited Peruvian poet Cesar Vallejo and American poet James Wright as the most important direct influences. Welch and Vallejo are similar in their ability to make disparate images live together in writing, in their effective use of colloquial speech, and in their gift for finding meaning in simple things. Perhaps this similarity is partially attributable to the fact that they are both mixed-bloods and have both lived among Native cultures and in white society. Welch has acknowledged the influence of his friend Wright, and the subject matter of Welch's and Wright's poems is often similar. An example is Wright's "Stages on a Journey Westward," wherein is found a predominantly rural setting and some of the favorite subject matter of Welch – sleep, horses, Indians, drunks, and bums.

It was with the publication of his first novel, *Winter in the Blood,* that Welch began to receive worldwide recognition. The book tells the story of a Native American man in his thirties coming to grips with his adult life on the Fort Belknap Indian reservation and how discovering the identity of his grandfather facilitates the process. Although the man appears to come to certain potentially helpful realizations about his life and himself, he does not undertake any specific action as the story draws to a close. This lack of a European-style ending is thought to be one of the strongest American Indian features of the text.

Early reviewers of the novel found a negative message therein, but in a seminar on *Winter in the Blood* during the 1977 Modern Language Association convention Peter G. Beidler concluded: "Although this issue abounds in provocative disagreements, it does appear that most of us agree, with varying degrees of conviction, that the narrator of *Winter in the Blood* does grow, and that he has achieved a measure of wisdom by the end of the novel." Beidler continues, "We have in these pages called into serious question that [nihilistic] reading of the novel . . . which is finally about life more than it is about death."

To this debate about the novel's message can be added Welch's own comments. Discussing *Winter in the Blood* in a 1982 interview, Welch addressed the narrator's potential: "He's a pretty bright guy and he could probably do all right. But for some reason he doesn't." Welch seems to be less interested in how the narrator's fortunes might improve as he learns about his grandfather than in the subject of people who do not try very hard to rise above what they are. He is also clear on the subject of humor in *Winter in the Blood:* in a 1984 interview included in Ron McFarland's *James Welch* (1986) he said: "I intentionally put comic stuff in there just to alleviate that vision of alienation and purposelessness, aimlessness." It is also important to note, however, that Welch specifically refers to Indian humor, which creates an opportunity to add to the Western notions of comedy that critics suggest are to be found in the novel.

In Welch's second novel, *The Death of Jim Loney* (1979), there is no room for speculation about the future of the central character, who orchestrates his own death at the hands of a tribal policeman. Like the narrator of *Winter in the Blood,* Loney has reached adulthood but is less equipped to deal with it. After a time of soul-searching and a pivotal event wherein he accidentally shoots a high-school classmate, he decides the life he is living is not worth continuing. In *Winter in the Blood* the narrator's grandmother provides him with valuable information, and Yellow Calf – who, he will discover, is actually his grandfather – nudges him into self-knowledge, but Jim Loney has no such helpers and as a result is unable to unmask the central mystery of his life.

The Death of Jim Loney begins with a scene of a high-school football game. As he watches the game, Loney recalls a biblical passage, "Turn away from man in whose nostrils is breath, for of what account is he?" The scene sets the tone of the novel, where faith and knowledge never really become clear, serving only to torture the protagonist.

The book's other main characters – Rhea, Loney's lover; Painter, the town cop; and Myron Pretty Weasel, Loney's friend – are also alienated for one reason or another, all living a kind of outpost existence on the margin of Native American culture. The desolate setting echoes T. S. Eliot's *The Waste Land* (1922), framing Loney's inability to put the pieces of his past and present together. He cannot imagine himself as Indian, but neither is he white. While in this state of mind he goes hunting with his high-school friend Pretty Weasel and accidentally shoots him. The event functions as the one clear sign Loney has ever had in his life – a sign that everything has gone wrong – and Loney decides to take control of his life by stopping the negative flow of events associated with it. He provokes a brutal tribal policeman, Quentin Doore, who finally shoots Loney.

Within this framework the critical debate is reduced to what it means to be a half-breed and the significance of Loney's pursuit of his own death. William Thackery said that "To live halfbreed is to be dead." Other reviewers, however, agreed that there is a positive element in Loney's death, even if it is only in the fact that Loney is in control of it. In his *Northwest Review* interview Welch said he agreed with the notion that Loney's suicide is a positive act because it is a creative act and that "all creative acts are basically positive." He again articulated his interest in individuals with self-limiting worlds, however: "Yeah, when [Loney] was a young boy he was very bright and he just sort of lost himself as he's gotten older. I'm fascinated with this type of person – I've seen him all over the Highline."

Fools Crow (1986) is significantly different from Welch's first two novels. The story revolves around events leading up to the Marias River Massacre of 1870. Fools Crow, the central character, is unable to prevent the massacre despite the fact that it has been revealed to him ahead of time by a spirit helper. Burdened with the knowledge of what will happen to his people, Fools Crow persists, achieving adult status in the tribal way, starting a family, and assuming the role of medicine man.

The protagonist is a full-blood living in a traditional Blackfeet world, a world white men are only beginning to enter as *Fools Crow* begins. The book is set in the late 1860s, a time when the Blackfeet are a strong and confident people. White Man's Dog – the childhood name of Fools Crow – is a member of

Dust jacket for Welch's historical novel set in the late 1860s

the Lone Eaters band of the Pikuni, or Piegans. His first opportunity to earn his adult name comes when he is invited along on a horse-stealing raid against the Crows. The raid is led by Yellow Kidney and Eagle Ribs, genuine Blackfeet tribal names. Fools Crow distinguishes himself during the raid, alienating his friend Fast Horse, who joins a renegade band. In an attempt to intercede Fools Crow explores the mythology of the Blackfeet, where he is given a glimpse of the future. The novel ends with a ceremonial procession through the Pikuni camp as the people celebrate the return of spring. Rain comes to the village, and Fools Crow thinks of all that will be lost but that the people will know their heritage by stories that will be handed down.

In *Winter in the Blood* Welch looks briefly into the Indian past; in *The Death of Jim Loney* the past is unknowable, making the future impossible; but *Fools Crow* is an extended journey through the past to the Blackfeet world of the late 1800s, merging actual events and characters with fictionalized recreation. Different as *Fools Crow* is, there is a continuance of a strand of thought from the previous two books: a concern with how Indian individuals and groups find ways to live fulfilling lives and with the consequences of the failure to do so. In the *Northwest Review* interview Welch remarked how such observation "could show how a group of people totally declines. These are really dramatic events, because after the massacre of 1870, the Blackfeet never fought white people again, ever. That was the end – they laid down their arms. And then in 1882 and 1883 they starved."

Not nearly as much has been written about *Fools Crow* or *The Death of Jim Loney* as *Winter in the Blood.* Excellent studies do exist, however, such as Nora Barry's *MELUS* essay " 'A Myth to Be Alive' " (Spring 1991–1992), wherein she argues that Welch transforms the events leading to the Marias River Massacre into a mythic, sustaining tale rather than a negative one. Welch's "prose epic," she argues, presents "a hero who must survive for his people, . . . and connects [this] hero to [traditional] Blackfeet myths and to historical events."

The Indian Lawyer (1990) is probably the least analyzed of Welch's fiction, possibly because it does not directly reflect the usual literary conventions. *The Indian Lawyer* is different from its predecessors, yet it continues to further a common theme that explores the ways Indian individuals and groups manage or fail to manage their lives in the postcolonial world. The novel expands the combination of In-

Dust jacket for Welch's novel about a successful middle-class Native American

dian and Western literary points of view, utilizing elements of psychology and social science Welch gained from his experience on the Montana Parole Board. The result is a narrative focused tightly on an Indian individual attempting to enter one of the most sacrosanct of Euro-American domains – the legal system.

An integral part of *The Indian Lawyer* is an examination of the transformation from insider to outsider of a member of the Blackfeet tribe. This type of change reflects a central issue, that of identity, in modern Native fiction. At a particularly telling point in the narrative, Sylvester Yellow Calf, the protagonist, reflects that "He had nightmares of waking up in the street, stark naked, alone in a crowd of strangers, not knowing where he was or what had happened, alone and naked and full of loathing of himself, his father, the strangers – and his mother." The passage illustrates the importance of the conflict between insider and outsider in the book.

The Indian Lawyer uses social science and psychology to move toward a new trend in Native fiction, as noted by Alan R. Velie in his 1992 article "American Indian Literature in the Nineties: The Emergence of the Middle-Class Protagonist": "Indian professionals who have achieved a great deal of success and prestige in the white world." This new direction of depicting middle-class Native American protagonists has value for those interested in how Indians actually deal with the modern world. Also, within the expansion of tribal settings common to earlier novels, identity remains a central issue.

The Indian Lawyer is the story of a man who has "progressed" in measurable modern ways but has left behind much of what he needs to be ultimately successful. Because he has allowed himself to become an outsider to family, landscape, and tribal identity, Yellow Calf is poorly equipped to cope with the challenges that arise. Finally, he begins to learn that he must start over in certain ways. The novel takes the reader far beyond the usual rural and urban Native communities found in earlier Native literature. The same concern with individual and tribal perception of identity found in Welch's earlier work, however, ties the book strongly to *Winter in the Blood, The Death of Jim Loney,* and *Fools Crow.*

Welch's most recent work, *Killing Custer,* coauthored with Paul Stekler, is a nonfiction retelling

Dust jacket for Welch and Paul Stekler's account of the Battle of Little Bighorn

of the Battle of Little Bighorn. In chapter 9 Welch intersperses the narrative with a characterization of his mother and father and tells how his mother provided him with government documents that gave him a connection to history when he was a young man. The interspersion is characteristic of Welch's style in the book, a style that personalizes a shopworn story, as well as providing Native American points of view toward events that are among the most celebrated in American history. The publication of Native American points of view toward such historic events represents a watershed in writing and other strategies of representation concerning the relationship between Euro-Americans and the indigenous people they encountered upon arriving on the North American continent.

The book, an extension of the Public Broadcasting System program "The American Experience: Last Stand at Little Big Horn" (1995), begins by pointing out how American history has often been distorted to justify the subjugation of Native people. A thorough discussion of the making and breaking of the treaty of 1868, which led to the Battle of Little Bighorn, follows. Welch then tells the history of the Black Hills area and of the people who have occupied that area, past and present. From the arrival of the horse to the American Indian Movement involvement that led to the modern-day Wounded Knee confrontation, the people known as the Sioux, or Lakota, are emblematic of what happened to all Native people in the United States.

The retelling of the battle, again from an Indian point of view, is fascinating, leading to archaeologist Richard Fox's conclusion that disorganization and panic characterized the white soldiers' actions. Thus is exploded one of the most powerful myths in American history, that of the novel and heroic "Custer's Last Stand." The denouement of Little Bighorn is a sad one, leading to the subjugation of the plains tribes and the treacherous murders of Crazy Horse and Sitting Bull. Welch's thorough research, personalization of the story, and attention to the input of individuals outside the academy represents an excellent model for the role of intellectuals in the struggle of minority peoples.

Within Welch's narratives are found the hero's journey, totem animals, the loss of a twin, and other Native elements. These elements coexist with academic scholarship, the use of comedy, the picaresque hero, Surrealism, and other Western literary conventions; social science and psychology are also reflected in Welch's work. This combination of elements is a helpful addition to the ways present-day readers comprehend Native cultures.

Interviews:

Bill Bevis, "Dialogue with James Welch," *Northwest Review,* 20 (1982): 163–185;

Joseph Bruchac, ed., *Survival This Way; Interviews with American Indian Poets* (Tucson: University of Arizona Press, 1987), pp. 311–321.

References:

Charles G. Ballard, "The Question of Survival in *Fools Crow,*" *North Dakota Quarterly,* 59 (Spring 1991): 251–259;

Ballard, "The Theme of the Helping Hand in *Winter in the Blood,*" *MELUS,* 17 (Spring 1991–1992): 63–74;

Nora Barry, "The Lost Children in James Welch's *The Death of Jim Loney,*" *Western American Literature,* 25 (May 1990): 35–48;

Barry, " 'A Myth to Be Alive': James Welch's *Fools Crow,*" *MELUS,* 17 (Spring 1991–1992): 3–20;

Peter G. Beidler, ed., "James Welch's *Winter in the Blood,*" special issue of *American Indian Quarterly,* 4 (May 1978): 93–172;

Seth Bovey, "Whitehorns and Blackhorns: Images of Cattle Ranching in the Novels of James Welch," *South Dakota Review,* 29 (Spring 1991): 129–139;

Rachel Barritt Costa, "Incommunicability: A Linguistic Analysis of Conversation Breakdown in *The Death of Jim Loney,*" *Forum* (Pisa), 1 (1989): 159–172;

David M. Craig, "Beyond Assimilation: James Welch and the Indian Dilemma," *North Dakota Quarterly,* 53 (Spring 1985): 182–190;

Ron Gable, "Sovereignty in the Blood: Cultural Resistance in the Characters of James Welch," *Wicazo Sa Review,* 9 (Fall 1993): 37–43;

Robert F. Gish, "New Warrior, New West: History and Advocacy in James Welch's *The Indian Lawyer,*" *American Indian Quarterly,* 15 (Summer 1991): 369–374;

Kenneth Lincoln, "Bad Jokes, Short Words, Stunted Psyches and Debatable Humor in *Winter in the Blood,*" *Forum* (Pisa), 1 (1989): 151–157;

Lincoln, "Blackfeet Winter Blues: James Welch," in his *Native American Renaissance* (Berkeley: University of California Press, 1983), pp. 148–182;

Denise Low, "A Healing Rain in James Welch's *Winter in the Blood,*" *Dionysos,* 2 (Fall 1990): 26–32;

Ron McFarland, " 'The end' in James Welch's Novels," *American Indian Quarterly,* 17 (Summer 1993): 319–327;

McFarland, ed., *James Welch* (Lewiston: Confluence Press, 1986);

Robert Nelson, *Place and Vision: The Function of Landscape in Native American Fiction* (New York: Peter Lang, 1993), pp. 91–131;

Roberta Orlandini, "Variations on a Theme: Traditions and Temporal Structure in the Novels of James Welch," *South Dakota Review,* 26 (Autumn 1988): 37–52;

John Purdy, "Bha'a and *The Death of Jim Loney,*" *Studies in American Indian Literatures,* 5 (Summer 1993): 67–71;

LaVonne Ruoff, "The Influence of Elio Vittorini's *In Sicily* on James Welch's *Winter in the Blood,*" *Forum* (Pisa), 1 (1989): 141–150;

Kathleen Sands, "Closing the Distance: Critic, Reader and the Works of James Welch," *MELUS,* 14 (Summer 1987): 79–85;

William Thackery, "Crying for Pity in *Winter in the Blood,*" *MELUS,* 7 (Spring 1980): 61–78;

Kathryn Vangen, " 'Only an Indian': The Prose and Poetry of James Welch," dissertation, University of Michigan, 1987;

Alan R. Velie, "American Indian Literature in the Nineties: The Emergence of the Middle-Class Protagonist," *World Literature Today,* 66, no. 2 (1992): 264–268;

Velie, *Four American Indian Literary Masters* (Norman: University of Oklahoma Press, 1982), pp. 91–103;

Dexter Westrum, "James Welch's *Fools Crow:* Back to the Future," *San Jose Studies,* 14 (Spring 1988): 49–58;

Peter Wild, *James Welch* (Boise: Boise State University Press, 1983).

Sarah Winnemucca

(1844 – 17 October 1891)

Ruth Rosenberg
Brooklyn College

BOOK: *Life among the Piutes: Their Wrongs and Claims,* edited by Mary Mann (Boston: Privately printed, 1883).

Edition: *Life among the Piutes: Their Wrongs and Claims,* foreword by Catherine S. Fowler (Reno: University of Nevada Press, 1994).

OTHER: Helen Hunt Jackson, *A Century of Dishonor,* appendix by Winnemucca (New York: Harper, 1881), p. 395.

SELECTED PERIODICAL PUBLICATION – UNCOLLECTED: "The Pah-Utes," *California: A Western Monthly Magazine,* 6 (September 1882): 252–256.

Sarah Winnemucca. The photograph is inscribed to her brother, Natchez (courtesy of the Nevada Historical Society)

Sarah Winnemucca's *Life among the Piutes: Their Wrongs and Claims* (1883) is generally acknowledged to be the first autobiography by a Native American woman. She formed an alliance with two New England activists and educators – Elizabeth Palmer Peabody and her sister, Mary Mann – who urged her to write her personal and tribal history in their rented rooms at 54 Bowdoin Street in Boston. Mann, who edited the autobiography, and Peabody, who raised the funds to have it printed, intended to use it to influence federal policy and legislation. To achieve this aim, Gae Whitney Canfield writes, "every effort was made by Sarah and her Boston friends to get the autobiography printed, bound, and out to the public before the next session of Congress." To help right the wrongs suffered by the Paiutes, Winnemucca founded the Peabody Indian School in the last few years of her life. Winnemucca's book presents four decades of injustices, beginning with the year of her birth. Her limited diction and simple syntax remind readers of her lack of formal education. To fulfill a request her grandfather had made on his deathbed in 1860, she and her younger sister were sent to a convent school in San Jose, California, but after three weeks, Winnemucca recalls, they were dismissed "when complaints were made to the sisters by wealthy parents about Indians being in school with their children."

Throughout her book Winnemucca uses the hesitant, nonconfrontational tone of her deferential opening sentence: "I was born somewhere near 1844, but I am not sure of the precise time." Her third chapter opens its discussion of an incident with the same note of caution: "This was in

Mary Mann, widow of the educator Horace Mann, and her sister, Elizabeth Palmer Peabody. Mary Mann edited Winnemucca's Life among the Piutes, *and Peabody raised funds to have it printed.*

the year 1858, I think; I am not sure." As a woman speaking before the time of female enfranchisement and as a Native American lacking any rights of citizenship, she is careful not to offend, not to recount whatever cannot be authenticated: "As I do not remember all the particulars," she writes of one incident, "I will not attempt to relate it."

Winnemucca also used a repertoire of stylistic devices from her oral tradition to compensate for her scanty literary background. One such feature of storytelling performance is a shift of voice, and each of the eight chapters of her book is narrated from a slightly altered perspective. These devices allow Winnemucca to indicate that her narrator is growing older and that she is increasingly assuming responsibility in situations that also grow increasingly worse.

The first chapter is told from the point of view of "a very small child when the first white people came." It relates the terror of a little girl born near Humboldt Lake in 1844 in what became the state of Nevada as Paiute land was invaded. Stories she had heard about cannibalism by white people seemed corroborated when Tuboitonie, her mother, fled from white people and buried Winnemucca in the sand for an entire day so that the little girl would not be eaten. Narrated in a conditional mode, chapter two uses an elegaic tone to tell of the courtship rituals in which she would have participated. Had the colonizers permitted the Numa to celebrate her puberty rites, Thocmetony – Winnemucca's name in the Northern Paiute language, which means "shell flower" – could have sung to her namesake flower as she danced wreathed in shell flowers.

After the narrative of the first chapter by a six-year-old, the third chapter is narrated by a thirteen-year-old from the home of Major Ormsby in Genoa, Nebraska, in 1857. She tells how there she helped Margaret Ormsby, the major's wife, and "learned the English language very fast." She also witnessed the humiliation of her cousin Numaga and her brother Natchez as well as the murders of three innocent Washo men brought in as sacrificial offerings by their sad chief.

more expensive to the government to restore order and quiet after the Indians have once broken out. and it does not require much provocation to make them do so. I know more about the feeling and prejudices of these Indians than any other Person connected with them & therefore I hope this petition will be received with favor. Sir I am the daughter of the Chief of the Piutes I am living at Camp McDermit and have been in the employ of the U.S. government for nearly three years as interpreter and guide. I have the honor to be, Sir, your

most obedient Servant
Sarah Winnemucca
Camp McDermit Nev

P S please answer this short Epistle if you consider me worthy and I promise you that my next letters will be more lenghty Direct to Camp McDermit Nev

Sarah Winnemucca
Augst 9th 1870

Last page of a letter from Winnemucca to Commissioner of Indian Affairs E. S. Parker (National Archives, Washington, D.C.)

The fourth chapter recounts events of 1860 from the perspective of a sixteen-year-old who has just lost her beloved grandfather, who had kept the peace until the outbreak of the Pyramid Lake War. The narrator of the fifth chapter is a twenty-one-year-old woman who has to assume the role of conciliator after being appointed as an interpreter for Captain Jerome at Fort McDermit. Following the massacre of 1865 Winnemucca's baby brother, sister Mary, and mother were dead, and her father, fleeing to the mountains, left Winnemucca to become the tribal leader by default. The tone of the narrative becomes mocking and satiric in caricaturing the corrupt agents of the reservations.

The second half of the sixth chapter, set at the Malheur Agency in Oregon, tells how the brutal W. V. Rinehart, a strict and humorless Baptist, replaced the beloved Indian agent Sam Parrish, to whom all the Indians had been devoted. Winnemucca was discharged as interpreter for having informed the commanding officer "about our *Christian* agent's doings." This agent had enriched himself by withholding rations, and in the winter of 1878 two delegations of Paiutes reported to Winnemucca that they were starving.

The beginning of the seventh and longest chapter, dealing with the Bannock War, relates how these delegations asked Winnemucca to intercede for them because "she can talk on paper."

The tone of the thirty-four-year-old woman who serves as Brevet Maj. Gen. Oliver Otis Howard's guide at the outbreak of hostilities contrasts dramatically with that of the tentative, self-effacing narrator of the preceding chapters. The assured Winnemucca savors the officers' banter, thoroughly enjoys the exploits on horseback, and earns the respect of the soldiers. She reports distances ridden, troop numbers, precise times and dates; and specifies the names and ranks of members of the headquarters' staff. Her information was so accurate that when Howard wrote his autobiography in 1907 he paraphrased or quoted from her book extensively. Ferol Egan's recounting of the Pyramid Lake War also validates her accuracy, and Dorothy Nafus Morrison finds that, where discrepancies exist between the accounts of Winnemucca and the reports of newspapers, research in the archives shows the journalists in error. In his collection of chronicles by Native Americans of Nevada, Jack D. Forbes shows how reliable Winnemucca's versions are.

Because Winnemucca had taken care to substantiate her claims, her book could not be faulted by those whose hypocrisy she unmasked. Because her text was unassailable, attempts were therefore made to discredit her character. Of the testimonials to her integrity that are appended to her work, the two most telling are the editorial sent by Judge Bonnifield, to expose the conspiracy against Winnemucca by the Department of the Interior, and the files mailed by Maj. Gen. Irvin McDowell, to prove that agent James Wilbur had lied to prolong the exile of the Paiutes at Yakima, Washington, and keep "these 'peaceable Indians' in the most 'wretched condition, with very insufficient food and clothing.' "

In the final tragic chapter Winnemucca is forced to tell the people whom she had rescued from the Bannocks and others whom she had convinced to surrender at Camp Harney that they were all being sent 350 miles across the mountains to Yakima. On the march that began on 6 January 1879, many froze to death. More died of starvation under Wilbur, the agent who threatened his interpreter with imprisonment if she did not stop agitating for the release of her people.

In November 1879 Winnemucca began telling the story of what the Paiutes had suffered to standing-room-only crowds in San Francisco theaters, and news of her performances reached Washington, D.C. In January 1880 a special agent was sent to escort her to the nation's capital, where Secretary of the Interior Carl Schurz gave her a letter permitting her people to return from exile. In exchange she was asked not to give any more talks. After a brief interview with President Rutherford B. Hayes, she announced with a flash of her humor that she was going to New York to lecture. "I only did this to make the man who was with us angry," she wrote, "because he was forever listening to what I was saying."

Winnemucca in the costume she designed for her 1883–1884 East Coast speaking tour (courtesy of the Nevada Historical Society)

Audiences responded to such jests with outbursts of laughter as she toured the East Coast and gave nearly three hundred lectures between April 1883 and August 1884. Canfield lists the many cities where Peabody had scheduled "innumerable speaking engagements," after which Winnemucca autographed copies of her book and circulated petitions seeking citizenship for Native Americans. According to Ellen Scordato these petitions "gathered a total of 5,000 signatures." Because of her popularity she was invited in 1884 before a Senate subcommittee headed by Sen. Henry L. Dawes to testify against the corruption of the reservation system.

Her stage appearance complemented the persona that she projected of a young girl daring to defy patriarchal authority. Short, with long black hair, and looking younger than she was in an intricately embroidered costume that she had made, Winnemucca seemed too vulnerable for the daring protests she had undertaken. One of these, in July 1879, may have been the first "sit-in." Wilbur had ordered her to keep her ragged and emaciated people out of the sight of a Methodist bishop, Erastus Otis Haven, who was visiting from Boston. She deliberately seated the Paiutes in the front pews reserved for "civilized and Christian Indians" to embarrass Wilbur by letting Haven see "how well we were treated by Christian people."

To show the ferocity and brutality of so-called "civilized" men and the unchristian behavior of ordained ministers, Winnemucca used a chiastic structure to organize her book: she contrasts their rapacity with the ethical behavior of so-called savages. The longest passages in the book concern the peacekeeping efforts of such leaders as Winnemucca's grandfather, Truckee; her father, Old Winnemucca; her cousin, Numaga, known as Young Winnemucca; her brother, Natchez; and herself. Each atrocity committed by the "civilized" requires the most persuasive oratory from such Native American leaders to keep the Paiute warriors from retaliating. According to A. J. Liebling, a letter to Governor Nye of Nevada confirmed the amity of the Paiutes despite "the grossest outrages upon them committed by villainous whites." The self-restraint of the Native Americans after their men were shot without provocation, their wives and daughters were violated, and their lands were taken is recounted in a series of scenes.

Authorial commentary follows the narration of events such as these, and Winnemucca shifts to second-person narrative that directly addresses readers in order to establish intimacy, elicit empathy, and appeal for redress. One significant incident, for example, is that of her brother's arrest for having protested that his people were not being issued the supplies that had been sent for them. The agent asked the Paiutes to sign a letter that he said requested "good clothing for them." In fact, it was a complaint against Natchez and resulted in his being sent to Alcatraz. "Dear reader," Winnemucca rhetorically asks, how can she and her Paiute people be "called bloodseeking savages" and such a man call himself "a Christian?"

The longest of Mann's footnotes anticipates this emblematic incident. She insists that "Indians are made to sign papers that have very different contents from what they are told," and she indignantly points out that agents deliberately hired incompetent teachers, because literate Native Americans would not have been so easy to manipulate if they had been well educated. In support of efforts to educate them effectively, on 11 February 1887 Mann left a small legacy for the school that Winnemucca had founded in Peabody's name on Natchez's land.

Winnemucca was married three times. Her first marriage, to Edward C. Bartlett, a Fort McDermit officer, was conducted on 29 January 1871 in Salt Lake City because interracial marriages were then illegal in Nevada. They separated after one month and formally divorced on 21 September 1876. She married Joseph Satwaller on 3 November 1876 in Carson City, Nevada; Satwaller abandoned her after a few weeks. On 5 December 1881 she married Lewis H. Hopkins of Virginia in San Francisco. He gambled away the $500 she had saved to go east on a speaking tour, cheated Natchez of the proceeds from his wheat harvest, and died of tuberculosis on 18 October 1887.

Peabody published a second edition of Winnemucca's autobiography in 1886 to raise funds for Winnemucca's school. To obtain federal recognition for the school Peabody also wrote a thirty-six-page pamphlet – *Sarah Winnemucca's Practical Solution of the Indian Problem* – that she mailed to members of Congress. Even though enrollment at the school doubled and reports showed that its students were making astounding progress, federal officials demanded Winnemucca's resignation as director in exchange for federal financial support: a woman could not be permitted to succeed where so many men had failed. Following passage of the Dawes Act in February 1887 all Native American children were required to attend white-administered schools such as Carlisle, where they could be shorn of their culture. Yet the inheritance that Winnemucca, a gifted teacher fluent in five languages, left to her students included pride in their own history, which she had so prominently helped to shape before she died on 17 October 1891.

For her authoritatively detailed history and its record of the traditions of the northern Paiutes for the instruction of future generations Winnemucca earned admission to the Nevada Writers Hall of

Fame in 1993. Her book serves as a significant bridge between cultures, because she had been, in the words of Patricia Stewart, "blessed with an intelligence capable of encompassing two cultures." *The New York Times* printed her obituary on the front page under the banner headline "Princess Winnemucca Dead: The Most Remarkable Woman among the Paiutes of Nevada."

She shared the dream of her contemporary fellow Northern Paiute, Wovoka, founder of the Ghost Dance religion, that peaceful coexistence would be possible in the millennium to come. General Howard memorialized her efforts in peacemaking, and in 1971 the state of Nevada erected its first historical marker honoring a woman. Engraved on the plaque at McDermit are her name and a memorial recognizing her hope for "the brotherhood of mankind." The republication of her autobiography by the University of Nevada Press in 1994 not only confers academic respect for her ideas but also makes them accessible to posterity.

Biographies:

George F. Brimlow, "The Life of Sarah Winnemucca: The Formative Years," *Oregon Historical Society Quarterly,* 53 (June 1952): 103–144;

Patricia Stewart, "Sarah Winnemucca," *Nevada Historical Society Quarterly,* 14 (Winter 1971): 23–38;

Katherine Gehm, *Sarah Winnemucca: Most Extraordinary Woman of the Paiute Nation* (Phoenix, Ariz.: O'Sullivan Woodside, 1975);

Catherine S. Fowler, "Sarah Winnemucca," in *American Indian Intellectuals,* edited by Margot Liberty (Saint Paul, Minn.: West, 1978), pp. 33–42;

Dorothy Nafus Morrison, *Chief Sarah: Sarah Winnemucca's Fight for Indian Rights* (New York: Atheneum, 1980);

Gae Whitney Canfield, *Sarah Winnemucca of the Northern Paiutes* (Norman: University of Oklahoma Press, 1983);

Ellen Scordato, *Sarah Winnemucca: Northern Paiute Writer and Diplomat* (New York: Chelsea House, 1992).

References:

H. David Brumble III, *American Indian Autobiography* (Berkeley: University of California Press, 1988);

Edward S. Curtis, "The Paviosto," in *The North American Indian,* volume 15, edited by Frederick Webb Hodge (New York: Johnson Reprint, 1970), pp. 66–88, 129–148;

Ferol Egan, *Sand in a Whirlwind: The Paiute Indian War of 1860* (Garden City, N.Y.: Doubleday, 1972);

Jack D. Forbes, *Nevada Indians Speak* (Reno: University of Nevada Press, 1967);

A. J. Liebling, "The Lake of the Cui-Ui-Eaters," *New Yorker,* 30 (1 January 1955): 25–30, 32–33, 36, 40; (8 January 1955): 33–36, 38, 40, 42, 44, 46–61; (15 January 1955): 32–36, 38, 40–44, 46, 48–50, 52, 54, 56–58, 60, 62–66; (22 January 1955): 37–38, 40, 42, 44, 46–47, 48, 50, 52–58, 60, 62, 64, 66–68, 70–73;

Elizabeth Palmer Peabody, *Sarah Winnemucca's Practical Solution of the Indian Problem* (Cambridge, Mass.: Wilcox, 1886);

A. LaVonne Brown Ruoff, "Nineteenth Century Autobiographers," in *Redefining American Literary History,* edited by Ruoff and Jerry W. Ward (New York: Modern Language Association, 1990), pp. 251–269;

Kathleen Mullen Sands, "Indian Women's Personal Narrative: Voices Past and Present," in *American Women's Autobiography: Fea(s)ts of Memory,* edited by Margo Colley (Madison: University of Wisconsin Press, 1992), pp. 268–294;

Margaret M. Wheat, *Survival Arts of the Primitive Paiutes* (Reno: University of Nevada Press, 1967).

Ray A. Young Bear

(12 November 1950 -)

David L. Moore
Cornell University

BOOKS: *Waiting To Be Fed* (Port Townsend, Wash.: Graywolf, 1975);

winter of the salamander: the keeper of importance (San Francisco: Harper & Row, 1980);

The Invisible Musician (Duluth, Minn.: Holy Cow!, 1990);

Black Eagle Child: The Facepaint Narratives (Iowa City: University of Iowa Press, 1992);

Remnants of the First Earth (New York: Grove, 1996).

RECORDING: *The Woodland Singers: Traditional Mesquakie Songs,* Canyon Records CR-6194, 1987.

For more than twenty-five years Ray A. Young Bear has offered the world a voice rich in his Meskwaki traditions, forceful in its individuality, and articulate and original in its poetic treatment of political and cultural questions. (His tribe's name is also spelled *Mesquakie,* but *Meskwaki* is the spelling Young Bear prefers.) The quietly compelling but radical imagination that animated his early work in the late 1960s has increased in intensity, and he has emerged as a master poet and novelist, one of the major Native American voices of the late twentieth century. Few of his Native American contemporaries – perhaps only Gerald Vizenor – so reshape the English language to fit so singular a voice. Young Bear challenges his readers to use language in new ways, to break away from habitual forms of knowledge, to accept new terms for reading across cultures. It is probably because of his unique approach to language, in fact, that critical response to Young Bear has been so infrequent. Although specialists recognize him as a pivotal figure in the explosion of Native American writing since the 1960s, few scholars or reviewers have been willing to engage his work. In what he describes in his autobiographical novel *Black Eagle Child: The Facepaint Narratives* (1992) as "creative emulation of thought through extraordinary, tragic, and comedic stories of an imagined midwestern tribal experience," many readers experience a kind of vertigo that spins them into new visions of American history and the American psyche.

Ray A. Young Bear

Born on 12 November 1950 in Marshalltown, Iowa, to Leonard and Chloe Young Bear, née Old Bear, Ray Young Bear was raised on the Meskwaki Tribal Settlement near Tama, Iowa, where he lives today with his wife, Stella Lasley Young Bear, whom he married in 1973. Young Bear's great-great-grandfather, Maminwanike, had purchased the settlement for his people in 1856 on ancestral lands along the Iowa River to prevent federal removal of the tribe to Kansas. Because of this unique history, Meskwakis do not live on a reservation. Young Bear's maternal grandmother, Ada Kapayou Old Bear, was a particularly great influence on him: "I'm grateful for my grandmother," he told John R. Milton, editor of the *American Indian II* (1971). "She is all of everything to me." A cofounder of the Woodland Song and Dance Troupe, a cultural performance group that tours on the powwow circuit and on the Arts Midwest lecture circuit, Young Bear frequently begins his poetry readings with songs, accompanied by a drum.

Young Bear's first language was Meskwaki, but he began writing seriously in English in his early teens: "From that day on in the seventh grade I tried to make it a point to learn the English language, write it, and think in it, while at the same time trying to present some aspects of Meskwaki culture – without dealing with sensitive material," he explained to Joseph Bruchac in a 1987 interview. Meskwaki ethical codes prohibit revealing such material, and these codes contribute to his aesthetic. His purpose is neither to reveal nor to conceal but to correct generations of misrepresentation.

At a poets' and writers' conference during a 1968 Upward Bound summer program, Robert Bly and David Ray introduced Young Bear, who by then had been writing poems seriously for two years, to their rigorous modes of revising poetry. David Ignatow also took interest in Young Bear's early work. Milton, who encouraged many Native American writers, published Young Bear's poetry in his anthologies *American Indian I* (1970) and *American Indian II* and organized a Native American writers' conference in the spring of 1971 at the University of South Dakota, where Young Bear met James Welch and Duane Niatum. He pursued his writing while studying at Pomona College in Claremont, California, from 1969 to 1971; at the University of Iowa in 1971; at Grinnell College in 1973; at Northern Iowa University in 1975–1976; and at Iowa State University in 1980.

In the interview with Bruchac, Young Bear mentions Diane Wakoski, Seamus Heaney, Galway Kinnell, and Charles Bukowski as being among the non-Native American poets "whose works I looked upon with great interest and respect. . . . I went to all their readings and tried to absorb some of what they were saying. But I discovered that they had limitations, such as the absence of one's roots – which Native Americans have. So I said, 'Well, maybe I can say something else a little better than what they're trying to do,' which was this aboriginal, primal sort of poetry."

Early in his career he wrote by thinking in Meskwaki and translating his thoughts into English. Although he no longer follows that procedure, he often writes in a heightened, formal style that echoes Mekwuaki oratory. In a revealing passage in *Black Eagle Child* Young Bear has the character Ted Facepaint playfully describe hallucinogenic mushrooms in verse lines that resemble a Young Bear poem: "Tomorrow evening, revived / by rain, thunder, and lightning, the new / Red-hatted Grandfather will stand / by the forest's edge." The narrator comments on Ted's parodic tone, explaining that he is "speaking in the reserved demeanor / of an elder." This reserved manner, simultaneously distant and intimate, characterizes much of Young Bear's poetry and prose. It includes natural and cultural references ("the forest's edge," "Red-hatted Grandfather"); a formal, heightened tone of starkly declamatory diction ("revived," "will stand,"); and an oratorical sentence structure of cumulative phrases, lists, and periodic climaxes ("rain, thunder, and lightning"). This reserved diction, rooted in cultural allusion and foregoing excessive language, generates potent aesthetic tension against the stunning leaps of imagistic association in many of Young Bear's texts.

Drawing on a tradition of oratory handed down from his ancestors' "divine leadership" (as he puts it in *Black Eagle Child*), Young Bear's highly personal voice moves between loneliness and community and between celebration and self-criticism. That voice is mobile and fluid, taking on various personae and points of view and relentlessly facing his own ruptures between faith and fear and between community and alienation – "waiting," as he writes in *winter of the salamander: the keeper of importance* (1980), "to be uplifted and shaken / from the fog."

Young Bear makes it clear that his wife is his partner in artistic expression. Stella Young Bear's beadwork adorns the covers of *Black Eagle Child* and his poetry collection *The Invisible Musician* (1990); *The Invisible Musician* is dedicated to her; in interviews he often mentions her and uses the first person plural in discussing his work; she often accompanies him to his readings; and she is the cofounder with him of the Woodland Song and Dance Troupe. In *Black Eagle Child* and in some of the poems in *The Invisible Musician* the autobiographical protagonist's wife, "Selene," is a vital and wise presence. Young Bear's emphasis

Dust jacket for Young Bear's novel about Edgar Bearchild and his friend Ted Facepaint

on Stella's presence is part of a crucial aesthetic: he does not locate his poetic persona in an individual ego, even though much of his work is intensely personal. Each poem is a collage of interior and exterior voices. To try to factor out final meanings from his poetry or prose is to miss the impressionistic values he so carefully constructs. Young Bear said in a 1992 interview, "when I collect ten or twelve dreams, I piece them together like a jigsaw puzzle and try to form some sort of statement." His work is thus like Stella's beadwork: it is an intricately woven collection of small moments, each with its own intensity, color, and sparkle but without meaning apart from the unique pattern in which it occurs, a pattern that itself is part of a larger cultural and historical context.

Young Bear's approach to his work, which he describes in *Black Eagle Child* as "a collage done over a lifetime via the tedious layering upon layering of images by an artist who didn't believe in endings," centers around what he calls "the philosophy of insignificance." A sense of human insignificance in the universe arises early in Young Bear's writing. In *winter of the salamander* he quotes his grandmother: "some people try to hide their lives / as long as they can, but we see them / and help them when members of their family / pass away. It doesn't work to feel important."

The philosophy of insignificance begins to take explicit form in *The Invisible Musician*. In the poem "Emily Dickinson, Bismarck, and the Roadrunner's Inquiry" Young Bear says that "traffic signs / overshadow the philosophy / of being Insignificant." In the afterword to *Black Eagle Child* he affirms this principle even more explicitly: "The philosophy that espouses cosmic insignificance, a belief that humans are but a minute part of world order, has shaped my words." It is a philosophy of humility and reciprocity derived from awe of the invisible forces of the world. The philosophy is not fatalistic but holistic; it is based on a sense of interrelations and of a connected cosmos. The Native American author Vine Deloria Jr. expresses a similar point of view in the revised edition of his *God Is Red* (1992) when he says that

> all inanimate entities have spirit and personality so that the mountains, rivers, waterfalls, even the continents and the earth itself have intelligence, knowledge, and the ability to communicate ideas. The physical world is so filled with life and personality that humans appear as

> one minor species without much significance and badly in need of assistance from other forms of life. Almost anyone can have almost any relationship with anything else. So much energetic potency exists that we either must describe everything as religious or say that religion as we have known it is irrelevant to our concerns.

This outlook reduces the significance of the human presence and the need for imposing human terms on the world, while it simultaneously recognizes the need for assistance from "other forms of life" that may speak in their own terms in poetry. This intricate polyvocality characterizes what critics have seen as "surrealistic" or "puzzling" in Young Bear's poetry, but his seemingly surrealistic leaps of association across images and cultures become realistic ones within this system of the insignificance of the human role in a living universe.

Young Bear is, however, alert to the stereotype of Indians as spiritual guides, and he frequently undercuts such images with raucous humor. For instance, the "Star-Medicine" scenes of a sacred peyote ceremony in *Black Eagle Child* are peppered with memories of the participants in former "lewd, drunken" moments. This technique, like that of the sacred clowns of various traditional societies, brings the reverential atmosphere of ceremonies "down to earth," where, in fact, it is strongest because spirit and matter are not separated. It strengthens the philosophy of insignificance even during the most significant ceremonial moments.

The need to elude cultural appropriation may be one reason that Young Bear rarely uses the term *spiritual* in describing the powers that visit, threaten, or nourish. Instead, in "The Language of Weather" and "Nothing Could Take Away the Bear-King's Image," in *The Invisible Musician,* he introduces a term with less New Age baggage: *ethereal.* The term describes a notion close to his aesthetic qualities of open-endedness and intuitive associations, and it also conveys a traditional sense of the loneliness of the lost souls who have not found their way to "walk towards / the west after death" (*winter of the salamander*). In the afterword to *Black Eagle Child* he explains:

> The most interesting facet in all of this has been the artistic interlacing of ethereality, past and present. As such there are considerations of visions, traditional healing, supernaturalism, and hallucinogen-based sacraments interposed with centuries-old philosophies and customs. Since these verities are still a prevalent part of modern tribal society, the divisions between dream and myth are never clear-cut.

It is telling that Young Bear does not speak of the common division between dream and reality. Instead, by linking individual dream with cultural myth, he affirms the continuing life of the Meskwaki community. That community life, with its poverty and its internal and external conflicts, is as "ethereal" as it is earthy. His own and his community's visions, healings, supernatural events, hallucinogenic trips, and echoes of ancient ways are interspersed with profanity, humor, feuds, beer, broken-down cars, billboards, neighboring rednecks, community dissension, and personal "apprehension and doubt." To read Young Bear's work is to plunge into an aesthetic experience carefully built to convey that ethereality even through the people's disenfranchisement, their "abyss of discontent" (*Black Eagle Child*).

Young Bear's *winter of the salamander* achieves a remarkable expansion of the English language beyond its usual cultural boundaries in eighty-three poems, many of considerable length, that are collected from publications such as *American Poetry Review, Northwest Poetry Review, Partisan Review,* and *South Dakota Review.* A bilingual epigraph in the introduction to the volume invites the reader to enter into linguistic play: "A gwi ma i • na ta wi • a sa mi ke ko • i i na tti mo ya nini • a yo shes ki • ne ko qua ta be ya i ke. There are no elucidations or foresights / merely / experiments with words." While the statement affirms the Meskwaki presence in the poems, it makes no promises to define what Meskwaki is. The poems include no capitalization and only loose punctuation. The title and subtitle of the work are explained in the poems "birds with tears in their bones," where it is "the spirit of the salamander who spread / news of death," and "trains made of stone," where the "keeper of importance" refers pejoratively to the speaker, who is "ignorant of the leaves changing color, / ignorant of where i stand." The four sections of *winter of the salamander* generally correspond to the seasons. The first section, "because the blue rain exists," includes a preponderance of winter images. The second section, "when we assume life will go well for us," may be identified with spring. The third section is "in the brilliance of summer daylight." The final section, "the sound he makes – the sound i hear," includes a many autumn images. Shifts of pronoun in the poems from first to second to third person and shifts of perspective from limited to omniscient weave through the voices of otters, fish, men, women, badgers, salamanders, grandmothers, grandfathers, horses, hummingbirds, and crows. Topics range from cultural loss to cultural celebration; from sacramental protections of family to death and loneliness on the railroad tracks; from alcoholism and racism to fishing rights: "grinning to the stars . . . / there is something about / trains, drinking, and being / an indian with nothing to lose."

winter of the salamander opens with one of Young Bear's most distilled poems, "grandmother," a paean to this principal figure in his life: "if i were to see / her shape from a mile away / i'd know so quickly / that it would be her. / the purple scarf / and the plastic / shopping bag." He mentions "her hands / warm and damp / with the smell / of roots," her voice "coming from a rock," and "her words" flowing inside him "like the light / of someone / stirring ashes / from a sleeping fire."

In the long poem "waiting to be fed," a pregnant woman swims in a river, in spite of "her mother's constant warning / about rivers." Soon the woman "felt twisted in a dream," "as if the sound / of water was also the sound / of rustling leaves." Malevolent forces seem not to have been properly appeased; the woman loses "all revenge to the giants / lifting their heads / in their watch / to her swimming over the cool / gushing spring." Things become confused, and death and silence are the result. The poem follows the woman through her death in childbirth and then moves into the new child's thoughts: "a smile on her face. / her arms and legs folded to her body. / the sun deep inside her eyes / walking to the river." Without dramatizing the events, the poem generates an intense human drama that is driven by mistakes like those of "insects . . . between shadow and sunlight / confused in their decisions." Young Bear's "experiments with words" become experiments with voices, and it is the voices of ethereal entities that shape the poem.

Young Bear occasionally shifts his focus in *winter of the salamander* to an attack on the intruding Euro-Americans. The poem "in disgust and in response to indian-type poetry written by whites published in a mag which keeps rejecting me" is a case in point, yet even here the explicit anger of the title is not repeated in the text. Instead, it boils under the surface of the two long stanzas. In the first stanza a quiet first-person-plural voice reviews the agonies that were foisted on the Meskwakis by whites: "feeling the strength and prayer / of the endured sacred human tests / we would set aside the year's / smallpox dead"; "They would carry our belongings / and families to the woodlands / of eastern iowa to hunt out food / separate and apart / from the tribe." The second stanza sets up a parallel between demonic possession and white co-optation of Indian traditions: "the method of entering / the spirit and body / of a turkey / to walk at night in suspension . . . to begin this line of witchcraft." Young Bear finally turns to the second person, directly addressing the intruders: "realize there is a point / when you stop being a people / sitting somewhere and reading / the poetry of others." The white poets claim to do what no Native writer presumes: "to feel yourself stretch / beyond limitation / to come here and write this poem / about something no one / knows about / no authority to anything." Whites are writing works about Indian values, of which they know nothing, but their publications may nonetheless take on a false authority. This poem expresses a skeptical Meskwaki view of both white ethnography and white poetry about Indians.

Another poem is about overt racial prejudice: "in viewpoint: poem for 14 catfish and the town of tama, iowa" recounts an incident in which Meskwaki ice-fishing rights were challenged by the local whites. Young Bear empathetically regards "the northern pike and the walleye fish," whose "realization that the end is near" has resonance for humans, as well. He has "unparalleled respect for the iowa river . . . but the farmers and the local whites / from the nearby town of tama and surrounding / towns, with their usual characteristic / ignorance and disregard, have driven noisily / over the ice and across our lands / on their pickups and snowmobiles, / disturbing the dwindling fish / and wildlife." The invective continues for six stanzas about the hypocrisy of white merchants who take Indian money but discriminate against their clientele and the hypocrisy of tribal leaders who are "so infected and obsessed / with misconceptions and greed" that they manipulate tribal funds for their own profit. The poem ends with an expression of Meskwaki pride: "in their paranoia / to compare us to their desensitized lives, / they will never progress into what they / themselves call a community, / or even for the least, / a human."

The final poem in the collection, "march eight/1979," mirrors the tribute to former generations found in "grandmother" by celebrating the birth of a new generation in Young Bear's nephew. The child, by whom the family is "bonded permanently," lies "on top / of grandmother universe." The poem includes an untranslated reference to the baby's name: "their red-faced son, elgin, *ba ke ka maa qwi,*" another linguistic affirmation of the cultural context. The poem and the volume end with a glance at Young Bear's internal struggle: "i pray for him that we shall one day / meet and talk in mutual good health / and i to explain to him my incredible joy, / how my mixed depression was momentarily / quelled."

The voice in *The Invisible Musician,* published ten years after *winter of the salamander,* is more consistent, and the book's structure and subject matter are more lucid; the many passionate and eloquent strands of *winter of the salamander* have matured and converged into a smaller number of more-compressed and polished poems – the book is less than half the length of its predecessor. The volume is not divided into sections, although it is structured around four bilingual transcriptions of Meskwaki love songs, veterans' songs, and celebration songs, placed at approximately quarterly intervals. Each of the songs reflects the topics of the poems that follow it. In contrast to his disavowal of "elucidation" in the epigraph of *winter of the salamander,* in this volume Young Bear provides clarifying endnotes to some of the poems. *The Invisible Musician* includes many of the same themes as the earlier work, as well as a few poems written prior to the publication of *winter of the salamander.*

"Ethereal" relations are a major theme of *The Invisible Musician.* The title refers to a frog whose songs enter into the book. In the poem "*Wa ta se Na ka mo ni,* Viet Nam Memorial," the speaker hears the "lone frog" singing on Veterans Day: "the invisible musician / reminded me of my own doubt. / The knowledge that my grandfathers / were singers as well as composers." The speaker admits that he lacks the "necessary memory or feeling / to make a *Wa ta se Na ka mo ni,* / Veterans' Song." Military service is an honorable vocation for young men in many Indian societies; medical and student deferments kept Young Bear out of the service during the Vietnam War, so he lacks a veteran's memories. Yet the poet has rallied himself to move beyond "country, controversy, and guilt" and to honor the names on the "distant black rock" of the Vietnam Memorial. Young Bear's song for the veterans is not included in the poem; he merely refers to it as the song the dead veterans "presently listened to along with my grandfathers." In the final line of the poem he claims that the song "was the ethereal kind which did not stop." The poem has described his complex struggle to live up to the tradition of the invisible musician.

The opening poem, "The Significance of a Water Animal," and its explanatory endnote establish a mythic link between Young Bear's great-great-grandfather's purchase of the Meskwaki Settlement and the role of the "Earthdiver," Muskrat, in "diving to make land available." In the Meskwaki creation story the muskrat returned from beneath the floodwaters with soil in his claws, and out of this soil the earth was built. The practical action taken by a nineteenth-century leader to assure the survival of his people is here invested with the importance of a cosmological event. Yet in the poem's last lines that survival continues to be threatened, "as my grandmother tells me / 'Belief and what we were given / to take care of, / is on the verge / of ending. . . .' " To counter that threat, in this poem "A certain voice of *Reassurance*" has referred to the mythical and historical creation stories.

Poster for a reading by Young Bear and a performance by his musical group

"The Language of Weather" is a portrait of the poet's constant efforts to read the ethereal language of the natural world. As he watches an approaching storm, "All in one moment, in spite / of my austerity, everything / is aligned: part-land, part-cloud, / part-sky, part-sun and part-self." He returns from his epiphany – "I am the only one to witness / this renascence" – to castigate himself for ingratitude: "no acknowledgement / whatsoever for the Factors / which make my existence possible." Yet the next line reverently describes his own ancestry, immediate and ancient. His parents in their potato garden call the family to " 'See that everyone in the household / releases parts of ourselves / to our Grandfathers.' " The storm is an ethereal sign of their balancing presence, while the closing image of a whirlwind, the endnotes explain, is a sign of a spirit out of balance, one of those "eternally trapped shadows or 'souls' of the deceased who have yet to be transferred ceremonially to the Hereafter." The poem concludes: "In the daylight distance, / a stray spirit whose guise / is a Whirlwind, spins and attempts / to communicate from its ethereal / loneliness."

Many of the poems in *The Invisible Musician* include a playful juxtaposing of polysyllabic and simple, unrefined words, as in the title of "The First Dimension of Skunk" and in one of that poem's lines: "In the midst of change / all it takes is one anachronism, / one otter whistle." This technique of bringing together the highly literate and the earthy reveals the interpenetration of these ostensibly separate categories of experience.

One of the most memorable and potent figures Young Bear has created is Bumblebee, a sort of trickster grandfather who appears in two long poems in *The Invisible Musician:* "A Drive to Lone Ranger" and "Race of the Kingfishers: In Nuclear Winter." "*Everyone knows the Indian's existence is bleak,*" the narrator says in an epigraph at the beginning of the first poem. "*In fact, there are people who have taken it upon / themselves to speak for us; to let the universe / know how we live, eat and think, but the Bumblebee – / an elder of the Black Eagle Child Nation – / thinks this sort of representation is repulsive.*" Entertaining the narrator and his wife during a midwinter visit to Bumblebee's earth lodge, "*after our car conked out,*" the old insect "confesses that he sleeps / with earphones attached to his apian body. . . . Over pheasant omelettes and wine / he offers an explanation about his obsession / with technology. / 'It may seem a contradiction, / but those cassette tapes on the wall / are the intellectual foundation / of my progeny.' " Bumblebee thus affirms the paradox of both continuity and change if Meskwaki culture is to survive, and the young narrator and his wife listen to him: "underneath our Transformation Masks / we respect the old man, Bumblebee, for he has retained the ability to understand / traditional precepts and myths. Moreover, / he understands the need to oppose / 'outside' mining interests." Bumblebee warns of a possible nuclear annihilation that will fulfill Meskwaki prophecies of "the true end," when the Northern Lights will reach to the South: "celestial messengers in green atomic oxygen, / highlighted by red – the color of our impending / nuclear demise." Yet he offers alternatives: "'In time we'll become prosperous, / or else we'll become martyrs.'" In the second poem the narrator is recuperating from a drunken, visionary, all-night discussion with Bumblebee at which spirit women raced in the winter wind, "holding silver saxophones" and dancing in "Kingfisher costumes." Bumblebee, "our metamorphic guest," proclaims that " 'Imported beer makes me philosophical' " and "narrates / the meaning of their intricate steps." This meaning proves to be another warning: " 'to apprise us of the Aurora Borealis / and how such lights will bring / the true end.' " Bumblebee's political world is changed with prophecy and humor.

In *Black Eagle Child* the first-person narration moves among at least seven voices: the protagonist, Edgar Bearchild; his uncle, Severt Principal Bear; his mother, Clotelde; his friend, Ted Facepaint; a Canadian Cree friend, Junior Pipestar; Junior's sister, Charlotte; and Edgar's great-uncle, Carson Two Red Foot. There are also extensive passages of third-person omniscient narration. The effect is to create a community of voices within a Meskwaki universe. Both a bildungsroman and an incisive social commentary, the novel mixes verse and prose in a remarkable blend of oral and literary forms.

Trying, not always successfully, to hearken to his grandmother's advice, Edgar Bearchild wanders in and out of danger among his Meskwaki friends, his enemies, and the "watery voices rising from the lakes and rivers" toward his eventual "salvation," a career as a writer. Young Bear paints vivid, relentlessly truthful, and unromantic narratives of contemporary Meskwaki life. In the afterword to the novel Young Bear says: "The Black Eagle Child Settlement is a fictitious counterpart of the central Iowa sanctuary where I am an enrolled, lifelong resident. The character of Edgar Bearchild mirrors in part my own laborious Journey of Words. . . . Ted Facepaint, on the other hand, is a composite of a dozen people met, known, and lost in the last forty years." The novel continues a pattern in Native American autobiography that was established in the nineteenth century by such writers as the Pequot William Apess, the Ojibwa George Copway, and the Dakota Charles Eastlake, in which personal, cultural, and historical narratives are balanced. Young Bear's combination of the cultural and the personal is a reaction against generations of anthropological and Hollywood representations of Indians, which Bumblebee found "repulsive."

Black Eagle Child is told relatively chronologically in sixteen chapters, though with many flashbacks as the various narrators come to the fore. Edgar recounts his early experiences with sacramental peyote, along with his trickster friend Ted Facepaint, in the opening chapters, "The Well-Off Man Church" and "Gift of the Star-Medicine"; he is surprised at the ceremony's successful mixture of Christianity and traditional ways and impressed by the intensity of the experience. The first chapter also sets up a key theme, that of internal tribal rivalries: "to denote tribal class, our Black Eagle Child / society was based on names." The tensions generated "around the hierarchy of clan names" eventually drive the free-spirited Ted away: "for anyone / who believed in the old labels would live / and plan their lives accordingly. / Facepaint knew this; he was the one / who said so." Not all traditions are represented as sacrosanct.

A sequence of three chapters, "The Precociousness of Charlotte," "The Brook Grassleggings Episode," and "A Circus Acrobat on the Grass," presents one of postmodern literature's most vivid portraits of reservation nightlife. Among peeling tires, tire-iron fights, a hailstorm, cultural commentary, and mythic memories, Edgar's and Junior's efforts to pick up girls explode into a cosmic allegory of Junior's ancestors' migrations as the Northern Lights blend in with the spinning lights of "police, ambulance, and assorted vigilantes" and the flashbulbs of reporters from the local redneck newspaper who are intent on embarrassing the Indians on their front page. Edgar's loss of innocence leads to the ninth chapter, "The Human Parchment Period," in which Edgar commits himself to writing: " 'Because no other voice should ever / can ever / replace the original voice of the American Indian / poet, especially one who resides at the place / of his birth and not in the city or academia, / I merely seek to compose meaningful narratives / as experienced within the Black Eagle Child Nation." The chapter includes a reworking of the poem "In the First Place of My Life" from *winter of the salamander;* Ted Facepaint's recounting of his hitchhiking escapades; and four bilingual songs by another old friend, Pat "Dirty" Red Hat. Both Pat and Ted die tragically yet transcendently in the novel. Young Bear juxtaposes their experiences with his own writing struggle in this chapter to place Edgar's solitary artistic experience within the deep and grievous bonds of friendship, and within the compelling commitment of both friends to their culture. The novel is a tribute to that friendship.

The second half of the book consists of samples of Edgar's writings. "How We Delighted in Seeing the Fat" is Edgar's great-uncle Carson Two Red Foot's story of Carson's mother's isolation with her children, "like a pack of breakaway clouds . . . in the snowy, turbulent hills and fields." This chapter prepares the ground for "The Supernatural Strobe Light," in which Edgar and his wife, Selene, encounter UFOs and ethereal spirits at their own isolated home at "*a ka me e ki,* distant forestland." "*During one warm October evening in 1981, Selene Buffalo Husband and I experienced an extraordinary but true encounter with a mysterious force that took the guise of owls, fireflies, and luminescent objects of the night. . . . To document what took place and to share it only means we are cognizant of invisible forces, especially the kind who have chosen to reveal themselves and interact momentarily with the unsuspecting lives of human beings.*" In both *Black Eagle Child* and *The Invisible Musician* Young Bear refers humorously to Iowa's Scandinavian immigrants as space aliens; thus, this episode, in addition to providing an extreme instance of ethereality, suggests how colonialism might seem as bizarre and terrifying to Meskwakis as an interplanetary invasion would appear to whites.

The final chapter, "The Man Squirrel Shall Not Wake," recounts Ted Facepaint's murder by a bigoted white emergency-room doctor who is so offended by Ted's wisecracking that he deliberately sets a plaster cast so tight on Ted's arm that the clotted blood pools and creates an aneurysm. As Ted gradually loses consciousness, earlier episodes in the novel reappear as his memories; finally, he leaves his body in the form of an eagle: "He peered out past the smoky hills before / unfolding and stretching his wingtips / upward to test them." This death imagery echoes that of Edgar's grandfather in the poem "In the First Place of My Life": "The music lifted above the crowd of dancers and stayed in place before lifting further, flying away, and then coming back to encircle us like an eagle whose powerful black and golden wingtips brushed our faces, waking us, telling us to see this dance through for my grandfather." By linking Ted imagistically in death with his revered grandfather, Edgar underlines the value he places on such an eccentric personality, "an imbrication of humanity, whose pieces belong to everyone." The eagle wings also evoke Ted's feeling for the pliant power of Meskwaki tradition: "Facepaint is a rare personality who is intrinsically attuned to the night sky, and he keeps an ever-present watch for any change, any subtle repositioning of the Orion constellation." *Black Eagle Child* concludes with this sense of soaring vigilance, symbolizing Meskwaki and Native American cultural renewal. Pouring out the stories of his youth, Young Bear has given the world one of the most nuanced and evocative portraits of contemporary Native American life yet published.

In moving from poetry to the novel to paint a broader view of Native American experience, Young Bear has followed a progression shared by such contemporaries as Vizenor, Welch, and Leslie Marmon Silko. Yet the larger canvas of Young Bear's fiction never loses the intimate precision of his poetry. As he approaches the height of his stylistic powers, Young Bear will assuredly draw more readers into his narrations and, like his colleagues, will help to revise America's story of itself.

Interviews:

Joseph Bruchac, "Connected to the Past," in his *Survival This Way: Interviews with American Indian Poets* (Tucson: University of Arizona Press, 1987), pp. 337-348;

David L. Moore and Michael Wilson, eds., "Staying Afloat in a Chaotic World: A Conversation with Ray Young Bear," *Akwe:kon Journal (Northeast Indian Quarterly),* 9 (Winter 1992): 22-26.

References:

Gretchen M. Bataille, "Ray Young Bear: Tribal History and Personal Vision," *Studies in American Indian Literatures,* 5 (Summer 1993): 17-20;

Vine Deloria Jr., *God Is Red: A Native View of Religion,* second edition (Golden, Colo.: North American, 1992), pp. 152-153;

Robert F. Gish, "Memory and Dream in the Poetry of Ray A. Young Bear," *Minority Voices,* 2, no. 1 (1978): 21-29;

Gish, "Mesquakie Singer: Listening to Ray A. Young Bear," *A: A Journal of Contemporary Literature,* 4, no. 22 (1979): 24-28;

Gish, "On First Reading Young Bear's *Winter of the Salamander,*" *Studies in American Indian Literature,* 6, no. 3 (1982): 10-15;

Richard Hugo, "Introduction," *American Poetry Review,* 2 (November-December 1973): 22;

John R. Milton, ed., *American Indian II* (Vermillion, S.Dak.: Dakota Press, 1971), p. 23;

David L. Moore, "Myth, History, and Identity in Silko and Young Bear: Postcolonial Praxis," in *New Voices in Native American Literary Criticism,* edited by Arnold Krupat (Washington, D.C.: Smithsonian Institution Press, 1993), pp. 370-395;

Robert Dale Parker, "To Be There, No Authority to Anything: Ontological Desire and Cultural and Poetic Authority in the Poetry of Ray A. Young Bear," *Arizona Quarterly: A Journal of American Literature, Culture, and Theory,* 50 (Winter 1994): 89-115;

James Ruppert, "Outside the Arc of the Poem: A Review of Ray Young Bear's *Winter of the Salamander,*" *Studies in American Indian Literature,* 6 (Summer 1982): 6-10;

Ruppert, "The Poetic Languages of Ray Young Bear," in *Coyote Was Here: Essays on Contemporary Native American Literary and Political Mobilization,* edited by Bo Schöler (Århus, Denmark: Seklos, 1984), pp. 124-133;

Studies in American Indian Literature, special issue on Young Bear, 6, no. 3 (1982).

Zitkala-Ša
(Gertrude Simmons Bonnin)

(22 February 1876 – 26 January 1938)

Margo Lukens
University of Maine

BOOKS: *Old Indian Legends, Retold by Zitkala-S̈a* (Boston & London: Ginn, 1901);
American Indian Stories (Washington, D.C.: Hayworth, 1921);
Oklahoma's Poor Rich Indians: An Orgy of Graft and Exploitation of the Five Civilized Tribes – Legalized Robbery, by Zitkala-Ša as Gertrude Simmons Bonnin, Charles H. Fabens, and Matthew K. Sniffen (Philadelphia: Office of the Indian Rights Association, 1924).
Editions: *American Indian Stories,* foreword by Dexter Fisher (Lincoln: University of Nebraska Press, 1979);
Old Indian Legends, Retold by Zitkala-S̈a, foreword by Agnes M. Picotte (Lincoln: University of Nebraska Press, 1985).

PLAY PRODUCTION: *The Sun Dance,* by Zitkala-Ša and William Hanson, Vernal, Utah, Orpheus Hall, 20 February 1913.

Zitkala-Ša was one of the first Native American women among her contemporaries to publish a collection of traditional tribal stories. Her command of English was refined, and her works are characterized by vivid imagery. She did not mince words, and her stories are emotionally charged – often angry, sometimes strident in directing accusations against white oppression of Indians. With her sense of her audience shaped largely by the Christian missionary schools she attended, her work expresses her discomfort in holding the status of a white-educated Indian, her love for Native American culture, and her concern for Indian self-determination.

Born at the Yankton Sioux Agency in South Dakota, Gertrude Simmons was the third child of Tate I Yohin Win (Reaches for the Wind), a full-blood Dakota, and a white man who left the family before the child's birth. Simmons learned the ways of her tribe until missionaries arrived in 1884 to recruit students for White's Manual Institute, a Quaker boarding school for Indians in Wabash, Indiana. Featuring orchards full of apples, their stories of the East may have persuaded the girl to leave for the distant school, despite her mother's fears. After completing six years of missionary education in 1895, she studied at Earlham College in Richmond, Indiana, from 1895 to 1897 and then accepted a teaching post at Carlisle Indian Industrial School in Pennsylvania in 1899.

Zitkala-Ša

As an Indian spokesperson at Carlisle, Simmons began to gain the attention of members of powerful literary and political circles in the East. Under the Lakota nom de plume Zitkala-Ša (Red Bird) she published her autobiographical stories in the first three monthly numbers of the *Atlantic Monthly* in 1900 and rapidly developed a literary reputation among readers of the magazine. (Others whose work appeared there in 1900 included Edith Wharton, former president Grover Cleveland, Henry James, Jack London, and John Muir.) At the turn of the century the *Atlantic Monthly,* which had been a culturally conservative magazine through the mid 1890s, was beginning to include politically and socially controversial material. Its publication of articles by Zitkala-Ša showed the influence of a popular movement that had begun in the 1880s and continued into the first decades of the twentieth century to reform U.S. policy toward Native Americans.

As Dexter Fisher says in the foreword to her 1979 edition of Zitkala-Ša's *American Indian Stories* (1921), Zitkala-Ša's autobiographical articles marked "one of the first attempts by a Native American woman to write her own story without the aid of an editor, an interpreter, or an ethnographer." In her freedom from such literary mediation she was able to criticize harshly the methods of the white culture in educating young Indians, the culturally genocidal intentions behind the inculcation of white culture in Indian students, and the mismanagement of Indian welfare by federal bureaucracies. She was also free to express the pain and discontent she felt as a white-educated Indian whose status put her, as she expressed it, "in the heart of chaos, beyond the touch or voice of human aid."

Although her writing, public recitations, and concerts were received with overwhelming public acclaim, Zitkala-Ša's forthright criticism of the Indian boarding school experience caused bad feelings between Zitkala-Ša and her employer at Carlisle. Deborah Welch notes that Richard Henry Pratt had founded the school in 1879 with the aim of acculturating Native American children, and, as Zitkala-Ša wrote in a letter to Carlos Montezuma, Pratt characterized her as "worse than pagan" and her stories as "trash." Montezuma, a Yavapai physician with whom she had developed a close relationship, was several years her elder, highly educated, and already experienced in political maneuvering among white people. As Montezuma warned, Pratt's displeasure with Zitkala-Ša's stories led first to her being reassigned as a recruiter – in effect, banished to the West and denied the support of her literary coterie – and eventually to the end of her service at Carlisle.

At Earlham College, Zitkala-Ša had begun to discover her musical talents, and she had performed as a violin soloist with the Carlisle Indian Band at the Paris Exposition of 1900. After she decided late that year to leave her position at Carlisle, she studied at the New England Conservatory during 1900 and 1901. Moving to Boston put her in touch with an intellectual and artistic community that supported her career as a writer and liberated her from the assimilationist demands of her Carlisle teaching experience.

Her literary popularity soon brought her a publishing contract with Ginn and Company, and to collect material for *Old Indian Legends* (1901) Zitkala-Ša returned to Yankton. There she struggled with the question of whether to insist that Montezuma join her and become a reservation doctor or to acquiesce in his wishes and pursue the Anglo lifestyle of a Chicago physician's wife. Eventually their relationship broke under this conflict between her pride in her heritage and his desire to show, by example, an Indian's capacity to excel in white society.

In a 1977 *American Indian Quarterly* article Fisher asserts that in publishing *Old Indian Legends* (1901) Zitkala-Ša sought "to become the literary counterpart of the oral storytellers of her tribe." The title page of the book supports this contention by including the words "retold by Zitkala-Ša," and the book's illustrations by Angel De Cora, a Winnebago artist, add a visual dimension to this published representation of traditional oratory. The legends include stories of Iktomi, the Dakota Trickster, and are traditionally told as entertainment rather than as sacred tales. Zitkala-Ša retells these tales with the intention of reaching a culturally diverse audience of young people. The work was popularly acclaimed, as a letter of 25 August 1919 from Helen Keller attests:

> I thank you for your book on Indian Legends. I have read them with exquisite pleasure. Like all folk tales they mirror the child life of the world. . . .
>
> Your tales of birds, beast, tree and spirit can not but hold captive the hearts of all children. They will kindle in their young minds that eternal wonder which creates poetry and keeps life fresh and eager. I wish you and your little book of Indian tales all success.

Dorothea M. Susag finds that the image of the trickster Iktomi informs not only *Old Indian Legends* but also Zitkala-Ša's autobiographical fiction and short stories. In representing the trickery of white people, Iktomi stories instruct Native American people to beware and not to be fooled by smooth talk.

Susag also sees Iktomi as embodying creative, powerful ways for Native American people to defend their cultural heritage by engaging in cultural trickery, as Zitkala-Ša did by seeming to accept the white world in which she excelled – while holding onto Dakota traditions with fierce pride.

Soon Zitkala-Ša's romance with the acclaim of the white eastern mainstream diminished: she wanted to live near her mother again, and she needed to support herself. After trying unsuccessfully to secure a reservation teaching job, she became an issue clerk at the Standing Rock Reservation, where she met Raymond Talesfase Bonnin, also a Yankton Sioux. She ended her engagement to Montezuma, and she and Bonnin were married on 10 May 1902. Later that year they transferred to the Uintah and Ouray Reservation near Fort Duchesne, Utah, where they spent the next fourteen years. Their son, Raymond O. Bonnin, was born there early in 1903.

Her move to Utah brought a hiatus in her writing career, as she found herself in a political and artistic backwater for nearly a decade. She was frustrated by the demands of motherhood and discouraged by conditions on the Ute reservation. She managed, however, to nourish her creative tendencies by collaborating in 1913 with William Hanson on an Indian opera, *The Sun Dance*. Her role in the composition was evidently extensive; as a result of her efforts, as Edward Ellsworth Hipsher writes, the opera presents "a sympathetic portrayal of the real Indian in a conscientious attempt to delineate the manners, the customs, the dress, the religious ideals, the superstitions, the songs, the games, the ceremonials – in short, the life of a noble people too little understood." Presented to appreciative audiences of whites and Indians alike, the opera would be chosen for performance by the New York Light Opera Guild as the American opera of the year in 1937.

In 1914 Zitkala-Ša became a member of the advisory board of the Society for the American Indian (SAI), which had been founded in 1911. The SAI required that its members be of Indian blood; it aimed to promote Indian self-determination, but it was essentially assimilationist. In 1916 Zitkala-Ša was elected secretary of the SAI, and to serve in that capacity she and her husband moved to Washington, D.C. Raymond Bonnin served in the army and later clerked at a Washington law firm.

As secretary of the society in 1918 and 1919 Zitkala-Ša also edited its journal, the *American Indian Magazine*. Following strenuous internal disagreements the SAI disbanded in 1920, and Zitkala-Ša began working with the General Federation of Women's Clubs to found the Indian Welfare Committee in 1921. She also collected her autobiographical stories and other previously uncollected short fiction as *American Indian Stories*. In addition to showing the Sioux from the inside, her stories reveal the cruelties that white schooling imposes on Indian children, as well as the feelings of alienation that this education had engendered in her.

As she relates in "The School Days of an Indian Girl," the missionary school was designed to strip children of their tribal cultures and replace these cultures with knowledge of the dominant one. At first Indians such as her mother thought that the offer of education began "to pay a tardy justice" for the theft of Indian lands and was necessary if their children were to advance in the white world; from the white culture, however, Gertrude Simmons discovered no compensation for her loss of Sioux culture and habits. Left angry and isolated, she was alienated from her family and decided to create her own name: Zitkala-Ša.

In the foreword to her 1985 edition of *Old Indian Legends* Agnes M. Picotte notes that, although Zitkala-Ša grew up speaking the Nakota (Dakota) dialect of the Sioux language, the name she chose was from the Lakota dialect. In Fisher's estimation Zitkala-Ša's act of self-naming asserted both her independence from and her ties to Sioux culture. That she chose a Lakota name, however, instead of one from her home dialect might indicate a profound dislocation from her family origins, as well as a conscious choice.

Zitkala-Ša tells of these origins in "Impressions of an Indian Childhood," the first piece in *American Indian Stories*. Sioux educational practices sharply contrast with those of her later experiences at a school run by white missionaries. Zitkala-Ša's early childhood appears to have offered her two modes of learning that she was to lose on entering the white school system – learning through experience and through imitating her mother and other older women of the tribe. Whether she attempted to create beadwork, which her mother insisted must be "sufficiently characteristic" in traditional styles, or to play with her girlfriends in imitating their mothers, the child learned to perpetuate the culture of her tribe. She was taught to respect her elders, to be a generous host to guests in her home, and to be concerned for the welfare of all members of her tribe, particularly the ill or unfortunate.

Zitkala-Ša represents her mother as a nearly prophetic voice of truth. When the mother yielded to her daughter's wish to leave for the missionary school, she did so partly because she wanted to acknowledge the "palefaces['] . . . large debt for stolen lands"; and, despite her knowledge that her "daughter must suffer keenly in this experiment," she let the girl go.

To characterize the white missionaries, Zitkala-Ša tells a story that occurred before she was old enough to be tempted to leave home with them. The incident is, significantly, set in winter, a time of confinement and probably of some deprivation. The missionaries had given her a bag of glass marbles, and the image of ice at the heart of the marbles prefigures the coldness that she later experienced when at the missionaries' hands. Later images describing the palefaces reiterate this image: the "glassy blue eyes" of white men stared at the Indian children on their journey to Indiana; "the snow still covered the ground, and the trees were bare" when she arrived at the missionaries' boarding school; and she found Earlham College students to be "a cold race whose hearts were frozen hard with prejudice."

Zitkala-Ša contrasts the way she was raised by her mother with the practices at the missionary boarding school in the second chapter, "The School Days of an Indian Girl." On her journey to Indiana in the company of the palefaces she was "as frightened and bewildered as the captured young of a wild creature," and after one day at White's Manual Institute she had become "only one of many little animals driven by a herder." Every activity of life, even eating meals, is now regimented in new, strange ways.

Zitkala-Ša repeatedly observes that the good intentions of the missionaries are wrongheaded, and in many cases the conventions of white culture affront well-brought-up Indians. The clothing she was required to wear at the school – dresses with tight-fitting bodices – struck her as terribly immodest, since she was used to concealing her figure in loose-fitting buckskin and a blanket. The hairstyle was even worse: for the Sioux, "short hair was worn by mourners, and shingled hair by cowards [i.e., captured warriors whose hair has been cut by the enemy]."

Zitkala-Ša narrates this cultural conflict in terms of a warrior's struggle because she recognizes the system of white education to be part of the violent destruction of her people and their culture. She tried to hide on the day her hair was to be cut, but she was found: "I felt the cold blades of the scissors against my neck, and heard them gnaw off one of my thick braids. Then I lost my spirit." She mourns the death of her Indian identity.

At Earlham College, Zitkala-Ša "hid" in her dorm room, "pined for sympathy," and "wept in secret." White students were slow to seek her out, doing so only when she won the Indiana State Oratorical Contest, where she was the sole representative of Earlham College in 1896. Zitkala-Ša tells of "the slurs against the Indian that stained the lips of our opponents" and describes "a large white flag, with a drawing of a most forlorn Indian girl on it. Under this they had printed in bold black letters words that ridiculed the college which was represented by a 'squaw.' " Zitkala-Ša characterizes this slur as "worse than barbarian rudeness" and puts the "savage" shoe on the white foot that she believes it truly fits.

Zitkala-Ša recounts her journey east in the third chapter of *American Indian Stories*. Carlisle Indian School in western Pennsylvania is the focus of this chapter, which is ironically titled "An Indian Teacher among Indians," for the only Indian with whom she interacted was her mother, during a brief visit to Yankton. There she discovered that her brother had been replaced as an Indian agent on the reservation, when her mother told her that "the Great Father at Washington sent a white son to take your brother's pen from him. Since then Dawee has not been able to make use of the education the Eastern school has given him." Dawee had risked becoming an advocate for his people, and, as his mother said, "The Indian cannot complain to the Great Father in Washington without suffering outrage for it here." Dawee's trouble helped to direct Zitkala-Ša toward her eventual life's work in Washington.

Zitkala-Ša's awareness of the intentions and corruptions of the Indian education system led her to reflect bitterly on her role as a teacher and on the "civilized" visitors who have passed through her classrooms as if they were going through a zoo. Her decision to leave her teaching post was predicated on the question that palefaces have failed to ask themselves: "whether real life or long-lasting death lies beneath this semblance of civilization," the white system of educating Indians. Having "forgotten the healing in trees and brooks," she characterizes herself as "a slender tree . . . uprooted from my mother, nature, and God . . . shorn of my branches. . . . The natural coat of bark . . . [has been] scraped off to the very quick." Though such a metaphor seems to bear little hope for the survival of the "cold bare pole" Zitkala-Ša feels that she had become, she extends and develops the metaphor to include the poles that bear long-distance telephone wires; through this trope she expresses her desire to communicate powerfully for her people in a new medium.

In much the same way that the dominant culture created the image of the white woman as the Christian "angel in the house," Zitkala-Ša depicts her mother as the bearer of tribal religion. Her mother, however, was not limited and enfeebled by being associated with her religion, as the white woman was by hers. Only when her mother was converted to Christianity did Zitkala-Ša cease to regard her as a source of power. Then, in the face of so much resistance, corruption, and disappointment, she temporarily lost her faith in the Great Spirit. "The Great Spirit does not care if we live or die!" she despaired. "Let us not look for good or justice: then we shall not be disappointed!" Despite having adopted Christianity, her mother replied, "Sh! my child, do not talk so madly. There is Taku Iyotan Wasaka, to which I pray." Zitkala-Ša adds a note on the name of this deity, which means "an absolute power," that implies that in later years she regained respect for the faith that she thought she had lost.

The second half of the book is a collection of essays and new stories. "The Great Spirit," originally published in the *Atlantic Monthly* as "Why I Am a Pagan" (1902), justifies her rejection of Christianity in favor of Native American religion. Zitkala-Ša describes herself as more religious than the converted Indian, whom she characterizes as a "distorted shadow," and insists that she is attuned to "the loving Mystery." She treats "the solemn 'native preacher' " with compassion and listens to him "with respect for God's creature, though he mouth most strangely the jangling phrases of a bigoted creed." In her knowledge of "natural forces" she has found the forthrightness and assurance necessary to discard Christianity, despite her missionary schooling. Since Christianity has justified the conquest of Native Americans, Zitkala-Ša's rejection of Christianity betokens her rejection of the imperialist impulse.

"The Trial Path," "A Warrior's Daughter," and "A Dream of Her Grandfather" present carefully constructed positive images of Plains Indian culture. "The Trial Path" is a tale of complex past relationships: an elderly grandmother tells how one of her two lovers killed his rival and had to stand trial, Indian-style. The trial involved a feat of pony riding; if the killer succeeded, he would be allowed to live. When the young man did succeed, he was adopted by the family of his rival as their new son, as the tradition of Indian justice prescribes. Indian justice preserves the structure of the family and the

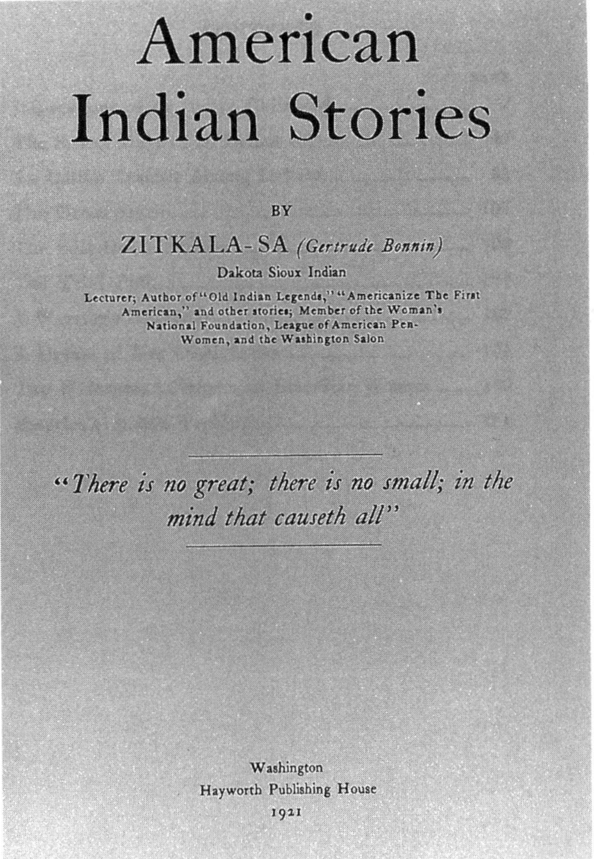

American
Indian Stories

BY

ZITKALA-SA *(Gertrude Bonnin)*

Dakota Sioux Indian

Lecturer; Author of "Old Indian Legends," "Americanize The First American," and other stories; Member of the Woman's National Foundation, League of American Pen-Women, and the Washington Salon

"There is no great; there is no small; in the mind that causeth all"

Washington
Hayworth Publishing House
1921

Title page for Zitkala-Ša's collection of her stories and essays

community instead of imposing an absolute rule that executes a murderer and thereby robs the community of his potentially valuable presence.

In "A Warrior's Daughter" Zitkala-Ša depicts a young woman of extraordinary strength, an unusual portrait when it was published in *Everybody's Magazine* in 1902. The woman's lover goes on a war party to get the scalp that her father requires before they can marry. The young man is captured, and the maiden, who has accompanied the older women following the war party, prays to the Great Spirit: "All-powerful Spirit, grant me my warrior-father's heart, strong to slay a foe and mighty to save a friend!" Disguised as an old woman, she infiltrates the enemy camp, kills the young man's captor, and frees her lover. The heroine's act perhaps exceeds ordinary Sioux expectations of women's behavior; but Beatrice Medicine points out that women warriors in Dakota society did participate in war "for glory as well as revenge, and some even led war expeditions."

"A Dream of Her Grandfather," published for the first time in *American Indian Stories,* depicts a young welfare worker in Washington, D.C., much like Zitkala-Ša, who derives hope for her people from a dream vision sent by her grandfather, a medicine man. The vision presents the nourishing quality of tribal life and traditions and emphasizes their necessity even in the lives of those who have assimilated to white culture. In her native Dakota language a message comes to her: "Be glad! Rejoice! Look up, and see the new day dawning! Help is near! Hear me, every one." She sees the dream as a sign that she is ready to perform a heroic task.

In "America's Indian Problem," the last piece of the collection, Zitkala-Ša writes, "Now the time is at hand when the American Indian shall have his day in court through the help of the women of America." She directs pointed questions to the readers: "Do you know what your Bureau of Indian Affairs, in Washington, D.C., really is? How it is organized and how it deals with wards of the nation?" Zitkala-Ša's aim is to arouse her readers' consciences.

In 1924 citizenship was finally granted to Native Americans. In the same year the Indian Rights Association assigned Zitkala-Ša to investigate alleged abuses of some Oklahoma tribes by the federal government. With two fellow investigators she co-authored *Oklahoma's Poor Rich Indians,* an exposé that resulted in the creation of the Meriam Commission.

In 1926 she founded the National Council of American Indians, serving as president until her death on 26 January 1938 of cardiac dilatation and kidney disease. She is buried in Arlington National Cemetery under a headstone inscribed "Gertrude Simmons Bonnin – 'Zitkala-Sa' of the Sioux Indians – 1876–1938."

Zitkala-Ša's works, like those of Sarah Winnemucca, have only begun to receive critical attention. Like Winnemucca, Zitkala-Ša wrote to revise the dominant white assessment of tribal culture. Like Winnemucca, Zitkala-Ša compares Sioux and white cultures and, through the comparison, shows the cruelty, ignorance, and superstition of the invading white nation. As Zitkala-Ša, Gertrude Simmons Bonnin wrote with the clear purpose of re-creating in the imagination of her mostly white audience the cultural identity of the people she had left behind her. Her life and letters exemplify the condition of a Native American writer in transition between two cultures. However, her literary achievement never overshadowed the truth that the source of her inspiration was in the traditional oral culture of the Sioux.

Biographies:

Mary E. Young, "Gertrude Simmons Bonnin," in *Notable American Women, 1607–1950,* edited by Edward T. James (Cambridge, Mass.: Belknap Press, 1971), pp. 198–200;

Frederick J. Dockstader, "Gertrude Simmons Bonnin," in his *Great North American Indians* (New York: Van Nostrand Reinhold, 1977), pp. 40–41;

Deborah Welch, "American Indian Leader: The Story of Gertrude Bonnin," dissertation, University of Wyoming, 1985.

References:

Martha J. Cutter, "Zitkala-S̈a's Autobiographical Writings: The Problems of a Canonical Search for Language and Identity," *MELUS,* 19 (Spring 1994): 31–44;

Dexter Fisher, "The Transformation of Tradition: A Study of Zitkala-Sa and Mourning Dove, Two Transitional American Indian Writers," in *Critical Essays on American Indian Literature,* edited by Andrew Wiget (Boston: G. K. Hall, 1985), pp. 202–211;

Fisher, "Zitkala-Sa: The Evolution of a Writer," *American Indian Quarterly,* 5 (August 1977): 229–238;

Margaret A. Lukens, "The American Indian Story of Zitkala-Sa," in "Creating Cultural Spaces: The Pluralist Project of American Women Writers, 1843–1902 (Margaret Fuller, Harriet Jacobs, Sarah Winnemucca, and Zitkala-Sa)," dissertation, University of Colorado, 1991, pp. 162–196;

Beatrice Medicine, *The Hidden Half: Studies of Plains Indian Women* (Lanham, Md.: University Press of America, 1983);

Dorothea M. Susag, "Zitkala-Sa (Gertrude Simmons Bonnin): A Power(full) Literary Voice," *Studies in American Indian Literatures,* 5 (Winter 1993): 3–24;

William Willard, "Zitkala-Sa, A Woman Who Would Be Heard," *Wicazo Ša Review,* 1 (1985): 11–16.

Papers:

Much of Zitkala-Ša's correspondence about Indian rights is housed in Record Group 75 of the National Archives in Washington, D.C., Central Files, 1907–1939, Bureau of Indian Affairs. Yale University is the repository of the John Collier Papers and the Richard Henry Pratt Papers, both of which include letters from her; more personal correspondence can be found among the papers of Carlos Montezuma at the Wisconsin State Historical Society. Documents relating to *The Sun Dance* are included among the William Hanson Papers at Brigham Young University.

Checklist of Further Readings

Allen, Paula Gunn. *The Sacred Hoop: Recovering the Feminine in American Indian Traditions.* Boston: Beacon, 1986; revised, 1992.

Allen, ed. *Studies in American Indian Literature: Critical Essays and Course Designs.* New York: Modern Language Association of America, 1983.

Bataille, Gretchen M., ed. *Native American Women: A Biographical Dictionary.* New York: Garland, 1993.

Bataille, and Kathleen Mullen Sands. *American Indian Women: Telling Their Lives.* Lincoln: University of Nebraska Press, 1984.

Beidler, Peter G. "Animals and Human Development in the Contemporary American Indian Novel," *Western American Literature,* 14 (Summer 1979): 133–148.

Bruchac, Joseph, ed. *Survival This Way: Interviews with American Indian Poets.* Tucson: University of Arizona Press, 1987.

Brumble, H. David III. *American Indian Autobiography.* Berkeley: University of California Press, 1988.

Brumble, comp. *An Annotated Bibliography of American Indian and Eskimo Autobiographies.* Lincoln: University of Nebraska Press, 1981.

Brumble, comp. "Supplement to *An Annotated Bibliography of American Indian and Eskimo Autobiographies,*" *Western American Literature,* 17 (November 1982): 243–260.

Chapman, Abraham, ed. *Literature of the American Indians: Views and Interpretations.* New York: New American Library, 1975.

Clayton, Jay. "The Narrative Turn in Recent Minority Fiction," *American Literary History,* 2 (Fall 1990): 375–393.

Colonnese, Tom, and Louis Owens, comps. *American Indian Novelists: An Annotated Critical Bibliography.* New York: Garland, 1985.

Coltelli, Laura, ed. *Native American Literatures.* University of Pisa Press, 1989.

Coltelli, ed. *Winged Words: American Indian Writers Speak.* Lincoln: University of Nebraska Press, 1990.

Cook-Lynn, Elizabeth. "The American Indian Fiction Writer: Cosmopolitanism, Nationalism, the Third World, and First Nation Sovereignty," *Wicazo Sa Review,* 9 (Fall 1993): 26–36.

Dorris, Michael. "Native American Literature in an Ethnohistorical Context," *College English,* 41 (October 1979): 147–162.

Drinnon, Richard. *Facing West; the Metaphysics of Indian-hating and Empire-building.* Minneapolis: University of Minnesota Press, 1980.

Espey, David B. "Endings in Contemporary American Indian Fiction," *Western American Literature,* 13 (August 1978): 133–139.

Evers, Lawrence. "Words and Place: A Reading of *House Made of Dawn,*" *Western American Literature,* 11 (February 1977): 297–320.

Fleck, Richard F., ed. *Critical Perspectives on Native American Fiction.* Washington, D.C.: Three Continents Press, 1993.

Forbes, Jack. "Colonialism and Native American Literature: Analysis," *Wicazo Sa Review,* 3 (Fall 1987): 17–23.

From This World: Contemporary American Indian Literature. Special issue of *World Literature Today,* 66 (Spring 1992).

Hanson, Elizabeth I. *Forever There: Race and Gender in Contemporary Native American Fiction.* New York: Peter Lang, 1989.

Hirschfelder, Arlene B., comp. *American Indian and Eskimo Authors.* New York: Association on American Indian Affairs, 1973.

Huntsman, Jeffrey F. "Native American Theatre," in *Ethnic Theatre in the United States,* edited by Maxine Schwartz Seller. Westport, Conn.: Greenwood Press, 1983, pp. 355–385.

Jacobson, Angeline. *Contemporary Native American Literature: A Selected & Partially Annotated Bibliography.* Metuchen, N.J.: Scarecrow Press, 1977.

Jahner, Elaine, ed. *American Indians Today: Their Thought, Their Literature, Their Art.* Special issue of *Book Forum,* 5, no. 3 (1981).

Jaskoski, Helen, ed. *Early Native American Writing: New Critical Essays.* New York: Oxford University Press, 1996.

Krupat, Arnold. *Ethnocriticism: Ethnography, History, Literature.* Berkeley: University of California Press, 1992.

Krupat. *For Those Who Came After: A Study of Native American Autobiography.* Berkeley: University of California Press, 1985.

Krupat. *The Turn to the Native: Studies in Criticism and Culture.* Lincoln: University of Nebraska Press. 1996.

Krupat. *The Voice in the Margin: Native American Literature and the Canon.* Berkeley: University of California Press, 1989.

Krupat, ed. *New Voices in Native American Literary Criticism.* Washington, D.C.: Smithsonian Institution Press, 1993.

Larson, Charles R. *American Indian Fiction.* Albuquerque: University of New Mexico Press, 1978.

Liberty, Margot, ed. *American Indian Intellectuals,* 1976 Proceedings of the American Ethnological Society. Saint Paul: West, 1978.

Lincoln, Kenneth. *Indi'n Humor: Bicultural Play in Native America.* New York: Oxford University Press, 1993.

Lincoln. *Native American Renaissance,* second revised edition. Los Angeles: University of California Press, 1985.

Littlefield, Daniel F. Jr. and James W. Parins. "Short Fiction Writers of the Indian Territory," *American Studies,* 23 (Spring 1982): 23–38.

Littlefield and Parins, comps. *American Indian and Alaskan Native Newspapers and Periodicals, 1826–1924.* Westport, Conn.: Greenwood Press, 1984.

Littlefield and Parins, comps. *A Biobibliography of Native American Writers, 1772–1924.* Metuchen, N.J.: Scarecrow Press, 1981.

Littlefield and Parins, comps. *A Biobibliography of Native American Writers, 1772–1924: A Supplement.* Metuchen, N.J.: Scarecrow Press, 1985.

Lyon, Thomas, and others, eds. *A Literary History of the American West.* Fort Worth: Texas Christian University Press, 1987.

Maddox, Lucy. "Native American Poetry," in *The Columbia History of American Poetry,* edited by Jay Parini and Brett C. Millier. New York: Columbia University Press, 1993, pp. 728–749.

Marken, Jack W., comp. *The American Indian: Language and Literature.* Arlington Heights: AHM, 1978.

Murphy, James E., and Sharon M. Murphy. *Let My People Know: American Indian Journalism, 1828–1978.* Norman: University of Oklahoma Press, 1981.

Murray, David. *Forked Tongues: Speech, Writing and Representation in North American Indian Texts.* Bloomington: Indiana University Press, 1991.

Nelson, Robert M. *Place and Vision: The Function of Landscape in Native American Fiction.* New York: Peter Lang, 1993.

Oaks, Priscilla. "The First Generation of Native American Novelists," *MELUS,* 5 (Spring 1978): 57–65.

Ortiz, Simon. "Toward a National Indian Literature: Cultural Authenticity in Nationalism," *MELUS,* 8 (Summer 1981): 7–12.

Owens, Louis. "Acts of Recovery: The American Indian Novel in the '80's," *Western American Literature,* 22 (Spring 1987): 53–57.

Owens. *Other Destinies: Understanding the American Indian Novel.* Norman: University of Oklahoma Press, 1992.

Ramsey, Jarold. "Tradition and Individual Talents in Modern Indian Writing," in his *Reading the Fire: Essays in the Traditional Indian Literatures of the Far West.* Lincoln: University of Nebraska Press, 1983, pp. 181–194.

Roemer, Kenneth M. "Contemporary American Indian Literature: The Centrality of Canons on the Margins," *American Literary History,* 6 (Fall 1994): 583–599.

Roemer. "The Heuristic Powers of Indian Literatures: What Native Authorship Does to Mainstream Texts," *Studies in American Indian Literatures,* second series 3 (Summer 1991): 8–21.

Roemer. "Indian Lives: The Defining, the Telling," *American Quarterly,* 46 (March 1994): 81–91.

Roemer. "Part One: Materials," in *Approaches to Teaching Momaday's The Way to Rainy Mountain,* edited by Roemer. New York: Modern Language Association, 1988, pp. 3–18.

Roemer. "Survey Courses, Indian Literature, and *The Way to Rainy Mountain,*" *College English,* 37 (February 1976): 619–624.

Rosen, Kenneth. "American Indian Literature: Current Condition and Suggested Research," *American Indian Culture and Research Journal,* 3, no. 2 (1979): 57–66.

Ruoff, A. LaVonne Brown. "American Indian Literatures: An Introduction and Bibliography," *American Studies International,* 24 (October 1986): 2–52.

Ruoff. *American Indian Literatures: An Introduction, Bibliographic Review, and Selected Bibliography.* New York: Modern Language Association, 1990.

Ruoff. *Literatures of the American Indian.* New York: Chelsea House, 1991.

Ruoff. "The Survival of Traditions: American Indian Oral and Written Narratives," *Massachusetts Review,* 27 (Summer 1986): 274–293.

Ruoff and Jerry W. Ward Jr., eds. *Redefining American Literary History.* New York: Modern Language Association, 1990.

Ruppert, James. *Mediation in Contemporary Native American Fiction.* Norman: University of Oklahoma Press, 1995.

Ruppert. "The Uses of Oral Tradition in Six Contemporary Native American Poets," *American Indian Culture and Research Journal,* 4, no. 4 (1980): 87–110.

Sarris, Greg. *Keeping Slug Woman Alive: A Holistic Approach to American Indian Texts.* Berkeley: University of California Press, 1993.

Schneider, Jack W. "The New Indian: Alienation and the Rise of the Indian Novel," *South Dakota Review,* 17 (Winter 1979–1980): 67–76.

Schöler, Bo, ed. *Coyote Was Here: Essays on Contemporary Native American Literary and Political Mobilization.* Special issue of *Dolphin,* 9 (April 1984).

Slapin, Beverly, and Doris Seale, comps. *Books without Bias: Through Indian Eyes,* second edition. Berkeley: Oyate, 1988.

Smith, Patricia Clark, and Paula Gunn Allen. "Earthy Relations, Carnal Knowledge: Southwestern American Indian Writers and Landscape," in *The Desert is No Lady: Southwestern Landscapes in Women's Writing and Art,* edited by Vera Norwood and Janice Monk. New Haven: Yale University Press, 1987, pp. 174–196.

Smith, William F. Jr. "American Indian Autobiographies," *American Indian Quarterly,* 2 (Autumn 1975): 237–245.

Stensland, Anna Lee, and Aune M Fadum, comps. *Literature by and about the American Indian: An Annotated Bibliography,* second edition. Urbana: NCTE, 1979.

Swann, Brian, and Arnold Krupat, eds. *Recovering the Word: Essays on Native American Literature.* Berkeley: University of California Press, 1987.

Velie, Alan R. *Four American Indian Literary Masters: N. Scott Momaday, James Welch, Leslie Marmon Silko, and Gerald Vizenor.* Norman: University of Oklahoma Press, 1982.

Velie, ed. *Native American Perspectives on Literature and History*. Norman: University of Oklahoma Press, 1995.

Vizenor, Gerald. *Manifest Manners: Postindian Warriors of Survivance*. Hanover, N.H.: Published for Wesleyan University Press by University Press of New England, 1994.

Vizenor, ed. *Narrative Chance: Postmodern Discourse on Native American Indian Literatures*. Albuquerque: University of New Mexico Press, 1989.

Warrior, Robert Allen. *Tribal Secrets: Recovering American Indian Intellectual Traditions*. Minneapolis: University of Minnesota Press, 1995.

Wiget, Andrew O. *Native American Literature*. Boston: Twayne, 1985.

Wiget. "Native American Literature: A Bibliographic Survey of American Indian Literary Traditions," *Choice,* 23 (June 1986): 1503–1512.

Wiget. "Sending a Voice: The Emergence of Contemporary Native American Poetry," *College English,* 46 (October 1984): 598–609.

Wiget, ed. *Critical Essays on Native American Literature*. Boston: G.K. Hall, 1985.

Wiget, ed. *Handbook of Native American Literature*. New York: Garland, 1996.

Witalec, Janet, ed. *Native North American Literature*. Detroit: Gale Research, 1994.

Wong, Hertha Dawn. *Sending My Heart Back Across the Years: Tradition and Innovation in Native American Autobiography*. New York: Oxford University Press, 1992.

Contributors

Julie LaMay Abner .... *California State University, San Bernardino*
Gretchen M. Bataille .... *University of California, Santa Barbara*
Peter G. Beidler .... *Lehigh University*
Kimberly M. Blaeser .... *University of Wisconsin – Milwaukee*
Elizabeth Blair .... *Southwest State University, Minneapolis*
Phyllis Cole Braunlich .... *Tulsa, Oklahoma*
Susan B. Brill .... *Bradley University*
Alanna Kathleen Brown .... *Montana State University*
William M. Clements .... *Arkansas State University*
Betty Booth Donohue .... *University of California, Los Angeles*
Roger Dunsmore .... *University of Montana*
Birgit Hans .... *University of North Dakota*
Helen Jaskoski .... *California State University Fullerton*
Sue M. Johnson .... *Vermillion, South Dakota*
Sidner J. Larson .... *University of Oregon*
Kenneth Lincoln .... *University of California, Los Angeles*
Margo Lukens .... *University of Maine*
David L. Moore .... *Cornell University*
Barry O'Connell .... *Amherst College*
James W. Parins .... *University of Arkansas at Little Rock*
Jarold Ramsey .... *University of Rochester*
Ann E. Reuman .... *Tufts University*
Julian Rice .... *Florida Atlantic University*
Kenneth M. Roemer .... *University of Texas at Arlington*
Gretchen Ronnow .... *Wayne State College*
Ruth Rosenberg .... *Brooklyn College*
A. LaVonne Brown Ruoff .... *University of Illinois at Chicago*
James Ruppert .... *University of Alaska – Fairbanks*
Susan Scarberry-García .... *Navajo Preparatory School*
Matthias Schubnell .... *University of the Incarnate Word*
Kathryn W. Shanley .... *Cornell University*
Michael D. Wilson .... *University of Wisconsin – Milwaukee*
Norma C. Wilson .... *University of South Dakota*
Raymond Wilson .... *Fort Hays State University*
Terry P. Wilson .... *University of California, Berkeley*
Hertha D. Wong .... *University of California, Berkeley*

Cumulative Index

Dictionary of Literary Biography, Volumes 1-175
Dictionary of Literary Biography Yearbook, 1980-1995
Dictionary of Literary Biography Documentary Series, Volumes 1-14

Cumulative Index

DLB before number: *Dictionary of Literary Biography,* Volumes 1-175
Y before number: *Dictionary of Literary Biography Yearbook,* 1980-1995
DS before number: *Dictionary of Literary Biography Documentary Series,* Volumes 1-14

A

B

C

D

E

F

G

Gibson, Charles Dana 1867-1944 ..... DS-13

H

I

J

L

M

Cumulative Index

N

O

P

Q

R

S

Cumulative Index

T

U

V

W

Y

ISBN 0-8103-9938-5

90000

9 780810 399389